What They Said
in 1981

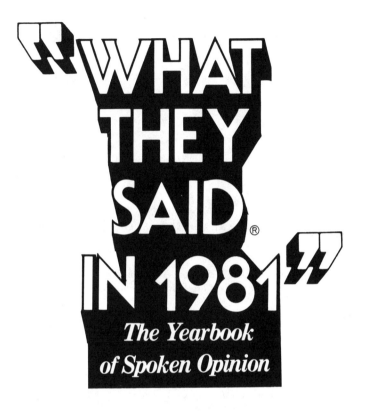

"WHAT THEY SAID" IN 1981

The Yearbook of Spoken Opinion

Compiled and Edited by

ALAN F. PATER

and

JASON R. PATER

Monitor Book Company, Inc.

To

The Newsmakers of the World . . .

May they never be at a loss for words

Preface to the First Edition (1969)

Words can be powerful or subtle, humorous or maddening. They can be vigorous or feeble, lucid or obscure, inspiring or despairing, wise or foolish, hopeful or pessimistic . . . they can be fearful or confident, timid or articulate, persuasive or perverse, honest or deceitful. As tools at a speaker's command, words can be used to reason, argue, discuss, cajole, plead, debate, declaim, threaten, infuriate, or appease; they can harangue, flourish, recite, preach, discourse, stab to the quick, or gently sermonize.

When casually spoken by a stage or film star, words can go beyond the press-agentry and make-up facade and reveal the inner man or woman. When purposefully uttered in the considered phrasing of a head of state, words can determine the destiny of millions of people, resolve peace or war, or chart the course of a nation on whose direction the fate of the entire world may depend.

Until now, the *copia verborum* of well-known and renowned public figures—the doctors and diplomats, the governors and generals, the potentates and presidents, the entertainers and educators, the bishops and baseball players, the jurists and journalists, the authors and attorneys, the congress-men and chairmen-of-the-board—whether enunciated in speeches, lectures, interviews, radio and television addresses, news conferences, forums, symposiums, town meetings, committee hearings, random remarks to the press, or delivered on the floors of the United States Senate and House of Representatives or in the parliaments and palaces of the world—have been dutifully reported in the media, then filed away and, for the most part, forgotten.

The editors of *WHAT THEY SAID* believe that consigning such a wealth of thoughts, ideas, doctrines, opinions and philosophies to interment in the morgues and archives of the Fourth Estate is lamentable and unnecessary. Yet the media, in all their forms, are constantly engulfing us in a profusion of endless and increasingly voluminous news reports. One is easily disposed to disregard or forget the stimulating discussion of critical issues embodied in so many of the utterances of those who make the news and, in their respective fields, shape the events throughout the world. The conclusion is therefore a natural and compelling one: the educator, the public official, the business executive, the statesman, the philosopher—everyone who has a stake in the complex, often confusing trends of our times—should have material of this kind readily available.

These, then, are the circumstances under which *WHAT THEY SAID* was conceived. It is the culmination of a year of listening to the people in the public eye; a year of scrutinizing, monitoring, reviewing, judging, deciding—a year during which the editors resurrected from almost certain oblivion those quintessential elements of the year's *spoken* opinion which, in their judgment, demanded preservation in book form.

WHAT THEY SAID is a pioneer in its field. Its *raison d'etre* is the firm conviction that presenting, each year, the highlights of vital and interesting views from the lips of prominent people on virtually every aspect of contemporary civilization fulfills the need to give the *spoken* word the permanence and lasting value of the *written* word. For, if it is true that a picture is worth 10,000 words, it is equally true that a verbal conclusion, an apt quote or a candid comment by a person of fame or influence can have more significance and can provide more understanding than an entire page of summary in a standard work of reference.

The editors of *WHAT THEY SAID* did not, however, design their book for researchers and scholars alone. One of the failings of the conventional reference work is that it is blandly written and referred to primarily for facts and figures, lacking inherent "interest value." *WHAT THEY SAID,* on the other hand, was planned for sheer enjoyment and pleasure, for searching glimpses into the lives and thoughts of the world's celebrities, as well as for serious study, intellectual reflection and the philosophical contemplation of our multifaceted life and mores. Furthermore, those pressed for time, yet anxious to know what the newsmakers have been saying, will welcome the short excerpts which will make for quick, intermittent reading—and rereading. And, of course, the topical classifications, the speakers' index, the subject index, the place and date information—documented and authenticated and easily located—will supply a rich fund of hitherto not readily obtainable reference and statistical material.

Finally, the reader will find that the editors have eschewed trite comments and cliches, tedious and boring. The selected quotations, each standing on its own, are pertinent, significant, stimulating— above all, relevant to today's world, expressed in the speakers' own words. And they will, the editors feel, be even more relevant tomorrow. They will be re-examined and reflected upon in the future by men and women eager to learn from the past. The prophecies, the promises, the "golden dreams," the boastings and rantings, the bluster, the bravado, the pleadings and representations of those whose voices echo in these pages (and in those to come) should provide a rare and unique history lesson. The positions held by these luminaries, in their respective callings, are such that what they say today may profoundly affect the future as well as the present, and so will be of lasting importance and meaning.

Beverly Hills, California

ALAN F. PATER
JASON R. PATER

Table of Contents

PART THREE: GENERAL

Editorial Treatment

ORGANIZATION OF MATERIAL

Special attention has been given to the arrangement of the book—from the major divisions down to the individual categories and speakers—the objective being a logical progression of related material, as follows:

(A) The categories are arranged alphabetically within each of three major sections:

Part One:	"National Affairs"
Part Two:	"International Affairs"
Part Three:	"General"

In this manner, the reader can quickly locate quotations pertaining to particular fields of interest (see also *Indexing*). It should be noted that some quotations contain a number of thoughts or ideas—sometimes on different subjects—while some are vague as to exact subject matter and thus do not fit clearly into a specific topic classification. In such cases, the judgment of the Editors has determined the most appropriate category.

(B) Within each category the speakers are in alphabetical order by surname, following alphabetization practices used in the speaker's country of origin.

(C) Where there are two or more quotations by one speaker within the same category, they appear chronologically by date spoken or date of source.

SPEAKER IDENTIFICATION

(A) The occupation, profession, rank, position or title of the speaker is given as it was *at the time the statement was made* (except when the speaker's relevant identification is in the past, in which case he is shown as "former"). Thus, due to possible changes in status during the year, a speaker may be shown with different identifications in various parts of the book, or even within the same category.

(B) In the case of a speaker who holds more than one position simultaneously, the judgment of the Editors has determined the most appropriate identification to use with a specific quotation.

(C) Nationality of the speakers is given only when it is relevant to the specific quotation.

THE QUOTATIONS

The quoted material selected for inclusion in this book is shown as it appeared in the source, except as follows:

(A) *Ellipses* have been inserted wherever the Editors have deleted extraneous words or overly long passages within the quoted material used. In no way has the meaning or intention of the quotations been altered. *Ellipses* are also used where they appeared in the source.

(B) *Punctuation and spelling* have been altered by the Editors where they were obviously incorrect in the source, or to make the quotations more intelligible, or to conform to the general style used throughout this book. Again, meaning and intention of the quotations have not been changed.

(C) *Brackets* ([]) indicate material inserted by the Editors or by the source to either correct obvious errors or to explain or clarify what the speaker is saying. In some instances, bracketed material may replace quoted material for the sake of clarity.

(D) *Italics* either appeared in the original source or were added by the Editors where emphasis is clearly desirable.

Except for the above instances, the quoted material used has been printed verbatim, as reported by the source (even if the speaker made factual errors or was awkward in his choice of words).

Special care has been exercised to make certain that each quotation stands on its own and is not taken "out of context." The Editors, however, cannot be responsible for errors made by the original source, i.e., incorrect reporting, mis-quotations, or errors in interpretation.

DOCUMENTATION AND SOURCES

Documentation (circumstance, place, date) of each quotation is provided as fully as could be obtained, and the sources are furnished for all quotations. In some instances, no documentation details were available; in those cases, only the source is given. Following are the sequence and style used for this information:

Circumstance of quotation, place, date/Name of source, date:section (if applicable), page number.

Example: *Before the Senate, Washington, Dec. 4/The Washington Post, 12-5:(A)13.*

The above example indicates that the quotation was delivered before the Senate in Washington on December 4. It was taken for *WHAT THEY SAID* from *The Washington Post*, issue of December 5, section A, page 13. (When a newspaper publishes more than one edition on the same date, it should be noted that page numbers may vary from edition to edition.)

(A) When the source is a television or radio broadcast, the name of the network or local station is indicated, along with the date of the broadcast (obviously, page and section information does not apply).

(B) An asterisk (*) before the (/) in the documentation indicates that the quoted material was written rather than spoken. Although the basic policy of *WHAT THEY SAID* is to use only *spoken* statements, there are occasions when written statements are considered by the Editors to be important enough to be included. These occasions are rare and usually involve Presidential messages and statements released to the press and other such documents attributed to persons in high government office.

INDEXING

(A) The *Index to Speakers* is keyed to the page number. (For alphabetization practices, see

Organization of Material, paragraph B.)

(B) The *Index to Subjects* is keyed to both the page number and the quotation number on the page (thus 210:3 indicates quotation number 3 on page 210); the quotation number appears at the right corner of each quotation.

(C) To locate quotations on a particular subject, regardless of the speaker, turn to the appropriate category (see *Table of Contents*) or use the detailed *Index to Subjects.*

(D) To locate all quotations by a particular speaker, regardless of subject, use the *Index to Speakers.*

(E) To locate quotations by a particular speaker on a particular subject, turn to the appropriate category and then to that person's quotations within the category.

(F) The reader will find that the basic categorization format of *WHAT THEY SAID* is itself a useful subject index, inasmuch as related quotations are grouped together by their respective categories. All aspects of journalism, for example, are relevant to each other; thus, the section *Journalism* embraces all phases of the news media. Similarly, quotations pertaining to the U.S. President, Congress, etc., are in the section *Government.*

MISCELLANEOUS

(A) Except where otherwise indicated or obviously to the contrary, all universities, organizations and business firms mentioned in this book are in the United States; similarly, references made to "national," "Federal," "this country," "the nation," etc., refer to the United States.

(B) In most cases, organizations whose names end with "of the United States" are Federal government agencies.

SELECTION OF CATEGORIES

The selected categories reflect, in the Editors' opinion, the most widely discussed public-interest subjects, those which readily fall into the over-all sphere of "current events." They represent topics continuously covered by the mass media because of their inherent importance to the changing world scene. Most of the categories are permanent; they appear in each annual edition of *WHAT THEY SAID.* However, because of the transient character of some subjects, there may be categories which appear one year and may not be repeated the next.

SELECTION OF SPEAKERS

The following persons are always considered eligible for inclusion in *WHAT THEY SAID*: top-level officials of all branches of national, state and local governments (both U.S. and foreign), including all United States Senators and Representatives; top-echelon military officers; college and university presidents, chancellors and professors; chairmen and presidents of major corporations; heads of national public-oriented organizations and associations; national and internationally known diplomats; recognized celebrities from the entertainment and literary spheres and the arts generally; sports figures of national stature; commentators on the world scene who are recognized as such and who command the attention of the mass media.

The determination of what and who are "major" and "recognized" must, necessarily, be made by the Editors of *WHAT THEY SAID* based on objective personal judgment.

Also, some persons, while not generally recognized as prominent or newsworthy, may have nevertheless attracted an unusual amount of attention in connection with an important issue or event. These people, too, are considered for inclusion, depending upon the specific circumstance.

SELECTION OF QUOTATIONS

The quotations selected for inclusion in *WHAT THEY SAID* obviously represent a decided minority of the seemingly endless volume of quoted material appearing in the media each year. The process of selecting is scrupulously objective insofar as the partisan views of the Editors are concerned (see *About Fairness*, below). However, it is clear that the Editors must decide which quotations *per se* are suitable for inclusion, and in doing so look for comments that are aptly stated, offer insight into the subject being discussed, or into the speaker, and provide—for today as well as for future reference—a thought which readers will find useful for understanding the issues and the personalities that make up a year on this planet.

ABOUT FAIRNESS

The Editors of *WHAT THEY SAID* understand the necessity of being impartial when compiling a book of this kind. As a result, there has been no bias in the selection of the quotations, the choice of speakers or the manner of editing. Relevance of the statements and the status of the speakers are the exclusive criteria for inclusion, without any regard whatsoever to the personal beliefs and views of the Editors. Furthermore, every effort has been made to include a multiplicity of opinions and ideas from a wide cross-section of speakers on each topic. Nevertheless, should there appear to be, on some controversial issues, a majority of material favoring one point of view over another, it is simply the result of there having been more of those views expressed during the year, reported by the media and objectively considered suitable by the Editors of *WHAT THEY SAID* (see *Selection of Quotations*, above). Also, since persons in politics and government account for a large percentage of the speakers in *WHAT THEY SAID*, there may exist a heavier weight of opinion favoring the philosophy of those in office at the time, whether in the United States Congress, the Administration, or in foreign capitals. This is natural and to be expected and should not be construed as a reflection of agreement or disagreement with that philosophy on the part of the Editors of *WHAT THEY SAID*.

Abbreviations

The following are abbreviations used by the speakers in this volume. Rather than defining them each time they appear in the quotations, this list will facilitate reading and avoid unnecessary repetition.

ABC:	American Broadcasting Companies
ABM:	anti-ballistic missile
ACLU:	American Civil Liberties Union
AFL-CIO:	American Federation of Labor-Congress of Industrial Organizations
AI:	Amnesty International
AT&T:	American Telephone & Telegraph Company
AVF:	all-volunteer force (military)
AWACS:	Airborne Warning and Command aircraft
BBC:	British Broadcasting Corporation
CBS:	Columbia Broadcasting System
CEO:	chief executive officer
CETA:	Comprehensive Employment and Training Act
CFL:	Canadian Football League
CIA:	Central Intelligence Agency
CNN:	Cable News Network
CPB:	Corporation for Public Broadcasting
CSA:	Community Services Administration
DOD:	Department of Defense
DOT:	Department of Transportation
EEC:	European Economic Community (Common Market)
EPA:	Environmental Protection Agency
ERA:	Equal Rights Amendment
FAA:	Federal Aviation Administration
FCC:	Federal Communications Commission
FDA:	Food and Drug Administration
F.D.R.:	Franklin Delano Roosevelt
FRG:	Federal Republic of (West) Germany
FTC:	Federal Trade Commission
GM:	General Motors Corporation

GNP:	gross national product
IBM:	International Business Machines Corporation
ILA:	International Longshoremen's Association
IRA:	Irish Republican Army
L.B.J.:	Lyndon Baines Johnson
MGM:	Metro-Goldwyn-Mayer, Inc.
MP:	Member of Parliament
NAACP:	National Association for the Advancement of Colored People
NASA:	National Aeronautics and Space Administration
NASL:	North American Soccer League
NATO:	North Atlantic Treaty Organization
NBA:	National Basketball Association
NBC:	National Broadcasting Company
NCAA:	National Collegiate Athletic Association
NEA:	National Endowment for the Arts: or, National Education Association
NFL:	National Football League
NFLPA:	National Football League Players Association
NIH:	National Institutes of Health
NOW:	National Organization for Women; or, negotiated order of withdrawal (bank account)
NRA:	National Rifle Association
NRC:	Nuclear Regulatory Commission
OMB:	Office of Management and Budget
OPEC:	Organization of Petroleum Exporting Countries
OSHA:	Occupational Safety and Health Administration
PAP:	People's Action Party (Singapore)
PATCO:	Professional Air Traffic Controllers Organization
PLO:	Palestine Liberation Organization
p.r.:	public relations
R&D:	research and development
SALT:	Strategic Arms Limitation Talks
SEC:	Securities and Exchange Commission
SWAPO:	South-West Africa People's Organization
TMI:	Three Mile Island
TV:	television
UAW:	United Automobile Workers of America
U.K.:	United Kingdom
UN:	United Nations
UNITA:	National Union for the Total Independence of Angola

U.S.:	United States
U.S.A.:	United States of America
USRA:	United States Railway Association
U.S.S.R.:	Union of Soviet Socialist Republics
VD:	venereal disease
WPA:	Works Progress Administration

Party affiliation of United States Senators, Representatives and Governors—

D: Democratic

R: Republican

The Quote of the Year

"My overwhelming observation is that history is neither the product of design nor of conspiracy but is rather the reflection of continuing chaos. Seen from the outside, decisions may seem clear and consciously formulated; inter-relations between governments may seem to be the products of deliberately crafted, even if often conflicting, policies. But one learns that so much of what happens—not only in the U.S. government, but in foreign governments too—is the product of chaotic conditions and a great deal of personal struggle and ambiguity. Sometimes you will find agreement on means but fundamental disagreement on ends; sometimes agreement on ends but disagreement on means. All this reinforces the impression of contingency and uncertainty which is inherent in the human condition and which is only magnified by the scale and intensity of the power one wields."

ZBIGNIEW BRZEZINSKI
*Professor of government, Columbia University;
Former Assistant to the President of the
United States (Jimmy Carter) for National
Security Affairs. In an interview.*

PART ONE

National Affairs

Presidential Inaugural Address

Delivered by Ronald Reagan, President of the United States, at the Capitol, Washington, January 20, 1981.

Senator Hatfield, Mr. Chief Justice, Mr. President, Vice President Bush, Vice President Mondale, Senator Baker, Speaker O'Neill, Reverend Moomaw, and my fellow citizens:

To a few of us here today this is a solemn and most momentous occasion. And, yet, in the history of our nation it is a commonplace occurrence.

The orderly transfer of authority as called for in the Constitution routinely takes place as it has for almost two centuries and few of us stop to think how unique we really are.

In the eyes of many in the world, this every-four-year ceremony we accept as normal is nothing less than a miracle.

Mr. President, I want our fellow citizens to know how much you did to carry on this tradition.

By your gracious cooperation in the transition process you have shown a watching world that we are a united people pledged to maintaining a political system which guarantees individual liberty to a greater degree than any other. And I thank you and your people for all your help in maintaining the continuity which is the bulwark of our republic.

The Economy

The business of our nation goes forward.

These United States are confronted with an economic affliction of great proportions.

We suffer from the longest and one of the worst sustained inflations in our national history. It distorts our economic decisions, penalizes thrift and crushes the struggling young and the fixed-income elderly alike. It threatens to shatter the lives of millions of our people.

Idle industries have cast workers into unemployment, human misery and personal indignity.

Those who do work are denied a fair return for their labor by a tax system which penalizes successful achievement and keeps us from maintaining full productivity.

But great as our tax burden is, it has not kept pace with public spending. For decades we have piled deficit upon deficit, mortgaging our future and our children's future for the temporary convenience of the present.

To continue this long trend is to guarantee tremendous social, cultural, political and economic upheavals.

You and I, as individuals, can, by borrowing, live beyond our means, but for only a limited period of time. Why, then, should we think that collectively, as a nation, we are not bound by the same limitation?

We must act today in order to preserve tomorrow. And let there be no misunderstanding—we're going to begin to act beginning today.

The economic ills we suffer have come upon us over several decades.

They will not go away in days, weeks or months, but they will go away. They will go away because we as Americans have the capacity now, as we have had in the past, to do whatever needs to be done to preserve this last and greatest bastion of freedom.

In this present crisis, government is not the solution to our problem; government is the problem.

From time to time, we've been tempted to believe that society has become too complex to be managed by self-rule, that government by an elite group is superior to government for, by and of the people.

But if no one among us is capable of governing himself, then who among us has the capacity to govern someone else?

All of us together—in and out of government —must bear the burden. The solutions we seek must be equitable, with no one group singled out to pay a higher price.

We hear much of the special interest groups. Well, our concern must be for a special inter-

3

est group that has been too long neglected.

It knows no sectional boundaries, or ethnic and racial divisions, and it crosses political party lines. It is made up of men and women who raise our food, patrol our streets, teach our children, keep our homes and heal us when we're sick.

Professionals, industrialists, shopkeepers, clerks, cabbies and truck drivers. They are, in short, "We the people." This breed called Americans.

Well, this Administration's objective will be a healthy, vigorous, growing economy that provides equal opportunities for all Americans, with no barriers born of bigotry or discrimination.

Putting America back to work means putting all Americans back to work. Ending inflation means freeing all Americans from the terror of runaway living costs.

All must share in the productive work of this "new beginning," and all must share in the bounty of a revived economy.

With the idealism and fair play which are the core of our system and our strength, we can have a strong, prosperous America at peace with itself and the world.

The Government

So as we begin, let us take inventory.

We are a nation that has a government—not the other way around. And this makes us special among the nations of the earth.

Our Government has no power except that granted it by the people. It is time to check and reverse the growth of government which shows signs of having grown beyond the consent of the governed.

It is my intention to curb the size and influence of the Federal establishment and to demand recognition of the distinction between the powers granted to the Federal Government and those reserved to the states or to the people.

All of us—all of us need to be reminded that the Federal Government did not create the states; the states created the Federal Government.

Now, so there will be no misunderstanding, it's not my intention to do away with government.

It is rather to make it work—work with us, not over us; to stand by our side, not ride on our back. Government can and must provide opportunity, not smother it, foster productivity, not stifle it.

If we look to the answer as to why for so many years we achieved so much, prospered as no other people on earth, it was because here in this land we unleashed the energy and individual genius of man to a greater extent than has ever been done before.

Freedom and the dignity of the individual have been more available and assured here than in any other place on earth. The price for this freedom at times has been high, but we have never been unwilling to pay that price.

It is no coincidence that our present troubles parallel and are proportionate to the intervention and intrusion in our lives that result from unnecessary and excessive growth of Government.

A Great Nation

It is time for us to realize that we are too great a nation to limit ourselves to small dreams. We're not, as some would have us believe, doomed to an inevitable decline. I do not believe in a fate that will fall on us no matter what we do. I do believe in a fate that will fall on us if we do nothing.

So, with all the creative energy at our command, let us begin an era of national renewal. Let us renew our determination, our courage and our strength. And let us renew our faith and our hope. We have every right to dream heroic dreams.

Those who say that we're in a time when there are no heroes—they just don't know where to look. You can see heroes every day going in and out of factory gates. Others, a handful in number, produce enough food to feed all of us and then the world beyond.

You meet heroes across the counter—and they're on both sides of that counter. There are entrepreneurs with faith in themselves and faith in an idea who create new jobs, new wealth and opportunity.

There are individuals and families whose

taxes support the Government and whose voluntary gifts support church, charity, culture, art and education. Their patriotism is quiet but deep. Their values sustain our national life.

Now, I have used the words "they" and "their" in speaking of these heroes. I could say "you" and "your" because I'm addressing the heroes of whom I speak—you, the citizens of this blessed land.

Your dreams, your hopes, your goals are going to be the dreams, the hopes and the goals of this Administration, so help me God.

We shall reflect the compassion that is so much a part of your makeup.

How can we love our country and not love our countrymen? And loving them reach out a hand when they fall, heal them when they're sick and provide opportunity to make them self-sufficient so they will be equal in fact and not just in theory?

Can we solve the problems confronting us? Well, the answer is an unequivocal and emphatic yes.

To paraphrase Winston Churchill, I did not take the oath I've just taken with the intention of presiding over the dissolution of the world's strongest economy.

In the days ahead I will propose removing the roadblocks that have slowed our economy and reduced productivity.

Steps will be taken aimed at restoring the balance between the various levels of government. Progress may be slow—measured in inches and feet, not miles—but we will progress.

It is time to reawaken this industrial giant, to get government back within its means and to lighten our punitive tax burden.

And these will be our first priorities, and on these principles there will be no compromise.

On the eve of our struggle for independence, a man who might've been one of the greatest among the Founding Fathers, Dr. Joseph Warren, president of the Massachusetts Congress, said to his fellow Americans, "Our country is in danger, but not to be despaired of. On you depend the fortunes of America. You are to decide the important question upon which rest the happiness and the liberty of millions yet unborn. Act worthy of yourselves."

Well, I believe we, the Americans of today, are ready to act worthy of ourselves, ready to do what must be done to insure happiness and liberty for ourselves, our children and our children's children.

And as we renew ourselves here in our own land, we will be seen as having greater strength throughout the world. We will again be the exemplar of freedom and a beacon of hope for those who do not now have freedom.

Foreign Policy

To those neighbors and allies who share our freedom, we will strengthen our historic ties and assure them of our support and firm commitment.

We will match loyalty with loyalty. We will strive for mutually beneficial relations. We will not use our friendship to impose on their sovereignty, for our own sovereignty is not for sale.

As for the enemies of freedom, those who are potential adversaries, they will be reminded that peace is the highest aspiration of the American people. We will negotiate for it, sacrifice for it; we will not surrender for it—now or ever.

Our forebearance should never be misunderstood. Our reluctance for conflict should not be misjudged as a failure of will.

When action is required to preserve our national security, we will act. We will maintain sufficient strength to prevail if need be, knowing that if we do so we have the best chance of never having to use that strength.

Above all, we must realize that no arsenal or no weapon in the arsenals of the world is so formidable as the will and moral courage of free men and women.

It is a weapon our adversaries in today's world do not have.

It is a weapon that we as Americans do have.

Let that be understood by those who practice terrorism and prey upon their neighbors.

I am told that tens of thousands of prayer meetings are being held on this day; for that I am deeply grateful. We are a nation under God, and I believe God intended for us to be free. It would be fitting and good, I think, if on each inaugural day in future years it should be declared a day of prayer.

Heroes of America

This is the first time in our history that this ceremony has been held, as you've been told, on this West Front of the Capitol.

Standing here, one faces a magnificent vista, opening up on this city's special beauty and history.

At the end of this open mall are those shrines to the giants on whose shoulders we stand.

Directly in front of me, the monument to a monumental man: George Washington, father of our country. A man of humility who came to greatness reluctantly. He led America out of revolutionary victory into infant nationhood.

Off to one side, the stately memorial to Thomas Jefferson. The Declaration of Independence flames with his eloquence.

And then beyond the Reflecting Pool, the dignified columns of the Lincoln Memorial. Whoever would understand in his heart the meaning of America will find it in the life of Abraham Lincoln.

Beyond those monuments to heroism is the Potomac River, and on the far shore the sloping hills of Arlington National Cemetery, with its row upon row of simple white markers bearing crosses or Stars of David. They add up to only a tiny fraction of the price that has been paid for our freedom.

Each one of those markers is a monument to the kind of hero I spoke of earlier.

Their lives ended in places called Belleau Wood, the Argonne, Omaha Beach, Salerno—and halfway around the world on Guadalcanal, Tarawa, Pork Chop Hill, the Chosin Reservoir, and in a hundred rice paddies and jungles of a place called Vietnam.

Under such a marker lies a young man, Martin Treptow, who left his job in a small town barber shop in 1917 to go to France with the famed Rainbow Division.

There, on the Western front, he was killed trying to carry a message between battalions under heavy artillery fire.

We are told that on his body was found a diary.

On the flyleaf under the heading, "My Pledge," he had written these words:

"America must win this war. Therefore I will work, I will save, I will sacrifice, I will endure, I will fight cheerfully and do my utmost, as if the issue of the whole struggle depended on me alone."

The crisis we are facing today does not require of us the kind of sacrifice that Martin Treptow and so many thousands of others were called upon to make.

It does require, however, our best effort, and our willingness to believe in ourselves and to believe in our capacity to perform great deeds; to believe that together with God's help we can and will resolve the problems which now confront us.

And after all, why shouldn't we believe that? We are Americans.

God bless you and thank you. Thank you very much.

The American Scene

Howard H. Baker, Jr.
United States Senator, R—Tennessee

1

A great deal has happened since the last Senate Republican majority 25 years ago. We have been embroiled in a tragic war. We have seen our countrymen—emissaries of the United States of America—taken captive and murdered abroad. We have seen our cities and towns explode in strife and violence. But we have also witnessed an absolute revolution in civil rights for minorities. We have been to the moon and we have witnessed a technological revolution so far-reaching we are still unable to appreciate its magnitude. We have the vision, the resources, the capabilities and, I believe, the leadership to make this land, once again, a beacon for all the world.

Washington, Jan 5/
Los Angeles Times, 1-6:(I)11.

Ray Bradbury
Author

2

The American people are a remarkable people. I think we're far more remarkable than we give ourselves credit for. We've been so busy damning ourselves for years. We've done it all, and yet we don't take credit for it. Everyone in the world is dressed like us. We're the center of the universe. If we opened the floodgates tomorrow, the whole world would pour in here. I'm always talking about the invisible revolutions—the things we've done that we don't take credit for. Last year we took in about a million people from other nations. Now, if we're as bad as we say we are, why are they coming here? To be corrupted, to be dumb, to be horrible, to be brutes—the way we describe ourselves to ourselves? No, they're coming here because we're excellent, because we offer freedom, because we offer opportunities.

At Harvey Mudd College commencement,
Claremont, Calif./Time, 6-15:55.

Jimmy Carter
President of the United States

3

We live in a time of transition, an uneasy era which is likely to endure for the rest of the century. It will be a period of tensions both within and between nations—of competition for scarce resources, of social, political and economic stresses and strains. During this period, we may be tempted to abandon some of the time-honored principles and commitments which have been proven during the difficult times of past generations. We must never yield to this temptation. Our American values are not luxuries but necessities . . . Our common vision of a free and just society is our greatest source of cohesion at home and strength abroad—greater even than the bounty of our material blessings.

Farewell address to the nation,
Washington, Jan. 14/
U.S. News & World Report, 1-26:34.

Marcus Cunliffe
Historian; University professor,
George Washington University

4

American society has a quite extraordinary, excessive fascination with novelty. The nation keeps chucking out old ideas and puts a premium on having bright, new ones. This is reflected in such phrases as "making a U-turn" in policy. This means that whatever the policy of the previous administration, the new administration assumes that it needs to do the opposite. So experts are rewarded for having an idea that is different from anyone else's. New ideas too often are exaggerated reactions to other ideas—with each, in turn, discarded as fashion changes. That is not a good way to operate.

Interview/
U.S. News & World Report, 9-7:66.

7

WHAT THEY SAID IN 1981

Oriana Fallaci
Italian journalist

1

[Universities in the U.S.] are filled with stupidity. You Americans go to the moon but you don't know the meaning of words like Marxism. You have all this technology but you have no culture, no history. You look at things in terms of black and white, you are so naive. I love America, but you don't bother to think any more; you just want entertainment. I feel like Cassandra when she said, "Troy is burning," and they said, "Oh, there she goes again!" But Troy *is* burning and you better hurry, because when *you* fall, Western civilization also falls.

Interview/Saturday Review, January:22.

David H. Fischer
Professor of history,
Brandeis University

2

. . . the scale of thinking in social science and public policy and politics [in America] is quite wrong—we normally don't deal with these problems until they become a crisis. We deal with them on a kind of interval scale which really doesn't allow us a depth of insight or a breadth of reforming. That's something new in America. The leaders of this society in the early republic, and even through the New Deal, were thinking about public problems not nearly for the moment—whatever the merits of their ideas. John Adams was thinking on a scale of centuries. Franklin Roosevelt had a very spacious sense of time. But liberals, conservatives, businessmen, politicians, social scientists today—everyone is working with blinders on. That's what's fatal to fundamental reform in this society.

Interview, Brandeis University/
The Christian Science Monitor, 9-24:13.

Ivar Giaever
Physicist, General Electric Company

3

. . . there is a lot of worry and pessimism in society that I am hard put to understand. People no longer seem to believe, as Americans once

did, that any sort of problem could be solved. Now people want to go back and live on the farm, without using fertilizers. They have all these romantic notions. People have time enough and have become rich enough to start worrying about problems that are almost nonexistent. Newspapers are full of stories, and people get scared about *this* and scared about *that*. Sometimes you are supposed to be fat and eat cholesterol, and sometimes you're supposed to be thin and stay away from it. People worry about chlorinated water because, presumably, under certain circumstances it can cause cancer. But you can't live without chlorinated water. If it does cause cancer, nobody has really found it out. But the United States is a very healthy society. I don't believe it is going down the drain—at least not in my lifetime.

Interview/U.S. News & World Report, 4-6:46.

Alexander M. Haig, Jr.
Secretary of State of the United States

4

The supreme American national interest is simple and compelling: We want a world hospitable to our society and our common ideals. As a practical matter, our national interest requires us to resist those who would extinguish those ideals and are hostile to our common aspirations. But there is a positive aspect to our national interest that should be stressed. Let us not make the mistake of allowing other peoples to believe that America and the Western world means nothing more than sophisticated technology and the consumer society. From its very beginning, the United States has been about life and liberty, not just the pursuit of happiness. Human rights are not only compatible with our national interest, they are an integral element of the American approach—at home and abroad.

Before Trilateral Commission,
Washington, March 31/The New York Times, 4-21:6.

Alfred Kazin
Critic; Professor of English,
Graduate Center, City University of New York

5

What has happened to the American mind these days? You have only to look at the mar-

(ALFRED KAZIN)

quees featuring one horror film after another, one more domestic drama, to wonder why a European film like *The Last Metro,* an Australian film like *Breaker Morant,* is so rare among us. There is not a single stage production on Broadway just now that bears in the slightest on our public condition. The favorite subjects on the book market are terrorism, how to slim down, and how to make a fortune in real estate.

At City University of New York
Graduate School commencement/Time, 6-15:55.

Jack Kemp
United States Representative, R—New York
1

. . . the social fabric of the nation is based upon good-will. And when the pie is shrinking, when you perceive that your gain must come at my expense or that my gain is coming at your expense, then this whole special-interest environment builds up. Blacks have to be more separate in order to organize themselves to protect themselves against what they perceive to be a threat to their survival. And labor unions must be more interested in their union membership in order to protect themselves against what they fear to be a shrinking of their piece of the pie. Business speaks only for business. The cities of the Northeast are pitted against the Sun Belt, and New York thinks it must advance by mugging another part of the country. I think much of the good-will in our society is based upon the belief that we can all advance together. Ultimately, the debates over busing and abortion and birth control, as important as they are to the country, will take place in an environment in which people don't have this perception that it's white versus black, rich versus poor, labor versus capital, and the Northeast versus the Sun Belt.

Interview/The Washington Post, 1-20:(A)21.

Edward I. Koch
Mayor of New York
2

We went through an era when middle-class values were dumped on. Honesty, integrity, hard work, patriotism, religiosity—all those were considered terrible things in the minds of some ideologues who are still out there. Not *me.* I always believed they were verities then. I think they're verities *now.*

Time, 6-15:28.

Arthur Levitt, Jr.
Chairman, American Stock Exchange
3

Today's fail-safe society seems to have generated a cult of mediocrity—a willingness to settle for whatever life provides instead of exerting every effort to get more, to reach the top, to have it all, or at least more of it than other folks have. The knowledge that no one in this country will be allowed to sink all the way to the bottom, that there will always be a helping hand, or even an entire arm, has . . . taken away one of our most precious rights—the right to fail as well as the right to succeed. Too many of us have lost the spirit of adventure, of risking all we have in order to have more.

At Texas A&M University commencement/
U.S. News & World Report, 6-15:35.

Louis Malle
French motion-picture director
4

One thing that is fascinating to a European is it seems that American economy and society and even psychology are very much for permanent change. It is striking to see the movement of people here from the Northeast to the Southwest, to see buildings go up that will last 20 years and then be torn down, to see objects that are manufactured to be obsolete in five years. There is still a pioneering spirit here, a basic believing in progress that is probably absent in Europe. If you go to the middle of the country, you still find people looking at their lives in terms of the future instead of the past.

Interview, New York/
The New York Times, 6-28:(2)1.

WHAT THEY SAID IN 1981

V. S. Pritchett
British author and critic

1

There is not half so much regard in America for what I would call "social obligation." In England the writer has a difficult time because everyone born in England is born inevitably with a strong consciousness of the society, his duties or his part in the society around him. It's going to interfere with his life, to impose obligations on him which are a great nuisance for a writer. It's partly because England is very small, incredibly small, immensely over-crowded. We have this social consciousness because we constantly have to bump our way down the street against each other. We simply cannot get away from each other. In America, obviously people can get away from each other to a greater degree. You [in America] have enormous space; the country appears to an outsider to be under-populated. Tennessee, I think, is remarkable: Four to five million people in a state of this size is fantastic. Therefore, the individual doesn't feel the same strict obligation to society. In America there's a curious sense of nonchalance: "I can go my own way when I like and do what I want. I'm floating free."

Interview, Vanderbilt University/
The Wall Street Journal, 6-12:24.

Ronald Reagan
President of the United States

2

It is time for us to realize that we are too great a nation to limit ourselves to small dreams. We're not, as some would have us believe, doomed to an inevitable decline. I do not believe in a fate that will fall on us no matter what we do. I do believe in a fate that will fall on us if we do nothing. So, with all the creative energy at our command, let us begin an era of national renewal. Let us renew our determination, our courage and our strength. And let us renew our faith and our hope. We have every right to dream heroic dreams.

Inaugural address,
Washington, January 20/
Los Angeles Times, 1-21:(I)16.

3

I believe the spirit of volunteerism still lives in America. We see examples of it on every hand—the community charity drive, support of hospitals and all manner of non-profit institutions, the rallying around when disaster or tragedy strikes. The truth is we've let government take away many things we once considered were really ours to do voluntarily out of the goodness of our hearts and a sense of community pride and neighborliness. I believe many of you want to do those things again, want to be involved if only someone will ask you or offer the opportunity. Well, we intend to make that offer.

Broadcast address to the nation,
Washington, Sept. 24/
The Washington Post, 9-25:(A)13.

David Riesman
Sociologist, Harvard University

4

Traditional American generosity—which is still stronger than in most of the world—is taking a beating. I've watched a rise in violence since the 1950s. By historical standards, the violence is not greater. But it is changing. It's a result of people feeling crowded by inflation, crowded by racial and ethnic issues. It's a general impatience, a surliness. I see it in the way people drive, taking frightful chances. There's always been a great deal of violence. But there was hope there would be less of it. There was more peer disapproval of violence. The great difference between 25 years ago and now is the lack of conviction of authorities or peers that it can be stopped.

The Christian Science Monitor, 4-16:7.

Robin M. Williams, Jr.
Professor of social science,
Cornell University

5

We [in the U.S.] live in the best-fed and healthiest era of recent history. Death rates are at all-time lows. The percentage of disposable income that the average consumer spends for food is 16.5 per cent in the U.S., 30 per cent in the U.S.S.R., and 65 per cent in the developing

10

(ROBIN M. WILLIAMS, JR.)

nations. We have an unprecedented level of scientific and technological knowledge, a high level of material comfort, fast and effective sys-tems of transportation and communication. But many people do not seem ready to accept this as a Golden Age. Pessimism is widespread.

The Washington Post, 11-29:(A)3.

Civil Rights . Women's Rights

Bernard E. Anderson
Director, social science division,
Rockefeller Foundation

1

... as a condition for their advancement up the corporate ladder, black managers, like whites, must accommodate themselves to the corporate value system. But unlike whites, black managers have had difficulty justifying those corporate values they've adopted because they recognize them to be inconsistent with the set of views and values articulated by the traditional civil-rights leadership and accepted by the black community at large. So they've been desperately searching for something which would give them and their views legitimacy in the black community.

Interview/
The New York Times Magazine, 10-4:23.

Harry Belafonte
Singer

2

Back in 1959, I fully believed in the civil-rights movement. I had a personal commitment to it, and I had my personal breakthroughs: I produced the first black TV special; I was the first black to perform at the Waldorf-Astoria. I felt if we could just turn the nation around, things would fall into place. And it actually happened. Because of the civil-rights movement, there were black reporters, black advertising on TV, black ballplayers. The country was in a renaissance. [But] the civil-rights movement ended [in the mid-1970s], and many blacks who had moved into the institutions of power were acting like their white predecessors. When I talked to members of the Black Caucus in Congress, I don't find much energy. It's business as usual, making deals with other members of Congress. They've had a taste of power, and they want to be re-elected.

Interview,
New York/The New York Times, 8-28:16.

Derek A. Bell
Dean, University of Oregon Law School;
Former civil-rights lawyer

3

[On the busing of schoolchildren for racial balance]: My contacts with blacks convince me that they want quality and effective schooling; they don't want the inconvenience of busing. [The earlier theory was that] if we put black kids where white kids are, the black kids would get what the white kids are getting. It didn't work. The needs and interests of the whites continued to come first, and the blacks got whatever was left.

The New York Times, 3-22:(1)14.

Terrel H. Bell
Secretary of Education
of the United States

4

[On predominantly white and predominantly black colleges]: None of these systems are functioning as segregated systems because whites are discouraged from attending traditionally black colleges, or vice versa. I say [they are] neither prohibited nor discouraged. I think that we have the degree of racial concentration there because of tradition; you know—"My parents went to this Florida A&M, so I go there," and I'm talking now as a black youngster. Because they feel more comfortable and more confident that they can make it at that institution. And I would hope that we [in government] can ... de-emphasize the stick in the closet—the cut-off of Federal money [to colleges with this kind of segregation].

Interview, Washington/
The Christian Science Monitor, 3-25:(B)4.

George Bush
Vice President of the United States

5

I know that many members of America's black community, along with other minority com-

(GEORGE BUSH)

munities, have serious concerns about the philosophy of the Reagan Administration on the paramount issues of civil rights and equal opportunity. Let there be no doubt among minority Americans regarding the commitment of this Administration to our nation's civil-rights laws ... Let the white hood and the swastika, those ugly symbols of hatred and bigotry, be buried in the past, for there is no room for racial or religious intolerance in America.

At Howard University convocation, May 9/
The Washington Post, 5-10:(C)1.

Joseph A. Califano, Jr.
Former Secretary of Health, Education and Welfare of the United States

1

[President] Reagan has clearly backed off from the commitment to do the hard thing, to bite the difficult bullet in the quest for racial justice. That has not involved any change in the law; it has involved [the Justice Department] not moving vigorously to enforce civil-rights laws; a change in attitude on the part of the Department of Education in terms of school integration; a change in enforcement by the Equal Employment Opportunity Commission. It is not necessary or appropriate to pull back on the government's moral, political and legal leadership in the area of civil rights. If that doesn't come from the President, it doesn't come from anywhere. We've learned that, ever since the Civil War.

Interview, Washington/
The New York Times, 9-18:10.

Patricia Carbine
Editor and publisher, "Ms." magazine

2

... it has probably been perceived by many people in the communications world that progress lies in the direction of seeing women pictured and portrayed in roles that have been previously perceived as male roles. A lineswoman working for AT&T. A pilot. A co-pilot. I'm not suggesting that these have not been

damned important to us, because they have been. But we're not going to get out of the Superwoman trap until we begin to see men integrated into roles that have been previously thought of as female roles, where we see men in roles in interaction with children, and where they are obvious inhabitors of space shared by more than one person.

Interview, Los Angeles/
Los Angeles Herald Examiner, 5-6:(D)5.

Charles E. Carter
Associate general counsel, National Association for the Advancement of Colored People

3

[On the forced busing of schoolchildren to achieve racial balance]: [To many people,] busing is an ugly word because it is used to help in carrying out the law of the land. The truth is that less than 3 per cent of the annual total cost of busing is spent on busing for desegregation. Busing is not the real issue. The people who cry the loudest about busing are not concerned with transportation. They really don't want integrated education. They don't want integrated communities or schools. They don't want it by bus, bicycle, walking or jogging. And any black person who mouths a lot of talk against busing at this time is playing into the hands of people who want to turn back the clock. The same goes for all this talk about the glories of the neighborhood school.

Chicago Tribune, 4-19:(2)4.

Nancy Chotiner
Chairman, Target '80s Committee

4

[Expressing concern over the small number of women appointed by President Reagan to important Federal positions]: The very conservative ... to the most liberal feminists are together on this. They are all concerned and worried. No one doubts [Reagan's] commitment, but he's had other things on his mind—like hostages and the economy. The problem is with his staff—the White House personnel operation. There is an insensitivity to the fact that there are all these

(NANCY CHOTINER)

women out there. It's the men's groups—the Old Boy network. The "you-pat-my-back-and-I'll-pat-yours." It's not a calculated plot, or an effort to block any woman's nomination. It's just the same old thing we've been fighting all these years. You'd think we could finally quit.

Los Angeles Times, 2-5:(V)1.

Kenneth B. Clark
Professor emeritus of psychology,
City College of New York;
New York State Regent

1

To say that blacks are more comfortable in black colleges is like saying the slaves were more comfortable with slavery. Black educators say that we need black colleges because black students can't compete with white students. That is a racist statement. If black students can't compete because they have had inferior secondary-school preparation, then let's subject them to a regime. You don't need black colleges—you need black preparatory academies.

The New York Times Magazine, 12-20:98.

Roy M. Cohn
Lawyer

2

. . . I'm not a feminist. I'm not a believer in the ERA. I'm not a believer in gay rights and all that stuff. What someone's sexual preference is is the business of that person. I have something inside of me that dictates against legislating these things. I think a lot of people who are really not against women's rights were turned off by watching those screaming parades. I think the ERA is dead, but I think women are doing fine. We have a woman on the United States Supreme Court. Women have remedies in the event of job discrimination and all of that. It's not a question of the underlying issue; it's a question of all the noise and agitation.

Interview,
Beverly Hills, Calif./
Los Angeles Times, 9-3:(V)22.

Robert F. Drinan
President, Americans for Democratic Action;
Former United States Representative,
D—Massachusetts

3

Over the past 50 years, no Administration prior to the one now in office [the Reagan Administration] has ever submitted legislation to weaken the enforcement of the nation's civil-rights laws . . . The decision of the Reagan Administration, with respect to education, at least borders on the ominous . . . Amazement has been expressed at the promise of Attorney General William French Smith that the Administration, rather than integrate schools, will seek to improve black schools; even if this were desirable, it cannot be done at a time when the Administration is drastically cutting back all Federal funds for education . . . The enemies of affirmative action have been energized by the reactionary policies of the Reagan Administration, and as never before have been proclaiming a war on hiring goals and timetables . . . Anger and indignation are heard more every day in the civil-rights community. Fears are expressed over what might happen when the full impact of the Reagan rejection of civil rights is understood by the nation.

The Washington Post, 11-19:(A)30.

Marian Wright Edelman
President, Children's Defense Fund

4

Clearly there's still racism in this society. People were gung ho for civil rights in the '60s, and some legislative victories were achieved. Then people tired in the '70s. Now that the '80s are here and blacks have a few affirmative-action jobs, people think blacks are doing okay—maybe even too well. So the poor and the minorities become scapegoats for the nation's economic problems.

Interview, Boston/
The Christian Science Monitor, 5-11:19.

Christopher Edley
Executive director,
United Negro College Fund

1

[On whether public universities should lower the admission standards for blacks]: I favor it. The demonstrated fact is that blacks do not score as well on certain standard tests because of cultural bias. Yet in case after case where performance is the test, the blacks have measured up and succeeded. There is no sin in giving a student an opportunity to prove whether he or she can make it in first-year college. I mean, the process of flunking students out is ruthless enough. We don't particularly need standardized tests to say this person will be banned in life from any opportunity to show that he or she can make it at the college level.

Interview/
Los Angeles Herald Examiner, 1-9:(A)17.

Jerry Falwell
Evangelist;
Chairman, Moral Majority

2

[It was] probably 1963, -4, -5 that I totally repudiated segregation. It was a carry-over from my heritage. I would say that 99 per cent of all Southerners—maybe Northerners, too, but certainly Southerners, I can speak for that—were segregationists. And once we became Christians, many of us were still in that cultural society—an all-white church and pastors who preached it as the gospel. I don't think they were guilty of racism. They just believed it was a scriptural position and sometimes misapplied Scripture to support it. It was only as I became a real student of Scripture that I saw it's not in the Bible. As a matter of fact, the opposite is there.

Interview, Los Angeles/
Los Angeles Times, 3-4:(I)14.

Dianne Feinstein
Mayor of San Francisco

3

There are times when I still have conflicts about having a career. Women are basically dif-

ferent from men; they have different needs. Society has yet to answer a lot of those needs. This is especially evident in the political arena, which is entirely tailored for men. Women in politics have a lot of adjusting to do. The accepted political style is a man's style; there is no real public image for a woman in public roles. They are constantly criticized for what they wear, how they speak, for being either too masculine or feminine. They are criticized for things a man doesn't have to face.

Interview, San Francisco/
The Christian Science Monitor, 7-14:18.

Arthur S. Flemming
Chairman,
United States Commission on Civil Rights

4

The re-emergence of the Ku Klux Klan and other proponents of hate ideologies serve as graphic reminders that virulent, overt bigotry has not disappeared from our political landscape. Discrimination also comes in many more subtle—but no less pernicious—forms. In virtually all sectors of society, massive social and economic inequalities between white males and the rest of the population persist . . . Our nation's civil-rights problems are as real and as profound as the national fiscal problems that have necessitated a complete review of the Federal budget. We believe that our nation should commit the resources that are required to assure progress—not retrogression—in the field of civil rights.

The Christian Science Monitor, 6-26:4.

5

[Supporting affirmative-action programs]: Built into the institutions of our society, whether it's a public agency or a private agency, is the factor of institutional discrimination. Unless you recognize its existence and do something about it, it will govern what happens to your agency in terms of opening up opportunities for minorities and women. Affirmative action is simply using the normal tools of management to achieve the objective that you want to achieve in the area of equal employment opportunity . . .

15

WHAT THEY SAID IN 1981

(ARTHUR S. FLEMMING)

Unless people in public office indicate that they believe that you must use affirmative action in order to achieve equal employment opportunity, equal employment is just going to be rhetoric and you are not going to see any real results.

> *Interview, Washington/*
> *The New York Times, 12-8:14.*

Betty Ford
Wife of former President of the
United States Gerald R. Ford

1

[Supporting passage of the ERA]: As a woman and as a Republican, I don't see how we can continue to stand up and be proud if we have not guaranteed the rights of half our population. We have gotten past the point of asking. We are at a point of demanding recognition of our right to equality.

> *At ERA rally, Washington, Oct. 12/*
> *The Washington Post, 10-13:(B)1.*

Betty Friedan
Founder,
National Organization for Women

2

[On the fight to get the ERA ratified]: It is going to take a miracle to get it, but the ERA is more important than it ever was. If we ever had any illusion that we didn't really need it, that it was just a symbol, that illusion was destroyed by the Supreme Court last week [when it ruled that a men-only military draft was legal and that divorced wives were not eligible to share in their former husbands' military pensions].

> *At ERA rally, New York, June 30/*
> *The New York Times, 7-1:9.*

3

It is necessary for feminists to be utterly serious and utterly realistic and realize we are *not* going to be able to hold on to the gains we've made in terms of the narrow rhetoric that too many feminists have locked themselves into, unless

we can deal with the situation that is faced by the majority of women in this country who *do* marry, who *do* have children, who *do* have needs for love, who express those needs for love, so far, in terms of men, who *do* have needs to be independent but who also have needs that remain *de*pendent. Anyone who wants to deny those needs in themselves or other women is not doing the basic cause of feminism a favor.

> *Interview, Beverly Hills, Calif./*
> *Los Angeles Herald Examiner, 11-4:(B)6.*

Ellen V. Futter
President, Barnard College

4

[Addressing the graduating class]: You [women] must not let yourself be trapped into trying to become superwomen—to being all things to all people at one time. The lesson of being a thoroughly modern liberated woman is, at least in part, that of transcending both traditional stereotypes of women's roles in society and more recent, but I believe equally stereotypical, concepts of what women should and should not do with their professional and personal lives.

> *At Barnard College commencement,*
> *New York, May 13/The New York Times, 5-14:17.*

David R. Gergen
Assistant to the President of the United States,
and White House Staff Director

5

[On the number of women to be appointed to top positions by the Reagan Administration]: We don't operate with a quota system here, so I can't tell you what the numbers will be. But I can say with authority that there is an accelerated effort underway to recruit women. They are out there. This is a subject of serious discussion here. We know there are some terrific women out there and we want them in this Administration. There are some good women in the White House with important jobs and you'll be seeing more in the departments and agencies.

> *Los Angeles Times, 2-5:(V)6.*

Barry M. Goldwater
United States Senator, R—Arizona

1

I voted against the civil rights bill [of 1964] for one reason . . . and that was they said you have to rent your home to anyone. I don't buy that. I'm old-fashioned. I think the right of property is one of the most sacred rights that we have. You try to tell me I have to rent my house to a drunken Irishman or a Communist, I'm going to tell you to go to hell . . . I have always believed that the only difference between a black man and a white man is his color. We both bleed red; we both breathe. We do the same damn things, but one of them is black and the other is white.

Interview, Washington/
The Wall Street Journal, 8-3:12.

Orrin G. Hatch
United States Senator, R—Utah

2

[On affirmative-action programs]: The original intent was not to allow any discrimination based upon race, color, sex, national origin or religion. And today we find through the affirmative-action programs that the government is itself becoming the discriminator by requiring mandatory discrimination based upon race or sex only. In the process, because the rules and regulations have become so burdensome, a number of employers are scared to death to hire the under-served, under-educated, under-skilled, under-privileged young black kids, and young women, by the way, because they're afraid they'll get ensnarled into a whole raft of affirmative-action-type interpretations that may ruin their businesses and cause them all kinds of unnecessary legal and other expenses.

Interview/The New York Times, 10-4:(4)19.

Paula Hawkins
United States Senator, R—Florida

3

I think it's rather ridiculous that women's organizations want to give you litmus tests on the Equal Rights Amendment. Everyone knows the overriding issue is inflation. We're all just grasping for every straw to survive today. If I can be a major force in taming inflation and restoring this country to economic soundness, then I've done the greatest job for women *and* men *and* children. Equality should be everyone's issue. There is no such thing as a woman's issue. I think the ERA is over.

Interview, Los Angeles, April 13/
Los Angeles Herald Examiner, 4-15:(B)5.

Benjamin L. Hooks
Executive director, National Association
for the Advancement of Colored People

4

[On the argument that race is no longer an obstacle to black advancement]: Well, I don't agree with that and I think all the evidence would go the other way. I could take an hour citing the evidence: Only 2 per cent of the doctors are black; 2 per cent of the lawyers are black; less than 1 per cent of the certified accountants; the black median family income is only 57 per cent of white family income; the unemployment rate is twice for the black community what it is for the white community; the percentages of blacks at or below the poverty level are much larger than for whites. I don't know of any evidence that does not point up that past pervasive racism has prevented blacks from achieving and being upwardly mobile.

Interview/The New York Times, 4-12:(4)5.

5

We shall not retreat [from demanding civil and economic rights for blacks]. We shall not equivocate, and we shall be heard . . . Until the victory of 400 years of intentional deprivation and subjugation are at par with the majority, the government must continue to make blacks whole . . . It is unconscionable that in the so-called enlightened '80s, our government is prepared to abandon this posture. We are not going to let the right-wing deodorize the stink of infection in the body politic . . . we counsel reconsideration and revision of the Federal budget because the cuts in

WHAT THEY SAID IN 1981

(BENJAMIN L. HOOKS)

social programs are born out of economic hocus-pocus.

At NAACP convention, Denver, July 3/
Chicago Tribune, 7-5:(1)4.

Frederick Humphries
President, Tennessee State University

1

Deep South and border states have made dramatic gains in improving opportunities for blacks in state-controlled higher education. But most of those gains have been posted in the area of increasing black student enrollment state-wide and have overshadowed many short-comings. With few exceptions, historically black colleges are finding their institutional missions changing very little as states map out new master plans for the 1980s, despite the fact that black students are pursuing their education in larger numbers at predominantly white colleges where they perceive educational opportunities to be broader. [Meanwhile,] black participation in the governance and policy-making process is still miniscule, and the hiring of blacks for teaching and administrative positions is still rare beyond the traditional confines of the black-college campus.

The New York Times, 9-3:11.

Jesse L. Jackson
Civil-rights leader, President, PUSH,
(People United to Save Humanity)

2

Every developing people use economics as a tool. People don't develop off of sociology or philosophy. People who have no economic strength with which to barter don't develop. We've [blacks] not put enough emphasis in late years on economic programs. And the thing that's amazing about it is the fact that the economic approach, when applied, has never failed us. In Montgomery [Ala.], it was economic withdrawal from the bus companies that got us the victory [desegregated buses] during the public-accommodations period. And we are compelled

to use the economic approach now more than ever before.

Interview/
Los Angeles Herald Examiner, 11-9:(A)7.

John E. Jacob
Executive vice president, and
president-designate, National Urban League

3

[On his being selected as the next president of the League]: Black people are hurting, and it is our mandate to do all we can to remedy that condition ... I am painfully aware that I come to office at a time of broad national withdrawal from civil-rights concerns and from issues such as the condition of the poor people and the cities. It means we must continue to raise our voice as advocates of the voiceless—the forgotten minority poor whose needs this nation must address.

News conference, New York, Dec. 7/
Los Angeles Times, 12-8:(I)7.

4

The realities of the '80s indicate that Americans must perceive civil rights as not solely a black problem, but also as an issue affecting white poor people. In the so-called glory days [the 1960s] of the movement, discrimination and racial bias stared black people in the face—"white" and "colored" water fountains, toilets, transportation, eating places, all labeled. Today the issues are jobs, inadequate housing, poor education, welfare. These are needs that affect even more white people than blacks ... The Urban League operates on four principles—advocacy, direct services, building bridges between the races and creating an open, pluralistic, integrated society. I plan to be forceful in seeking these same goals.

Interview, Boston/
The Christian Science Monitor, 12-11:14.

Vernon E. Jordan, Jr.
President, National Urban League

5

What are the new ideas the [Reagan] Administration is ramming down the throats of the

(VERNON E. JORDAN, JR.)

nation?—get government off our backs; give power and programs to the states; Federal programs have failed; rely on the free-enterprise system; build more missiles. These are not ideas, they are slogans. Like most slogans, they contain a grain of truth. And like most slogans, they oversimplify and distort. They reinforce the meanest instincts of selfishness. They cut society loose from its moral bearings. But black people don't need to be told that government is on our backs because we know it has been by our side, helping to counterbalance the vicious racism that deprived us of our lives, our liberty and our rights . . . Black people want economic growth. We know that in this America we will not get our fair share unless there is more for everyone. But we also know that we will not get our fair share just because there is more. America has managed to push us from the table of prosperity in good times and in bad times.

At National Urban League conference, Washington, July 19/The New York Times, 7-20:8.

Jack Kemp
United States Representative, R—New York

1

[On how the Reagan Administration should go about getting support from blacks]: I think clearly by identifying the Republican Party once again as a party of civil rights. There's no doubt in my mind that our Party has to make sure that those doors that have been opened by the law are not closed by the economy in the '80s. So, in effect, the civil-rights strategy for the Republican Party in the '80s is to protect those legal gains that have been made by minorities, but then shift the emphasis in the civil-rights strategy toward an expanding pie. That means reaching out to the cities in terms of establishing high levels of economic growth and opportunity and social justice in the inner cities.

Interview/ The Washington Post, 1-20:(A)21.

Nannerl Keohane
President, Wellesley College

2

I think a feminist is someone who: is sensitive to the special situation of women in the past, interested and curious about what life was like for women in all sorts of cultures and societies; cares about fighting for equal opportunity for women in the present so that particular kinds of disadvantages or discriminations can be overcome, giving women full opportunity to realize their goals and talents as individuals; and is concerned to work for a future society in which both men and women will be able to take advantage of social opportunities and push to fulfill themselves without barriers to discrimination by sex. That's a definition which makes it possible for men to be feminists, too. I think that's important.

Interview, Wellesley College/ The Christian Science Monitor, 11-4:(B)15.

John W. Mack
President, Los Angeles chapter, National Urban League

3

[On the California Supreme Court's ruling upholding an order ending forced school busing for racial integration]: It appears that the California Supreme Court has succumbed to the ugly conservative mood that's sweeping our state and this country and as a result has made a political decision that's tragedy because it reaffirms separate and historically unequal education for students of different racial backgrounds.

March 12/Los Angeles Times, 3-13:(I)18.

Joseph E. Madison
Director, voter education department, National Association for the Advancement of Colored People

4

The technical [black] militant of the old days, say during the days of the Montgomery [Ala.] bus boycott, was the domestic worker who would work all day with swollen feet and ankles but would be militant in thought so that when it came to participating in the civil-rights move-

WHAT THEY SAID IN 1981

(JOSEPH E. MADISON)

ment, she would not ride the bus home but would walk. We've got to develop technical militants out of these middle-class affluent blacks who have received training, acquired good educations and have worked themselves into the mainstream of economic life in this country. Today there are blacks who work 40-hour-a-week desk jobs, drive to and from work, who maintain or control or direct multi-million-dollar computer organizations; but they won't volunteer their services or talent to local political organizations, churches or the NAACP. We don't have enough technical militants who will use their ability to do things for their people.

At legislative weekend sponsored by Congressional Black Caucus, Washington/ The New York Times, 9-30:12.

Benjamin E. Mays
Former president, Morehouse College; Former dean, Howard University School of Religion

1

"Desegregation" means the absence of segregation. To "integrate" means to unite together to form a "more complete, harmonious or co-ordinate entity." In an integrated society, fellowship, comradeship and neighborliness have no limits or boundaries based on nationality, race or color. Associations will be formed mainly in the realm of spiritual, mental and cultural values ... Integration is largely spiritual. It is even possible for a married couple to live in the same house bearing and rearing children, fussing and feuding, without ever becoming thoroughly integrated, without ever being unified in their purposes and outlook on life. Although there is a vast difference between desegregation and integration, desegregation is an indispensable step in the march toward integration. All barriers that keep integration from developing must be destroyed. Desegregation creates the atmosphere, plants the seed, tills and fertilizes the soil so

that integration can sprout and grow in a normal fashion.

At University of the District of Columbia commencement, May 9/ The Washington Post, 5-21:(A)26.

Walter F. Mondale
Former Vice President of the United States

2

In difficult times economically, it becomes easier to ignore the needs of others who are less fortunate. In difficult times, bigotry and intolerance find fertile ground—and are even justified in the name of "morality." But let there be no mistake: In this country there is a "majority"—and it opposes racism, it opposes anti-Semitism, it opposes the arrogation, by any group, of the right to define what is "moral." And it always will.

At Brandeis University commencement/ The Christian Science Monitor, 6-17:14.

Benjamin F. Payton
President, Tuskegee Institute

3

You end black colleges and youngsters will end up as serious social misfits. It will cost far more to keep them in prison than to develop their competencies. If the American people understood better what we are talking about, they would see that it is less costly, more humane and contributes more to the welfare of society to educate [black] people [in black colleges] than to neglect them.

The New York Times Magazine, 12-20:98.

Samuel R. Pierce, Jr.
Secretary of Housing and Urban Development of the United States

4

There is an uneasiness in the black community today. There seems to have developed a fear that

(SAMUEL R. PIERCE, JR.)

the Reagan Administration will turn back the clock [on racial matters.] I have heard these concerns, and I recognize how deeply they are felt. I want to work with you in finding solutions to those problems before a storm flowing between the black community on one shore and the Reagan Administration on the other. With a biblical phrase in mind, I say, "Come let us reason together."

At NAACP convention/
The Christian Science Monitor, 7-7:5.

Ronald Reagan
President of the United States

1

This Administration is going to be dedicated to equality. I think we've made great progress in the civil-rights field. I think there are some things, however . . . that may not be as useful as they once were, or that may even be distorted in the practice—such as some affirmative-action programs becoming quota systems. And I'm old enough to remember when quotas existed in the United States for the purpose of discrimination. And I don't want to see that happen again.

News conference, Washington, Jan. 29/
The New York Times, 1-30:10.

2

[Saying he has not yet decided whether to extend the 1965 Voting Rights Act]: But until a decision is announced, you should know this: I regard voting as the most sacred right of free men and women. We have not sacrificed and fought and toiled to protect that right so that we can now sit back and permit a barrier to come between a secret ballot and any citizen who makes a choice to cast it. Nothing will change that as long as I am in a position to uphold the Constitution of the United States.

At NAACP convention, Denver, June 29/
Chicago Tribune, 6-30:(1)3.

William Bradford Reynolds
Assistant Attorney General,
Civil Rights Division, Department of
Justice of the United States

3

[On the busing of schoolchildren to achieve racial balance]: Forced busing has, in the final analysis, largely failed in two respects. It has failed to gain needed public acceptance and it has failed to translate into enhanced educational achievement. Blind allegiance to an experiment that has not withstood the test of experience obviously makes little sense . . . We must ensure, whatever the ultimate racial composition in the classroom, that all students attending public schools—regardless of race, color or ethnic background—have an opportunity to receive an education. We are concerned, quite frankly, much less with student relocation than we are with student education.

Before Education Commission of the States,
Chicago, Sept. 27/
Chicago Tribune, 9-29:(1)7.

Richard Richards
Chairman, Republican National Committee

4

[Saying the Republican Party has written off many U.S. black leaders]: It's a waste of our resources to go out and try to get votes from people who have shut the door on us. The Reagan program is good for the black man in this country just like it's good for the white man and everyone else. These leaders who are attempting to build their own coffers, build their own organizations, or whatever, by attacking President Reagan are making a mistake. So-called black leaders, civil-rights movement leaders and others [have done blacks an injustice] because they have drawn them away from the Republican Party . . . they make them a one-party people. [Because black leaders have rejected the Republican Party,] Democrats don't have to bargain for them—they know they've got them.

Radio interview, Atlanta, Aug. 13/
The Washington Post, 8-15:(A)4.

Phyllis Schlafly
President, Eagle Forum

1

Sexual harassment on the job is not a problem for virtuous women, except in the rarest of cases. Men hardly ever ask sexual favors of women from whom the certain answer is no. Virtuous women are seldom accosted.

Before Senate Labor Subcommittee,
Washington, April 12/Time, 5-4:29.

2

The most cruel and damaging sexual harassment taking place today is the harassment by feminists and their Federal government allies against the role of motherhood and the role of the dependent wife.

Before Senate Labor Subcommittee,
Washington, April 21/
Los Angeles Herald Examiner, 4-22:(A)2.

Eleanor Smeal
President, National Organization for Women

3

[Saying NOW will continue to push for ratification of the ERA despite many setbacks]: If you had given up on suffrage, or any other major right, in any kind of adverse times, we wouldn't have any rights. We have never thought this would be easy, but the fight for equality will never end until it's reality. There isn't going to be any artificial time limit, nothing that's going to say magically, "Oh, forget it; accept your status as second-class citizens, accept your lesser paychecks and your lesser opportunities. It's okay, it's over with." The drive for women's rights will continue until there is justice, and the social conditions of our times, the changed role of women, fuels it. Right now, when it's getting tougher and tougher to survive, I don't think people can with calmness accept the fact that women get half as much Social Security. Right now, heating oil is 47 per cent of the budget of the average elderly woman. Our job is to constantly make the connection between these economic realities and the fact that programs such as Social Security, which is a Federal program, discriminate on the basis of sex.

Interview, Los Angeles/
Los Angeles Times, 3-5:(V)10.

4

[Criticizing the Supreme Court decision upholding an all-male military draft]: We believe it is a tragedy. The decision says women can be discriminated against, that there is going to be yet another exception made. [The Court is] perpetuating the myth of this country that all men are better than all women.

June 25/The Washington Post, 6-26:(A)2.

5

[On President Reagan's opposition to the ERA]: We have been saying for 10 years we can go backwards, and now people see President Reagan taking the first steps to move us back. That has brought out a fighting spirit and bolstered the *esprit de corps* [of the women's movement] as nothing ever before . . . There are hundreds of laws that discriminate against women, and if we are to go, case by case, to the courts, asking that these laws be overturned, it will take a couple of hundred years to get them off the books. But that is the route that President Reagan favors. Women won't stand for going backwards or taking centuries to accomplish what can be accomplished by the ERA.

Los Angeles Times, 12-11:(I-B)9.

William French Smith
Attorney General of the United States

6

[Declaring an end to the Justice Department's support for mandatory busing of schoolchildren for racial balance and the use of racial quotas in employment]: Just as we have compromised the principle of color-blindness through overreliance on mandatory busing to desegregate our schools, we have come perilously close in recent years to fostering discrimination by establishing racial quotas in other areas . . . A bedrock principle [of the Constitution] is that the government

(WILLIAM FRENCH SMITH)

should treat all citizens fairly and equitably. [But] it would be a serious mistake to interpret this change of focus at the remedial level as a signal that the Justice Department will not vigorously prosecute any governmental attempts to foster segregation. We will not countenance any retrenchment here. We will not permit any of our citizens to be stigmatized by government as the result of their race . . . If the government had violated the free-speech rights of a particular group, the effective remedy would be to secure those rights for both groups. But it would not be consistent with our traditions or our laws to impose free-speech restraints on the previously advantaged group. [The goal] must always be genuinely color-blind state action. The time has come in America when more can be accomplished by emphasizing the aspiration most Americans have in common irrespective of race: a high quality of education for their children and the opportunity to make the most of their individual abilities.

Before American Law Institute,
Philadelphia, May 22/
The Washington Post, 5-23:(A)1,9.

Thomas Sowell
Economist; Senior fellow,
Hoover Institution, Stanford University

1

As I've looked at affirmative action, I do not see blacks or Hispanics rising relative to the general population under affirmative action. I think there are a lot of assertions and foregone conclusions that are stated over and over again, but repetition is not a substitute for facts. The fact is that under affirmative action Puerto Rico income, for example, has fallen from 60 per cent of the national average to 50 per cent of the national average. Mexican-American income has fallen from 76 per cent to 73 per cent of the national average. Black income has fluctuated right about where it was before affirmative action. When you break down the figures further, what you find is that those blacks who have education, who have years of experience on the job, are rising abso-

lutely and relative to whites, but that those who are average and who don't have that level of education, they are falling relative to whites, so they are falling behind from before.

Broadcast interview/
"Meet the Press," NBC-TV, 9-20.

David S. Tatel
Former Director, Office for Civil Rights,
Department of Health, Education and
Welfare of the United States

2

[On Reagan Administration efforts against forced busing of schoolchildren for racial integration]: We are now seeing an even more serious attack on desegregation than under the Nixon Administration. What this Administration is doing is a serious threat to desegregation. But desegregation is not dead. While the Federal government has made it clear that it will not insist on school desegregation, there are enough responsible city, state and school officials and courts who will take their responsibility seriously.

The New York Times, 7-18:6.

William L. Taylor
Director, Center for National Policy Review,
Catholic University of America School of Law

3

[Supporting the forced busing of schoolchildren to achieve racial integration in the classroom]: The Supreme Court has found that busing is an indispensable tool in some communities to eliminate the wrong that has been done to minority students through enforced segregation . . . despite all the furor over it, busing has been a very useful educational tool, as well as a legal tool in correcting wrongs. Researchers tend to agree that when you establish classrooms in which advantaged children are in the majority, there is a favorable educational environment for all children. Busing makes this possible.

Interview/U.S. News & World Report, 6-22:49.

Franklin A. Thomas
President, Ford Foundation

4

Some black people in the last decade have clearly seen extraordinary progress and oppor-

23

(FRANKLIN A. THOMAS)

tunity. Some black high-school graduates are already demonstrating equal opportunity in employment. They now have access to fields that historically were not open, such as banking and finance. [But] there is a group within the black community—and I don't know its size—for whom the reality of life in the last 10 years or so has not measurably improved. And this is clearly the larger of the two groups. The opportunities either have not presented themselves, or even when they have, they have not been taken advantage of.

Interview, New York/
The Christian Science Monitor, 10-26:4.

Strom Thurmond
United States Senator, R—South Carolina

1

[On the busing of schoolchildren to achieve racial balance]: The courts have gone entirely too far on the busing question. The *Brown vs. Board of Education* decision provided that government cannot deny a child of any race the right to attend any school. But since that decision, the courts have gone 180 degrees the other way and now contend that in order to integrate schools—or to desegregate schools, whichever you want to call it—the government must pick up a child in one place and transport him 25 or 30 miles to force a racial balance. That was not the intention of the *Brown* decision.

Interview/U.S. News & World Report, 3-23:41.

Paul E. Tsongas
United States Senator, D—Massachusetts

2

As a group, women office workers are not paid what they deserve. Many working women are mistreated in a manner that no one deserves . . . Discrimination is wrong; it is unacceptable. But if reason alone could cure it, we wouldn't be here today [discussing this subject]. In the 1980s, we must be even better-organized to attack it effectively. We must use all the tools of politics, law and economics to win decent salaries and

professional treatment for working women . . . The fact is that discriminating against a working woman is unjust, illegal—and economically irrational. It means artificially holding someone below her potential to produce. Discrimination against a working woman is a tragic waste of a human resource.

At Second Convention of Working Women/
The Washington Post, 4-23:(A)26.

Robert S. Walker
United States Representative,
R—Pennsylvania

3

[Advocating a bill that would prohibit numerical quotas for women and minority groups in hiring and school enrollment]: [This amendment to the Civil Rights Act would] return this landmark law to its original intent of making it illegal to use race as a factor in denying employment. This bill is an attempt to assure continuance of those things we have already regarded as best within our society; namely, treatment of individuals as equal under law, not as nameless, faceless members of a group to be arbitrarily disadvantaged.

Washington, May 6/
The New York Times, 5-7:11.

Marilyn Waring
Member of New Zealand Parliament;
Fellow, Institute of Politics, Harvard University

4

Every issue is a woman's issue—illiteracy, hunger, poverty, peace, development, migration, refugees—and yet what is really frightening is the absence of women from these debates, the physical invisibility of women around tables in the world where these issues get discussed. Women are just not there. And even when they are, government briefs do not include a woman's perspective.

Interview, Boston/
Los Angeles Times, 8-14:(V)3.

Eddie N. Williams
President, Joint Center for Political Studies
1

Contemporary devotees of the philosophy that the best government is one that governs least surely misunderstand or ignore the fact that for decades the protection and advancement of black people have depended on the laws and enforcement powers of the Federal government. Would we have achieved even a modicum of equal opportunity in education without busing and affirmative action? Would the political rights of blacks and Hispanics have been won and sustained had there been no Voting Rights Act? In every phase of human endeavor, who can say that blacks and other minorities would be better off today had there not been the visible hand of the Federal government in the lives of American citizens?

The Washington Post, 3-11:(A)22.

Walter E. Williams
Professor of economics,
George Mason University
2

[Arguing against the forced busing of schoolchildren to achieve racial balance in schools]: As a black person and an American, I'm for high-quality education. But it is not clear to me that, to get high-quality education, black people have to go out and capture a white kid for their children to sit beside. I'm not suggesting I'm for segregated schools, but I'm saying there's considerable evidence that you can improve black education without busing. The classic and most publicized example is Marva Collins [who runs a black private school] in Chicago. In the horrible slums of Chicago, her kids are reading one, two and perhaps three years above grade level. They are doing math at or above grade level. She didn't go out and capture white kids; there's no busing involved. Perhaps more important, she does it for $60 a month [per child]. So it says two things: You can improve black education without busing and without huge financial resources.

Interview/
The New York Times, 4-12:(4)5.

Andrew Young
Candidate for Mayor of Atlanta; Former
United States Ambassador/Permanent
Representative to the United Nations
3

In 1964, I was in the middle of a civil-rights demonstration in St. Augustine, Florida, where people were getting clobbered, and I yawned. Being cool has always been a means of survival in controversial situations for blacks. As a child, my daddy used to shadow-box with me to teach me not to have a temper. "Don't get mad," he used to say, "get smart."

The Washington Post, 9-13:(A)2.

Commerce . Industry . Finance

Malcolm Baldrige
Secretary of Commerce of the United States

1

[Saying he favors relaxing U.S. corporate bribe laws as they affect foreign sales of U.S. products]: Whether we like it or not, many countries are underpaying some of their government people, such as customs agents, with the implicit assumption that they make up the difference in pay by accepting relatively small gifts . . . That's sometimes called "grease," it's something called "facilitating-payments," but it means you are not trying to bribe anybody to do anything outside the law or change their payment on buying your product or accepting their product. You're just trying to get your product that you've already sold through the system to its final destination.

Interview, Washington/
Chicago Tribune, 3-23:1:(1)1.

2

. . . poorly run [U.S.] industries that cannot survive foreign competition will fall by the wayside in the '80s and beyond . . . I don't think it's labor productivity that's a problem. It's management. And I speak as a former manager. Management has been too fat, dumb and happy in the past 10 years. Management hasn't been sharp enough or hungry enough or lean enough.

Before U.S. Chamber of Commerce executives,
Springfield, Mass., Sept. 30/
Los Angeles Times, 10-1:(IV)1.

William Baxter
Assistant Attorney General, Antitrust Division,
Department of Justice of the United States

3

The freedom to make [corporate] mergers, large and small, is a very, very important part of the economy [and] essential to the health of our capital markets. Whether any particular merger is a good thing or a bad thing is a question one can answer only after one takes a very careful look at the markets the two companies participate in. In general, merger activity is a healthy thing . . . In an enormous economy, a growing economy, it is quite appropriate from time to time that we will have merger proposals between very large companies. So I do expect to see more. I would expect over the course of the years that some of them probably would be challenged and other won't be. Of course, to the extent that the merger rules are relatively clearly articulated by the Justice Department, we can expect that the companies won't even attempt to engage in mergers that violate those rules.

Interview/Chicago Tribune, 7-19:(5)3.

4

. . . I see nothing wrong with large [corporate] mergers simply because they're large. But we will look to see whether there are areas of horizontal overlap—where the merging companies are both in the same business. If there are overlaps, we will not let the mergers go forward unless these problems are cured. Of course, it is not always necessary to block an entire merger in order to cure an area of horizontal overlap. Often a merger can be saved by pruning one or the other of the partners, carving out a subsidiary prior to the merger. For example, if a steel company wanted to purchase an auto firm, that deal would normally be allowed because it would be a vertical arrangement—the acquisition of a manufacturer, in this case the auto firm, by a supplier, the steel company. However, if that auto firm

(WILLIAM BAXTER)

also owned a big steel-making operation, the acquisition would take on horizontal aspects, and that steel operation would probably have to be sold before the acquisition would be allowed.

Interview/
U.S. News & World Report, 8-3:51.

Bob Bergland
Former Secretary of Agriculture
of the United States

1

[On an Agriculture Department report citing the increase in big farms and the decrease in smaller, family-owned farms]: It may be the thing to do. Maybe the public would be best-served by continuing with the trends we have. We subsidize large-scale farming and we do it in many ways. Mostly it's hidden. It's found in tax policy, research policy, commodity price-support policy, in the credit field, and a whole host of others. We support these very large farms, but we hide it. What we're saying is that maybe the public will be best-served by having a trend in this direction, that maybe 300,000 to 400,000 farms could produce everything we need and want in the United States and still be competitive in the world. I'm not saying that ought to be stopped. I'm saying that that's where we are headed. We're getting there because our policies contribute to that end. And if we want to preserve the family farm as an institution—and there are reasons for doing so that go far beyond simply some old-fashioned, romantic attachment—then we'll have to consider what this report provides.

Interview/
Chicago Tribune, 1-22:(4)2.

John R. Block
Secretary of Agriculture
of the United States

2

If you don't put priority Number 1 on agriculture and provide a climate for health and prosperity in the farming end of agriculture,

nothing else can build upon that effectively. That's where it all starts. We have all kinds of programs that relate to the farming industry all the way out to the food programs that are feeding people, people who need food. But it all starts on the farm, even the school lunch . . . It all starts back on a farm, and so that's where we have to have prosperity and strength.

Interview, Chicago/
The Christian Science Monitor, 3-17:8.

3

The new [Reagan Administration] farm bill will virtually eliminate farm subsidies. Farmers will be living with the free-market system. There will be no artificial supports that would force the price higher than what the market dictates. Take the dairy program. The existing program supports dairy prices at 80 per cent of parity—a figure that's designed to give farmers prices for their commodities in line with prices they must pay for production and living expenses. That's too generous. It is costing taxpayers $2-billion a year to buy up surplus dairy products resulting from this program . . . The Administration also wants to eliminate target prices for feed grains, wheat, rice and cotton. Under the existing program, the Treasury makes direct payments to farmers if the market price falls short of the target prices. We don't think the government should make direct payments to farmers to support prices.

Interview/
U.S. News & World Report, 8-17:46.

Frank Borman
Chairman, Eastern Air Lines

4

[On the Reagan Administration]: A basic difference in this Administration is that business is not viewed as an adversary from the instant we walk in the door. That is very refreshing. The people now in government recognize that cooperation is required. That doesn't mean that they are going to do anything that is not in the country's best interest; but they do realize that in some areas it is in the country's best interest to

(FRANK BORMAN)

go forward with programs that are beneficial to business. That view was lacking in the past.

Interview/
U.S. News & World Report, 11-2:78.

Bill Brock
Special Trade Representative for the
President of the United States

1

I do think that there are times, when a major domestic industry is in serious trouble, that you have the right to seek from your trading partners around the world some understanding of that problem, and some restraint on their part. [But] I think it would be very difficult to support legislated quotas [on imported products] when, sometimes, you can get a much more rational agreement through negotiations.

To reporters, Bal Harbour, Fla./
The Washington Post, 2-18:(D)8.

Arthur Burck
Business consultant

2

Some [corporate] mergers are necessary. Every firm must change ownership sooner or later. There are many reasons why a business should be sold. To name a few: death of the owner or founder, technological obsolescence of the firm's product, changing markets, need for greater economics of scale and the inability to obtain sufficient investment capital. Generally speaking, it is only the smaller companies that really need to be sold or merged. The real test of a merger's necessity should be need, not greed.

Interview/
U.S. News & World Report, 12-21:64.

Fletcher L. Byrom
Chairman, Koppers Company

3

We [in the U.S.] are devoting a smaller share of gross national product to capital investment, savings, research and development than our competitors. We are losing markets to foreign competitors. A crisis is coming unless the trend line is changed. To presume that this nation can proceed to be a competitive contributor to the well-being of world society without any understanding of what it is trying to do is sheer nonsense . . . Right now, antitrust policy, a consumption-oriented fiscal policy and the presumption that you can distribute wealth before you have created it are liquidating the capital base of the United States economy. What we need are actions that encourage capital formation, for without such actions there is no hope of turning around this country's habit of spending and consuming into a habit of productive growth and saving.

Interview/
The New York Times, 10-11:(12)5.

A. W. Clausen
President, Bank of America;
President-designate, International Bank for
Reconstruction and Development (World Bank)

4

[On those who say he has run Bank of America in a dictatorial manner]: I can say I'm the nicest guy in the world, but if the perception is something different, well, the world runs on perceptions. A chief executive officer has to discover what is effective—how he can make people listen, how he can be persuasive, how he can lead and motivate. If a CEO can't, then he's not very good—he'll be eaten up by the troops.

Interview, San Francisco/
San Francisco Examiner & Chronicle, 4-19:(D)1.

John Danforth
United States Senator, R—Missouri

5

The Reagan Administration, in my view, has demonstrated a singular lack of interest in the enforcement of antitrust laws. This, in my opinion, is a mistake. Free and open competition is at the heart of Republican philosophy, and diligent enforcement of the antitrust laws

(JOHN DANFORTH)

is important to the maintenance of a competitive marketplace.

At Senate Commerce Committee hearing on the confirmation of James Miller to chair the FTC, Washington, July 31/ The Washington Post, 8-1:(D)7.

Amitai Etzioni
Director, Center for Policy Research, George Washington University

1

[Saying the government should not bail out financially ailing Chrysler Corporation]: . . . I personally own a $20,000 Chrysler bond which comes due in five months, [but] I still think the government should sink Chrysler. And so not only the country would be out of pocket, but I personally would make my contribution. If you're going to cleanse America of inefficiencies and obsolete industries so we can put our resources to work in a true reindustrialization, then the symbol of it all is definitely letting Chrysler find its own fate without public funds. Reindustrialization doesn't mean going back to the same old stuff, but rather going back to the priorities of economic growth. As to the consequences, first of all I don't believe that all the Chrysler people will be unemployed. Chrysler is making tanks, so somebody is going to buy that plant and keep making tanks. So I don't think those people will be out of work.

Interview/Chicago Tribune, 1-18:(5)3.

William Fellner
Former member, Council of Economic Advisers to the President of the United States (Richard M. Nixon)

2

[Arguing against a return to the gold standard]: I feel strongly that it cannot be done in the now-foreseeable future, because the price of gold will prove too unstable. That is another way of saying that in the present circumstances you can't have stability in the dollar price of gold and a stable general price level at the same time. If

you try to keep the price of gold stable, the general price level will change . . . An essential point to remember about the days when the gold standard worked is that it was not considered respectable for governments to change the gold price. It really happened very rarely . . . [Today you can] set the "right" gold price according to market preferences at the time. But from there on, it is apt to become too low. The demand for gold will grow as world population and living standards increase. International uncertainty will create demand, too. Demand will increase faster than the current gold output would increase the gold stock.

Interview/ U.S. News & World Report, 9-7:72.

John Kenneth Galbraith
Professor emeritus of economics, Harvard University

3

. . . I don't join the crusade against multinational corporations. There is some reason to worry about the conglomerates because they add another layer of business. But I've never been persuaded of the usefulness of legislation to stop it. My friend [industrialist] Norton Simon says we need this system [of large companies buying small ones] to rescue businesses from incompetent management and revive failing corporations . . . So while I'm not sure the trend is always beneficial, I'm unsure about what should be done about it. I don't approve legislation to stop it. I see big business as inevitable. Organizations can lack competence, as was the case with Chrysler, but they can be very competent, such as AT&T and IBM.

Interview, San Francisco/ San Francisco Examiner & Chronicle, 5-17:(Review)5.

Clifton C. Garvin, Jr.
Chairman, Exxon Corporation

4

[On the current rash of corporate mergers]: I am not opposed to it. If you believe in our economic system, you are not opposed to mergers

WHAT THEY SAID IN 1981

(CLIFTON C. GARVIN, JR.)

and acquisitions. The history of our economic growth has been based on those kinds of things. A free economy, for obvious benefits, permits those kinds of things to go through. And there are antitrust rules that are subject to a certain amount of interpretation by government officials. That's what they get paid for, and they'll do it.

Interview / The Wall Street Journal, 7-27:21.

George Gilder
Program director, International Center for Economic Policy Studies, New York

1

If progress is to occur in a capitalist system, new industries must rise to displace the old ones. But the political order will almost inevitably support the old capital formations rather than the companies of the future, because the future has yet to manifest itself and, hence, has no voice. So when government grows, it tends to reinforce the power of the established economic configuration. The crucial conflict in every economy is between the established companies and the new ones.

*Interview /
U.S. News & World Report, 4-6:53.*

Barry M. Goldwater
United States Senator, R—Arizona

2

Business has become more a system of conglomerates that will make anything, any item and any different variety of items, with the sole idea being to make some money. Nobody has pride in what they're doing; they just want to show a little profit. Now, there's nothing wrong with making money. But I think there's something to be said for a manufacturer learning how to make what he started out to make and doing it well.

*Interview, Washington /
The Wall Street Journal,
8-3:12.*

Alan Greenspan
Former Chairman, Council of Economic Advisers to the President of the United States (Gerald R. Ford)

3

[On President-elect Reagan's incoming Administration]: It would be better to describe them as pro-free enterprise than as pro-business. If you're asking, "Will this Administration seek to improve the over-all business climate and business incentives," the answer is emphatically yes. If you're saying, "This is an Administration that will cater to special business interests with subsidies and direct government assistance," generally I would say no.

*Interview /
The New York Times, 1-11:(12)16.*

Jerry Harvey
Professor of management science, George Washington University

4

Business education reflects exactly what people in the business world want. We've designed organizations that reward people who think very narrowly and behave very narrowly. Why aren't management textbooks funny? It's because they don't have much realism to them. If they had much realism to them, they'd be funny as hell.

Time, 5-4:58.

Geoffrey C. Hazard
Professor of law and dean, School of Organization and Management, Yale University

5

Every [company] CEO I've ever talked to, once pushed into a corner with two martinis, will tell you that though the myth is that he stands with the reins of power in his hands, his big question is not "How shall I drive this marvelous chariot?" but "How the hell can I get these goddam horses to move their asses at all?"

Time, 5-4:61.

Walter W. Heller
Professor of economics, University of Minnesota;
Former Chairman, Council of Economic
Advisers to the President of the United States
(John F. Kennedy)

1

[On Reagan Administration plans to lessen government regulations on business]: There's a lot of evidence in the polls that the American people don't want their rivers and air polluted, that they want protection from deceptive marketing practices and packaging, and fraud. In the rush to give away the store, we may not be considering the costs and risks. We have to be sure that not all of life is economic life. It's a question of gross national welfare as well as gross national product.

Interview/Chicago Tribune, 7-19:(5)1.

Frederick G. Jaicks
Chairman, Inland Steel Corporation

2

Perhaps in some ideal world we'll create a society where every one of us will have an opportunity to get the best possible education and training before we enter the job market. Today that isn't the case. Given that reality, we need an economic system that doesn't automatically relegate the unskilled to menial positions, but instead gives them opportunities to earn a good living while learning valuable skills. A basic industry such as steel does just that. And I suggest that when critics talk about the declining importance of industries such as steel in this nation's economic system, they're overlooking that role so crucial to the economic well-being and development of Americans.

Upon accepting Humanitarian Service Award of
Abraham Lincoln Center/
Chicago Tribune, 2-26:(4)10.

Reginald H. Jones
Chairman, General Electric Company

3

More and more, strategic planning is no longer just a buzz phrase or paperwork exercise. At GE, we entered the 1970s getting 80 per cent of

our earnings from electrical equipment. By 1979, that was down to 47 per cent. If you take this longer-term strategic approach, it will get you more capital investment, increased productivity and take you out of dying industries and into ones that are growing.

Interview/The New York Times, 1-27:26.

4

I think the top business schools do a good job. But they could do better at teaching communication skills. And if the schools could concentrate on a little instruction in humility it would be helpful. You just don't come fresh out of business school ready to run a large corporation.

Interview/The New York Times, 1-27:26.

Jerry Jordan
Dean, Robert O. Anderson School of
Management, University of New Mexico

5

"Think-tanks" probably don't have a great track record about the future, but they have a pretty good record at identifying the range of probable future events. The business community has a tendency to start with the present and think in terms of changes from there out, rather than get its minds in the future and think backwards. [A think-tank] can contemplate draining the swamps instead of having to hit the alligators over the head. There's some merit in not having to think about this quarter's earnings.

The New York Times, 1-11:(3)4.

Donald P. Kelly
President, Esmark, Inc.

6

Our role in business is to profitably grow business, and that provides jobs. When we in the private sector create jobs, I think we're contributing something to the social good of the country ... If we don't produce jobs and we don't reduce inflation, then we've failed. Any time that we have over-all profits in business that afford business an opportunity to grow and to invest in

(DONALD P. KELLY)

business, it helps everybody—or else the free-enterprise system is worthless and we've got to junk it.

Interview/Chicago Tribune, 7-19:(5)1.

William Kieschnick
President, Atlantic Richfield Company

1

We've always felt we had an obligation to not only bring home the bacon to our stockholders, and to do that aggressively as well, but also to be a good national citizen. We'll continue to behave with that sense. First of all, it's the right thing to do. After all, we ought to be a part of the solution, not the problem. And secondly, we live in a country that from time to time has challenged the validity and usefulness of large companies, and I think we have to demonstrate to them that we're valuable institutions, not only to generate jobs and pay taxes but also to be good corporate citizens.

Interview, Los Angeles/
Chicago Tribune, 2-18:(4)10.

Kiyoaki Kikuchi
Deputy Foreign Minister of Japan

2

My theory is that Communism and agriculture will never go together. Farmers have felt since time immemorial that they owned the land. The Communist penchant for collectivizing agriculture will always produce failure.

Newsweek, 10-26:39.

Lane Kirkland
President, American Federation of Labor-Congress of Industrial Organizations

3

[Urging cuts on exports of U.S. technology and restrictions on imports]: The United States must continue to be a diversified nation with a broad and firm industrial base. It cannot stake its future on the successes or failures of a handful of industries, nor can it continue its slide into an economy that provides only services, while other nations provide the manufactured goods. [The AFL-CIO believes] the United States must continue to share its markets, [but] that international trade must be fair trade—fair to all nations ... America needs an economy that works in the real world, not one that satisfies textbook theorems that are not practiced in day-to-day business. The countries that are out-performing the United States economically have most certainly not relied on so-called free-market *laissez-faire* policies.

At Japan Institute of Labor, Tokyo, Jan. 27/
Los Angeles Times, 1-28:(IV)2.

Otto Lambsdorff
Minister of Economics of West Germany

4

[On automobile companies which say they need protectionism or other government favors]: [To these companies I say,] "I'm sorry. When I look back at the beginning of each year, typically, you gave a pay increase, and two weeks later you had a price increase. That game is over—there's competition in the market from the Japanese and others—and you should ask yourselves, 'Why are they successful?' And I do not play the game of being the Economics Minister, taking care of the economy, and losing sight of the consumer. So what you have to do in my view," I tell them, "is go ahead, do capital spending, develop better techniques, build better cars, do more innovation—and do it yourself. Government subsidies are out of the question. For if we start government subsidies in the auto sector, where do we end?"

Interview, Washington/
The Washington Post, 3-26:(A)17.

Tom Lantos
United States Representative, D—California

5

[On the attempts by Mobil Oil and U.S. Steel to take over Marathon Oil]: This is one of those dramas where we have only villains. We have the villain of Mobil, taking those tremendous profits and not using them to find one new barrel of oil

(TOM LANTOS)

. . . We have Marathon fighting righteously but offering its voluptuous sizes and shapes and attractions to Texaco. We have U.S. Steel not modernizing but using its resources to buy up Marathon and, again, not adding one barrel of oil to our energy independence.

The Washington Post, 11-20:(A)9.

Lewis E. Lehrman
President, Lehrman Institute;
Member, United States Gold Commission

1

[Advocating a return to the gold standard]: A gold standard would . . . encourage one of the greatest economic booms ever. Under the managed paper currency of today, nobody saves any more. People stop saving because the future purchasing power of the currency is in doubt. What the gold standard does is give working people confidence in the future purchasing power of their saved wages. I would predict that true savings committed to productive investments would double within one year after the establishment of a gold standard. Therefore, businesses would have an enormous pool of savings from which to draw capital to invest in new plants and new equipment. This investment would create a huge demand for labor, end unemployment and lead to the creation of new wealth and economic opportunity for the poor.

Interview/
U.S. News & World Report, 9-7:71.

Abbott B. Lipsky, Jr.
Deputy Assistant Attorney General,
Antitrust Division, Department of
Justice of the United States

2

[On criticism that the Reagan Administration is too lenient in enforcing antitrust laws]: Our own view is that the changes likely to occur will differ only incrementally—not radically—from the policies of our predecessors. My purpose is to remind you that despite the arguments—over merger policy, for example—there remains

agreement that the most fundamental purpose of the antitrust laws—the prevention of private cartel activity—is still endorsed without reservation by this Administration, and that this purpose is still strongly supported from nearly every point of the political compass.

Washington, July 31/
The Washington Post, 8-1:(D)7.

Jean Mayer
President, Tufts University; Nutritionist

3

. . . the public [must understand] better how the 3 per cent of our population on farms is living. We are reaching a danger level in the number of people practicing our major industry . . . The income of our farmers has to be sustained and we have to have more farmers than we need at the minimum. We have to give more glamour to agriculture because we are now bucking 2,000 years of depreciation of agriculture.

Before House Agriculture Committee,
Washington, July/The Washington Post, 8-17:(A)3.

F. James McDonald
President, General Motors Corporation

4

I don't believe that advertising ever gets you a quality reputation. If you don't have it, advertising won't help you a bit. And if you do have it, word of mouth is enough.

Interview, Los Angeles/
Los Angeles Times, 2-10:(IV)3.

John F. McGillicuddy
Chairman,
Manufacturers Hanover Corporation

5

[President-elect] Reagan must take steps to improve capital formation in this country. Unless the U.S. does something to restore savings as a viable concept, we're going to lose the cornerstone on which financial markets are built and which has been one of the great strengths in U.S. development.

Interview/U.S. News & World Report, 1-12:52.

WHAT THEY SAID IN 1981

Marvin Meek
National chairman,
American Agriculture Movement

1

[Criticizing the Reagan Administration's plan to cut Federal farm loans]: A lot of people think we are over-reacting, but if they stick to these budget cuts, we are going to lose from 20 to 30 per cent of our producers. On the heels of one of the worst droughts in history, they simply can't cut the operating and ownership loans.

The Washington Post, 3-26:(A)6.

Arjay Miller
Dean emeritus, Graduate School of
Business, Stanford University;
Former president, Ford Motor Company

2

I don't think anyone over 70 should be a chief executive of a large corporation. It's hard for anyone to know when he starts slipping. Corporations recognize that the pressures on a chief executive have increased dramatically. There's a global pressure that just wasn't there before. The travel can be exhausting, and technology changes very quickly. Executives burn out more, so it's appropriate to lower the mandatory retirement age for the boss. Ex-chiefs, however, do make good directors. It also helps the morale of a corporation to have turnover at the top; there are a lot of young bucks waiting to be chief.

Interview/The New York Times, 2-8:(3)4.

Akio Morita
Chairman, Sony Corporation (Japan)

3

[Comparing companies in Japan and the United States]: In Japan we don't pay a bonus to the management, we pay the bonus to employees. At Sony, I say management should not worry about year-by-year profit. Maybe every three years I review management wages . . . In this country [the U.S.], I think the problem exists on the management side. The manager feels he is the one who runs the company, therefore he is the man who makes a profit. But that is not true. Profit is generated through the cooperation of all the people [in the company]. Why should only the top management take all the money? I think such a system is a big mistake in this country. My concept is that a company is a fate-sharing body, so to make a good business we have to work together. If we face a recession, we should not lay off employees; the company should sacrifice a profit. It's management's risk and management's responsibility. Employees are not guilty; why should they suffer?

Interview, Washington/
The Washington Post, 4-12:(G)1.

Willard Mueller
Professor of economics,
University of Wisconsin, Madison

4

Large companies are not innovative. Hugeness destroys initiative.

Time, 8-3:45.

Roger Nightingale
Chief economist, Hoare Govett Ltd.,
London brokerage house

5

If I were advising [U.S. President] Reagan, I'd push very hard to get fair treatment for U.S. agricultural products in world markets. The Americans have been incredibly generous: You let the rest of the world sell their manufactures freely in the U.S. market even though you aren't very competitive against them. Yet in an area where the U.S. does have a massive advantage, agriculture, you let the Europeans and Japanese close their doors to you. If you have more external markets for U.S. food, you could produce more and keep prices up—and you'd earn foreign exchange to buy capital equipment and increase productivity. It would be a windfall gain of sorts.

Interview, London/Forbes, 2-16:46.

Julius K. Nyerere
President of Tanzania

6

The price at which cotton is bought and sold in the world is determined by the workings of the international free market. Countries in the south

34

(JULIUS K. NYERERE)

learn what the prices will be by listening to reports from Britain, U.S.A. and Europe. The cost of producing that cotton is completely irrelevant; so is the cost of living of the worker or peasant in the cotton fields. On the other hand, the prices of lorries [trucks], tractors, railway wagons, fertilizers, et cetera, are all determined by the producers, the transnational corporations and other firms. The result is that poor countries almost always buy dear and sell cheap.

At Commonwealth Conference,
Melbourne, Australia, Oct. 2/
The New York Times, 10-3:6.

Edward I. O'Brien
President,
Securities Industry Association

1

The sharp increase of foreign participation in United States markets reflects significant growth in confidence, not only in the securities markets, but in United States economic prospects generally. We think that this is based on overseas perception of the change in American public policy toward a more pro-investment posture.

The New York Times, 3-17:35.

David Ogilvy
Former chairman,
Ogilvy & Mather, Inc., advertising

2

There's a big difference between American and European ads. In America a commercial may be crass but it's been tested, whereas here [in France] there's very little testing. French advertising is much more sophisticated because it's not researched.

Interview, Bonnes, France/
The New York Times, 8-23:(1)22.

Ronald Reagan
President of the United States

3

Today, this once-great industrial giant of ours has the lowest rate of growth in productivity of

virtually all the industrial nations with whom we must compete in the world market. We can't even hold our own market here in America against foreign automobiles, steel and a number of other products. Japanese production of automobiles is almost twice as great per worker as it is in America. Japanese steelworkers out-produce their American counterparts by about 25 per cent. This isn't because they are better workers. I'll match the American working-man or woman against anyone in the world. But we have to give them the modern tools and equipment that workers in the other industrial nations have. We invented the assembly line and mass production, but punitive tax policies and excessive and unnecessary regulations plus government borrowing have stifled our ability to update plant and equipment. When capital investment is made it is too often for some unproductive alterations demanded by government to meet various of its regulations.

Broadcast address to the nation, Washington, Feb. 5/
The New York Times, 2-6:8.

4

The result [of over-regulation of business by government] has been higher prices, higher unemployment and lower productivity growth. Over-regulation causes small and independent businessmen and women, as well as large businesses, to defer or terminate plans for expansion, and, since they are responsible for most of our jobs, those new jobs aren't created. We have no intention of dismantling the regulatory agencies —especially those necessary to protect the environment and to assure the public health and safety. However, we must come to grips with inefficient and burdensome regulations—eliminate those we can and reform those we must keep.

Before joint session of Congress,
Washington, Feb. 18/The New York Times, 2-19:14.

5

There are a number of [Federal] subsidies to business and industry I believe are unnecessary.

WHAT THEY SAID IN 1981

(RONALD REAGAN)

Not because the activities being subsidized aren't of value, but because the marketplace contains incentives enough to warrant continuing these activities without a government subsidy.

Before joint session of Congress,
Washington, Feb. 18/
The New York Times, 2-19:14.

Donald T. Regan
Secretary of the Treasury
of the United States

1

We do not look with favor on government's rescuing companies that have gotten into trouble as a result of mismanagement or as a result of true market forces—unless, of course, it's a public-utility type of business, the sole supplier of service, and therefore has to be supported, or if it has a major defense role that must be preserved. The fact that over 200 automobile companies went out of business at one time or another without government intervention doesn't seem to strike anybody as odd. Yet the Chrysler Corporation, for some reason, seems to be unique [in that many people are calling for government to support the financially-ailing Chrysler]. I don't follow that logic. Nonetheless, when our Administration came in, the Congress had already approved a financial-aid package for Chrysler, and we had to uphold the law. But I don't think that in the future we would be persuaded too quickly that a large rescue operation ought to be mounted.

Interview/U.S. News & World Report, 3-9:27.

2

We, the Federal government, cannot produce much on our own, and much of what we produce is useless anyway. Business is what produces, and business has to take over. That's going to be the biggest challenge to American business since World War II: how to carry out this [economic] program once you're free of the fetters that you've been decrying for so many years. Business has been saying, "Turn me loose, let me do it." All right, we're going to turn you loose in six months. Are you ready for it? Can you stand the shock of competition? Are you sure your clients understand what they're going to be asked to do? You'd better start telling them about it, because if they fail, we fail. We cannot do this job on our own. We can get the bills through Congress, we can get the President to sign them. But then business has to take over, and it's American business that's going to make our program succeed or fail.

At Chamber of Commerce of the United States,
Washington, March/Nation's Business, April:52.

3

[Charging that business has failed to tangibly back President Reagan's economic program]: We have carried through on our commitments . . . but where is the business response? Where are the new research and development initiatives? Where are the new plants? Where are the expansion plans? It's like dropping a coin down a well—all I'm hearing is a hollow clink.

Before Economic Club of Indianapolis, Sept. 14/
The Washington Post, 9-15:(C)14.

Norman Robertson
Senior vice president and chief economist,
Mellon Bank, Pittsburgh

4

[On the recent strong demand for business loans and the wildly fluctuating prime rates]: As one who has learned from terribly bitter experience over the last year, my advice is don't get carried away by one week's number—or even one month's number. They are all subject to massive revisions at a later date. It's all part of this bloody mess we economists find ourselves in trying to monitor the Fed.

The Wall Street Journal, 1-5:2.

David Rockefeller
Chairman, Chase Manhattan Bank

5

It will come as a surprise to some of you, but annual meetings aren't the favorite task of most

(DAVID ROCKEFELLER)

corporate chairmen. Indeed, some of my colleagues have assured me that the greatest benefit of retiring is never having to face another.

At his final annual meeting before retiring as chairman, New York/ The Wall Street Journal, 4-22:4.

David Rockefeller
Former chairman, Chase Manhattan Bank

1

The chief executive's ability to influence the corporation is by no means absolute. Fifty years ago, many chief executives were very dominant figures who could do just about anything. That really has changed. No chief executive today can very long take measures that go contrary to strong views within the organization or the wishes of the board of directors. He might get away with it for a bit, but sooner or later it would catch up with him, and he would find himself out of a job. Having said all that, an active and effective executive can guide the direction in which a corporation is headed and can probably have an impact on the pace at which steps are taken to achieve the goals that he helps to establish. In the end, he has to make the last decision and accept the responsibility for the results—good or bad.

Interview/U.S. News & World Report, 6-15:38.

John S. R. Shad
Chairman, Securities and Exchange Commission of the United States

2

Broad stock ownership, like home ownership, is very important [to an economy]. It brings economic and political stability. Capital flees areas of economic and political instability. Also, greater equity investment is essential to improve our rates of growth and productivity and the standard of living of all Americans. About 28 million individuals now own stocks directly, and many more own stocks and bonds indirectly through their banks, insurance policies, pension and mutual funds. The mass of Americans have a real stake in the nation's future.

Interview/U.S. News & World Report, 9-14:81.

3

[On the existence of "insider" activity in the stock market]: It's definitely a major problem and it requires a major assault by the SEC, the Bar and the industry—and that's what I'm trying to support. But to suggest that the billions of dollars of securities that change hands daily in America are on insider trading is irrational—it's only a tiny fraction of 1 per cent of the volume of trading. I think it's wrong to suggest that the public is playing a game for which the dice is loaded against them. To say that insider trading is the rule rather than the exception, that it's a common act, is just not true.

To reporters/The New York Times, 10-26:23.

Irving S. Shapiro
Former chairman,
E.I. du Pont de Nemours & Co.

4

Credibility is the Number 1 ingredient in successfully running a major corporation. Any chief executive officer has a whole series of consistency groups—employees, stockholders, the community, the press, fellow businessmen. With each of those groups, you have to have a credibility that means that your views will be given serious consideration. There is no way you can lead a large organization unless your people have independently come to a judgment that you're trustworthy, have a good sense of values and don't hand them a lot of baloney.

Interview/U.S. News & World Report, 6-15:39.

Gil Slonim
President,
Oceanic Education Foundation

5

The fourfold increase in Soviet merchant ships in 17 years results from national policies that create shipbuilding capabilities, strong maritime markets, a pool of trained seamen, and ships. A peacetime merchant marine can keep sea lanes open, crews updated in technological improvements, and ensure an immediate backup for military purposes.

The Christian Science Monitor, 10-20:8.

WHAT THEY SAID IN 1981

William French Smith
Attorney General of the United States

1

We must recognize that bigness in business does not necessarily mean badness, and that success should not be automatically suspect. Some have argued that competition is synonymous with a large number of competitors. Economic reality, however, is more complex. In some industries, competition yields a large number of competitors—in others, only a few—depending upon the economics of scale, distribution costs and other factors . . . In an economy based on unfettered competition as the rule of trade, efficient firms should not be hobbled under the guise of antitrust enforcement.

Before District of Columbia Bar Association,
Washington, June 24/
Los Angeles Herald Examiner, 6-25:(A)1.

2

It is true that there are a host of [corporate] mergers going on right now, but mergers have a way of coming in surges, and nobody knows why that is the case. A company may be cash-rich, it may be searching for a bargain, finds one, or it may be in a condition such as the oil industry is, where there are shortages of oil-drilling rigs and therefore they look in other directions to invest. It may be a mature industry, such as the tobacco industry, where there's no future in investing in that industry, so they look elsewhere—all kinds of reasons why mergers take place. As far as any effect that may have on our [antitrust] enforcement policy—let me make this very clear, and that is that in those areas which go to the heart of antitrust activity, namely, price-fixing or market division or bid-rigging, this Administration is going to be very, very vigorous in enforcing the law in those areas. By vigorous, I mean we're going after criminal sanctions, not civil: we're going after prison sentences, not fines. In that area, which we think is where damage can occur to our free competitive-enterprise system, we are going to be very vigorous.

Broadcast interview/"Meet the Press," NBC-TV, 8-2.

Albert T. Sommers
Chief economist, The Conference Board

3

The question of government and free enterprise is one of our cardinal weaknesses. Our tradition of free enterprise is very limiting. In the past it has paid off in entrepreneurial vigor. But if we're moving into a deliberate industrialization policy, it will require capital investment induced and supported by government, with much more collaborative relations between government and business.

U.S. News & World Report, 3-9:60.

Zenko Suzuki
Prime Minister of Japan

4

Protectionism [in trade] would, in the final analysis, be nothing short of a suicidal act. Its only outcome would be the loss of vitality and the stagnation of the free economic system of the West. The combined economic capacity of Japan, the United States and Western Europe at present amounts to more than half that of the entire globe. If that were to collapse, the human race would be plunged into dire distress.

Before Royal Institute of International Affairs,
London, June 17/Los Angeles Times, 6-18:(IV)2.

Barbara S. Thomas
Commissioner, Securities and
Exchange Commission of the United States

5

In my judgment, our responsibility is not to prevent investors from high-risk investments. Our responsibility is to ensure that all of the risks are adequately disclosed. However, I am quite concerned that an overly detailed disclosure document, although completely fair and accurate, can, in fact, obscure effective disclosure . . . I believe we should risk an experiment with a requirement that two separate documents be distributed to investors. One would consist of the traditional disclosure material, pared down as much as possible. The second would be a short-form prospectus in large type and in as few words as possible. The

COMMERCE / INDUSTRY / FINANCE

(BARBARA S. THOMAS)

short form would provide only the most relevant information and a broad warning about the risks of the venture.

News conference, Los Angeles, July 7/
Los Angeles Herald Examiner, 7-8:(A)9.

David A. Thomas
Dean, School of Business,
Cornell University

1

I find that [business] students spend too much time worrying about their rank in class and their marks. If they are not in the top 10 per cent they get complexes. I say: "Look, I have been here over 25 years. When I hear that one of our graduates has been made a chairman or a president of a company, I look up the records. They frequently were average students but had other things—personality, courage, the ability to handle people, and the ability to withstand uncertainty. I think that is Number 1—the ability to handle uncertainty."

The New York Times, 8-26:39.

Maurice Valente
Former president, RCA Corporation

2

[On the increasing number of top executives fired by major companies]: There's been a rash of these things. I think that when one happens, or two, those responsible for making the decision feel very hesitant to do so. But then there're three, then four and five, and suddenly everyone finds great strength in being one of several who had to fire somebody . . . I don't think there's been a time in American management history when that many have happened so quickly.

Interview/The New York Times Magazine, 3-8:24.

Jay Van Andel
Chairman, Amway Corporation

3

To some degree, large companies are not as flexible as small companies. They suffer

more from erroneous decisions. They can't quickly decide to change their own direction if they make the wrong product, for instance. A small company can probably get out of that decision. A big company has got such long commitments that it would be years before they get out.

Interview/The Christian Science Monitor, 2-19:11.

Karl H. Vesper
Professor of business administration,
University of Washington

4

There are six critical things you've got to have before you can get a company going. You need a concept of the enterprise in terms of the product or service you're going to deliver. You must have technical knowhow in the business you're getting into; at least, *somebody* in the company must have it. You have to have physical resources. Frequently you attain them with money, but sometimes you don't; for example, they might already be in your basement shop. That's why I don't say "capital." You have to have contacts. That is totally neglected in the business literature. Everybody knows you have to have bankers, lawyers and accountants. But not only those. If you want to be successful, you can't operate in a vacuum. You have to have other people to put pieces into it. It's important for the would-be entrepreneurs to know that. Many of them want their own businesses because they hate everybody and want to be alone. They want to be successful hermits, and you can't do that. Then, next, you have to have customer orders. As obvious as that is, students don't think of it when I ask what things you need. Those five characteristics are in my book. The sixth was pointed out to me by a student. And it should have been so obvious because it has thwarted me personally. And that is *time*.

Interview/Forbes, 3-2:100.

Paul A. Volcker
Chairman, Federal Reserve Board

5

[On government banking regulations]: Banks, of course, must be free to take risks—and to fail.

WHAT THEY SAID IN 1981

(PAUL A. VOLCKER)

Through the years we have developed an elaborate official "safety net" designed to prevent the transmission of failure through the system. That "safety net" has served us well, but we should be alert to the other side of the coin. To the extent the "safety net" comes to be viewed as a substitute for discipline and prudence of the individual banker, we will end up with a fragile and vulnerable banking system.

Before American Bankers Association,
San Francisco, Oct. 7/Chicago Tribune, 10-8:(4)1.

Ross Webber
Professor of management, Wharton School,
University of Pennsylvania

1

[Saying older chief executives should not be automatically retired]: I think we exaggerate the flexibility and freshness of young people. Advanced age can be conducive to conceptual skills that are extraordinarily important. Experience obviously helps, except when it causes us to see new events as mere repetitions of the past.

Interview/The New York Times, 2-8:(3)4.

Murray L. Weidenbaum
Chairman-designate, Council of
Economic Advisers to the
President of the United States

2

Free trade can't be a one-way street. However much as I oppose protectionist measures, I have to call attention to the very real barriers erected by other countries against the U.S. I don't think we can blithely follow a position of free trade without encouraging our trading partners to do the same.

At Senate Banking Committee hearing
on his confirmation, Washington/
The Wall Street Journal, 2-6:3.

Murray L. Weidenbaum
Chairman, Council of Economic Advisers
to the President of the United States

3

[Opposing special Federal aid for ailing industries]: The best thing we can do for the auto industry, the steel industry and other industries presently suffering financial difficulties, is to restore a vigorous and less-inflationary rate of growth in the American economy. We mustn't make the mistake of taking steps for particular segments of the economy which could jeopardize the economic well-being of the entire country.

At Woodrow Wilson International Center,
Washington/The Wall Street Journal, 3-13:31.

4

[On imports that hurt domestic U.S. industries]: We should recognize that any form of trade restraint to help a specific industry really is an internal transfer of income and wealth to that industry from U.S. consumers, and from American workers and owners of our export industries. The emphasis in trade-adjustment policies should be just that, adjustment, not preservation of an uncompetitive industrial structure.

Before Senate Finance subcommittee, Washington/
The Washington Post, 11-29:(F)6.

Howard L. Weisberg
Director of international trade policy,
Chamber of Commerce of the United States

5

[U.S.] law provides criminal penalties for business conduct which is often common practice and sometimes necessary in order to do business in certain foreign markets.

The New York Times, 2-8:(12)20.

Harold M. Williams
Chairman, Securities and Exchange
Commission of the United States

6

[Saying business is being increasingly taken over by institutional stockholders as opposed to traditional individual investors and are thus becoming more interested in short-term gains and lack much accountability]: The corporate system has become structured so that, in many instances, important participants in it may have an interest in milking American business, or, at least, an insufficient interest not to . . . It has

(HAROLD M. WILLIAMS)

become rare to find a major public corporation controlled, in the absolute sense, by anyone.

Before Securities Regulation Institute,
Coronado, Calif. Jan. 22/
Los Angeles Times, 1-23:(IV)2.

1

[On government regulation of ethics in business]: As regulation expands, the room for individual ethical values shrinks proportionately. To be ethically sound, a person or institution must have the freedom to develop . . . internal mechanisms consistent with the expectations of society, and not merely be subject to externally imposed directions.

Chicago Tribune, 2-5:(1)18.

William S. Woodside
Chairman, American Can Company

2

It's not so much that the quality of U.S. products is dropping as it is that standards elsewhere [in the world] have been increasing more rapidly, due in great part to more-modern plants. I look at our country's aging industrial base, and I'm absolutely certain that it has something to do with product quality and the people's perception of quality. In addition, even though standards for many products are as good as ever, controversy over quality is the result of stricter government policies on recalling products and from the publicity that goes with recalls.

Interview/U.S. News & World Report, 5-11:83.

Lewis H. Young
Editor-in-chief, "Business Week" magazine

3

The short-term success in the 60s of the Jimmy Lings, the Saul Steinbergs, the Harry Figgies, the J. B. Fuquas and even the Harold Geneens promoted a radical change in executive training and behavior. With their noses buried in numbers, executives have become risk-aversive and short-run oriented. They are building corporate hierarchies and bureaucracies that are every bit as lethargic, obstructive and non-productive as those in government about which people complain so bitterly. This obsession has shown up in declining competitiveness in world markets, a lack of innovation in new products and shrinking R&D efforts.

To partners of Ward Howell International/
The Wall Street Journal, 5-6:22.

Crime . Law Enforcement

David L. Bazelon
Senior Judge, United States Court of Appeals for the District of Columbia

1

Accepting the full implications of what we know about street crime might require us to provide every family with the means to create the kind of home all human beings need. It might require us to afford the job opportunities that pose for some the only meaningful alternatives to violence. It would assure all children a constructive education, a decent place to live, and proper pre- and post-natal nutrition . . . A genuine commitment to attacking the roots of crime might force us to reconsider our entire social and economic structure. And, like the short-term approach, it might conflict with other deeply held values. Can we break the cycle at crime's roots without invading the social sphere of the ghetto? Would this require the state to impose its values on the young? Are we ready to substitute the state for the ghetto family? If we really want a lasting solution to crime, can we afford not to?

Before Western Society of Criminology, San Diego, Feb. 28/The Washington Post, 3-1:(A)2; The Wall Street Journal, 5-8:26.

Griffin B. Bell
Co-Chairman, Federal Task Force on Violent Crime; Former Attorney General of the United States

2

We long since have stopped being serious about violent crime. If we were serious, violent criminals would be charged, would not be admitted to bail, and would be tried quickly and incarcerated. We are going to have to build more prisons. We have listened to these prophets for so long who say that prisons are bad and we shouldn't put anyone in them because they don't reform people. Well, you put a criminal in prison to punish him. You don't put him there to rehabilitate him. You also lock him up to protect the rest of the public. We have a situation here where a quarter of a per cent of the population is terrorizing the rest of us. And that is a very bad thing.

Interview, Washington/Chicago Tribune, 3-29:(1)5.

Walter Berns
Resident scholar, American Enterprise Institute

3

At the sight of crime, law-abiding citizens feel —and ought to feel—a righteous anger. That kind of anger is absolutely essential for a decent, just society. Like love, and unlike greed, for example, anger is a passion that can reach out to other people. We'd all be lost if everyone reacted as people did in the case some years ago of a woman who was screaming because she was being mugged and murdered—no one even bothered to pick up the phone and call the police. Righteous anger should be satisfied by punishing the criminal. In this way, by rewarding it, you may promote law-abidingness, which is a general deterrent to all kinds of crime. And in the case of particularly heinous crimes, the anger is rightly so intense that only punishment by [the death penalty] will satisfy it.

Interview/U.S. News & World Report, 4-20:50.

Harold A. Breier
Chief of Police of Milwaukee

4

If we have to build more prisons, so be it. Some criticize prisons as bad because they don't reform. It seems to me that the purpose of a jail sentence is to punish a criminal and protect the public from him. If there is to be any rehabilitation, it can come after he has served his time.

Interview/The Christian Science Monitor, 4-2:7.

David R. Brink
President, American Bar Association

1

[Criticizing the Reagan Administration for its emphasis on preventive detention]: I think it's right that none of us is presumed guilty until we're tried and found guilty beyond a reasonable doubt. There should be a darned good reason before we lock a person up, and it ought to be based on current evidence [that the suspect is likely to intimidate witnesses], and not on the general feeling that what this person is accused of is terrible and therefore the person is dangerous and should not be released.

Interview, Nov. 16/Los Angeles Times, 11-17:(I)7.

Edmund G. Brown, Jr.
Governor of California (D)

2

[On gun control]: I was reading an article yesterday that it would take a transcontinental magnet to pick up all the guns that presently exist, as many as 100 million. So a proposal for some kind of unilateral disarmament on the part of the citizens would probably meet with utter frustration. So, in absence of a house-to-house search or the invention of a transcontinental magnet, I have not yet seen the proposal of how we get these guns out of people's hands. We've banned heroin; there still seems to be a lot of it around. The proposal is to register the guns. As a former [California] Secretary of State, I can tell you what a lot more paper will produce—it'll produce a lot more clerks. Whether it will reduce the number of people who commit crimes, I have my doubts.

Los Angeles/
Los Angeles Herald Examiner, 1-6:(A)1.

3

Certainly the anonymity and mobility in our society, coupled with the breakdown of certain values, has led to an increase in crime. You look at a place like Japan, with a much lower crime rate—we find a country where the neighborhood polices crime and where a stranger is relatively

rare. People can't just walk down the street without being noticed or identified. And the connection between the police and citizens is very close. We [in the U.S.] have a different kind of society and we'll have to take that into account.

News conference, San Francisco, April 7/
Los Angeles Times, 8-8:(I)23.

Warren E. Burger
Chief Justice of the United States

4

[The fight against crime] will call for spending more money than we have ever before devoted to law enforcement. [But this money] will be less costly than the billions in dollars and thousands of blighted lives now hostage to crime. It is as much a part of our national defense as the Pentagon budget . . . Over-all violent crime increased from 1979 to 1980, continuing a double-digit rate. More than one-quarter of all households in this country are victimized by some kind of criminal activity at least once a year . . . Our rate of casual, day-to-day terrorism in almost any large city exceeds the casualties of all the reported "international terrorists" in any given year. Why do we show such indignation over alien terrorists and such tolerance for the domestic variety? Are we not hostages within the borders of our own self-styled, enlightened, civilized country?

Before American Bar Association, Houston, Feb. 8/
Los Angeles Times, 2-9:(I)1,19.

5

[On preventive detention]: A startling amount of crime is committed by persons on release while awaiting trial. [There should be added to] all bail-release laws, state and Federal, the crucial element of future dangerousness, based on the evidence before the court and the past record of the accused, to deter crime-while-on-bail.

Before American Bar Association, Houston, Feb. 8/
The New York Times, 2-25:11.

WHAT THEY SAID IN 1981

(WARREN E. BURGER)

1

I have long believed—and I have frequently said—that when society places a person behind walls and bars it has a moral obligation to take some steps to try to render him or her better-equipped to return to a useful life as a member of society. Now, I say "try," and I use the term "moral" obligation, not legal, not Constitutional. The Constitution properly mandates due process and it mandates certain protective guarantees, but it mandates nothing concerning the subject of punishments except that they not be "cruel and unusual." To make these people good citizens is also for our own proper self-interest.

At George Washington University School of
Law commencement, May 24/
The Washington Post, 5-26:(A)19.

Kenneth B. Clark
Professor emeritus of psychology,
City College of New York

2

[Saying stiff punishment will not deter violent crime, and may in fact increase it]: [Violent crimes are committed by] individuals who have given up on any possibility of a quality of life that is positive. They operate on the assumption that they don't have a damn thing to lose. In some cases, they have a moment in the sun in the case of being caught. [Countering the surge in violent crime] is not as easy as severe punishment, building more jails, having tougher police who shoot first and ask questions later. All these things do is increase the adversary relationship between the underclass and [the rest of] society. In fact, we're perpetuating a kind of guerrilla warfare . . . What I'm advocating is that if you are really going to do something about crime, society will have to address itself to the roots of violence, to the roots of racially related crime. You will have to do something extremely difficult—namely, a total re-examination of some of the givens, assumptions and explanations of the society of which we are a part. I do not believe this is going to happen. I think we are going to

deal with the problem in a way that will intensify it . . . The middle class understandably wants to protect itself from the manifestations of desperation of the underclass.

Before House Criminal Justice Subcommittee,
Washington, March 4/Los Angeles Times, 3-5:(I)1,16.

Thomas Coughlin
Commissioner of Corrections of
New York City

3

Not that [prisons are] going to improve anybody . . . [But] what we have to do is to take the mass of people, the 9,000 people that we get every year, and we have to say, "Here are the range of options. If you don't speak English, we'll teach you English as a second language. If you don't have a fifth-grade education, we're going to try to give you a fifth-grade education. If you want to go to school, college, we'll provide a college program for you. If you want to learn a skill, we'll provide a skill for you." Now, that's what a prison system's supposed to do. You can't just lock them up 23 hours a day, because when you do that, prisons blow up . . .

The New York Times Magazine, 3-8:60.

Jeremiah Denton
United States Senator, R—Alabama

4

There is a new threat which is not recognized and remains essentially unaddressed, threatening the survival of freedom here and elsewhere. This new and most insidious threat is terrorism . . . If we continue to ignore the threat, the sand in which we bury our heads will eventually bury our nation.

San Francisco Examiner & Chronicle, 9-13:(A)16.

George Deukmejian
Attorney General of California

5

Criminals today believe that crime pays; that they can commit a crime, that the chances of getting caught are rather small, and that if they do get caught, the chances of not receiving very strong punishment are in their favor.

News conference, Sacramento, Feb. 11/
Los Angeles Times, 2-12:(II)4.

Steven Duke
Professor of criminal law, Yale University
1

[On preventive detention—the jailing of defendants considered dangerous if let out on bail]: It is unconstitutional, it is wrong and it is idiotic. [It is] fundamentally unfair to imprison a person on a prediction of dangerousness when he hasn't been adjudicated guilty of a crime . . . Any thoughtful person who proposes preventive detention must realize that what they are headed for is a system of punishment without conviction. [Such a system would] just put people in jail, and not bother with criminal procedure at all, just let the police and judge handle it. The implications are mind-boggling. If they can put away somebody that they suspect of being a rapist, they can put away somebody that they suspect of being a Communist, or a rabble-rouser, or a left-winger, or a right-winger.
The New York Times, 2-25:11.

John P. East
United States Senator, R—North Carolina
2

Under the 1976 guidelines, in order for the FBI to investigate an individual or an organization to determine potential for violence and terrorism, it must show that acts of violence have been committed or are about to be committed. So it's a Catch-22 situation, where it has to prove at the outset of the investigation the very thing the investigation is designed to prove. That unduly restricts the FBI and gives an enormous advantage to individuals who flirt with violence and terror. Elements of this kind don't play by the queen's rules. But we have the FBI in the position of merely being firemen, or merely reacting to crisis and not being able to prevent the crisis.
Interview/U.S. News & World Report, 11-16:33.

Don Edwards
United States Representative, D—California
3

[Arguing against the easing of restrictions that limit intelligence efforts of the FBI to investigate terrorism]: . . . terrorism in the United States is declining. The terrorist bombings that

once occurred at the rate of 100 a year went down to 20 in 1980. And the FBI's priorities list now has domestic terrorism at Number 12 or 13. The problem is steadily getting smaller in this country, I'm happy to say. Before the current rules [placing restrictions on FBI methods of investigation] were put into effect, there were terrible abuses. A General Accounting Office audit of the FBI's domestic-intelligence activities from 1952 to 1975 found there had been hundreds of thousands of investigations. It was a terrible waste, taking about 20 per cent of the FBI's time for no good reason. Nothing good ever came of it. Very few criminals were caught. All for crimes not connected with internal security. All that happened was that Americans' rights were violated.
Interview/U.S. News & World Report, 11-16:33.

Don Feder
Executive director, National Rifle Association
4

I have never seen statistical data that objectively proves that gun-control works, that it either keeps guns out of the hands of criminals or the type of sociopaths who commit violent acts . . . I don't think you can prevent a crime by controlling the instrumentality of a crime. I view guns in the same way that I view alcohol or drugs or pornographic material: There is no commodity that people want that can be effectively prohibited, because the human mind is ingenious in devising ways around prohibitions . . . The danger comes whenever a person's right to self-defense is lessened. I'm a libertarian. I believe it's wrong for the government to try to regulate people's conduct when the conduct doesn't involve harming another person. If you grant people the right to defend themselves, then they must have the means to defend themselves.
Interview, Chicago/Chicago Tribune, 8-25:(1)9.

Dianne Feinstein
Mayor of San Francisco
5

Crime can be as paralyzing as any autocrat if, as it increasingly does, it imprisons citizens in their homes because they fear to venture outside.
Time, 3-23:21.

WHAT THEY SAID IN 1981

Lawrence Z. Freedman
Psychiatrist, University of Chicago

1

[On the recent attempted-assassination shootings of President Reagan and Pope John Paul II]: For us in the last part of the 20th century, the recent rash of assassinations and attempted assassinations seems shocking. I think we will have more attempts of this kind. The presence of marginal personalities with a real or fancied hatred of people in power is endemic. The ability to carry out assassination attempts is greatly increased by the availability of handguns. Any person willing to risk death is able to carry out such an act because basically it is impossible to completely protect public figures.

Chicago Tribune, 5-17:(1)2.

Keith M. Gaffaney
President, National Rifle Association

2

I plan to embark on a campaign of educating the public that gun-control does not equate with crime-control. There is a serious need for reformation of our justice system. Guns are already controlled, being registered several times. And the buyer registers when he buys a firearm. Both state and Federal officials are notified of the transaction. There is a waiting period before the buyer can pick up a handgun; thus officials are able to check on his qualifications. But what good does it do for a police officer to apprehend a suspect, help get him convicted for misuse of a firearm and then have the courts give the person a minimal sentence or probation instead of a sentence according to the statutes? It is punishment, swift and with certainty, in accordance with the law, that is a deterrent to crime. But there are too many deals made, too much plea-bargaining, in my opinion.

Los Angeles Herald Examiner, 6-9:(D)5.

Rudolph W. Giuliani
Associate Attorney General, Department of Justice of the United States

3

Poverty and unemployment—at least I always believed—have an affect on crime rates. But there are studies that purport to show just the opposite. The most dramatic example is the fact that the crime rates during the Depression were quite low. It teaches us something about the problem of crime: that it is more complicated than just the unemployment rate or poverty.

Panel discussion/The New York Times, 8-9:(4)21.

Daniel Glaser
Sociologist, University of Southern California

4

If gun-control does occur, it will not be a panacea for a number of reasons: A gun can be easily hidden, and people won't report their guns to the police department because they have strong feelings about the gun as a protection. But actually, a gun in the house is six times more likely to kill a member of the household or a guest than an intruder—by accident or family quarrels or suicide. I think that if we had controls over the sale and importation of guns, and more controls over who could get them, we could very slowly reduce the readiness with which guns are accessible—and it would make some contribution. But gun-control is certainly not a quick source of drastic change.

Interview/Los Angeles Herald Examiner, 4-2:(A)9.

Billy Graham
Evangelist

5

[On the attempted-assassination shooting of President Reagan]: This shocking event is a grim reminder that violence has become part of daily life in America. We have lost sight of what is right and wrong, and we have come to value life cheaply.

Los Angeles Herald Examiner, 3-31:(A)7.

Edward V. Hickey, Jr.
White House Chief of Security

6

There are those who claim that crime is primarily a product of poverty and racism. The liberal intellectuals who repeat that tired old cliche are the ones who've dominated legal thinking for decades. It has been under their tutelage

(EDWARD V. HICKEY, JR.)

that crime grew from a problem in the back alleys to a monster marauding through the downtown and residential streets of almost every American city.

Before American Society for Industrial Security, New Orleans, Sept. 3/ The Washington Post, 9-4:(A)8.

James Jardine
Chief Inspector, London Metropolitan Police; Chairman, Police Federation of England

1

It frightens me to death to be in America. Personally, I wouldn't want to be a policeman in this country because of the use of guns. We [British police], of course, are an unarmed force —and want to remain so. I think it's very dangerous, for both the public and the police, for the police to be armed . . . The British police are held in very high [public] esteem, and this is partly because of how we go about our duties— unarmed, unassuming and with helmets on. Our police cars are not flashy like you have [in the U.S.], and we don't go screaming to incidents, and we don't jump out and make people put their hands up. We don't need this.

Interview, Los Angeles/ Los Angeles Herald Examiner, 4-11:(A)2.

Brian Jenkins
Director, program on political violence, Rand Corporation

2

Perhaps the greatest danger posed by terrorism, and indeed sometimes its intended effect, is that it creates an atmosphere of fear and alarm in which a frightened populace will clamor for draconian measures, totalitarian solutions. Terrorism should be fought with even more democracy. I know it sounds trite, but it represents a recognition that a certain amount of political violence is a price paid for a free and open society. Terrorism, or at least public knowledge of it, is absent only in totalitarian states, and even there not entirely. Combating terrorism is a tough task in a democracy. I get nervous when people start talking about eradicating terrorism.

Interview/ The Washington Post, 2-1:(C)7.

D. Lowell Jensen
Assistant Attorney General, Criminal Division, Department of Justice of the United States

3

While sociological studies have reached differing conclusions, common sense tells us that the death penalty does operate as an effective deterrent for some crimes involving premeditation and calculation. Society does have a right— and the Supreme Court has confirmed that right —to exact a just and proportionate punishment on those individuals who deliberately flout its laws.

Before Senate Judiciary Committee, Washington, April 10/ The Washington Post, 4-11:(A)3.

B. K. Johnson
Chief of Police of Houston

4

The fear of crime is slowly paralyzing American society. We have allowed ourselves to degenerate to the point where we're living like animals. We live behind burglar bars and throw a collection of door locks at night and set an alarm and lay down with a loaded shotgun beside our bed and then try to get some rest. It's ridiculous.

Time, 3-23:16.

J. Bennett Johnston
United States Senator, D—Louisiana

5

The most efficient way to catch a criminal is to search everyone and everything, to use the massive power of the state to extract a confession through intense and prolonged questioning. But we know enough about human nature to know that unless the power of those in a position of power is carefully circumscribed, the possibility of tyranny is great . . . A legal system that permits even the nastiest, the dirtiest criminal to be searched, coerced or have his liberty curtailed threatens everyone else with the wideranging punitive powers of the government. It is not too much to say that the substantial rights

WHAT THEY SAID IN 1981

of mankind are hammered out in cases involving not very nice people.

At Tulane University School of Law commencement/
The Washington Post, 6-3:(A)22.

Edward M. Kennedy
United States Senator, D—Massachusetts

1

[On the attempted-assassination shooting of President Reagan]: I am saddened, as I am sure all Americans are, at the news of the attack on President Reagan ... All of us who care about this country and who care about our fellow citizens bear an important responsibility in whatever way we possibly can to rid America of the kind of violence and hatred that we have seen today and so often in recent years.

Los Angeles Herald Examiner, 3-31:(A)2.

2

The President [Reagan] is . . . calling for a new war against crime. The war has been declared again and again—and it has been lost over and over. If this latest war is to be more than words, more than a partisan slogan for the coming political year, then it is time for the Administration to put its money where its rhetoric is. Talking tough is not enough. We are told these days that national defense is vital, and it is. But national defense begins in our own neighborhoods, where we must stop the reign of aggression by the muggers, the thieves, the robbers and the rapists. We cannot fight crime on the cheap—which is the hard lesson we should have learned in earlier years.

At Senate Judiciary Committee hearing,
Washington, Sept. 28/
The Washington Post, 9-29:(A)2.

Edward I. Koch
Mayor of New York

3

I'm not a sociologist and I am not going to tell you why crime occurs. We know it is there. I do not accept the premise that crime is basically caused by poverty. Poverty is a factor, but most poor people do not commit crimes. I believe that people commit crimes because the odds of getting away with the crime are better than they are at the track and we have to cut those odds down. The way you cut those odds down is to have speedy trials and the certainty of punishment if you are convicted. We don't have either. We are getting there. Our jails are filling up. Judges are sending more people to jail. People are asking me if I am responsible for that, and I say I hope so.

Interview, New York/
The Wall Street Journal, 3-10:22.

Myron Leistler
Chief of Police of Cincinnati

4

The law has lost its credibility. We have to put respect back into it by reinstating its premise that you will get the punishment prescribed for the crime—none of this business of suspended sentences and other shortcuts. The people who violate the law have learned how to use the system to defeat the system and often escape retribution altogether. People see others violating the law with impunity, and those obeying it are beginning to lose respect for it as well.

Interview/The Christian Science Monitor, 4-2:7.

Bonnie Lee Martin
Judge, Los Angeles Superior Court

5

There is a great deal of frustration and fear among members of the public that somebody should be able to do something to control crime. We often hear the criticism that soft judges cause crime. Nothing could be further from the truth. Judges do not cause crime. The social factors which cause a lot of other problems in society cause a person to become a criminal. We deal with crime after it happens. And if criminals are punished for their behavior, maybe they'll change and maybe they won't change. I firmly believe that the change has to come from within the individual, that very little a judge says to the convicted criminal, very little that the pro-

(BONNIE LEE MARTIN)

bation officer tries to do or the parole officer tries to do, has any effect.

*Interview, Los Angeles/
Los Angeles Herald Examiner, 1-5:(B)1.*

Paul N. McCloskey, Jr.
United States Representative, R—California

1

[Advocating gun control]: This recent rash of killings, coupled with what happened yesterday [the shooting of President Reagan], might cause the National Rifle Association to rethink its position [against gun control]. They can now see that it can happen to one of their own, a conservative [Reagan]. All my advisers have told me that you can never take a strong position on gun control. But what happened yesterday has convinced me to take a strong position, win or lose.

*Washington, March 31/
Los Angeles Times, 4-1:(I)B.*

Edwin Meese III
*Counsellor to the President of the United States;
Former Assistant District Attorney,
Alameda County, California*

2

We ought to take the person who has committed a crime, been convicted of a crime, and if he or she is willing to participate in his or her own rehabilitation, to give the person every benefit to return as a useful citizen to society. That to me is the best kind of crime prevention, because you have taken a person with clear, demonstrated proclivities toward crime and you've turned that person around, and I think we don't do nearly enough toward providing adequate prisons, toward providing humane prisons or toward providing rehabilitation. Now, there are some who believe there is no hope of rehabilitation. I don't believe that. I believe there is some percentage—and no one knows for sure what it is—of those who've been convicted of crime that, given the right kind of assistance and treatment, will never commit another crime. But

right now we have kind of a Gresham's law of criminality and penology—that is, the worst people are setting the tone for the prisons.

Interview/The Washington Post, 7-7:(A)15.

W. Walter Menninger
*Senior staff psychiatrist,
Menninger Foundation*

3

[On the attempted assassination of President Reagan]: Every society produces its alienated persons who try to carry out their own agenda, but some characteristics of ours increase the potential risk. For one thing, more guns are available than ever before—and these are the main weapons in assassination as well as violent crime, of which we have more than any other Western civilized nation. We also have a tradition of individual freedoms—and more resistance to limits on those freedoms. Another thing is affluence. Potential assassins can easily go to where their target is.

Interview/U.S. News & World Report, 4-13:32.

Norval Morris
*Professor of law and criminality,
University of Chicago*

4

America has always had a very high crime rate. We have traditionally had a culture of violence here. It's the dark side of fierce independence and skepticism of government and authority. It's the dark side of an insistence to have freedom, especially the freedom to have handguns.

The Christian Science Monitor, 2-19:13.

Patrick V. Murphy
*President, Police Foundation; Former
Police Commissioner of New York City*

5

The people are upset about the level of crime, and they're looking for an answer. The truth is, there is no quick fix. All of the police officers in the world can do only one thing, which is to make an arrest and a charge. But what about the capacity of the remainder of the system? Maybe you need more prison cells, maybe you need

WHAT THEY SAID IN 1981

(PATRICK V. MURPHY)

more judges, maybe you need more district attorneys, and maybe you need more police. We don't know much yet about what is the right balance.

Interview/Los Angeles Times, 3-9:(I)3.

1

People who can afford expensive lawyers can beat the system when it comes to the death penalty as well as other kinds of punishment. Also, I'm a bit of a cynical New York cop. I have found in the weeds the bodies of mob guys bumped off by other guys in the mob. Those are the coldest, most calculating kinds of murderers—the mob hit-men. Their crimes are well planned, very hard to detect—and witnesses don't talk, so those are not the people who get executed for murder. The ones who do get executed are often pathetic, mentally defective people, or are people who killed a wife, a husband, a lover in the heat of passion . . . How do we deal with crime? I'm looking for the right answers—but I honestly don't believe the death penalty is one of them.

Interview/U.S. News & World Report, 4-20:50.

Charles J. Orasin
Executive vice president, Handgun Control, Inc.

2

[On the attempted-assassination shooting of President Reagan]: Are people just exhausted by all this violence? What is it? Are they so inured to violence in their neighborhoods that they expect it? Are they so used to seeing national leaders fall they don't react any more? Have we accepted shooting as a way of life? Do we have to bury another President? Is that what it's going to take to get people angry enough to do something about it? What's going to get them angry enough to pick up the phone, call their Congressman, and demand they pass a gun-control law now and stop this madness? The gun lobby has got the Congress afraid to do anything, and the problem is the Congress here in Washington. That's why we've got to find a million new members [of Handgun Control, Inc.], people who are really

mad. We want to channel that anger where it belongs and get them willing to tell their Congressmen, "Enough of this! We want an end to this!"

The Washington Post, 4-1:(A)8.

Ronald Reagan
President of the United States

3

. . . my concern about gun-control is that it's taking our eyes off what might be the real answers to crime; it's diverting our attention. There are, today, more than 20,000 gun-control laws in effect—Federal, state and local—in the United States. Indeed, some of the stiffest gun-control laws in the nation are right here in the District [Washington] and they didn't seem to prevent a fellow, a few weeks ago, from carrying one down by the Hilton Hotel [and shooting the President]. In other words, they are virtually unenforceable. So I would like to see us directing our attention to what has caused us to have the crime that continues to increase as it has and is one of our major problems in the country today.

*News conference, Washington, June 16/
The New York Times, 6-17:13.*

4

At the very same time that crime rates have steadily risen, our nation has made unparalleled progress in raising the standard of living and improving the quality of life. It's obvious that prosperity doesn't decrease crime—just as it's obvious that deprivation and want don't necessarily increase crime. The truth is that today's criminals, for the most part, are not desperate people seeking bread for their families; crime is the way they've chosen to live. Some of these people are poor. Some of them are driven crazy with desire for stuff they'll never be able to afford. But not all of them are poor, not by a long shot. A lot of them are making as much money or a great deal more than you or I do. They do it because it's easy. They do it because they believe no one will stop them. They do really believe that they're better than the rest of us, that the world owes them a living, and that those of us who

50

(RONALD REAGAN)

lead normal lives and earn an honest living are a little slow on the uptake.

Before International Association of Chiefs of Police, New Orleans, Sept. 28/The New York Times, 9-29:13.

1

Controlling crime in American society isn't simply a question of more money, more police, more courts, more prosecutors. It is ultimately a moral dilemma, one that calls for a moral or, if you will, a spiritual solution . . . The solution to the crime problem will not be found in the social-worker's files, the psychiatrist's notes or the bureaucrat's budget; it's a problem of the human heart, and it's there we must look for the answer.

Before International Association of Chiefs of Police, New Orleans, Sept. 28/ The Christian Science Monitor, 9-30:1,7.

2

Contrary to a distorted image that emerged during the last decade, there is no inherent conflict between the intelligence community and the rights of our citizens. This is not to say mistakes [by the CIA] were never made and that vigilance against abuse is unnecessary. But an approach that emphasizes suspicion and mistrust of our own intelligence efforts can undermine this nation's ability to confront the increasing challenge of espionage and terrorism.

Announcing his easing of restrictions against U.S. intelligence agencies, Washington, Dec. 4*/ The Washington Post, 12-5:(A)1.

Milton Rector
President, National Council on Crime and Delinquency

3

By building more [prison] cells, we're committing society to the incarceration of low-income, uneducated and unskilled offenders . . . We're perpetuating the myth that the criminal-justice system will stop the [crime] problem . . .

If cells are built, you can be sure the states will fill them.

Newsweek, 3-23:54.

William H. Rehnquist
Associate Justice, Supreme Court of the United States

4

[Criticizing the Supreme Court for delaying the carrying out of capital-punishment sentences]: I do not think that this Court can continue to evade some responsibility for this mockery of our criminal-justice system . . . This Court, by constantly tinkering with the principles laid down in the five death-penalty cases decided in 1976, together with the natural reluctance of state and Federal habeas judges to rule against an inmate on death row, has made it virtually impossible for states to enforce with reasonable promptness their Constitutionally valid capital-punishment statutes. When society promises to punish by death certain criminal conduct, and then the courts fail to do so, the courts not only lessen the deterrent effect . . . they undermine the integrity of the entire criminal-justice system . . . There can be no doubt that delay in the enforcement of capital punishment frustrates the purpose of retribution . . . In the nation's capital, law-enforcement authorities cannot protect the lives of employees of this very Court who live four blocks from the building in which we sit and deliberate the Constitutionality of capital punishment [a reference to the recent murder of a Supreme Court messenger].

Exchange among justices, Washington, April 27*/ The Washington Post, 4-28:(A)10.

Daniel Robinson
Professor of psychology, Georgetown University

5

The current wave of violent crime, of which assassinations are merely the most celebrated, strikes me as unique in perhaps the past two centuries of Western experience. What we have, I think, is a growing inability of the established democracies to take a firm position on the function of the law and its connection with civil-

WHAT THEY SAID IN 1981

(DANIEL ROBINSON)

ized life . . . It seems to me that the rhetoric of the left, coupled with the Hitler experience, has made the governments of the Western democracies extremely defensive and inclined to measures that invariably fall short of anything that might be called oppressive. And if your objective is never to risk condemnation as an oppressor, you will soon be in a position of not being able to control the ordinary affairs of social life.

Interview/U.S. News & World Report, 5-25:25.

Ruth Rushen
Director, Califorma Department of Corrections

1

If you're talking about violent, senseless crime, I don't think we know what would stop that. And the sad thing is, we're not trying to find out. You're dealing with a very different person from your ordinary criminal when you deal with the man or woman who points a gun at you and says, "Give me your money," so you give him the money and he blows your head off. That's not the kind of person any prison term is going to deter. If you are talking about, though, the criminal in the classic sense, we can recognize certain characteristics of those people. They are usually poor; they are usually in the ethnic minority; they are usually in that category of, "What have I got to lose?" A lot of people don't want to hear that, but we have to look at it if we're talking about prevention or controlling crime.

Interview/
Los Angeles Herald Examiner, 3-26:(A)2.

Henry Schwarzchild
Director, Capital Punishment Project,
American Civil Liberties Union

2

[Arguing against capital punishment]: Killing human beings is an act so awesome, so destructive, so irremediable, that no killer can be looked upon with anything but horror, even when that killer is the state.

Before Senate Judiciary Committee, Washington/
The New York Times, 6-14:(1)15.

Whitney North Seymour
Chairman, special committee on
criminal justice, New York Bar Association

3

The deterrent effect of the criminal laws is directly proportional to the promptness and sureness of sanctions.

Time, 3-23:24.

William French Smith
Attorney General of the United States

4

Last year 30 per cent of all households in the United States were touched by some serious crime. Since 1970, the incidence of violent crime in this country has increased 59 per cent, while the population has increased less than 10 per cent. In the single year from 1978 to 1979, violent crime increased 11 per cent, and the preliminary data for 1980 indicate that violent crime increased an additional 10 per cent. There has been no comprehensive examination of the Federal role in this area for many years. The climate of crime today makes such a review necessary.

News conference, Washington, March 5/
Los Angeles Herald Examiner, 3-6:(A)7.

5

Probation should be recognized as a penalty rather than as the absence of penalty . . . Every felon granted probation should for the first time receive a discernible penalty—he should be required to make restitution to his victims, to work in community service or to pay a fine . . . Imprisonment should no longer involve the imposition of terms that create the illusion of substantial punishment, but that in fact will be significantly shortened at the discretion of parole authorities.

Before House judiciary Subcommittee on
Criminal Justice, Washington, Oct. 28/
The Washington Post, 10-29:(A)10.

Strom Thurmond
United States Senator, R—South Carolina

6

Crime is primarily the responsibility of the states and local communities. We must not make

52

(STROM THURMOND)

it appear that the Federal government is going to take over criminal-law enforcement. But there are a number of things we can do. [There is] the Federal death penalty. Another is speedy trial. When we do not have speedy trials, that encourages crime. Determinant or fixed sentencing could be important. A man who is waiting to be sentenced would know that he will not be put on probation or parole. Federal bail reform is important, too. At present, judges cannot consider danger to the community before releasing someone on bail. That should be changed.

Interview/U.S. News & World Report, 3-23:42.

Stansfield Turner
Former Director of Central Intelligence of the United States

1

[Criticizing President Reagan's order permitting the CIA greater latitude in intelligence collecting in the U.S. as well as overseas]: The very fact that you now have permitted it in an executive order engenders suspicions among the public, [especially among] the people who think the fillings in their gold teeth were put there by the CIA . . . It's not just that none of us wants to undermine the right of privacy . . . The CIA is not trained to operate within the constraints of American law. The FBI is. You are being unfair

to a CIA officer when you put him in that environment where he's more likely to make a mistake.

To reporters, Washington, Dec. 8/
The Washington Post, 12-9:(A)2.

William H. Webster
Director, Federal Bureau of Investigation

2

I wish I had been more successful [during the past three years since taking office] in turning around the shrinkage of the Bureau, because we're being steadily asked to do more and more things and we're ending up with fewer and fewer people to do them. The problem facing the country today is fear, and the fear is of violent crime. Fear has a way of getting in the way of national momentum, so there ought to be an increased effort to improve our ability to cope with violent crimes. But you give me a hard choice when you say would I be willing to cut into our organized-crime program, in order to increase the other. [Nevertheless,] that may be the choice.

Interview, Washington/The New York Times, 2-26:7.

3

If the people support the police, the police can make a difference. Information is the most important part of law enforcement, and information depends on people.

Time, 3-23:24.

Defense . The Military

Lew Allen Jr.
General and Chief of Staff,
United States Air Force

1

[The Reagan Administration's intention is] to confront the Soviet Union quickly with clear indications of the resolve and determination of the American people to match the Soviet threat and to show that resolve in an unambiguous way prior to resuming arms-limitations discussions . . . The B-1 [bomber] offers a way of doing that which is incredible and early and which will be noticed by the Soviet Union in a very major way.
Interview, Washington, June 30/
The Washington Post, 7-1:(A)8.

2

[Saying cutbacks in Federal spending to aid the economy must not adversely affect the military]: We must and will reject the false economies of neglecting [armed-forces] people-oriented programs or of procuring supposedly cheaper weapons systems that are not adequate to the missions we are required to fulfill . . . We fully recognize that a strong economy is essential to a strong defense. [But] whatever the fiscal constraint, the Air Force must protect the quality of its forces. [Unless Americans] are willing to bear the burden, the risk of significant United States inferiority is very real and the dangers associated with such inferiority ominous. The sacrifice is clearly bearable. American spending on alcoholic beverages has exceeded Air Force expenditures in each of the past five years, and casino gambling revenues are running double the Air Force's annual fuel bill.
Before Air Force Association, Washington,
Sept 15/The New York Times, 9-16:16.

Richard V. Allen
Assistant to the President of the United States
for National Security Affairs

3

We detect now some in Europe who believe that the arms-control negotiations [with the Soviet Union] can somehow substitute for, rather than complement, the modernization efforts in our weapons systems. They believe that we can bargain the reduction of a deployed Soviet weapons system for a promise not to deploy our own offsetting system. Common sense, as well as the long history of arms negotiations with the Soviet Union, tells us that this is illusory. The only way to deal with the Soviet Union is from a strong position. Only if it is absolutely clear then that we are in the process of fielding weapons of our own will they agree to serious bargaining on their weapons. We will negotiate, but we will negotiate while we modernize. [If the negotiations should fail] we want to be sure that we will have a stable balance anyhow and that we will offset growing Soviet strength with our own.
At Conservative Political Action Conference,
Washington, March 21/
The New York Times, 3-22:(1)8.

Les Aspin
United States Representative, D—Wisconsin

4

It is nothing short of insane, not to mention economic suicide, for the United States to take upon itself an even greater share of the Western [defense] burden while Japan and, to a lesser extent, Western Europe . . . pump their capital into industries that are starved in the United States because of the defense umbrella.
Chicago Tribune, 5-25:(1)7.

54

(LES ASPIN)

1

[Agreeing with the Reagan Administration's plan to install missiles in stationary silos rather than continuously moving them around as a way of protecting them]: [Stationary silos are] the most workable and realistic way to build a new U.S. intercontinental-ballistic-missile force that can survive a Soviet surprise attack. That, along with the capability of the MX to destroy Soviet missiles quickly, will force Russia's leaders to become serious about arms control once again. There is no perfect solution to our basic problem: the vulnerability of land-based missiles to increasingly accurate Soviet warheads. All our plans are flawed, some more than others. But we have to choose the best way to begin closing this "window of vulnerability."

Interview/U.S. News & World Report, 11-2:47.

James A. Baker III
Chief of Staff to the President
of the United States

2

[President Reagan's plans for a buildup of U.S. military forces is necessary to match] the most massive buildup in military arms by the other side that man has ever seen. We recognize that the Soviets are now seizing on America's buildup to launch a major propaganda offensive against us and that some of our friends are nervous. But we are convinced that the only way to achieve a more stable, peaceful world is to engage in a steady, long-term strengthening of our military forces.

Before National Press Club, Washington, July 16/
The Washington Post, 7-17:(A)6.

Julius W. Becton, Jr.
Lieutenant General, United States Army;
Commander, U.S. Army VII Corps

3

[On the all-volunteer armed forces]: If we reverted to the draft tomorrow, the draft would not help me one iota for soldiers. We are getting the numbers we need, at least in VII Corps. What I need is a greater retention of my buck sargeants,

my staff sargeants, my sargeants-first-class, that middle management of non-commissioned-officer leadership. I think it's clear, however, when you talk about a volunteer force, you've got to talk about the active Army, the National Guard and the U.S. Army Reserve. And if the Guard and the Reserve are hurting for numbers of people, then we are hurting, because they are the ones we rely upon for reinforcements. For the active-duty forces, I see no problem.

Interview, Stuttgart, West Germany/
Chicago Tribune, 4-27:(1)4.

Christoph Bertram
Director, International Institute for
Strategic Studies, London

4

Skeptics, although often paying lip service to true arms control, feel certain that effective arms control in the sense of serving the security interests of the West is simply illusory so long as the Soviet Union and the United States are locked in continuing rivalry. The international environment does not now seem to lend itself to serious compromise. Current and future strategic concerns seem to find too little reflection in the present arms-control approach. Successful arms control requires a favorable international climate, domestic support and credible instruments of agreement. The present situation is lacking in all three.

Los Angeles Times, 1-18:(I)8.

5

For the past 30 years or so, you were able to combine the other priorities in public expenditure with defense. [But today] the perimeters of economic experience which have governed European society for 30 years are no longer valid... At a time when you are trying to combat recession and fight inflation by reducing public expenditures, you can't keep the defense budget un-

WHAT THEY SAID IN 1981

(CHRISTOPH BERTRAM)

touched ... Defense, by trying to be a sacred cow, at a time when everything else is being cut, is risking becoming more and more controversial.

The Wall Street Journal, 4-1:24.

Rolf Bjornerstedt
Chairman, Stockholm International
Peace Research Institute

1

1980 was certainly not a very good year for disarmament, and the outlook at the start of 1981 is not much better. But on the other hand, the whole history of disarmament is one of slow and patient diplomacy to sort out areas of potential agreement, bits and pieces of understanding which can then suddenly be fitted together when the political moment is right. So a great deal has been going on which could be quickly translated into agreement when the political will and timing are there. For the moment, we think that everything depends on the tone and attitude which the new [U.S. Reagan] Administration in Washington adopts. Like it or not, it is the superpower relationship which really controls almost everything that happens in the disarmament field.

Los Angeles Times, 1-18:(I)7.

J. T. Bowlin
Colonel, and Commandant of the
Recruit Training Regiment,
United States Marine Corps.

2

We're still turning out hard and competent Marines, but we're doing it by motivating a recruit, not by scaring him half to death. There's plenty of stress without adding fright. Today, the drill instructor sets an example. American society won't stand for [the overly harsh treatment of recruits that] went on here in the '50s and '60s.

U.S. News & World Report, 1-12:61.

Willy Brandt
Acting chairman, West German Social
Democratic Party; Former Chancellor of
West Germany

3

[On his recent discussions with Soviet President Leonid Brezhnev]: [What the Soviets] expressed was the self-assurance of a big power that is determined to keep pace if the other big power in the world tries to gain the upper hand in the possession of weapons of mass destruction. My experience has been—and, by the way, this was pointed out in Moscow—that in the course of history the lapse of time between the discoveries of one side and the other is becoming shorter all the time. First, in the case of the atom bomb, then the hydrogen bomb, and then the other weapons systems. The idea of driving the other side to ruin by arming is not realistic in my view.

Interview/Chicago Tribune, 7-17:(1)9.

Leonid I. Brezhnev
President of the Soviet Union; General Secretary,
Soviet Communist Party

4

For our part, we are prepared to continue the relevant [SALT] negotiations with the United States without delay, preserving all the positive elements that have so far been achieved in this area. It goes without saying that the negotiations can be conducted only on the basis of equality and equal security. We will not consent to any agreement that gives unilateral advantage to the U.S.A.

At Soviet Communist Party Congress,
Moscow, Feb. 23/
U.S. News & World Report, 3-9:29.

5

Bellicose-minded militaristic circles, headed by American imperialism, launched an arms race unprecedented in scale. The Soviet Union does not threaten anyone, does not seek confrontation with any state in the West or East ... History has taught a stern lesson. The people have paid too big a price for the failure to prevent war, to avert in time the threat hanging over the world.

(LEONID I. BREZHNEV)

A repetition of the tragedy must not be allowed. The world has already been saturated with weapons of mass annihilation. But their stockpiling continues.

*Before Supreme Soviet, Moscow, June 23/
Los Angeles Herald Examiner, 6-23:(A)4.*

1

[On a possible U.S. offer to refrain from deploying new nuclear missiles in Europe if the Soviets would dismantle a number of their existing missiles]: Those in the United States who advance this kind of "proposal" apparently do not for a minute expect that the Soviet Union might agree to them. Most probably the authors of such "proposals" do not really want [arms-control] talks, let alone successful talks. What they need is a breakdown of the talks, which they can use as a sort of justification for continuing the planned arms race.

Interview/The New York Times, 11-19:9.

Harold Brown
*Secretary of Defense of the
United States*

2

[A pitfall] that I would urge a new Secretary of Defense to avoid involves the consensus about defense, which I think is real and has grown over the past two or three years. But it is fragile—more fragile than may appear on the surface. I believe the American people want more defense and are probably willing to pay for some more of it. But there are limits to their willingness to give up other government benefits or to accept the prospect of a higher deficit or rate of inflation in order to get an unlimited amount of defense expenditure. The intellectual consensus behind defense, although real, is fragile. People who agree that we should be stronger militarily don't all necessarily agree on how that military strength should be expressed and used. They don't agree on particular programs—which is normal—nor do they agree on our attitudes toward the Soviets, toward

our allies, toward the Chinese, toward other parts of the world. If that is not kept in mind, the pro-defense consensus could, if not fragment, then certainly erode.

Interview/U.S. News & World Report, 1-26:28.

Harold Brown
*Former Secretary of Defense
of the United States*

3

If you are trying to limit Soviet military capability, arms control clearly is one way to do it. It's a very important facet of national-security policy. It is not true, in my judgment, that the Soviets are always able to outnegotiate us or that they always have outnegotiatied us. It is worth noting that the [Reagan] Administration's defense program does not include any substantial program that we were constrained from deploying by the unratified SALT II treaty. That suggests that the people who negotiated that treaty took pains to see that U.S. options were not greatly limited, although Soviet options clearly were limited. I don't offer that as a pat on the back for the Carter Administration or criticism of the Reagan Administration; I offer it only as a way of showing that arms control can—and, properly handled, does—improve U.S. security.

*Interview/
U.S. News & World Report, 9-28:24.*

Zbigniew Brzezinski
*Assistant to the President of the United States
for National Security Affairs*

4

I am convinced that we will enjoy greater security if we proceed with the [SALT II] treaty and the military programs allowed by the treaty than if we proceed with the programs without the treaty. A treaty is a bilateral arrangement. Many things in it could be improved upon. But then we would have to negotiate the treaty with ourselves, and implement it unilaterally. The treaty enhances our security—of that I am absolutely certain.

Interview/U.S. News & World Report, 1-26:28.

WHAT THEY SAID IN 1981

Zbigniew Brzezinski
Professor of government, Columbia University;
Former Assistant to the President of the
United States (Jimmy Carter) for
National Security Affairs

1

I approve increased defense spending. I approve the [U.S.] determination to make the Soviets realize they have to exercise restraint in the Third World. But words are not enough. One has to make basic decisions. For example, the delay in the MX [missile] deployment is going to widen the window of opportunity for the Soviets in the course of the 1980s and give them strategic leverage which otherwise they may not have. In brief, rhetoric is not a substitute for substance.

Interview/Los Angeles Herald Examiner, 6-7:(A)12.

James L. Buckley
Under Secretary for Security Assistance,
Department of State of the United States

2

[On U.S. arms sales abroad]: The Carter Administration adopted [limiting] policies toward the transfer of arms to friends and allies that substituted theology for a healthy sense of self-preservation. [It] had the net effect of lessening U.S. influence over the arms policies of other nations by encouraging them to seek weapons they needed from other suppliers. This [Reagan] Administration believes that arms transfers, judiciously applied, can complement and supplement our own defense efforts and serve as a vital and constructive instrument of American foreign policy.

Before Aerospace Industries Association,
Williamsburg, Va., May 21/
Chicago Tribune, 6-22:(1)2.

Kelly H. Burke
Lieutenant General, and Deputy Chief of Staff
for Research and Engineering,
United States Air Force

3

[Saying the U.S. needs a new manned bomber, like the proposed B-1]: Ballistic missiles cannot attack the Red Army. They can attack an army

garrison or installation; but if you hypothesize a Soviet first strike, the Red Army is not likely to be sitting in the barracks waiting for our retaliatory strike. We also need a manned bomber to succeed the B-52s in non-nuclear roles—for the kind of confrontations that may develop in the Persian Gulf or Mideast, for missions like dropping conventional bombs in the Vietnam war.

Interview/Los Angeles Times, 1-19:(I)8.

George Bush
Vice President of the United States

4

One thing I could never stomach . . . were the vicious attacks [in recent decades on the military]. And thank God we seem to have put behind us those far-too-frequent attacks on those who are willing to serve their country . . . If we value freedom and if we value peace, we must also value those who wear the uniform of our country.

At U.S. Naval Academy commencement, May 27/
The Washington Post, 5-28:(A)2.

5

[On the Reagan Administration's decision to increase the military budget]: How many billions would we have gladly paid to avoid Pearl Harbor? Ten billion? Twenty billion? Thirty-five billion dollars? Who's going to step forward and say, "My children's lives are not worth that much"?

Before Veterans of Foreign Wars,
Philadelphia, Aug. 17/The New York Times, 8-18:2.

Frank C. Carlucci
Deputy Secretary of Defense
of the United States

6

[The] steady and cumulative expansion [by the Soviet Union] of conventional, chemical and theatre-nuclear forces has been accompanied by a long-term and major shift in the strategic nuclear balance, from one of unquestioned U.S. superiority to essential equivalence, and the prospect, if appropriate steps are not taken, of

(FRANK C. CARLUCCI)

possible inferiority. The twin results of this shift are that the United States no longer enjoys a strategic edge to compensate for other deficiencies and that Soviet ability to use the threat of conventional force for political purposes could be significantly enhanced. On all levels of military capability, the trends are ominous.

At military policy conference, Munich, Feb. 21/
The New York Times, 2-22:(1)8.

Jimmy Carter
Former President of the United States

1

I felt the "black bag" [of secret nuclear codes] was in good hands when it was in my possession. Anyone who runs for the Presidency sooner or later comes to realize that is one of the responsibilities that you volunteer to assume—the necessity of using atomic weapons under certain circumstances to protect the security of our country. I crossed that bridge during the early stages of my decision to run for President. I was prepared to do it, if I had to. But I was prepared to avoid the necessity . . . that was ever-present in my mind.

Interview, Plains, Ga./
The Washington Post, 3-16:(A)2.

2

This SALT process had been pursued not just to reduce the nuclear threat and alleviate tension between the pre-eminent leaders of the East and West, but also to convince our allies and other nations that we seek peace and are committed to the process of nuclear arms control. Now we have seen a radical American departure from this long-prevailing policy. From my successors [the Reagan Administration] there have been mixed signals, at best, even involving the acceptability of limited nuclear wars and demonstration nuclear warning shots. These have aroused consternation here and in Europe and have dealt the unity of NATO a most damaging blow.

Before Council on Foreign Relations,
New York, Dec. 17/The New York Times, 12-18:4.

William D. Clark
Acting Assistant Secretary for Manpower,
Department of Defense of the United States

3

I don't think it is a question of whether we should have women in the Army or not. I think it is a question of the degree of reliance that we place upon women. We are hesitant, as a matter of fact reluctant, to continue with the increasing number of women as has been directed by the Defense Department until such time as we have a better understanding [of their effect on readiness]. So we are trying to hold the line on the number of women.

Before Senate Armed Services Manpower and
Personnel Subcommittee, Washington, Feb. 26/
Los Angeles Times, 2-27:(I)8.

William S. Cohen
United States Senator, R—Maine

4

[On the Reagan Administration's plans for increasing military spending]: Once the public becomes aware of the realistic cost of the programs—the MX [missile], the cruise missile, the B-1 [bomber], the 600-ship fleet, the pay raise that will be necessary to keep qualified personnel—and then see what we are going to do to the budget to achieve that, [then the] euphoria will dissipate in the land.

Newsweek, 6-8:29.

John M. Collins
Senior specialist in national-security affairs,
Congressional Research Service

5

[Criticizing a Defense Department study on Soviet military power]: It is not an assessment of the Soviet threat. It is not even an assessment of Soviet capabilities. It is not a review of trends in Soviet force posture. What it really is is a snapshot of Soviet military power at this particular point in time, and that's all. A threat assessment has to appraise what capabilities pose the greatest danger in what priority. That means you've got to have some feel for intention as well as capabilities. People in the defense

WHAT THEY SAID IN 1981

(JOHN M. COLLINS)

community don't want to discuss intentions because intentions are transitory states of mind, where capabilities are facts that you can measure . . . I want to make very clear that I am not even intimating that this military power being displayed by the Soviet Union should be disregarded by the United States. [But we should not] gaze at this mass of Soviet power indiscriminately but try to put it into some kind of perspective.

Interview, Washington/
The New York Times, 10-10:8.

Alan Cranston
United States Senator, D—California

1

It is beyond imagination that the Soviet Union would actually feel that it could successfully launch a first strike that would so cripple all the various parts of our triad, all the various ways we have to strike back at the Soviet Union, so successfully that we would give up and not devastate them in a second strike. It's ridiculous to think that could occur.

Los Angeles Times, 9-28:(I)12.

William L. Dickinson
United States Representative, R—Alabama

2

[Saying the U.S. should build the B-1 bomber rather than rely on upgrading the aging B-52]: In the final analysis, it comes back to credibility and what is sufficient for deterrence. And now even if you enhance the capability of the B-52 sufficiently to have a penetration capability, the cost is tremendous. And you still have a 30-year-old bird. So this is part of the equation; I don't think it's ever discussed: If you don't build a B-1, what are you going to do? . . . Also, if we give our enemies a new weapons system to worry about—a B-1 bomber—then this complicates their problems. They [the Soviets] want to protect Moscow and their other cities. They believe in having a redundancy of defenses that won't wait. We force them to spend that much more on defense with a new weapon. Then if

you come on later with the Stealth [plane], you've given them still more to worry about. They'll be outspending us 5-to-1 just to counter what we're doing. And whatever they spend on defense takes away from what they can spend on offensive weapons.

Interview/The New York Times, 10-11:(4)5.

John Erickson
Director of defense studies,
University of Edinburgh

3

[On chemical warfare]: Soviet interest in chemical weapons is steeped in an assumption in Soviet military doctrine that, in a "decisive" clash between socialist and capitalist systems, the "logic of war" may inveigh against any restraints on the use of available weapons.

Los Angeles Times, 8-2:(I)2.

J. J. Exon
United States Senator, D—Nebraska

4

They're talking over there now in the Pentagon about a $10,000 bonus for an 18-year-old youngster if he'll serve in the infantry. To me, when people over there in that Pentagon are thinking such thoughts they aren't thinking about the survival of the United States. They're thinking about political survival—not having the guts to say that maybe this [all-volunteer force] isn't going to work.

Chicago Tribune, 4-27:(1)7.

Newt Gingrich
United States Representative, R—Georgia

5

You can take every quote by President Reagan about bureaucracy in general, every quote about its waste, its silliness, its lack of direction, and you can apply them to the Pentagon. The reality is that the Pentagon is the largest, most sophisticated bureaucracy in this city; that for the last 35 years it has systematically and steadily developed an ability to do less and less while spending more and more with greater and greater complexity.

Before the House, Washington/
Chicago Tribune, 12-13:(2)3.

Barry M. Goldwater
United States Senator, R—Arizona
1

[Criticizing the plan to reactivate some World War II U.S. battleships]: With the modern weapons available to the Soviets, I would not give the battleship a chance of survivability of more than 20 or 30 minutes in hostilities . . . The Soviet Navy is not sailing around in old battleships that fought in World War II. They are sailing around in new modern cruisers, new modern fast ships that can outmaneuver that big ship any day of the week. So, Mr. President, I am going to vote against this battleship [the U.S.S. *New Jersey*]. Even though I love to watch them sail through the water, I do not like to see them go down, and that is where this one would go in a big, fat hurry.
Before the Senate, Washington/
Los Angeles Times, 7-26:(V)3.

Daniel O. Graham
Lieutenant General, United States Army, (Ret.);
Former Director, Defense Intelligence Agency
2

[Advocating the stationing of U.S. ABMs in space orbit]: [Military] superiority is a perfectly reasonable thing for our side to have. One day, one nation or . . . a consortium of nations is going to establish the same kind of domination out there [in space] that the British once had over the high seas . . . [A U.S. space-borne defense] would be doing more for our allies than any other single program that we can think of. Japan and Europe [would] get defended whether they like it or not. [And such a system would show NATO that] this country is not in a position to be blackmailed by the Soviet Union . . . [A program to build that kind of system can be embarked upon] with fewer dollars, in less time and with a great deal more public support than [can] the incremental approach of trying to catch the Soviets in some tail chase for numbers of missiles, planes, tanks, ships and so forth. And we have the advantage of the [space] shuttle. The shuttle is a railroad train into

space. It is my view that the Soviets lag us badly in creating any such system
At defense forum, Washington, May/
The Christian Science Monitor, 5-28:12.

Harry J. Gray
Chairman, United Technologies Corporation
3

If there were a national emergency today, I seriously doubt that our nation could mobilize its industrial base in time to make an appreciable difference in sustaining a war effort. It might take as much as two years before we'd see any real increase in production of war materiel.
San Francisco Examiner & Chronicle, 12-6:(E)1.

Andrei A. Gromyko
Foreign Minister of the Soviet Union
4

The ruling circles of a number of NATO countries now worship but one God: an unrestrained arms race. Everything that serves this end is acceptable to them . . . decisions are taken on a huge increase in military expenditures such as history has never known. An urge to expand the military presence wherever possible has now acquired the element of bacchanalia, with half a million U.S. troops stationed in more than a dozen countries . . . The whipping up of the arms race is madness. This has been repeatedly recognized by many political and public figures in the world—scientists and men of culture. And mankind must be saved from this. The present balance of military power is fully in line with the interests of peace and international stability. Our country has never sought, nor is it seeking, military superiority. But we will not permit others to become superior to us.
At United Nations, New York, Sept. 22/
The New York Times, 9-23:6.

Alexander M. Haig, Jr.
Secretary of State-designate of the United States;
Former Supreme Allied Commander/Europe
5

I have always been somewhat skeptical about the long-term desirability of the all-volunteer

(ALEXANDER M. HAIG, JR.)

[armed forces] concept. In practice, some of this skepticism has not proven unjustified; some of it has. It's clear that there are a number of worrisome indications on the horizon with respect to the long-term manpower needs of the United States in the security sphere. And this becomes increasingly worrisome as you project the trends into the 1980s. Having said that, I see no basis today for a panicky approach. Nor, I must add, do I see a political consensus existing which would permit, in practical terms, an immediate return to the draft.

Interview/
U.S. News & World Report, 12-29('80)-1-5('81):7.

Alexander M. Haig, Jr.
Secretary of State of the United States

1

It has been my experience that achieving arms control is never the product of rhetoric or idealistic hopes. It is always the product of pragmatic reality.

Interview/Los Angeles Times, 2-9:(A)11.

2

Arms control can be only one element in a comprehensive structure of defense and foreign policy designed to reduce the risks of war. It cannot be the political centerpiece or the crucial barometer of U.S.-Soviet relationships, burdening arms control with a crushing political weight. It can hardly address such issues as the Soviet invasion of Afghanistan, the Iran-Iraq war, the Vietnamese invasion of Cambodia, the Libyan invasion of Chad or the Cuban intervention in Africa and Latin America. Our first principle is that our arms-control efforts will be an instrument of, not a replacement for, a coherent allied security policy . . . we will seek arms-control agreements that truly enhance security. We will work for agreements that make world peace more secure by reinforcing deterrence. On occasion, it has been urged that we accept defective agreements in order "to keep the arms-control process alive." But we are seeking much more than agreements for their own sake.

We will design our proposals not simply in the interest of a speedy negotiation but so that they will result in agreements which genuinely enhance the security of both sides. That is the greatest measure of the worth of arms control, not the money saved nor the arms eliminated. Indeed, valuable agreements can be envisioned that do not save money and do not eliminate arms. The vital task is to limit and to reduce arms in a way that renders use of the remaining arms less likely.

Before Foreign Policy Association,
New York, July 14/The New York Times, 7-15:7.

3

We are debating today how to prevent the Soviet military buildup from upsetting the balance of power. It is agreed by all knowledgeable students that our margin of safety has narrowed. But the democracies are torn by the argument that our security will actually be compromised by greater defense efforts. We are told that the resources required for defense will come at the expense of social peace. A dollar more for the military, so goes the argument, in my own country as well as here in Europe, is a dollar less for welfare, for health and for other necessary benefits. We have heard this reasoning before. Its premise is a lack of confidence that a democratic society can provide for both social progress and an adequate defense. Yet the democracies have proven time and time again since the Second World War that they can achieve these objectives. The West has been able to defend itself. And behind that shield, we have registered extraordinary social progress. Clearly the two are complementary. If we are not prepared to defend ourselves, then we shall lose the chance to reform our societies; and if we are not prepared to seek social justice, then we shall lose the will—and the reason—to defend ourselves.

Before Berlin Press Association,
West Berlin, Sept. 13/The New York Times, 9-14:8.

Gary W. Hart
United States Senator, D—Colorado

4

[Arguing against the proposed B-1 bomber]: We don't have the Stealth technology yet so you

(GARY W. HART)

can't build it into the B-1 bomber. That's the Achilles heel of the B-1 bomber. It is an obsolete technology, given both existing and projected Soviet defensive capabilities. It will be obsolete by the time it's deployed. Stealth is a breakthrough. It would leapfrog technology instead of challenging technology. What the B-1 bomber does is accept a certain given of Soviet technology and say, "We're going to go right at it and try to defeat it." And that's its fatal flaw. Stealth says, "We know what that technology is going to be and we're going to leapfrog it by sophisticated counter-technology." B-1 would offer no particular threat or challenge to the Soviets; Stealth makes obsolete what they have and what they will have, and forces them into a defensive mode which requires an enormous capital investment.

Interview/The New York Times, 10-11:(4)5.

Mark O. Hatfield
United States Senator, R—Oregon

1

[Arguing against further funding of the MX missile and the neutron bomb]: I'm going to stand in the schoolhouse door on things like the MX missile and the neutron bomb because I cannot support that when we have people problems . . . We cannot create any sacrosanct agencies. I want to assure you that the cost-effectiveness we all want out of everything—food stamps, welfare programs that are so necessary—must be applied as well to military spending and to the Pentagon.

Before Los Angeles City Council, Feb. 10/
Los Angeles Times, 2-11:(I)6.

2

[Calling for a reduction in defense spending]: I don't know of any school of economics that contends we can do all those things President Reagan wants to do—tax cuts, raising employment, reducing inflation—without at least some cuts on the defense side . . . We Republicans damned [the late President Franklin] Roosevelt

for years for throwing money at problems . . . Now we're doing the same thing by saying if you escalate dollars, you escalate security. You can't prove that on a cost-benefit ratio.

Interview, Washington, March 5/
The Washington Post, 3-6:(A)8.

Thomas B. Hayward
Admiral and Chief of Operations,
United States Navy

3

In the naval area today your country is over-exposed and under-insured. Our margin of comfort is totally gone. We are operating at the ragged edge of adequacy when it comes to our globally disposed naval forces. We have been able to manage only because our forces have not been subjected to the added stress of combat anywhere in the world. Were contingency requirements superimposed on the equation, we would clearly have to reassess our priorities, and forego our presence in some areas that we now consider essential . . . In summary, our naval forces are covering all the geography that matters today, but not in numbers that give us the degree of confidence we would like, and at a high cost in terms of wear and tear on our people and material. I see nothing downstream that promises significant relief from the commitments we are now experiencing. If anything, the trends are in the opposite direction. While I am pleased with the high quality of ships, aircraft and weapons entering the fleet, my enthusiasm is notably tempered by the pace of modernization displayed by the Soviets. On a comparative basis I would have to say that while we had a very good year in 1980, the Russians had a spectacular one.

Before Senate Armed Services Committee,
Washington, Feb. 5/
The Christian Science Monitor, 3-31:26.

Ernest F. Hollings
United States Senator, D—South Carolina

4

[On the all-volunteer armed forces]: [Without a draft,] our nation's defense burden would rest with the poor, the black and the disadvantaged

(ERNEST F. HOLLINGS)

for years to come. Almost one-quarter of all new recruits are black—double their proportion in population. The number of other minorities, especially Hispanics, is growing. And, more than a racial problem, it is a class problem. For even the white recruits are drawn from the poorer and less-educated segments of society.

News conference, Washington, March 23/
Chicago Tribune, 3-25:(1)2.

1

This [Reagan] Administration is uncertain about where it is going on defense policy. Not only does it lack plans for implementing the programs, but it is unclear as to the program priorities. We are told of all the many programs DOD would like to buy. So Congress inevitably comes face to face with the fundamental question: Can we afford all of the programs that the President and DOD have said are necessary to make significant improvements in our armed forces? I believe the answer is resoundingly "no" if we assume adoption of the President's economic and tax program and when consideration is given to the flawed estimates of the Administration concerning inflation in the defense business and to the uncontrolled management and spending of the DOD.

Before the Senate, Washington/
The Washington Post, 8-6:(A)28.

Richard H. Ichord
United States Representative, D—Missouri

2

. . . there has been a serious decline in the nation's defense industrial capability that places our national security in jeopardy. An alarming erosion of crucial industrial elements, coupled with a mushrooming dependence on foreign sources for critical materials, is endangering our defense posture at its very foundation.

Before House Armed Services Committee,
Washington/
The Christian Science Monitor, 5-27:11.

John Paul II
Pope

3

It has been estimated that about half of the world's research workers are at present employed for military purposes. Can the human family morally go on much longer in this direction? Can we remain passive when we are told that humanity spends immensely more money on arms than on development, when we learn that one soldier's equipment costs many times more than a child's education?

Hiroshima, Japan, Feb. 25/
Los Angeles Times, 2-25:(I)12.

Herman Kahn
Director, Hudson Institute

4

Land-based missiles give America a true war-fighting nuclear force. What I'm saying is this: If we want to deter war, we must prepare for the chance that deterrence may fail—meaning we must be ready to actually fight a nuclear war and win. I call this "thinking the unthinkable." If we are unwilling to make this leap of imagination, our deterrent system is not credible. *Minutemen* [missiles] are by far the best weapons we have for this mission. They're the most accurate, flexible, controllable, reliable—you name it. The MX missile is even better.

Interview/U.S. News & World Report, 9-21:54.

George F. Kennan
Co-chairman, American Committee on
East-West Accord; Former United States
Ambassador to the Soviet Union

5

We [the U.S. and Soviet Union] have gone on piling weapon upon weapon, missile upon missile . . . helplessly, almost involuntarily, like the victims of some sort of hypnosis, like men in a dream, like lemmings headed for the sea [until the total numbers have reached] such grotesque dimensions as to defy rational understanding.

Upon accepting the Albert Einstein Peace Prize,
Washington, May 19/
The Washington Post, 5-20:(A)14.

(GEORGE F. KENNAN)

1

What I would like to see the President [Reagan] do, after due consultation with the Congress, would be to propose to the Soviet government an immediate across-the-boards reduction by 50 per cent of the nuclear arsenals now being maintained by the two superpowers —a reduction affecting in equal measure all forms of the weapon, strategic, medium range and tactical, as well as all means of their delivery —all this to be implemented at once and without further wrangling among the experts, and to be subject to such national means of verification as now lie at the disposal of the two powers. Whether the balance of reduction would be precisely even—whether it could be construed to favor statistically one side or the other—would not be the question; once we start thinking that way, we would be back on the same old fateful track that has brought us where we are today. Whatever the precise results of such a reduction, there would still be plenty of overkill left—so much so that if this first operation were successful, I would then like to see a second one put in hand to rid us of at least two-thirds of what would be left.

Upon receiving the Albert Einstein Peace Prize,/ Washington, May 19/ The Christian Science Monitor, 6-1:23.

Gene R. LaRocque
Rear Admiral, United States Navy (Ret.); Director, Center for Defense Information

2

We are moving away from political solutions [to world problems]. We are being driven by the military. The military in the United States is the dominant force in our society. We criticize our clergy, our judges, even our wives—but never the Joint Chiefs of Staff.

At Conference on Nuclear War in Europe, Groningen, Netherlands/ The New York Times, 4-28:6.

3

I think there are two pervasive myths: The first is that the United States is not strong and is growing weaker, and the second is that the Soviet Union is strong and growing stronger . . . We are far stronger militarily than the Soviet Union. We have more nuclear weapons and have always had more nuclear weapons than the Soviet Union. Our Navy is much better than the Soviet Union's. We have nearly 540,000 men in our Navy and the Soviets have about 450,000. We have 5,000 operating aircraft in the U.S. Navy, and the Soviets have 1,600. We have 4,400 major naval bases scattered around thr world. The Soviet Union has six naval bases—all in the Soviet Union—and three of them freeze up in the wintertime . . . The United States has 188,000 Marines; the Soviet Union has 12,000 marines. We have more Marines in the United States Navy than all the countries in the world put together. The United States has a large Coast Guard; the Soviet Union has no coast guard. Our ships are younger, more modern than all the Soviet ships. The average age of a Soviet warship is 24½ years. The Soviet Union has 100 less submarines today than it had 15 years ago. The Soviet Union has less ships in total today than it did 15 years ago. Having said that, the Soviet nuclear-powered submarines could make devastating attacks on our Navy and our merchant marine in time of war. But any war we get into with the Soviet Union will be a nuclear war, and both sides will be destroyed.

Interview/ Los Angeles Herald Examiner, 6-9:(A)12.

John F. Lehman, Jr.
Secretary of the Navy of the United States

4

. . . our national strategy requires naval superiority without euphemism or hedge words. Maritime superiority is necessary because America, unlike the Soviet Union, is an island nation. Geographic location can be a great advantage, no doubt. But Alfred the Great learned from his struggles with the invading Danes that "there is no advantage in living on an island unless you control the waters that wash its

(JOHN F. LEHMAN, JR.)

shores." That is an embryonic appreciation of the importance of seapower. We now know that there is no advantage—in fact there is great disadvantage—to living in an island nation, unless you control the seas that wash its shores and the sea lines of communication that sustain it. Maritime superiority means that we must be capable—and be seen to be capable—of keeping our sea lines of commerce and communications secure in those areas of the world where our vital interests depend on them. If we are to survive as a free nation, our access to our allies, our energy sources and our trading partners cannot be hostage to the offensive power of any combination of adversaries. We must have the Naval and Marine Corps power to defeat militarily any attempts to interfere with such access.

At Naval War College, April/
The Christian Science Monitor, 4-15:23.

1

[On why the Navy wants to reactivate two World War II battleships]: Because that is the best way quickly to restore real offensive firepower to our Navy. With battleships, we can do it faster, better and at far less expense than we could by any other means. A battleship is an impressive sight, but it is impressive because it can do so much damage to an enemy. The visual impact of a United States battleship on the horizon springs from its ability to put Soviet ships on the bottom of the sea and to put devastating firepower ashore ... These ships—the *New Jersey* and the *Iowa*—are as fast as any on the oceans today. They are as fast as our *Nimitz* aircraft carrier or Russia's *Kirov* battle cruiser. They're also tougher than any ship in anybody's navy. They were built to hold up against Japanese naval gunfire—2,700-lb artillery shells from 18-inch naval guns fired at three times the speed of sound. That's a far more formidable threat than any conventional warhead the Soviets can throw against us. In the old days, you had to take hits and keep on fighting. That's the way these ships were built.

Interview/U.S. News & World Report, 5-4:37.

Carl Levin
United States Senator, D—Michigan

2

There is growing resistance to spending so much on defense at the same time there is a lack of effort to get at [Pentagon] waste ... I think the public wants to be strong [militarily]. Nonetheless, the public also wants us to eliminate some waste. There's no budget this size that doesn't have substantial waste in it. They see an effort made to eliminate waste and fat in domestic programs, but they don't see that same effort being made in the defense budget.

The Washington Post, 4-17:(A)10.

Scott M. Matheson
Governor of Utah [D]

3

If our resources were limitless, we would not be forced to ask ourselves what economic and social opportunities are foregone by making massive investments in armaments. But viewed in the context that national security is defined by a strong economy, stable energy markets, social well-being and military preparedness, perhaps we must conclude the race against the Soviets to build and deploy gold-plated weaponry can be won only by starving other vital components of that national security.

At West Desert High School commencement,
Partoun, Utah, May 21/
The New York Times, 5-23:8.

Edwin Meese III
Counsellor to the President
of the United States

4

[On President Reagan's rejection of former President Jimmy Carter's plan to shuttle MX missiles among many different shelters as a means of protecting them against attack]: [President Reagan] was looking at the issue of survivability. The key was that, no matter how many shelters you have, the Russians can manufacture warheads faster and cheaper than you can build shelters for missiles. The President didn't want to waste a lot of money and use resources we didn't

(EDWIN MEESE III)

have, like real estate, for a system that was no more survivable than the one we have now. On that basis, he made the decision to place the missiles in existing shelters and to proceed with research into three other modes of deployment. He was choosing the greatest protection at the earliest possible time, to the limits of available technology.

Interview, Washington, Oct. 3/
The New York Times, 10-4:(1)18.

Walter F. Mondale
Former Vice President of the United States
1

Everyone agrees we must meet the Russian challenge to improve our defenses. But that . . . is essentially a challenge to American technology. There is no way that we would or should try to match American bulk for Soviet bulk. They have more people under arms; they are producing more tanks than we do. Our advantage lies in our ability to be far superior to them in terms of sophistication, high technology, advanced business and industrial methods. All of this is a direct and indispensable product of quality education.

Before National Education Association,
Washington, April 30/
The New York Times, 5-1:10.

Sam Nunn
United States Senator, D—Georgia
2

[Warning against using tax exemptions and bonuses to attract volunteers to the military]: We must address the question of who will serve and who will not serve in the armed forces. I do not believe the American people want to be protected by a praetorian guard or an army of Gurkhas. Our entire history and tradition supports the concept of citizen-soldiers serving the nation —not soldier-mercenaries served by the nation . . . Creative ideas are needed. But the grab-bag and "throwing money" approach indicated [by] the Administration thus far is not in the best

long-term interests of this nation or our citizen-soldiers.

Before the Senate, Washington, May 8/
Los Angeles Times, 5-10:(1)22.

Verne Orr
Secretary of the Air Force of the United States
3

Our military forces in Vietnam served as well as any in our history. They were denied the cup of victory, not because they lacked any of the merits of veterans of earlier wars, but because of the political tenor of the times in which they served. They returned home to no parades, no bands, no waving flags. There was no outpouring of public gratitude for the sacrifices of those who had sweltered in the jungles 8,000 miles from home. Nor was there any outpouring of public sympathy for the families of those who failed to return from those jungles. The United States was sadly remiss . . . That situation must be corrected, and President Reagan is determined that it will be.

At ceremony marking National Day of Recognition
for Veterans of the Vietnam Era,
Washington, April 26/
The Washington Post, 4-27:(C)3.

Leon E. Panetta
United States Representative, D—California
4

[Saying it is important for armed-forces personnel to be well-versed in foreign languages]: If we had to suddenly take a division into the Middle East, or into an African nation, we would have very little capacity for people who are knowledgeable of the language . . . There has to be recognition of this as meeting a very real national-security need—as important as development of a weapon, as important as the training of a man to fight in hand-to-hand combat.

Los Angeles Herald Examiner,
1-18:(A)13.

67

WHAT THEY SAID IN 1981

William J. Perry
Chief of Research and Engineering,
Department of Defense of the United States

1

[On whether or not to go ahead with a new manned bomber, such as the proposed B-1]: The primary question is whether this is the appropriate time to bring this weapon system into the operational inventory . . . Even if money were unlimited, other resources are not. The aerospace industry is already overtaxed due to defense and commercial orders. We already have a 2- to 2½-year order time for some parts. And in this overheated situation, inflation is running 15 per cent to 20 per cent, some 5 per cent over the national level. Adding a new B-1 procurement would greatly aggravate the situation.

Los Angeles Times, 1-19:(I)9.

Robert Pirie
Assistant Secretary for Manpower Reserve
Affairs and Logistics, Department of Defense
of the United States

2

All-volunteer-force-versus-draft debates have cropped up periodically throughout the 1970s. They are founded on a lopsided argument in which an enormously complicated structure like the AVF is pitted against a slogan and a sentiment called "the draft." I am certain we could design some peacetime drafts . . . We could prohibit volunteers, or draft according to racial quotas to ensure a representative force; we could draft according to occupation to fill our needs for skilled technicians; we could eliminate all deferments or give them to all who apply, depending on what social theory we favor; we could pay conscripts next to nothing to reduce costs and in the process increase the number of applications for discharge because of hardship. This is the critical point. Those who are quick to find answers to all of our manpower questions in a peacetime draft are conspicuously silent on these questions: What kind of draft? Of whom? With what budgetary and social cost?

Interview/
The Washington Post, 7-22:(A)20.

Melvin Price
United States Representative, D—Illinois

3

In the event of a war, the U.S. defense industry would find it almost impossible to expand its weapons production suddenly and dramatically in the numbers necessary to sustain a prolonged conflict. The [Armed Services] panel's findings reveal that the U.S. defense industrial base lacks the capacity, manpower, skills and critical materials required to swing into crisis productions.

Washington, Jan. 4/Los Angeles Times, 1-5:(I)1.

David Pryor
United States Senator, D—Arkansas

4

[Arguing against the U.S. producing more chemical weapons]: We don't know what the Russians have in chemical weapons, how sophisticated their supplies are, or how extensive their stockpiles might be. We should have this intelligence before moving in reaction to supposition. We don't know for sure, as some have suggested, that the U.S.S.R. has used nerve gas in Afghanistan and Laos. In fact, the best evidence we have shows that they have used only riot-control agents and not lethal gas at all . . . Finally, we are left with the simple issue that nerve gas is inhumane. It doesn't kill soldiers who are equipped with masks and protective clothing that can make them invulnerable. It kills civilians who would have no protection from aerosol clouds that cause fatalities many miles from their detonation points. It goes against everything our country stands for.

Before the Senate, Washington/
The Christian Science Monitor, 7-22:23.

5

Let me make it clear that I don't trust the Russians. None of us trusts the Russians. But what's the alternative to serious and genuine arms limitations? Given the basic truth that we are suspicious and distrustful, do we then spend ourselves into exhaustion—in pursuit of weapons that would destroy us all? The truth? We all

(DAVID PRYOR)

know it: Neither side can purchase invulnerability . . . My concern today might be expressed in one simple and time-worn term: escalation. We harden the [missile] silos, and the Russians build bigger missiles with larger loads. The dog chases its tail. Inevitably, we face a catastrophic result. President Reagan should try for another arms treaty—now. Before it's too late.

Before the Senate, Washington/
The Washington Post, 11-8:(C)6.

Ronald Reagan
President of the United States

1

I believe my duty as President requires that I recommend increases in defense spending over the coming years. Since 1970, the Soviet Union has invested $300-billion more in its military forces than we have. As a result of its massive military buildup, the Soviets now have a significant numerical advantage in strategic nuclear delivery systems, tactical aircraft, submarines, artillery and anti-aircraft defense. To allow this imbalance to continue is a threat to our national security.

Before joint session of Congress,
Washington, Feb. 18/The New York Times, 2-19:14.

2

[On possible U.S.-Soviet arms-control talks]: I have repeatedly said that I am willing to negotiate if it's a legitimate negotiation aimed at verifiable reductions—in particular, the strategic nuclear weapons. And I also made it plain that I think at such a negotiation table—if and when this takes place—there should be other considerations, what has been termed by [Soviet leader] Brezhnev as "linkage." I think that you can't just deal with one facet of the international relationship. You've got to deal with all of the problems that are dividing us.

News conference, Washington, Feb. 24/
Los Angeles Times, 2-25:(I)11.

3

A Chinese philosopher, Sun Tzu, 2,500 years ago, said winning a hundred victories in a hundred battles is not the acme of skill; to subdue the enemy without fighting is the acme of skill. A truly successful army is one that, because of its strength and ability and dedication, will not be called upon to fight because no one will dare to provoke it. There have been four wars in my lifetime; none of them came about because the United States was too strong.

At U.S. Military Academy commencement, May 27/
The New York Times, 5-28:8.

4

In much of the '70s, there was a widespread lack of respect for the uniform, born perhaps of what has been called the Vietnam syndrome. The result was inevitable: the falloff of enlistments, but even worse, a drop in re-enlistments resulting in a great loss of experienced noncommissioned officers. A cry for a draft arose to a crescendo. Well, I still believe there is another way, one more in keeping with our system of rewarding those who work and serve on a scale commensurate with what we ask of them. I don't suppose we could put an exact price on the sacrifice that we ask of those who guarantee our safety, but one thing is certain: They deserve better than a bare subsistence level.

At U.S. Military Academy commencement, May 27/
The New York Times, 5-28:8.

5

[On the neutron bomb]: This weapon was particularly designed to offset the great superiority that the Soviet Union has on the Western front against the NATO nations—a tank advantage of better than 4 to 1. And it is purely, as I say, a defensive weapon. And maybe that is why it's so painful to the Soviet Union to realize that this could offset their great advantage there . . . this is something that seems to be overlooked in all the

WHAT THEY SAID IN 1981

(RONALD REAGAN)

propaganda that's now being uttered [against] this weapon, and that is that the present tactical battlefield weapons stationed in Europe are nuclear weapons far more destructive, far longer in rendering areas uninhabitable because of radioactivity than the neutron weapon . . . there's no mention made [by critics of the neutron bomb] of 200 SS-20s, strategic [Soviet] nuclear weapons of medium range that are aimed at the cities of all of Europe today, and that are not being considered in any of the talk of reduction of theatre forces . . . So let's remember the SS-20s before we start worrying too much about the [neutron bomb].

News conference, Santa Barbara, Calif., Aug. 13/
The New York Times, 8-14:8.

1

[On the Soviet Union's criticism of the U.S. decision to manufacture neutron bombs]: What we are in is a situation where we're being realistic about their military buildup, which has gone on unchecked in spite of all of the meetings having to do with arms-control. I can understand their anguish. They are squealing like they are sitting on a sharp nail, simply because we now are showing the world that we are not going to let them get to the point of dominance where they can someday issue the free world an ultimatum of "surrender or die." And they don't like that.

News conference, Santa Barbara, Calif., Aug. 13/
The New York Times, 8-14:8.

2

We are going to continue to urge [the Soviets] to sit down with us in a program of strategic-arms reductions. It will be the first time that we have ever sat on our side of the table and let them know there is a new chip on the table. And that chip is that there will be legitimate, verifiable arms reductions, or there will be an arms race which they can't win.

Before Illinois Forum, Chicago, Sept. 2/
Los Angeles Times, 9-3:(I)5.

[On whether a nuclear exchange could be limited or would inevitably escalate]: I don't honestly know . . . There never has been a weapon that someone hasn't come up with a defense. But it could . . . and the only defense would be, well, you shoot yours and we'll shoot ours. And if you still had that kind of stalemate, I could see where you could have the exchange of tactical weapons against troops in the field without it bringing either one of the major powers to pushing "the button" . . . I do have to point out that everything that has been said and everything in their manuals indicates that, unlike us, the Soviet Union believes that a nuclear war is possible and they believe it is winnable.

To newspaper editors, Washington, Oct. 16/
Chicago Tribune, 10-21:(1)1.

Bernard W. Rogers
General, United States Army;
Supreme Allied Commander/Europe

4

[NATO's] relative ability to counter the Soviet threat is declining. There is no question about that in my mind . . . In every key area that we use as a measurement, the Warsaw Pact continues to outnumber NATO by 2 to 1 or greater. I am talking about divisions, tanks, artillery, tactical aircraft and submarines. Added to that is the fact that in the 1970s they overcame the technological lead that we have had in the quality of our weaponry and upon which we had depended to overcome their traditional quantitative lead. My conclusion is that the Warsaw Pact has now surpassed—or soon will surpass—NATO in every category of war-fighting capability required to implement our strategy. That is why I think NATO nations must strengthen their defenses while there is still time.

Interview/U.S. News & World Report, 6-15:26.

Eugene V. Rostow
Director-designate, Arms Control and
Disarmament Agency of the United States

5

Many look to arms-control agreements as magical guarantees of peace. The history of the

(EUGENE V. ROSTOW)

subject should persuade us to accept more modest expectations. Fair, balanced and verifiable arms-control agreements can play a significant role both in achieving and in maintaining peace. They cannot do so themselves. But despite the disappointments and the setbacks, our foreign policy since President Truman's time has never stopped trying for effective international controls to minimize the risk of nuclear war and encourage the peaceful use of nuclear energy. Under President Reagan, this will emphatically continue ... [But] unless effective containment [of Soviet expansion] is restored, we cannot expect to pursue detente and arms control fruitfully. The restoration of containment should be the predicate for useful arms-control agreements with the Soviet Union, which could then reinforce the policy and help to sustain it during periods of stress. Even competing nations have common interests in peace, if they can be brought to accept them. It should be possible, whatever the difficulties, to translate those interests into agreements to limit and control armaments. And such agreements, in turn, could reduce the risk of war by inadvertence, moderate arms competition and promote political cooperation.

At hearings on his confirmation before
Senate Foreign Relations Committee,
Washington, June 22/The New York Times, 6-23:6.

Edward L. Rowny
Lieutenant General, United States Army (Ret.);
Special Representative for Arms Control and
Disarmament Negotiations for the
President of the United States

1

[The Soviets] want an [arms-control] treaty [with the U.S.], and they need a treaty, and they'll come around and they'll do business with us in the end. But we'll do business better if we negotiate from strength than if we negotiate from weakness. We're going hand in hand with a two-track approach, showing that we've got the will and the commitment, as Churchill said, to "arm to parley" ... [The Soviets] are realis-

tic people, they understand international politics and they understand the correlation of forces. I think that they're finding in this [Reagan] Administration a formidable adversary ... I think that now they've got to say to themselves, "Look, we're dealing with somebody who's got some idea of where he's going ... and he's not going to be pushed around." They understand strength in weapons and they understand strength in people.

Interview, Washington/
The Christian Science Monitor, 8-17:1,9.

2

[The Soviets] believe nuclear weapons are there to be used. They believe their civil-defense system would allow them to get away with "only" about 13 million casualties—5 per cent of their population—fewer than they suffered in World War II. So we must think about nuclear exchanges not because they will ever occur necessarily, but because as long as the Soviets believe they're possible, they will have the power of blackmail over us.

Time, 8-31:16.

James R. Schlesinger
Former Secretary of Defense
of the United States

3

Nuclear forces are a backdrop against which other forces and diplomacy operate. If other countries, particularly our allies, see the Soviets having the probable capacity to inflict damage on our ICBM fields—and we lack the capacity to do the same to them—then perceptions will have been altered in such a way that the political will of both the U.S. and our allies may be less firm. We may be more willing to yield to pressure [from the Soviets].

Time, 8-31:14.

Helmut Schmidt
Chancellor of West Germany

4

[Criticizing the spread of pacifism in his country]: Any German who tried to talk the

WHAT THEY SAID IN 1981

(HELMUT SCHMIDT)

West into disarming, assuming he had any success with our own people, would forfeit the trust and solidarity of the allies on whom we depend for our security . . . The young people and adult theologians who would decide on our behalf for surrender rather than defense . . . are acting irresponsibly in the true sense of the word, for they are not responsible for the consequences . . . And these same people nonsensically suggest that if one renounces defense, there is no need for fear. That is absurd.

Interview/Chicago Tribune, 3-31:(1)4.

Gard Schmueckle
General, West German Army (Ret.); Former Deputy Supreme Allied Commander/Europe

1

[Supporting the U.S. decision to produce neutron bombs]: I believe the stationing of the neutron weapon in Europe would be more useful than the other atomic weapons. Besides, [Soviet President Leonid] Brezhnev himself said years ago that the Soviet Union was testing the neutron weapon, and I presume Moscow will soon have one of its own. Many of those [Europeans] currently cursing the Americans will be the first to call for the neutron weapon in case of war.

Interview/Los Angeles Times, 8-12:(I)19.

Patricia Schroeder
United States Representative, D—Colorado

2

President Reagan's war on waste, fraud, abuse and mismanagement [in government] has, up until now, been limited almost entirely to domestic social programs. Victory cannot be won, however, if our army of auditors and investigators is prevented from crossing the river and attacking waste, fraud, abuse and mismanagement at the Pentagon.

Before Senate Appropriations Committee, Washington, July 9/The New York Times, 7-10:8.

Eleanor Smeal
President, National Organization for Women

3

[All-male draft registration] says to every woman, "The government doesn't need you in time of national emergency." It says that the worst-qualified man is better than any woman. [By excluding all women, the Selective Service Act] reinforces the stereotype that she's unable to defend herself and is weak. [Moreover, the male-only rule means that] every man is at risk and is [therefore] entitled to more benefits.

Interview, Washington/ The Christian Science Monitor, 3-23:7.

Arlen Specter
United States Senator, R—Pennsylvania

4

The arms race makes little sense, but unpreparedness makes even less sense. In light of the potentially catastrophic consequences of being unprepared, it is my personal judgment that we must be militarily strong. It is a form of insurance policy. This particular insurance is very expensive; but, as with any insurance, the insured prefers to pay the premium and not to collect rather than incur the risk-event and collect.

The New York Times, 12-4:15.

John G. Tower
United States Senator, R—Texas

5

[Criticizing Reagan Administration plans to install MX missiles in stationary silos rather than continuously moving them around as a way of protecting them]: The most critical strategic problem facing the U.S. today is the vulnerability of our land-based missile forces to a Soviet knockout strike. The President's plan does nothing to remedy this weakness. The hard truth is this: By stuffing the MXs into fixed silos, we're creating just so many more sitting ducks for the Russians to shoot at. The MX missiles in these silos will be exposed targets, like our *Minuteman* ICBMs are today. The "window of vulnerability" will remain open to the

(JOHN G. TOWER)

Soviet first-strike threat. True, the MX missile itself will be more powerful, more accurate—and we need that kind of weapon. But it's of little use to us unless the Soviets are convinced that it can survive an attack. Without that, the Russians will have no incentive to start serious arms-control talks.

Interview/U.S. News & World Report, 11-2:47.

Robert L. Walters
Vice Admiral and Deputy Chief of Operations for Surface Warfare, United States Navy

1

[On the plan to reactivate some World War II battleships]: The phenomenon of naval presence is often difficult to quantify, but it is clearly that the ability to operate naval forces around the world is a highly effective political and diplomatic tool. In this role, the battleship will be impressive and intimidating.

Before Congressional subcommittee, Washington/
Los Angeles Times, 7-26:(V)3.

Paul C. Warnke
Chairman, Committee for National Security; Former Director, Arms Control and Disarmament Agency of the United States

2

The way the United States can deter Soviet attack is to build the most survivable forces possible. And the way you do that is to strengthen and modernize the diverse nuclear arsenal we now have. Diversity causes uncertainty, and uncertainty makes the concept of a pre-emptive strike seem very, very dangerous. That's the major reason why the Soviets would have to be out of their minds to contemplate an attack on our ICBM force.

Interview/U.S. News & World Report, 9-21:54.

3

[On Soviet civil-defense efforts to protect themselves in a nuclear war]: What kind of civil-defense program is going to protect you against 6,000 nuclear warheads? It depends upon whether you want to die in the field or die in a hole. Would you rather be roasted or boiled? It doesn't make any real difference. There *is* no civil defense against the number of warheads that we and the Soviet Union have deployed against one another . . .   [And] what happens when the people come out of the holes, those that have survived? Where do they go? What do they do? Where do they work? Where do they find food? We lack imagination when we talk about a "limited" nuclear war in which either the Soviet Union or we would emerge as the winners.

Interview/Los Angeles Times, 9-29:(I)10.

Thomas J. Watson, Jr.
Former United States Ambassador to the Soviet Union

4

I believe that the United States is living currently in a world of fantasy. We have been since the beginning of President Johnson's Administration. You cannot fight major wars in distant places on a guns-and-butter basis. You've got to have higher taxes, all sorts of things like universal military service, a standing army, etc. And you've got to do it with a modest pay scale. What does a Swiss get when he goes into his service? Cigarettes and chewing-gum money. I think the first step is the draft. I think it's ridiculous for the U.S. Army to compete for people at business-type pay scales.

Interview, Moscow/Los Angeles Times, 1-18:(V)5.

5

I believe that thermonuclear weapons are good for two things—for deterrence or for suicide. Other suggested uses are pure fantasy. Scenarios for trying to use limited nuclear war to advance the interests of the United States lack understanding of the weapons or common sense or both.

Before Arms Control Association,
Dec. 9/
The New York Times, 12-22:14.

WHAT THEY SAID IN 1981

Caspar W. Weinberger
Secretary of Defense of the United States

1

One of the most disturbing developments we confront is the continuing deterioration of the balance in intercontinental nuclear arms. We must make large investments in this area to deter the ultimate catastrophe. It is unacceptable to find ourselves today facing the prospect of Soviet strategic superiority and to watch the Soviet Union mass-producing both land-based missiles and a manned-bomber fleet, while the United States has an open production line for neither. Our descent from a position of clear strategic superiority to the present perilous situation coincided with our strenuous attempt to bring the arms competition under control through negotiated agreements with the Soviet Union. Rarely in history have we or any great nation pursued such noble goals, risked so much, and yet gained so little.

Before Senate Armed Services Committee, Washington, March 4/The New York Times, 3-5:10.

2

[On allied support for U.S. defense responsibilities]: Our people will not want to march alone. If our effort is not joined by all who are threatened, by all who face the common danger, we in the United States could lose at home the critical public support for which we have labored long and hard.

Before NATO defense ministers, Bonn, West Germany, April 7/The New York Times, 4-8:6.

3

[Saying President Reagan will refrain from instituting a military draft as long as he can]: . . . the draft is a very hard thing to administer fairly, and if it isn't administered fairly, isn't perceived to be, you have all kinds of trouble, even if you don't have a Vietnam war. [The selection process] causes all kinds of trouble. Usually everybody in school is exempt, and that causes problems. And then you have all the rich and poor and inequity and all of that business. So he wants to avoid it just as long as he can,

and I think there's a possibility he can avoid it . . . [But] if it develops two or three or four months running that we're just falling way, way behind and we're not able to realize the added strength that we want, then I would just go to the President and say, "I'm very much afraid it looks as if we're going to have to do something to get more men in, and women." And I would think he would probably reluctantly agree.

Interview, Washington/Los Angeles Times, 5-20:(I)11.

4

We welcome the opportunity to have discussions with the Soviets about genuine arms limitations and a real reduction in strategic arms. SALT II did not have what I considered anything resembling an effective limitation on arms. It is important to have these talks, but not at any price and not necessarily at the precise time the Soviets want them. But I think it's essential that when we go into negotiations of that kind it be correctly perceived by the Soviets that we have completely changed our policies, that we have started to add, and plan to continue to add, no matter what happens, the strength to get us back to a balance that can secure the peace through deterrence.

Interview, Washington/ Los Angeles Herald Examiner, 5-24:(A)1.

5

We do not seek military power for its own sake. But the fact is, the Soviets' military build-up has been anything but defensive in nature. It would have been naive to expect the Soviets, should they achieve a clear superiority, not to exploit it even more fully than they currently are. We have no choice but to assume some purpose behind their huge allocation of resources to the military at the expense of other needs, which have gone unmet for so long, in their state-run economy. The facts are that for several years, as Soviet military power has increased, so has their aggressive activity around the world.

At University of San Diego commencement/ U.S. News & World Report, 6-15:35.

(CASPAR W. WEINBERGER)

1

[On President Reagan's decision to begin manufacturing the neutron bomb]: Given the record of vacillation [on the neutron bomb by the former Carter Administration] a few years ago, and given the reaction it caused—in Europe and the Soviet Union—of a weak, divided America and given the direction of the Congress to do this, had we done anything other than go ahead with it, it would have contributed enormously to the impression that the United States was doing business at the same old vacillating stand.

News conference, Washington, Aug. 10/
Los Angeles Times, 8-11:(I)9.

2

[On calls for cuts in the defense budget in order to aid the general economic recovery]: There is no way to wish aside the realities in the world which demand that we rearm America and do it expeditiously. Defense of the country comes first. There won't be much economy if the nation is not strongly defended . . . We all want better defense at lower cost, but as anyone who has ever seen war knows, war is a terribly costly and savagely destructive human activity. These are the bitter truths and we cannot look away from them. No strategic or technological trick can change these truths nor can sleights of hand make our ability to deter aggression anything but an expensive affair.

Before American Legion, Honolulu, Sept. 3/
Los Angeles Times, 9-4:(I)1,20.

3

[On the risks of supplying advanced U.S. military equipment to ostensibly friendly countries, when that equipment might fall into the hands of unfriendly nations through accidents or unauthorized transfers]: There's always going to be a risk. We simply have to make the decision as to whether we want sales of our equipment to countries which we think share our ideals, whether we want to thereby help the defense of freedom throughout the world, or whether we want to become a self-contained island and not make any sales to anyone.

Stockholm, Oct. 18/
The Washington Post, 10-19:(A)22.

4

The principal problem that we have in the world stems from the fact that we [the U.S.] did cut defense in the past. We are perceived as unreliable and not willing to make the sacrifices necessary to sustain the strength we need in this kind of dangerous world. What we must do now is regain that strength. It takes time, and it takes a very steady resolve to do it. I am sure that we will be under pressure. But those who bring the pressure do not have a reasoned set of recommendations. It's simply a desire to cut defense because other things are being cut. Those who call for cuts in defense don't take into account the results in terms of the nation's security.

Interview/U.S. News & World Report, 11-23:29.

Leonid M. Zamyatin
Director, International Information
Department, Soviet Communist Party
Central Committee

5

We rule out the possibility of "limited" nuclear war. In a nuclear war, whether supposedly limited or unlimited, it will be difficult to tell the victor from the vanquished. We're not advocates of a strategy of preventive war, and we're not looking for a nuclear duel with the U.S. We want to return to businesslike cooperation, reduce the level of confrontation, including the nuclear area. Yet we can't sit idly by and do nothing when one great power [the U.S.] accuses another [the Soviet Union] of a policy of limited war. If the U.S. insists on an arms race, all right. Maybe we'll be put to the test. We will endure it. But, we assure you, America will not attain superiority.

Interview, Moscow/Time, 11-2:35.

75

The Economy . Labor

William J. Abernathy
Professor, school of business,
Harvard University

1

[The Japanese] productivity advantage comes from a multitude of factors, but mainly from the fact that they have a work force that's "turned on," willing to work and is excited about making cars. Whereas our work force, because of the long adversarial history we've had, has been hostile to management and managers have been hostile to the work force. We have a different basic productivity position in this country, and it's because of a lot of minutia. It's not the sort of thing that can be corrected by investment policy, by a higher rate of savings. It's going to have to be fixed by management and labor together. And that's a tough and long problem, to correct this relationship between the management and labor.

Interview/Forbes, 2-2:65.

William L. Armstrong
United States Senator, R—Colorado

2

[On the proposed cuts in Federal spending initiated by the Reagan Administration]: Today is just the first step, not just in improved budgeting, but in revitalizing the nation's economy. We're not talking about cutting back to the '40s or '50s or '60s. This year's budget will be bigger than last year's, and next year's will be bigger than this year's. We're making a very, very modest reduction in programs that have grown at a very rapid rate.

Washington, March 19/
The New York Times, 3-20:11.

Thorne G. Auchter
Assistant Secretary for Occupational
Safety and Health, Department of Labor
of the United States

3

Safety and health is a subject that involves everyone at the workplace. There are no white hats and black ties, as far as this subject is concerned, because *everyone* wants to see workers return safe and sound to their families each day ... We don't look upon safety and health as an antagonistic process where one side loses if the other side wins. If hazards are kept out of American workplaces we all are winners. And this Administration intends that OSHA will serve as a catalyst, a unifying force for bringing people together to protect our workforce... Regulatory reform means a different way of doing business for America's regulatory agencies. It means government will work with the private sector to find common solutions to pressing problems instead of simply imposing its will by regulation. And it means that we will act upon the basis of fact—hard, objective data—whenever we make a decision.

The Washington Post, 8-27:(A)30.

James A. Baker III
Chief of Staff to the
President of the United States

4

[Blacks] have got a better shot at a job under the Reagan economic program than they have had historically in this country. This problem of black unemployment is not a problem that has been occasioned by Reagan—by President Reagan's economic program. It's something that's been with us through the days of the Great

(JAMES A. BAKER III)

Society and through the days of all the programs that were enacted in order to try and deal with it. It's something the President deplores. But if we can—if the program does succeed, it will create 13 million new jobs by 1986, three million more than would be created without the program. Clearly, black employment will gain from that.

Broadcast interview/
"Meet the Press," NBC-TV, 11-8.

Moe Biller
President,
American Postal Workers Union

1

Denying Federal-government employees the right to strike becomes a sort of refuge for government bureaucrats. They can ignore problems for years and then repress workers who seek to change the bad conditions through collective bargaining . . . I've always maintained that if government workers had the legal right to strike, you would see fewer strikes. I am convinced that there would be a greater feeling of responsibility all around and more sophistication—less need for people to show how macho they are.

Interview/U.S. News & World Report, 8-24:18.

Kenneth T. Blaylock
President, American Federation
of Government Employees

2

[On the current illegal strike by air-traffic controllers and the resulting dismissals and fines imposed by the government]: The events leading up to this confrontation, and the repressive measures taken since, lead to the unmistakable conclusion that the Reagan Administration is intent on breaking PATCO and all it stands for. If FAA were operating in the private sector, they would have faced charges of failure to bargain in good faith from the National Labor Relations Board. Instead, they enjoy the full force of Federal legal machinery and the judicial system in attempting to stifle the legitimate demands of PATCO and the workers it represents. We must ask who is the more blatant lawbreaker.

The Washington Post, 8-6:(A)8.

3

. . . unless mechanisms are developed to address the problems that public workers have, there will be strikes [by government employees]. I've been saying for many years that unless this country comes to grips with, one, the types of service it wants from government, and then deals with establishing fair personnel practices, policies, economic conditions and so on, that there would be workers' strikes and work stoppages, et cetera, in this country with public workers.

Broadcast interview/"Meet the Press," NBC-TV, 9-6.

W. Michael Blumenthal
Chairman, Burroughs Corporation;
Former Secretary of the Treasury
of the United States

4

[On the business community's skepticism about President Reagan's economic policy]: I think this Administration has done rather well for the business community, and business is grateful. Whatever skepticism is being voiced is done so very reluctantly. So I don't think that President Reagan is being picked on by the business community. But they're now concerned that the numbers don't add up. It's pretty clear that the loss of three quarters of a trillion dollars in tax receipts to the Treasury in the next five years [due to the Administration's lowering of tax rates] represents a gap that no one can see being bridged very easily.

Interview, Detroit, Oct. 1/
The Washington Post, 10-3:(D)10.

Edmund G. Brown, Jr.
Governor of California (D)

5

The very essential issue is economic prosperity and the problems of not attaining it. It has to be recognized that the underlying problem is that our economic growth is reaching a plateau. The real question is, will [President] Reagan be able to deal with that issue? I think there is a serious question about whether he will. If he doesn't, people are going to look around for some other political ideas. And I am attempting to conceptualize those ideas. There are those people who

(EDMUND G. BROWN, JR.)

say, well, the New Deal doesn't work; but they have no positive agenda. I have a positive agenda that involves technological innovation, resource investments and innovative education and training.

Interview, Sacramento, Calif.
The Christian Science Monitor, 2-12:12.

1

The 7.5 per cent unemployment [rate in the U.S.] reflects a bankrupt job-training philosophy and program in the United States. And the challenge is not just to help the people—which we ought to do out of compassion and human commitment—but the challenge is to recognize that America is going to decline as an economically powerful nation unless all our citizens are brought up to their level of talent.

Before House Subcommittee on
Employment Opportunities, Los Angeles, Aug. 14/
Los Angeles Times, 8-15:(I)30.

George Bush
Vice President of the United States

2

[On whether President Reagan's economic program of tax cuts and large government-spending cuts is an experiment, since it has rarely been done in the past]: Perhaps that's true. When you have an economy that is in an unprecedented state, you have to say that any medicine is an experiment to some degree. But there is a record of tax cuts accompanied by spending restraints that was set in the 1960s—and it worked. So it is not totally an experiment. But I will readily concede that there were some different economic ingredients then—rates of inflation, rates of unemployment, and a different economy. Still, whenever you chart an economic course in troubled economic seas like these, there is a certain amount of inexactitude in the science of prediction. But having said that, I think that the need for acceptance of this program—which is threefold: spending constraints, tax relief and regulatory relief—is unarguable. Now, you can

argue with where the tax cuts should go; some Congressmen will be arguing about it. But the reason I think the President has this popularity is because the people still perceive he is trying to do something about the economy—and trying to take some drastic action.

Interview/The Christian Science Monitor, 3-3:7.

Robert C. Byrd
United States Senator, D—West Virginia

3

There are two reactions to the new President [Reagan]. The first one, now, is good. You'll see another reaction later on, when people start to get hurt economically, when state taxes have to be increased, when inflation is not down to what they predict, or there's an energy shortage and they have no program except higher prices. That may be 18 months down the road, or a year.

Interview, Washington, March 13/
The New York Times, 3-14:8.

Jimmy Carter
Former President of the United States

4

[Criticizing President Reagan's tax-cut program]: Well, it's a wonderful tax program for rich people and special-interest groups, and one of the things that I learned was that there's a tremendous momentum to pass a bill like that at any time. The only thing that stands between a bill like that for special-interests and its passage is the President, protecting the interests of the average working families of our country. I think the Democrats did the best they could to have a bill more tailored for the working families of the country, and they failed. I don't find fault with anybody because of the outcome.

Atlanta, Aug. 7/
The Washington Post, 8-8:(A)4.

Tony Coelho
United States Representative, D—California

5

[On public support of President Reagan's economic program]: There was almost a religi-

(TONY COELHO)

ous belief in the beginning. People didn't want to listen to specifics; they were taking it on blind faith that the guy was right. I heard the same thing repeatedly—that the Democrats had been in for 40 years, and it was time to give the other guys a chance. But now, after six months, things are worse, and they're no longer willing to accept things on faith. They're scared.

The New York Times, 9-10:10.

Roy M. Cohn
Lawyer
1

I think the use of tax money is absolutely outrageous. It's not the very rich I would worry about; they always have tax shelters. The poor are all supported by government programs—food stamps and welfare and 50,000 other things. It's the middle class that is being slowly wiped out. You tell me today how somebody making $20-30,000 a year can pay taxes, send a couple of kids to college, have a car, buy food, buy fuel. I think that's one of the major things that was responsible for the Reagan Presidency. It was the middle class, the blue-collar worker, being taxed to death. And what for? Substantially to pay for people who are just as capable of working as they are. The "works" in this country are supporting the "don't-works."

Interview, Beverly Hills, Calif.
Los Angeles Times, 9-3:(V)22.

Thomas Donahue
Secretary-treasurer, American Federation of Labor-Congress of Industrial Organizations
2

[Saying he expects anti-labor action from the Reagan Administration]: Even if he wants to, I doubt that Reagan will be able to keep the right-wing political animals caged up for more than six months to a year before he has to throw them pieces of raw meat.

Los Angeles Times, 1-29:(I)1.

Raymond J. Donovan
Secretary of Labor of the United States
3

[Saying that government should stop making it easier for people to be unemployed and instead should be concentrating on creating jobs]: We have become fat, lazy and unconcerned in America. Our compassion has been misguided. It's time we admit that an unemployment check is a poor substitute for a paycheck. [America was built by] lean, hard-working self-reliant people. Facing a vast, unknown continent with the sea at their backs and no government to save them from their mistakes—they created a nation.

Before National Press Club, Washington, April 23/
The New York Times, 4-24:9.

4

[Saying he will seek heavy fines against "sweatshop" operations]: And when I say sweatshops, I'm not just talking about the garment industry. I'm talking about any of the multitude of businesses in which workers are abused and exploited. That this nation has allowed these shops —and the lawbreakers that run them—to stay in business is a national disgrace.

Before Business Roundtable, May 19/
Los Angeles Herald Examiner, 5-20:(A)5.

5

[On his background as a building contractor]: Of course I'm not from academia nor big labor, as some of my predecessors were. But maybe it's time we had someone with the practical experience of having been an employer as well as a union member. Every single predecessor has left behind the same problems I face now. I say the best social programs in the world are jobs. And I will trade pushing paper in this Department for jobs any day of the week.

Interview, Washington/The New York Times, 10-1:12.

Peter F. Drucker
Professor of social science, Claremont (Calif.) College Graduate School
6

Who is responsible for the plight of the automobile [industry]? Make it 50 per cent union, 30

WHAT THEY SAID IN 1981

(PETER F. DRUCKER)

per cent government, and the rest is management. [The late auto-labor leader] Walter Reuther foresaw this. He was very conscious of the danger of the American automobile industry outrunning the productivity base. He didn't know how to stop it, but he was very worried about it. And his sucessors, who are not great men, now realize that we have the first union-made unemployment. Union-made largely because 85 per cent of the value added goes out to the wage fund in one way or another, and that means that there is no capital formation... Notice this—the most automated capital-intensive industry we have is commercial agriculture, and agriculture is our star performer in exports.

Interview/Forbes, 5-25:46.

Otto Eckstein
Economist;
President, Data Resources, Inc.

1

[Arguing against monetary systems going back on the gold standard]: To tie the world economy to an asset that represents such a small part of the monetary system is really impossible. You could as well stabilize the world economy on the cabbage standard. It is absurd.

Time, 6-22:64.

Stuart E. Eizenstat
Assistant to the President of the United States for Domestic Affairs

2

The election of 1980 sent an unmistakable message. The taxpayers of America—the great American middle-class—are frustrated at persistent high inflation and its corrosive impact on their incomes and savings, their inability to buy a home, to plan for tomorrow, to retire when they hoped and once retired maintain a reasonable standard of living... Many believe the Democratic Party has lost touch with their concerns.

The New York Times, 1-11:(12)12.

Thomas S. Foley
United States Representative, D—Washington

3

We [Democrats] think that it would be inflationary and dangerous to go into a three-year, across-the-board tax cut [as proposed by President Reagan]. We think it's also inequitable. Do we want to see some form of economic program work? Of course. This country needs to have job stimulation and relief from inflation. We need to have a greater savings rate and re-industrialization of our key industries. We're for those things. The Democrats are going to cooperate to develop a program that can do that. But we want to see the program work, and we don't feel it's fair just to stand back and wait and allow the President to have any program he wants to send up. Most of the American people think it would be wrong for us to obstruct the President's program, and I think it would be. It's also wrong for us merely to rubber-stamp it ...

Broadcast interview/"Meet the Press," NBC-TV, 5-10.

Douglas A. Fraser
President,
United Automobile Workers of America

4

We're not disposed right now to open negotiations with Ford or GM before our contract expires in 1982. But if they should ask for concessions, whether it be now or in '82, they'd better be ready to talk about a whole range of things. They won't be able to just come to us and say, "Well, look here, we'd like you all to do for us what you did for Chrysler." It won't be that easy. They'd better be willing to talk about more representation on boards of directors, more worker input at the plant level—not necessarily in that order—but things like profit-sharing and financial disclosure, agreements to stop giving union work to outside contractors ... They'd better be willing to talk about a lot of things formerly considered the exclusive prerogatives of management.

The Washington Post, 2-17:(A)8.

(DOUGLAS A. FRASER)

1

[Saying in the future there will be more active ownership of companies by workers]: I know a lot of people in the labor movement are cool to the idea. I think sooner or later—and unfortunately, probably later—as time goes on and the complexity of society increases and economic shifts take place more regularly and profoundly, any labor leader has to start thinking it's not enough to be in a position to challenge decisions already made and irreversible. The only way workers can have a voice in their own destiny and the future is to have a voice in the decision before —not after—it's made.

The Washington Post, 3-8:(F)7.

2

[Saying union leaders should have a strong code of ethics]: We must be above suspicion, like Caesar's wife. Anybody [in labor leadership] who is indicted should stand aside until that is cleared up . . . The labor movement can't turn its back on corruption. Every time a teamster or longshoreman is indicted, we all get tarred with the same brush. It hurts the image of the entire labor movement.

To reporters, Washington, May 27/ Los Angeles Times, 5-28:(I)19.

Milton Friedman
Economist; Senior fellow,
Hoover Institution, Stanford University

3

I have always in the past argued for the gradual approach [in economic policy]. That has seemed to me desirable on theoretical grounds. But I have been shaken in my faith about that by empirical observation. The successful cases of controlling inflation that I know of have all involved moving at once.

Panel discussion sponsored by Western Economics Association, San Francisco/ The Wall Street Journal, 7-28:27.

John Kenneth Galbraith
Professor emeritus of economics,
Harvard University

4

[On the Reagan Administration economic program]: I would advise everyone to reserve judgment and not allow their enthusiasm to carry them away. I would venture the thought it will look less well a year from now than it does today. There's a basic contradiction in the Reagan economics that has nothing to do with ideology. On the one hand, it proposes to have a large expansion in the economy that will drown out inflation; on the other hand, it proposes to increase the budget deficit and make greater use of monetary policy. Monetary policy works only as it restricts employment. Unemployment makes for idle capacity. So the program calls on the one hand for an expansion of supply and on the other for a contraction of supply, and those are rather hard to reconcile.

Interview, San Francisco/ San Francisco Examiner & Chronicle, 5-17:(Review)4.

John W. Gardner
Founder, Common Cause

5

For a long time we believed that the great American pie would keep expanding, with more for everyone, and that nothing could ever go wrong for America. It takes time and there will be conflicts as we try to work ourselves out of our present situation—but we're coming down to earth.

U.S. News & World Report, 3-9:60.

John Glenn
United States Senator, D—Ohio

6

We, the Democratic Party, moved tens of millions of people from [the] lower status up into pretty good living—a camper, a little white house in the suburbs, the kids in a pretty good school. Not too shabby. Pretty good. And all at once those folks are very much concerned about what their money's going to be worth and where their jobs are going to come from because they've

81

(JOHN GLENN)

seen several hundred thousand jobs in this country go to Japan, Germany. We're now being outcompeted in some fields and that's a new experience for Americans—that we're not the innovators. We're not leading in research and we're not coming up with the new ideas that, in a capitalistic system, provide all these jobs. So where are they going to come from? Well, they're not going to come because we're starting new WPA programs at this stage and still have the economy that we've known in the past. If, in our period of time, we have to shift directions to address what are now the greatest needs of the greatest number of people, well, so be it. We have to shift gears and get on with it.

Interview/The Washington Post, 5-18:(A)13.

Barry M. Goldwater
United States Senator, R—Arizona

1

A major factor today is that we have such a large percentage of our population living off the rest of the population. The question is: Will the [President] Reagan economic policies turn out to hurt these people to the point that they will unite against the President or any Republican? But balancing that, I think, is that a growing number of people, of both liberal and conservative persuasion, realize that either we change our way of economic life or this country is going to cease to exist as we have known it.

Interview, Washington/
The Wall Street Journal, 8-3:12.

Peter Grace
Chairman, W. R. Grace & Co.

2

[On the Reagan Administration economic program, which includes tax cuts just approved by Congress]: We are thrilled. We've finally turned things around. There is a limit on the amount of money you can take from hardworking people under the guise of compassion. Sure the tax cut benefits the rich, but it is also going to benefit a lot of people who aren't rich. I am more interested in the prosperity it implies for the average family than the impact it will have on business. We're in the retail and restaurant business. We are not going to sell anything if people are not going to buy it.

Interview/The New York Times, 7-31:25.

Phil Gramm
United States Representative, D—Texas

3

[Supporting a 10 per cent across-the-board cut in tax rates, saying that it would, in reality, increase the actual amount of taxes collected while at the same time stimulate the economy]: . . . people in the upper quarter of the income distribution find themselves with marginal [tax] rates that induce them to try to avoid taxes by finding shelters. They often take a real economic beating in finding those shelters. So when we cut the maximum rates, we are going to raise revenues as they move out of those shelters into ordinary income sources, and we are going to collect more tax. We did it with the Kennedy tax cut; we did it with the Mellon tax cuts in the 1920s. Every year in the Mellon tax cut the upper quarter of the income distribution paid more taxes and we cut the rates from 77 per cent to 25 per cent over five years. And people making over a million dollars paid twice as much tax at that 25 per cent as they did at 77 per cent.

Interview/The Wall Street Journal, 4-30:22.

C. Jackson Grayson, Jr.
Executive director,
American Productivity Center;
Former Chairman, Federal Price Commission

4

Productivity is not speed-up, it is not sheer numbers, and it is not the same thing as profits. You can have high productivity and low profits or high profits and low productivity—for a short time. Productivity equals output versus input; output in terms of both quality and quantity and input including employees, equipment, buildings, energy and materials, and not just labor. In the last three years the U.S. has had negative productivity growth. We are still the most pro-

(C. JACKSON GRAYSON, JR.)

ductive, but others are outgrowing us, including Japan. We are below the United Kingdom in productivity growth. Japan, which is 99 per cent dependent on outside oil, is at the top in productivity growth. Unless we move, Japan is going to catch up to us.

At Executive Conference sponsored by CNA Insurance Companies, Chicago/ Chicago Tribune, 9-11:(2)1.

Alan Greenspan
Former Chairman, Council of Economic Advisers to the President of the United States (Gerald R. Ford)

1

[On the Federal government's debt reaching a trillion dollars]: The trillion-dollar figure is, in and of itself, not important. It is important because it is symbolic—as a clue to the fact that we have accumulated an awful lot of non-productive Federal borrowing. Government debt, by its very nature, is not used for productive purposes. The absolute size of that debt is not critical. What is is the change from year to year in the proportion of new savings that are taken up by Federal borrowing. That has been increasing steadily and is, in my judgment, the major force which is propelling the inflation in this country.

Interview/U.S. News & World Report, 8-3:67.

Louis Harris
Public-opinion analyst

2

If by this time next year, inflation is not below 10 per cent, the prime rate on borrowing is not down to 11 or 12 per cent, if capital investment is not up sharply, if new technology is not being infused into the industrial process, and if the Federal budget is not well on its way to being balanced, then the patience of the American people [with the Reagan Administration] will be stretched to the breaking point.

At Yale Political Union, New Haven, Conn., Sept. 11/ Los Angeles Herald Examiner, 9-11:(A)14.

Gary W. Hart
United States Senator, D—Colorado

3

[Criticizing the Reagan Administration's tax cuts]: I have never felt . . . a groundswell in support of an inflationary tax cut. What good does it do the average American to get $200 or $300 or $400 or even $500 in tax cuts if the rate of inflation, fueled by a budget deficit in part, takes away spending power of $1,000 or $1,500 at the same time? The American people are very smart. They're very intelligent. They have a great deal of common sense, and they know just cutting taxes, if it doesn't help solve the inflationary problem or even contributes to it, is a no-win situation, and, in fact, a lose situation.

Broadcast interview/"Meet the Press," NBC-TV, 7-12.

Orrin G. Hatch
United States Senator, R—Utah

4

[Organized labor is] the most powerful special-interest group in this country. And I don't know that I want to change it [labor's power]. I believe in a strong, viable union movement even though they accuse me of being the Number 1 enemy of labor. Without unions, we would have only a rich and a poor class in America. Unions are necessary economic levelers. And I admire both Mr. [Lane] Kirkland and Mr. [Thomas] Donahue AFL-CIO leaders]. Both are honest men.

Interview, Washington/Los Angeles Times, 1-29:(I)18.

Mark O. Hatfield
United States Senator, R—Oregon

5

[Criticizing President Reagan's budget cuts]: We are accelerating the erosion of the infrastructure of our society. We are weakening our education system—they want to cut the Fulbright program in half; we are endangering health care, transportation, resource management. What we are saying is that we can let it deteriorate because we are building more bombs. But if we don't have a strong economy and a strong people, what is our national security?

Interview, Washington/ The Washington Post, 11-3:(A)3.

WHAT THEY SAID IN 1981

Paula Hawkins
United States Senator, R—Florida

1

I stay in touch with reality by buying groceries at midnight. You see the difference of inflation on people then—their faces show it. Every Senator should be sentenced to grocery shopping.

U.S. News & World Report, 3-16:51.

Walter W. Heller
Professor of economics, University of Minnesota; Former Chairman, Council of Economic Advisers to the President of the United States (John F. Kennedy)

2

President Reagan's [economic] promises were unrealistic and inconsistent. He misled the Congress and the country into thinking you could have gains without pains. That's not how the economy works. You have to give up some things to get other things. To lower inflation and interest rates, Reagan gave up economic growth for the current recession. But there's a real time bomb in the Reagan program. Those reckless tax cuts pose huge deficits for 1984 and beyond. Unless he makes a major midcourse correction to cut those deficits, we're in for a lot of trouble ... The simplest thing would be to rescind the third year of the individual tax cut. If we earn it by appropriate spending cuts and lower inflation, I'd say go ahead. But without that, the third-year tax cut and the indexing of the tax code in 1985 are out of bounds.

Interview/U.S. News & World Report, 12-28:72.

Norman D. Hicks
United States Representative, D—Washington

3

[Criticizing the House's voting approval of President Reagan's budget proposal]: We may have lost the battle, but we'll be better off in the long run. Now the Republicans take the responsibility for what happens to prices, interest rates, jobs and housing starts. I think in six months we can show people we [who voted for an amended budget] offered a very conserva-

tive, cautious, constructive program, and that Reagan's was the radical alternative.

Washington, May 7/
The Washington Post, 5-8:(A)2.

Walter E. Hoadley
Senior fellow, Hoover Institution, Stanford University; Former executive vice president and chief economist, Bank of America

4

My feeling is that the [Reagan economic] program can work and it should work, but it hinges entirely on whether there is a response in the kitchens and in the boardrooms of America over the next few months. Response is critical: The whole Reagan program hinges on people reacting to an incentive. What's happening now is that the professionals are playing down the field. There's a lot of second-guessing as to whether they're playing a good ballgame or not. The American public and business leadership are sitting in the bleachers. So far, they've been asked to do nothing but sit and wait and watch the results. In order to win the game, we have to get them out of the bleachers.

Interview/U.S. News & World Report, 11-23:50.

Benjamin L. Hooks
Executive director, National Association for the Advancement of Colored People

5

... I would hope [President] Reagan could break the back of inflation and create jobs. My worst fear is that the Administration's programs simply will not work. And if they don't, the country will be infinitely worse off at the end of a period of it not working than before. I think the Reagan Administration has, for some reason, chosen not to address the two major issues, inflation and joblessness, and has dealt with the third, balancing the budget, because of the sense, I guess, that it's something they feel they can do, while inflation is so pervasive, so widespread and there are so many systemic causes for it, that to deal with it demands a lot of ingenuity and imagination and it's not subject to simplistic answers.

Interview/The New York Times, 4-12:(4)5.

Jacob K. Javits
Former United States Senator, R—New York

1

I thought [former President Jimmy] Carter economics didn't remotely have a chance, but I believe [current President] Reagan economics are a lot closer to the mark. We do have cuts to make in the cost of government. But that will only give us the *opportunity* to aid the economy—it won't do it itself. Government, as big as it is, does not represent *that* appreciable a part of the economy. Government represents on the Federal side about $600-billion. We're running an economy which is at least four times that—$2.5-trillion. Therefore, by government demands alone, we can't make it or break it. What [Reagan's economic policy] can do is to inspire confidence in the business and investing community.

Interview/Los Angeles Herald Examiner, 8-31:(A)8.

James R. Jones
United States Representative, D—Oklahoma

2

[Critcizing President Reagan's refusal to reduce the inflation-indexing of Federal benefits]: I think one of the major shortcomings [in Reagan's economic program] is that he's completely ducked the issue of indexing. Just the indexing portion of the budget is almost $50-billion in cost-of-living adjustments. In every country that expanded indexing to as much or greater extent as we have, indexing itself becomes one of the driving forces for inflation.

Los Angeles Times, 3-6:(I)17.

3

The elections of 1978 and 1980 demonstrated dramatically that inflation has become the dominant issue, and, in most districts, your attitude on inflation is measured by your attitude on [government] spending . . . This is just like Vietnam. When public opinion decides that something has to change, it changes. The interest groups that supported the war faded away in the face of that change, and the same thing is happening now to the interest group that supported all this domestic spending. They're

just fading away. It speaks for the genius of our system.

The Washington Post, 3-15:(A)11.

Vernon E. Jordan, Jr.
President, National Urban League

4

[Criticizing the Reagan Administration economic program as it affects the poor]: "A rising tide lifts all boats" is no answer. A rising tide lifts only the boats in the water . . . and we know we will be stranded on dry land. [Reagan's program amounts to] a massive transfer of resources from the poor to the rich. We agree with them that inflation must be curbed. We agree with them that blacks do better when the economy is better. We agree with them that America must produce more and create more jobs in the private sector. But . . . what are black and poor people supposed to do in the meantime?

At National Urban League annual meeting/
The Wall Street Journal, 7-31:19.

Henry Kaufman
Chief economist,
Salomon Brothers, investment bankers

5

One of our great problems that we have had all year long is the imbalance in government [fiscal] strategy. A policy based on substantial tax cuts, substantial increases in defense expenditures, and [with] large budget deficits, does not show discipline or restraint on the fiscal side. This places an extraordinary burden on the financial markets and on interest rates.

Interview/Newsweek, 9-21:32.

Jack Kemp
United States Representative, R—New York

6

[On the Reagan Administration economic program]: Personally, I don't think bringing inflation down and interest rates down and trying to provide the type of new tax system in this country and regulatory relief that's necessary is going to be all that painful. Why should it be

(JACK KEMP)

painful to tell the American people that the outlook for their investment in savings and work is going to be brighter in the future? Why should it be painful to tell small business and farmers that interest rates can start to come down when we stabilize the fiscal and monetary policy of this country? I think, frankly, when you stop hitting yourself over the head with a hammer, it's going to feel immediately better; and the American people have had a hammer blow against the head of this economy over the last, if not eight, at least 10 to 12 years . . .

Broadcast interview/"Meet the Press," NBC-TV, 2-2.

1

There are two uses of income: consumption and savings. And there are two uses of time: leisure and work—i.e., production. In effect, the price of leisure is the amount of income you forgo by not working, and the price of consumption is the amount of income you forgo in the future by not saving. Today, the price of leisure is very low, given the fact that in many instances labor and capital forgo very little income by not being as productive as they possibly can, and the price of consumption is very low because the reward for savings is so low. Lowering all tax rates will instantaneously modify economic behavior by increasing rewards for savings and work.

Interview/U.S. News & World Report, 2-16:21.

Edward M. Kennedy
United States Senator, D—Massachusetts

2

[On President Reagan's proposed economic program of reduced Federal spending and reduced taxes]: This program of unfair sacrifice and unequal benefit is based on an untested and uncertain economic theory. The Administration has gambled our future on a dubious plan that does not deal directly with the relentless spiral of rising prices, wages and interest rates. I believe that every industry and worker would respond patriotically to a policy of even-handed price and wage restraint. I believe that all of us would support fair tax reductions for average families, and carefully targeted tax incentives for major enterprise and for small business. And I believe that all of us are ready to bear a fair share of the burden to bring the Federal budget into balance over time . . . Fairness is what we as Democrats will demand in the weeks and months ahead. Our commitment is not to outworn programs, but to old values that will never wear out.

Television broadcast to the nation,
Washington, Feb. 28/
San Francisco Examiner & Chronicle, 3-1:(A)2.

Charles P. Kindleberger
Professor emeritus of economics,
Massachusetts Institute of Technology

3

I have a view that, to be stable, the world needs a stabilizer—someone who takes responsibility for worrying about the world economy and for trimming the excesses when the markets get too tight or too loose. But no country is taking that responsibility. America used to do it, but now we're copping out . . . the world was fairly stable up to 1914 because the British stabilized it; it was stable from 1945 to about 1971 because America stabilized it. But the 1929 Depression was such a disaster because everyone was looking after himself: Devil take the hindmost, and beggar thy neighbor. And that seems to be the case today. It is particularly true that the U.S., which used to feel the strongest responsibility for the world economy, is doing less and less. Just look at the American position on foreign aid or Japanese imports, and you see a neo-mercantilism creeping in.

Interview/Forbes, 9-14:104.

Lane Kirkland
President, American Federation of Labor-
Congress of Industrial Organizations

4

[Criticizing President Reagan's economic program which includes massive government spending cuts]: Today we are being told that these cuts represent the will of the people. We are told that we [critics] are running against the

(LANE KIRKLAND)

popular mood. We are told that the Administration has a mandate won on Election Day. It is my view that the President has no such mandate. If the President has any popular mandate, it is a mandate to bring down inflation and unemployment, to spur economic growth, to improve the productivity and competitiveness of the American economy, to broaden the horizons of opportunity for all Americans, and to rebuild our national defense. It is not a mandate for monetarism. It is not a mandate for the meat ax. It is not a mandate to perform occult economic experiments on the American people. We are not a nation of guinea pigs who can be expended in the interest of testing unproven economic hypotheses.

At AFL-CIO regional conference, Chicago, March 19/
Chicago Tribune, 3-21:(1)3.

1

[On the current illegal strike by air-traffic controllers]: I respect the law. [But] when working people feel a deep sense of grievance, they will exercise what I think is a basic human right, the right to withdraw their services, not to work under conditions they no longer find tolerable. I think that is the right that is inherent and one that's not adequately addressed by legislative remedies simply saying that it's against the law.

News conference, Chicago, Aug. 3/
The New York Times, 8-4:10.

2

[Addressing U.S. labor-union members and criticizing Reagan Administration economic policy]: You are the people who do the work of America. You run its factories and offices, work its farms, transport its produce, maintain its buildings, teach its children, nurse its sick, clean its streets and fight in its defense. When something goes wrong in America, you feel it first, before the politicians or the more securely placed. Something has gone wrong and you know it all too well. Labor is here in its one

hundredth year to deliver a simple message to the Administration and to the Congress. We have come too far, struggled too long, sacrificed too much, and have too much left to do, to allow all that we have achieved for the good of all to be swept away without a fight. We are out front and we shall not fall back to hide and wait for better political weather. But the winds are changing, as they always do. The winter's chill is approaching and the bloom is fading from false mandates.

At Solidarity Day rally, Washington, Sept. 19/
The New York Times, 9-20:(1)16.

3

I think the inherent strength of the [labor] movement is not so much broad public relations, because I think by the nature of our role in society—certainly in American society—we're never going to rely on popularity. The things one would have to do to be wildly popular, to be well received by organs of opinion, the establishment generally, would be a guarantee of our ultimate consignment to oblivion. We have to do things that are inherently unpopular to effectively represent our people.

Interview/The New York Times, 11-16:12.

4

We [unions] frequently say we represent a growing percentage of the work force—we represent far more, many times the number of people who actually pay dues and carry a union card. We represent everybody who works at the minimum wage, because we're the only people who have pushed through, from time to time, some increase in the minimum wage. They don't pay dues, for the most part. We represent everybody who's in a shop where we have bargaining rights but no union shop. We're obligated to represent everyone in that establishment, whether they're paying dues or not. We represent everyone who only get their increases when the union gets its increase. We represent everyone where the management gives an increase to keep the union out, or pays a premium to keep the union out. You can probably develop that into some sort of figure that we, the

(LANE KIRKLAND)

trade-union movement, represent 50 million, 60 million people in this country. It's just that only maybe a little over 20 million pay dues. It's remarkable that that many do when they can get so many of the benefits without having to do it.

Interview/The New York Times, 11-16:12.

Andrew Knight
Editor, "The Economist" (Britain)

1

For the first time [in the world], economic issues are becoming political in people's minds. People discuss economics and believe that it matters in a way they never did before. The issues of the pocketbook and inflation and the balance of society between the private and public sectors, and management and the unions, are so vivid that they have been politicized.

Interview/World Press Review, June:6.

Edward I. Koch
Mayor of New York

2

The fight for justice is never an easy one, and the struggle of American labor has been no exception. From Samuel Gompers, George Meany to the leaders gathered here today, the efforts are the same, just as the labor movement has been one in bringing about the process of change in American life. And, over those years, there have been those who said that changes brought about by the labor movement for the American freedom would harm our economic development. What actually happened, of course, is that America grew into the most enlightened and productive nation in the world, and that growth took place because America is a nation of laws. It is our laws that were adapted to embrace the reasonable objective of the labor movement.

*Labor Day address, New York, Sept. 7/
The New York Times, 9-8:14.*

Arthur Laffer
*Professor of economics,
University of Southern California*

3

You never make a poor person well-to-do by taxing the hell out of a rich person.

Newsweek, 6-29:11.

4

[On President Reagan's economic program]: There is a major change coming in this country, and I feel very good about having been a part of that [by way of his theories being used in the program]. I think you're going to see enormous economic growth in the country, with real prosperity returning. I think we're going to cut our tax rates and bring them back to a more reasonable tax structure. I think we're on the verge of an American Renaissance . . . Just because something's simple doesn't mean it's wrong. More and more people are understanding the role of incentives and their importance. The last person you should ever have run the country is a professor of economics. But the next silliest mistake you could make is not to listen to one.

*Interview, Los Angeles/
Chicago Tribune, 8-10:(4)8.*

Reed Larson
President, National Right to Work Committee

5

[Supporting right-to-work laws which limit compulsory labor-union membership for employees]: If there is no compulsory membership, the unions must be careful to tend to the interests of those they represent. Voluntary membership means that unions have to perform or die.

Nation's Business, June:38.

Wassily Leontief
Nobel Prize-winning economist

6

[On the effect on the economy of Reagan Administration plans for large increases in defense spending]: If handled improperly, these huge jumps in military spending will mean higher

(WASSILY LEONTIEF)

inflation, a worsening balance-of-payments gap, a drain on productive investment, soaring interest rates, increasing taxes, a debased currency and, in the longer term, more unemployment. Reagan proposes to leap across—rather than bridge—the nation's economic gap. What worries me is that, if you jump even 5 inches short, you face economic calamity. It is a very great gamble . . . America's economy is so vast and its problems are so deeply ingrained that any turnaround will take years. The military bills come due much more quickly. Reagan hopes our gross national product will expand so much that we will be able to pay for higher defense spending without raising taxes. This is not likely to happen. In fact, I personally guarantee that it will not happen.

Interview/U.S. News & World Report, 3-16:26.

David J. Mahoney
Chairman, Norton Simon, Inc.

1

I propose that America's 1,000 largest corporations immediately implement a job-creation program targeted to the disadvantaged. I propose that each of our companies add 1 per cent to budgeted manpower costs to hire and train people for entry-level jobs. And I propose that larger local and regional companies adopt a similar "1 per cent plan" in the communities where they operate. That 1 per cent would not represent a burden for most companies . . . And a "1 per cent plan" would help penetrate the alienation that grips so many Americans by holding out the prospect of real jobs, real training and real paychecks.

The Washington Post, 11-11:(A)26.

Charles T. Manatt
Chairman, Democratic National Committee

2

It is an open secret in Washington that the basic economic assumptions that underlie the entire Reagan [economic] program were arrived at through a series of jockeying and maneuvers among the President's advisers that resembled

the haggling of rug merchants at a bazaar more than a serious economic analysis. Under the pressure of a deadline, the numbers were produced that no Administration official can justify. When you look hard at all the Reagan Administration's fundamental assumptions about economic growth, inflation, interest rates and savings—the bedrock upon which their entire economic program is built—they disappear like numbers written in the sand after the tides wash . . . Much as I wish the President's economic assumptions could somehow come true, I'm afraid that the Administration's program contains the seeds of disaster for our country. And I take no comfort in that prospect, whatever short-term political advantage it might bring.

*Before Commonwealth Club, San Francisco/
The Washington Post, 6-2:(A)18.*

Sam P. Mazza
*Commissioner, Federal Mediation
and Conciliation Service*

3

When I started in the labor movement, there were no such things as [worker] holidays, vacations, sick leave, seniority or hospitalization. Absolutely nothing. In those days you hid your union button inside your shirt or your cuff. Today a young guy walks in, gets a job, and is handed a full contract that may have taken 40 years of negotiations. The first thing he says, "What have you done for me lately? That's not enough." One of the hardest jobs of a union official is to convince a young worker that current wage levels and the fringe benefits did not come overnight. How much more can union leaders deliver? Today more and more fringes are being introduced to satisfy the wants of the members.

Interview/Chicago Tribune, 9-3:(2)5.

Allan Meltzer
*Professor of economics,
Carnegie-Mellon University*

4

[On the Reagan Administration economic program, which includes tax cuts and budget cuts]: I think it's terrific. There is going to be a

(ALLAN MELTZER)

very positive improvement in the long-term productivity of the economy. I don't think there is anything inflationary about it. Even the most straightforward Keynesian wouldn't argue that a cut in taxes matched by a cut in spending is inflationary. It is hard to see how taking money from the government and giving it to the taxpayer can possibly increase total spending. The government spends 115 per cent of its income, while an ordinary taxpayer spends only 92 per cent of his.

Interview, July 30/
The New York Times, 7-31:32.

Francois Mitterrand
President of France

1

There is a currency war, an economic war, and this is one of the most disquieting points for the future of Western relations. Today, it is every man for himself. The U.S., so it says, needs a very high interest rate. That's its business. But it cannot ignore the fact that this measure exacerbates already dangerous movements of capital. Likewise for the fluctuations in the dollar exchange rate. This disorganizes the Western economic system. Since each nation is undergoing a crisis, they all tend toward egotism. Each country first wants to rescue itself, whereas they will only be rescued together.

Interview, Paris/Time, 10-19:57.

Walter F. Mondale
Former Vice President of the United States

2

[On President Reagan's economic program]: We had an Administration that came into office saying, "There's no problem here. All we do is reduce taxes by a trillion dollars, and everything gets better. Inflation drops, interest rates drop, the economy picks up, the budget deficit is reduced by the revenues derived from increased growth." The fact is, however, it hasn't worked at all. It was a simple answer that in fact has been a disaster. Interest rates are at an all-time high.

We're slipping into a recession that could be substantial. The housing industry is dead. The auto industry is dead. The Reagan economics have clearly been rejected by the financial markets both here and abroad. It's been a terrible mistake, and I think that the Democrats have the right to point out that most of us, including myself, argued for two and three years that this so-called Kemp-Roth tax cut, which is really now called Reaganomics, has been one of the most serious mistakes ever introduced into our economy.

Broadcast interview/"Meet the Press," NBC-TV, 10-25.

Daniel P. Moynihan
United States Senator, D—New York

3

The Economic Recovery Act is too expensive. The Act is expected to cost the Treasury nearly $750-billion in lost revenue over the six years from 1981 to 1986... When Congress committed itself to the bill, it did so on the assumption that there would be a small budget surplus of about $1-billion in 1984. The Republican staff now says to expect a deficit in 1984 of $78-billion ... Do we really want a decade in which *the* issue of public discourse, over and over and over, will be how big must the budget cuts be in order to prevent the deficit from being even bigger? What a dismal and dispiriting prospect. Do we really want to be forced to choose between strengthening the national defense or continuing to pay Social Security benefits we have promised elderly Americans? No other areas in the budget offer large savings ... My concept is that [we will] wake up to an empty Treasury, with the grimmest consequences. This need not happen. There is still time to prevent it.

The Washington Post, 9-20:(C)6.

Richard M. Nixon
Former President of the United States

4

Politics rears its ugly head when the economy goes down. Bad times ahead; bad unemployment numbers; predictions of doom. It is going to take a cold winter to have a good spring, when we can move up again sharply. [President] Reagan has

(RICHARD M. NIXON)

set the right directions. Now is the time that he must stay, as former House Minority Whip Les Arends used to say, "steady in the buggy" . . . Reagan must succeed or we will have a country bloated by inflation, a government that gets bigger, people who get less productive . . . Our economy is the best thing going for us in the world. We can beat the hell out of the Soviets; economically they are dead. But we can lose to the Japanese, the French, the Germans.

Interview/Time, 11-2:30.

Leif H. Olsen
Chairman, economic policy committee, Citicorp/Citibank

1

It appears that the counterattack on the Reagan Administration's economic program has served to obscure further the process of change toward less inflation that is now under way. Those who are unhappy with the ideology of the Administration have in their public criticism disregarded the evidence of accepted theory to put the worst possible face on the outlook for fiscal policy. This, of course, has helped to promote the general uproar in the credit markets which the critics then cite in support of their contentions . . . The indispensable ingredient of inflation is on overly expansionary monetary policy, and that has been ruled out—not just by the Administration's strategy but by the financial markets' extreme reaction to it . . . But people believe what they want to believe, and right now shifting business strategies to accommodate less inflation is too painful for many to contemplate . . . But the change toward less inflation, which we are not locked into, is advancing. How far it will proceed remains to be seen, but it should not be ignored.

The Washington Post, 9-17:(A)26.

Thomas P. O'Neill, Jr.
United States Representative, D—Massachusetts

2

[On the House's voting approval of the Reagan Administration's budget proposals]: I guess the monkey is off the Democrats' back. The cuts,

as brutal as they are, are Reagan's cuts. The deficit is Reagan's deficit. The high interest rates . . . are Reagan's interest rates. The inflation rate—and most economists tell us it's going to soar—is Reagan's inflation rate.

Washington, May 7/
The Wall Street Journal, 5-8:3.

J. F. Otero
International vice president, Brotherhood of Railway and Airline Clerks; Public member, Federal Select Commission on Immigration and Refugee Policy

3

We fully recognize that the overwhelming majority of illegal aliens come to America to support themselves and to take a responsible role in society. However, too often, unscrupulous employers prey upon these newcomers, forcing upon them low wages and substandard conditions in an atmosphere of abuse and fear. These problems are of acute concern to the U.S. labor movement, which insists on safeguarding its hard-won standards of life and work . . . This is not a view shared only by those of us in the leadership of organized labor. National awareness of the illegal-immigration problem . . . comes at a time of increasing scarcity, when very large numbers of people in this country are hard pressed to find jobs, to pay their bills or to maintain their standard of living . . . Though issues of race and xenophobic reaction should have no place in U.S. immigration policy or practices, they must be sharply distinguished from feelings of deep economic insecurity and a concern for one's own welfare.

The Washington Post, 1-20:(A)20.

Clarence M. Pendleton
President, San Diego Urban League; Chairman-designate, United States Commission on Civil Rights

4

You want to get as free as you can, and the best social program is a job. If people really want to be free, they have to develop their own asset base and income stream, and there will never be

WHAT THEY SAID IN 1981

(CLARENCE M. PENDLETON)

enough government money to do that . . . If we can encourage the private sector to employ people, that's what America is all about.

Interview/The Christian Science Monitor, 11-19:8.

Samuel R. Pierce, Jr.
Secretary of Housing and Urban Development of the United States

1

[Supporting President Reagan's economic program]: The fact is, before we can accomplish much else we must bring inflation under control and get the economy moving forward again. The fact is that reliance on government programs, no matter how well-intentioned, simply hasn't worked, and it is time to try something new. The fact is that revitalizing the economy will benefit everyone; and indeed, minorities and the poor have the most to gain.

Before National Association for the Advancement of Colored People, Denver, July 2/ The New York Times, 7-3:8.

Donald Ratajczak
Director, economic forecasting project, Georgia State University

2

[On the current recession]: You could argue that a recession was necessary to make the transition from a consumptive economy, with its high interest rates and inflation, to the savings and investment economy that [President] Reagan projected. By this logic, the Reagan program is still on track, and we should take the pain and not mess with it. But there is another school of thought that says the Reagan program is not now working and never will. There are some disquieting signs to this effect, particularly the sharp drop in capital-equipment orders at a time when investment should be rising. Because of the decline in sales and high interest rates, producers are foregoing expansion. But without a growth in capital investment, you will not get the growth in productivity, employment and savings that the Reagan program hinges upon.

The New York Times, 11-8:(1)14.

Ronald Reagan
President-elect of the United States

3

A reduction in the tax rates should not be interpreted as automatically meaning a cut in revenues [for the government]. We know from experience proper cuts in rates can also have another effect—a feedback effect—of more revenues due to more prosperity, to more people working and so forth . . . Every time you add a percentage point to the rate of unemployment, you add billions of dollars to government cost—reduced taxes on one side and increased outgo on the other. I think the over-all policies of the last few decades have been based on false economic philosophy that government can go on endlessly spending more than it takes in without coming to a day of reckoning. We've come to that day of reckoning. It must stop.

Interview, Jan. 7/ U.S. News & World Report, 1-19:23,24.

Ronald Reagan
President of the United States

4

We suffer from the longest and one of the worst sustained inflations in our national history. It distorts our economic decisions, penalizes thrift and crushes the struggling young and the fixed-income elderly alike. It threatens to shatter the lives of millions of our people. Idle industries have cast workers into unemployment, human misery and personal indignity. Those who do work are denied a fair return for their labor by a tax system which penalizes successful achievement and keeps us from maintaining full productivity. But great as our tax burden is, it has not kept pace with public spending. For decades we have piled deficit upon deficit, mortgaging our future and our children's future for the temporary convenience of the present. To continue this long trend is to guarantee tremendous social, cultural, political and economic upheavals. You and I, as individuals, can, by borrowing, live beyond our means for only a limited period of time. Why then should we think that collectively, as a nation, we're not bound by that same limitation?

Inaugural address, Washington, Jan 20/ Los Angeles Times, 1-21:(I)16.

(RONALD REAGAN)

1

. . . in all these years of government growth, we've reached—indeed surpassed—the limit of our people's tolerance or ability to bear an increase in the tax burden. Prior to World War II, taxes were such that on the average we only had to work about two and a half months each year to pay our total Federal, state and local tax bills. Today we have to work about five months to pay that bill. Some say shift the tax burden to business and industry, but business doesn't pay taxes. Oh, don't get the wrong idea; business is being taxed—so much so that we are being priced out of the world market. But business must pass its costs of operation, and that includes taxes, onto the customer in the price of the product. Only people pay taxes—all the taxes.

Broadcast address to the nation,
Washington, Feb. 5/
The New York Times, 2-6:8.

2

. . . inflation results from all that [government] deficit spending. Government has only two ways of getting money other than raising taxes. It can go into the money market and borrow, competing with its own citizens and driving up interest rates, which it has done, or it can print money, and it's done that. Both methods are inflationary. We're victims of language. The very word, "inflation" leads us to think of it as high prices. Then, of course, we resent the person who puts on the price tags, forgetting that he or she is also a victim of inflation. Inflation is not just high prices; it is a reduction in the value of our money. When the money supply is increased but the goods and services available for buying are not, we have too much money chasing too few goods.

Broadcast address to the nation,
Washington, Feb. 5/
The New York Times, 2-6:8.

3

[On critics of his tax-cut proposal who say the plan will be inflationary]: They never answer one question that I keep asking, and you probably heard me ask it: Why is it inflationary if the people keep their own money and spend it the way *they* want to, and it's not inflationary if the government takes it and spends it the way *it* wants to? . . . Our opponents want more money from your family budget so they can spend it on the Federal budget and make it remain high. Maybe it's time that you and millions like you remind them of a few simple facts: It's your money, not theirs. You earned it, they didn't. You have every right to keep a bigger share than you've been allowed to keep for a great many years now. And when they insist we can't reduce taxes and spending and balance the budget too, one six-word answer will do: Yes we can, and, yes we will.

To a group of his supporters, Washington, June 11/
The New York Times, 6-12:28.

4

[On criticism that his economic policies favor the rich because he and his advisers do not identify with working people]: [When I was a boy,] we didn't live on the wrong side of the railroad tracks, but we lived so close to them we could hear the whistle real loud. And I know very much about the working group. I grew up in poverty and got what education I got all by myself and so forth. And I think it is sheer demagoguery to pretend that this economic program which we've submitted is not aimed at helping the great cross-section of people in this country that have been burdened for too long by big government and high taxes. The [group] from $10,000 to $50,000 to $60,000 covers, certainly, all the middle class, and they pay 72 per cent of the tax, and 73 per cent of our tax relief or more is going to that bracket of workers. And we're going to do our utmost to keep that bottom rung of the ladder clear for those people that haven't yet started to climb.

News conference, Washington, June 16/
The New York Times, 6-17:13.

WHAT THEY SAID IN 1981

(RONALD REAGAN)

1

[On the imminent Congressional vote on his tax-cut proposal]: In a few days, the Congress will stand at the fork of two roads. One road is all too familiar to us. It leads—ultimately—to higher taxes. It merely brings us full circle back to the source of our economic problems—where the government decides that it knows better than you what should be done with your earnings and, in fact, how you should conduct your life. The other road promises to renew the American spirit. It's a road of hope and opportunity. It places the direction of your life back in your hands—where it belongs . . . I ask you to trust yourselves. That's what America is all about. Our struggle for nationhood, our unrelenting fight for freedom, our very existence—these have all rested on the assurance that you must be free to shape your life as you are best able to—that no one can stop you from reaching higher or take from you the creativity that has made America the envy of mankind. One road is timid and fearful. The other, bold and hopeful.

Broadcast address to the nation, Washington, July 27/
The New York Times, 7-28:36.

2

[On the current illegal air-traffic controllers strike]: I respect the right of workers in the private sector to strike. Indeed, as president of my own union, I led the first strike ever called by that union [the Screen Actors Guild]. I guess I'm the first one to ever hold this office [the U.S. Presidency] who is a lifetime member of an AFL-CIO union. But we cannot compare labor-management relations in the private sector with government. Government cannot close down the assembly line; it has to provide without interruption the protective services which are government's reason for being. It was in this recognition that the Congress passed a law forbidding strikes by government employees against the public safety.

To reporters, Washington, Aug. 3/
The New York Times, 8-4:10.

3

To some of those who opposed our budget reduction, let me point out that we haven't cut spending back to less in 1982 than it was in the year of 1981. We have reduced the *increase* in spending from 14 per cent each year to 6.5 per cent. Now, this is hardly cruel and inhuman deprivation. We're not, as some have said, trying to turn back the clock; we're just trying to make the rate of increase in spending about half of what it has been.

Before United Brotherhood of
Carpenters and Joiners, Chicago, Sept. 3/
The New York Times, 9-4:7.

4

[On the increasingly difficult job of reducing Federal spending in the hopes of balancing the budget by 1984]: We never promised it would be easy and we never promised it would be quick. We can't be stampeded now by frustration or fear. We have to stay on a steady, long-term course . . . I know it's a hell of a challenge. But ask yourselves, "If not us, who? If not now, when?"

To his Cabinet officers, Washington, Sept. 10/
Los Angeles Times, 9-11:(I)1.

5

[Criticizing Wall Street's worries about his economic program]: Now, I have listened to those Chicken Littles who proclaim the sky is falling, and those others who recklessly play on high interest rates for their own narrow political purposes. But this concern about a plan not even in effect yet is nothing more than false labor . . . Let me say we did not sweat and bleed to get the economic package passed [by Congress] only to abandon it when the going gets a little tough . . . It took us years of fiscal mismanagement to get where we are today and our economic recovery program is not designed to provide instant gratification.

Before National Federation of
Republican Women,
Denver, Sept. 18/
Chicago Tribune, 9-19:(1)1,16.

(RONALD REAGAN)

1

[On the current recession and those who blame his Administration for it]: Our [economic] program has only been in effect for some 40 days, and you can't cure 40 years of problems in that short time. But we believe we've laid a firm foundation for economic recovery in 1982 . . . It's ironic that those who would have us assume blame for this economic mess are the ones who created it. They just can't accept that their discredited policies of tax and tax, spend and spend, are at the root of our current problems. We will not go back to business-as-usual. Our plan for economic recovery is sound; it was designed to correct the problems we face. I am determined to stick with it, stay on course, and I will not be deterred by temporary economic changes or short-term political expediency.

News conference, Washington, Nov. 10/
The New York Times, 11-11:14.

2

Only when the human spirit is allowed to invent and create, only when individuals are given a personal stake in deciding economic policies and benefiting from their successes— only then can societies remain economically alive, dynamic, prosperous, progressive and free. "Trust the people." This is the one irrefutable lesson of the entire post-war period, contradicting the notion that rigid government controls are essential to economic development. The societies which have achieved the most spectacular, broad-based economic progress in the shortest period of time are not the most tightly controlled, nor necessarily the biggest in size, or the wealthiest in natural resources. No, what unites them all is their willingness to believe in the magic of the marketplace. Everyday life confirms the fundamentally human and democratic ideal that individual effort deserves economic reward. Nothing is more crushing to the spirit of working people and to the vision of development itself than the absence of reward for honest toil and legitimate risk. So let me speak bluntly: We cannot have prosperous and successful development without economic freedom. Nor can we preserve our personal and political freedoms without economic freedom.

Before Board of Governors of World Bank and
International Monetary Fund, Washington/
The Wall Street Journal, 12-14:22.

3

[On his promise, in last year's election campaign, to balance the Federal budget by 1983, which now appears impossible]: . . . I said what was our goal, not a promise. But when I first announced my economic plan—and this is when those dates were used—was in September of 1980, during the campaign. The deterioration in the economy was so great between September and January [1981] that taking office we had to revise our own estimates and our own figures and plan. And I have confidence in our plan; that it is the right solution to the present problem. But again, like so many, we were caught— while we always said that the economy would be sluggish and soft for the balance of the year and in 1982, we did not foresee a recession, and I don't think anyone else did . . . this is not a case of a broken promise; this is a case of circumstances beyond our control, whose foundation has been laid over the last several decades . . . The only proper way to balance the budget is through control of government spending, which we haven't had for some 20-odd years or more, and increasing prosperity and productivity for all. And that's what our program is aimed to do, and I have every confidence it is going to do it.

News conference, Washington, Dec. 17/
The New York Times, 12-18:16.

Donald T. Regan
Secretary of the Treasury
of the United States

4

Inflation is primarily a monetary phenomenon. Stable prices are impossible if money growth rates outstrip the growth of goods and services year in and year out, as they have done, on average, for more than a decade. The major contribution of the Federal Reserve must be to

WHAT THEY SAID IN 1981

(DONALD T. REGAN)

bring down the growth rates of the monetary aggregates, reducing inflation, inflationary expectations and interest rates. There is no alternative to this fundamental reform. The President's tax, spending and regulatory program cannot succeed unless inflation is brought under control.

Before Congress,
Washington/
The Christian Science Monitor,
2-13:14.

1

[On whether he accepts President Reagan's supply-line economics]: Who won this election? Ronald Reagan. Why did he win this election? The people liked his program. What is his program? His program calls for supply-side-type tax cuts and a strong monetary policy—that is, slow growth. Why not, then, give the President what he wants at the Treasury? . . . Having been selected as the Secretary of the Treasury, I assure you that I will carry out the President's policy. The more I examine supply-side economics, the more I find I've always been on this side. But I thought it was just old-fashioned conservatism: "Let people have their own money; let me spend my money the way I want; let me invest it the way I want. The best government is the least government." I thought sentiments like this were just old-fashioned. Turns out that's supply-side.

Interview/
U.S. News & World Report, 3-9:27.

2

[On the recent increase in the prime interest rate]: Temporarily, we'll have a slowdown in business while these high interest rates are enforced. It's a bitter medicine to have to take. It's not going to taste that good. But it sure as hell will improve the health of the patient.

To reporters,
Washington, May 6/
Los Angeles Times,
5-7:(I)14.

3

The President [Reagan] sees no need to change his [three-year, 30 per cent tax-cut] program. We have seen no other program that achieves these same objectives. If we can be shown something that is superior, in other words with more bang for the buck, we'd be more than willing to take a look at that . . . Ultimately, it is the people who must restore growth through increased work, savings and investment. We therefore must adopt a tax policy that reduces the tax barriers to their efforts.

Before Senate Finance Committee,
Washington, May 13/Los Angeles Times, 5-14:11.

4

Our current tax system is headed in a dangerous direction that will cripple our economy unless we take immediate action. Up to this point, inflation has pushed taxpayers into higher tax brackets, making it less profitable to earn more. Tax rates on extra earnings have risen very sharply for most taxpayers in the last few years. For example, the percentage of tax returns in or above the 25 per cent tax bracket, the 30 per cent bracket—and most of the other tax brackets that used to be reserved for the rich—has more than tripled in the last 10 years. If nothing is done, virtually any family that now pays taxes—even those at the lowest marginal rate of 14 per cent—will be in the top 50 per cent tax bracket on their earned income by the year 2000, less than 20 years from now. What kind of incentives do these projections give Americans to work harder and save more?

Interview/Nation's Business, June:32.

Henry S. Reuss
United States Representative, D—Wisconsin

5

When you come to think of it, there is no particular reason why the Reagan [economic] program should work. Essentially, it is a proposal to transfer income from the poor and the middle classes to the top 5 or 10 per cent of Americans. Reaganomics derives its economic justification from just about every freakish economic theory

(HENRY S. REUSS)

that ever came out of the land of gurus and swamis. Its supply-siders say that budget deficits do not matter because Americans will immediately start working harder and investing more. The Reagan monetarists proclaim that money alone matters, and that high interest rates will somehow go away before they kill us all. The Reagan rational expectations wistfully hope that money men will embrace the Reagan program, and immediately reduce their interest rates—exactly the opposite of what they are doing. Put them all together, as the Administration does, and you have a recipe for disaster.

Before the House, Washington/
The Washington Post, 5-10:(B)6.

Paul Craig Roberts
Assistant Secretary-designate for Economic
Policy, Department of the Treasury
of the United States

1

The tax rates in the United States are extremely high on all forms of productive activity . . . Part of the reason we have 10 per cent inflation is that we have been following a fiscal policy which encourages increase in demand, or spending, but automatically discourages production incentives. It was sort of a rule-of-thumb assumption that supply would respond automatically to demand. What was overlooked is that the responsiveness of supply is a function of the rate of return. As you go from 0 to 100 [in the tax rates], the responsiveness of supply to increases in demand continually falls off.

Interview/The New York Times, 2-8:(3)2.

Felix G. Rohatyn
Chairman, Municipal Assistance
Corporation of New York

2

The economic aims of the Reagan Administration are impeccable: reduce government spending, reduce taxes, reduce interest rates, strengthen our defense, balance the budget. Although I hope for its success, the probabilities are against it because of their inherent contradiction. The result may well be continued in-

flation and slow growth, combined with greater and greater disparities as oil, defense and sunshine favor half the country, while the other half drifts more and more into the shadows. No democracy, not even one as large as ours, can survive half suburb and half slum.

At Hofstra University School of
Business commencement/
U.S. News & World Report, 6-15:35.

Dan Rostenkowski
United States Representative, D—Illinois

3

The President [Reagan] wants us to close our eyes for the next three years and trust his economists, who haven't been right thus far. He's asking us to forget the big deficits and a balanced budget. He's asking us not to worry about Social Security . . . In the end, it always comes down to the same $50,000 question: Should we give the largest share of the tax cut to families earning less than $50,000—that working American who has a big share of the American economy? Or should we give the big tax break to those people making over $100,000? It's just that simple. We believe the Democrat plan [giving a bigger tax cut to those earning under $50,000] works for the working American family.

TV broadcast, July 27/
The New York Times, 7-28:37.

4

[On Federal Budget Director David Stockman's magazine interview which was critical of President Reagan's economic program]: David Stockman's candid admission that the President's entire economic plan rests on the foundation of wishful thinking, the fact that hundreds of billions of dollars in spending and tax cuts are based on phony assumptions, boggles the mind. Here we are, speeding down a wet road at 75 miles an hour, and suddenly we learn a few lug nuts are loose and the tires on which we are riding are bald.

Before National Association of Realtors,
Miami Beach, Fla., Nov. 13/
Chicago Tribune, 11-15:(1)2.

WHAT THEY SAID IN 1981

John Rutledge
Director, Claremont Economics Institute

1

[Saying there should be a steady, predictable fiscal and monetary policy by government]: Our view of the world is that it is expectation-driven. The only value the past has is in teaching people to think about the future. What you need to do is to provide them with signals that they view as reliable, and they will organize their lives around those signals.

Interview/The Washington Post, 2-12:(A)19.

Paul A. Samuelson
Economist

2

For 40 years, since Roosevelt's New Deal, America has been seeking a more humane society —a welfare state. Conservatives have hated this. Now [President] Ronald Reagan seeks to end that trend. Yes, Reagan's [economic] program does attempt a radical break with the past. A radical-right crusade is being sold as a solution for an economy allegedly in crisis. There is no such crisis! Our people should join this crusade only if they agree with its philosophical conservative merits. They should not be flim-flammed by implausible promises that programs to restore 1920s inequalities will cure the inflation problem.

Interview/U.S. News & World Report, 3-2:33.

John S. R. Shad
Chairman, Securities and Exchange Commission of the United States

3

A lot of people don't know what capital formation means. It means, among other things, savings invested in modern equipment, which increases worker productivity. For example, earth-moving equipment instead of a shovel. And, of course, the greater a worker's productivity, the greater his pay and the higher his standard of living. And in fact, the nation's productivity and growth and standard of living are simply the sum of its citizens. So this is a terribly important activity . . . Within the brief span of

a generation, America's tax, fiscal and regulatory policies have become antithetical to capital formation, [with] mounting regulatory burdens, rising inflation, corporate and individual taxes, inadequate depreciation allowances, double taxation of dividends, 70 per cent taxes on dividends and interest, and one of the highest effective rates on capital-gains taxation in the industrialized free world . . . As a result, America's rate of capital formation has plummeted from among the highest to among the lowest in the industrialized nations . . . If we are to maintain the standard of living of all Americans— the nation's leadership in the competitive world community—it is essential that these adverse trends be reversed.

Interview/The Washington Post, 7-26:(F)7.

Leon Shull
*Executive director,
Americans for Democratic Action*

4

[President] Reagan's reactionary economic program constitutes a massive transfer of income from workers, the middle class and the poor . . . to the wealthy and corporations . . . Despite his lip service to equity and equal sacrifice, the President places the burden of resolving our economic difficulties on the backs of those . . . already suffering the most from our current high inflation and high unemployment.

The Washington Post, 2-19:(A)1.

Alan K. Simpson
United States Senator, R—Wyoming

5

We have huge numbers of illegal aliens coming into this country. The laws and regulations we have now, which provide for visa checks, deportation and so on, seem ineffective in keeping them out. Most come not to escape political persecution, but because they can work and make money here. And we know there are Americans who make extensive use of illegal-alien labor, and profit from it. We have to get tough and send out a signal throughout the world that the U.S. is no longer a place where illegal aliens can get a

(ALAN K. SIMPSON)

job. That could restrain millions of people abroad from coming to the U.S. without permission, and it might also induce many of the millions of aliens already here illegally to leave. There is discussion about giving amnesty or legal status to illegals who have already settled here. Well, the American people won't buy that unless they can be assured that, at the same time, new millions won't be coming.

Interview/U.S. News & World Report, 3-23:51.

Roger B. Smith
Chairman, General Motors Corporation

1

To me, this is a good time for the [employee] profit-sharing plan, because if the UAW guy gives up the wage concessions, then he has a right to share in the profits of his labor. It makes him a partner in the business in a more complete way. But then you may ask why you didn't give him profit-sharing five years ago. There's no point putting profit-sharing on top of high wages. What we need to do is substitute profit-sharing for a portion of those wages and get the wages competitive. Then if our income goes up, he'll get back a portion of what we earn. It seems to me the time is ripe for profit-sharing. It's going to keep us honest and keep him honest. That makes ultimate sense to me and I haven't heard anybody in the UAW say that it isn't right, either.

Interview, Detroit/Los Angeles Times, 4-26:(V)3.

David A. Stockman
*Director, Federal Office of
Management and Budget*

2

[On critics of the Reagan Administration's tax-cut proposal]: I can't for the life of me understand how people conclude that cutting taxes—thereby restoring incentives, leaving more of the income produced by firms and individuals in their own hands—is inflationary . . . the economists [who think that] have been wrong in the past and I think they're wrong now . . . We've tried the majority's approach for the last decade and the inflation's gotten worse, the financial disorder has gotten worse and the government

spending and deficits have gotten worse. I don't think we ever can hope to turn around our economic condition by following the threadbare advice of establishment economists.

*Interview, Washington, Feb. 20/
The New York Times, 2-22:(4)2.*

3

I'll take [Federal] budget cuts any way I can get them. But budget cuts alone won't solve the problem. We need tax cuts, because the tax burden is too high on the productive apparatus in our economy, whether it's individuals or firms. If you want to restart the engines of growth, investment, entrepreneurship, you've got to lower the tax rates. It's that basic.

Interview/U.S. News & World Report, 3-9:24.

4

[On the Federal spending cuts the Reagan Administration has proposed]: We have to deal with the facts of life. The Federal deficit is too big. The Treasury is borrowing too much money. It's elbowing everyone else out of the market and driving interest rates up to intolerable levels. Congress is going to have to take action to reduce that deficit . . . I think, given the kind of fiscal situation that we face, a budget that just has enormous momentum, that we can never promise that a program won't be cut. The government has been running a credit card for 10 years and the bills are now coming in. If it takes cuts in areas that we had hoped to avoid before, then we are going to have to make those cuts. We can't spend what we don't have.

Interview/"Face the Nation," CBS-TV, 9-27.

5

[On the Reagan Administration's economic program]: The hard part of the supply-side tax cut is dropping the top rate from 70 to 50 per cent—the rest of it is a secondary matter. The original argument was that the top bracket was too high, and that's having the most devastating effect on the economy. Then, the general argu-

WHAT THEY SAID IN 1981

ment was that, in order to make this [the 70-to-50 cut] palatable as a political matter, you had to bring down all the brackets. But, I mean, Kemp-Roth [the Administration's plan] was always a Trojan horse to bring down the top rate . . . . It's kind of hard to sell "trickle down," so the supply-side formula was the only way to get a tax policy that was really "trickle down." Supply-side is "trickle-down" theory.

Interview/The Atlantic Monthly, December:46,47.

1

[On the Reagan Administration's formulation of its economic program]: The reason we did it wrong—not wrong, but less than the optimum—was that we said, "Hey, we have to get a program out fast." And when you decide to put a program of this breadth and depth out fast, you can only do so much. We were working in a 20- or 25-day time-frame, and we didn't think it all the way through. We didn't add up all the numbers. We didn't make all the thorough, comprehensive calculations about where we really needed to come out and how much to put on the plate the first time, and so forth. In other words, we ended up with a list that I'd always been carrying of things to be done, rather than starting the other way and asking, "What is the over-all fiscal policy required to reach the target?"

Interview/The Atlantic Monthly, December:54.

2

[On the *Atlantic Monthly* interview he gave in which he expressed misgivings about President Reagan's economic program]: . . . my poor judgment and loose talk [have] done him and his program a serious disservice; worse, they have spread an impression that is utterly false. President Reagan believes with every ounce of his strength in his program for economic recovery and the better opportunities it will bring to all Americans. Never, ever, has he attempted to mislead the Congress or the American people or say things which weren't true . . . I would not be here now, nor would I have worked 16 hours per day for nearly a year, if I did not believe in the

President and his policies. Honest people may worry about how best to advance our vision for getting the messed-up economy we inherited back on track and the overgrown budget under control. I have worried, but too publicly, and I deeply regret any harm that has been done . . . I grew up on a farm, and . . . my visit to the Oval Office [today] for lunch [and discussion of the interview] with the President was more in the nature of a visit to the woodshed after supper. He was not happy with the way this has developed—and properly so. He was very chagrined that these interpretations have been developed and these questions have been raised about his purposes, his intent and his belief.

*News conference, Washington, Nov. 12/
The New York Times, 11-13:38.*

3

[Saying he believes in President Reagan's economic program, despite voicing misgivings about it in an *Atlantic Monthly* interview]: I believe, absolutely believe, the supply-side theory is workable. Its essence is the assumption that incentive affects economic behavior and that if you improve the incentive for all of those ingredients to determine whether an economy grows, whether investment grows, whether productivity improves, you're going to get a better economy, you're going to get more jobs, you're going to get a higher standard of living. I believe that. I have never doubted it and I think this program will work. I guess what has happened is that I've also become more realistic about the phasing and the timing and the enormous amount of inertia that we have inherited as we attempt two goals at once: to squeeze inflation out of the economy because inflation was too high and to stimulate growth from an economy that was stagnant and declining, and to attempt . . . to do that all the while we're coping with the budget that reflects the momentum of spending over a 20-year period. But I think we're going to get it done. It won't be achieved—the literal accounting—down in 1984. But I think the public wants it done and I think we're going to get it done . . .

*News conference, Washington, Nov. 12/
The New York Times, 11-13:38.*

John Sweeney
President, Service Employees
International Union

1

A [labor] union should seek the best possible contract for its members. But you have to keep the employer healthy or you negotiate yourself out of a job.

U.S. News & World Report, 9-14:62.

Margaret Thatcher
Prime Minister of the
United Kingdom

2

I'm afraid that in the early stages bringing down inflation means that you have increasing unemployment, and I don't know any other way of doing it. Unemployment is much worse if your work force demands larger pay than is warranted by productivity. I have the impression that in the United States your pay increases are very much more modest, much more in step with productivity [than in Britain]. You also do not have the same number of public-sector industries that we have. I think [U.S.] President Reagan is more likely to be able to reduce inflation and still have not as much increased unemployment as ours. Never, never, never, I beg of you, go the way of incomes policies [wage and price guidelines] in the sense that you say, "You can only have X per cent." You build in all sorts of rigidities. Never go that way, because you'll spend the next two years unwinding the distortions. And they always unwind upward.

Interview, London/Time, 2-16:36.

3

My policy is a perfectly simple one: You keep the amount of money in line with the goods and services which back it. That is why I say the kind of money and financial policies I like are the moral ones. If you ever start to print money as a government, you're saying to every saver, "I am deliberately taking away a proportion of the value of your savings."

To reporters, London, Nov. 6/
San Francisco Examiner & Chronicle, 11-8:(A)21.

Leslie C. Thurow
Professor of economics, Massachusetts
Institute of Technology

4

When people voted for [President] Reagan, they weren't saying they had suddenly become more conservative on economic policy. They were saying they wanted a higher standard of living. The traditional Democratic program was designed to keep the lower class up with the middle class. But that doesn't solve today's problem, which is that the middle class is falling.

The Wall Street Journal, 2-27:18.

5

In the United States, we save $5 and spend $95 of every $100 we earn. If Kemp-Roth [the Reagan Administration's proposed economic plan] goes through and the average American family is given a $100 tax cut, it is true that it will increase savings and investment. Savings will rise by $5.50 but consumption will rise $94.50. Military spending is consumption spending. It doesn't augment our ability to produce more goods. If you're going to have a supply-side program, you have to take the tax off savings and investment and put it on consumption. Real supply-side economics would be to slap on a big value-added tax. A 10 per cent value-added tax would have yielded about $235-billion in revenue in 1980. This would have been more than enough to replace both the corporate income tax and the Social Security tax. The value-added tax is on consumption. If you don't consume, you don't pay the tax.

Interview, Cambridge, Mass./
"W": a Fairchild publication, 4-24:8.

Paul A. Volcker
Chairman, Federal Reserve Board

6

It is critically important that tax reduction proceed in harness with [government-] spending restraint, and as a practical matter, the credibility of that approach will depend on early Congressional action to deal with spending. A large cutback from projected increases in spend-

(PAUL A. VOLCKER)

ing in coming years is a crucial linchpin in an effective over-all economic program. I know how difficult that will be to accomplish in practice. Many people support cutbacks in general but not in their favorite program—and virtually every program is somebody's favorite.

Before Congressional
Joint Economic Committee,
Washington, Feb. 5/
Los Angeles Times, 2-6:(IV)1.

1

Curbing inflation will require persistent restraint on the growth of money and credit. An attempt to escape from high interest rates and strains on financial markets and institutions by abandoning that restraint would be self-defeating. [Easing up on restraint] would soon stimulate even more borrowing, further reduce incentives to save and ultimately result in still higher interest rates and more economic difficulty.

Before House Banking Committee,
Washington, July 21/
Los Angeles Times,
7-22:(I)1.

2

[On President Reagan's economic program and the Federal Reserve's tight-money policies]: There is no safe, painless alternatives to the fiscal and monetary objectives we have set for ourselves. Indeed, a sense of retreat would not only aggravate the present problems, but could set back the prospects for restoring growth and stability for years to come . . . We have been at critical junctures before in the fight on inflation, and the bleak reality is we have not had the foresight and the courage to stay on course. That is why we have gradually come into the grip of the most prolonged and debilitating inflation in our entire economic history.

Before Senate Budget Committee,
Washington, Sept. 16/Chicago Tribune, 9-17:(3)1.

Henry C. Wallich
Governor, Federal Reserve Board

3

We have neglected the supply side [of the economy] to the point where productivity gains have fallen and fallen over a period of 15 years until, for the last two years or so, they have been zero or negative. We have continuously favored the interests of the consumer to the detriment of the producer. We have expropriated the saver to subsidize the borrower. As a result, investment and savings in the American economy are among the lowest of major industrialized countries. Our growth has fallen far behind that of other countries that save and invest more. This trend must be reversed if the United States is to maintain its position in the world. That is the function of supply-side economics.

At St. Cloud (Minn.) University/
The Wall Street Journal, 4-24:22.

4

[On past eras when the gold standard was accompanied by low inflation and low interest rates]: That was the situation in the dim past— the 19th century, then in a modified way after World War II. But to get from our present situation to that blessed condition will take more than some mechanical decision to implement [the gold] standard. The transition to stability would be just as difficult as it would be without the gold standard. You have high inflation, you have expectations, you have wage contracts, you have interest rates that were high and built into the system; and to get away from that will require substantial adjustments no matter how you do it. If you got back to stable conditions it would be more feasible to have a gold standard. But I still am very doubtful that a gold standard would allow us to maintain that stability.

Interview, Washington/
The New York Times, 9-6:(4)4.

Glenn Watts
President, Communications Workers of America

5

[On the illegal air-traffic controllers strike during which the government fired striking con-

(GLENN WATTS)

trollers]: For the President [Reagan] to justify his rigid, uncompromising stand on the basis that the controllers' strike is "illegal" is simplistic and anachronistic. How would he have reacted 11 years ago in President [Richard] Nixon's place when 175,000 postal workers walked off the job? The Nixon Administration . . . expressed great outrage over the illegal strikes but was wise enough to leave the door open a crack for negotiation. When the crisis was resolved, both sides were congratulating each other for their responsible approach.

Los Angeles Herald Examiner, 8-30:(A)10.

Murray L. Weidenbaum
Chairman, Council of Economic Advisers to the President of the United States

1

It's our strong desire in the Administration to avoid involving the Federal government in collective bargaining and wage-and-price decision-making. We want to set in motion an economic policy that puts pressure on labor and management to develop, on their own initiative, wage and price patterns that are conducive to a lower rate of inflation, rather than using jawboning. The last time jawboning was very successful was in the Old Testament when Samson killed his enemies with one.

Interview/U.S. News & World Report, 4-13:51.

2

We expect to see a major expansion in the savings rate, for a variety of reasons. One, of course, is the expectation, borne out in the past, that cutting individual and family income-tax rates across the board will generate a more-than-proportionate increase in savings. Technically, I'm referring to the permanent-income hypothesis. What will make that shift more durable is a shift in inflationary expectation. The major reason that the savings rate is so depressed is the average citizen's belief, quite properly, that in recent years it hasn't paid to save because of inflation. Our total program—looking at the

monetary policy, the fiscal policy, the regulatory policy—pushes toward a diminished rate of inflation.

Interview/The New York Times, 4-19:(4)3.

Roy L. Williams
President, International Brotherhood of Teamsters

3

[Saying maybe unions should tone down wage demands in order to restore the jobs of laid-off workers]: I'm not trying to scare nobody, [but] we have been around a long time and have built our vacations, our holidays, our sick leaves. Maybe we should cool down a little bit. Get our people back to work. Maintain our wages. Work it out in such a way so we stay even with what we got and get the trucking industry in a position where they can't raise hell with us for raising the rates . . . Our people are wanting to go back to work. Somebody's going to have to do something to put our people back to work.

At Teamsters Union western conference, San Diego, Sept 1/Los Angeles Times, 9-2:(II)8.

James C. Wright, Jr.
United States Representative, D—Texas

4

[On President Reagan's call for a 10 per cent income-tax cut in each of the next three years]: The Reagan tax proposals are literally regressive because they would redistribute the wealth upward. I can't understand how the President can be so persuasive that he can get people pleading for a program that his own Vice President has called voodoo economics, and which give a family of four with a $10,000 annual income a $40 tax cut. You can't reduce taxes under the Kemp-Roth bill, increase defense spending by $34-billion and other expenses by $41-billion, and still balance the budget. The supply-siders are forcing the government into a bind. They're willing to risk deficits only if the deficits are caused by tax cuts. The monetarists believe a balanced budget is essential and takes precedence over tax cuts. Sooner or later, President

WHAT THEY SAID IN 1981

(JAMES C. WRIGHT, JR.)

Reagan is going to have to come to grips with these two competing cults.

Washington, March 6/
San Francisco Examiner & Chronicle, 3-8:(A)11.

1

[On President Reagan's veto of financing legislation passed by Congress, thereby halting many government operations, saying it calls for too much spending]: It's theatre, it's play-acting [by Reagan], to create a new diversion as a means of carrying out their cynical formula [of] . . . "When things go wrong, blame Congress" . . . The Reagan deficit is enormous, in the range of $90-billion, as a result of his excessive tax cuts for the wealthy and the deep decline in the economy. Therefore, he's got to find a scapegoat to blame it on. He's got to posture himself in an attitude of holding down the deficit. But the piddling amounts involved are nothing compared to the billions in deficits the Administration's policies have brought about.

Washington, Nov. 23/The New York Times, 11-24:12.

Jerry Wurf
President, American Federation of State,
County and Municipal Employees

2

We [government workers] face a challenge that's bigger than one person, even a [U.S.] President. We face a rising and disturbing national political mood that threatens our livelihoods and our futures as public employees . . . Public employees have to care about auto workers, and auto workers have to care about textile workers, and all of us have to care about the quality of life in the society as a whole. We have some tough years ahead. We have to face them united.

Chicago Tribune, 1-8:(4)5.

Edward Yardeni
Chief economist, E.F. Hutton & Company

3

[On the recent plunge in stock market prices]: There's a gnawing feeling that, while the [Reagan Administration's economic] policies sound great in theory, it may be a lot tougher to make them work. Another factor in the current disenchantment on Wall Street is that there seems to be a growing lack of consensus within the Administration about where we go from here —stories that the supply-siders are breaking ranks with the monetarists are disconcerting . . . The financial markets have seen—too often— Administrations underestimate their budget deficits. The recent concession by the Administration that the deficit will be larger than anticipated raises disquiet in the hearts and minds of investors.

The New York Times,
8-26:33.

Mortimer J. Adler
Educator; Chairman, board of editors,
Encyclopaedia Britannica

1

I once thought that the colleges would save us from educational decline by providing liberal general schooling. I now realize that's impossible. You can't reform education from the top down; change has to start at the bottom in elementary school. That's a recent reformation on my part. When I was at the University of Chicago in the 1930s and '40s, president Robert Hutchins and I were trying to produce general education at the college level. But given the age at which most young people attend college—18 to 22—and under the pressures of contemporary life, many students are understandably concerned with how they're going to earn a living. So the period of liberal general schooling must start much earlier.

Interview/U.S. News & World Report, 7-13:73.

Joann Albright
Director of career counseling and placement,
University of Denver

2

[On the increase in older persons and retirees enrolling in college]: They are people who may be feeling restless, bored, or are living with unfulfilled dreams. They have always wanted to do something and are now financially able to underwrite an education. It is enriching, doing something they have always wanted to do; a desire to continue growing.

Interview/The Christian Science Monitor, 1-26:(B)10.

Benjamin Alexander
President, Chicago State University

3

The history of some minorities and poor whites in this country is replete with stories of accomplishments despite long odds. This is why I deeply lament the efforts by too many educators to lower educational standards in order to accommodate the disadvantaged. Minorities, like any other group, must be able to perform competently according to the standards prevalent in the larger society. Curricula that do not prepare students toward this end are dishonest and criminal.

Before National Industrial Recreational Association, Chicago/Chicago Tribune, 7-22:(1)9.

Alexander W. Astin
Professor of higher education,
University of California, Los Angeles

4

[On the drop in the number of students scoring well on SAT tests]: There's no reason to suppose that there's been any rapid decline in inborn abilities. But it does seem that students are taking fewer hard academic courses in secondary school and taking more peripheral courses where As and Bs are easier to get . . . The schools are just less demanding than they used to be, and [students] are lazy up and down the ability spectrum. The gifted are as lazy as the others. They're not all driven, and when they're asked for less, they do less.

The Washington Post, 3-2:(B)4.

5

During the 1970s many of our public institutions made the mistake of assuming that students would be attracted to a program that made it easy to get a college degree: live at home, hold a full-time job and merely commute to campus for a

(ALEXANDER W. ASTIN)

few hours a day to take classes. This point of view often carried over into the classroom, where it was assumed that students would be alienated by courses that made too many demands on them. In effect, such attitudes encourage students not to be involved. Our research indicates that students are actually turned off by such an approach, and that they are more likely to drop out of an institution that does not challenge them. Students who invest their time and energies attending college —and especially those who live on the campus and whose parents are willing to foot the bill for a private-college education—do not want to feel that they are wasting their time and their parents' money. They may complain about being worked hard, but they expect it and they want it.

Before Lutheran Education Conference of
North America/
The Christian Science Monitor, 8-17:16.

Stephen K. Bailey
Professor of education, Harvard University;
President, National Academy of Education

1

[On the active recruiting of students by colleges to keep up enrollments]: When there are great pressures to get students, there are great pressures to keep them once they are there . . . There's a whole series of subtle self-interests [by faculty]: You do it in the name of remediation or of giving [students] a second chance. But the result is a loss of standards that has changed the nature of higher education from a serious pursuit with quality control and high standards to a custodial function . . . If you [the prospective student] receive a hundred fancy colored brochures, it has to make you a little bit cynical and ask the question, "If they have to push the product so hard, there must be something wrong with it."

The Washington Post, 2-11:(A)8.

Grace Baisinger
Former president, National
Parent-Teacher Association

2

[Criticizing proposals to grant tax credits for private- and parochial-school tuition]: Tuition tax credits are a bad idea. They would be bad economic policy, bad education policy, and bad public policy. They would undermine the funding base of public education by providing a form of Federal welfare to a small segment of our population, which includes those among us who are the most well-off financially.

June 1/Los Angeles Times, 6-2:(I)5.

William S. Banowsky
President, University of Oklahoma

3

The people I really empathize with . . . are the public-school teachers. I think they've been getting a bum rap. When I was a young man going to public schools, nobody was more honorable than our teachers. It was a great thing to be a teacher. Now people look down on teachers. We pay garbage-collectors more than teachers. We pay rock singers scandalous salaries, baseball players. And the people who are charged with transferring the wisdom and the values of the ages to our children are treated terribly.

Interview/Los Angeles Herald Examiner, 10-24:(A)7.

Terrel H. Bell
Secretary of Education of
the United States

4

[Saying the Reagan Administration is canceling proposals made by the Carter Administration requiring non-English-speaking children to be taught in their native language]: The [bilingual] rules are fiercely opposed by many, supported by few. Nothing in the law or the Constitution anoints the Department of Education to be National School Teacher, National School Superintendent or National School Board. I would like to use this regulation, symbolic of many of the ills that have plagued the

(TERREL H. BELL)

Federal government and this fledgling Department, to telegraph a message of change to the American people.

Washington, Feb. 2/Los Angeles Times, 2-3:(I)1.

1

... we need more discipline, more rigor in our education system. I think we need standards, and I think we need to stand by them more vigorously than we have ever done in the past ... I feel that we have not held to standards; we've not demanded arrival at a certain level of accomplishment before you can be promoted. Parents, especially in the inner city, have been expecting automatic promotions, automatic awarding of diplomas, and what we really have is an education system that's academically quite flabby. As I have said before, I think it's time to shape up in academe.

TV-radio interview/
"Meet the Press," National Broadcasting Company,
3-15.

2

We have been moving steadily and almost relentlessly toward more and more Federal control over education in this country ... And this [Education] Department has been promulgating regulations that violate the autonomy of states, state legislators, state boards of education and local school boards. And if we don't reverse the trend, we could be moving unwittingly toward a Federal ministry of education, and that would be a disaster ... If you get a Federal ministry, your inclination is to tighten up the control and have everybody singing out of the same page of the hymn book.

Interview, Washington/
The Christian Science Monitor, 3-25:(B)5.

3

When school superintendents around the country try to implement higher academic standards, they are frequently undercut by school boards that are afraid to back up tougher policies. That's why I zero in on the school board. It is the chief policy-making body in a school system. I don't think these boards are doing their duty in this country by setting less-than-rigorous standards. Parents and taxpayers have a right to know that students must attain a minimum-competency level, or they will not be able to progress from one grade to the next. If the school boards would set that kind of policy and require it of everyone, I think we'd start to solve this very complex problem.

Interview/U.S. News & World Report, 6-8:61.

Richard E. Berendzen
President, American University

4

[Addressing freshmen students]: If your principal motivation for coming to this university at this time is simply to get away from mom and dad and to party and play for four years, do not unpack today—go elsewhere ... You will waste your own time, your parent's money and our institutional reputation. We are concerned about serious business here. And we want you to be, too. Of course, university life should be fun; indeed, learning itself can be one of life's greatest joys, along with the pleasures of sports, friendships and romances. Still, your central purpose should be the pursuit of knowledge, not the quest of parties.

The Washington Post, 9-11:(A)18.

5

[Criticizing the U.S. for lagging behind other countries in funds spent for international educational exchange programs]: The Soviets view exchanges as a branch of foreign policy. We are spending something like one-tenth of what the Soviets spend on this in Latin America, and about one-twelfth what they spend on Africa. Both these areas are important to us. I should think the present government should note this.

The New York Times, 11-29:(1)6.

Bruno Bettelheim
Psychologist

6

The worst aspect of the system is that we try to make education easier and easier. To become

(BRUNO BETTELHEIM)

educated isn't easy; it's hard work. Our attitude that it should be easy is detrimental. When education is presented as fun, the child who succeeds gets little feeling of accomplishment, and the child who fails is defeated, since he can't do what he is told is easy to do; so he thinks, "I'm no good." When I taught children, I always told them, "This is difficult, but if you work hard, you can learn it." Under those conditions, if children fail, they're not defeated, since they have been warned that it is difficult. But if they succeed, they have a wonderful feeling.

Interview/The Washington Post, 7-19:(C)5.

David W. Breneman
Senior fellow, Brookings Institution

1

[On the stepped-up recruiting of students by colleges and universities]: Higher education has had a fixation with growth. Now they're after almost anything that's breathing, and there's a danger that there's a qualitative downgrading of the whole enterprise . . . A handful of institutions remain highly selective and still seem to be delivering high quality, but many others seem to be competing themselves down to the lowest common denominator.

The Washington Post, 2-11:(A)8.

George Burnham
Director of admissions,
University of Colorado, Denver

2

[On the increase in older persons and retirees enrolling in college]: The higher the age, the greater the motivation. It could be from a variety of aspects. The older student tends to have this desire toward accomplishment, toward completing something, and naturally he brings to it a great deal of experience. Once he finds that what he has been doing feeds into what he is now trying to learn, this in itself provides an ever-expanding area of motivation.

Interview/
The Christian Science Monitor, 1-26:(B)10.

John E. Coons
Professor of law,
University of California, Berkeley

3

[On a voucher plan by which the government gives flat grants of money to parents so they can send their children to the public or private school of their choice]: The voucher idea can revive free public education as a reliable vehicle for the training of children for at least a decade to come. And it can save private education, too . . . We do not advocate tax credits for people who send their kids to private schools. Our idea is to give the poor, blacks, Hispanics and other disadvantaged people a choice of schools for their children, rather than shackle them to inadequate public schools. They may select another public school system or a private school. This would improve both public and private education.

The Christian Science Monitor, 1-22:10.

Christopher Edley
Executive director,
United Negro College Fund

4

People look for glittering, shiny solutions to our problems—but education is the single most effective tool in overcoming our social ills. And when you educate a student from the ghetto, you're doing more than educating the individual. You're educating his cousins, nieces, aunts, children—everyone is uplifted by that. It gives hope to a whole spread of family and friendship connections. We've lost some of what existed when I was attending public school, where the teachers drilled the importance of education into us time and time again. We let something creep into the education system, which is a so-called value-free public school education. I don't give a darn about a value-free education system.

Interview/Los Angeles Herald Examiner, 1-9:(A)17.

Lloyd H. Elliott
President, George Washington University

5

Every corner, nook and cranny [of higher education] has been affected by Federal regulations.

(LLOYD H. ELLIOTT)

Most of their goals are defensible, but, on net, they have hurt the universities. The amount of time and resources they consume have detracted immensely from our primary goals, which are teaching and research . . . The red tape is strangling.

The Washington Post, 3-30:(A)2.

R. Buckminster Fuller
Engineer, Author, Designer

1

[On whether the educational system hinders original thinking]: No question about it. Every child is born to be a comprehensivist. The mind deals with what you can't see as well as what you can. But how do we teach the children? When a child asks, "Why do the galaxies do what they do?" the daddy answers, "Wait until you get to school." Then the school says, "Never mind about the universe. Let's talk about whether you're going to get an A or a B or a D." We have learned in biology and anthropology that extinction has been the consequence of over-specialization, and our specialization is leading to the extinction of the species. The only thing humans need is the ability to think. Unfortunately, they think mostly about how to make a living and get along in the system rather than about what the universe is trying to tell us.

*Interview, Pacific Palisades, Calif./
Los Angeles Times, 3-15:(Home)43.*

A. Bartlett Giamatti
President, Yale University

2

America cannot allow itself to transform the public schools into warehouses for the angry. Let us remember that the partnership of parents and neighbors, civic leaders and politicians must agree that the schools are the most important single asset the community holds in common. Let us assert that the duty of that partnership is to decide that the first priority for public money is the school system. And let us insist that schools have a role and obligation in the treasured com-

mon life beyond just schooling. When we have reassembled a vision of the purpose of school and of the means of education, then we can pass to the rebuilding of what is both a system and a process of civility.

*At Atlanta University commencement/
Time, 6-15:55.*

Paul E. Gray
*President,
Massachusetts Institute of Technology*

3

Universities, like civilization itself, are most precious. It takes forever to create them and but a moment to lose them and everything they represent . . . Surely there must be reductions in Federal spending. But I am troubled that some programs—such as many related to defense—are receiving little or no apparent scrutiny, while others—having to do with education or social service, for example—are being proposed for major reductions.

*At MIT commencement/
The Christian Science Monitor, 6-17:16.*

Norman Hackerman
President, Rice University

4

[On cuts in Federal aid to higher education]: Now that we have real economic pressure on us, maybe we [colleges and universities] will concern ourselves and come to a solution—a deliberate and reasoned solution rather than the inadvertent conclusions we came to, when if we didn't solve a problem one way one day, we could always get a patch of a million dollars [from the government] and try another way. [The new situation] doesn't sound bad to me. It's hard, but it's not necessarily bad. No doubt individuals will be hurt, not only on the student side but also on [the] scholarly side. Individuals who have been used to being supported will not be. [But] those who are really bound and determined to become scientists and engineers will do so. So we will maybe turn out fewer of them, but they will certainly be the most highly motivated.

*Interview, Houston/
The Christian Science Monitor, 12-31:7.*

WHAT THEY SAID IN 1981

Samuel Halperin
*Director, Institute for Educational Leadership,
George Washington University*

1

Sure, there are some excesses in Federal regulation [of higher education]. But it's not just make-work and bureaucratic silliness. It's done to protect vulnerable groups ... Real progress has been made in higher education because of these laws. I don't think the groups that made these social gains can be put back into the bottle and corked up again.

The Washington Post, 3-30:(A)2.

Warren Heemann
*Trustee, Council for Advancement and
Support of Education*

2

Public schools have begun to develop full-scale staffs active in fund-raising. Whereas they may have had one or two people chipping away at it in the past, they're now developing a complement of skilled staff members that more closely resembles what private institutions have. Public institutions are getting their act together more and more in terms of private fund-raising. They've seen what private schools are doing and have identified those missed opportunities.

The Christian Science Monitor, 5-19:7.

Theodore M. Hesburgh
President, University of Notre Dame

3

If a college president means anything, he has to stand up for the integrity of the institution. The university is a kind of sacred place. Nobody can be allowed to interfere—not the state, not the benefactors, not the church ... The name of the game in the 1980s is quality. We must get back out of the wild growth of the curriculum and get back into some core of knowledge—history, philosophy, theology, language, literature, mathematics, science, art and music. Otherwise, we are just graduating trained seals ... Higher education and every other enterprise moves forward when there is good leadership; otherwise it stagnates. We need people

with vision, elan, *geist*, people who have standards and a certain toughness. How to get leadership gets down to every single college president who is chosen, people who do more than raise money. Of course, you need money. But if you have money and no vision, you just squander it.

Interview/The New York Times, 10-13:20.

Ernest F. Hollings
United States Senator, D—South Carolina

4

[Arguing against special tax credits for parents who send their children to private schools that charge tuition]: It's an obligation of the government to support public schools and not get involved in private education. Our great task today is to rebuild public education ... But this tuition-credit proposal would instead materially contribute to the final demise of public education by starting us off on a tangent of financing private schools ... Tuition credits would indirectly subsidize the "protest schools"—private white-flight schools built to avoid racial integration. Here we're trying to build a unitary school system providing equal opportunity, and suddenly we are going to make things easier for protest schools. Many such academies don't have money for a chemistry lab or a gym. Tax credits for parents would boost enrollment, enabling the protest schools to expand their facilities with the tax money of the very people in whose faces they slam the door.

Interview/U.S. News & World Report, 1-19:70.

Charles Huggins
*Professor of surgery,
University of Chicago*

5

A decline in education is the greatest problem the United States faces. We sugarcoat our education and bring it down to a low level. In many places, students who can't read get their high-school diplomas anyway. This effort to bring everything down to a palatable level is a cancer on the society. What we have to do is make more room for the highly talented elite of our country —the boys and girls of 10 to 18—who can study

(CHARLES HUGGINS)

calculus and the like. The more we care for and nurture our talented people, the better off we will be. At the same time, of course, we have to provide education facilities for the rest of the young.

Interview/U.S. News & World Report, 4-6:45.

Roger H. Hull
President, Beloit (Wis.) College

1

[Saying students should have a moral rather than a legal obligation to repay scholarship loans]: A student would be given a scholarship and be told he has a moral, but not legal, obligation to repay . . . All students receiving moral-obligation scholarships would get special counseling and be informed that the scholarships are intended as a revolving fund for future students. Though there would be no legal obligation to repay, there would be a moral obligation to do so—and the college would assist the student in developing, along the lines of existing loan programs, gift repayment schedules and measures of the real cost of the scholarship over time . . . The program, we believe, will lead to a revolving fund that eventually will be larger than what was put in by the initial donors, because scholarship recipients will probably continue giving long after thay have paid their moral debt.

Chicago Tribune, 12-13:(1)10.

Alfred Kazin
Critic; Professor of English, Graduate Center, City University of New York

2

[Criticizing the notion that private universities are important because they are the only independent universities]: In the midst of a terrible Civil War, July 2, 1862, the Congress of the United States provided that the Federal government give portions of the land it owned within the states to the states themselves for state universities. The Morrill Act is virtually the most important piece of legislation on behalf of

American education ever passed. Thirteen million acres of the public domain were given to the states. To imagine America today without the benefits of the great universities of California, Michigan, Minnesota, Indiana, Iowa, etc., etc., is impossible. To think that any private university . . . is more "quote independent" than a great state university, with its healthy pluralism of religious and non-religious inspirations, its concern for the public weal, its basis in the Constitutional separation of church and state, is to recognize, among other signs, that the American mind in high places is going backward these days.

At City University of New York Graduate Center commencement/The New York Times, 6-13:17.

Donald Kennedy
President, Stanford University

3

Current proposals before Congress include tax deductions for industrial contributions to university research and provisions for a new comprehensive Federal patent policy that would help universities and small business realize income from research discoveries. These efforts are laudable, and both should be enacted . . . but the emphasis on commercialization incentives is producing some farther-reaching institutional innovations that should be examined carefully for side effects . . . Scientists who once shared prepublication information freely and exchanged cell lines without hesitation are now much more reluctant to do so . . . One casualty surely is the accessibility of a large body of significant work to young investigators and graduate students . . . Perhaps even more important, the fragile network of informal communication that characterizes every especially active field is liable to rupture.

The Washington Post, 1-18:(C)6.

Nannerl Keohane
President, Wellesley College

4

A college has a double stance in the world. One is a kind of special place apart where people can come and have an opportunity and space to develop their minds and personalities

WHAT THEY SAID IN 1981

(NANNERL KEOHANE)

. . . But college also has a responsibility for satisfying the hunger of people who are not a part of this group set apart in a residential way, but who have an interest and need for talking about ideas, being mentally refreshed, excited and stimulated by the things a college stands for. To me, both stances are important.

Interview, Wellesley College/
The Christian Science Monitor, 11-4:(B)17.

Donald Klein
First Assistant Superintendent of Schools,
Cook County, Ill.

1

The whole permissive attitude that has pervaded our society has obviously slipped into the schools. There's much more hassle today. In many cases teachers find themselves acting as highly paid police or babysitters. Very little education is going on.

Chicago Tribune, 2-1:(1)10.

Arthur Kornberg
Professor of biochemistry,
Stanford University

2

Biochemists and geneticists, who were finding it difficult to locate a job, suddenly have sex appeal in the industrial world. But virtually everything being done in an industrial setting originated in an academic environment. There is a danger that if the bright young people are siphoned off into industry, then the new developments that we will need to work on for the next 20 years will not be going on in university laboratories and research institutes. There is a risk of killing the goose that lays those golden eggs.

Interview/U.S. News & World Report, 3-16:74.

Ernest R. Leach
Dean of student affairs, Prince George's
Community College (Maryland)

3

[On the active recruiting of students by colleges to keep up enrollments]: We have an obli-

gation to make education available to as many people as we can. We try to find out what it is that the customer needs, and we will build a service that that customer needs . . . If colleges continue to build Chryslers, they'll all go bankrupt.

The Washington Post, 2-11:(A)8.

Robert Linnell
Professor of chemistry, and director of
institutional studies,
University of Southern California

4

A university is supposed to be free of the pressures of the marketplace, a place where experts can debate the great questions of our age, like nuclear energy or gene-splicing. But now you can't find a leading [faculty member] in these fields who isn't involved doing research for a private company or even president of the company. There's no objectivity left. They've all sold their souls.

The New York Times, 11-16:13.

William N. Lipscomb
Professor of chemistry, Harvard University

5

Our schools offer no conception of the scientific process of discovery. They do not encourage creative thought. In fact, they stifle it through too much rigidity in teaching. If we set out to give as little help as possible to originality in science, we could hardly devise a better plan than our educational system. Youngsters ought to be told what is unknown about ourselves and our universe as well as what is known. But our schools have deteriorated to the point that it's almost impossible to do so. Part of the problem is that people are asking much more of the schools. They are asking them to deal with all kinds of desirable and worthwhile social phenomena—from integrating the races to babysitting. And, at the higher levels of education, they're asking that research be immediately useful. Yet if we turn all of our attention to applied science, I'm afraid that we will not have fundamental discoveries.

Interview/U.S. News & World Report, 4-20:85.

Bernard McKenna
Evaluation specialist,
National Education Association

1

The public assumes that "alternative schools" are wild places where kids do their own thing in storefronts. But students have shown that the strongest part of their curriculum is in the basic skills . . . Alternative schools are much more needed than in the past. Parents today want different things for their children for different purposes and feel they should have different alternatives for their children. I hope that the alternative-education movement becomes more healthy for the survival of the public educational system . . . With a broader range of students in today's schools, alternative institutions need to be nourished.

The New York Times, 11-15:(12)27.

Floretta D. McKenzie
Superintendent of Schools-designate
of the District of Columbia

2

One of the problems in an urban school system is the largeness, the largeness and depersonalization that takes place in a city. It appears sometimes that parents are not as supportive of youngsters in their schooling in a city. And sometimes it appears that city schools are not anxious to have parents involved . . . This is caused by the diverse population in a city, by the large number of disadvantaged young people. So when you put that situation on top of the real purpose of a school—to teach a child to read and write, to speak effectively and to have some sense of aesthetics and citizenship —well, you don't have all the things going for you that you might in a rural situation where there are closer family ties, or even a suburban school where the school is the center of community social activity.

Interview/The Washington Post, 6-22:(A)15.

Floretta D. McKenzie
Superintendent of Schools of the
District of Columbia

3

We are very much for reading, writing and computation skills, but we are also very much for

teaching young people about their bodies, about being good citizens and about the arts. All of it makes for an educated person . . . While test scores are very important, we also want to know that kids can perform well by other indications, like attendance and good grades, and that they can apply to real-life situations that we teach them . . . I am suggesting that reading and math are not the only subjects to be taught . . . There has been so much concern with reading and writing that I've discovered some schools don't have any program, say, in vocal music.

Interview/The Washington Post, 9-8:(A)10.

Edwin Meese III
Counsellor to the President
of the United States

4

[During the Vietnam era,] the universities were plunged from being citadels of the best that America has to offer to the worst that America had. As a result, the universities no longer enjoyed the respect and support of a majority of Americans. Whether it was the free-speech movement or the filthy-speech movement or the war in Vietnam or whatever, taxi-drivers came to no longer revere our universities . . . It turned people against the institutions of our society—anti-police, anti-university—all because of students who were willing to close down a university. And in fact, it wasn't just students. It was a lot of adults who were at fault too, adults who did not have the courage to stand up to the students . . . I don't think you have these same undesirable and anti-education elements on the campuses [today]. Students and faculties are more mature than they were in the '60s. The faculties particularly have learned a lot . . . In the 60s, faculty members encouraged demonstrators and protestors.

Interview/The Washington Post, 3-15:(A)10.

Thomas P. O'Neill, Jr.
United States Representative, D—Massachusetts

5

Investment in education is an investment in the long-term health of our economy and our

WHAT THEY SAID IN 1981

(THOMAS P. O'NEILL, JR.)

society. Education has made the American dream a reality for millions. Now is not the time to question that investment . . . This country will not be served by drastically cutting student financial aid and limiting opportunities for the hard-pressed middle- and lower-income students to attend private colleges and universities . . . As a nation, we are faced with increasing our military expenditures by nearly 50 per cent between 1981 and 1983. We are trying to curb Federal spending to reduce Federal deficits and lower inflation. Naturally, we face hard choices. One choice that we must avoid is that of crippling higher education and denying our youth equal access to educational opportunity.

At Boston College commencement/
The Christian Science Monitor, 6-17:12.

Bob Packwood
United States Senator, R—Oregon

1

[Supporting a special tax credit for parents who send their children to private schools that charge tuition]: The bulk of those who go to private schools go to church-affiliated schools and are from families with total incomes under $25,000 a year. Relatively few families can afford to send their children to Exeter or Groton, and for those who can afford it, a maximum credit of $250 or $500 isn't going to make much difference when the tuition is $4,000 or $5,000 a year. This proposal is really designed to help those who go to private schools charging tuitions of from $500 to $800 a year. I want to start out with a relatively modest credit to establish the principle . . . The tax reduction provided by this bill is about $4-billion a year. That, I think, is not too big a price to pay to support the diversity and competitiveness represented by private education—by providing a simple, non-bureaucratic form of assistance to parents who want to take advantage of it.

Interview/
U.S. News & World Report, 1-19:70.

Peter Peyser
United States Representative, D—New York

2

[Addressing Education Secretary Terrel Bell on Reagan Administration plans to cut student financial-aid programs]: I feel sorry for you. I feel you are involved in destroying a program, and hundreds of thousands of young Americans are going to be affected. You are probably the only one in the Administration aware of what this is going to do. Certainly President Reagan doesn't know and [Budget Director] David Stockman doesn't care. Stockman is sort of like the bomber pilot flying high who doesn't have to see the faces of the people he destroys.

At House Subcommittee on
Postsecondary Education hearing, Washington/
Chicago Tribune, 3-27:(1)4.

Edward Phelan
New York Academic administrator

3

[On the trend toward non-Catholic students enrolling in Catholic schools]: In the inner city schools where many residents are not Catholic, many parents want the benefits of Catholic education—values, discipline and academic excellence. Catholic schools have traditionally been neighborhood schools; we are there to serve the population of that particular neighborhood. That is "catholic."

Chicago Tribune, 4-26:(1)15.

George Rainsford
President, Kalamazoo (Mich.) College

4

[On the intense competition among colleges to attract top students to their campuses]: There is a premium on academically talented kids. A student with good grades and high test scores can heat his house with college catalogues and brochures.

San Francisco Examiner & Chronicle,
4-26:(This World)24.

Ronald Reagan
President of the United States

1

. . . some have protested there must be no reduction of [Federal] aid to schools. Let me point out that Federal aid to education amounts to only 8 per cent of total educational funding. For this the Federal government has insisted on a tremendously disproportionate share of control over our schools. Whatever reductions we've proposed in that 8 per cent will amount to very little of the total cost of education. It will, however, restore more authority to states and local school districts.

Before joint session of Congress,
Washington, Feb. 18/The New York Times, 2-19:14.

2

Where there are predominantly students speaking a foreign language at home, coming to school and being taught English, and they fall behind or are unable to keep up in some subjects because of the lack of knowledge of the language, I think it is proper that we have teachers equipped who can get at them in their own language and understand why it is they don't get the answer to the problem and help them in that way. But it is absolutely wrong and against [the] American concept to have a bilingual-education program that is now openly, admittedly dedicated to preserving their native language and never getting them adequate in English so they can go out into the job market and participate.

Before National League of Cities, Washington/
Los Angeles Herald Examiner, 3-3:(A)7.

3

. . . education is the principal responsibility of local school systems, teachers, parents, citizen boards and state governments. By eliminating the [Federal] Department of Education less than two years after it was created, we can not only reduce the budget but ensure that local needs and preferences—rather than the wishes of Washington—determine the education of our children.

Broadcast address to the nation, Washington,
Sept. 24/The Washington Post, 9-25:(A)13.

Robert M. Rosenzweig
Vice president for public affairs,
Stanford University

4

[Defending standardized college entrance tests]: The contribution of standardized tests to the democratization of American education is hard to over-estimate. The use of reliable testing instruments has made it all but impossible to overlook intellectual ability as the main criterion for college admission. Equally important, it has made it possible for college admissions offices to find talent in places in which its existence is a rare nugget rather than a rich lode. Tests have removed the worst kinds of subjectivity from admission decisions—subjectivity based on racial, ethnic, religious and class bias. Moreover, because they provide reasonably reliable evidence of academic ability, tests have made it safer to exercise a healthier subjectivity based on the assessment of disabilities overcome, leadership ability, non-academic achievements and a host of other qualities that mark successful human beings.

At meeting of National Council of Higher Education
and Loan Programs and National Association of
State Scholarship and Grant Programs,
San Diego, Calif./The Wall Street Journal, 7-17:26.

Albert Shanker
President, American Federation of Teachers

5

[Today] we have a public which is as well-educated or more educated than the teachers. Instead of looking up at teachers, they can look straight at them or down on them. Teachers are surrounded by parents who feel they could do as good a job teaching their children if they weren't too busy making more money.

Newsweek, 4-27:78.

6

[Criticizing proposals to grant tax credits for private- and parochial-school tuition]: Citizens do not have the right to come and say: "I don't like your public drinking-water—pay for my

Perrier." The question we face is whether we want to have a publicly funded public school system or whether the public school system becomes a charity ward.

News conference, June 1/
Los Angeles Times, 6-2:(I)5.

John R. Silber
President, Boston University

1

It is often said, and said mistakenly, that students at graduation go into the "real world." That is an expression of escapism. It suggests that we were avoiding the real world all the time we were in school and in college. No world is more real than the world of ideas in which students are, or should be, immersed from kindergarten through college.

At Boston University commencement/
The Christian Science Monitor, 6-17:12.

2

What you need in the schools is educated people, and education will happen automatically. If I wanted to improve a school system, I wouldn't worry about testing the students; I would test the teachers. There has got to be a way of certifying a teacher as a qualified teacher without making her take all that stuff that they try to cram into somebody at a school of education. They don't approach literature with any great understanding . . . When it comes to teaching history, what you want there is somebody who knows some history and has a natural flair for telling stories. It's very important to have someone who is engaging and has an interesting mind.

Interview/Chicago Tribune, 8-4:(1)20.

3

The quality of education that [high-school] graduates get today is substantially inferior to that of students 50 or even 20 years ago . . . Quite simply, today's high-school diploma is a

fraudulent credential. It doesn't guarantee a level of literacy for the graduate. It doesn't imply anything about the person's ability to do ordinary arithmetic—much less algebra, solid geometry or trigonometry. It doesn't certify competence in science, world or American history, or anything else. What the high-school diploma tells you is that a student was institutionalized for about 12 years. That's all. You wouldn't know whether the student had been in a prison colony, a reform school or a place for mental defectives . . . We've seen a denuding of the curriculum, largely driven by professional educators who wanted to design a program in which no one could fail. But the consequence was that no one could succeed. The standards had been set so low that gifted and average students met those standards with ease and, as a result, were never pushed to the level of achievement of which they were genuinely capable. We suffer from that to an appalling degree.

Interview/U.S. News & World Report, 9-7:53.

4

In the 1950s, when I was a young assistant professor of philosophy at Yale, becoming a professor was like taking a secular vow of poverty. You gave up money for time, time to do your own work. [But now,] the profile of many academics more closely resembles that of a businessman. They will spend time to make money, like cutting down on office hours for students. Some people no longer go into academic life for intellectual rewards.

The New York Times, 11-16:13.

Paul Simon
United States Representative, D—Illinois

5

We [in the U.S.] are doing almost nothing to promote fluency in the increasingly critical languages of Arabic, Chinese, Japanese, Persian, Swahili, Urdu and Polish. Some 300 million people [in the world] speak Hini, but fewer than 300 Americans are studying that language . . . If we don't have a national will to express

(PAUL SIMON)

ourselves in something other than the mother tongue, then we might as well erect a sign at each port of entry into the country reading, "Welcome to the United States—we cannot speak your language."

U.S. News & World Report, 4-27:57,58.

Joseph J. Sisco
Chancellor, American University, Washington

1

[Saying he is resigning as head of the university]: I'm very pleased with what I did at American University. I think it's a better school academically, and we brought some visibility to the place . . . But frankly, a lot of what I did was high-level sophisticated begging, and I'm just absolutely fed up with doing any more fundraising. I've had enough of it.

Interview/The Washington Post, 1-16:(B)1.

Michael I. Sovern
President, Columbia University

2

Surely at this critical time, our nation should not be so shortsighted as to embark on the false economy of cutting financial aid to students . . . We are risking waste of our most precious national resource, stunting of individuals, and serious damage to independent colleges and universities—all for savings that amount to a fraction of 1 per cent of the Federal budget.

*At Columbia University commencement/
The Christian Science Monitor, 6-17:14.*

Thomas Sowell
*Economist, senior fellow,
Hoover Institution, Stanford University*

3

[On whether he favors government aid to private schools]: I'm for anything that will add choice of schooling—such as tax credits or vouchers—anything that will allow people who don't have much money to have a voice in how their kids are educated. Whether they send them

to private school isn't that important, but the fact that public schools know they might, could be a major factor in improving education. If a kid can't read, it's not going to matter what other policies are followed—he won't be able to find a job.

Interview/Forbes, 9-14:104.

Shirley Stanton
*Director of conferences,
Williams College*

4

We feel that liberal arts is important as a means of training people to think, make decisions and order their time in a more efficient way. There are lots of schools that can tell you how to read the bottom line, and this is important, but an executive needs to take 12 different strands of information and put them together into a decision.

The New York Times, 8-30:(12)23.

Albert N. Whiting
*Chancellor, North Carolina
Central University*

5

I propose that black colleges do a massive redesigning of their cultural orientation, that they broaden their scope to appeal to white students. Black public colleges can make a choice—act to survive, or talk politics to pacify egos. The choice is yours.

The Christian Science Monitor, 3-27:12.

Fred Zuker
*Director of admissions,
Tulane University*

6

[On the competition among colleges to attract top students to their campuses]: High achievers define the intellectual tone of the school. You have to have these students to challenge the faculty and stimulate classroom activity.

*San Francisco Examiner & Chronicle,
4-26:(This World)24.*

WHAT THEY SAID IN 1981

James H. Zumberge
President,
University of Southern California

1

We [the university] are essentially a conglomerate. We are in the hotel business, the restaurant business, the entertainment business, the research industry and more . . . The president must coordinate all of this. His most difficult job is to convince the members of the conglomerate that they exist to serve the interest of the university. They do not exist unto themselves.

Interview, San Marino, Calif./
Los Angeles Times, 2-17:(II)1.

The Environment . Energy

Ansel Adams
Photographer; Conservationist

1

[On Secretary of the Interior James Watt]:
This [Reagan] Administration, with Mr. Watt
spearheading the effort, seems bent on desecration and exploitation of our public lands. They
know the price of everything and the value of
nothing, and would casually encourage transfer
of priceless public possessions to private wealth
. . . In all my years, there has never been a
Secretary of the Interior so arrogant and intractable toward the land and its natural beauty.
It is incomprehensible how such a person with
such an attitude toward the Earth could be appointed guardian of our nation's natural resources.

News conference, Washington, Nov. 16/
Chicago Tribune, 11-17:(1)3.

Cecil D. Andrus
Former Secretary of the Interior
of the United States

2

[On the loss of 3 million acres of farmland
every year through urban sprawl, construction,
highways, etc.]: What we have is a tough but
manageable set of bad tendencies. The question,
as it is with energy, is whether we will act while
our depletion of agricultural land can still be
halted, or whether we will wait until a set of
troublesome tendencies becomes a full-blown
emergency. We tolerate the conversion of prime
farmland because we have a substantial reserve.
Cropland now in production amounts to 413
million acres, and we have another 127 million
potential for a total of 540 million acres. This
would appear to be a sufficient cushion to
guarantee future farm production and still permit further commercial development.

At National Agricultural Lands Conference,
Chicago, Feb. 9/Chicago Tribune, 2-10:(1)2.

3

[Interior Secretary James] Watt has set himself
up as the supreme judge of resource decisions.
He ignores the Congress of the United States
and the will of the majority of American people
in order to be a development zealot of the highest degree. His approach seems to be—if Mobil
or Exxon [oil companies] want it, they can have
it . . . There were 300 million visitors to the
[national] parks last year. They are crowded;
that's the problem. And here is this man [Watt]
saying there should be no more acquisition of
parkland, that we should not have urban parks.
He says he doesn't like to walk or paddle. That's
the wrong philosophy for the Department of the
Interior.

Interview, July 17/
The New York Times, 7-19:(1)15.

Malcolm Baldrige
Secretary of Commerce
of the United States

4

[On whether the U.S. should sell its oil and
natural-gas technology to the Soviet Union]:
One question you have to ask: Might it be better
to help Russia with its own energy development
so that the [Soviet] temptation to meddle in the
Persian Gulf area is lessened? Sometimes you
have to avoid backing the other fellow in the corner, where he just has no way to go except to
come out clawing.

Interview/U.S. News & World Report, 5-4:48.

WHAT THEY SAID IN 1981

Hans Bethe
Professor emeritus of physics,
Cornell University

1

Energy is the nation's greatest long-range problem. We are not going to lick inflation permanently unless we solve the energy problem. Finding a solution will take time, and we will need cooperation from many parts of society. I would propose to deal with our soil problem in three distinct ways. First: Produce synfuels. Second: Conserve. And third: Substitute other fuels for oil. My goal would be to stop importing oil altogether in 10 years.

Interview/U.S. News & World Report, 4-6:40.

Peter A. Bradford
Commissioner, Nuclear Regulatory
Commission of the United States

2

[On criticism that his agency has been too slow in licensing nuclear power plants]: Since I've been here [four years] the NRC has licensed about 20 plants, just about as many as exist in any other country in the world. The slowdown in nuclear growth is traceable to the accident at Three Mile Island and to simple economics. With today's capital and construction costs, nuclear plants are just too expensive a way of supplying energy.

Los Angeles Times, 6-6:(I)2.

Lester R. Brown
President, Worldwatch Institute

3

A Soil Conservation Service study done in Iowa concludes that if farmers there whose land is eroding excessively were to adopt the practices needed to stabilize their soils—such as terracing the land, rotating crops, minimum tillage—the short-term costs would be three times as great as the benefits. But if they don't take these steps, their land eventually will become worthless. It means the farmer who is losing topsoil at an excessive rate has two choices: go bankrupt in the short run, or go bankrupt in the long run. That's not a very pleasant set of alternatives.

Interview/U.S. News & World Report, 11-2:58.

Humberto Calderon Berti
Minister of Energy and
Mines of Venezuela

4

[On why oil-exporting countries such as his own have increased the price of their oil exports]: [There are] 30 countries, industrialized countries having housing, food, clothing, access to education. They have everything they need. On the other side, we have 120 countries. Some of them don't have anything. They don't have access to education. They don't have housing facilities. Food—very limited quantities of food . . . Before 1970, the oil companies paid whatever they wanted for this oil. They established the price. But the industrialized countries didn't ask *us* how much we wanted to pay for their cars, their refrigerators, the things we imported from them. What's really happening now? We're recovering what we lost before. Nothing else.

Interview, Caracas/
The Washington Post, 1-26:(A)15.

Jimmy Carter
President of the United States

5

There are real and growing dangers to our simple and most precious possessions: the air we breathe, the water we drink and the land which sustains us. The rapid depletion of beauty, the blight of pollution, the demands of increasing billions of people—all combine to create problems which are easy to observe and predict but difficult to resolve. If we do not act, the world of the year 2000 will be much less able to sustain life than it is now. But there is no reason for despair . . . We can meet the resource problems of the world . . . if we tackle them with courage and foresight.

Farewell address to the nation,
Washington, Jan. 14/
U.S. News & World Report, 1-26:34.

Mary E. Clark
Professor of biology,
San Diego State University

1

In just a few decades, we have used up half the world's fossil-fuel supplies, which took millions of years to be created. We are rapidly depleting the ground water that was deposited during the Ice Age. Topsoil is draining out of the Mississippi River at a rate of 15 tons per second. None of these resources will ever be replaced. One of the lessons biology teaches is that no population can long exceed the carrying capacity of its environment without a crash.

Interview / U.S. News & World Report, 8-17:48.

A. W. Clausen
President, International Bank for
Reconstruction and Development (World Bank)

2

Conservation, in its broadest sense, is not a luxury for people rich enough to vacation in scenic parks. Rather, the goal of economic growth itself dictates a serious and abiding concern for resource development . . . awareness is spreading that environmental precautions are essential for continued economic development over the long run.

Before Conservation Foundation, Washington, Nov. 12/The Christian Science Monitor, 11-13:7.

Henry L. Diamond
Co-Chairman, President Ronald Reagan's
Transition Task Force on the Environment

3

The old conservation movement still lives, and may have some important lessons in a resource-short era. Those lessons involve husbanding resources and wise use of what we have. When Lyndon Johnson left a light on in a room, his daddy asked if he owned stock in the power company, and made him go back and turn it off. The country laughed when he did that in the White House. In fact, that's energy conservation; and the remarkable thing is that it seems to be one of the few aspects of the energy program that is working. The old-style conservation precepts of

wise use as opposed to single-purpose and single-minded use may also work now. A society without limits to its capabilities can afford to dedicate vast resources to a single limited use such as wilderness or strip-mining. It can demand absolutely pure affluents from cities and industries. But a society with limits must allocate its resources among competing meritorious uses. This is what the old-style conservation taught and it may be an extraordinarily appropriate lesson for today.

Before Environmental Industry Council/ The Washington Post, 4-21:(A)18.

Charles DiBona
President,
American Petroleum Institute

4

[Supporting the Reagan Administration's proposals to open up more public land for development of resources]: The public perception is that we've now got an Interior Department that's going to be giving away public lands willy-nilly; but that's simply not true. What you've got is an Administration that is trying to strike some balance. Sure, it's a sharp shift in policy, but it's a shift from one extreme [against any development of public lands] to the center.

San Francisco Examiner & Chronicle, 4-5:(A)14.

Thomas L. Dineen
President, Allis-Chalmers-Coal
Gas Corporation

5

Perhaps the most ominous obstacle to the development of a shale-oil industry in the United States today is the need for some rather difficult political decisions related to possible environmental problems around the major shale deposits. While favorable decisions will probably be reached, the question of when is very difficult to answer.

The Christian Science Monitor, 1-30:14.

121

WHAT THEY SAID IN 1981

William Drayton
Former Assistant Administrator,
Environmental Protection Agency
of the United States

1

[On EPA budget cuts being considered by the Reagan Administration]: If these budget cuts go forward, there is no hope, for example, to control toxics before the end of the decade—none. Human exposure levels to environmental hazards are expected to double over the next decade. And so this is not really just about budget cuts. This is really about a society's decision about whether to curb the dangerous side effects of the chemical revolution.

Los Angeles Times, 10-1:(I)9.

Rene Dubos
Professor emeritus of microbiology,
Rockefeller University

2

Nature is very resilient, and so I am optimistic about the ability of the environment to recover from the damage that people inflict on it. I have seen enormous amounts of destruction in my native France during two wars—and I have seen how completely the land can come back from such destruction even though it was thought that everything was lost. There is phenomenal resiliency in the mechanisms of the earth. A river or a lake is almost never dead. If you give it the slightest chance by stopping pollutants from going into it, then nature usually comes back. When we deal gently with the earth—even when we have thoughtlessly damaged it—we can repair our friendship with it.

Interview/U.S. News & World Report, 2-23:72.

Ted Eck
Chief economist,
Standard Oil Company (Indiana)

3

Oil is still the cheapest portable form of easily transportable energy, and there is no synthetic-fuels challenge at the present price level. The competition from alternative energy sources is not there, so we will have to rely on normal supply-and-demand economics. And that means relying on OPEC, or, in reality, on Saudi Arabia.

The Washington Post, 6-15:(A)4.

James B. Edwards
Secretary of Energy of the United States

4

I am a strong supporter of nuclear energy. As you look across the horizon to find the answers to our energy problems, there's no real place to turn in the next 30 years other than nuclear to help keep us from being all hostages to foreign countries.

To reporters, February/The New York Times, 3-8:(3)1.

5

[Criticizing the Nuclear Regulatory Commission for hampering the development of nuclear power by delaying licensing of nuclear power plants]: It's not fair to the public, it's not fair to the utilities, it's not fair to the stockholders, and particularly not fair to people who are trying to switch to electricity from oil and gas ... No industry has ever been so controlled, and the safety record has never been as great as the nuclear industry.

Interview, Washington, June 5/
Los Angeles Times, 6-6:(I)2.

Thomas Eisner
Professor of biology, Cornell University;
Chairman, biology section, American
Association for the Advancement of Science

6

[Saying protection against extinction should be given to lower forms of life as well as to the larger species]: The emphasis now appears to be toward giving attention to the larger species—the grizzly bear or the California condor—and deciding that protection of plants and lower animals is of no significance. That's crazy. The exact opposite is what is needed. The real reservoir is in the lower animals and plants. Most of the chemicals for production of future food supplies, chemicals, medicines and other compounds are probably within those millions of

(THOMAS EISNER)

systems. If we lose genetic diversity, especially in the short run to satisfy some need or even greed, like chopping down a forest for lumber, then we may be driving into oblivion those things on which our long-range survival depends.

Los Angeles Times, 12-30:(I)1.

Brock Evans
Associate executive director, Sierra Club

1

[Criticizing Reagan Administration plans to open wilderness and other Federal land areas for mineral exploration]: It's a myth that public land areas aren't open to mineral exploration [as the Administration claims]. Only 80 million of 760 million acres of public lands are totally closed—primarily national parks, defense-department reservations and lands set aside for particular uses, such as oil-shale mining or reservoirs. The bulk of the lands that are completely closed are in Alaska. [Environmentalists don't object to tapping public land] when the national security is truly at stake and not just the profits of the mining companies . . . The mining people are far more rabid than anybody else about the issue of public lands. They just can't stand to see land sitting there not being used. They'll use any argument [to justify opening up public lands].

The Washington Post, 3-15:(H)2.

Mervin Field
Public-opinion analyst

2

There's a lot of latent, more than latent, feeling for the environment. It's a real kinetic force that any despoiling of the environment would touch off. There's plenty of data to show that now the public really doesn't think it has to trade off environmental safeguards for energy, or anything else. They really believe they can have both.

The Christian Science Monitor, 5-11:3.

Clifton C. Garvin, Jr.
Chairman, Exxon Corporation

3

The requirements for energy are so large that even if our needs grow by 1.5 per cent to 2 per cent a year from now on, you go out to 50 years and it builds up to a hell of a big increase in energy requirements. Coal and nuclear power can compete if society accepts them. What we'll have is a combination of all forms of energy. By the middle of the next century, it is hard for us to see a society that's not based pretty much on electrical use, and it is hard to see that without large nuclear contributions. But we don't accept nuclear because some people say they're scared to death from it, and they don't accept coal because of acid rain. These kinds of folks would argue for the soft-energy approach from renewable sources such as the sun. I say I'm with them, except that it is not feasible to turn this country in 25 years into relying completely on soft energy. It takes a lot of time, money and technological know-how. We will also need synthetic fuels. When you look ahead, your grandchildren have only got the sun. I've no quarrel with that, but you've got to find a way to get there smoothly and at a cost society can afford.

Interview/The Wall Street Journal, 7-27:30.

Victor Gilinsky
Commissioner, Nuclear Regulatory Commission of the United States

4

There is too little evidence that the nuclear [-power] industry, which was never very good at calculating its own interest, is seriously contemplating the effect of another [reactor safety incident such as at] Three Mile Island on its future—or its fortunes. The industry has already returned to complaints that the safety bureaucracy is nitpicking it to death, running up contruction costs and delaying licenses. The latest complaint is that, in the aftermath of the TMI accident, NRC diverted safety reviewers to deal with operating reactors and fell behind in approving new licenses. There is a kind of tunnel-vision in the failure to see the connection between safety and the special financial risk in-

(VICTOR GILINSKY)

volved in nuclear investment. To use the current energy crisis to avoid safety requirements is to ignore the fact that safety is essential to protecting the heavy investment in nuclear power. Some hope lies in the fact that although the industry thinks safety requirements are a pain in the neck, they may be forced to look on them as an investment in financial public relations to alleviate the bankers' skepticism.

At Michigan State University/
The Wall Street Journal, 5-21:24.

1

[On nuclear power]: Do you really think the industry can regulate itself? I don't. Irritating as it may be, NRC performs a badly needed service, not just for the public but for the industry as well. We help keep your [nuclear power] plants safe and thus help protect the enormous investment they represent. Whether we are doing enough is another question. I think we have not been nearly tough enough. I must tell you that, if I had my way in the past, enforcement would have been swifter, and more severe . . . So far as I can see, it's just not in the cards for the nuclear enterprise to grow much beyond the number of current firm projects. There is no point in trying to balloon that number or argue about where all those earlier rosy forecasts went. It's mostly the work of Adam Smith. Let's try to make sure that the reactors we are building and operating are built right and work right. NRC is an essential element. It can only do its job if the industry and the Administration work with it, not against it.

Before Washington section,
American Nuclear Society/
The Washington Post, 11-20:(A)30.

Barry M. Goldwater
United States Senator, R—Arizona

2

People criticize [Interior Secretary] Jim Watt, but he is a Westerner and the Department of Interior is nothing but the West. I think I could

put every inch of ground that the Department controls east of the Mississippi in this office. But in the West the Department of Interior owns the land, runs the land, takes money from our states, and here we have a man [Watt] who knows the trouble.

Interview, Washington/
The Wall Street Journal, 8-3:12.

Alan Greenspan
Former Chairman, Council of Economic Advisers to the President of the United States [Gerald R. Ford]

3

[Until last year or so,] we believed ourselves to be on a continuous treadmill whereby any resumption of growth would be choked off by an associated explosion of oil prices. This outlook has changed dramatically with the extraordinary and unexpected slowing in oil consumption throughout the Western world, which surprised even the optimists. The net result is a significant decline in the projected demand for OPEC-supplied oil over the next decade.

At Pace College commencement/
The Washington Post, 6-15:(A)4.

S. I. Hayakawa
United States Senator, R—California

4

[Saying more wilderness areas should be opened to potential development]: We can no longer afford land-management paralysis. Our country needs timber, minerals, oil, gas and recreation sites, and it's up to us to decide just how these demands can be met with the limited resources we have available to us.

Los Angeles Times, 4-22:(I)16.

Douglas F. Henderson
Director, public lands department, American Petroleum Institute

5

We [in the oil-exploration and refining business] don't intend to denigrate any wilderness area, be they present wilderness areas or ones

(DOUGLAS F. HENDERSON)

proposed. Our activities are very compatible with the wilderness concept... we think we do an awfully good job of husbanding those environmental values that people like. We are convinced that in 99 per cent of the areas in the United States, including both Alaska and the Outer Continental Shelf, we could go in and explore for oil and gas, find it, produce it, and cover our tracks after we finish that process. In a relatively few years, why, you wouldn't be able to tell we were there.

Interview/Chicago Tribune, 3-1:(5)3.

Jack Kemp
United States Representative, R—New York

1

... I think the United States has as much control over the price of oil as does [Saudi Arabian Oil Minister] Sheik Yamani. Our land-use policies, our domestic price controls, our steady devaluation of the U.S. dollar have done as much to cause and aggravate our energy problem as anything the Saudis have done.

Interview/The Washington Post, 1-20:(A)21.

George F. Kennan
Co-chairman, American Committee on East-West Accord; Former United States Ambassador to the Soviet Union

2

... I am referring to the environmental problems: the question whether great industrial societies can learn to exist without polluting, exhausting and thus destroying the natural resources essential to their very existence. These are not only problems common to the two ideological worlds [of East and West]; they are ones the only solution of which requires each other's collaboration, not each other's enmity.

At Second World Congress on Soviet and East European Studies, Garmisch, West Germany/ Chicago Tribune, 2-15:(2)5.

William Kieschnick
President, Atlantic Richfield Company

3

I feel good about being in the energy business. It's an industry that's so fundamentally important to our country that you have to feel that you're doing something valuable, and everybody wants to do something they feel is good and valuable. And secondly, besides feeling that it's a very socially valuable business, I have treasured the entrepreneurial, risk-taking, scientific adventures that can happen in an energy industry. It's fulfilling to invent things or discover things or to plan forward, and those things are permitted and necessary in the energy business.

Interview, Los Angeles/ Chicago Tribune, 2-18:(4)10.

Polykarp Kusch
Professor of physics, University of Texas, Dallas

4

What troubles me is a world population that is increasing exponentially. A rational way of running the world would be to reduce the number of people. Without controls on population growth, the ability to provide a reasonable allotment of resources for every individual will diminish ... Nonetheless, there remains a general mood of optimism—a feeling that no matter what happens we can save ourselves. But many of our resources are finite. We're not going to improve anything if our population continues to grow. If we could somehow reduce the rate of increase in population, many of our problems would disappear.

Interview/U.S. News & World Report, 4-6:40.

Jonathan Lash
President, Energy Conservation Coalition

5

During the 1970s a dozen major environmental statutes were passed. Those lay out mandatory duties for the Federal government and for individuals and private enterprise. In the year that the conservatives were supposed to have taken over [1981], that the country was supposed to

WHAT THEY SAID IN 1981

(JONATHAN LASH)

have retreated from environmental values that we were getting hard-headed and only looking at business—not one of those statutes has been changed in any way. The Congress, after it began hearing the public response, has refused to pass a single amendment to enviromental legislation.

The Christian Science Monitor, 12-17:6.

Jerry McAfee
Chairman, Gulf Oil Corporation

1

... the best way to deal with major [oil] supply interruptions in the future is to learn from our experience as to what has not worked and as to what has worked ... We've demonstrated in spades, in both '73 and '79, that [price and allocation control] does not work ... The National Petroleum Council study, in which we concur, says basically that for relatively minor—which could still be significant—interruptions, the best thing to do is to rely on the marketplace to make adjustments. But when a really serious interuption occurs ... the government [should] have the authority to step in, but with major, significant, meaningful industry involvement.

Interview, Pittsburgh/
The Washington Post, 7-19:(F)3.

Gaylord Nelson
Chairman, Wilderness Society

2

What substance is there, if any, to Interior Secretary James Watt's strident rhetoric alleging that there is a "lock up" of vast amounts of minerals, gas and oil on public lands, that wilderness areas must be opened now to mineral exploration? And that ranchers should have a freer hand in grazing cattle on public lands, that the Strip Mining Act should be substantially weakened and, finally, that past Congresses and Presidents alike, Democrats and Republicans alike, have pursued policies inimical to the best interests of the nation and that Interior Secretaries have been inadequate stewards of our public lands and their resources? This is the thrust of Mr. Watt's

assault, and it is vital to the interests of the nation that issue be joined with him ... His philosophy, policies and rhetoric make it clear that he basically rejects the major conservation and environmental laws of the past two decades, and that he disagrees with the public lands-management policies of past Administrations and Congresses. Mr. Watt's objections to the conservation policies of the past 20 years are substantive, not cosmetic.

The Washington Post, 9-13:(C)6.

J. Allen Overton, Jr.
President, American Mining Congress

3

[Supporting Interior Secretary James Watt's proposals for opening up more public lands for development of resources]: [Give President] Reagan and Mr. Watt an "A" for the course—a first-rate performance in terms of recognizing the problem and doing something about it ... Look, these natural resources were placed in nature by a bountiful Creator for the use of mankind. He didn't put them in the earth to lock them up so they could never be used. In some areas, this country has established restrictions that are so severe you can't do a damned thing with the land except look at it.

San Francisco Examiner & Chronicle, 4-5:(A)14.

Russell W. Peterson
President, National Audubon Society;
Former Chairman, Federal Council on
Environmental Quality

4

We are going to maximize our grass-roots clout and do it in partnership with other environmental and citizen groups, labor organizations and church groups. Power is with the people, and we are potentially one of the most powerful citizens groups, with 422,000 members and 457 chapters around the country ... There has been such a radical and extreme change in Washington. Most environmental leaders were concerned about President Reagan's taking over because of his obvious lack of enthusiasm for the

(RUSSELL W. PETERSON)

environment. But I don't think any of us realized how bad it was going to be.

The New York Times, 4-19:(1)13.

Clem Rastatter
Senior associate, Conservative Foundation

1

[On proposed Reagan Administration cuts in funds for clean-water programs]: We believe that a shift in financial responsibility away from the Federal government, if properly managed, could help avoid the over-designed, high-cost and unreliable systems which now are troubling so many communities. It is quite clear to us that budget-cutting is not inconsistent with national goals for clean water.

Before Senate subcommittee, June/
The Christian Science Monitor, 6-30:5.

Ronald Reagan
President of the United States

2

[On criticism of Interior Secretary James Watt by environmental groups]: Jim Watt has been doing what I think is a common-sense job in the face of some environmental extremism that we've suffered from. And I can assure you Jim Watt does not want to destroy the beauty of America. He just wants to recognize that people are ecology too.

News conference, Santa Barbara, Calif.,
Aug. 13/The New York Times, 8-14:8.

Nathaniel Pryor Reed
Director, Nature Conservancy, and
Florida Audubon Society;
Former Assistant Secretary of the Interior
of the United States

3

[Criticizing Interior Secretary James Watt's environmental policies of increasing development of natural resources]: They are attempting to turn the clock back to the pre-[Theodore] Roosevelt era, when everyone supposed natural

resources were inexhaustible. I cannot sit idly by and watch this lame-brained, outmoded philosophy take hold and stain my [Republican] Party's image . . . It causes me great pain to criticize the [Reagan] Administration as I am about to do. But my quarrel is not with Ronald Reagan. I think he will be a good President and a notable environmentalist. The problem as I see it is that some of his appointees—and particularly James Watt—have broken faith with the Republican Party and betrayed their President . . . [Regarding Watt's plan to deeply cut the Land and Water Conservation Fund,] butchering the fund . . . is a senseless act. Since open space is disappearing at a horrendous annual rate, many of the state and local park opportunities will be lost forever. Since the price of land will surely escalate, no money is being saved. Since many endangered species must be rescued now or never, no time is being bought. Why does Watt support such a looney proposal?

Before Sierra Club, San Francisco, May 2/
San Francisco Examiner & Chronicle, 5-3:(A)17.

Donald T. Regan
Secretary of the Treasury
of the United States

4

. . . one of the first things this [Reagan] Administration did was to decontrol oil [prices]. The reason for the decontrol was to get more supply. We think that if you let a free market operate, that the free market will actually go out there and find oil because they have the incentive to do it. Under the past program, where you were keeping a lid on prices, there was no incentive to do it. That's the main part of the philosophy that most people have missed: The Reagan economic program will put incentives back to work.

TV-radio interview/"Meet the Press,"
National Broadcasting Company, 2-22.

Raymond Robinson
Assistant Deputy Minister, Environment Canada

5

How the United States chooses to deal with the tradeoffs involved in addressing air or other

WHAT THEY SAID IN 1981

kinds of pollution is a matter for the United States to decide. Canada has no desire to enter your domestic debate on that issue . . . On the other hand, when your practices, both present and contemplated, threaten Canada's environmental and economic integrity, we believe we have a duty to bring our concerns to your attention. In other words, pollutants, especially those released into the air, respect no political boundaries and each country therefore has a right to insist that the other's legislation and related practices are adequate to protect its neighbor.

Before House Energy Subcommittee on Health and the Environment, Washington, Oct. 6/ Chicago Tribune, 10-7:(1)3.

John D. (Jay) Rockefeller IV
Governor of West Virginia (D)

1

[Encouraging more use of coal as a fuel for power plants and industry]: This country's dangerous dependence on foreign oil has profound implications for our national security and represents a threat to our quality of life just as real as the dangers of unregulated air pollution. The modern coal-fired plants and industrial boilers being built now are clean and safe. Industry has learned how to burn coal cleanly and efficiently.

At Congressional hearings on the Clean Air Act, Washington, May 20/Los Angeles Times, 5-21:(I)15.

Larry Rockefeller
Staff attorney,
National Resource Defense Council

2

[Criticizing the government's encouragement of people settling on barrier islands with such subsidies as low-cost flood insurance, disaster relief and bridge and highway development]: It's folly to continue the current policies. I suppose you can say we had advance notice way back in the Sermon on the Mount. Jesus said, and there it is in the Bible, not to build on the sand. And here we are, not only building on the sand, but asking

the general taxpayer to subsidize it . . . We're not proposing a regulatory bill that would prevent development, just a move to cut off the subsidies. It should have substantial appeal to a government that is considering cutting food stamps and a number of other items which are important to people in need. And these subsidies benefit the well-to-do in the building of their condominiums on the beaches.

Interview, New York/ The Christian Science Monitor, 3-4:(B)5.

R. Neil Sampson
Executive vice president, National Association of Conservative Districts

3

We [in the U.S.] are wasting soil and water at a rapid rate. We are running farmers out of business at a steady pace, and many of those that remain, while they are getting bigger, are getting more deeply in debt. They have had to leverage the inflation-pushed value of their land into adequate capital to operate in an agriculture that has become cash-addicted and which needs more and more capital each year. As a result, farmers push their land as hard as possible, trying to get every dime possible. The land is not getting the type of care it needs to regenerate itself, and, as a result, soil productivity is falling . . . When we decide that the economic, environmental and political costs of letting the current situation continue are higher than the political and economic costs of changing the system, we will move to do so.

Before American Society of Agricultural Engineers, Chicago, Dec. 16/Chicago Tribune, 12-17:(1)3.

Russell L. Schweickart
Chairman, California Energy Commission;
Former American astronaut

4

I consider myself an environmentalist in the larger sense, but many of my environmental friends view space as an anathema. Space exploration and NASA are all high-tech, big-business, military centralization to them, populated by all the bogeymen they all fear and

(RUSSELL L. SCHWEICKART)

hate. I don't see it that way and would carry the analogy of Earth mother a step further. We first begin to understand loving our mother *after* birth, not before. Before, we don't even know mother is mother. The knee-jerk reaction from some environmentalists is a fear of moving off Earth into space, because they think it means we're not interested in taking care of this planet. But in moving off Earth is our only hope of maintaining Earth as a life-enhancing environment . . . We rip up the earth for coal, molybdenum, chromium and steel, but space is saturated with energy and resources. Once you've paid the price of getting out of earth's gravity, it's cheap to bring in asteroids, park them next to your orbital factory, and extract materials. If we don't get off the earth and start recognizing that space can provide these nutrients for the growth of this organism, then we are going to eat ourselves alive.

Interview, Sacramento, Calif./
The Christian Science Monitor, 4-29:(B)4.

Gerald D. Seinwill
Acting director,
Water Resources Council

1

Water is the most serious long-range problem now confronting the nation—potentially more serious than the energy crisis. By the turn of the century, almost every section of the country faces water shortages unless the nation recognizes that we cannot continue to waste and mistreat a precious, finite resource.

U.S. News & World Report, 6-29:34.

Lee M. Talbot
Director general, International
Union for Conservation of Nature

2

In the past 10 years, the world has spent billions and billions of dollars on development [in poor countries]. Yet, more people today are hungry, and less land is available for human development because of environmentally un-

sound development . . . In the past, the ideas of development and conservation were antagonistic. The message of the World Conservation Strategy [a conservation program] is two-fold: You can't have development without conservation. The other is, you can't have conservation without development.

Interview, Nairobi, Kenya/
Los Angeles Times, 8-23:(I)15.

William A. Turnage
Executive director, Wilderness Society

3

The new Secretary of the Interior, James Watt, is essentially a fanatic in terms of his views on energy development. His views seem to be even stronger than those of most of the oil-company executives—that we've got to go out and develop every inch of America to find energy. Our view is that there are a lot of other values that have to be considered. There are some places in America that are so beautiful and so special that they shouldn't have oil derricks over them.

Interview/Chicago Tribune, 3-1:(5)3.

Mack Wallace
Member,
Texas Railroad Commission

4

[On the decontrol of oil prices]: If we are going to be paying 5 cents to 15 cents a gallon more for gasoline, then the American public is entitled to have that money spent on exploration and drilling right here at home. I have long been an advocate of decontrol. I believe it is best for the country. To me, it has nothing to do with oil-company profits. The salient issue is the security of our country. It is therefore incumbent on the petroleum industry to put these new investment dollars into an all-out energy exploration and production program here on our continent . . . Only 2 per cent of America has ever been explored by a drill bit and only 3 per cent of the outer continental shelf has ever been offered for lease . . . I think the American public wants to hear the drill bits turning in America.

The Wall Street Journal, 3-10:22.

James G. Watt
Secretary of the Interior-designate
of the United States

1

It has been my argument that this country must commit itself to a reasoned, environmentally conscious program for developing and utilizing the tremendous energy resources our nation possesses. Unless we have such a program, economic, social and political pressures will grow to such an extent that the Federal government will be forced, in a crisis situation, to mount a crash program to develop coal, uranium, oil shale, tar sands and oil and gas. All too often, the Federal government moves in a crisis, not with the precision of a surgeon's scalpel, but with the force of a meat ax. Those of us who love and are committed to preserving the beauty and values of our environment fear this possibility. We want the right kind of development to come over time, not the wrong kind of development to come in a crisis. I am a concerned Westerner, a concerned American. I want the Federal and state governments to strike a balance between the development and protection of our natural resources. We can have reasonable development of our energy resources, and preserve our natural environment, if we are given an opportunity to phase in, with proper safeguards, the expansion being demanded by the nation.

At Senate Energy and Natural Resources Committee
hearing on his confirmation, Washington, Jan. 7/
The New York Times, 1-8:11.

James G. Watt
Secretary of the Interior
of the United States

2

Failure to know our potential, to inventory our resources, intentionally forbidding proper access to needed resources, limits this nation, dooms us to decline, foreshortens creative energy and damages our right as a people to dream heroic dreams. With all of America's greatness, we still do not understand our own wealth. We must inventory our lands. Today we do not know the full extent of our mineral values, our agricultural potential, or our oil and gas reserves.

Unfortunately, the only way at this time to inventory our lands to determine the quantities of oil and gas is to drill [in some environmentally sensitive areas].

Before House Subcommittee on the
Environment, Washington, April 28/
The New York Times, 4-29:12.

3

The state of the National Park System is sickening to me. To see the deterioration and degradation because we have not been good stewards hurts . . . I am appalled at the condition of the National Park System. What the Reagan Administration has inherited is shameful. As Secretary of the Interior, I owe an apology to the American people for the fact that the National Park System has not been maintained.

Before Senate Energy and Natural Resources
subcommittee, Washington, May 7/
The Washington Post, 5-8:(A)5.

4

The present drought [in areas of the U.S.] may be the best thing that could ever happen. Hopefully, it will make us wake up to the problem of the '90s—water shortages. I considered energy to be the extreme problem of the '70s. Minerals are going to be the problem of the '80s. And water will be the problem of the '90s. It will probably take a traumatic experience to get America's attention. And we [at the Federal level] don't have that capability to be the referee, and the states are going to have to focus on it and go back and build storage facilities. And a hue and cry [against building them] is going to come up from these preservationists [environmentalists].

Interview/The Washington Post, 5-24:(C)7.

5

. . . there is an absolute conflict built into the Department of the Interior. I am called, on one hand, the chief environmental officer for the nation, and the special-interest groups refuse to look at anything else. I suppose I might also be called the chief miner on Department of the Interior lands, the chief harvester of timber, the chief

(JAMES G. WATT)

Indian. And these missions, outlined by statute, are contradictory in many instances. To the various special-interest groups, the Secretary has a statutory duty to do A, B and C, but they refuse to look at any of the other responsibilities of the office. That's why I'm so critical of the narrow special-interest groups on both the development and the preservation sides. I must search for balance. Yet, if I do an effective job, I will receive criticism at different times from different groups.

Interview/
Nation's Business, September:39.

1

[On his credentials as an environmentalist]: I suppose I could go back to birth. I am a native of Wyoming. I grew up on a ranch. I am a man of the soil. I've lived with the environment good and bad. I've enjoyed the spring and the growth that comes with it. I've ridden 14, 15 miles a day to pump water for cattle who would be dying from lack of water. I've known the dust; I've fixed the fence; I've fought the blizzard. I've known the land. Those who grew up in a fragile environment such as the West learn to live with the environment. Did we alter the land? Of course we did. We wanted to improve it, enhance it.

Interview/
The New York Times, 1-10:9.

William W. Winpisinger
President, International Association
of Machinists

2

In terms of economics, nuclear power is the most expensive, most inefficient and most government-subsidized way to boil water ever designed by man. In terms of the nation's health, each nuclear power plant, with its potential for radiation release and on-site nuclear waste dump, is a communal cause of cancer.

News conference, Washington, Oct. 9/
The New York Times, 10-10:9.

James C. Wright, Jr.
United States Representative, D—Texas

3

We have said that we are going to make this country of ours energy independent again, so that we will not be any longer dependent upon nations which have values far different from ours. If we blow the trumpet of retreat after having so recently made that commitment, I think it gives the wrong signal to the world. President Valery Giscard d'Estaing of France said, two years ago, that on the day the United States makes a true commitment to the development of synthetic fuels—on that day the world situation will change dramatically. I think that was prophetic.

TV-radio interview/"Meet the Press,"
National Broadcasting Company, 2-15.

Foreign Affairs

Elliott Abrams
Assistant Secretary for Human Rights,
Department of State of the United States

1

[On the human-rights aspect of U.S. foreign policy]: If your human-rights policy consists mostly of public speeches, then everyone will see what you're doing and you will get a great deal of credit for your efforts. In a sense, whether or not they work, you get an "A" for effort. [That] is not a human-rights policy. It's a p.r. policy . . . I don't have any predilection for any particular tactic—public condemnation [of foreign governments' human-rights violations], diplomatic efforts, security and economic sanctions. The question is: What is likely to have the desired effect? . . . [In many areas of the Third World, the choice] is not between paradise and an existing and troubled regime. It is between the regime in power and a much worse regime. If you replace a repressive regime with a more repressive regime, in many cases with a Communist regime, you have not helped the human-rights situation.

To reporters, Washington/
San Francisco Examiner & Chronicle, 12-27:(A)15.

Richard V. Allen
Assistant to the President of the
United States for
National Security Affairs

2

If it makes any sense—and I speak personally —that we maintain ties with totalitarian nations and build bridges of understanding to them, then it makes equal sense that we have to maintain ties to people who do not profess to be our enemies and with whose systems we may differ radically. I personally don't consider an improvement of relations with South Africa as any stamp of approval of the system of apartheid, of which I do not approve and which I believe deserves to be roundly condemned. [The U.S. has] no obligation to embrace every facet of the internal system of countries with which we do business . . . I firmly reject the notion that doing business with someone—particularly a country that recognizes its friendship for us—is necessarily an endorsement of a system which governs from within.

At Conservative Political Action Conference,
Washington, March 21/
San Francisco Examiner & Chronicle, 3-22:(A)24.

James A. Baker III
Chief of Staff to the
President of the United States

3

[On President Reagan's recent hard-line statements aimed at the Soviet Union]: They [the Soviets] should be thinking that there is a President of the United States today who is going to be realistic with respect to the Soviet Union, and not naive . . . I guess the message is that it's not going to be business as usual, you're [the Soviets] not going to have preferred status unless your actions around the world are such as to justify it, that this business of getting along is not a one-way street and we're going to judge you by your actions and not your words.

Broadcast interview, Washington/
"Face the Nation," CBS-TV, 2-1.

(JAMES A. BAKER III)

1

The President [Reagan] doesn't feel you have to lay out in chapter and verse what his [foreign] policy is. He feels that what you then do is limit your options. No one has a crystal ball to see two, three, four years down the road. He believes you don't have to spell out a foreign policy in order to have a foreign policy.

Interview, Washington/
The Christian Science Monitor, 10-26:22.

Vere C. Bird
Prime Minister of
Antigua and Barbuda

2

[On U.S. aid to developing countries]: Already the U.S. ranks very low in the list of Western aid-giving nations in terms of aid as a proportion of its GNP . . . Now there are plans to reduce aid even further, with representatives of the U.S. [Reagan] Administration on record as saying that developing countries must pull themselves up by their own bootstraps. None of us disagree with that concept; but first we must have the straps by which to pull up the boot. And we will never have the straps if the order of priority does not place the required aid at the forefront.

At Miami Conference on the Caribbean,
Key Biscayne, Fla., Nov. 30/
The Christian Science Monitor, 12-2:7.

Charles W. Bray III
Former Deputy Director,
International Communication Agency
of the United States

3

The first requirement for a competent foreign policy is to possess a historical perspective. It is not merely that those who do not recall the past are condemned to repeat it. Knowledge of history provides individuals and nations with a sense for the ebbs and flows of events, reminds them that civilizations, our own included, rise and decline —and can be extinguished if not tended to— gives one a sense of identity and purpose,

teaches patience, and provides object lessons in the value of persistence—surely not our longest national suit in foreign policy. Americans are historical illiterates. Our education provides us with anecdotes about our own past and virtually no knowledge of the history of others. Yet we cannot hope to manage history-in-the-making— and that ultimately is the purpose of foreign policy—without a knowledge of history-as-it-was-made.

At world affairs conference, San Francisco/
The Christian Science Monitor, 3-24:26.

Leonid I. Brezhnev
President of the Soviet Union;
General Secretary,
Soviet Communist Party

4

It is universally recognized that in many ways the international situation depends on the policy of the U.S.S.R. and the U.S. As we see it, the state of relations between them at present, and the acuteness of the international problems requiring a solution, necessitate a dialogue, and an active dialogue, at all levels. We are prepared to have this dialogue. Experience shows that the crucial link here is meetings at the summit level. This was true yesterday and is still true today. The U.S.S.R. wants normal relations with the U.S. There is simply no other sensible way from the point of view of the interests of both our nations and humanity as a whole.

At Soviet Communist Party Congress,
Moscow, Feb. 23/The Washington Post, 2-24:(A)1.

5

Imperialists have no regard either for the will of the people or the laws of history. The liberation struggles cause their indignation. They describe it as "terrorism." [Imperialists] use any pretext for interference in others' affairs, for military expansion; and when there are no such pretexts, they create them artificially. Recall . . . how official Washington used the question concerning a group of American diplomats who were detained some time in Iran. They have long since returned home, but the powerful Navy

(LEONID I. BREZHNEV)

brought to the Indian Ocean and Persian Gulf allegedly for the rescue of the "hostages" is to this day sailing in those waters, threatening neighboring states and universal peace.

Welcoming Libyan leader Muammar el-Qaddafi to Moscow, April 27/ The Washington Post, 4-28:(A)14.

Zbigniew Brzezinski
Assistant to the President of the United States for National Security Affairs

1

. . . to conduct foreign policy without being willing to use military power, including occasionally the use of it as a deterrent—and deterrence is in part a bluff—is to deny oneself the ability to influence constructively an adversary who is prepared to use military power. Diplomacy not backed by power is an exercise in good-will. But that may not be sufficient for a world in which power is still an important asset.

Interview, Washington, Jan. 17/ The New York Times, 1-18:(1)3.

Zbigniew Brzezinski
Professor of government, Columbia University; Former Assistant to the President of the United States (Jimmy Carter) for National Security Affairs

2

My overwhelming observation is that history is neither the product of design nor of conspiracy but is rather the reflection of continuing chaos. Seen from the outside, decisions may seem clear and consciously formulated; interrelations between governments may seem to be the products of deliberately crafted, even if often conflicting, policies. But one learns that so much of what happens—not only in the U.S. government, but in foreign governments too—is the product of chaotic conditions and a great deal of personal struggle and ambiguity. Sometimes you will find agreement on means but fundamental disagreement on ends; sometimes agreement on ends but disagreement on

means. All this reinforces the impression of contingency and uncertainty which is inherent in the human condition and which is only magnified by the scale and intensity of the power one wields.

Interview/The New York Times, 4-22:25.

3

We in the [Carter] Administration did not do well enough [to explain foreign policy to the people]. The President was disinclined to make formal and comprehensive speeches. He was superb in direct, personal interviews; but these do not generally give one the opportunity to lay out one's philosophy. Secretary of State [Cyrus] Vance had various strong qualities, but an inclination to engage in a sustained effort to educate the public was not among them. [Vance's successor as Secretary of State, Edmund] Muskie tried to do some of that, but it was too late in the game. To some extent, *I* was pushed into that role, but my own ability to try to explain what we were doing was limited by the fact that the very assumption of the role was controversial, not to speak of the circumstance that my emphasis on "the need to restore American power in the world" was strongly opposed by some sectors of the bureaucracy . . . I do believe that we did perform adequately on the level of decisions—Panama, Central America, the Middle East, Israel and the Arabs, or the Chinese. But we failed to some extent to explain all this to the public and to mobilize popular support.

Interview/The New York Times, 4-22:25.

4

It seems to me that either we have a system under which the Assistant for National Security Affairs is predominant [in foreign policy]— and this is largely the case when the President himself is very much involved in foreign affairs —or we have a system in which the Secretary of State is predominant. Either system is a respectable one and works well, for ultimately any decision-making system has to be suited to the President's preferences. Some Presidents, like Kennedy, Nixon and Carter, were deeply involved in foreign affairs and they could not

(ZBIGNIEW BRZEZINSKI)

be therefore excluded. What perplexes me is that we do not have today [in the Reagan Administration] visible personal leadership in the area of foreign policy from the White House, and yet the Secretary of State has not been given the opportunity to fill that vacuum. In other words, [Secretary of State Alexander] Haig has not been permitted to become [a Dean] Acheson or a [John Foster] Dulles. And no one in the White House has emerged in the role of a [McGeorge] Bundy or a [Henry] Kissinger or a Brzezinski.

Interview/Los Angeles Herald Examiner, 6-7:(A)12.

Thomas Buergenthal
*Dean, Washington College of Law,
American University*

1

[Reagan Administration] spokesmen criticize and reject a strong human-rights [foreign] policy because they see it as having purely moral but very little, if any, political significance. They view it as a propaganda tool to be used against the Soviets, but not to criticize our allies. They argue that totalitarianism of the left is worse than the repression of the right practiced by some of our allies. They contend that the United States faces a formidable adversary in Soviet expansionism and cannot afford the luxury of being the moral policeman of the world . . . that the United States needs allies and cannot afford to alienate friendly anti-Communist governments even if they are repressive. In short, they contend that what we need is to balance our commitment to human rights against foreign-policy assets. A sound human-rights policy provides the United States with an ideology that distinguishes us most clearly from the Soviet Union and seriously undercuts the ideological appeal of Communism . . . And those who do not grasp its significance do not know much about the world we live in and the forces that shape it.

*The Washington Post,
4-15:(A)22.*

George Bush
*Vice President of the
United States*

2

This [Reagan] Administration is pledged to human rights [in foreign affairs]. We will work to effect changes to help improve human rights, but we're going to do it quietly. We will not be selective in our indignation. Some feel we must shout from the rooftops and beat our breasts and humiliate countries in order to effect change. [But we will] exert our influence in the area of rights by quiet diplomacy and persuasion. Results are what count, not rhetorical confrontation.

*At University of Virginia commencement,
May 24/The New York Times, 5-25:3.*

3

The specialized agencies [of the UN] have lost touch with economic reality. They have been living in a dream world, immune from the economic problems of the donor countries, from inflation or privation, or harsh budget-cutting . . . There is quite simply a large amount of fat in most [UN] agency budgets. There is too much travel, too many conferences, too much misuse of resources and too little cutting off of dead wood.

*Before United Nations Association of the
United States/Los Angeles Times, 6-6:(I)7.*

Jimmy Carter
Former President of the United States

4

In the four corners of the earth today, thousands of people are alive and millions more have hope for the future because the United States [during the Carter Administration] did not turn its back on human rights [in its dealings with other countries]. We have not kept silent when people in other nations have been tortured for their political or religious beliefs, or thwarted in their desire to be united with their own families. Just since 1976, 150,000 Soviet Jews have come to live in freedom here and in Israel

135

(JIMMY CARTER)

because this nation did not keep silent. We did not keep silent while hundreds of thousands, if not millions, of innocent people were driven from their homes and often killed in Cambodia; nor when the freedom-loving people of Afghanistan were brutally invaded and suppressed by their powerful neighbor [the Soviet Union]. We have not kept silent when Jews and others in Latin America have been arrested in the night, many never to be heard from again. And we dare not keep silent [today] when American women missionaries are murdered in El Salvador or when a government is sustained and nurtured by racism in South Africa. The one thing oppressive governments fear everywhere is that the civilized world will *not* remain silent—that it will speak out and condemn the denial of basic human rights.

Before New York Board of Rabbis, May 17/
The New York Times, 5-18:13.

1

Though it is politically popular to condemn everything about the Soviets today, I was convinced then and I still am convinced that [Soviet President Leonid] Brezhnev desires peace. I could see in his remarks and his attitude a deep memory of the 20 million Russians who were killed during World War II and a deep desire to avoid another world conflict.

Interview, Xi'an, China, Aug. 29/
The Washington Post, 8-31:(A)10.

2

Our commitment to [detente] cannot be lightly abandoned if the word means the easing of tension between our two nations [the U.S. and Soviet Union]. Both superpowers must exercise restraint in troubled areas and in troubled times and must search for better understanding of one another. The importance and complexity of Soviet-American affairs require that our national policy be thoroughly and frequently proclaimed to the public. Repeatedly, in news conferences and in major speeches, we [the Carter

Administration] made clear our eagerness to cooperate with the Soviets whenever possible, but our willingness to compete with them when necessary. A one-sided [U.S.] attitude of belligerence toward the Soviet Union may be politically attractive for a time, but it is not an adequate basis for American policy because it precludes cooperation and generates fear among those who would avoid a superpower confrontation.

Before Council on Foreign Relations, New York,
Dec. 17/The New York Times, 12-18:4.

Fidel Castro
President of Cuba

3

I am deeply concerned that the group which constitutes the main core of the U.S. [Reagan] Administration is Fascist. Its thinking is Fascist. Its foreign policy is Fascist. Its contempt for world peace is Fascist. Its intransigent refusal to seek for and find an honorable coexistence among states is Fascist. Its haughtiness, its conceit, its arms race, its quest for military support at all costs, its attachment to violence and domination, its methods of blackmail and terror, its shameless alliance with South Africa, its threatening language and its lies are Fascist.

At meeting of Interparliamentary Union,
Havana, Sept. 15/Los Angeles Times, 9-16:(I)18.

Anna Chennault
Widow of Claire Lee Chennault,
Commander of American Flying Tigers
in World War II

4

In politics and in international affairs, you must keep an open mind and keep on learning and look at the world in reality. Today, we recognize that the United States cannot afford to be isolated. We want to deal with all international issues realistically. My way of looking at the world in the '60s was different from the '50s; and in the '70s it was different from the '60s; and now we are coming into the '80s. We have to reassess our positions, broaden our base, be humble enough to learn and have the courage to change our positions . . . If you don't learn,

(ANNA CHENNAULT)

you stay put in the same positions and look at the world in an unrealistic way.

Peking, Jan. 4/Los Angeles Times, 1-5:(I)1.

Warren M. Christopher
Former Deputy Secretary of State
of the United States

1

[Saying human rights should be an important aspect of U.S. foreign policy]: Unquestionably, Communism and terrorism are enemies of order. But we deceive ourselves if we think human misery is not as great an enemy, for it gives the others places to flourish. A strong human-rights policy enhances our security. Stable societies make stronger, better allies. Of course, we cannot say that our influence will always make a difference, or that a human-rights strategy will prevent turmoil. But surely it is preferable to exert what influence we can for peaceful, constructive change, even as we stand ready for military action when our vital interests are threatened and there is no other choice.

At Bates College commencement/
The Christian Science Monitor, 7-14:23.

William E. Colby
Former Director of Central Intelligence
of the United States

2

I think if we analyze our threat, we have to start with the only nation in the world that can destroy us, the Soviet Union. It has the weaponry; it has the force with which to do it . . . But I think we have to examine the most effective Soviet weapon used against us in recent years, which has been unarmed transport aircraft, full of Cubans and East Germans sent to exploit the turmoil in the Third World. We must be secure against that kind of weapon as well as the nuclear. We must devote ourselves to developing the tools, the forces and the weapons to meet the challenge of the economic and sociological differences and demogogy that we see in much of the world. We have to transform those dif-

ferences into mutual growth, friendship and peace. The tools to do this are diplomacy, trade and aid, not military force alone.

Before Committee for National Security/
The Washington Post, 2-22:(C)6.

3

. . . we [the CIA] hurt ourselves because we frightened a lot of people around the world with the mass of publicity that we turned out in 1975. We convinced a lot of people that they couldn't share sensitive matters with us because we couldn't keep secrets. That convinced a lot of people that they didn't dare work with us as agents—that it wouldn't be safe to do so. Now, I think in fact we did protect those identities. We did protect our relationship with certain foreigners in our groups. But nonetheless the impression was given by all the publicity, all the spectacular breast-beating and recriminations and all the rest of it that the Americans had rejected intelligence. So if you were an individual foreigner asked to help us, would you feel confident in doing so? No, you wouldn't. And so in that respect we have hurt ourselves in the past few years. I think we can heal the wounds. Frankly, it's going to take a little time and it's going to take some specific actions. The major specific action I think is necessary is a law that would send people to jail who leak the secrets of intelligence.

Interview, Washington/
Los Angeles Herald Examiner, 3-22:(A)14.

Richard N. Cooper
Professor of economics, Harvard University;
Former Under Secretary for Economic Affairs,
Department of State of the United States

4

The Reagan Administration has really not yet formulated a policy toward the Third World. They have taken a view on foreign aid—which has been more a byproduct of their concerns with the U.S. budget—which gives foreign aid a seat in the caboose of the train. And that is not good. Per dollar spent, foreign aid represents a very good investment by the United States and

WHAT THEY SAID IN 1981

(RICHARD N. COOPER)

by the West in general. For us now to retrench on what are relatively small numbers of dollars compared with, for example, the contemplated increases in the defense budget, may well cost us many times more in defense expenditures in 10 or 15 years.

Interview/The New York Times, 7-5:(4)4.

Robert B. Delano
President,
American Farm Bureau Federation

1

[On the U.S. embargo of grain exports to the Soviet Union]: We applaud President-elect Reagan's promise to end the embargo, and without attempting to bind the hands of the new President, we ask that this be given high priority. A full embargo of all trade, technology, services and cultural contacts might be useful if Soviet aggression continues in Poland or elsewhere. Short of this, we see piecemeal economic sanctions [such as the grain embargo] as nothing more than a measure of national weakness.

News conference, New Orleans, Jan. 11/
Chicago Tribune 1-12:(1)2.

Patricia M. Derian
Assistant Secretary for Human Rights,
Department of State of the
United States

2

[Criticizing incoming Reagan Administration statements that human-rights factors will be played down as major determinants of U.S. foreign policy]: What Reagan and his people have been saying about human rights is not based on reality—on knowledge of the situation, the law and the methods and machinery that the law imposes on this government. My hope is that once they've pondered the law and gotten a good fix on the situation, they'll drop all this strange talk, face the fact that human rights have become a fact of life in foreign policy and start thinking about what has to be done to make the policy better and more consistent . . .

My hardest task was to make that clear to a bureaucracy that for 100 years had been weaned on the idea that American political, commercial or security interests were the only things that counted in diplomacy. I tried to make them see that human rights was something that wouldn't tarnish their polished and exquisite view of classical diplomacy, but that could actually serve as a powerful new weapon for American interests.

Interview, Washington/
The Washington Post, 1-17:(A)3.

Patricia M. Derian
Former Assistant Secretary for Human Rights,
Department of State of the
United States

3

[On those who say that human rights is an internal matter for each country and that therefore the U.S. should not take it into account when dealing with other nations]: I can't believe that in 1981 anyone would advance such an argument. Internal matters affect the world community. Was it none of our business when Hitler decimated the Jews? When Stalin, who killed millions inside the Soviet Union, was, in the name of *Realpolitik*, effectively given Eastern Europe? And when today many people who want to leave the Soviet Union are still prevented from doing so? Or when millions were killed in mainland China? Curiously, I find people applying this argument of "none of our business" only to right-wing dictatorships—not to the Soviet Union. In addition, a roomful of documents makes human rights a matter of international law and concern: the Helsinki Final Act of 1975, the Inter-American Declaration of the Rights and Duties of Man, the United Nations Universal Declaration of Human Rights.

Interview/U.S. News & World Report, 3-2:49.

Miguel D'Escoto
Foreign Minister of Nicaragua

4

You cannot have a revolution, not in Central America or elsewhere, that is not home-grown.

Newsweek, 3-16:43.

Alan Dixon
United States Senator, D—Illinois

1

[On the use of trade embargoes in foreign policy]: There has been considerable controversy over whether embargoes succeed in the short-term. Over the longer term, I think the answer is clearer. Embargoes are generally poor public policy.
Washington, Feb. 3/Chicago Tribune, 2-4:(1)6.

Martin Ennals
Secretary-general, Amnesty International

2

Every society is capable of providing and does provide examples of violations of the rights its constitution guarantees. All nations have contradictions within their systems which create the tensions which lead to human-rights abuses. AI makes no attempt to offer solutions to economic or political problems, but works to make the violation of human rights more difficult in any political system.
Interview/The Christian Science Monitor, 7-1:(B)16.

Malcolm Fraser
Prime Minister of Australia

3

I am convinced that our generation of leaders will ultimately be judged largely in terms of their success or failure in reconciling the interests of the rich and poor countries of the earth. In my mind, those who fail to recognize the gravity and drama of the issues disguised by the bland term "North-South dialogue" are guilty of a serious failure of historical imagination.
At Commonwealth Heads of Government meeting, Melbourne, Australia, Sept. 30/ The Washington Post, 10-1:(A)26.

Carlos Fuentes
Author; Former Mexican Ambassador to France

4

The nations of Africa, Asia and Latin America do not want to be pawns in a chess game played by two players only [the U.S. and Soviet Union].

More and more, each nation clearly perceives its own national and regional interests. Nigeria or Mexico, Poland or Venezuela, Zimbabwe or Pakistan, Hungary or Algeria, China or Brazil —none of the emerging nations wants to be caught in the East-West conflict that serves the United States or the U.S.S.R., but not their own peoples.
At the New School, New York/ The Washington Post, 5-3:(C)4.

Jeffrey B. Gayner
Director of foreign-policy studies, Heritage Foundation

5

[Opposing lifting the U.S. grain embargo against the Soviet Union, which was initiated in response to Russia's invasion of Afghanistan]: In diplomatic parlance, lifting the embargo would send the wrong signals to the Soviet Union and our allies. It would demonstrate, as the Carter Administration did previously, that the U.S. does not have a coherent policy in dealing with the Soviet Union. Lifting the embargo would make it appear that we have accepted the Soviet invasion of Afghanistan. And it would make a mockery of the strong language used recently by President Reagan and Secretary of State Haig in response to the Soviet support for terrorism that was evident in the Iranian hostage ordeal.
Interview/U.S. News & World Report, 2-16:25.

Andrei A. Gromyko
Foreign Minister of the Soviet Union

6

[Soviet policy is aimed at]: reduction of both nuclear and conventional armaments . . . settling the existing conflicts and crisis situations and preventing new ones, deepening detente and developing peaceful cooperation among nations. We are prepared for a dialogue and cooperation with all responsible political and social forces, with all those who share the concern over the present state of world affairs and seek to strengthen peace and security.
New York, Sept. 17/Chicago Tribune, 9-19:(1)5.

WHAT THEY SAID IN 1981

(ANDREI A. GROMYKO)

1

Washington is ever more often heard speaking about the American leadership of the world—though no one has entitled the United States to such leadership. Nobody. The architects of that course see as their main instrument for achieving these objectives the whipping up of international tensions, as well as resorting to what they themselves call methods of force in politics. Even when they occasionally talk about the possibility of a diplomatic alternative, they hasten to make it clear that diplomacy, unless it relies on force, does not suit them.

At United Nations, New York, Sept. 22/
The New York Times, 9-23:6.

Alexander M. Haig, Jr.
Secretary of State-designate
of the United States

2

The central strategic phenomenon of the post-World War II era [is] the transformation of the Soviet military power from a continental and largely defensive land army to a global offensive army, navy and air force capable of supporting an imperial foreign policy.

At Senate Foreign Relations Committee hearing
on his confirmation, Washington, Jan. 9/
The Washington Post, 1-10:(A)6.

3

The President needs a single individual to serve as the general manager of American diplomacy. President-elect Reagan believes that the Secretary of State should play this role. As Secretary of State, I would function as a member of the President's team, but one with clear responsibility for formulating and conducting foreign policy, and for explaining it to the Congress, the public and the world at large. The Assistant to the President for National Security would fill a staff role for the President.

At Senate Foreign Relations Committee hearing
on his confirmation, Washington, Jan. 9/
The Washington Post, 1-10:(A)8.

4

. . . the task of statesmanship is not simply to react to events . . . The task of statesmanship is to master these problems, and thus minimize the necessity for ricocheting from crisis to crisis.

At Senate Foreign Relations Committee hearing
on his confirmation, Washington, Jan. 9/
The Washington Post, 1-10:(A)8.

5

. . . we must behave reliably. American power and prestige should not be lightly committed. But once made, a commitment must be honored. Our friends cannot be expected to share in the burdens and risks of collective action if they cannot count on the word of the United States. Our adversaries cannot be expected to exercise prudence if they perceive our resolve to be hostage to the exigencies of the moment. Those whose posture toward us remains to be determined cannot be expected to decide in favor of friendship if they cannot confidently assess the benefits of association with us . . .

At Senate Foreign Relations Committee hearing
on his confirmation, Washington, Jan. 9/
The Washington Post, 1-10:(A)8.

6

The assurance of basic human liberties will not be improved by replacing friendly governments which incompletely satisfy our standards of democracy with hostile ones which are even less benign.

At Senate Foreign Relations Committee hearing
on his confirmation, Washington, Jan. 9/
Chicago Tribune, 1-10:(1)3.

7

I've never been anything but convinced that the Soviet leadership is influenced by tough, clear, concise Western policy. They understand it. I would also suggest that they are never influenced by Western rhetoric. They are influenced by Western deeds, and . . . that involves the expenditure of capitalist resources to support policies, whatever they may be, preparing

(ALEXANDER M. HAIG, JR.)

our defense forces, supporting a developing nation. Deeds are the *bona fide* in the Soviet calculations of true Western intentions, but never our words.

*At Senate Foreign Relations Committee hearing
on his confirmation, Washington, Jan. 14/
The New York Times, 1-15:12.*

Alexander M. Haig, Jr.
Secretary of State of the United States

1

International terrorism will take the place of human rights in our concern because it is the ultimate abuse of human rights. And it's time that it be addressed with better clarity and greater effectiveness by Western nations and the United States as well.

*News conference, Washington, Jan. 28/
The New York Times, 1-29:6.*

2

A French statesman once remarked that the true business of government was to foresee problems and to administer appropriate remedies while time remained. In our approach to foreign affairs, we have sought to distinguish between the symptoms of the problem and the problem itself, the crisis and its cause, the ebb and flow of daily events and the underlying trend.

*Before American Society of Newspaper Editors,
Washington, April 24/
The New York Times, 4-25:5.*

3

The developing countries, sometimes grouped together as the Third World, are a vastly varied multitude of states, most of them beset by severe economic and political problems. What once united them—the memory of colonialism—is fading. The new emphasis is the future, not the past. The West in general and the United States in particular hold the key to that future. It is we who demonstrate by our own history how to

combine freedom and development, political stability and economic progress. Two guidelines should govern our actions: We must show that friends of the United States benefit from that friendship, even in the face of Soviet-supported intervention. We must offer hope that the United States and its allies are not some form of closed club, hostile to the problems and frustrations attending development.

*Before American Society of Newspaper Editors,
Washington, April 24/The New York Times, 4-24:5.*

4

If we are seriously interested in a world where there can be peaceful change, where nations can settle disputes short of war, then we must act to restrain the Soviet Union. Soviet actions or the actions of Moscow's surrogates threaten Western strategic interests. Even more importantly, it is Soviet reliance on force and the threat of force to create and exploit disorder that undermines the prospect for world peace.

*At Syracuse (N.Y.) University commencement,
May 9/
San Francisco Examiner & Chronicle, 5-10:(A)10.*

5

. . . we must be discriminating in our actions [toward countries that violate human rights] with an eye to the source of the violation and the impact of our protest on the violator. We should distinguish between the so-called totalitarian and authoritarian regimes. The *totalitarian* model unfortunately draws upon the resources of modern technology to impose its will on all aspects of a citizen's behavior. The totalitarian regimes tend to be intolerant at home and abroad, actively hostile to all we represent and ideologically resistant to political change. The *authoritarian* regime usually stems from lack of political or economic development and customarily reserves for itself absolute authority in only a few politically sensitive areas. I am not making a case for the excellence of authoritarian government; I am making a case that such regimes are more likely to change than their totalitarian counterparts. It should be our ob-

WHAT THEY SAID IN 1981

(ALEXANDER M. HAIG, JR.)

jective to hold forth ourselves as a model worthy of imitation as that change occurs and to help the evolution of authoritarian government toward a more democratic form.

Before Trilateral Commission/
The Christian Science Monitor, 5-15:23.

1

[On criticism of President Reagan's lifting of the U.S. grain embargo against the Soviet Union]: To understand the grain-embargo decision and the signal it sent, I think you have to adopt a different perspective. It is well-known that I did not favor an end to the grain embargo. But I had the luxury of being able to look at the problem strictly in terms of foreign-policy considerations. In that sense, there obviously was a cost. But the President had to take into account other considerations. First, he had made a commitment to lift the embargo—not once or twice but dozens of times. In foreign policy, as in all other things, a commitment cannot be taken lightly. This President is not going to devalue his words. And he had good grounds for opposing the embargo. Before the election [last year], I opposed it, too. Such narrowly based sanctions do not work over the long haul. Second, even in the foreign-policy area, the embargo was problematic. Not all of our allies had joined us; some of those who had cooperated with the embargo wanted it to end. We were beginning to run the risk of allied disunity, in which American farmers would be bearing the burden almost alone, supporting a policy that was not as effective as the disadvantages it brought. The short-term problems presented by the decision to lift the embargo can be managed without great harm. Furthermore, there should be no doubt on this point: Once the President made his decision, I supported it. I support it today.

Interview/U.S. News & World Report, 5-18:29.

2

We are seeking a more just and responsible relationship with the Third World. The de-

veloping states are beginning to see the difference between the offers of the East and the offers of the West. The Soviets bring weapons, a pervasive presence, and eventually a client-state relationship. The West brings economic development, science, technology and humanitarian assistance. We will encourage the movement toward association with the West. It is in our interest to do so and it offers the best hope for the developing states themselves.

At Hillsdale (Mich.) College commencement/
The Christian Science Monitor, 6-17:13.

3

The President's [Reagan] view on summitry is that summitry for its own sake can be self-deluding and can result in euphoric expectations which quite often historically have not been realized. So he believes that summitry must be preceded by the most careful preparation on every one of the issues which are likely to arise, and that there is some indication that that summitry would result in progress. This does not suggest that summitry must be abandoned in any situation in which that preparation and that anticipated outcome is not there, but it means in general that that would be the President's approach, and I expect he'll live by that.

Interview/The Wall Street Journal, 7-9:22.

4

I'm not one who accepts the thesis that if we don't help the Soviets in one category or another, including energy, that they are going to then be motivated to pursue aggressive policies. I think that's a very specious approach to this otherwise extremely complex problem. What we must always ask ourselves is, "Are the policies we are pursuing in fact going to achieve the objectives which meet over-all American interests?" Therefore, you cannot pursue them in narrow, functional categories. There are always pros and cons to every one of these questions. In fact, I am not one who would be a rigid opponent of no contacts with the Soviet Union in commercial terms and trading terms and technology transfer. It's not in our interest to pur-

(ALEXANDER M. HAIG, JR.)

sue that kind of rigid approach. On the other hand, I think it would be equally fallacious to believe that political relationships are exclusively determined by economic relationships. History would suggest quite the contrary.

Interview, Washington/
The Christian Science Monitor, 8-24:14.

1

. . . growth for development [in developing nations] is best achieved through reliance on incentives for individual performance. The individual is the beginning, the key element and the ultimate beneficiary of the development process. Suppression of economic incentives ultimately suppresses enthusiasm and invention. And the denial of personal freedom can be as great an obstacle to productivity as the denial or reward for achievement. History cautions against regimes that regiment their people in the name of ideals, yet fail to achieve either economic or social progress. Those governments that have been more solicitous of the liberties of their people have also been more successful in securing both freedom and prosperity.

At United Nations,
New York, Sept. 21/
The New York Times, 9-22:6.

Armand Hammer
Chairman,
Occidental Petroleum Corporation

2

Trade is part of the dialogue between the United States and Russia and it is crucial that we keep this dialogue going. The Soviet leadership is gradually coming to see trade, rather than confrontation with the West, as the way to improve economic conditions. If we are going to have peace, we should encourage the Soviet leadership in this direction. In any event, if the United States refuses to sell the Soviet Union the products it needs, other countries will.

The New York Times Magazine, 11-29:122.

W. Averell Harriman
Diplomat;
Former United States Ambassador
to the Soviet Union

3

. . . the Russian objective is to have as much of the world Communist as possible. This is their ideological goal. They think security will be best enhanced by Communist countries—dictatorships, as we call them—whereas we believe that our security and our best interest is best served by democratic governments, namely, some form of government that is responsible to the will of the people; and that's an irreconcilable difference . . . [But] we needn't have come to as vigorous a difference at different times if we had been a little more understanding of a very simple fact: that these [the Soviets] were competitors of ours and that they were not necessarily doing things because they were our enemies, but because of their ideology. I think if there had been a little more of that understanding in our government, we might not have had quite as vigorous a difference [with them].

Interview/
The Washington Post, 11-15:(C)1,4.

Ulric St. Clair Haynes, Jr.
United States Ambassador to Algeria

4

[On being an Ambassador]: . . . when it comes to any job, we all come to the job with the sum total of our backgrounds. One element of my background is the fact that I am black, that I am a first-generation American—my parents are immigrants, came from a Third World country, Barbados in the West Indies. All of these things are at least as important in my getting the job done and being able to communicate with leaders of the Third World as my blackness. That doesn't mean that I am one-up on an intelligent and perceptive white diplomat. A lot depends on your personality, a lot depends on the way you apply your background, a lot depends on, indeed, the professional qualifications which your host country's leaders perceive that you have. I think that the day of the unqualified political appointee as

WHAT THEY SAID IN 1981

(ULRIC ST. CLAIR HAYNES, JR.)

Ambassador is over. The Third World is as sensitive as is the developed world to the qualifications of the man that a country sends to represent it.

Interview, Algiers/
The Christian Science Monitor, 2-11:(B)15.

Max M. Kampelman
Chief United States delegate to the
Madrid conference on the
1975 Helsinki human-rights accords

1

. . . you cannot have detente while you have the Soviet Union, in effect, acting in complete violation of its human-rights commitments under the 1975 Helsinki Final Act, and becoming increasingly repressive in the area of human rights. Secondly, we have said that we do not see detente while the Soviet Union is using its troops in Afghanistan in complete violation of the Helsinki Final Act. And we have said that in both of these areas—human rights and Afghanistan—the United States requires specific movement of the Soviet Union before we would be prepared to say that detente can be achieved.

Interview/
U.S. News & World Report, 2-9:38.

Jack Kemp
United States Representative, R—New York

2

I don't want to overstate my economic thesis. And I'm not suggesting that [for example] the Iran-Iraq problem would be cured by the United States' conducting sound monetary policy. But I think our strengthening our own economy would once again allow the United States to conduct a sounder foreign policy. We would have more credibility. People would have more faith in our word. The more progress we could show for the United States as well as some of our allies and friends and democracies in the West and throughout the Third World, the more illiberal the Soviet model would look.

Interview/The Washington Post, 1-20:(A)21.

George F. Kennan
Co-chairman, American Committee on
East-West Accord; Former United States
Ambassador to the Soviet Union

3

[Saying foreign governments sometimes find it difficult to conduct relations with Washington]: There is, for example, the extensive fragmentation of authority throughout our government—a fragmentation that often makes it hard for a foreign representative to know who speaks for the American government as a whole. There is the absence of any collective Cabinet responsibility, or indeed of any system of mutual responsibility between the Executive and Legislative branches of government. There are the large powers exercised, even in matters that affect foreign relations, by state, local or private authorities with which the foreign representative cannot normally deal. There is the susceptibility of the political establishment to the emotions and vagaries of public opinion, particularly in this day of confusing interaction between the public and the various commercialized mass media. There is the inordinate influence exercised over American foreign policy by individual lobbies and other organized minorities. And there is the extraordinary difficulty a democratic society experiences in taking a balanced view of any other country that has acquired the image of a military and political enemy— the tendency, that is, to dehumanize that image—to oversimplify it, to ignore its complexities.

At Second World Congress on Soviet and East
European Studies, Garmisch, West Germany/
Chicago Tribune, 2-15:(2)1.

4

[On U.S.-Soviet relations]: I recognize that this [the Soviet Union] is a regime with which it is not possible for us to have a fully satisfactory relationship. There are a number of Soviet habits and practices which I deeply deplore, and which I feel we should resist firmly when they impinge on our interests. I recognize that there has recently been a drastic and very serious

(GEORGE F. KENNAN)

deterioration of Soviet-American relations—a deterioration to which both sides have made their contributions. [But the prevailing view of the Soviet Union in the U.S. is] so extreme, so subjective, so far removed from what any sober scrutiny of external reality would reveal, that it is not only ineffective but dangerous as a guide to political action . . . [Americans must recognize that there is] another great people, one of the world's greatest, in all its complexity and variety, embracing the good with the bad—a people whose life, whose views, whose habits, whose fears and aspirations, are the products, not of any inherent inequity but of the relentless discipline of history, tradition and national experience . . . If we insist on demoralizing these Soviet leaders—on viewing them as total and incorrigible enemies, consumed only with their fear or hatred of us and dedicated to nothing other than our destruction—that, in the end, is the way we shall assuredly have them, if for no other reason than that our view of them allows for nothing else, either for us or for them.

At Dartmouth College, Nov. 16/
The New York Times, 11-18:6.

Jeane J. Kirkpatrick
United States Ambassador/Permanent
Representative to the United Nations

1

[Criticizing former President Jimmy Carter's emphasis on human rights as a determinant of U.S. foreign policy]: Our position in the Western Hemisphere has deteriorated to the point where we must now defend ourselves against the threat of a ring of Soviet bases being established on and around our borders. I'm not saying that the Carter human-rights policy was the only factor in bringing this about, but it certainly played a role. One reason for the failure of the Carter policy was the belief that you can influence governments and people more effectively by hitting them over the head with a two-by-four, excoriating and humiliating them publicly and treating them like moral pariahs than by using quiet persuasion and diplo-

macy . . . Speaking generally, we must make it perfectly clear that we are revolted by torture and can never feel spiritual kinship with a government that engages in torture. But the central goal of our foreign policy should be not the moral elevation of other nations, but the preservation of a civilized conception of our own national self-interest.

Interview/
U.S. News & World Report, 3-2:50.

2

[Saying U.S. influence at the UN is trivial]: . . . I would describe the United Nations as our greatest challenge because it is the major arena of world politics. I do not favor our withdrawal from the UN. But it does seem to me that we don't want to keep losing, to be humiliated, to be powerless. From one perspective, we can't hope for too much from the UN. But from another, it is surely one of the greatest challenges to us in foreign affairs.

Interview/
U.S. News & World Report, 11-9:37.

Andrew Knight
Editor, "The Economist" (Britain)

3

There are two ways to rally American opinion [in foreign policy]. One is with some saber-rattling against an identifiable enemy like the Soviet Union. The other is to invoke American idealism, as [former President Jimmy] Carter did over human rights. I think human rights are an instrument of public policy. What [President] Reagan needs to do is to sound both militant and idealistic. For example, he needs to tell El Salvador, "We will support you [against the rebels], but you must realize that if you continue running a dictatorship our support will be worthless because you cannot change people's hearts and minds with a gun. You can only change them with a better system." Policy must allow for the possible use of force, but it should also encourage regimes to seek popularity in their own countries.

Interview/World Press Review, April:24.

WHAT THEY SAID IN 1981

Irving Kristol
Professor of social thought,
New York University; Senior fellow,
American Enterprise Institute

1

We have to start trying to create what we have never had in this country: an intellectual conservative framework for foreign policy. Conservative foreign policy for decades has veered all over the place—from isolationism to containment, to a little foray by [the late Secretary of State] John Foster Dulles into something called liberation, back to containment again, then into quasi-isolation, then into detente, then into anti-detente. The truth is, as the liberal framework for foreign policy has slowly been crumbling, the conservatives have not come up with something in its place—not yet. More than that, Republicans, on the whole, have never been much concerned with thinking about foreign policy.

Interview/U.S. News & World Report, 7-20:50.

Richard Lamm
Governor of Colorado (D)

2

[Saying U.S. immigration laws should be tightened]: The economic pie is not growing and the day of the frontier is over. America cannot become the lifeboat of all of the excess population floating around.

Time, 5-18:26.

G. Gordon Liddy
Former Special Assistant to the Secretary
of the Treasury for Organized Crime;
Convicted Watergate conspirator

3

[Contrasting the relative safety of a little old lady with a purse and an armed football offensive tackle to illustrate how the U.S. should preserve its safety and freedom]: Freedom, the absence of intrusion, is something you will have only as long as you're prepared to defend it . . . [The freedom of the football tackle] will be respected [by potential criminals]. Why? They're not crazy. They're going to wait for the little old lady. [Around the world, the U.S. is] beginning to look less and less like that big offensive tackle and more and more like that little old lady. You are dealing with the nature of man, and the nature of man is not just gratuitous in respect of everybody else's freedom. That's not the way it works out there.

Lecture, University of Pittsburgh/
The Wall Street Journal, 1-19:18.

Joseph Luns
Secretary General,
North Atlantic Treaty Organization

4

[U.S.] President Carter has been far too strongly attacked in the American media and by American public opinion. Carter was far from being a hypocrite. He was a very sincere man, and an idealistic man, and a religious man. He made mistakes, which are probably due to his too-idealistic view of world affairs, and an under-estimation of the use of power. I might say that the new President [Reagan] seems more aware of the importance of the power factor and, furthermore, we have the impression that the people of his staff are more knowledgeable, more experienced and are more united than the Carter staff. So, on the whole, the reaction in Europe to the election of Mr. Reagan has been very good—just as there has been a shift in American public opinion, there has been a shift in European public opinion in its judgment of Mr. Reagan.

Interview, Brussels/
Chicago Tribune, 1-19:(1)4.

Charles McC. Mathias, Jr.
United States Senator,
R—Maryland

5

[Criticizing President Reagan for giving too many Ambassadorships to outside political appointees rather than selecting Ambassadors from the career Foreign Service]: Our national security is too important to be subordinated to the patronage requirements of partisan politics. Morale is undermined when many of the most

(CHARLES McC. MATHIAS, JR.)

responsible and prestigious foreign assignments are given to neophytes in foreign affairs.

The Christian Science Monitor, 12-4:2.

Donald F. McHenry
Former United States Ambassador/
Permanent Representative to the
United Nations

1

A recent study reveals that your knowledge is significantly short when it comes to the world in which you live . . . You live in a time when knowledge of world affairs is no longer simply nice to have or a luxury. It is essential to our well-being. Long-term strategy requires a political consensus. Without consensus we are vulnerable to uninformed simplistic appeals, heavy on jingoism and misguided patriotism.

At University of Missouri-Columbia commencement/
Time, 6-15:55.

Robert S. McNamara
President, International Bank for
Reconstruction and Development
(World Bank)

2

The United States contribution to development assistance [for Third World countries] is disgracefully low; it has declined in relation to national income 90 per cent since the Eisenhower Administration at a time when national income in real terms per capita has more than doubled. It is today the 15th lowest [contribution] among the major industrialized nations. There is no other large industrialized nation providing as low a proportion of its national income to development assistance; it is disgraceful . . . We [at the World Bank] and others have failed to inform the people of the industrial countries of the nature and magnitude of the changes in the relationships among nations, economically and politically, over the last decade, [especially their great interdependence]. For that reason, we have failed to show them where their own narrow interests lie. We have failed to convince them that there is a plus-sum game as part of

which they can move to assist the developing countries to achieve economic and social advance, with benefits to both the developing and industrialized countries . . . it is that failure which I think is leading to less than rational action by many of the nations, particularly the United States.

Interview, Washington/
The New York Times, 6-21:(1)16.

M. Peter McPherson
Administrator, United States Agency
for International Development

3

We will continue to have a foreign-aid program that addresses the various humanitarian and development needs of the world. But we feel—and feel strongly—that problems are not going to be solved solely by the massive transfer of resources from the West. Problems will be solved, first and foremost, by Third World countries exercising their own sovereignty and coming to grips with their own difficulties.

Interview/U.S. News & World Report, 10-26:24.

Edwin Meese III
Counsellor to the President
of the United States

4

[On speculation that Secretary of State Alexander Haig has been too independent of President Reagan in foreign affairs]: I think that really Al Haig has done exactly what the President has wanted him to do: strong spokesman for the foreign policy of this country, primary developer of the foreign-policy options that have to be decided by the President. And then to implement that policy through the State Department. I think he has done that very well— and I think the President feels the same way . . . I think that on some occasions the President made decisions that were different than what Secretary Haig wished, just as that would be true with virtually every Cabinet member—because nobody is going to agree 100 per cent of the time with everybody else.

Interview, Washington/
The Christian Science Monitor, 5-1:11.

147

Francois Mitterrand
President of France

1

There is no international system for pursuing a far-reaching [economic] policy, no international monetary system. A number of ideas for aiding the Third World have been put forward, particularly by the Brandt Commission, by the European Community, by the Havana non-aligned conference, by OPEC; but neither the World Bank nor the International Monetary System allow for such a policy. I am convinced that the balance between the two parts of the world, the industrialized nations and the others, will be one of the causes of the most serious tragedies at the end of the century—to be explicit, of world war.

Interview, Paris, June 1/
The New York Times, 6-4:6.

Walter F. Mondale
Vice President of the
United States

2

. . . one of the most grievous inadequacies of our present system is that the President of the United States, who has to conduct American foreign policy, is left enfeebled in terms of a crucial foreign-aid and military assistance [situation]. I could give you a hundred examples. It took us a year to get the little help we got in Nicaragua. Whatever you think of what's going on down there, certainly the President ought to be able to act decisively. With Pakistan we could only come up with a small amount—they called it peanuts. You can say the same of the situation in Liberia, in El Salvador. I feel very deeply about that, and I wish we'd give a President a fund that he could use quickly, expeditiously, albeit requiring accounting, so that he could be effective and decisive in a crucial area where he cannot be today.

Interview/The Washington Post, 1-20:(A)21.

Walter F. Mondale
Former Vice President of the United States

3

I'm very worried about U.S.-Soviet relations. I cannot understand—it just baffles me—why the Soviets these last few years have behaved as they have. Maybe we have made some mistakes with them. Why did they have to build up all these arms? Why did they have to go into Afghanistan? Why can't they relax just a little bit about Eastern Europe? Why do they try every door to see if it is locked?

The Christian Science Monitor, 3-10:4.

4

Some [Reagan] Administration spokesmen now say that there is a difference between right-wing authoritarianism and left-wing totalitarianism, and that we must tolerate the terror of the one, but must condemn that of the other. [But] torture is torture, and terror is terror. And whether it occurs in Cuba, Russia, Vietnam, Argentina, Chile or El Salvador, we in America should oppose it, condemn it, and do our best to stop it.

At Brandeis University commencement/
Time 6-15:54.

Edmund S. Muskie
Former Secretary of State
of the United States

5

. . . we must arrive at a greater appreciation of the human and physical resources of our planet. There are 13 million people on the move right now in places like Afghanistan, Somalia and Indochina. Homeless, hungry, desperately searching for life. We must help them in their search. We must close the gap between the wealth which resources bring and the desperation which war and scarcity create. Doing so will require more disciplined use of our resources and a better global mechanism for sharing them.

Before Maine Legislature, Augusta/
The Christian Science Monitor, 2-20:23.

Enos Nkala
Minister of Finance of Zimbabwe

6

[Criticizing the U.S. for imposing tough conditions on financial assistance to Third World

(ENOS NKALA)

countries]: By laying overemphasis on the private sector, the American government is trying to transpose its own policies onto other people. My view is that it's going to rebound on the Americans because an anti-American attitude is beginning to emerge [in developing countries. The Americans] are too arrogant. They want to dictate what people should do . . . There has been some foolish thinking in the American Administration that they are everything to everybody. There are many alternatives. One alternative is to say, "Out with the Americans," and to look for other friends elsewhere. The world does not consist of the Americans. America is not the only wealthy country in the world.

Interview, Salisbury, Oct. 9/
The Washington Post, 10-10:(A)19.

Michael Novak
Chief United States delegate to United
Nations Commission on Human Rights

1

[The "new terrorism" of today is] exported cynically by other states for their own national interests and purposes . . . All nations must be concerned about the training camps for rings of international terrorists, about the weapons, the passports, and funds which make it possible for the terrorists to survive. Many states, while criticizing the use of violence, themselves provide arms, training, funding and logistical support to terrorist groups. Concrete and effective measures must be developed, therefore, to deny to terrorists the benefits of their acts. Nations must not give in to blackmail and must take firm steps to sanction those who violate the basic norms of international behavior.

At meeting of U.N. Commission on Human Rights,
Geneva, Feb. 9/Chicago Tribune, 2-10:(1)7.

Muammar el-Qaddafi
Chief of State of Libya

2

We put the production of nuclear weapons at the top of the list of terrorist activities. As long

as the big powers continue to manufacture atomic weapons, it means they are continuing to terrorize the world; also the deployment of military bases on other countries' territories; also deploying naval fleets around the world. This is one reason why the U.S. is a top terrorist force in the world.

Interview/Time, 6-8:31.

Ronald Reagan
President of the United States

3

[Warning against future holding of American hostages by foreign terrorists]: Let terrorists be aware that when the rules of international behavior are violated, our policy will be one of swift and effective retribution. We hear it said that we live in an era of limits to our powers; but let it be also understood—there are limits to our patience.

At ceremony welcoming home 52 Americans who were
held hostage by Iran for over a year, Washington,
Jan. 27/Los Angeles Times, 1-28:(I)1.

4

. . . so far, detente's been a one-way street the Soviet Union has used to pursue its own aims. I don't have to think of an answer as to what I think their intentions are: They have repeated it. I know of no leader of the Soviet Union, since the revolution and including the present leadership, that has not more than once repeated in the various Communist Congresses they hold, their determination that their goal must be the promotion of world revolution and a one-world Communist-socialist or Communist state—whichever word you want to use. Now, as long as they do that and as long as they, at the same time, have openly and publicly declared that the only morality they recognize is what will further their cause—meaning they reserve unto themselves the right to commit any crime, to lie, to cheat, in order to obtain that, and that is moral, not immoral, and we operate on a different set of stand-

WHAT THEY SAID IN 1981

(RONALD REAGAN)

dards—I think that when you do business with
them, even at a detente, you keep that in mind.

News conference, Washington, Jan. 29/
The New York Times, 1-30:10.

1

[Saying future terrorist activities against the
U.S., such as Iran's holding 52 Americans hostage, will not be tolerated in the future]: People
have gone to bed in some of these countries that
have done these things to us in the past confident
that they can go to sleep, wake up in the morning
and the United States wouldn't have taken any
action . . . anyone who does these things, violates
our rights in the future, is not going to be able to
go to bed with that confidence.

News conference, Washington, Jan. 29/
Los Angeles Times, 1-30:(I)20.

2

[Announcing his decision to lift the embargo
on U.S. grain shipments to the Soviet Union]: As
a Presidential candidate, I indicated my opposition to the curb on sales because American
farmers had been unfairly singled out to bear
the burden of this ineffective national policy . . .
In the first few weeks of my Presidency, I decided
that an immediate lifting of the sales limitation
could be misinterpreted by the Soviet Union. I
therefore felt that my decision should be made
only when it was clear that the Soviets and other
nations would not mistakenly think it indicated
a weakening of our position. I have determined
that our position now cannot be mistaken: The
United States, along with the vast majority of
nations, has condemned and remains opposed to
the Soviet occupation of Afghanistan [which
prompted then-President Jimmy Carter to impose the embargo] and other aggressive acts
around the world. We will react strongly to
acts of aggression wherever they take place.
There will never be a weakening of this resolve.

Washington, April 24*/
The New York Times, 4-25:6.

3

Theodore Roosevelt said that the Presidency
was a bully pulpit. Well, I, for one, intend that
this bully pulpit shall be used on every occasion,
where it is appropriate, to point a finger of shame
at . . . wherever it takes place in the world, the
act of violence or terrorism, and that even at the
negotiating table, never shall it be forgotten for
a moment that wherever it is taking place in the
world, the persecution of people, for whatever
reason—persecution of people for their religious
belief—that is a matter to be on that negotiating
table or the United States does not belong at that
table.

At "Day of Remembrance" ceremony for
victims of the Holocaust, Washington, Apr. 30/
The New York Times, 5-1:4.

4

There seems to be a feeling as if an address on
foreign policy is somehow evidence to have a
foreign policy, and until you make an address
you don't have one, and I challenge that. I'm
satisfied that we do have a foreign policy. I have
met with eight heads of state already, representatives of nine other nations. The Secretary of State
is making his second trip and is now in China
and is going to meet with the Asian nations in
the Philippines and then go on for a meeting in
New Zealand. The Deputy Secretary of State has
been in Africa and is now returning by way of
Europe. I have been in personal communication
by mail with [Soviet] President Brezhnev. I don't
necessarily believe that you must, to have a
foreign policy, stand up and make a wide declaration, this is your foreign policy.

News conference, Washington, June 16/
The New York Times, 6-17:13.

5

Basically, good foreign policy is the use of
good common sense in dealing with friends and
potential adversaries.

At Republican fund-raising dinner,
Chicago, July 7/
Los Angeles Times, 7-8:(I)10.

(RONALD REAGAN)

1

The Executive Branch is more or less entrusted with foreign policy because you can't run foreign policy through legislation. And while there may be some safeguards that should remain—I wouldn't be averse to that; we do have a multiple kind of government—I do think that the President has got to have some leeway with regard to negotiations. And some ability to say across a table, "this is what we will do or what we won't do," and those that he's dealing with know that he has the authority to say that.

To group of editors, Washington, Oct. 16/
The Washington Post, 10-18:(A)9.

2

[Saying that a U.S.-Soviet summit meeting is likely in 1982]: I've always recognized that ultimately there's got to be a settlement, a solution [to U.S.-Soviet differences]. The other way—if you don't believe that—then you're going to find yourself trapped, in that in the back of your mind [you will accept] the inevitability of a conflict some day . . . That kind of conflict is going to end the world.

Interview, Washington/
San Francisco Examiner & Chronicle, 12-27:(A)4.

Benjamin S. Rosenthal
United States Representative, D—New York

3

[On Reagan Administration foreign policy]: They've got us on this roller-coaster, zigging and zagging every day. Nicaragua is up, Nicaragua is down; El Salvador is up, El Salvador is down; SALT is up, SALT is down; Poland is up, Poland is down. We almost need a Valium for the country.

Newsweek, 3-30:20.

Loret Miller Ruppe
Director, United States Peace Corps

4

There are too many people across the United States who, when Peace Corps is mentioned,

say: "Oh, is that still around? I haven't heard of it in years." To say that this is a matter of concern for us would be to characterize it too lightly. This is of grave concern. This loss of knowledge of the work of our volunteers, I fear, has made us lose several generations of potential American volunteers at a time when they are needed more than they ever were . . . This is a government program that has worked. This is a cost-effective venture that you, as American taxpayers and American business people, can be proud of . . . But when it all really hits home is when, after hours of bouncing around on dirt roads [in an undeveloped country], traversing mountainsides where no such thing as a guardrail exists, you come to a small village where one or two Americans have been serving. Suddenly, the whole village assembles at the adobe schoolhouse and you join them, sitting on kindergarten chairs on a dirt floor, no glass in the window spaces, little children, old people, farmers, animals mingling as family—the entire population pours in, and a spokesman stands up and says, "We want to thank America for this helper you have sent us. We know we are poor, but this person is helping us and our children to have a better life." How I would love to bring a film crew with me, and bring these scenes back to the American taxpayer via national television! The taxpayers deserve to know that their gift and the gift these volunteers bring is appreciated.

Before Commonwealth Club, San Francisco/
The Christian Science Monitor, 10-22:23.

Anwar el-Sadat
President of Egypt

5

I advise Americans not to seek [military] bases either in Egypt or in any other part of the world. It only leads to hatred. The era when it was possible to maintain military bases in the Third World is past. They are reminiscent in our minds of the old colonialism. Today they only bring hatred to the one who gives the base and to those who are given it.

Interview, Washington/
San Francisco Examiner & Chronicle,
8-16:(A)23.

151

WHAT THEY SAID IN 1981

George P. Shultz
Former Secretary of the Treasury
of the United States

1

Around the world, the perception is gaining ground that a market-based economy—even under authoritarian conditions—does more for people generally than does a state-directed one. The flow of facts has demolished the Communist side of the argument. In operational terms, we have won . . . The only reason we haven't swept the board is the Soviet's awesome military power, and total brutality in willingness to use it.

Zale lecture, Stanford University/
The Wall Street Journal, 9-29:26.

Norodom Sihanouk
Former Chief of State of Cambodia

2

[On what the late U.S. Secretary of State John Foster Dulles told him in 1958]: "Prince Sihanouk [Dulles said], you are very young. You must choose between the free world and the Communist world." Today I pay homage to his grave. John Foster Dulles was right: There is no non-alignment.

Singapore, Sept. 4/The New York Times, 9-5:3.

Alan K. Simpson
United States Senator, D—Wyoming

3

[Saying U.S. immigration laws should be tightened]: Our policies have made us the laughter of the world. Immigration is a game of numbers, and somewhere along the line we are going to have to deal with those numbers, or else we will be overwhelmed . . . If there is nothing else I get done, I intend to send a signal to the world that you have to have some kind of identification before you work here. Right now we are the patsies of the earth.

Time, 5-18:24,27.

Donald B. Sole
South African Ambassador
to the United States

4

. . . there is a great deal said that the United States must choose between black Africa and South Africa—in the same way as it is argued that the United States must choose between Arabs and Israel, between Taiwan and the People's Republic of China. But our approach . . . is that for a superpower to allow itself to be forced into a position where you have to choose between the one or the other is basically an admission of weakness. A superpower has interests in all these areas of either actual or potential conflict, and the superpower must draw the balance.

Interview/
Los Angeles Herald Examiner, 6-1:(A)11.

Zenko Suzuki
Prime Minister of Japan

5

[Criticizing U.S. President Reagan's decision to lift the embargo of U.S. grain shipments to the Soviet Union and of not consulting Japan about it]: The grain embargo was the major pillar of U.S. sanctions [in response to the Soviet invasion of Afghanistan]. I recall that Reagan declared during the Presidential election campaign that the grain embargo would have to be lifted sooner or later. But at this time the outlook for the future in Poland is not yet clear and there remain other sources of anxiety [about Soviet actions] that have not at all been eliminated. Japan felt that lifting the grain embargo at such a time was unexpected. Japan, among the Western nations—including the United States—earnestly and sincerely cooperated with the United States in carrying out economic sanctions against the Soviet Union . . . [But the U.S. lifting of the embargo was taken without asking our opinion in advance or consulting with us or explaining why the action was being taken at this time. [Nor did the U.S.] consult with Japan on what Japan should do concerning its economic sanctions against the Soviet Union or attempt to make any adjustments [with Japan] on those sanctions.

News conference, Tokyo, April 28/
Los Angeles Times, 4-29:(I)1.

Margaret Thatcher
Prime Minister of the United Kingdom

1

[U.S.] President Reagan and his Administration have understood the challenge [from the Soviet Union]. If we are safe today, it is because America has stood with us. If we are to remain safe tomorrow, it will be because America remains powerful and self-confident.

News conference, London, Feb. 16/
The New York Times, 2-17:3.

Pierre Elliott Trudeau
Prime Minister of Canada

2

. . . global confidence in the United Nations may be eroding dangerously, principally because the fine words spoken from countless UN podiums have too seldom been translated into concrete expressions of the unity of purpose we often profess.

At United Nations Conference on New and
Renewable Sources of Energy, Nairobi, Kenya,
Aug. 11/The New York Times, 8-12:4.

Cyrus R. Vance
Former Secretary of State
of the United States

3

. . . the issue of human rights is an issue that is international in its nature. This has been recognized by most of the nations of the world, by their signing of various agreements which indicate that they recognize that that is the fact. Therefore, I think what we should be doing now is not trying to downgrade the issue of human rights but to continue to have it as a central part of our foreign policy. It is necessary that we keep this issue very much at the forefront of our foreign policy, and it is important as to how we are perceived by other nations in this regard. We ought to stand in the world for human rights and not merely for human rights when human rights is convenient.

Broadcast interview/"Meet the Press," NBC-TV, 6-21.

Ben J. Wattenberg
Senior fellow, American Enterprise
Institute; Chairman, Coalition for
a Democratic Majority

4

. . . I, for one, kind of like the idea of an American President [Reagan] standing up and saying, "Communism as an idea is over the hill and we are the wave of the future." There is still a great war of ideas, of values, going on in the world. In that sense, [this stance] buys Reagan a lot of trouble. On the other hand, people around the world and in the United States say, "By God, we're standing up for what we believe in again, and we're not just cookie-pushers." And that's healthy in a foreign policy.

Interview/The New York Times, 8-2:(4)3.

Murray L. Weidenbaum
Chairman, Council of Economic Advisers
to the President of the United States

5

[On whether he is sympathetic to the economic plight of Third World countries that ask for aid from the West]: You know, lots of nations have a different life-style from what they scorn as the materialism of the West—a life-style they have chosen not to adopt. They point to the serious social costs of our materialistic life-style. But the idea that they want to share the benefits—but not the costs—of our life-style leaves me cold. Of course, you don't have to go abroad—you can find parallels in our own country, like the drop-outs who don't mind showing up for their monthly checks. I take a hard line on domestic claimants on our budget, so my attitude on foreign claimants is not discriminatory.

Interview/The Washington Post, 8-16:(E)7.

Charles Z. Wick
Director, International Communication
Agency of the United States

6

[On the future direction of Voice of America broadcasts]: Whatever we do will in no way change or skirt the charter of the Voice of

(CHARLES Z. WICK)

America . . . The greatest weapon we have is truth . . . to give verifiable truth. The greatest asset that the Voice of America has, and the BBC, is credibility. Without credibility, you don't have an audience. Therefore, it is of paramount importance that the credibility be maintained.

Interview/The Washington Post, 11-10:(A)10.

Andrew Young
Former United States Ambassador/
Permanent Representative to the
United Nations

1

[Criticizing the Reagan Administration's deemphasis of human rights as a determinant of U.S. foreign policy]: Here is an Administration that has come to power without really understanding the basis of the American dream and the American ideal for mankind, which is based, to me, on the Constitution and a notion that human rights is basic to everything that this country has been working for for 200 years . . . If you're going to have economic alliances with the African continent, you've got to respect majority rule and human rights. If you're going to have continued economic alliances with the Arab world, there's got to be some recognition of Palestinian rights. If you're going to have alliances economically with Central America, there's got to be respect for the rights of the people in El Salvador to own land.

Interview, Los Angeles, Feb. 24/
Los Angeles Times, 2-25:(I)7.

Edward Zorinsky
United States Senator, D—Nebraska

2

[Saying the U.S. should lift its grain embargo against the Soviet Union, which was initiated in response to Russia's invasion of Afghanistan]: The grain embargo should be lifted for many reasons. It has not been effective, other than to harm the farmers of America. Candidate [Ronald] Reagan made farmers a promise to end the embargo during the [Presidential] campaign. And now that he is President, it would be a loss of credibility for his Administration to do otherwise. The embargo has destroyed the credibility of the United States as a reliable supplier of agricultural goods. With the embargo, this country pointed a gun at the Soviet Union and shot the U.S. farmer in the foot.

Interview/U.S. News & World Report, 2-16:25.

Government

Thomas L. Ashley
United States Representative, D—Ohio

1

[On lobbyists' dealings with Congressmen]:
It used to be that these lobbies had to hire their
own hall, but now they get rooms in the Ray-
burn House Office Building. They [the lobby-
ists] give you only the finest in food, smoked
Irish salmon and caviar. And they're not serving
cheap scotch; it's all Chivas Regal and better.
Los Angeles Times, 3-2:(I)7.

Les Aspin
United States Representative, D—Wisconsin

2

In the old days, you had the ward heeler who
cemented himself in the community by taking
care of everyone. But city machines died once
Franklin D. Roosevelt brought in the Federal
government to take care of everybody. Now the
Congressman plays the role of ward heeler—
wending his way through the bureaucracy,
helping to cut through red tape and confusion.
U.S. News & World Report, 3-2:39.

Bruce E. Babbitt
Governor of Arizona, (D)

3

My basic case against the Federal government
is that it is into everything, and in the process
is destroying the vitality and independence of
state and local governments while neglecting
the things it ought to be doing.
The Washington Post, 2-21:(A)8.

Howard H. Baker, Jr.
United States Senator, R—Tennessee

4

The difference between the loyal opposition
and the majority [in Congress] is very real.
There is less room for individual initiative when
you have the responsibility for moving a legislative package. When you're in the opposition,
you can find one piece of high ground and
snipe away very effectively. But when you are a
chairman and in the majority, there's a different
set of imperatives.
The Washington Post,
1-20:(Inauguration '81)21.

5

[Saying he would like to eliminate all-night
Senate sessions]: I have a strong view that legislation passed after midnight is almost never
good legislation to begin with. Too often I have
seen bills passed in the wee small hours of the
morning when you didn't have the vaguest idea
of what was in the thousand-page document on
your desk.
Chicago Tribune Magazine, 2-15:12.

6

[Advocating the televising of Senate proceed-
ings]: I think it is important because a fundamental part of the parliamentary system of
government, which includes our own Congressional forum, is public access to the means
and methods by which public policy is formulated. I think that had radio and television
existed at the time of the framing of the Constitution and the design of our structure of
government by our founding fathers, that they
would have included electronic access as well
as personal access to the public galleries. In
my view, radio and television access is a
simple extension of the public galleries in the
House and Senate chambers . . . It's hard to
conceive of any of us becoming more verbose
[because of the TV cameras] than circumstances
permit. And we must concede in our most
private moments that all of us are prima don-

(HOWARD H. BAKER, JR.)

nas. But I don't think it will increase that one bit. On the contrary, I think it will diminish it. One of the values of television, I have always thought, is that you can spot a phony.

Interview, Washington, Oct. 29/
The New York Times, 10-31:9.

Edward P. Beard
Former United States Representative,
D—Rhode Island

1

[Comparing being in Congress with being a bartender as he is now]: In the Congress, they always ran into deficit spending. As a bartender, I need to show a surplus. Since I bought this place, I found out if you do just the opposite of what they do in Congress, everything will be great.

Interview, Central Falls, R.I./
U.S. News & World Report, 9-7:46.

Paul F. Boller, Jr.
Professor of American history,
Texas Christian University

2

A balanced attitude toward life requires a sense of humor, so I'm a little afraid of Presidents who are humorless people—individuals who are too uptight, too badly earnest about themselves and everything else. Jimmy Carter and Richard Nixon are among several Presidents who fall into that category. I don't want to establish too close a relationship between having a nice sense of humor and being a competent Chief Executive, but I'd like to think that a humane and decent President is a person with some deep feeling for the incongruities of life as well as its seriousness. Presidents with a sense of humor tend to have a better understanding of what life is all about. As a result, they have better relationships with Congress and with others.

Interview/
U.S. News & World Report, 10-19:62.

Zbigniew Brzezinski
Assistant to the President of the
United States for National Security Affairs

3

The external world's vision of internal decision-making in the government assumes too much cohesion and expects too much systematic planning. The fact of the matter is that, increasingly, policy-makers are overwhelmed by events and information . . . a great deal of decision-making is done through implementation by the bureaucracy, which often distorts it. Part of the dilemma of the last four years was that often what the President [Carter] said publicly, and what I would then echo him on, would not be implemented in the same spirit or with the same intent or with the same determination.

Interview, Washington, Jan. 17/
The New York Times, 1-18:(1)3.

James MacGregor Burns
Historian

4

[On the reluctance of Presidents to take hard action against their staffs for wrongdoing]: This is very standard Presidential behavior—in that lies the fascination. What to outsiders would seem rational, quick action that exorcises the problem very early—that is not done. It goes back to the almost family feeling that develops in the White House, and the terrific feeling of us-against-them, of mutual protection . . . This was a great criticism of F.D.R., that he had people he was having trouble with or who were disloyal. Roosevelt's technique was usually to avoid confrontation, not to take action. He got away with it because there were broad political things working in his favor.

The Christian Science Monitor, 12-7:4.

George Busbee
Governor of Georgia (D)

5

[There is] the alarming tendency so prevalent in the minds of some people in Washington of seeing Federalism as a way for the Federal

(GEORGE BUSBEE)

government to dispose of its excess fiscal baggage. I fear it's only a matter of months before some of our friends in OMB attempt to impose . . . a sorting-out process guided by one sole criteria: What makes it easiest to balance the Federal budget? From the point of view of budgetary tunnel vision, Federalism becomes an easy matter. Just pick out the most expensive, the most difficult to manage, the most politically controversial Federal program, and hand them over to the states and localities with a heart-felt sigh of relief.

At National Governors Association conference,
Atlantic City, N.J., Aug. 11/
The Washington Post, 8-12:(A)16.

George Bush
Vice President of the United States

1

I have taken a low-profile approach, because I think that the way you become an effective Vice President—have something substantive to do—is to have the confidence of the President. And if you are always out there in the newspapers or in some news conference and talking about your close relationship with the President—well, it just won't work. It might work for a while. But the President's staff will look at you differently . . . I really feel that stories are going to be written on "whatever happened to George Bush? Where is he?" Stories along that line. That will not bother me. The way I see this relationship, that story almost has to be written. But if I'm out there with a high profile, holding press conferences, putting my spin on whatever it is, I won't have this kind of relationship with the President.

Interview/The Christian Science Monitor, 3-3:7.

2

The power of government to do that which individuals cannot do for themselves can play a vital role in guaranteeing the inalienable right to life, liberty and equal opportunity for citizens of a free, just society. But paternalism

that saps the power of individual decision and self-reliance—no matter how well-intentioned such paternalism might be—has in recent years become the problem, not the solution, for millions of Americans who really crave and seek those blessings.

At Tuskegee Institute's Founders Day and
Centennial Celebration, Tuskegee, Alabama,
April 12/Chicago Tribune, 4-13:2.

3

[Presidential] leadership calls for difficult decisions. And it isn't always a matter of winning a popularity contest. Our best Presidents, our true national leaders, have always kept uppermost in their minds that their compact is with the people.

At Republican fund-raising dinner, Los Angeles,
April 23/Los Angeles Times, 4-24:(I)3.

4

Do people really feel there has been too much regulation [by government]? The answer, in our view, is a resounding "Yes"—at the Federal level, the state level and the local level . . . Not all regulations are mischievous. If there has to be regulation, the best place to regulate is at the local level. The more that can be done at that level, when it needs to be done, the less the Federal government will come charging in.

Nation's Business, September:32.

5

[On President Reagan]: Does this President rely heavily on aides? Yes, he does. Do good executives, the best executives in America, delegate authority? Yes, they do. But he doesn't sign away his responsibilities as President. He does delegate. And he does put trust in top people. If that's what [people] are saying, then that's a fair observation. If they are saying it in a bad sense—I don't think so.

Interview, Washington/
The Christian Science Monitor,
11-27:14.

157

WHAT THEY SAID IN 1981

Joseph A. Califano, Jr.
Former Secretary of
Health, Education and Welfare
of the United States

1

I think the President's [Reagan] proposals for deregulation in many areas make a lot of sense. Is the government into American life too intimately? Yes. I would probably differ with Reagan on environmental values and in areas of social justice and social services. But the idea of trimming back that forest of regulations is sensible and overdue.

Interview, Washington/
The New York Times, 9-18:10.

Hugh L. Carey
Governor of New York (D)

2

State governments find themselves burdened by the rising costs of implementing Federally mandated programs, while at the same time they must comply with constitutions that require balanced budgets and deal with popular demands for tax reductions. Too, the proliferation of Federal programs that completely bypass state governments has made effective planning and program integration almost impossible.

Nation's Business, March:65.

Jimmy Carter
President of the United States

3

Because of the fragmented pressures of special interests, it is very important that the office of the President be a strong one, and that its Constitutional authority be preserved. The President is the only elected official charged with representing all the people. In the moments of decision, after the different and conflicting views have been aired, it is the President who then must speak to the nation and for the nation.

Farewell address to the nation,
Washington, Jan. 14/
The New York Times, 1-15:12.

Jimmy Carter
Former President of the United States

4

. . . now there is a heightened skepticism about what government can or should accomplish. There are even those who argue that the main business of government should be to do nothing—to abandon those who need help and to retreat from the field of political battle, especially on the most controversial issues. These are not new; for the time being they are only louder.

Accepting the Harry S. Truman Public
Service Award, Independence, Mo., May 8/
The Washington Post, 5-9:(A)3.

5

I don't think anyone who has not served [as President] can adequately appreciate the continuity of problems and challenges and decisions. The things that [former President] Gerry Ford decided when he was in office affected me daily. Even the things that [the late President] Harry Truman decided 30 years before I went into office affected me daily. You can make modifications of a previous President's policies, but there is a stream of decisions and ideals and goals and hopes and dreams and problems and disappointments that transcends the identity of the President in the Oval Office. They come from the American people themselves. We share that.

Interview aboard Air Force One, Oct. 10/
The Washington Post, 10-12:(A)2.

William J. Casey
Director, Central Intelligence Agency
of the United States

6

[Arguing against what he calls the "bureaucratic instinct for consensus" in advising the President]: The President does not need a single best view, a guru or a prophet; the nation needs the best analysis of the full range of views and data it can get . . . The time has come to recognize that policy-makers can easily sort through

158

(WILLIAM J. CASEY)

a wide range of opinions but cannot consider views and opinions they do not receive.

U.S. News & World Report, 6-1:36.

William P. Clements, Jr.
Governor of Texas (R)

1

The Federal government for many years has grossly interfered with our states' business . . . That's true whether it's in the area of energy, education, highways, the environment or whatever. The more we can reduce this Federal-government interference, the better off we'll all be. I'm convinced that . . . we [in the states] can do a better job of making and enforcing regulations without interference from Washington.

Interview/
U.S. News & World Report, 12-14:65.

William S. Cohen
United States Senator, R—Maine

2

There must be a redefinition of the role of Congressmen. We have held ourselves as being everything, ombudsmen and legislators. I would dare say 60 per cent of our work is casework, which is far more important to constituents than any bills we're considering. Frankly, we've encouraged that. It's good politics. But there has come a point where we're so preoccupied with constituent services that we simply don't have the time to reflect. One study said Congressmen had 17 minutes a day to think.

Interview/Chicago Tribune, 3-18:(1)4.

Archibald Cox
Chairman, Common Cause

3

[On the process of confirmation by the Senate of Presidential appointees]: Common Cause has worked to do what we can to make the confirmation process a serious inquiry, and will continue to work for that. There's a tendency at the beginning of a President's term to say, "Well,

unless there's something that totally disqualifies a man, the President ought to be able to choose who he wants to choose—particularly the Cabinet officers." But when the confirmation process comes to judges, for example, there should surely be a very serious inquiry into a man's qualifications and into whether he has the ethical standards that are important to the judge.

Interview/
Los Angeles Herald Examiner, 1-19:(A)2.

Ed Davis
California State Senator (R);
Former Chief of Police of Los Angeles

4

[On what makes government tick]: Special interests. About 90 per cent of all legislation is conceived by special interests. It is merchandised by special interests. And probably less than 5 per cent is inspired by Governors, by individual legislators, by government itself. You say, "Oh, isn't that evil!" The answer is, hell no, it isn't evil. That's what a democracy is all about; and the special interests are the labor unions and management associations, chambers of commerce, agricultural interests and farm workers. What's happening in the [state] legislature and what's happening in Washington is the elitists are on their way out and the pragmatists—the ones who believe in representing the people—are in, and they're going to be in more and more. The people are tired of elitists.

Interview, Sacramento/
Los Angeles Times, 1-19:(I)18.

Byron L. Dorgan
United States Representative,
D—North Dakota

5

. . . I find Congress much like any other collection of Americans; I've found a generous dose of the best and the brightest and also some of the dull and dullest. I've discovered that there aren't any higher truths in Washington. The Congress is fairly closely controlled; a lot of us run around and a few run Congress. And we

(BYRON L. DORGAN)

have to try and get some attention to try and make a dent in the consciousness of the few who determine the agenda and the issues.

Panel discussion, Washington/
The New York Times, 6-14:(4)5.

Thomas J. Downey
United States Representative, D—New York

1

The lobbying process is fueled by campaign contributions. The correlation between contributions and [law-makers'] votes is remarkable.

U.S. News & World Report, 2-23:26.

Peter F. Drucker
Professor of social science, Claremont (Calif.)
College Graduate School

2

The old saw by which government has operated—"If at first you don't succeed, try, try again"—is a recipe for malfunction. The statistical laws say, "If at first you don't succeed, try once more—and then do something else." Government needs to act in accordance with this law, and that is beginning to happen. A more realistic view of the need to abandon programs is developing because nobody really believes any more that government delivers. Even in matters of defense—the purpose for which government was instituted among men—no government can promise any longer that it can protect civilians and that they are not going to be harmed by wars. And government can no longer control the economy, because the world economy controls all of us. National governments have become totally impotent. The only ones that do reasonably well are those that take their cue from the world economy, like Japan.

Interview/U.S. News & World Report, 12-21:75.

David Durenberger
United States Senator, R—Minnesota

3

[Criticizing President Reagan's "new Federalism" program of turning powers back to state

and local governments]: [The Reagan Administration has] been cutting and capping and blocking with no sense of where we are going. And we aren't going back to Bunker Hill and the Boston Tea Party. There is more to the Federal role than defense and interstate commerce. I hope we haven't lived two centuries with the genius of the Federal system to forget the things it can accomplish. Do we remember the struggle for civil rights to bring minorities and the handicapped into the mainstream of our society? Do we remember what Federal research funds have accomplished to improve the health of our citizens? Do we remember that higher education has been a national purpose...?

Before National League of Cities,
Detroit, Dec. 1/
Los Angeles Times, 12-3:(I)16.

Bobbi Fiedler
United States Representative, R—California

4

There's far too much legislation and not enough plain gut work being done around here [in Washington]. I resent the fact that my time, which I consider to be valuable, is wasted running back and forth to the House chamber for routine votes. We could perhaps meet fewer days of the year and concentrate our workload. It's much too fragmented now.

Panel discussion, Washington/
The New York Times, 6-14:(4)5.

Gerald R. Ford
Former President of the United States

5

[The threat of assassination is] part of the job [of being President]—the peril of the profession, if you will. There's no way you can get 100 per cent security unless you sit in the White House immunized. But you can't isolate yourself. The job entails certain responsibilities. One of those responsibilities is moving around, seeing people and appearing in public. If you're in the job, you have to accept that gamble.

Interview/Time, 4-13:37.

Mark S. Fowler
Chairman,
Federal Communications Commission

1

Simply stated, we will eliminate all unnecessary regulations and policies. The functions of the FCC need radical surgery. Without question there are rules and programs at the Commission that are either anachronistic or otherwise irrelevant in light of changes in the technological and social environment. The continued enforcement of pointless rules and policies imposes costs on business, discourages individual initiative and weighs down the government. The common thread that runs through these objectives like a bright, scarlet ribbon, is what I call—perhaps ungrammatically—"unregulation." Insofar as a regulatory philosophy of government, we shall not be moving toward 1984, but away from it.

At National Cable Television Association
convention, Los Angeles, May 31/
The Washington Post,
6-1:(Washington Business)3.

John Kenneth Galbraith
Professor emeritus of economics,
Harvard University

2

There is no way to run a modern economy without a large number of bureaucrats [in government]. So just as I don't join in the crusade to get rid of the big corporations, I don't join the crusade to get rid of the bureaucrats. We should always bear in mind in the Federal government and state governments . . . and in city governments . . . there are a very large number of hard-working, devoted people, and I don't think we do ourselves or them any good by these attacks [on government bureaucracy]. I've said many times that attacking bureaucrats is the only form of racism allowed in the United States and I'm not in favor of it. I think our public servants are generally good people.

Interview, San Francisco/
San Francisco Examiner & Chronicle, 5-17:(Review)4.

Clifford A. Goldman
State Treasurer of New Jersey

3

[On the Reagan Administration's proposal to cut Federal aid to states but change to block grants instead of categorical grants]: The flexibility offered by the block-grant concept is excellent. We can adjust the funds to where they are needed without having to make applications to Washington, and we can respond to local conditions more rapidly. However, the cuts in funding will remove some of that flexibility and create crisis situations that will take a great deal of time to iron out. The program is a mixed blessing, and, on balance, we'd be better off with the way we are with 100 per cent financing.

The New York Times, 3-22:(1)18.

Donald Haider
Professor of public management,
Northwestern University

4

It's hard to think of a major function of state or local government today that does not involve Federal money and regulations. Today, state and local governments receive about 23 per cent of their funds from Washington. Twenty years ago, that figure was only 13 per cent. With this funding has come all the attendant Federal mandates, requirements and cross-cutting conditions that erode state and local authority. The Federal government tends to take over policy leadership in nearly every area where it provides assistance. Even where funds haven't been provided, Congress has mandated responsibilities upon state and local governments—drinking-water standards, handicap requirements and contributions to unemployment compensation, to name a few. These are examples of Federal regulations being imposed without accompanying Federal support.

Interview/
U.S. News & World Report,
5-11:59.

Alexander M. Haig, Jr.
Secretary of State-designate
of the United States

1

[The Constitution and the Presidency] are intimately related in every sense of the word. I have witnessed two, three or maybe even four Presidents at reasonably close range, and the point I'm trying to make is that the office itself, the institution of the Presidency, is an extremely important safeguard for our people. [That often] has lead less than perhaps perfect men constantly to feel the weight of that office itself and to inevitably make judgments in terms of how they are going to be judged by history.

At Senate Foreign Relations Committee hearing
on his confirmation, Washington, Jan. 9/
The Washington Post, 1-10:(A)7.

Ernest F. Hollings
United States Senator, D—South Carolina

2

. . . it was government that really instituted the land policy that opened up the frontier and gave homesteads to millions of Americans. And when it became difficult to travel, it was the government that instituted the land grants that brought the railroads to the West. And it was government, when it became difficult to bring products to market, that developed the waterways and the ports. When we had the industrial revolution, it was the government that put the legal underpinnings to corporate America so they could compete. And at the time of the Depression, when the only question was the economic survival of this country, it was government programs that saved this nation . . . we should be proud of government and quit scaring the American people with all this tommyrot about deregulation, decontrol and get-rid-of-government.

Interview/The Washington Post, 5-18:(A)13.

Harold E. Hughes
Former United States Senator, D—Iowa

3

. . . if you have an alcoholic in Congress, the results of that disease are transmitted to more people than in any other capacity I can think of . . . Congressional alcoholism needs more attention because their [the legislators'] decisions have far more effect on people's lives and their safety than decisions elsewhere.

Los Angeles Times, 3-2:(I)7.

E. Pendleton James
Special Assistant to the President
of the United States for Personnel

4

[On regulations governing conflicts of interest and ethics in the appointment of government personnel]: We have no quarrel with the intent of the law, which is that the men and women chosen to serve in the senior levels of government have no conflicts of interest. My argument is that the law was written in the post-Watergate hysteria to purify government. It was written in haste and should be cleaned up. We could achieve the same results and not slow down the process of these appointments . . . I fully understand the need to investigate the financial background and holdings of a candidate for appointment to ensure there is no conflict in his financial personal wealth that might interfere with his judgment on issues coming before him in his government job. But to allow that to become a public document that everybody has access to, other than those authorized to examine such documents, is clearly an invasion of privacy.

Interview/Nation's Business, August:29.

Vernon E. Jordan, Jr.
President, National Urban League

5

[On the attempted-assassination shooting of President Reagan]: Even the most outspoken opponents of his economic program, including myself, like him as a human being, respect the office he holds, and abhor violence of any kind, especially violence of the sort we witnessed in Washington. I want to back him when I think he is right. And I want to oppose him when I think he is wrong. I want the opportunity to educate him to my way of thinking and, if I fail,

(VERNON E. JORDAN, JR.)

want to know that I must respect his views with the same tolerance with which he must respect mine. And in a democracy, I do not want a man with a gun to deprive me of my President, for, right or wrong, he is my President and the symbol of my nation's authority and leadership. America chose Ronald Reagan to be its President, and all Americans want him to serve his term in the White House for the next four years. The President is the President of all of the people, and all of the people have a stake in his ability to discharge the functions of his office. We all have a stake in the stability of the government. We all realize that our freedoms are endangered when dangerous weapons in the hands of people with twisted minds replace the political process.

Before National Urban League, April 3/
The Washington Post, 4-5:(C)7.

Jack Kemp
United States Representative, R—New York

1

[On what can get in the way of a government implementing its policies]: . . . the word that came to my mind was "timidity." Trepidation. Defeatism. The status quo. President-elect Reagan said many times that *status quo* was Latin for the mess we're in . . . Once you take power, the forces that say, "Don't change, don't follow out your agenda," seem to take over. But the one thing I think those of us who want to move quickly and dramatically and boldly have going for us is Ronald Reagan himself. I believe he is committed—intellectually, emotionally, politically and in every other way—to that type of decisiveness that [Douglas] MacArthur talked about when he said that in order to establish authority, precipitate action immediately.

Interview/The Washington Post, 1-20:(A)21.

Susan B. King
Former Chairman, Consumer Product Safety Commission of the United States

2

The question isn't the number of [government] regulations but the quality and subject of regulations. One of my greatest concerns has been that a statute normally is passed at a time of crisis, and often entire agencies are created to respond to a specific problem. For every law you pass, that's only the beginning of the questions to come . . . There are too many regulations because of questions from the private sector: "Can we do this? Can we do that?" Industry wants an answer. They don't care what it is, just an answer. Industry has a desire for certainty . . . We have to respond to all of them, and the vast majority are from industry. Then everybody starts criticizing the agency for saying too much . . . This controversy over whether an agency had over-extended its authority or violated its Congressional mandate would not have arisen if Congress had exercised its power through the appropriations, authorization and oversight process to look at the agencies. It's hard work, and they've avoided it for 15 years. It's in their power to say, "We don't want you to be doing this."

Interview, Washington/
Chicago Tribune, 7-12:(1)12.

Richard Lamm
Governor of Colorado (D)

3

For 200 years, our nation had a Federal system of government as opposed to a central government. Dual sovereignty was intended to buttress our system of checks and balances and to provide through the states a level of government that was closer to the people while far enough away to avoid being captured by parochial interests. Today, the states stand in danger of being eclipsed by the Federal government they created. The past 50 years have witnessed an increase in the concentration of financial and policy-making responsibilities at the Federal level. Erosion of the states' role threatens to undermine a truly Federal system of governance whose diversity and strength have been critical to the success of the American democratic experiment.

Interview, Denver/
U.S. News & World Report, 3-2:80.

WHAT THEY SAID IN 1981

Elliott Levitas
United States Representative, D—Georgia

1

We have not only created an imbalance between Federal and state government, but we have exacerbated the imbalance by placing so much power in the bureaucracies with their regulatory and enforcement power . . . We've created an animal that is much more powerful than the Congress and the President.

U.S. News & World Report, 5-11:48.

George M. Low
President,
Rensselaer Polytechnic Institute

2

. . . today we have made it nearly impossible for our best people to join their government without enormous sacrifice. Chances are that if they have worked for an oil company, they will not be asked to work for the Department of Energy; or if they are asked, they will have to run the gauntlet of trial by the media and endless hearings, and will be accused of all kinds of mischief; and finally, they will foreclose the possibility of returning to their industry, and earning a living, after service. It is curious to note that, by our current standards, it is a conflict for a businessman to work in an agency of government that deals with the industry he comes from; yet it is not a conflict for a consumer advocate to work in an agency that has as its primary goal the protection of the consumer . . . We now have to re-establish the view that government service is a high calling, and at the same time we must see to it that those who accept the responsibility of service are accorded fair treatment. If we don't, we will forgo excellence in favor of the mediocre.

Before American Society of Mechanical Engineers,
Chicago/The Wall Street Journal, 2-2:17.

Theodore J. Lowi
Professor of American institutions,
Cornell University

3

The theory of American democracy has been changed drastically in the past generation. As we became a big government centered on the Presidency, our civic education was changed accordingly. We've been led to believe that if government centers in the Presidency, therefore it's effective. Yet we have every indication that it's not. It's like the dinosaur—an enormous body and a tiny head. We believe that the head of this dinosaur is so potent and so wise that it can make appropriate and effective choice. But it cannot.

Interview/U.S. News & World Report, 2-2:24.

Charles T. Manatt
Chairman, Democratic National Committee

4

The fundamental difference between the [Democratic and Republican] parties quickly reasserts itself, and classically so, in a Republican Reagan era. Republicans believe the government that governs least governs best. You can see that in their approach to the "safety net" [for needy people] that he [President Reagan] talks about and then violates with his proposed changes in Social Security. The Democratic vision is that government is a concept of cooperation whereby people collectively can achieve more of the greater good acting together than they can as individuals.

Interview/The Washington Post, 5-18:(A)13.

Mike Mansfield
United States Ambassador to Japan;
Former United States Senator, D—Montana

5

Out here [as Ambassador] I have a chance to think things through and arrive at considered judgments, good or bad. That was impossible in the Congress. One of the reasons I left the Senate was because the pressures were getting to be too many, and all too often I voted without knowing what I was voting on and therefore I made many mistakes. From what I see of the Senate, it hasn't gotten any better, and I'm more glad than ever that I left when I did.

Interview, Tokyo/
Los Angeles Times, 11-27:(1-A)3.

Charles McC. Mathias, Jr.
United States Senator, R—Maryland

1

[On problems President Reagan has had with his aides David Stockman and Richard Allen regarding their judgment and alleged improprieties on their part]: [The Stockman and Allen affairs are] following a distressingly familiar pattern. [Former President Jimmy] Carter had it in his first year and never recovered from it. If you put the records of recent Presidents on a graph, the whole thing would be very similar. It's part of the first-year shakedown cruise. The real test is whether a President recovers from it, whether he recognizes the problem and deals with it.

Los Angeles Times, 11-19:(I)7.

Robert P. Mayo
President, Federal Reserve Bank of Chicago; Former Director, Federal Office of Management and Budget

2

[On the Reagan Administration's intent to cut Federal spending]: Every agency and every constituency being hurt by the reductions will scream bloody murder. But the motto for a successful [Federal] Budget Director has to be to try to be unfair to everyone.

Interview, Chicago/Chicago Tribune, 2-16:(4)7.

James A. McClure
United States Senator, R—Idaho

3

[Supporting broadcast coverage of Senate proceedings]: It has been suggested that if television and radio broadcasting were begun in the Senate, it would open a Pandora's box. Senators, wishing to gain wider national reputations or possibly improve their standing in the polls, would be tempted to abuse the broadcasting system ... Another often-expressed argument against bringing cameras and microphones into the Senate relates to the image Americans will see during the course of the day's activities. It has been suggested that if the public observes a chamber of empty chairs, they may assume that the Senators are not working. And those against the idea of TV coverage have pointed out that this inaccurate interpretation of their government could further erode the reputation of individual Senators and the body as a whole ... [But] if there are empty chairs and empty rhetoric, the people have a right to know. The Senate is not a private club created to serve its members' needs. It's a duly-elected legislative body meant to serve at their behest—and at the pleasure of the American people.

Before Senate Rules Committee, Washington/ The Washington Post, 5-20:(A)22.

Charles McDowell
Washington columnist, "The Richmond (Va.) Times Dispatch"

4

To be a good American, you're supposed to respect the law, pay your taxes and assume that Congress is just a bunch of boobs ... But for those of us who've been around Washington a long time, Congress is just filled with really interesting people, and there's humor and humanity all around you.

The Washington Post TV Magazine, 9-6:3.

George S. McGovern
Former United States Senator, D—South Dakota

5

I think we'll go through a period where conservatives are kind of the vogue thing of the day, but my guess is that the problems of this country are going to demand more, rather than less, activity on the part of the government. And people will see this as we grapple with the continuing problems of energy development, the decline of our transportation system, the growing challenge of crime, the environmental dangers. Those are all problems that are not going to be resolved purely by private business—they are going to require a very strong role by the government, too. So my guess is that we'll go through a period of tightening up government programs—which is not all bad; some of them probably do deserve to be tightened up—and

(GEORGE S. McGOVERN)

then we'll begin to see there are certain other initiatives we have to take through the government to meet our problems. And that's where the liberals come back into power.

Interview/
Los Angeles Herald Examiner, 3-16:(A)11.

Edwin Meese III
Counsellor to the President
of the United States

1

I would say that the [Reagan Administration's] use of "Cabinet government" has been done very effectively. The Cabinet members like it. They have fully realized the authority and responsibility that goes with their offices. The President does hold them accountable for what happens in their departments. The Cabinet meetings have been worthwhile. Cabinet members who have served in prior Administrations have indicated they have been the most successful and substantive Cabinet meetings they have ever attended.

Interview, Washington/
The Christian Science Monitor, 4-6:12.

James C. Miller III
Associate Director for Information and
Regulatory Affairs, Federal Office of
Management and Budget

2

[The problem with government regulation often stems from the fact that] the legislation is faulty in many cases. Sometimes it tells people to do things that don't make sense, and at other times it gives agencies a great deal of discretion to promulgate meddlesome regulations that have little basis in fact and are extremely costly relative to their marginal benefits.

Interview, Washington/
Los Angeles Herald Examiner, 2-2:(A)6.

William G. Milliken
Governor of Michigan (R)

3

In my 12 years as Governor, I've seen a general and steady movement of power, authority and responsibility to the Federal government. I've seen Washington set up standards and requirements that complicate the job of efficient administration by states. One of the most disturbing trends is the shift away from broad-based grants toward narrow, categorical programs. In the last five years, categorical grants have grown by about 65 per cent and general-purpose grants have dropped by nearly 30 per cent. It is essential that we reverse this trend.

Interview/U.S. News & World Report, 5-11:55.

Walter F. Mondale
Vice President of the United States

4

. . . a President, in my opinion, starts out with a bank full of good-will, and, slowly, checks are drawn on that, and it's very rare that it's replenished. It's a one-time deposit. And you have to be careful. The more you do to encourage public trust, the longer those reserves are there. And a President's power is not to be found much in the law or in the institutional strength of the President. It's there, but it's almost totally a matter of public confidence and trust. When that exists, everything is possible, overseas and at home.

Interview/The Washington Post, 1-20:(A)21.

Walter F. Mondale
Former Vice President of the
United States

5

[On being Vice President under Jimmy Carter]: If I disagreed with other advisers or even the President on something serious, I'd always make my argument alone, in private, with him. I didn't want to be in a position where these things were reported, where he couldn't talk to me in candor and might have to read about it in the paper. To be effective, you have to be willing not to get public credit. You must keep the

(WALTER F. MONDALE)

President's confidence. If I couldn't support something. I just told him I didn't want to talk about it. He never pressed me to do it. Looking back on the arrangement, I didn't ask myself why it had succeeded, but why it hadn't happened so much earlier? The President has so much to do, this country has so much work to do—to waste that office [the Vice Presidency] is an abomination. We can't afford it.

Interview/
The Saturday Evening Post, September:62.

Daniel P. Moynihan
United States Senator, D—New York

1

. . . we [Democrats] have embodied a great idea, which is that an elected government can be the instrument of the common purpose of a free people; that government can embrace great causes, and do great things . . . We *believe* in American government and we fully expect that those who denigrate it, and even despise it, will soon or late find themselves turning to it in necessity, even desperation.

At Gridiron Club, Washington/
The Washington Post, 5-18:(A)13.

David R. Obey
United States Representative, D—Wisconsin

2

[On the Reagan Administration's plans to shift Federal programs to the states]: I'm not against turning over to the states a good deal more responsibility than they have now. But there are national interests that must be defended by the national government, or they will not be defended by anybody. Our natural resources, for instance, very often cross state lines. Transit problems often involve more than one state. A poorly educated child moves around and can provide serious burdens for other areas besides the one in which he was educated. Some of our basic civil rights guaranteed by the United States Constitution have not always been upheld by local jurisdictions. Water is a natural

resource every bit as important to our long-term national survival as oil, coal and food. And there are others. We have to be very careful about whether we transfer totally to states those programs meant to guarantee that the national interest is served. There has to be Federal guidance in the way these problems are addressed, so that you don't have jurisdictions stumbling over one another.

Interview/
U.S. News & World Report, 12-14:65.

J. E. Olson
Vice chairman, American
Telephone & Telegraph Company

3

Many of our most pressing problems right now in this country stem from our own willingness to sink into the soft security—or what many of us assume to be security—of growing government stewardship of our lives. In essence, we have simply taken [the late President] John Kennedy's call of the early '60s, "Ask not what your country can do for you; ask what you can do for your country," and turned it around. We asked what our country could do for us. And government responded, as governments are wont to do, by trying to do it all.

At DePauw University commencement/
The Christian Science Monitor, 6-17:14.

Thomas P. O'Neill, Jr.
United States Representative,
D—Massachusetts

4

[Criticizing President Reagan's budget proposals]: Sure, in the 1970s my [Democratic] party made mistakes. We over-regulated. There was too much red tape and probably too much legislation. And we paid for it at the ballot box last year . . . [But] do you want to meat-ax the programs that made America great? Or do you want to go slow in correcting the errors of the past?

At House debate on budget, Washington/
Newsweek, 5-18:39.

Ronald E. Paul
United States Representative, R—Texas

1

Everybody's real optimistic that [President] Reagan is going to turn off the [spending] spigot of government. But I'm less optimistic. The momentum of big government is so strong that even good intentions and big words are not going to be enough. Turning off the spigot is much more difficult than people realize.

Interview, Washington, Jan. 20/
The Washington Post, 1-21:(A)31.

Prince Philip
Duke of Edinburgh

2

Many democracies have voted themselves into the hands of bureaucracies; it does not always need a revolution in the name of the working class to create a dictatorship by a bureaucracy. And all bureaucracies are inevitably middle-class. Once started, such a process is difficult to reverse, and it usually only comes to an end when it founders under the weight of its own inefficiency.

Interview/U.S. News & World Report, 2-9:45.

Jerrold Post
Founding member, International
Society of Political Psychology

3

It is striking to observe the number of countries in our modern world which are led by men well in their late 60s and 70s. Particularly in Oriental societies such as China and Japan, where age is venerated, gerontocracies are the norm rather than the exception. Part of it is the value these societies place on wisdom. Particularly if an individual has had a rewarding and self-actualizing career, he may in old age contribute a dispassionate wisdom based on a lifetime's experience.

Los Angeles Times, 5-16:(I)1.

Ronald Reagan
President-elect of the United States

4

For a long time we've lived with the fallacy

that the people demand this or that, and therefore Congress or government has only done what the people have wanted. But most legislation is spawned by government agencies. They volunteer programs, and once this is done, then you create a group that is getting a benefit from the government at the expense of their fellow citizens. They want to keep getting that benefit, and they don't realize that as those special-interest groups have spawned, everybody is benefiting at the expense of someone else.

Interview, Pacific Palisades, Calif./
Newsweek, 1-26:51.

Ronald Reagan
President of the United States

5

From time to time we have been tempted to believe that society has become too complex to be managed by self-rule, that government by an elite group is superior to government for, by and of the people. But if no one among us is capable of governing himself, then who among us has the capacity to govern someone else?

Inaugural address, Washington, Jan. 20/
Los Angeles Times, 1-21:(I)16.

6

We are a nation that has a government—not the other way around. And this makes us special among the nations of the earth. Our government has no power except that granted it by the people. It is time to check and reverse the growth of government which shows signs of having grown beyond the consent of the governed. It is my intention to curb the size and influence of the Federal establishment and to demand recognition of the distinction between the powers granted to the Federal government and those reserved to the states or to the people. All of us need to be reminded that the Federal government did not create the states; the states created the Federal government. And, so there will be no misunderstanding, it's not my intention to do away with government. It is rather to make it work—work with us, not over us; to stand by our side, not ride on our back. Government can

(RONALD REAGAN)

and must provide opportunity, not smother it; foster productivity, not stifle it.

Inaugural address, Washington, Jan. 20/
Los Angeles Times, 1-21:(I)16.

1

[I have] made mention of changing categorical [Federal] grants to states and local governments into block grants. We know, of course, that categorical-grant programs burden local and state governments with a mass of Federal regulations and Federal paper-work. Ineffective targeting, wasteful administrative overhead—all can be eliminated by shifting the resources and decision-making authority to local and state governments. This will also consolidate programs which are scattered throughout the Federal bureaucracy.

Before joint session of Congress, Washington,
Feb. 18/The New York Times, 2-19:14.

2

[On waste and fraud in government]: One government estimate indicated that fraud alone may account for anywhere from 1 to 10 per cent—as much as $25-billion of Federal expenditures for social programs. If the tax dollars that are wasted or mismanaged are added to this fraud total, the staggering dimensions of this problem begin to emerge . . . No Administration can promise to immediately stop a trend that has grown in recent years as quickly as government expenditures themselves. But let me say this: Waste and fraud in the Federal budget is exactly what I called it before—an unrelenting national scandal, a scandal we are bound and determined to do something about.

Before joint session of Congress, Washington,
Feb. 18/The New York Times, 2-19:14.

3

[It must be remembered] that government has certain legitimate functions which it can perform very well; that it can be responsive to the people, that it can be humane and compassionate; but that when it undertakes tasks that are not its proper province it can do none of them as well or as economically as the private sector . . . We forgot to challenge the notion that the state is the principal vehicle of social change; or that millions of social interactions among free individuals and institutions can do more to foster economic and social progress than all the careful schemes of government planners.

At University of Notre Dame commencement,
May 17/The Christian Science Monitor, 5-18:13.

4

Today the Federal government takes too much taxes from the people, too much authority from the states and too much liberty with the Constitution. One of our next goals is to renew the concept of Federalism. The changes will be as exciting and even more profound in the long run than the changes produced by our economic package . . . The Founding Fathers saw the Federalist system as constructed something like a masonry wall. The states are the bricks, the national government is the mortar. For the structure to stand plumb with the Constitution, there must be a mix of that brick and mortar. Unfortunately, over the years many people have increasingly come to believe that Washington is the whole wall—a wall that leans, sags and bulges under its own weight.

Before National Conference of State Legislators,
Atlanta, July 30/
Chicago Tribune, 7-31:(1)1,3.

5

We've instituted a Cabinet system of government, and I think this has been very successful. Now, you might say, "Well, we've always had had a Cabinet"—but not a Cabinet that met regularly and debated and discussed, like a board of directors. The only difference between what we have and a board-of-directors meeting is that we don't take a vote. When I've heard enough of the debate to satisfy my needs about knowing, then *I* make the decision. I believe in

(RONALD REAGAN)

this because it is really the only way to execute a job this big. The trap you could fall into would be trying to keep your finger on every single detail.

Interview, Washington/
U.S. News & World Report, 12-28:26.

Donald T. Regan
Secretary of the Treasury
of the United States

1

[On the cut-back in government services as a result of spending limitations]: Our test is going to be whether or not the average person in the U.S., looking at all the things that he or she is engaged in, will sublimate the one or two things that are important to them for the over-all good of everything . . . It is going to take time to get it over. With the government cutting back, people are going to say, "Well, gee, you know, what am I going to do? Is my county government going to do it? Is my state government going to do it? Who is going to do this for me?" And pretty soon it's going to dawn on them that an awful lot is going to have to be done by themselves.

Time, 3-23:14.

Warren Rudman
United States Senator,
R—New Hampshire

2

The rules of the Senate do not give you the opportunity to be really informed on some of the issues that are being debated . . . People elected us to come down here and use our best judgment on issues facing the country. Unfortunately, because of the system of hearings and other duties, you become heavily reliant on committee staffs and your own staff. As a result, I think staffs, particularly committee staffs, play far too important a role in the running of the Senate.

Interview/
U.S. News & World Report, 10-5:46.

Patricia Schroeder
United States Representative, D—Colorado

3

Some new legislators come here [to Washington] with a grade-school civics-class notion about Congress being the greatest debating body in the free world. Instead, they discover the workload is so enormous that lawmaking sometimes has to be put aside.

U.S. News & World Report, 3-2:39.

Charles E. Schumer
United States Representative, D—New York

4

Brooklyn [his district] is a very urban environment. It's very dependent on government services. My constituents need mass transit to get to work. The private housing market doesn't work without government help. They want more police to keep down crime. There's no breathing room. In Phoenix, people might feel they can do things on their own; but in Brooklyn, government is a necessity.

Interview, Washington/
The New York Times, 1-18:(1)10.

Irving S. Shapiro
Chairman, E. I. du Pont
de Nemours & Company

5

Obviously, there are fields in which regulation is a necessity, and only government can do it. On the other hand, government has no self-restraint. Once it has power, it tends to exercise its maximum power without reservation. That's the heart of the problem. No one would argue that the Food and Drug Administration shouldn't control drugs. The issue is really, how do you do it, how much control do you exercise, what tradeoffs do you consider? And government isn't very good at dealing with those kinds of issues . . .

Interview/
The Washington Post, 2-8:(G)1.

Joe Silbey
Professor of American history,
Cornell University

1

The breakdown of the [political] parties means that we now have a society constantly at war with itself, resolving issues not by coalition-building and compromise but by confrontation. The spirit of coalition says that you don't ride tractors down Constitution Avenue in Washington to win specific farm prices. It says that you do not go out into the streets on behalf of a set of social ideas. But those approaches are now attractive to people because they see no alternatives. And if the society is frightened enough, it gives in to demonstrators. The result is a massive program of government activities that culminate in permanent inflation, permanent government extravagance.

Interview/
U.S. News & World Report, 5-25:74.

Richard A. Snelling
Governor of Vermont (R)

2

I think it's very clear that the Federal government has intervened in many areas where they need not intervene in order to assure people of their Constitutional rights and to promote the general welfare . . . [But] if [President] Reagan means that there is no cause for governmental support of programs at the Federal level to assure equality of opportunity and of capacity across the state borders, then I would say simply that I see no Constitutional justification for that. That view was absolutely rejected by the Federalist papers . . . I frankly believe that the Constitution's call for power to implement the Bill of Rights, with respect to the common welfare, requires the Federal government to assist the states when the states do not have the capacity to afford the citizens their Constitutional rights.

Interview/
The New York Times, 12-6:(4)3.

Larry Speakes
Deputy Press Secretary to the
President of the United States

3

[On the functioning of the White House in the wake of the shooting of President Reagan]: Basically, there is no division of authority. The President remains the President. The White House did not skip a beat. The government did not skip a beat. The White House performed effectively. There was not a single ripple.

Washington, March 31/
Los Angeles Times, 4-1:(I)B.

Stuart M. Statler
Acting Chairman, Consumer Product
Safety Commission of the United States

4

The concept of independent regulatory commissions needs rethinking: Independence from whom and for what purpose? The theory underlying the independent commission was enlightened; but changing economic and political circumstances can make obsolete even the boldest of ideas . . . The vaunted independence of these agencies already has been very much diluted. Today, one must question its continued value when viewed against a growing public mandate for more-efficient, coordinated and less-burdensome government . . . Good government suggests that the President be able to direct and implement national policy to the greatest extent possible. The President must be able to successfully pursue the goals for which he was elected. But to prevent the President from tackling large sectors of the economy that are regulated by a host of independent regulatory commissions . . . may well be self-defeating.

The Washington Post, 4-30:(A)22.

David A. Stockman
Director, Federal Office of
Management and Budget

5

I don't believe that there is any entitlement, any basic right to [government-financed] legal services or any other kind of services. And the

(DAVID A. STOCKMAN)

idea that's been established over the last 10 years that almost every service that someone might need in life ought to be provided, financed by the government as a matter of basic right, is wrong. We challenge that. We reject that notion.

Broadcast interview/"Issues and Answers,"
American Broadcasting Company, 3-22:

Richard L. Strout
Political columnist,
"The Christian Science Monitor"

1

The public really doesn't understand the office of the Presidency. Again and again, they create a superman. Then when the people discover that he can't put into effect the things everybody wants, they're apt to destroy him. I fear that if this country really gets into a jam—a nuclear confrontation or something of that sort—our Constitution would make it possible for us to become a dictatorship more easily than other democracies. In time of war, we just automatically turn to the President. He can gather powers that are not acceptable in peacetime because of his vested authority as Commander-in-Chief. Abraham Lincoln, perhaps our greatest President, took extra-Constitutional measures during the Civil War. It's easy to see how, if you get someone like a [former President Richard] Nixon in office, it would be possible in a time of crisis to fall into a pattern in which it would be hard to distinguish the President from the proverbial man on horseback.

Interview/U.S. News & World Report, 7-20:59.

James L. Sundquist
Senior fellow, Brookings Institution

2

Rarely have so many Americans been so thoroughly convinced that their national government has not been working well. Public confidence in our leaders and our institutions has fallen to appalling levels.

Los Angeles Times, 1-9:(I)1,16.

Margaret Thatcher
Prime Minister of the United Kingdom

3

We believe that governments serve the people and not the other way around, [and] that governments are instituted to secure the rights of men. We will not allow bureaucratic convenience to be given priority over personal liberty. In his inaugural address, the [U.S.] President [Reagan] said that, in the present crisis, government is not the solution, it is the problem. I warmly agree. The results of the last elections in our two countries have shown that our people agree.

Before Pilgrims Society, London, Jan. 29/
Los Angeles Times, 1-30:(I)15.

4

Never let it be said that a person of my political beliefs . . . does not want strong government. We do; strong in the things that government, and only government, can do. The government has to be strong in defense, strong in upholding and enforcing the rule of law, strong to maintain the value of the currency, strong to protect the integrity of the nation, the individual and his freedom. Only government can do those things. But it must not intrude too much on the things which the people do better than government.

Interview, London/Time, 2-16:36.

Strom Thurmond
United States Senator,
R—South Carolina

5

. . . the [Federal] budget has been balanced only one time in 20 years. Congress has not shown the courage to do it. There are so many special forces converging on Congress for appropriations and special consideration that the pressures are tremendous. It is better for the public and better for Congress, too, if a balanced budget is mandated by a Constitutional amendment . . . This amendment would limit Federal spending to a certain pecentage of the gross national product and would provide that the

(STROM THURMOND)

government cannot spend more than it takes in unless 60 per cent of the House and Senate agree to it. I don't know if Congress will approve it. But there is strong sentiment for it if the Administration recommends and supports it.

Interview/
U.S. News & World Report,
3-23:41.

Richard S. Williamson
Assistant to the President of the United States
for Intergovernmental Affairs   1

The tremendous growth of the infrastructure of state and local governments has created a greater sophistication and ability for problem-solving that just did not exist 30 years ago. [President] Reagan does not believe that wisdom and compassion is a monopoly on the banks of the Potomac. He feels that state and local officials are closer to the people and therefore more accountable.

The Christian Science Monitor, 5-18:13.

Law . The Judiciary

Floyd Abrams
Constitutional lawyer

1

[On television broadcasting of trials]: I believe that it will lead to a better judiciary. The added scrutiny of the camera will help us deal with problems of corrupt prosecutors, of defendants who are too close to judges, or judges who have a tendency to doze off. Television will be an additional check on governmental abuse and, as such, a good thing.

San Francisco Examiner & Chronicle,
3-1:(This World)24.

F. Lee Bailey
Lawyer

2

The legal profession is a business with a tremendous collection of egos. Few people who are not strong egotistically gravitate to it. If they do, they wind up in the archives or doing tax returns, or they stay as junior partners in a law firm for the rest of their lives. To get ahead, you've got to assert yourself. That's the lawyer's stock in trade.

Interview/U.S. News & World Report, 9-14:73.

Melvin Belli
Lawyer

3

Contrary to what a lot of people think, we [lawyers] don't coach witnesses. We do tell them how to say things so they're more palatable, but I don't ask a guy if he's guilty, because it's such a mixed question of ethics and fact. I think it's the silliest thing a lawyer could ask a client, because you're guilty only if the jury says you're guilty. The good criminal lawyers that I know don't say that they have to believe in their client. I think that there's never a deed so foul that something couldn't be said for the guy

and that's why there are lawyers, to try to do something for that poor bastard.

Interview, Los Angeles/
Los Angeles Times, 12-18:(V)31.

Thomas Buergenthal
Dean, Washington College of Law,
American University

4

The study of law is the search for justice, for the equitable resolution of conflict, for tolerance. The search for justice is not easy. That is why the study of law cannot and should not be easy; that is why we ask more questions than we know the answers to.

To first-year American University law students,
Washington/The Washington Post, 8-30:(C)6.

Warren E. Burger
Chief Justice of the United States

5

No one questions that a criminal conviction should always be open to correct a miscarriage of justice. But no other system in the world invites our [U.S.] kind of never-ending warfare with society, long after criminal guilt has been established, beyond reasonable doubt, with all the safeguards of due process. Our system has moved thoughful, sensitive observers who are dedicated to individual liberty to ask: "Is guilt irrelevant?"

At George Washington University School of Law
commencement, May 24/
The Washington Post, 5-26:(A)19.

Archibald Cox
Professor of law, Harvard University

6

[Saying he opposes the Reagan Administration's plan to dismantle the Federal Legal

(ARCHIBALD COX)

Services Corporation]: I oppose it because I think it would surely result in denials of equal justice under law. A humane and rich society like ours ought to be able to provide equal access to justice to all people and not just to the wealthy. The Legal Services Corporation last year served 1½ million clients. It's an exceedingly cost-effective operation: Less than 2 per cent of its funds go to overhead. If the program were not funded at near its present level of $321-million a year, the poor would not receive equal justice.

Interview/U.S. News & World Report, 8-3:33.

Ed Edelman
Chairman, Los Angeles County
Board of Supervisors

1

The grand jury is set up not to be a captive of any department. In county government, all authority is vested in the Board of Supervisors. There is no check by an executive branch, as there is in city government. The grand jury acts as a check. It is also the eyes and ears of the public. It brings to the light of day areas that need to be exposed.

Los Angeles Times, 2-2:(I)14.

Dennis Edwards, Jr.
Acting Justice, New York State
Supreme Court

2

Certainly, the plea-bargaining process is a recognized concept of our court structure. Its desirability is not for me to debate. It is here—a necessary, realistic fact of life, in light of the number of matters coming into the criminal side of the court and the problem with the number of judges and the court personnel and court facility.

New York, Aug. 24/
The New York Times, 8-31:22.

Kevin Forde
President, Chicago Bar Association

3

We have to attract and retain on the bench the best of the law profession. And the best have some great opportunities in private practice. They are willing to make sacrifices, but there is a limit to how much they should be expected to sacrifice.

Chicago Tribune, 9-3:(1)11.

Stephen Gillers
Teacher of legal ethics,
New York University Law School

4

[On law firms that use public-relations organizations instead of advertising]: Public relations is advertising for elite law firms. Small-firm lawyers advertise; Park Avenue and Wall Street lawyers hire public-relations firms. You're not going to have Cravath, Swaine & Moore or Paul Weiss, Rifkind, Wharton & Garrison take out ads saying, "We handle mergers and acquisitions." Those firms recognize the business-getting potential of publicity, and they want in on it, too, but their self-image doesn't allow advertising. They get to their audience by being mentioned in the business sections of the newspapers, and the way you get mentioned is not by buying space but by buying entree.

The New York Times, 3-20:14.

Ira Glasser
Executive director,
American Civil Liberties Union

5

The Bill of Rights was added to the Constitution to secure the rights of individuals by setting limits on government power. But the problem is that it's not self-enforcing. If a legislature or a President or a governor or a police chief or a school principal exceeds the limits of his power and violates the rights of an individual, there is no self-executing mechanism to remedy that. The judicial system, the

WHAT THEY SAID IN 1981

(IRA GLASSER)

courts, are really the institution that does that, but the courts cannot initiate action. Somebody whose rights are violated has to go to the courts and make a claim that this government official violated his or her civil rights. The ACLU basically came into existence to be that private organization outside of government which helps initiate those kinds of actions and helps, therefore, to enforce the Bill of Rights, and aims to do so without respect to political belief, religion, color, creed or anything else.

Interview, New York/
Los Angeles Times, 12-4:(I-A)4.

1

[Criticizing the Reagan Administration plan to cut back the Legal Services Corporation]: . . . in cutting off the Legal Services Corporation, they are telling poor people in a society that is so dependent on laws and, therefore, on lawyers—and where you must pay fees to hire lawyers—that the system of laws is not for you if you're poor. The problem is that a lot of middle-class people can't afford lawyers, either . . . most legal-services cases have to do not with Constitutional issues but with issues like divorce, landlord-tenant disputes, things like that. If you don't have a lawyer, you can't use the laws, and, in a fundamental way, you're being denied equal protection of the laws. You're being denied access to the system itself.

Interview, New York/
Los Angeles Times, 12-4:(I-A)8.

Joel F. Henning
Former assistant director of communication,
American Bar Association

2

Unquestionably the [legal] profession is held in low esteem [by the public]. Our entire social system seems to be disintegrating into a series of one-on-one squabbles, and people identify lawyers with that disintegration.

The Wall Street Journal,
2-6:44.

Michael J. Horowitz
Special Counsel, Federal Office
of Management and Budget

3

[On the Reagan Administration's desire to cut government-supported legal services to the poor]: The legal profession has indicated in its operative canons of ethics that the principal responsibility for the representation of people unable to afford legal fees ought to be placed on the profession itself. We think that's right; the bar has a fundamental responsibility to undertake that which its own set of ethics imposes. And we do think it somewhat troublesome that a bar whose members' total gross income now substantially exceeds $20-billion a year needs to lobby for a wholly Federally funded program in order to exercise its own admitted responsibility to represent the poor.

Interview, Washington/
The New York Times, 6-28:(4)5.

Henry J. Hyde
United States Representative, R—Illinois

4

[Calling for the revision of the exclusionary rule, which prohibits use of evidence obtained illegally]: If the officer [who obtained the evidence] was intentionally off-base, he should be disciplined. But the evidence should be used against the defendant, for it directly bears on his guilt or innocence . . . The liberal community, as well as the criminal-defense bar, view a technical violation of search and seizure law—even a good-faith violation—as every bit as reprehensible as breaking down a door without a warrant. The evidence is suppressed. And the guilty go free . . . We drew on the finest legal minds in the country. And there was almost universal accord that the rule must be modified. There is no reason that a balance cannot be reached so that the obviously guilty cannot walk out of courtrooms because of what may have been a technicality. Unreasonable search and seizure must not be permitted. But the exclusionary rule does not discipline the policeman who has violated the law. Instead, it frustrates justice. So society is doubly ill-served.

Chicago Tribune, 8-9:(1)5.

J. Bennett Johnston
United States Senator, D—Louisiana

1

Criticism of the legal profession is popular. But much of it proceeds from a basic misconception of the role of lawyers. Lawyers are advocates in an adversary system. Centuries of the common law have shown that the best way of getting at the truth is through an adversary proceeding. It is not the job of the lawyer, under our system, to reveal weaknesses of his case nor to argue with even-handed impartiality the pros and cons of both sides. It is an empirical observation, tested through the centuries, that truth best emerges when opposing sides are vigorously represented and fairly judged.
At Tulane University School of Law commencement/
The Washington Post, 6-3:(A)22.

Edward I. Koch
Mayor of New York

2

America is a nation of laws . . . The law is not always an easy friend, because the law does not play favorites. But for those who seek justice in a society of responsible citizens, the law will always be an ally.
New York, Sept. 7/
Los Angeles Times, 9-8:(I)16.

Robert J. Kutak
Chairman of American Bar Association
commission to establish a new code of
ethics and standards of conduct
for lawyers

3

If we [lawyers] don't get our house in order, if we don't make our rules clear and acceptable to the bar and to society, somebody is going to write the rules for us [such as the Supreme Court]. I don't think anyone wants that.
The Wall Street Journal, 2-6:44.

Thurgood Marshall
Associate Justice, Supreme Court of
the United States

4

The task of interpretation is the cornerstone of the judicial process. As we undertake it, we [judges] must strive for neutrality. None of us is perfect, and I recognize that neutrality is more ideal than real. Each of us brings along to the judicial role certain preconceived biases. It is, I suppose, impossible to make a decision totally uninfluenced by them. But we as judges must try to do so to the extent we possibly can. This ideal of neutrality is particularly hard to maintain in times such as these, when our society faces major unresolved problems. Indeed, we judges are frequently criticized these days for our neutrality . . . Our central function is to act as neutral arbiters of disputes that arise under the law. To this end, we bind ourselves through our own code of ethics to avoid even the appearance of impropriety or partiality. We must handle the cases that come before us without regard for what result might meet with public approval. We must decide each case in accordance with the law. We must not reach for a result that we, in our arrogance, believe will further some goal not related to the concrete case before us . . . We must never forget that the only real source of power that we as judges can tap is the respect of the people. We will command that respect only as long as we strive for neutrality. If we are perceived as campaigning for particular policies, as joining with other branches of government in resolving questions not committed to us by the Constitution, we may gain some public acclaim in the short run. In the long run, however, we will cease to be perceived as neutral arbiters, and we will lose that public respect so vital to our function.
At 2nd Circuit Judicial Conference/
Chicago Tribune, 8-15:(1)11.

Robert J. McGuire
Police Commissioner of New York

5

In the criminal courts, cases are being trivialized in ways independent of the evidence. In-

(ROBERT J. McGUIRE)

stead of the system being geared to treat each individual case as a manifestation of anti-social behavior, the main impetus is to dispose of it. No one is talking about the morality of crime.

Newsweek, 3-23:53.

Walter McLaughlin
Lawyer; Former Chief Justice,
Supreme Court of Massachusetts

1

[On what he found most striking upon returning to private law practice]: The [legal] fees. They are outrageous. With the cost of litigation these days, I think clients would often be better off if they just met in the halls and threw dice. Certainly it would be cheaper.

Time, 7-27:68.

Edwin Meese III
Counsellor to the President of the
United States; Former Assistant District
Attorney, Alameda County, Calif.

2

Do away with the insanity defense in criminal cases. A good portion [of criminal trials] is taken up with hot-and-cold running psychiatrists for both sides telling all the things wrong with the accused. The way psychiatrists are now pushed and tugged and, in effect, compromised with their medical standards in order to provide testimony for one side or the other—this is a disgrace to their profession.

Before California State Sheriff's Association,
San Rafael, Calif., April 15/
Los Angeles Times, 4-16:(I)15.

3

[On the Reagan Administration's plan to dismantle the Federal Legal Services Corporation]: . . . we're not abolishing legal services for the poor; we're just seeking a better system. I think that local bar associations have a responsibility to provide legal services to the poor. There would still be funds provided by the Federal

government. These funds could be utilized through a variety of programs in each state, and they would probably be more effectively utilized than they are now through the Legal Services Corporation. We're also talking about making sure that the kinds of legal services that are provided are those that really meet the needs of individuals. We don't want money going for promotion of social causes and other things that have actually siphoned off funds from those who might need them.

Interview/U.S. News & World Report, 8-3:34.

Glen Mowrer, Jr.
President, California State Public
Defenders Association

4

[Supporting the right of defendants to have their preliminary hearings closed to public and press]: To me it's always been ironic that I never heard the people who complain about closed preliminary hearings complain about the closed grand-jury process. On a philosophical basis, a person should not have to be publicly identified and subject to the abuse and ridicule that those charges are going to bring until it is shown there is sufficient cause for that process to be filed. In those cases, we feel it is better the proceeding be held privately. The other part of it is there are some types of hearings in which it seems a person gets a more fair hearing when the public is not allowed to be there to pressure the system.

San Francisco Examiner & Chronicle, 3-22:(A)6.

Malcolm Muir
Judge, United States District Court for
the Middle District of Pennsylvania

5

The toughest part of this job is sentencing. I've lost all kinds of sleep over sentences. I find it dreadful . . . When I took this job, I wanted to render what I felt was a real service—not to the lawyers but to the people. I find this an extremely lonely job. Regrettable as it is, I think it's the right way. I'm not running a popularity contest.

San Francisco Examiner & Chronicle, 3-8:(B)11.

Sandra Day O'Connor
Associate Justice-designate,
Supreme Court of the United States

1

As a citizen, as a lawyer and as a judge, I have, from afar, always regarded the [Supreme] Court with the reverence and the respect to which it is so clearly entitled because of the function it serves. It is the institution which is charged with the fiscal responsibility of insuring that basic Constitutional doctrines will be continually honored and enforced. It is the body to which all Americans look for the ultimate protection of their rights. It is to the United States Supreme Court that we all turn when we seek that which we want most from our government: equal justice under the law.

At Senate Judiciary Committee hearing on her
confirmation, Washington, Sept. 9/
The Washington Post, 9-10:(A)1.

2

I do not believe it is the function of the judiciary to step in and change the law because the times have changed. I do well understand the difference between legislating and judging. As a judge, it is not my function to develop public policy.

At Senate Judiciary Committee hearing on her
confirmation, Washington, Sept. 9/
The Washington Post, 9-10:(A)1.

Howard Phillips
National director,
Conservative Caucus

3

Since the mid-1960s, first through the Office of Legal Services at the U.S. Office of Economic Opportunity, and now, by means of the Legal Services Corporation, Congress has compelled me and millions of other Americans to furnish contributions of money [via taxes], through the Internal Revenue System, for the propagation of opinions which we disbelieve and abhor . . . Whatever the issues—be it OSHA, busing, transsexual benefit claims, quotas, election law, expunging arrest records, private schools,

conscription, economic policy, and even national defense—the poverty lawyers are being subsidized at public expense to propagate their private views of what is good for the poor and what is good for the country . . . If the American Bar Association, for all its whining, is unable to find from among its 275,000 members the interest in aiding the poor which is now supposedly concentrated in 5,500 legal-services lawyers, why should the legal profession's lack of social conscience be laid upon the backs of taxpayers who, themselves, lack the resources to sue or lobby at will?

The Washington Post, 5-1:(A)18.

Tom Railsback
United States Representative, R—Illinois

4

[Criticizing Reagan Administration plans to eliminate government legal services to the poor]: Every lawyer in this body, and in the nation for that matter, is fully aware of the fact that to successfully use our system of justice, you need the assistance of an attorney—and to deny these [poor] people their assistance is the very same as denying them access to our system of justice. If we do this, then I believe the consequences may be serious, not just for the poor, but for our entire system of government.

Before the House, Washington/
The Washington Post, 6-24:(A)21.

Ronald Reagan
President of the United States

5

[Announcing his nomination of Sandra Day O'Connor as the first woman Supreme Court Justice]: . . . without doubt, the most awesome appointment a President can make is to the United States Supreme Court. Those who sit on the Supreme Court interpret the laws of our land and truly do leave their footprints on the sands of time, long after the policies of Presidents, Senators and Congressmen of a given era may have passed from the public memory . . . As the press has accurately pointed out, during my campaign for the Presidency, I made a com-

(RONALD REAGAN)

mitment that one of my first appointments to a Supreme Court vacancy would be the most qualified woman I could possibly find. That is not to say I would appoint a woman merely to do so. That would not be fair to women, nor to future generations of all Americans whose lives are so deeply affected by the decisions of the Court. Rather, I pledged to appoint a woman who meets the very high standards I demand of all court appointees . . . [Judge O'Connor] is truly a "person for all seasons," possessing those unique qualities of temperament, fairness, intellectual capacity and devotion to the public good which have characterized the 101 "brethren" who have preceded her.

News conference, Washington, July 7/
The New York Times, 7-8:8.

1

Our freedom is secure because we are a nation governed by laws, not by men. We have the means to change the laws we find unjust or onerous. We cannot pick and choose the laws we will or will not obey.

Before United Brotherhood of Carpenters and
Joiners, Chicago, Sept. 3/
Los Angeles Times, 9-3:(I)1.

2

What is especially disturbing about our failure to deal with crime is the erosion it has caused in public confidence in our judicial system. This decline in public confidence in our courts and in the legal profession remains a threat to one of our most important traditions, traditions as Americans: the heritage of our independent judiciary, free from public or political influence, and a legal profession with a reputation for high, unassailable ethics.

Before International Association of
Chiefs of Police, New Orleans, Sept. 28/
The New York Times, 9-29:13.

Suzanne Saunders
Member, Commission of Advertising,
American Bar Association

3

I think that those [lawyers] who advertise have proven to provide lower-quality services. You have a lower-caliber attorney who is sometimes more interested in attracting clients than in being a perfectionist. Over-all, while there are groups that recognize the right to advertise, the vast majority of lawyers still disapprove of the practice. They haven't accepted it. They merely tolerate it because for so many years it was considered appalling and degrading.

Los Angeles Times, 9-17:(I-A)8.

William French Smith
Attorney General of the United States

4

This Administration is fully aware of the difficulties arising from the growth of law in recent years. Both the number and complexity of laws have diminished public understanding of their own government. Only recently, when the full negative effects of our 15-year lawmaking spree began to be generally felt throughout our economy, did the public stir. As the product of that public stirring, the Reagan Administration has earnestly begun the process of returning law and government to the real world. We recognize the limits of governmental action, but also the need for effective government action in many spheres. We recognize the need for realistic laws, but that no law can prove effective without public understanding and support. We recognize that few laws are self-executing and that the best of laws must be firmly enforced. Any nation is only as great as its laws and its will to enforce them. We intend to do everything in our power to ensure more realistic laws and their widespread observance.

Before American Bar Association/
The Washington Post, 8-21:(A)28.

5

We are seeking women and minorities [for Federal judgeships], but we are not going to

(WILLIAM FRENCH SMITH)

sacrifice basic qualifications for that purpose. Our two principal criteria are quality and a general agreement with the President's [Reagan] judicial philosophy—that a judge's function is to interpret and apply the law and not to make it. The President feels very strongly that people who make the law should be people elected by and responsible to the electorate, and not people who are appointed to lifetime positions and who are not really responsible to anybody except themselves.

Interview/
U.S. News & World Report, 10-26:34.

1

In recent decades, Federal courts have engaged in . . . judicial policy-making. The Justice Department will focus upon the doctrines that have led to the courts' activism. We will attempt to reverse this unhealthy flow of power from state and Federal legislatures to Federal courts, and the concomitant flow of power from state and local governments to the Federal level . . . The extent to which the Federal courts have inappropriately entered legislative terrain can be seen most clearly, and felt, in their attempts to fashion [equitable remedies] for perceived violations. Federal courts have attempted to restructure entire school systems in desegregation cases. They have asserted similar control over entire prison systems and public housing projects. They have restructured the employment criteria to be used by American business and government, even to the extent of mandating numerical results based on race and gender. No area seems immune from judicial administration.

Before government lawyers, October/
The New York Times, 11-1:(4)8.

William Reece Smith, Jr.
President, American Bar Association

2

[Criticizing the Reagan Administration's plan to eliminate Federal funding of legal services

for the poor]: [The decision is] unsound, unwise and not in the nation's best interest. Eliminating this important program, committed to assuring access to justice for the nation's poor, will in the long run cost our society far more than any immediate dollars we may save.

March 6/The Washington Post, 307:(A)6.

Potter Stewart
Associate Justice, Supreme Court of the United States

3

[On whether a woman should be appointed to replace him on the Court, now that he is retiring]: It's an insult to the Court, to the appointee and to the American public to appoint somebody just because he or she is not a white male. There is nothing more antithetical [to the process of finding a good judge than] to think it has something to do with representative democracy . . . As far as I'm concerned, the mark of a good justice or a good judge is an opinion you can read and have no idea whether it was written by a man or a woman, a Republican or a Democrat, or a Christian or a Jew . . . The most important thing is quality and competence and temperament and character and diligence.

News conference, Washington, June 19/
The Washington Post, 6-20:(A)1,9.

Margaret Thatcher
Prime Minister of the United Kingdom

4

Government . . . can make the law. Police and courts can uphold the law. But a free society will only survive if we, its citizens, obey the law and teach our children to do so.

Broadcast address to the nation,
London, July 8/
The New York Times, 7-9:1.

Strom Thurmond
United States Senator, R—South Carolina

5

I believe people resent the attempts of Federal judges to reorganize American society through

(STROM THURMOND)

court-made law. In my view, judges should be removed from the business of imposing their view of social organization on the people and should be returned to their traditional role of deciding civil cases and controversies and trying criminal prosecutions . . . In other words, it is not the business of the judiciary to legislate. We have three branches of government: Congress to make the law, the Executive Branch to administer the law and the judicial system to interpret the law. Each should be restricted to its own functions. But as you know, judges in recent years have handed down decisions that are equivalent to legislating.

Interview/U.S. News & World Report, 3-23:42.

Mark O. Tobriner
Justice, Supreme Court of California

1

As far as the public is concerned, I think the court has always been criticized—perhaps for being what some people think is soft on criminals. It's true of the United States Supreme Court and it's true of most courts over the whole history of courts. Very often, the courts have been used as a scapegoat. At the time of Theodore Roosevelt the same thing occurred. People criticized the courts because they were thought to be too soft on criminals . . . The trouble with that is that it looks at the courts as the factor that is going to correct the crime problem.

Interview/
San Francisco Examiner & Chronicle, 9-27:(B)1.

Politics

John B. Anderson
Former United States Representative,
R—Illinois; 1980 independent
candidate for President

1

[Saying he may run for President again in 1984]: [The difference in the campaign then would be] to structure it more formally, in a third party, not just simply go charging around as an independent. I think you would have to have a party structure—to give people the feeling that they were not just dealing with a kind of ephemeral figure who would rise and fall and flower and fade, but something they could sink their teeth into. We'd have a national convocation, a national convention, call in people, lay the foundations . . . I'm still haunted by the fact that less than 53 per cent voted, and that millions and millions of people didn't see in what I was doing the kind of definite effort that encouraged them to participate. Maybe it's because it wasn't a third party. Maybe it's because we didn't single out one issue or two issues and hammer away more at them. Maybe we were too diffuse in our approach, too centrist. Maybe you've got to become a little bit more—almost apocalyptic. I think we to a fault tried to carefully eschew the right and the left and to posture ourselves right in the center. Maybe there are some issues where you have to take a position that's a little bit farther in one direction or the other.

Interview, Pasadena, Calif., Feb. 3/
Los Angeles Times, 2-4:(I)18.

James A. Baker III
Chief of Staff to the President
of the United States

2

[On how President Reagan has become so politically potent]: First of all, the President's judgment in political matters is superb. He has wonderful political instinct. But I think it is probably something more than that. I think that the country desperately wants the President to succeed. There have been some Presidential failures in the recent past. And there has been a diminution of strength in the Executive Branch. The prerogatives of the President have been watered down. Really, there is a feeling among a lot of Americans that they'd like to see a strong President and a successful Presidency. They're putting a lot of faith and stock in this President's actions. Whether you are seeing something more than just the transitory tolerance of a new President—call it honeymoon or whatever—I think it is a little premature to tell. Although I'll say this: We'll take another five months like the first five if you would offer it to us.

Interview, Washington/
The Christian Science Monitor, 7-1:5.

Roger Baldwin
Founder,
American Civil Liberties Union

3

[The ACLU] can be a watchdog, but it can't be a force—the force has to lie in the public awareness of an issue. The public has to want the same things we do. People who become aware of a democratic society have to want it. Some may think we're surrounded by conservatives [in the U.S. now], but you're not surrounded by people who don't want to change things. They may want to change them backwards—but they still want to change things.

Interview, Oakland, N.J./
Los Angeles Times, 2-23:(V)5.

WHAT THEY SAID IN 1981

Alfred Balitzer
*Director, Republican National
Committee Outreach Program*

1

. . . there's a large black working class in America, people who go to work at 9 and leave at 5, have union cards and share the concerns of most other Americans about crime in the streets, the character of their neighborhoods, how to pay the grocery bill. I believe that the black working class should be a major concern of our Outreach Program . . . Black volunteers in the Reagan-Bush [Presidential] campaign represent neither the intellectual class nor the wealthy class in the black community but the real folk in their constituencies . . . Against all popular rhetoric, I believe the Republican Party is the party of the working-man. I believe it's the principles and programs of the Republican Party that are most desired by the working-man today.

Interview/The Washington Post, 7-26:(D)6.

Anthony C. Beilenson
United States Representative, D—California

2

[On the prospects for the Reagan Presidency]: I think he's wrong on every issue. He is enormously, extremely, completely conservative . . . He doesn't work very hard; he doesn't immerse himself in issues . . . He doesn't spend a lot of time thinking about things . . . What bothers me most is that he seems not to be educable. You couldn't sit him down for an hour or two [when Reagan was Governor of California] and explain what you were trying to do in your bill. He was an adequate Governor. He had good subordinates. The state was all right after he left. But I'm not convinced he'll be an adequate President. I don't think the jobs are comparable. The problems, the issues, the decisions . . . are so much more complex . . . [But] he may just turn out to be awfully good. Maybe the pressures of the Presidency are so great that a person like Reagan—ironical as it may seem—may be the only kind of person who may be successful in the Presidency today. Truman was like that. He'd make a decision and then

go to sleep. I can't sleep. I make a decision and then I lie there, wondering, "Did I do the right thing?" Maybe [Reagan] doesn't have to be educated. I don't know.

Interview/Los Angeles Times, 1-22:(IX)1.

Dale Bumpers
United States Senator, D—Arkansas

3

People think that [the Republican election victory in] 1980 was some kind of wild abberation that's not likely to ever be repeated again, and in one sense it was. That is, it all seemed to come together at one time. But you have to understand that this conservative tide in this country about government spending and government deficits and government waste and inflation really began back with [the Administration of] Richard Nixon in 1968 to one extent or another. And you can't say that Jimmy Carter was an interlude because Jimmy Carter ran on precisely the same platform that Ronald Reagan did—and promised the same things and delivered nothing.

Interview/The Washington Post, 5-18:(A)1.

William P. Bundy
Editor, "Foreign Affairs" magazine

4

[President Reagan] has shown both a capacity to speak persuasively to the American people and a skill and organization in dealing with Congress that have not been seen in Washington since at least the days of John Kennedy or the Lyndon Johnson of 1964-65. Moreover, whereas Kennedy could speak but not twist arms, and Johnson could twist arms but not speak, Reagan, it appears, can do both, perhaps to a degree for which one would have to go right back to Franklin Roosevelt for a parallel, and in a way that hits observers all the harder as it comes after a President [Jimmy Carter] who could do neither . . . Both potential domestic critics and foreign statesmen have seen a combination of personal charm and firmness of purpose that are bound to make them think twice before taking him on, at least head to head.

*At policy study seminar, July 31/
The Washington Post, 8-2:(A)8.*

George Bush
Vice President of the United States

1

[After the defeat of the Democrats in last year's national election,] you'd think that the President's [Reagan] opposition might come up with some new approach to our country's problems— the problems they helped create. But they have no new approach. They're back at the same old stand. Let's face it—the big-government, big-spending special interests haven't had an original idea in half a century. They call themselves "liberals," but their minds are shut to everything but their own dogma.

Before Young Republican National Federation Leadership Conference, Washington, March 28/ San Francisco Examiner & Chronicle, 3-29:(A)10.

Robert C. Byrd
United States Senator, D—West Virginia

2

The last election [which made Ronald Reagan President] was a referendum on frustration . . . People voted for a change, and it's important we Democrats give the new President a fair trial of his policies. But that pendulum will swing back. People will tire of the far-right, ultra-conservative, single-issue politics. They will see through it soon.

Interview, Washington/ The Washington Post, 2-15:(C)7.

Jimmy Carter
President of the United States

3

Today, as people have become more doubtful of the ability of the government to deal with our problems, we are increasingly drawn to single-issue groups and special-interest organizations to insure that, whatever else happens, our own personal views and our own private interests are protected. This is a disturbing factor in American political life. It tends to distort our purposes because the national interest is not always the sum of all our single or special interests. We are all Americans together and we must not forget that the common good is

our common interest and our individual responsibility.

Farewell address to the nation, Washington, Jan. 14/ The New York Times, 1-15:12.

Clark M. Clifford
Former Secretary of Defense of the United States

4

[President] Jimmy Carter was a man who came from nowhere, flashed across the political firmanent, had some solid accomplishments in his four years, but ultimately failed to establish a political base. Then, the people, at their first opportunity, returned him to Georgia. There was nothing exceptional about it, no new theory of government was presented. It was just one of those rare moments that historians will rack their brains to understand and explain.

The New York Times, 1-8:11.

William S. Cohen
United States Senator, R—Maine

5

[Former] President [Jimmy] Carter enjoyed being President. But he didn't enjoy politics. He didn't enjoy cultivating friendships, stroking egos, doing whatever had to be done to build a reservoir of good-will [in Congress]. Whenever someone disagreed with the merits of his proposals, he had no cushion of good-will to fall back on, not even in his own party. [President] Reagan will use his lines of communications and I think we'll see less antagonism on the Hill than we have in the last decade. Ronald Reagan is not a mean-spirited or vindictive man. That's the difference. Carter had that streak and it came through.

Interview/Chicago Tribune, 3-18:(1)4.

Archibald Cox
Chairman, Common Cause

6

[On public financing of Presidential campaigns]: I think it's done three important things in the Presidential elections. First, it's virtually

(ARCHIBALD COX)

eliminated special-interest money. In 1972, before the public funding—if my memory's right —153 individuals put up something like $20-million for Richard Nixon. And one wonders, after the election is over, whose vices will be pardoned. That sort of doubt and skepticism in the electoral processes are eliminated. Second, public funding opens up the process so that the people have more to choose from. It's questionable whether Jimmy Carter would have been able to run without public funding. And third, candidates are relieved of spending enormous amounts of money and enormous amounts of time trying to solicit money. If public financing is extended to races for Senators and Congressmen, I think that they, too, will have some kind of ceiling put on the aggregate of campaign spending . . . the more money the candidate raises from special-interest groups, the more sense of obligation—I'm not suggesting he was *bought*—but the more sense of obligation there is to those who put you in.

Interview/Los Angeles Herald Examiner, 1-19:(A)2.

Alan Cranston
United States Senator, D—California

1

[On the Democratic Party's attitude toward President Reagan's economic program.]: The attitude among Democrats here is that we can't be in the position of preventing him from trying what he was elected to do. We can't go along on every detail, but if we obstructed everything, it would be bad for the country and bad for the Democrats. The voters would remove a lot more of us.

Time, 3-2:14.

Walter Cronkite
Anchorman, CBS News

2

I don't [vote] unless I feel strongly about something. I don't necessarily believe in this business of "get out the vote." I think unless you have a *reason* to vote, there's no purpose in just putting an "X" in one box or another.

Interview/Chicago Tribune Magazine, 3-15:22.

Richard DeVos
President, Amway Corporation

3

[President-elect Reagan] is and will continue to be an optimistic person, believing in America. That is in contrast to President Carter, who started out on a positive note, but ended up being negative, telling people they would have to make do with less. Reagan is an achiever, and he appears to be surrounding himself with people who are achievement-minded.

Interview/U.S. News & World Report, 1-12:50.

Christopher J. Dodd
United States Senator, D—Connecticut

4

Single-issue politics and the PACs [political action committees] are extremely destructive to the two-party system, which is the glue basically of this society. The facts speak for themselves. Last year 75 million eligible voters failed to participate. And I think in large part that was due to single-issue politics and to the really obscure cost of campaigns. Dick Bolling [chairman of the House Rules Committee] may have said it best in a debate several years ago: Too many people in Congress have come to believe that the sum of the special interests equals the national interest. It does not. And the fact is that's destroying our ability to act as legislators; it's making it almost impossible for an overwhelming number of people to participate in the political process as candidates. I think it's driving a significant number of people away from the polls on election day.

Panel discussion, Washington/
The New York Times, 6-14:(4)5.

5

I think this Congress is far more political, far more partisan, than anything I've ever seen before. Whatever else any Democrat may have to say about the [Reagan] Administration, the Congressional Republicans' discipline and cohesiveness far outstrips anything I've seen in the Democratic Party.

Panel discussion, Washington/
The New York Times, 6-14:(4)5.

John T. Dolan
Chairman, National Conservative
Political Action Committee

1

I think [President] Reagan has chosen to surround himself with people who simply do not share the same vision of America that he has. It's mind-boggling that conservative, pro-Reagan activists are being bumped off lists, while people who have no commitment to Ronald Reagan are being given jobs ... To say that Reagan has to employ country-club, silk-stocking [Vice President] George Bush Republicans is garbage. That didn't win him the election. He won by broadening his base to the ethnics, the blue-collar vote, the born-again Southern Democrats. Reagan has a commitment to these people and he's got to live up to it. He didn't win by being a centrist; he won because he's conservative.

The New York Times, 1-25:(1)15.

Byron L. Dorgan
United States Representative,
D—North Dakota

2

One-issue politics is the scourge of the system. I think it's going to ruin politics some day unless we start getting people to understand you have to have a broader view. The fund-raising that goes along with it, and all the pressures brought to bear on every politician of every philosophical stripe are, I think, a real disservice to politics.

Panel discussion, Washington/
The New York Times, 6-14:(4)5.

Lee Sherman Dreyfus
Governor of Wisconsin (R)

3

We're going back to a kind of oral tradition in American politics that we haven't had since the days of the founding of the Republic. At that time, politics on a local level was strictly oral. Leaders would speak, and people would make judgments of them. Today, because of television, people are back to trusting their

own judgment about human beings—candidates and officials—they can see and hear.

Interview/Chicago Tribune Magazine, 8-23:30.

Robert F. Drinan
President, Americans for Democratic
Action; Former United States
Representative, D—Massachusetts

4

An American liberal does not say "get government off our backs." He says that government is needed in the economy in certain circumstances. He does not believe in free enterprise, as if that is going to solve everything. He believes that we need the minimum wage; he knows that we need very tough environmental standards; and he wants a strong OSHA because there are still thousands of industrial accidents. Furthermore, in the area of helping the poor and the disadvantaged, he believes in the social programs that we have. He thinks that housing is so expensive that virtually everyone needs a good deal of help. Fundamentally, he believes in government as an entity by which the last and the lowest and the least should in fact be assisted. Likewise, in the area of civil rights and civil liberties, the liberal is the expansionist, if you will, with regard to the Bill of Rights. He would generally believe in enhancing and increasing and implementing human rights or civil liberties, as the Supreme Court has done. On the international level, the liberal seeks to carry on that bi-partisan consensus that brought about a strong defense with the accent on foreign aid and with a good deal of idealism as well as protecting our interests. All of these things are now being challenged. And the liberal, frankly, is frightened.

Interview/The Washington Post, 6-28:(A)3.

Peter F. Drucker
Professor of social science,
Claremont (Calif.) College Graduate School

5

We are in an age of the adventurous in politics. Leaders such as [Prime Minister] Margaret Thatcher in England and [Presidents] Jimmy

WHAT THEY SAID IN 1981

(PETER F. DRUCKER)

Carter and Ronald Reagan in the U.S. fall into that category. They are people who do not fit the traditional mold. They have not risen to the top through normal institutional processes; instead, they started at the top without a sponsor. This is a relatively new phenomenon. Right through Dwight D. Eisenhower, the routes to the Presidency were few and very clearly demarcated—the successful General, the successful Senator, the New York Banker, the lawyer. But then we got into [Richard] Nixon, Carter and Reagan. Nixon looked conventional, but he wasn't. And Carter and Reagan are total outsiders; they have no sponsor and exploited the fact that the traditional parties have no cohesion and no leadership. The rise of the adventurer can be advantageous in that traditional restraints on the ability of people to move ahead rapidly are gone. But it can also represent a tremendous danger because restraints are removed for the demagogue, too. The impact, finally, is unpredictable.

Interview/U.S. News & World Report, 12-21:74.

E. J. (Jake) Garn
United States Senator, R—Utah

1

I think conservatives make a very big mistake when they say, "If I can't have the whole pie, I don't want any of it." I don't think that's the responsible way. Rather than stating, "If I don't get three-fourths [of conservative legislation passed], I'll take nothing," I'd rather get a fourth. Those conservatives who stand on one point and demand the whole hog are not going to get anything.

The Washington Post,
1-20:(Inauguration '81)21.

David R. Gergen
Assistant to the President of the
United States for Communications

2

It is not my job to make [President] Ronald Reagan, the man, look good. He is more than capable of taking care of himself in that regard. It is my responsibility, along with others, to help Ronald Reagan, the President, convey to people what it is he is trying to do for the country. In the past, there have been occasions when we have tried to package our Presidents almost as you might package detergents, to put it in the worst light. That is something we have not engaged in in this White House. We don't have a White House bubble-machine trying to help Ronald Reagan the man.

Interview/U.S. News and World Report, 12-7:26.

A. Bartlett Giamatti
President, Yale University

3

If a society presumes its politicians are venal, stupid or self-serving, it will attract to its public life as an ongoing self-fulfilling prophecy the greedy, the knavish and the dim. If . . . a culture like ours has wrongly persuaded itself that power is really mere force, and the use of power in its public or private life simply the exercise of force, then that culture will attract to leadership those who misunderstand power and who therefore cannot possibly use it correctly or well. How power is conceived in a society has the most to do with determining who is attracted to positions of power. A healthy society must never wish to have as its public servants people who only hunger to be in public life, who, thinking power is a natural force, believe they will become immortal if they can tap into its sheer, natural flow. The best way to avoid such people is to avoid such an idea of power.

At Yale University commencement/
The Washington Post, 5-28:(A)19.

Ira Glasser
Executive director,
American Civil Liberties Union

4

. . . the meaning of liberal and conservative in this society is so crazy. I like to go places like Kansas and Nebraska and say that the ACLU is the most conservative organization in America; but who else is running around talking as their

(IRA GLASSER)

sole purpose is life protection of an 18th-century document [the Constitution] and taking the position that it shouldn't change? That, by definition, is what you mean by conservative; what we're seeking to conserve are the values that were established in the Constitution 200 years ago. People who want to make radical changes in those values and that Constitution, who sort of take the position that they're out-moded, those are the ones who are anything but conservative. And yet, in this country, people calling themselves conservative want to over-turn those traditional values, and people who are seen as vaguely radical want to conserve those traditional values.

Interview, New York/
Los Angeles Times, 12-4:(I-A)7.

Thomas W. Gleason
President, International
Longshoremen's Association

1

There was a time you couldn't go to mass on Sunday if you didn't vote the straight Demo-cratic ticket. Those days are over. There are no such things as all bad Republicans or all bad Democrats.

At AFL-CIO convention, Bal Harbour, Fla./
Chicago Tribune, 3-1:(2)10.

John Glenn
United States Senator, D-Ohio

2

In the past, the Democratic coalition has been looked on too often as only labor, lower-income levels and special-interest groups. And we al-ways tried to represent the least advantaged in our society. All that is good, and should continue, but I think we've got a much broad-er tent. I think we have to concentrate on the issues of today: inflation, high interest rates, jobs. You can take in a large coalition of voters by finding long-range solutions to those problems.

Interview/U.S. News & World Report, 9-28:34.

Barry M. Goldwater
United States Senator, R—Arizona

3

[On the spectacular and expensive inaugura-tion festivities for President Reagan]: I've seen seven [inaugurations]. And I say that when you've got to pay $2,000 for a limousine for four days, $7 to park and $2.50 to check your coat, at a time when most people in this country just can't hack it—that's ostentatious!

Chicago Tribune, 1-25:(12)2.

4

I don't think a conservative today is any dif-ferent than a conservative has been since the days of the Greeks. We want to make progress on the proven values of the past. Our constitu-tional government is the finest thing ever devised by man. Why screw around with it? Our American free-market system has produced more goods for more people than all the other systems of the world put together. Now, why should we follow Lord Keynes and go back to the days of socialism? In other words, don't fool around with things that don't work.

Interview, Washington/
The Wall Street Journal, 8-3:12.

Henry F. Graff
Professor of history,
Columbia University

5

While the stars of television entertainment rehearse, then are taped and retaped, the politi-cal luminaries are shown *au naturel*, unim-proved, and "live." The politicians' quips and jokes—being less taxing to viewers than ideas —are amply reported, thus assimilating the pols to the professional comedians, who, alas, are served by abler writers. The fumbles and stumbles of our leaders, moreover, are frequent fare on the evening news. The effect on the Presidency has been withering. Television, indeed, must bear important responsibility for the fall of the last four chiefs.

Chicago Tribune, 4-21:(1)13.

189

WHAT THEY SAID IN 1981

Alexander M. Haig, Jr.
Secretary of State-designate
of the United States

1

[Saying he was not involved in the Watergate scandal while he was White House Chief of Staff under President Richard Nixon]: I never went along with or supported anything I believed to be illegal. Suggestions came up from time to time. And on every occasion I fought it, rejected it or prevented it. What is it you want me to say? What is it you're after? Nobody has a monopoly on virtue, not even you, Senator. I have not ever indulged in something that is wrong or illegal . . . Others did. That's clear. The record is clear. We saw the volumes of it . . . Do you expect me to endorse what was done? No way.
Addressing Senator Paul S. Sarbanes while testifying at his confirmation hearing before Senate Foreign Relations Committee, Washington, Jan. 13/
Los Angeles Herald Examiner, 1-13:(A)1.

Gary W. Hart
United States Senator, D—Colorado

2

There are essentially three tides in the Democratic Party. One is to preserve the status quo—that is, protect the New Deal and the Great Society. The other is essentially "let's become more Republican," particularly on military and foreign policy. That's the neo-conservative movement. The third, and perhaps the most interesting and most difficult, is the actual redefinition of the Democratic Party. In shorthand, that means to try and figure out non-bureaucratic, non-programmatic methods of dealing with the realities of the '80s and '90s in ways that do not abandon the fundamental principles of the Democratic Party. Now, that is difficult. It is complicated. In some sense, it's profound because you're trying to do almost what [former President] Franklin Roosevelt did without the economic cataclysm to operate as a catalyst forcing these things to happen.
Interview/
The Washington Post, 5-17:(A)12.

Peter D. Hart
Democratic Party
public-opinion analyst

3

[On the Republican Party's 1980 national election victory]: In 1980 a series of specific issues —each of which tended to favor the Republicans —dominated the campaign dialogue and shaped the ultimate results. If support for a stronger national defense, less government spending and a businesslike approach to inflation are replaced by different priorities in future elections, the gains the Republicans made in the last election are likely to be transient . . . The key to the 1980 election is the fact that 75 million Americans chose not to participate. If a truly . . . long-lasting realignment is to occur, those Americans under the age of 40 who have never voted, or do so only occasionally, must be included. At present, these people are on the sidelines.
The Christian Science Monitor,
3-3:11.

S. I. Hayakawa
United States Senator, R—California

4

[Calling for a simultaneous closing of polls around the country so that early projections of voting results in the East will not affect voting in the West]: The biggest loser [last] November 4 was not any single candidate but the American political system. We have been told that hundreds of thousands of Californians did not vote as a result of early media projections of a Presidential winner. It is not the numbers that are important . . . [It] is that voters in the Western states believed that voting was a useless exercise . . . There is a tendency . . . [for some to think] that if the East has made up its mind, the country has made up its mind. By God, the East is not the country. It's only part of it.
Washington, May 7/
Los Angeles Times, 5-8:(II)8.

Tom Hayden
Political activist; Candidate for
the California Assembly
1

If you're a typical politician in the state of California, you seek high name identification, and you seek to avoid engagement with any issue where there's division of public opinion. I do exactly the opposite because I see no point in popularity contests . . . There is no way that a non-controversial person can get anything done. During one's lifetime, one's effectiveness is measured up to a point by having a divided constituency. If you have 100 per cent of the people against you, obviously you've made a fundamental mistake. But it should be 50-50.
Interview, Santa Monica, Calif./
The Christian Science Monitor, 12-18:14.

Jesse A. Helms
United States Senator, R—North Carolina
2

[Criticizing President Reagan for not adhering to the hard-line conservative approach demanded by many of his constituents]: The people who fought and bled and died for Reagan have not been listened to. He's got to remember who took him to the dance.
Time, 5-4:21.

Henry M. Jackson
United States Senator, D—Washington
3

I am convinced that one reason we Democrats lost the [1980 national] election was the Republican success in pre-empting the historic stance of the Democratic Party on issues of defense and foreign policy. The Republicans struck at the heart of our Party—the tradition of Franklin Roosevelt and Harry Truman, champions of a strong and resolute America, leader of the free world, proud of its greatness . . . Too many of our fellow Democrats misjudged the mood of the country. We were told it was out of bounds for good Democrats to sound patriotic. We were told that to call America a great country was passe. Well, the recent

vast and tumultuous outpouring of unabashed patriotism [when American hostages were released by Iran] should put that myth to final rest. What a chance we Democrats missed!
Before Coalition for a Democratic Majority/
The Wall Street Journal, 3-3:22.

Forrest James
Governor of Alabama (D)
4

[On his dealings with special-interest groups]: We are all part of some special-interest group. . . . there's nothing wrong with that. But the Governor, above all, has got to draw a circle and within the circle he's got to say this is the *public* interest. A Governor's got to say [to special interests], "You've got a real place in this society and we love you, but you ain't going to cross that circle if I've got anything to do about it. If it makes you mad, we still love you, but that's the way it is." I've tried to consistently do that every time I saw that threat approach. If that makes some people mad, I think you know how much sleep I lose over that.
Interview, Montgomery, Alabama/
Los Angeles Times, 12-11:(I-C)15.

Jacob K. Javits
Former United States Senator, R—New York
5

[On his being a liberal]: . . . I have always been very proud of being identified with that word. "Liberal" means not only living in the present and not only learning from the past, but not being tied to the past and looking to the future. I was very liberal humanistically—that is, when it came to the underlying hazards of life: unemployment, ill health and similar vicissitudes not the fault of the person who was their victim. But I'm very hardheaded about money, very conservative. I always felt that when you contracted a bill, you had to pay it.
Interview/Los Angeles Herald Examiner, 8-31:(A)1.

Jack Kemp
United States Representative, R—New York
6

Real [political] leadership is predicated upon a concern for not just the whole, but the least

(JACK KEMP)

unto that whole—the stray, the indigent, the handicapped, poor and oppressed. I would like to see my [Republican] Party not be a party of just the middle class, but a party of consensus.

Interview/The Washington Post, 1-20:(A)21.

Edward M. Kennedy
United States Senator, D—Massachusetts

1

One thing that concerns me about the Democratic Party: Is the Democratic Party trying to be another Republican Party? This nation doesn't need two Republican parties. Any time the Democrats have tried to be like the Republicans and have gone before the American people, the American people have selected the real thing. That's going to happen in the future. And that's why I think it's so important that Democrats stand for their constituencies now, because their constituencies are being threatened [by the current Republican Administration]. It's going to be imperative in the rebuilding process that those groups understand who is speaking for them.

Interview/The Washington Post, 5-18:(A)13.

Lane Kirkland
President, American Federation of Labor-Congress of Industrial Organizations

2

The vote of the people might not always produce the proper results, but it isn't too bad if you don't take those results either as the ultimate dawn of a new day or the ultimate cataclysm, and remember you always have another shot at at in the next election.

Los Angeles Times, 1-29:(I)19.

Jeane J. Kirkpatrick
United States Representative/Permanent Representative to the United Nations

3

[Criticizing recent swings to the ultra-left by many in the Democratic Party]: We [Democrats]

were there when a new kind of liberalism spread through our Party like the plague . . . a plague that involves a particular kind of arrogance, that tends to elitism, utopianism of a sort that is prepared to trade real goods for symbolic ones.

At meeting of Coalition for a Democratic Majority, Washington, Feb. 2/ The Washington Post, 2-3:(B)4.

Andrew Knight
Editor, "The Economist" (Britain)

4

[On the U.S. electoral process]: I would like to see a return to the smoke-filled rooms in the selection of candidates. The steeplechase course of primary elections projects media stars rather than people who know how to operate in the world of politics. I would not like to see primary elections disappear altogether, but I would like to see a return to the caucus system, or possibly a single national primary, plus state caucusing. The two parties need to get back to selecting candidates who know what the art and business of government are about.

Interview/World Press Review, April:23.

Edward I. Koch
Mayor of New York

5

I speak to everybody the same way, whether black, white or brown, and whether Christian, Jewish or Moslem. I think it's the height of pandering to speak differently to different groups of people. To do that, as far as I'm concerned, is real discrimination, real polarization. I believe in being truthful about what I am and who I am.

The New York Times Magazine, 2-1:66.

6

[On which Democratic candidate he will support for President in 1984]: If I support [Senator] Ted Kennedy, there would be cruises, jet-set parties and long, lazy summers at Hyannis Port.

[EDWARD I. KOCH]

If I were to support [former Vice President] Fritz Mondale, there would be winter in Minnesota. It's a tough choice.

Time, 11-2:93.

Jim Leach
United States Representative, R—Iowa

1

To some degree, the Republican Party is now identified as jeopardizing the security of the elderly, offending the young on environmental issues, as aggressive abroad, alienating blacks and alienating labor. Among constituencies, there aren't very many left a base could be built on.

The Christian Science Monitor, 12-15:8.

Patrick J. Leahy
United States Senator, D—Vermont

2

Single-issue politics of either the left or the right destroys the concept of a pluralistic nation, destroys the idea of representative democracy.

Washington, Sept. 15/
Los Angeles Times, 9-16:(1)6.

Charles T. Manatt
Chairman,
Democratic National Committee

3

We [Democrats] cannot be seen as the party whose simplistic response to every problem is more government and more regulation. We must convince people we can manage government as well as we can create it. We cannot be viewed as dewy-eyed spendthrifts or incompetent administrators. The voter must be convinced we spend money carefully and manage the business of government in a way that accomplishes their goals without endless red tape.

Before Democratic National Committee,
Washington, Feb. 27/
Los Angeles Herald Examiner, 2-28:(A)5.

4

. . . I would not couch our [Democratic Party] comeback on the success or failure of the Reagan economic program or foreign policy. Remember, only a few years ago—after the Watergate scandal—things looked great for us and bleak for the Republicans. Then we let the Republicans get far ahead of us in mechanization and techniques. We've got a lot of catching up to do, and we've got to do it at the state party level . . . We need to reassert ourselves with working people. We also must concentrate on younger people. We have to be very aware of growth regions in the South and Southwest. And we'll do all these things. In the 1982 election, we fully expect to increase our majority in the House and gain seats—if not control—in the Senate.

Interview/U.S. News & World Report, 5-25:44.

J. Edwin Matz
Chairman, John Hancock Mutual
Life Insurance Company

5

One problem that President Carter had from the beginning was that he moved into Washington determined to run the government as though it were Plains, Georgia. Carter is as much an alien to the Washington establishment now that he's leaving office as he was when he came in. [President-elect] Reagan, however, has really made a lot of impact by going to Washington and making a lot of friends in the weeks before his inauguration. That's all for the good.

Interview/U.S. News & World Report, 1-12:51.

James A. McClure
United States Senator, R—Idaho

6

We [Republicans] have 18 months to convince the American public that what we are trying to do is going to work and that what we are doing promises them a better future. If the people are convinced of that 18 months from now, then we are going to fare well in the next elections. Otherwise, it will be farewell . . . The conservative movement is strong and vital, but it's got to produce. The American people are very prag-

WHAT THEY SAID IN 1981

(JAMES A. McCLURE)

matic. They want something that works. When you look at this last election, I'm mindful of the tremendous Electoral College sweep that [President] Reagan had. But there were an awful lot of those states that he barely carried. Out of the 22 Republican Senators who were elected or re-elected, 11 were elected with 52 per cent or less of the vote. All of this tells me that the mandate was very broad but it wasn't very deep and was not a commitment to Reagan or the Republicans or the conservatives.

Interview, Washington/Los Angeles Times, 2-10:(I)6.

Harry C. McPherson, Jr.
*Lawyer; Former Special Counsel to
the President of the United States
(Lyndon B. Johnson)*

1

Ultimately, Jimmy Carter came across to the public as a political bookkeeper. He never displayed that "fire-in-the-belly" quality that people want in a political leader. The public never knew where he lived, what he really cared about. They finally decided that his overriding, driving purpose was to stay in office, so they turned him out. That's not the stuff of history.

Chicago Tribune, 1-16:(1)13.

2

The Democratic Party, like a silhouette painting, will begin to take its shape by what the Republicans do. This is not unlike 1960. John Kennedy's campaign was made up mostly of programs that [Dwight] Eisenhower had either vetoed or threatened to . . . [President] Reagan is not your laid-back Republican conservative, a nice old fellow who likes to play golf—or a young Democrat's image of Eisenhower back in the '50s. His [Reagan's] Administration has more in mind than merely sitting in neutral. On a number of programs, it wants to put the car in reverse. With that strong activism, a [Democratic Party] shape will come about as Democrats begin to rally round.

Interview/The New York Times, 8-2:(4)2.

Robert H. Michel
United States Representative, R—Illinois

3

[On his job as House Republican leader]: Each member [of the House] is a separate entity. You can't treat two alike. I know what I can get and what I can't, when to back off and when to push harder. It's not a matter of twisting arms. It's bringing them along by gentle persuasion. Sometimes they don't realize they're being brought into the orbit. You get down to the end of the walkway and you say, "Hey, we aren't 2 cents apart, are we?" and he says, "Well, I guess we aren't."

Interview/The Washington Post, 8-10:(A)5.

Walter F. Mondale
Former Vice President of the United States

4

I believe that [outgoing] President Carter is going to be treated much more generously by history than some might suggest. He stayed out of war. We did this other little thing: We told the truth and obeyed the law. And the President took on every miserable issue conceivable. From water policy to energy policy, Civil Service reforms, he did it. I think he deserves credit for it.

Interview/The Washington Post, 1-20:(A)21.

5

It takes a long time to understand the meaning of the past. Sometimes you must look more than once. If we look back on the [President Lyndon] Johnson years—and on the years of [Franklin] Roosevelt, [Harry] Truman and [John] Kennedy before, and [Jimmy] Carter after—we [Democrats] can capture a meaning that may have eluded us as we were going along. What through the haze of history stands out boldly today—more than the programs we passed, the regulations we wrote, the measures we framed—is a commitment we made. What we achieved as a people was to fundamentally commit ourselves to building a just society. That commitment is forever. I have never regretted it. And I'll never back off it.

*At Lyndon Johnson School of Public Affairs,
Austin, Texas/The Washington Post, 5-25:(A)18.*

Daniel P. Moynihan
United States Senator, D—New York
1

My feeling about the Congress is not that we [Democrats] lost the last election but that we seem to have persuaded ourselves that we've lost the next election. People are acting in anticipation of not just more losses, but of a continuation of the trend of the last few years. That has immobilized us. The Democratic members of the Senate are not a coherent group; they're not an energized group. They expect worse before ever there will be better.
Interview/The Washington Post, 5-17:(A)12.

Richard Neustadt
Professor of government, Harvard University
2

[President Reagan] and his top team had been severely underrated as government politicians. I look at the way he performs operationally—it seems awful good; and I look at the top people around him, and it's an impressive little crowd. In the short run, you're tempted to say "wow" ... [But] it's too early to tell what's transient from what's characteristic or enduring.
The Christian Science Monitor, 5-1:10.

Lyn Nofziger
Special Assistant to the President of the United States for Political Affairs
3

[Saying President Reagan will run for the Presidency again in 1984]: I kid you not, it'll be the same guy. If anybody has any doubts about Ronald Reagan's not thinking down the road four years and eight years, get it out of your head. If you're [other Republicans] lurking out there thinking, "Boy, in four years I'm going to get to run for President," you'd better change your [party] registration.
At California Republican state convention,
Sacramento, Feb. 8/
Los Angeles Herald Examiner, 2-9:(A)6.

Thomas P. O'Neill, Jr.
United States Representative,
D—Massachusetts
4

During the last 50 years, the Democratic Party has built up America, especially middle America. The record is out there. America was dilapidated. And we built it up. But we did make mistakes. There was a lack of productiveness in our programs; too much idealism; too many regulations; we went too far.
To reporters, Washington/
The Christian Science Monitor, 4-13:23.

5

[On President Reagan]: I think he's going to remain popular, to be perfectly truthful with you. People like him as an individual, and he handles the media better than anybody since Franklin Roosevelt, even including Jack Kennedy. There's just something about the guy that people like. They want him to be a success. They're rooting for him, and of course they're rooting for him because we haven't had any Presidential successes for years—Kennedy killed, Johnson with Vietnam, Nixon with Watergate, Ford, Carter and all the rest.
The Washington Post, 11-8:(A)1.

Rudolph G. Penner
Resident scholar,
American Enterprise Institute
6

While our current era is more conservative than the late 1960s and early 1970s, the power of special-interest groups has soared to disturbing levels since that time. The groups representing the elderly are especially powerful and their numbers are growing rapidly. They might lobby successfully for huge discretionary benefit increases that would be higher than those provided by the current automatic system. Yet, I believe that even the special interests are beginning—admittedly at a glacial pace—to face up to some constraints. They are starting to realize that if they continue to abuse their substantial political power to exploit the ordinary taxpayer, they

(RUDOLPH G. PENNER)

could provoke such an extreme political reaction that their benefits could be cut in a punitive manner. If I am wrong and they do not recognize this danger, we are in serious trouble. At worst, if the special interests do not begin to restrain themselves, they may eventually be restrained legally in ways that are not consistent with the precepts of a free society.

Before Senate Appropriations Committee,
Washington, Jan. 29/
The New York Times, 2-1:(3)2.

Shimon Peres
Chairman, Israeli Labor Party

1

Democracy is a school with endless classes, a permanent education. I know it's extremely difficult, because basically people look at politics for drama, for a kill, a bullfight.

Interview, Jerusalem/Time, 5-18:40.

Ronald Reagan
President-elect of the United States

2

As far as ethics are concerned, I believe the halls of government are well-nigh as sacred as a church or a cathedral or temple—that people shouldn't require a code of ethics if they're going to be in government. They should be determined, themselves, that their conduct is going to be beyond reproach. There can be no double standard in politics. This is one of the things that's wrong in our country today—that people who are so honest that they'd walk back to give back 2 cents in change if they were undercharged, at the same time are prone to say, "Well, you know, in politics it's different." Well, politics has no right to be different.

Interview, Jan. 7/U.S. News & World Report, 1-19:26.

Ronald Reagan
President of the United States

3

Every judgment [by the senior White House staff] will be made on the basis that no one is

going to be seeking office ever again. Now, I don't say that we won't seek office ever again, but the decisions will be made on what is good for the people . . . with no political considerations entering in.

At swearing-in ceremonies for his staff,
Washington, Jan. 21/
Los Angeles Times, 1-22:(I)18.

George E. Reedy
Dean, school of journalism, Marquette University; Former Press Secretary to the President of the United States (Lyndon B. Johnson)

4

[Former President Jimmy] Carter's main achievement was to slow the country down a bit after the shock of Watergate. Times were not right for much more than that. This was one of those periods when Presidents tend to disappear into the woodwork, like 1848-1860. We all remember Lincoln, but what can you recall about Zachary Taylor?

Los Angeles Herald Examiner, 1-11:(A)6.

Richard Richards
Chairman, Republican National Committee

5

We're [Republicans] still a minority, but the gap between us and the Democrats is closing fast. All my life the Democratic Party has lived on the myth that it was the party of the little guy, and the Republican Party was the party of the rich. But four years of Jimmy Carter exploded that myth, when unemployment and inflation hit the little guy the hardest. We know that many of our 44 million votes last November came from blue-collar workers, who no longer go to the union hall to get the word on how they are going to vote . . . We [Republicans] stand for values that we feel are important: working for what we get; making the family an important institution in our lives; getting government out of places where it has no business; creating economic opportunities for everyone. We've now got a great opportunity to show that our programs work.

(RICHARD RICHARDS)

If we fail, those people who joined us in 1980 will say, "It really doesn't make any difference who is in charge; everything is going to come out the same." We're confident we can show it does make a difference.

Interview/
U.S. News & World Report, 5-25:44.

John D. (Jay) Rockefeller IV
Governor of West Virginia (D)

1

. . . I don't think either major political party is ever going to be the power it was 20 or 30 years ago. Take the Republican victory in 1980. Did the big election sweep really represent a long-term revival of the Republican Party? Or did a particular coalition of voters, for a temporary set of reasons, vote Republican in just this one election? There's a big difference, and I think it was just a temporary shift. Reagan went over in the South last year, but that does not make it permanent, any more than the West is here and forevermore Republican. As for my [Democratic] Party, I continue to feel that the majority of people are closer to the Democrats and usually vote Democratic. They simply didn't do it last year.

Interview/U.S. News & World Report, 9-28:33.

Felix G. Rohatyn
Chairman, Municipal Assistance
Corporation of New York

2

. . . liberalism will not become a needed counterweight to current trends until it comes back to the real world, the bread-and-butter world of jobs and growth, of urban blight and energy independence, of the realistic need for American power in a chaotic world; until it returns to the notion that democracy requires equality of opportunity, but not an egalitarianism resolutely blind to the question of merit. Gay rights and national health insurance may be important to some. But they are not the country's first priority. It is liberalism's fascination with secondary issues that has created the reaction which now sees the Moral Majority intimidating politicians and advertisers, and the

Congress trying to determine the beginning of life [for abortion legislation].

At Hofstra University School of Business
commencement/The Washington Post, 5-28:(A)19.

Clay Shaw
United States Representative, R—Florida

3

Every conservative becomes a liberal when he talks about his own district.

Interview, Washington/
The New York Times, 1-18:(1)10.

Leon Shull
Executive director,
Americans for Democratic Action

4

The current Democratic [Party] syndrome—"Let him [President Reagan] have everything he wants; we'll pick up the pieces after he's failed"—is a massive failure on the part of the Democratic leadership on the Hill and in the Party. Me-tooing the President is no way back to political power. Privately, the Democrats on the Hill say Reagan's program is madness. But publicly they go along with it. It's very sad. I have more respect for the Republican Party leadership. At least over the years they stood up against the Democrats and fought.

The Christian Science Monitor, 5-5:3.

Theodore C. Sorenson
Historian; Former Special Counsel to the
President of the United States (John F. Kennedy)

5

The Carter Administration will go down in history as proof of the inability of those who have no experience in national or international issues to govern the country effectively. The President came in with the best of intentions and a high-quality Cabinet, but the lack of experience and sensitivity that he and some members of his White House staff displayed so undermined his effectiveness at the start that he never overcame.

Chicago Tribune, 1-16:(1)13.

Robert S. Strauss
Former Chairman,
Democratic National Committee

1

I could go into the major lobbying firms in this town [Washington] and stock an entire government. I could put a quality government in place, with substantive people, people who know the issues, and know how to get things done.

Los Angeles Times, 2-9:(I)11.

Michael L. Synar
United States Representative,
R—Oklahoma

2

I've come to the conclusion that outside of the three big issues—energy, the economy and government regulation—the major issue of the '80s will be the impact of special interests on this country. They have become such a dominant force in politics, financially and information-wise. They have better grass-roots organizations than most Congressmen.

Interview, Washington/
The New York Times, 1-11:(1)13.

James R. Thompson
Governor of Illinois (R)

3

The policies of today are negative. It is not so much who you elect, its who you throw out.

Chicago Tribune Magazine, 7-26:9.

Gore Vidal
Author

4

There is a violent feeling against [President] Ronald Reagan in the movie business, where I make a living. It's not sour grapes, but the people out there [Hollywood] know actors. Reagan is an actor, and the one thing actors are paid for is to be plausible. There's nothing much in his head. There doesn't have to be; other people write the things for him to say. Actors are pas-

sive all their lives; they are moved around by directors like pieces of furniture. We probably should have elected [director] Billy Wilder. He'd move the country around and we'd have some good jokes, and he's only 73 years old.

Interview, Washington/
The Washington Post, 5-4:(B)13.

Lech Walesa
National chairman, Solidarity
(independent Polish trade union)

5

[On politics in Western countries]: . . . all those political parties which don't know what they want, and one disturbs the other, doesn't let the other work, yet one supports the other—what kind of brothel is that? It seems a brothel to me and nothing else . . . [Western parties] waste their time biting each other, insulting each other, accusing each other, collecting gossip on each other: He goes to sleep with her, she goes to sleep with someone else. It doesn't seem to me that your parties have done much, and in all that brothel I see only one indisputable fact: They say they want something and they do the reverse.

Interview/The Washington Post, 3-8:(C)4.

Kevin H. White
Mayor of Boston

6

We politicians are seldom described as sane men. But you have to have mental health to survive in government. The political environment itself seems insane.

Chicago Tribune, 9-27:(2)6.

James C. Wright, Jr.
United States Representative,
D—Texas

7

I am not at all sure the Democrats were whipped very badly [in last November's national elections]. The Democrats retained control of the House by a margin of 51 seats, and the House is and always has been the

(JAMES C. WRIGHT, JR.)

closest of any entity of government to the American people. Ironically, while the Republicans were gaining control of the Senate, there were actually more votes cast for Democratic Senatorial candidates throughout the nation than there were for Republican Senatorial candidates.

Broadcast interview/
"Meet the Press,"
NBC-TV, 2-15.

Social Welfare

James F. Bere
Chairman, Borg-Warner Corporation

1

Corporations today feel an absolute obligation both to help the economically underprivileged and to aid a wide range of activities that we hope will advance our society. Although the amount of money and time contributed by business in the last decade have risen sharply, business can probably afford more than it has been giving . . . We all need what only private philanthropy can offer. We need its compassion. We need its understanding of human frailty; its availability in time of stress, of danger and of deprivation. We need its concern for the poor, the weak, the uncertain, the frightened. But above all, we need philanthropy to be useful, not simply to be there.

Before Chicago Community Trust/
The Christian Science Monitor, 10-19:22.

Edmund G. Brown, Jr.
Governor of California (D)

2

Since Franklin Roosevelt signed the Social Security Act into law in 1935, there has been a national commitment—during Republican and Democratic Administrations alike—that one of the duties of government is to help older Americans live in dignity. That promise has been broken in the name of Reaganomics . . . The message we receive from Washington [the Reagan Administration] is that Reaganomics has little concern for the elderly, little appreciation for what it is like to be poor, sick and old and in need of help.

Before California delegates to White House
Conference on Aging, Los Angeles, Nov. 24/
Los Angeles Times, 11-25:(I)3.

Dale Bumpers
United States Senator, D—Arkansas

3

What happened in this country—and I know you've heard this before—the New Deal and the Fair Deal and all those things really worked almost too well. Now it's kind of "pull-up-the-ladder-Jack-I'm-aboard." So many people have gotten on board that they're not quite as sensitive. They forget those people who are still reaching for the first rung on the ladder. It's not very trendy right now to say that you're sensitive to the plight of the poor folks and the people who still haven't made it.

Interview/
The Washington Post, 5-18:(A)13.

George Bush
Vice President of the United States

4

Everyone involved in [the debate over President Reagan's proposed reduction in Social Security benefits] . . . agrees that if the Social Security System continues along its present path, it will self-destruct in a matter of a few years. Something has to be done . . . The charge was made that President Reagan lacked compassion in dealing with the problems facing our country's Social Security recipients . . . That charge is baseless . . . He is in fact faced with a crisis largely brought on by the actions over the years of many of the very critics now attacking him. Is the question of how we can best salvage Social Security debatable? Certainly. And, to his credit, the President has from the first indicated an open mind on this issue.

At University of Virginia commencement,
May 24/The Washington Post, 5-25:(B)8.

(GEORGE BUSH)

1

I hope we can move forward in a non-partisan way on the whole question of entitlement programs. I'm not talking about adversely affecting the earned benefits of people on Social Security. However, I don't know a Democrat or a Republican in Congress who doesn't think there's a need to review the broad field of entitlements. Look at some of the increases in the last 10 years: Social Security pensions up 281 per cent, Medicare up 400 per cent, Federal-employee retirement up 370 per cent, unemployment compensation up 420 per cent, food stamps up 1,416 per cent. If the American people took a look at these figures, they'd say: "Wait a minute. That's too much in 10 years." You must concede that a massive part of the Federal budget is uncontrolled.

Interview/
U.S. News & World Report, 12-14:21.

Robert N. Butler
Director, National Institute on Aging
of the United States

2

The very fact that there are so many older women now means we should be paying more attention to their health, housing, economic and social needs. These older women are the poorest of the poor in our society. We must realize that they already are what the younger women of today will be in the future . . . Our rapidly expanding population of older women is due primarily to medical advances that have reduced the number of women who die during childbirth. We believe men have been dying sooner than women because men have traditionally had a harder life-style, have been harder drinkers, have worked on more dangerous jobs and played hazardous sports and have been killed in war. That explains about 60 per cent of the reasons why women are living longer than men. The other 40 per cent is beyond our knowledge at this time.

The Washington Post,
4-20:(A)4.

Robert C. Byrd
United States Senator,
D—West Virginia

3

[Criticizing President Reagan's proposed reduction in Social Security benefits]: The President's proposals constitute a retreat from his campaign rhetoric and statements he made subsequent to the inauguration. There has been a breaking of promises . . . We are told that Social Security was one of those sacred parts of the safety net. The suddenness with which this action would be taken would be unduly hurtful of those who would be affected.

News conference, Washington, May 15/
The New York Times, 5-16:9.

Samuel Cornelius
Deputy Director, Community Services
Administration of the United States

4

[Saying he is happy that his agency is being eliminated]: Come September 30th, we're not just going to be cut back, we're going to be cut out. I was in on the attempt to cut CSA 10 years ago. I think the states ought to be coming up with the solutions to poverty. I reject the notion that people in Washington are the only ones with any brains.

At National Conference of Blacks in Government,
Washington/The Washington Post, 8-28:(B)2.

Robert F. Drinan
President, Americans for Democratic Action;
Former United States Representative,
D—Massachusetts

5

There is no reason why we have to turn our back on the poor. There is no reason we should take the social programs that passed overwhelmingly by large margins all through the years and cut them back by 25 per cent. Even in the name of the ideology of the economics of this [Reagan] Administration, it's not going to cure inflation. They are transferring virtually all of this money from the poor to the Pentagon. Federal spending is not diminished. The budget will not go down.

The Washington Post, 7-12:(H)4.

Marian Wright Edelman
President, Children's Defense Fund

1

[On the Reagan Administration's cuts in aid for the poor]: The Administration is engaged in a wholesale attack on existing programs without specifically examining what is working and what is not, what can be improved and what cannot, who needs help and who does not. In the process, they are dismantling the fundamental national commitment to groups too long excluded from American society.

Washington, Feb. 19/
The New York Times, 2-20:9.

Bob Elias
Director of government and industrial relations, Action for Boston Community Development, Inc.

2

[Criticizing the Reagan Administration's proposal to end the Community Services Administration]: I'm not saying CSA is infallible. It clearly is not. I'm not even saying don't cut the anti-poverty funds. If the Federal budget has to be cut, we can take our share of cuts. All I'm saying is that we need to save CSA as an indication of continuing Federal concern for the poor. This is the only government agency whose only concern is poor people. To eliminate it is to deny the country's commitment, its basic way of thinking and feeling about the poor. It is like taking away a ladder that has been constructed piece by piece over the last 50 years that offers a way up and out of the quicksand of poverty.

Interview, Washington/
The Washington Post, 4-17:(A)13.

Walter E. Fauntroy
Delegate to the United States House of Representatives, D—District of Columbia

3

[On President Reagan's proposed economic program of cutting taxes and government spending]: It is apparent to those of us in the [Congressional] Black Caucus that the burden of fighting inflation and balancing the budget is to be placed on the shoulders of those who can least afford to bear it. I have come to tell you today that the Reagan Administration is failing the moral test of government . . . [Senator] Jesse Helms of . . . North Carolina represents his constituents well. His theory is that government is over-feeding poor children on what amounts to 86 cents a day. Eighty-six cents. Now what you gonna eat with eighty-six cents? . . . Their rationale is that people who are working ought to buy their own food. But some people would have to stop working if they didn't have the extra help food stamps provide. They will go back on welfare, and pay no taxes either. Now, isn't that *stupid*? But you know, there are a lot of people out there who really think our problem in America is all those poor people. Probably they haven't looked at Mr. Reagan's $2.9-billion public-welfare program which he calls the oil-depletion allowance . . . Right now, the oil companies are so rich that they don't have anything better to do with their money than run around and buy up Montgomery Ward stores. *But they need help.* And Ronald Reagan and Jesse Helms *want* to help them by taking food away from some little child who's mama gets food stamps and who may get a free meal at school.

At rally sponsored by D.C. Food Stamp Coalition,
Washington, March 7/
The Washington Post, 3-8:(B)1,2.

David H. Fischer
Professor of history,
Brandeis University

4

The problem with Social Security is part of a huge problem with our social-welfare system generally. Just as we're finding it increasingly difficult to afford Social Security, we're having the same problem with education, with health, with almost every kind of public service. Either we have to increase our spending in the public sector—and it could be increased; we lag behind many European nations in that respect—or we could reduce the level of spending in these areas, or we could try to reform the system in some fundamental way. Those are the only three pos-

(DAVID H. FISCHER)

sibilities. We're now doing one and two. I think the nature of individual values in our society is such that Number 1 is not a political possibility in the future. The American voters will say, "No more!"—as in fact they are beginning to do. Numbers 1 and 2 are much less constructive solutions than 3.

Interview, Brandeis University/
The Christian Science Monitor, 9-24:12.

George Gilder
Program director, International Center for
Economic Policy Studies, New York

1

One of the more irritating ideas is that anybody who criticizes the welfare system wants people out on the streets. It is the welfare system that breaks down families and drives fathers into the streets. The fact is that the chief enemies of a rational welfare system are people who refuse to reduce the current level of benefits. They continually cut back on the fringes of the system in the belief that there are some deserving poor who should receive very great benefits—twice as great as the income from a job at the minimum wage—while there are all these undeserving poor out there whom the government can identify and kick off the rolls. This always means that the government behaves in a very brutal way while at the same time creating huge incentives for the poor to wildly destroy their lives in order to qualify for benefits that are far greater than any job could yield them. This is not compassionate; it's the most immoral aspect of American liberalism.

Interview/U.S. News & World Report, 4-6:54.

John V. Graziano
Inspector General, Department of
Agriculture of the United States

2

Food stamps have become a secondary currency. They are as negotiable as regular currency is. People have learned, unfortunately, that you can use a food stamp to buy a lot of things besides food.

Time, 10-12:44.

Milton Gwirtzman
Chairman, National Commission
on Social Security

3

At some time during [1982], it [the main Social Security trust fund] would be well below the level required to meet the benefit payments becoming due shortly after the end of [each] month . . . When we talk about Social Security having "cash flow" problems, it is a gentle way of saying that if nothing more is done, sometime next year Social Security checks will just not go out.

Before House Social Security Subcommittee,
Washington, Feb. 17/Chicago Tribune, 2-18:(1)3.

Paula Hawkins
United States Senator, R—Florida

4

I'd like to redo the food-stamp program so it's fair and can be easily enforced. I want to feed more people with the same amount of money. I want to restore dignity to the project. I regret that a program which had such worthy beginnings and a great cause of feeding people who could not feed themselves ended up being a gravy train for crooks. I don't like cheaters. Above all things, I like justice. Mercy is great, but justice is better.

Interview, Los Angeles, April 13/
Los Angeles Herald Examiner, 4-15:(B)5.

Jesse A. Helms
United States Senator,
R—North Carolina

5

[On the food-stamp program]: I believe we owe it to the taxpayers to take every precaution available to us to make sure that one of the most outrageously expensive and most abused programs in the history of the country will be brought under control. I do not begrudge helping any of the truly needy; but anybody who tries to pretend that this program does not need radical reform is just cockeyed.

Before the Senate,
Washington, June 26/
The Washington Post, 7-6:(A)3.

WHAT THEY SAID IN 1981

Benjamin L. Hooks
Executive director, National Association for the Advancement of Colored People

1

[On President Reagan's proposed government spending cuts]: We of the NAACP have concluded that the Administration's economic proposals will, if enacted, wreak havoc and devastation on the bottom end of our society, on the poor and working poor. As to the budget cuts, we feel that they are unjustified, unnecessary, skewed against the poor and tilted toward the rich. We will mobilize public opinion to dramatize that President Reagan does not have a mandate to wreck these social programs of the last 50 years.

News conference, Washington, March 9/
Los Angeles Times, 3-10:(I)7.

Dwight Ink
Director, Community Services Administration of the United States

2

[Saying the imminent dissolution of his agency will not mean less government service to the poor, only a change to different, more local, hands]: I do not accept the idea that the Federal government is highly efficient and the states are inefficient, that people at the Federal level are compassionate and the states ignore people and social problems.

Interview/The Washington Post, 9-18:(A)27.

Vernon E. Jordan, Jr.
President, National Urban League

3

Even the wildest optimist knows it will take years for the President's [Reagan] program to produce the prosperity he promises. What do we do until then? How do poor people survive without the basic programs they need until then? . . . The real issue is the grand design of substituting charity for entitlements, local tyranny for Federal protection, and unbridled, law-of-the-jungle capitalism for a balanced cooperation between the public and private sectors. Thus, the real issue is the nature of our society.

News conference, Washington, July 19/
The Washington Post, 7-20:(A)9.

Keith Joseph
Secretary for Industry of the United Kingdom

4

The best friend of the afflicted, whether the elderly, the handicapped, or other groups, are the profits earned in the competitive marketplace, because these profits are the direct and indirect sources of the tax revenues needed to pay for social programs.

Interview, Chicago/
The Christian Science Monitor, 7-7:10.

Edward M. Kennedy
United States Senator, D—Massachusetts

5

[Criticizing Reagan Administration proposed budget cuts]: Real human beings will suffer from untreated illnesses as a result of unfair budget cuts. Real workers will be put out of work. The elderly on Social Security will be left next winter with a cruel choice between food on their tables and heat in their homes. Children will be born retarded because of cuts in protein for their mothers. They deserve a better chance in life than to join the body count of [Federal Budget Director] David Stockman's budget.

Before Women's National Democratic Club,
Washington, June 8/
Los Angeles Times, 6-9:(I)12.

6

[On Reagan Administration plans to trim Social Security benefits as a way of keeping the system solvent]: This Administration has launched an unprecedented assault on Social Security. They want these cuts not to save the system from bankruptcy but to try to save the rest of the budget from deficit. You should say to [Federal Budget Director] David Stockman, "Keep your budget-cutting hands off the Social Security system."

At Social Security rally,
Washington, July 21/
Los Angeles Times, 7-22:(1)11.

Lane Kirkland
*President, American Federation of Labor-
Congress of Industrial Organizations*

1

[The Reagan Administration has] drained the public purse [to] lavish welfare on the greedy rich, in the name of "incentive." They have stripped the poor and jobless of welfare, food stamps and unemployment insurance, also in the name of "incentive." That is known as the carrot-and-stick policy: for the rich, the carrot; for the poor, the stick.

*At AFL-CIO convention, New York, Nov. 16/
Chicago Tribune, 11-18:(1)8.*

David J. Mahoney
Chairman, Norton Simon, Inc.

2

Now we are faced with a phased withdrawal of Federal funds from social programs and the communities they serve ... We [in business] are presented with a unique opportunity to demonstrate that we can meet society's needs more efficiently, more wisely and more effectively than the government can ... If every American corporation donated just 5 per cent of taxable income—half of what is allowed—there would be $10-billion additional available to provide a meaningful shock absorber in this time of changed Federal priorities. That would represent a sound investment in meeting the critical needs of our communities. And it would be a positive, active assertion of business' responsibility to the society that sustains us.

The Washington Post, 11-11:(A)26.

Iris Mitgang
*Chairman,
National Women's Political Caucus*

3

[Criticizing President Reagan's sweeping cuts in Federal spending]: Women recognize that a serious economic condition exists, and we agree with the critical need to reduce inflation, lower unemployment, increase productivity and reduce the tax burden. But this must be accomplished through an economically sound policy

that is also compassionate and fair. The Reagan proposal is neither ... When the government calls for a new relationship between citizen and Federal government, it is calling for drastic social change. The tax cut, when combined with the budget cuts, will insure the distinction between the rich and everyone else—and will limit opportunities for social mobility for all.

March 26/Los Angeles Times, 3-27:(V)1,11.

Walter F. Mondale
Vice President of the United States

4

... one of the things that was pretty much off the stage [during the recent Presidential election] I think will be back up front in '84, and that will be the issue of social justice in America. The American people are very fair-minded, and if the [newly elected President] Reagan people are betting that they're not, they're going to find out they're wrong. To abandon this shared commitment of over 50 years to social justice in America will, I think, bring about a prompt and dramatic public response that will put that issue back up front ... I'm talking about everybody in America who is in a position where just a minimum decent life is not possible. That can be old people, handicapped people, poorly educated children, a small-businessman who can't get along. It also includes civil-rights.

Interview/The Washington Post, 1-20:(A)21.

Walter F. Mondale
Former Vice President of the United States

5

[Criticizing President Reagan's proposals to reduce Social Security benefits as a way of dealing with the system's fiscal problems]: When it comes to Social Security, you cannot keep your bargain with working Americans by eliminating the minimum benefit, by canceling student benefits, by telling those who choose early retirement to get along on 55 per cent of their basic benefit, by cutting more than a million disabled people. A House committee tells us that over the next five years this Administration's proposal will cut benefits by 10 per cent for 18 million people; one-third for the seven million who choose early retirement. And 1.3

million disabled people who get nothing at all. The point is this: When you work a lifetime, and raise a family, and the time comes to retire, that Social Security check—and the way it is figured —should be as sure as the sun coming up in the morning.

At Lyndon Johnson School of Public Affairs commencement, Austin, Texas/ The Washington Post, 5-25:(A)18.

1

[Criticizing Reagan Administration budget cuts and policies toward public-assistance programs]: It is not only what they are doing that offends a decent sense of fairness. It's how they are doing it. Someone told me the other day he thought it might be necessary to cut money for handicapped children, but at least our leaders shouldn't look like they are enjoying it ... We achieved so much as a people because we have listened so closely to our conscience. We've been true to our history because we led with our values. What worries me today is that just when America is hitting its moral stride, there are those who would stop our progress dead in its tracks ... The tragedy is that we could do what needs to be done—tighten the budget and reduce our deficits—and we could do it fairly. Our needed programs would have to be constrained with the others, but they could go forward ... Wherever there's a chicken coup, [the Administration] has found a fox to guard it. To promote human rights, they proposed an opponent of human rights. To watch over lands and water, they found the right person to befoul them. [Budget Director David Stockman] may know how to cut a budget, but I wouldn't trust him to draw a line between poverty and wealth, or meanness and fairness in America.

Before National Urban League, Washington, July 22/ The Washington Post, 7-23:(A)18,19.

J. Richard Munro
President, Time, Inc.

2

I know that business executives are not supposed to disapprove of the [Reagan] Adminis-

tration's spending program. Polls show support among us hovering around 90 per cent. That's a phenomenal vote of confidence. I support the new policies that promote growth, new investment and greater productivity. Yet, in the rush to fight inflation and stimulate investment, I fear that we have cut too deeply, that we have put too high a burden on the poor and elderly, and that we are jeopardizing the long-term goals of this program and the interests of business. I am especially concerned about the cuts in social spending. They have gone too far, too fast. And too few of us understand their impact ... You can go down the line—education at all levels, jobs and training programs, Medicaid, housing aid, food stamps, school nutrition, support for poor families with children, energy assistance, unemployment insurance, and numerous other social services. Every one of these received major spending cuts, adding up to $25-billion of the $35-billion total cut from the budget this summer ... The budget cuts are leaving some serious and immediate human needs unmet. And if the budget cuts continue as scheduled, the problems of the poor will worsen intolerably. As business executives, I don't think we should stand by and let this happen.

Before Union League Club of New York, November/The New York Times, 11-15:(3)2.

Ralph Nader
Lawyer; Consumer-rights advocate

3

[President Reagan is a] cruel man with a steady smile ... We're dealing here with a philosophy of anarchy and reactionism ... Reagan is moving to destroy legal services for the poor ... to drastically cut antitrust actions ... and to remove the major advances in workplace standards. These are only a few illustrations of a constant theme—to pursue the Exxon and GM policy lines, regardless of who is hurt ... There is more and more grass-roots opposition. Neighborhoods and community groups are organizing themselves to prevent the destruction of the quality of life in America ... The Reagan policies are doomed to failure.

News conference, Santa Monica, Calif., March 29/ Los Angeles Times, 3-30:(I)11.

Thomas P. O'Neill, Jr.
United States Representative,
D—Massachusetts

1

The President [Reagan] may be hard as nails when it comes to programs that help poor people. He may be a real tightwad when it comes to programs that help working families. He may be a real Ebenezer Scrooge when it comes to programs like student loans that offer opportunity to the young middle class. But when it comes to giving tax breaks to the wealthy of this country, the President has a heart of gold . . . That's a great philosophy—for the people living in Beverly Hills. But it's not the philosophy that built this country . . . and will rebuild America in the 1980s.

Before Communications Workers of America,
Washington, July 7/
Los Angeles Herald Examiner, 7-8:(A)6.

J. A. (Jay) Parker
Director, Lincoln Institute

2

Public housing and urban-renewal programs . . . have destroyed more dwelling units than they have constructed. Urban renewal has destroyed viable neighborhoods, driving the poor from their homes to even less-satisfactory and often more-expensive housing.

Interview, Washington/
The Christian Science Monitor, 2-11:4.

Claude Pepper
United States Representative,
D—Florida

3

[On Social Security]: There are many voices sounding the call of retreat . . . Social Security, they say . . . must be slashed . . . in order to make it possible to cut the taxes of many . . . who hardly need tax reduction as much as the elderly need the benefits they are receiving.

Before the House,
Washington, February/
The New York Times Magazine, 11-29:126.

Charles B. Rangel
United States Representative,
D—New York

4

[On President Reagan's proposal to cut Federal spending]: The consequences of the President's program on the needy and the working poor will be terrible, catastrophic and swift. The stakes are simply too high for children and elderly, the disadvantaged, the unemployed and the working poor for us to be swept blindly along in a rising wave of budget-slashing hysteria.

Before House Public Assistance Subcommittee,
Washington, March 11/
Los Angeles Times, 3-12:(I)9.

Ronald Reagan
President of the United States

5

[On his proposed Federal budget cuts]: We will continue to fulfill the obligations that spring from our national conscience. Those who through no fault of their own must depend on the rest of us—the poverty stricken, the disabled, the elderly, all those with true need—can rest assured that the social safety net of programs they depend on are exempt from any cuts. The full retirement benefits of the more than 31 million Social Security recipients will be continued along with an annual cost-of-living increase. Medicare will not be cut, nor will supplemental income for the blind, aged and disabled. Funding will continue for veterans' pensions. School breakfasts and lunches for the children of low-income families will continue as will nutrition and other special services for the aging. There will be no cut in Project Head Start or summer youth jobs. All in all, nearly $216-billion providing help for tens of millions of Americans will be fully funded. But government will not continue to subsidize individuals or particular business interests where real need cannot be demonstrated.

Before joint session of Congress,
Washington, Feb. 18/
The New York Times, 2-19:14.

WHAT THEY SAID IN 1981

(RONALD REAGAN)

1

. . . the main goal in any of these reductions [in government spending for social services] is still aimed at correcting those abuses that come about through the interpretation of regulations to allow people who do not have real need that justifies their imposing on their fellow citizens for sustenance—for them to still be able to take advantage of these programs. The person with real need we still want to help. At the same time, when you say to force someone to go out and seek work—I think that the whole target of some of our social reforms, like welfare, always should have to find a way to salvage those people and make them self-sustaining. Instead of perpetuating them unto the third and fourth generation as wards of the government.

News conference, Washington, Nov. 10/
The New York Times, 11-11:14.

2

This is a very diverse country. The problems of the welfare client in New York City are far different than those from one in some small town in the rural areas in the Middle West, or something in more rural states. I believe that there is much more chance of waste and of fraud in trying to run it from the national level than there is in running it at the local level. These are your neighbors there that you are trying to help, and you are better able to know what to do for them than Washington is, 3,000 miles away.

Interview, Washington, Nov. 19/
The New York Times, 11-22:(1)14.

3

[On critics of his handling of the Social Security issue]: There has been political demagoguery and outright falsehood and, as a result, many who rely on Social Security for their livelihood have been needlessly and cruelly frightened. Those who did the frightening either didn't know what they were talking about or they were deliberately lying. [During last year's Presidential election campaign, I pledged

to] try to restore the integrity of Social Security and do so without penalty to those dependent on that program. I have kept that pledge, and intend to keep it—both parts of it. We will not betray those entitled to Social Security benefits, and we will—indeed, we must—put Social Security on a sound financial basis.

At White House Conference on Aging,
Washington, Dec. 1/
Los Angeles Times, 12-2:(1)1.

Richard S. Schweiker
Secretary of Health and Human
Services of the United States

4

The Social Security System must be maintained in a manner that insures its long-term financial integrity. Current Social Security recipients must be assured they will continue to receive benefits and that benefit levels will not erode over time. Just as important, those who contribute their hard-earned dollars to the Social Security System must have confidence that security is guaranteed when retirement comes. To restore this confidence will be my top priority as Secretary.

Before American Hospital Association,
Washington, Feb. 2/The New York Times, 2-3:8.

5

The current Congressional budget process makes it clear that there really are not any uncommitted Federal revenues present to turn to for [funding] Social Security. Any general revenues for this purpose would have to come from new or increased taxes of other types. This would mean that additional taxes would need to be paid by—and be a burden on—the same people who now pay Social Security taxes . . . The remaining option of slowing the growth of the benefit outgo under the program [trimming benefits] is the only real choice. [Reagan Administration proposals] will overcome Social Security's serious funding problems by eliminating excessive incentives to claim benefits early, by removing penalties for continued work ef-

(RICHARD S. SCHWEIKER)

forts, and by lessening the emphasis on the social, adequacy or welfare aspects of the system at the expense of its basic purposes . . . No matter whose economic forecasts or assumptions you use, the basic Social Security program is going to be unable to meet its commitments to millions of Americans unless some legislative action is taken, and taken soon.

Before Senate Social Security Subcommittee,
Washington, July 7/
Los Angeles Times, 7-8:(I)12.

Fortney Stark
United States Representative, D—California

1

[On Reagan Administration budget cuts]: For the first time we are being asked to take food from poor families, educational projects from the retarded, protection from the elderly. These cuts are being made so [the Administration] can provide a 30 per cent tax break for someone who makes $200,000. I want to help the President cut spending and balance the budget, but I have no stomach for achieving that by taking 150,000 children out of day-care centers or cutting assistance to 1.3 million children in the poorest families.

At House Ways and Means Committee hearing,
Washington/Chicago Tribune, 3-27:(1)4.

John A. Svahn
Commissioner, Social Security Administration of the United States

2

The Social Security program is a little bit like the Constitution. It gets reinterpreted every so often. Originally, it was to be a base for a foundation for retirement—not a retirement system unto itself, but a partial replacement for wages lost as a result of retirement. It was then expanded to provide a partial replacement for wages lost by reason of death of the worker. The last big component was intended to be a partial replacement for wages lost as a result of disability of the worker . . . We don't want to go

to general [government] revenue [to support Social Security], because once you eliminate the fiscal discipline of the trust fund and the dedicated tax, it becomes all too easy to finance the program out of the deficit, so to speak. Print more money. That fuels inflation, and inflation hits people who are retired and disabled much harder than it does other people.

Interview/The New York Times, 5-31:(4)4.

3

I think we have to face up to the fact that we have, over the past 10 years, over-developed Social Security. That's just in the last 10 years. For 30 years before that, it did fairly well. But in the last 10 years, we just over-developed it. We have now a system that is geared to increasing payments for more and more people at a rate that's far richer than we can afford. What we have to do is dampen that benefit growth in the future. A small adjustment now with time for people to plan in the future will solve the long-range problem.

Interview/
Los Angeles Herald Examiner, 7-29:(A)14.

Franklin A. Thomas
President, Ford Foundation

4

There is a growing need for foundations to play a connective role in society—to link private-sector resources with the energies of people in a community who are trying to address problems, whether these people are in community groups or social agencies that work for the public's benefit. Foundations are making explicit efforts to link these sectors and to focus attention on particular social issues. To achieve this, more than good-will and intelligence are needed; you have to bring dollar resources with you. The more you have, the greater your ability to act as a catalyst.

Interview/
U.S. News & World Report, 3-23:62.

WHAT THEY SAID IN 1981

Ben J. Wattenberg
*Senior fellow, American Enterprise
Institute; Chairman, Coalition for a
Democratic Majority*

1

The Great Society—the mixed economy, welfare state, whatever you want to call it—is going to survive. It's probably gone too far; it's going to be rationalized; it's going to be shaved. But [the Reagan Administration is] not—rhetoric notwithstanding—going to destroy the good part. And they couldn't get away with it if they tried.

Interview/The New York Times, 8-2:(4)2.

Transportation

Malcolm Baldrige
Secretary of Commerce
of the United States

1

[On charges that limiting Japanese car imports by the U.S. would be an act against free trade]: There is no completely free trade in automobiles anywhere in the world, and I defy you to show me a country that has it. Italy limits imports to less than 1 per cent of all autos. France allows no more than 3 per cent. Japan has a tax that amounts to 20 per cent in addition to non-tariff barriers. Countries like Mexico and Brazil demand that 50 to 60 per cent of a car be domestically produced. I look at free trade as an ideal that we should strive for and gradually work up to. But I do not believe in the United States unilaterally disarming itself because of a theory that nobody else is following.
Interview/U.S. News & World Report, 5-4:48.

Moe Biller
President,
American Postal Workers Union

2

[On the illegal air-traffic controllers strike during which the government fired striking controllers]: There are compassionate ways to end this strike. This is a strong nation, and compassion and understanding should have a place in public policy. Don't we all admire the Solidarity trade-union movement in Poland for essentially doing the same thing as the air-traffice controllers—striking against their own government? There was no action taken against them, I might add. Now the Poles are struggling for food and for basic freedoms, but it was all begun in the shipyards by union people. The U.S. does not have a dictatorial government, but in a very real sense the controllers felt repressed by an agency [the FAA] that would not treat them fairly.
Interview/U.S. News & World Report, 8-24:18.

Robert Blanchette
Administrator, Federal
Railroad Administration

3

The DOT is opposed to dismembering Conrail. We want to reintegrate it with the private-sector railroad industry, maximizing the lines that will be retained and improving service going to shippers in the Northeast and Midwest. To me, dismemberment is kind of a fire-sale scenario, in which it's catch-as-catch-can and good businesses are "cherry-picked" [and unprofitable lines passed over] . . . The DOT position is a middle ground between Conrail as a nationalized company, which it would be if it continues in its corporate form, and a scenario depicted in a USRA report of a "fire-sale" in which 45,000 people are unemployed and massive miles of track abandoned. We propose an orderly transfer of Conrail's services, lines and employees to the private sector so that the government can get out of the railroad business . . . We're not going to recapture the $7-billion investment taxpayers have made so far in Conrail's lines . . . If Conrail continues as a nationalized railroad, the bill for the taxpayers could be another $4-billion over the next five years.
Interview/Chicago Tribune, 4-12:(5)3.

Douglas A. Fraser
President, United Automobile
Workers of America

4

[On Japanese automobile exports to the U.S.]: . . . I think the Japanese are taking unfair ad-

(DOUGLAS A. FRASER)

vantage of this market. The [U.S.] auto industry is an undustry in trouble, and what we need is time, time to turn this industry around. People have to start looking at the cost of unemployment. A lot of economists estimate that because of the downturn in the auto industry, we lost something like $11-billion last year. This is a cost of losing the taxes from the auto workers who were unemployed and the people who are dependent upon the auto industry ... Restraint [in Japanese exports] is not a long-term answer. The long-term answer is to get the Japanese to put some capital where their market is. This is a $10-billion market for the Japanese, and they should make some cars where their sales are.

Broadcast interview/"Meet the Press," NBC-TV, 3-22.

John Galipault
President, Aviation Safety Institute

1

[On the illegal air-traffic controllers strike during which the government fired striking controllers and is now using supervisors, military controllers and non-striking controllers]: I've talked to a lot of pilots in the last few days. The majority have told me: "We don't care if the [fired] controllers never come back ... We're getting great service [now] and being treated very nicely, with no bad-mouthing." It raises the question of how many people you really need to do that job. I know of one control tower that would tip over if you put one more person in it.

The Christian Science Monitor, 8-7:12.

David Girard-diCarlo
Chairman, Southeastern Pennsylvania Transportation Authority

2

[On the country's deteriorating public-transit system]: The most likely scenario is things will get worse around the country before they get better ... We may indeed have more systems around the country that will shut down. The entire industry has funding problems, whether you are talking about cities that have subway systems or mass transit in general. There is less than adequate commitment by the Federal and local government. We are still on the horns of a dilemma in this country. If we are to be in the public sector, someone will have to bite some tough political bullets and give us an adequate funding base to do the job that has to be done.

Los Angeles Times, 3-9:(I)18.

Lee A. Iacocca
Chairman, Chrysler Corporation

3

We need to get the word out that things [at Chrysler] are not as stormy as they look. We'd be off to the races if it wasn't for the gnawing problem that a lot of people out there still lack confidence in us. We don't expect to go bankrupt. There's too much pent-up demand for fuel-efficient cars ... We're not going to be in the GM market, replacing the big cars with front-wheel-drive, because it's a program we just couldn't afford. But I don't know if we should be. You look at the intermediate [car] market today and it's going to hell in a handbasket. If we had a billion dollars, I don't think with what we're seeing happen that we'd reinstitute that program.

*Interview, Detroit/
Los Angeles Times, 3-17:(IV)2,3.*

Lane Kirkland
President, American Federation of Labor-Congress of Industrial Organizations

4

[On the illegal air-traffic controllers strike during which the government fired striking controllers]: The air-traffic control system is purely a subsidized service the government is providing for the private airline industry. Under the [President] Reagan doctrine of getting government off people's backs, you'd think they might try to turn the whole thing over to the industry to run instead of using the might and majesty of government to suppress a strike.

*The New York Times,
8-16:(3)24.*

Drew Lewis
*Secretary of Transportation
of the United States*

1

I feel stronger about cutting Amtrak than any other part of my budget. In my judgment, it must be cut back; it must be cut back drastically. Amtrak is a monument to bureaucracy . . . It's a mode of transportation from a bygone day.

*Before House Appropriations Subcommittee on
Transportation, Washington, March 16/
Chicago Tribune, 3-17:(1)6.*

2

. . . every single auto-maker in this country except General Motors is in trouble, and GM is not as strong as it once was. Ford's working capital has gone from about $3-billion to less than half a billion, on $37-billion of sales. You can't carry sales levels of that magnitude with so little working capital. If I were Philip Caldwell, chairman of the board of Ford, and didn't see some immediate change in the burden of government regulations, some rollback in imports and some wage concessions by the UAW, I would start shutting down plants in this country as promptly as possible, cut losses in America and start investing in Mexico and Japan and wherever else I could. I'm definitely concerned about what will happen if nothing is done to address the problems of this industry.

Interview/U.S. News & World Report, 3-30:25.

3

There is no free trade in automobiles anywhere, except in the United States. I think it's fine to have free trade. But when we ship a U.S. automobile to Japan, by the time Japanese duties and tariffs and transportation costs are added, the price is doubled. Italy restricts Japanese imports to about 2,200 vehicles. France has restrictions; so does Great Britain. Right now, the Japanese are increasing their auto-making capacity by 20 per cent. The most viable market for those added cars is the United States.

*Interview/
U.S. News & World Report, 3-30:25.*

4

[On the illegal air-traffic controllers strike, during which the government fired striking controllers]: . . . when [controllers-union president Robert Poli] left the [negotiating] table on the 3rd of August, he was asking for $681-million, or $40,000 additional cost per controller. When he talks about resigning, he said he would resign if we could go back where we were at that time. Well, the people of this country are not going to pay controllers $40,000 more, in view of the fact they're already making an average of $33,000, and some are making up to $55,000. They're some of the best-paid public employees we have.

*Broadcast interview/
"Meet the Press," NBC-TV, 8-23.*

5

[On the illegal air-traffic controllers strike, during which the government fired striking controllers]: These people signed an oath to support the Constitution of the United States and not to strike against the Federal government, because their jobs affected safety and the public welfare. Now we're in a position that the very core of this democracy—the very system of law that we've developed over the last 200 years —is in jeopardy. The President [Reagan] has to support the Constitution and cannot be in a position of permitting these people—a few people in a country of more than 200 million—to blatantly violate the law while expecting other people to support the law . . . Once we get by what we're going through now, we must recognize that there are problems with this group [controllers], and that some of those problems have to be dealt with by the FAA. This thing has been festering for 10 years. I asked Robert Poli of PATCO to sit down and talk about the difficulties his people have with the FAA, but all he wanted to talk about was money. He talks about idealism when he gets on television, but when it comes down to real negotiations, all he talks about is money.

*Interview/
U.S. News & World Report, 8-24:19.*

Sassy N'Diaye
Africa director, International
Air Transport Association

1

An airline isn't a luxury. It's a foreign-currency earner; it's vital to communications; it's vital to development; and in a crisis of any nature, it's your link with the world.

The Wall Street Journal, 8-25:1.

Donald E. Petersen
President, Ford Motor Company

2

. . . if we can't manufacture competitively in the United States—then we will be forced to manufacture more and more products off-shore where costs are lower, and perhaps ultimately to produce complete automobiles. That would be a bad move for America . . . [The Japanese] have a whopping $1,500 cost advantage on small cars shipped to and landed in the United States. The overwhelming source of Japan's cost advantage is in labor costs, both salaried and hourly—a combination of compensation levels and productivity. [Import restraints of the right dimension] would increase volume for U.S, producers, provide some of the capital for the $80-billion investment program to develop and produce smaller and more fuel-efficient cars, and put many of our employees back to work.

Before Los Angeles World Affairs Council,
April 21/
Los Angeles Herald Examiner, 4-22:(A)12.

Sergio Pininfarina
Automobile designer

3

[Comparing European automobiles with U.S. models]: In Europe, we used to make very different cars—smaller, because of the much higher price of petrol, narrow roads, old cities, mountains, no speed limit. But you [in the U.S.] have wide roads, petrol for nothing. It was natural you had big cars. But the concept of an American car and a European car were very different. And now, you see, with the energy crisis, the two schools come together . . . Dimensions

[in future cars] will change. There must be a different ratio between inside and outside. It's going to change; it's already changing, and materials will, too. We made a car for the Geneva auto show that was like a laboratory, using materials with no weight. The new technology is fascinating. The car was an old object and is becoming young again.

Interview/The New York Times, 5-31:(1)21.

Robert E. Poli
President, Professional Air Traffic
Controllers Organization

4

[On the illegal air-traffic controllers strike, during which the government fired striking controllers]: These people had a job that paid reasonably well and they struck over some serious issues. I'm not a pied piper. They cared about the issues. They were worried about job problems, especially the spouses, who were saying, "Better not to have a job like this at all than to come home a wreck every night." I still think they [the government] will sit down with us. Both sides have to save face, not to mention that the system is going down the tubes, and the reduced traffic is going to cause economic chaos . . . Everybody thinks we wanted $10,000 pay increases. What we were really talking about was the health and future of our members, and the safety of every person in this country who flies a plane. We endorsed [President] Ronald Reagan because he said he was going to rebuild the air-traffic control system. Then they start talking to us about blue-ribbon committees. We've heard that for 10 years.

Interview, Washington/
The Washington Post, 8-14:(C)6.

5

[On the illegal air-traffic controllers strike, during which the government fired striking controllers]: The truth of the matter is that it has hurt the aviation community, the public, very, very much. The unreasonableness that has been displayed [by the government], the attempts to break our union, the insensitive

(ROBERT E. POLI)

attitude toward what our issues were, the promises that we had received prior to going into negotiations, and the failure of the government to address our particular issues leaves us with only one position. I've talked to many members around the country. We're as strong now as we were the first day [of the strike]. We believe that reasonableness will prevail.

Broadcast interview/
"Meet the Press," NBC-TV, 8-23.

Ronald Reagan
President-elect of the United States

1

Government is literally dictating what should be done and how cars should be built. Air bags are just one example of what has been hanging over the automobile industry and hanging over all of us. I'd be very uptight driving down the road and knowing that thing could pop out and hit me on the face if something went wrong. And something usually does go wrong —with anything. Or consider our great effort in taking the weight out of automobiles and building smaller automobiles. I'm wondering what's going to happen when we take a look at the fatality rate down the road a few years and find out how much it has grown.

Interview, Jan. 7/
U.S. News & World Report, 1-19:24.

Ronald Reagan
President of the United States

2

[On the illegal air-traffic controllers strike]: I must tell those [controllers] who failed to report for duty this morning they are in violation of the law, and if they don't report for work within 48 hours, they have forfeited their jobs and will be terminated . . . I hope you'll emphasize the possibility of termination, because I believe that there are a great many of those people who have been swept up in this and probably have not really considered the fact that they have taken an oath [not to strike], the

fact that this is now a violation of the law. I hope they will remove themselves from the lawbreaker situation by returning to their posts.

To reporters, Washington, Aug. 3/
Chicago Tribune, 8-4:(1)1,24.

Leonard Ronis
President, American Public
Transportation Association

3

[On Federal cuts in aid to local transportation systems]: Additional cuts could mean local communities, still reeling from the last round of budget adjustments, will be forced to raise transit fares beyond the means of many citizens and cut service levels to the point where public transportation becomes inefficient, inconvenient and ineffective. Employers will find it more difficult to match jobs with workers, retailers will find dwindling sales in many locations, and urban land will lose the values resulting from good access by mass transportation.

At American Public Transit Association meeting,
Chicago/The New York Times, 10-11:(1)17.

Robert Rose
Professor of psychiatry, University of
Texas Medical Branch, Galveston;
Former leader of government-contracted
team studying air-traffic controllers

4

[On the illegal strike by air-traffic controllers]: I believe the strike is a result of the alienation of the controllers from their management. Most of the time when something goes wrong, the controllers are not supported by their supervisors—they are left out there all alone. They have no reward for doing a good job; there is no positive reinforcement. All they get is negative reinforcement if something goes wrong . . . There are a series of things that suddenly can go wrong that can change a routine operation into a high-stress operation. The weather can deteriorate, the amount of traffic congestion can suddenly build up, a private pilot won't understand a command, planes get too close

(ROBERT ROSE)

together. A controller knows that something very horrible could happen in seconds . . . and that's always hanging over his head. Life-and-death situations don't happen continuously, but they happen often enough.

The Christian Science Monitor, 8-7:12.

Irving S. Shapiro
Chairman, E. I. du Pont
de Nemours & Company

1

I can remember when General Motors started to produce the Chevette. It had trouble giving those cars away. That shows the market wasn't ready for a small car. Then when the [energy] crisis started to move very vigorously, the country finally decided we really did have an energy crisis, and everybody wanted a small car overnight. The industry couldn't produce that many small cars in a hurry. And so there was an obvious market opening for the Japanese and the Germans and others, and they very adroitly seized it with good products and good marketing. Now, the fact is that the Japanese, particularly, have been making small cars for a long time because Japan always knew it had an energy problem and so their automotive needs were different. They just happened to have the right product at the right time for the American market.

Interview/The Washington Post, 2-8:(G)1.

Bud Shuster
United States Representative,
R—Pennsylvania

2

I support tightening Conrail's belt, but I oppose tightening a noose around its neck. To cut off Federal funding after fiscal year 1982 would be economically wasteful and would severely cripple a vital transportation network.

Before House transportation subcommittee,
Washington, March 19/
The Washington Post, 3-20:(A)34.

Roger B. Smith
Chairman, General Motors Corporation

3

People don't want small cars—what they want is fuel-efficient cars. Our long-term game-plan is: You can have any kind of car you want. If you need a big station wagon, it will have a diesel engine for the fuel economy.

Interview, Detroit, March 17/
The New York Times, 3-18:29.

Zenko Suzuki
Prime Minister of Japan

4

[On his country's decision to place limitations on its auto exports to the U.S.]: I would be less than truthful if I pretended my decision was painless. Nonetheless, I sincerely believe that the pain is worth enduring if this temporary arrangement contributes in the long run to preserving and strengthening the free-trade system.

At National Press Club, Washington, May 8/
Chicago Tribune, 5-9:(1)3.

Jerry Wurf
President, American Federation of State,
County and Municipal Employees

5

[On the illegal air-traffic controllers strike, during which the government fired striking controllers]: We can't stand still and watch these decent people [the controllers] being thrown out of their jobs and blacklisted for Federal employment with less due process than would be accorded a person with a record of 80 arrests accused of raping a 93-year-old-woman. [President] Reagan's over-reaction against the air controllers could bring terrible misery for the whole labor movement, public and private, unless we recognize the gravity of the challenge and muster the solidarity to reverse it.

The New York Times, 8-16:(3)1.

Urban Affairs

Marion S. Barry, Jr.
Mayor of Washington

1

The problems [of Washington] aren't unique. They're traditional problems: unemployment, housing, human services, transportation, economic development. But the solutions to those problems are made more difficult because of the unique arrangement the District of Columbia has with the Federal government. The local citizens contribute 80 per cent of the tax revenue for our local budget. The Federal government contributes 20 per cent of the revenue even though they own over 55 per cent of the taxable land. The President and the Congress have the authorization to make 100 per cent of the decisions over our annual budget. It means our priorities are shifted to meet the priorities of the Congress.

*Interview, Washington/
The New York Times, 10-3:11.*

Helen Boosalis
*Mayor of Lincoln, Neb.; President,
United States Conference of Mayors*

2

[Saying Reagan Administration budget policies will make cities more dependent on states]: States will be part of the urban solution, but it's critical that we move slowly and only after a major national debate on all the pitfalls involved. We must have some indication of state intentions and capabilities, for it could just end up creating another expensive layer of bureaucracy . . . Cities have to become part of the decision-making process.

*Louisville, Ky./
The Christian Science Monitor, 6-18:9.*

Edmund G. Brown, Jr.
Governor of California (D)

3

[President] Ronald Reagan can sit in the White House and talk about how he's cutting the budget, but in truth [his economic program is] shortchanging the cities and states of America. It's a tax shift, not a tax reduction. If there's going to be a shell game here, responsibility will have to rest in Washington, where it began. The Federal budget has not been cut to any significant degree. Rather, local governments have been asked to bear a burden that they have not suffered before.

*At meeting of National Governors Association,
Atlantic City, N.J., Aug. 11/
Los Angeles Times, 8-12:(I)1.*

George Busbee
Governor of Georgia (D)

4

[On state-city relations]: State legislators have long since been reapportioned, state work forces professionalized, state revenue-sharing capacity expanded, state administrative and planning systems modernized. The states . . . now represent the best hope for the future of our communities great and small.

The Christian Science Monitor, 5-29:4.

5

Federalism must be a two-way street. State and local officials are willing to take on greater responsibilities if there is a carefully conceived plan to sort out appropriate roles for each level of government and to balance those with adequate resources. In the absence of such a con-

(GEORGE BUSBEE)

sensus, further efforts to shift new responsibilities to state and local governments will meet with firm resistance from the states.

At meeting of National Governors Association,
Atlantic City, N.J., Aug. 8/
The New York Times, 8-9:(1)12.

Richard E. Carver
Mayor of Peoria, Ill.

1

Too many states have a benign attitude toward central cities, and, until they change, it is inappropriate to funnel money to states without minimum requirements. This is not a partisan issue. It is a fundamental issue of intergovernmental relations.

The Christian Science Monitor, 5-29:4.

2

I've said for a long time that, give a strong economy to any city, and you've got a city that can take care of itself. If you get a growing job base, a growing tax base, growing revenues coming into your city from the local community, the need for Federal assistance is substantially reduced. I've urged very strongly that the [Reagan Administration] budget cuts are a necessary part of restoring our economy, which will in effect give us that kind of strength. I don't care if it's steel mills in Gary [Ind.] or Caterpillar Tractor in Peoria, Illinois; it's those new *private* job opportunities, that new tax base, that expanding economy that I think is going to be important to all American cities in the 1980s.

Broadcast interview/
"Meet the Press," NBC-TV, 7-5.

Dianne Feinstein
Mayor of San Francisco

3

One reason there has been a taxpayers' revolt is that people have found it easy to separate public services from their own costs. Once you have free parks, libraries and a cheap transit system, it's very easy to take them for granted. It isn't until they are faced with losing these things that the connection is all too apparent.

Interview, San Francisco/
The Christian Science Monitor, 7-14:18.

Richard G. Hatcher
Mayor of Gary, Ind.; President,
United States Conference of Mayors

4

Every Mayor in the country wants to help President Reagan and the Congress bring inflation under control and restore full employment. [But] many of the budget cuts he has proposed will make it harder. The President has asked us to renew our cities through private investment and private jobs. But his Administration now wants to cut many of the programs we need to attract and keep private industry. We hope the Administration does not believe the way to restore the economy of our country is to ravage the economics of our cities. Millions of distressed people depend on these economies . . . A tighter-run, more targeted program of aid to our cities and their people would win support from Democratic and Republican Mayors across the country.

The Washington Post, 3-1:(C)6.

5

It's not just the Mayors who say that the relationship between cities and states has not been the best in the past. The Advisory Commission on Intergovernmental Relations just came out with a report recently which found that there were only a handful of states which had in fact worked out useful relationships with the local governments under their jurisdiction. So, clearly, there is a problem in terms of historical relations. I don't think that we are saying that states are inhumane. I think what we're basically saying is that a state government's interests, at least as it views its interests, in many instances is different from that of local government.

Broadcast interview/"Meet the Press," NBC-TV, 7-5.

Edward I. Koch
Mayor of New York

1

[Criticizing President Reagan's statement that those in cities who are dissatisfied with the way the city is managed should say so at the polls or move somewhere else]: The middle class and the wealthy may "vote with their feet" by leaving. The poor, who don't have mobility . . . will remain in the cities, without opportunities and as hostages of the public doles. If urban America —70 per cent of the population—is satisfied with the promise of today's economic and domestic policy, vote for it. If not, paraphrasing the President, "vote with your feet"—let them take you to the voting booth, because this so-called "New Federalism" [President Reagan's plan to give more power to state and local governments] is a sham and a shame.

Before National League of Cities, Detroit,
Dec. 1/Los Angeles Times, 12-2:(I)11.

Henry W. Maier
Mayor of Milwaukee

2

I say to you that if you say [cities] can live without Federal help, God bless you. Some of us are on the brink of catastrophe. You don't believe me, go look at those bond ratings . . . We have city after city on the verge of collapse. Now we're being told, as we are about to be booted down the hill further, that we ought to allow them to boot us—take it in good grace—and I have only one thing to say to you: To hell with that! . . . I think the most ignorant damn people in America are the media because you're all middle-class. Most of you come from middle-class homes, and you really don't get the smell of these central cities and the problems of these central cities. If you did, your Number 1 priority, like ours, would be to make damn sure our funding isn't cut back; because if it is cut back, the domestic tranquility—I promise you—is going to be very seriously disturbed.

At meeting of U.S. Conference of Mayors,
Washington, Jan. 19/
The Washington Post, 1-20:(A)7.

3

[On Reagan Administration plans to give cities more responsibility in handling their own affairs]: My concern is that the Administration's promised land of milk and honey may turn out to be a desert of rocks and dust for this city and the other older central cities of America . . . What have we gained if we trade Federal red ink for municipal red ink or—worse—blood in the streets?

U.S. News & World Report, 6-1:22.

Ronald Reagan
President of the United States

4

. . . for many of this country's major cities, economic stagnation is not a recent phenomenon. Interestingly, while power centralized in Washington, D.C., many great urban areas declined. Many cities cannot even remember a time when they were economically healthy. Local officials who once saw the local voters as boss now look to Washington, D.C., before considering a move. And what once was a Federal helping hand is quickly turning into a mailed fist. Instead of assistance, the Federal government is giving orders—they call them "mandates." More often than not the command comes from Washington, but few funds to implement the order can be found in the envelope. Mayor Koch of New York has detailed the problem of mandates better than anyone. Last year he said his city was driven by 47 Federal and state mandates, with a total cost of $711-million in capital expenditures, $6.25-billion in expense-budget dollars and $1.66-billion in lost revenue. And people wonder why New York sings the economic blues.

Before National League of Cities, Washington,
March 2/The New York Times, 3-3:10.

Carl E. Reichardt
President, Wells Fargo & Company

5

We have been very wasteful over the years with our land resources and have created unplanned sprawling suburbs, often taking prime

WHAT THEY SAID IN 1981

(CARL E. REICHARDT)

agricultural land out of production to do it. This wasteful, unplanned use of the land spread out farther and farther from the inner city, which virtually destroyed American cities and created serious transportation problems for workers . . . [But from today's] bad news about soaring prices on single-family detached homes, as well as skyrocketing oil prices, we have some good results—the return of and rejuvenation of our cities, and increasing focus on new, efficient and non-polluting methods of public transit. I question whether history will view these new trends as a lowering of our living standards.

Before Colorado Cattle Feeders, Vail, Colo./
Chicago Tribune, 10-13:(1)11.

Felix G. Rohatyn
Chairman, Municipal Assistance
Corporation of New York

1

I like big cities. Civilization grows there. Religion develops in open air, I suspect. But civilization—that is in the cities.

Interview, New York/Newsweek, 5-4:26.

Charles Royer
Mayor of Seattle; Vice President,
National League of Cities

2

Upheavals in state and Federal governments are creating mayhem for those of us in cities. Our tax base falls victim to a sluggish economy; our traditional state and Federal support dries up. It's all happening too fast, with too much uncertainty about the future. We have little time to adjust, and we have few tools to bring to bear on local solutions.

At League of California Cities conference,
San Francisco/Los Angeles Times, 10-22:(IX)1.

Vincent Schoemehl, Jr.
Mayor of St. Louis

3

[On President Reagan's plan to give cities more responsibility in welfare, housing, education, etc.]: You can't lay these responsibilities

on the older cities in this country like Chicago, St. Louis and Cleveland and expect them to supply the resources for it. We don't have the tax base. The question is whether the cost is going to fall on those not able to pay. [President Reagan's] "New Federalism" is the choice between progressive and repressive government. The wealth of this country has to be redistributed, or we have to abandon our goals.

The Christian Science Monitor, 12-3:1.

Donna Shalala
President, Hunter College

4

[Saying cities need to spend for law enforcement, education, street cleaning, social services, etc., and that may not be possible with a balanced budget]: A city with a balanced budget may be a fine business. But a good business is not necessarily a good city.

Interview, New York/
The Washington Post, 2-24:(A)13.

Kenneth Slapin
Chairman, transportation committee,
National League of Cities

5

The Federal government tends to be more understanding of city needs than some state governments are. You don't eliminate the public-sector cost or save money by passing the buck from Washington to the states.

The Christian Science Monitor, 5-29:10.

Richard S. Williamson
Assistant to the President of the United States
for Intergovernmental Affairs

6

. . . the biggest thing that [President] Reagan can do for the cities is to give us a healthy economy. A year from today, there will be a significant economic growth for the first time in many years and the cities and rural areas will be the beneficiaries.

The New York Times,
8-30:(3)17.

Andrew Young
Candidate for Mayor of Atlanta; Former
United States Ambassador/Permanent
Representative to the United Nations

1

[People] see being Mayor as a big step down from being Ambassador. People think I need to go higher. I don't evaluate life that way. The cities are the future of this country. That is where the challenge is in government . . . Being UN Ambassador was fun, but not the challenge that running a thriving, dynamic city would be.

San Francisco Examiner & Chronicle,
9-6:(A)11.

PART TWO

International Affairs

Africa

Richard V. Allen
Assistant to the President
of the United States for
National Security Affairs

1

I personally don't consider an improvement in [U.S.] relations with South Africa as any stamp of approval on the system of apartheid, of which I don't approve and which I believe deserves to be roundly condemned.

The Wall Street Journal, 3-23:5.

John B. Anderson
Former United States Representative,
R—Illinois; 1980 independent candidate
for President

2

[On U.S. relations with South Africa]: I have not seen, and others have not seen, the kind of progress toward human rights in this country [South Africa] that would entitle [U.S.] rapproachment with the present government . . . No alleged strategic interests in either the minerals or the Cape shipping routes around South Africa should blind the [U.S.] government [to the impossibility of rapproachment]. . . . the vast bulk of petty apartheid still remains three years after promises that it would be abandoned. My impression is there has been no fundamental change . . . and that this will continue to be a society based on white domination.

News conference, Johannesburg, Aug. 23/
Los Angeles Times, 8-24:(I)5.

Pieter W. Botha
Prime Minister of South Africa

3

[Criticizing U.S. Assistant Secretary of State-designate for Africa, Chester Crocker]: I have certain reservations after Dr. Crocker's visit to Africa and even earlier. I don't like the way he referred to SWAPO. I think it is an attempt to create an atmosphere in which he can talk to SWAPO's friends. Well, it doesn't suit us; we don't like SWAPO. We know that SWAPO is Communist-controlled and they have one idea only, and that is to subordinate South-West Africa by brutal force.

Interview/The Washington Post, 4-17:(A)19.

Roelof F. Botha
Foreign Minister of South Africa

4

[Saying the UN is biased in favor of SWAPO in the controversy over independence for Namibia]: Unless the United Nations, at least the Western governments, adopt a more reasonable attitude and display greater fairness, and accept the anti-SWAPO parties as equals to SWAPO in any negotiations . . . I consider the chances of a successful peaceful solution as just about zero. South Africa will continue to remain true to its standpoint that the Namibian parties should decide their own future, no matter what the consequences are. We are committed to the creation of a democratic state in South-West Africa, and we do not want us or the internal parties to be burdened by threats and intimidation. The world must learn that such tactics cannot and will not work.

Jan. 14/Los Angeles Times, 1-15:(I)10.

5

[On the poor relations between his country and the rest of Africa]: I think the geographic and economic imperatives of southern Africa will play an important part in the road ahead irrespective of present differences. There is no way you can get away from the fact that we are

(ROELOF F. BOTHA)

part of the African continent. And if the facts indicate that Africa is dying economically, that the railways don't function, the ports, the roads, that net food exporters have become importers . . . Africa's trade deficit this year is $20-billion. There are 63 million Africans unemployed—45 per cent of the labor force. A French expert told me recently that he had given up all hope—[that] the combined resources of the U.S., Europe and the Soviet Union could not stop the decline of Africa. But we are sincerely ready to help. That is why we are for regional development. The idea that you can put chimneys in the bush doesn't work. Politicians can't change the rules. Investors want railroads, clean water, freedom of expression.

Interview/The New York Times, 2-8:(4)21.

George Bush
Vice President of the United States

1

[On Libyan Chief of State Muammar Qaddafi]: He's an egomaniac who would trigger World War III to make the headlines. He's the world's principal terrorist and trainer of terrorists. He's the protector of the likes of [former Uganda leader] Idi Amin. He's dangerous to Egypt, to Israel, and he's dangerous to peace.

At National Press Club, Washington, Oct. 9/
The New York Times, 10-10:6.

Chester A. Crocker
Assistant Secretary for African Affairs,
Department of State of the United States

2

In South Africa, the region's dominant country, it is not our task to choose between black and white. In this rich land of talented and diverse peoples, important Western economic, strategic, moral and political interests are at stake. We must avoid action that aggravates the awesome challenges facing South Africans of all races. The [U.S.] Reagan Administration has no intention of destabilizing South Africa in order to curry favor elsewhere. Neither will

we align ourselves with [South African] apartheid policies that are abhorrent to our own multi-racial democracy.

Before American Legion, Honolulu, Aug. 29/
The New York Times, 8-30:(1)10.

3

The activities of the Soviets and their partners threaten the security of Africa in every corner of the continent, and in accordance with our objectives the United States is working to frustrate these activities and to help African states resist them . . . As leader of the West, the United States has a responsibility to help shape the strategic context that impinges on Africa. It is time for us Americans to recognize this reality and cease indulging in the romantic illusion that Africa is somehow uniquely buffered from the effects of destabilization, whether it is of external or regional origin.

Before American Legion, Honolulu, Aug. 29/
The New York Times, 8-30:(1)10.

Luis Jose d'Almeida
Angolan Ambassador to France

4

[On South African claims that Soviet personnel are helping to train the Angolan Army]: We have never made any secret of the fact that our Soviet friends are training our army to help Angola defend its territory. You cannot train an army with a correspondence course . . . We are determined to continue cooperating with our Soviet and Cuban friends as long as necessary to assure our security and to train the Angolan Army so it can defend our territory. That is a right we acquired through our sacrifices in our long struggle [against Portuguese colonial rule].

News conference, Paris, Sept. 2/
Los Angeles Times, 9-3:(1)11.

Vennacio do Moura
Vice Foreign Minister of Angola

5

The problem on U.S. relations isn't on the Angolan side. Those who are preoccupied by the

(VENNACIO do MOURA)

presence of foreign [Cuban] troops in Angola must first be preoccupied by the presence of South African troops in Angola, because the Cuban presence is a consequence of Angola's efforts to counter South African troops.

The Washington Post, 9-21:(A)18.

Gerald R. Ford
Former President of the United States

1

[On Libyan Chief of State Muammar Qaddafi]: This man is, in my judgment, a cancer in that area of the globe, and he has to be treated as a person that is not interested in peace, but is interested in some extent in his own personal aggrandizement, his own ambition to be a ruler beyond his own borders. And the world as a whole cannot tolerate that kind of continuous activity.

Interview aboard Air Force One, Oct. 10/
The Washington Post, 10-12:(A)2.

Brand G. Fourie
Director General, Department of
Foreign Affairs of South Africa

2

[Arguing against the threat of economic sanctions against his country because of its policies in South-West Africa]: [A boycott of South Africa] would in effect amount to sanctions against the countries of southern Africa, whose economies are so closely interrelated. The ripple effect of sanctions, if ever applied, would therefore be ruinous. Tolerance and understanding are required in deliberations on the future of South-West Africa, not threats by the United Nations or any other quarter.

At United Nations, New York, April 22/
The New York Times, 4-23:4.

Andre Goncalves Pereira
Foreign Minister of Portugal

3

When dealing with matters of southern Africa, it is our position that racism is unac-

ceptable, and this has to be said almost every time these issues are mentioned. Very often people who think this forget to state it, and this leads some African countries to think there is more support for apartheid than there really is.

To reporters, Washington, Oct. 2/
The New York Times, 10-3:2.

Alexander M. Haig, Jr.
Secretary of State of the
United States

4

We want an independent Namibia—internationally recognized, genuinely non-aligned, free of external military presence, with a regularly exercised mandate from the people and with guaranteed rights for minorities. One element of such an approach might be to incorporate these guarantees into a constitutional framework that would set the basic course for an independent state.

Interview/U.S. News & World Report, 5-18:30.

5

We look at the Libyan situation not only in a regional context but in a global context. They have directly invaded neighboring Chad. They are threatening neighboring states throughout the Northern African region, and beyond that into South Africa. They train, fund and espouse radical revolutions in a global sense. And it is our view that if the vast resources being expended by [Libyan leader Muammar] Qaddafi today for external mischief-making were applied to the welfare of the still deprived—and I would say harshly deprived—populations of Libya, that we would be prepared to respond in a constructive way in the direction of normalization. Unfortunately, thus far that hasn't been the case.

Interview, Washington/
The Christian Science Monitor, 8-24:14.

6

We abhor apartheid and oppose continued South African occupation of Namibia. None-

WHAT THEY SAID IN 1981

(ALEXANDER M. HAIG, JR.)

theless, our objective has been to achieve results, rather than to engage in arguments. We have attempted to persuade the South Africans that their true interests lie in a peaceful settlement. Acting through quiet diplomacy with our allies, South Africa, Nigeria and frontline states, we have shown that we are prepared to push for a balanced Namibian settlement . . . Pretoria has agreed to work on a phased approach to resolve the remaining issues, thus clearing the way for tangible movement in 1982. At long last we see the prospect of real progress toward an independent Namibia.

Before House Foreign Affairs Committee,
Washington, Nov. 12/
The New York Times, 11-13:4.

1

[On reports that Libya has sent a "hit squad" to assassinate top U.S. government officials]: It is clear that the United States has been made the focal point . . . of specifically targeted terrorist activity, and we enjoy through a host of sophisticated intelligence collection ability a rather up-to-the-minute access to what is going on in Libya. Each nation is entitled to draw its own conclusions with respect to Libyan activity. But for our part, we no longer believe that a double standard with respect to international lawlessness and terrorism, especially when it is targeted against American officials, is a contributor to international peace and stability and the rule of law.

News conference, Brussels, Dec. 11/
Los Angeles Times, 12-11:(I)6.

J. Bennett Johnston
United States Senator, D—Louisiana

2

[On the recent dogfight between U.S. and Libyan planes over international waters claimed by Libya]: Frankly, I think we sent a fleet in there [the contested waters] to provoke an incident, and provoke an incident we did. And we, in effect, won. I think that's very proper we

did it, and if we'd just draw the line with some of those dictators [such as Libya's Qaddafi] we'll cut down their influence in the world.

Aug. 20/Los Angeles Times, 8-21:(I)11.

Paolo T. Jorge
Foreign Minister of Angola

3

I don't see any possibilities of what American officials talk of as reconciliation [between his government and Jonas Savimbi, leader of UNITA]: We do not accept reconciliation with traitors and terrorists. Savimbi represents nothing in my country. It is shocking to hear the President of the United States say that UNITA controls one-half of Angola when it does not control a single province. UNITA can infiltrate, can sabotage, but that is all. Just as the United States cannot control all of its border with Mexico, we cannot control all of our frontier.

Interview, United Nations, New York, April 23/
The Washington Post, 4-25:(A)22.

Gerald Kalk
South African Consul-General in Chicago

4

[On his leaving the post of Consul-General]: I most certainly have come to understand that, beneath imperfections which are only too apparent, there is an American society and institutions, a greatness and strength, a vigor, a goodness and a compassion. I would hope, and I believe, that you have come to realize that much-maligned South Africa, with its own only-too-apparent imperfections, in its society and institutions has also a greatness, a strength, a vigor and a compassion which will correct these imperfections . . . Speaking as the private citizen I am about to be, I believe that it is an effective summary of the philosophy and the policy of my government and my countrymen to say that we work and shall continue to work for equality of opportunity for all human beings.

At farewell party, Chicago/
Chicago Tribune, 3-2:(1)6.

Henry A. Kissinger
Former Secretary of State
of the United States

1

[On Libya]: If you cannot take care of a country of 2 million that is threatening all its neighbors—marching armies into Chad, threatening Uganda, threatening Morocco, active in the Sudan—if all the neighbors cannot find a way to get such a rogue, criminal country under control, then we are living in a world in which all restraints have disappeared.

Broadcast interview/
"Good Morning America," ABC-TV, 10-7.

Edem Kodjo
Secretary General,
Organization of African Unity

2

Our continent is a theatre of political commotion. It is necessary for Africa to remain united. We must do away with the image of an Africa that is weak and dependent on the outside world.

Before OAU-member Foreign Ministers,
Nairobi, Kenya, June 16/
The New York Times, 6-17:3.

Senyi Kountche
Head of State of Niger

3

[On Libyan leader Muammar Qaddafi's designs on Niger and other countries]: The behavior of Qaddafi toward Niger is not behavior toward only one country but is part of a global strategy for West Africa. The case of [Libya's military intervention in] Chad is not only a tragedy, but a humiliation and really a shame for any human being who is considered to be civilized and free.

Interview/The Washington Post, 3-26:(A)32.

Jaap Marais
Leader, Herstigte Nasionale Party
of South Africa

4

Our contention is that whatever policy you follow in South Africa, . . . there is one absolute

imperative: The whites must form the core. We quite accept that there is a large black population who contend they are part of South Africa and should be treated on an equal basis with whites. But once you concede that, then you must be prepared to concede that they will be a majority and it would end in a one-man-one-vote system. This would be the end of all stability and progress in South Africa. It would be the end of the white nation in South Africa. As far as the Afrikaners are concerned, my forebearers fought two wars of independence for this country and we are not prepared to concede that we have lost this country, that we will lose this country in a sort of bloodless coup.

Interview, Pretoria, South Africa/
The Washington Post, 7-8:(A)18.

Donald F. McHenry
Research professor of diplomacy and international affairs, School of Foreign Service, Georgetown University; Former United States Ambassador/Permanent Representative to the United Nations

5

. . . the U.S. must seek to promote change in the last remnant of a colonialism-type question in Africa—that is, the racial apartheid policies within South Africa . . . Our options are very limited. The best thing we can do is demonstrate that South Africa stands isolated from the world community so long as it pursues its present policies. South Africa wants to be accepted as Western, anti-Communist, pro-capitalist, Christian. We must make it clear that they are, in many respects, none of those things. Their policies promote Communism. Their values are not Western in any way. We need to drive that reality home.

Interview/U.S. News & World Report, 8-31:35.

Hal Miller
Managing director, Argus Printing and Publishing Company (South Africa)

6

[On the banning by the government of his company's two black newspapers]: We have no

(HAL MILLER)

power to prevent the government's action, no redress against the course it has chosen to follow. We think that by acting this way it diminishes us all—that another bar has been added to the cage which is beginning to circumscribe our freedom.

The Christian Science Monitor, 1-21:10.

Francois Mitterrand
President of France

1

The refusal of apartheid [in South Africa] is important, not only on moral grounds, but also on political grounds. I have a fairly good knowledge of black Africa, with which I have had numerous contacts throughout my political career. It would in my view be unwise to encourage practices, such as apartheid, that are liable to cause serious problems for the continent. I would be against all racisms. You see, one has to accept the pre-eminence of great universal principles or abandon any hope of making progress in world society.

Interview, Paris, June 1/
The New York Times, 6-4:6.

Daniel arap Moi
President of Kenya

2

[Calling on African nations to give more financial and military aid to guerrillas fighting to free Namibia from South African control]: Let me emphasize that Africa does not seek the wastage and bitterness of military conflict. But as the record has shown in my own and other countries, armed struggle with all its costs and sacrifices may be the only ultimate way of achieving independence.

Before Organization of African Unity
foreign ministers, Nairobi, Kenya, June 15/
The New York Times, 6-16:5.

Peter Mueshihange
Secretary for foreign affairs,
South-West Africa People's Organization
(SWAPO)

3

[On attempts by Western nations to draw up new plans for the independence of Namibia from South Africa]: [It is a] well-calculated strategy to win yet another stay of execution for the Fascist South African regime and to continue to safeguard the vested interests of the capitalist powers and their giant transnational corporations in southern Africa.

At United Nations, New York, April 23/
Los Angeles Times, 4-24:(I)21.

Robert Mugabe
Prime Minister of Zimbabwe

4

All who challenge the authority of my government and the people of Zimbabwe by force of arms, or who mutiny or revolt, declare themselves the enemies of the people, and I am determined to descend on them with a hammer.

Before Parliament, Salisbury/
The Washington Post, 2-18:(A)12.

5

I must say it would be most regrettable and harmful to the good relations which have hitherto existed between us and the United States if, in the circumstances in which South Africa is consistently proving herself to be a regional aggressor and delinquent, the [U.S.] Reagan Administration were to lend its support to the South African regime and its policies of apartheid and regional hostilities. We hope sanity will prevail in Washington.

At luncheon honoring the President of
Sierra Leone, Salisbury, March 18/
The Washington Post, 3-19:(A)25.

Denis Norman
Minister of Agriculture of Zimbabwe

6

East, north and west of us they're all short of grain. My guess is that they'd rather buy from us

(DENIS NORMAN)

than from South Africa. But our railway system is mainly single-track; we are short of rail cars; road transport is limited. And to get to a port we have to use the South African or Mozambique railways, which have limited capacity . . . We have the land, we have the water, we have the people. All we need is the capital. I get excited when I think of the potential. But you have to bring the peasant sector up, not the commercial down. If the white farmers left, the economic fabric would fall apart. They grow 80 per cent of our food, and 1.3 million people live on those farms.
Interview, Salisbury/The New York Times, 1-29:21.

Sam Nujoma
President, South-West Africa
People's Organization

1

SWAPO's preoccupation right now is to fight for the liberation of Namibia from South African colonial domination. Once this is achieved, it will be the responsibility and duty of the Namibian people to decide what sort of social system they will have politically, internal as well as external. I won't be able right now to elaborate in detail what will be the position of the National Assembly of the future independent Namibia. We will, of course, gear all the means of production, whatever we produce in Namibia, to uplifting the living standard of our people. With regard to our foreign policy, a SWAPO government would pursue a policy of non-alignment, for we are already full members of that movement. Namibia is a small country with a small population. It would not be in a position ideologically, politically or economically to influence any other country.
Interview, Geneva/The New York Times, 1-18:(4)3.

2

We [in SWAPO] never studied Marxism-Leninism. We met the Communists outside our country [Namibia]. They are friendly to us, therefore we are friendly to them. Certainly we are not going to be capitalists . . . It is capitalists who are giving arms to South Africa to kill our people. Ideology is for America and the superpowers. Those of you who are already free, you have the privilege and time to study ideology. Our preoccupation is to free our people.
Interview, Salisbury, Zimbabwe, June 5/
The Washington Post, 6-8:(A)12.

3

The successive governments in Washington, and the Reagan Administration in particular, have, in their selfish pursuit of world domination and access to strategic minerals, allied themselves with racists in South Africa, and regrettably this new Administration in Washington has embraced a terrorist state . . . This is a very serious and very dangerous development which, if not confronted right away in a serious manner, may engulf this entire continent of Africa in an East-West conflict, with disastrous consequences for the entire world.
At meeting of Organization of African Unity,
Nairobi, Kenya, June 24/
The New York Times, 6-25:3.

4

The people of Namibia are yearning for peace, but are prepared to fight . . . if a negotiated settlement [to the problem of Namibian independence from South Africa] can't be found. SWAPO is a democratic organization and we believe in free and fair elections. We are challenging the Pretoria [South Africa] regime to free and fair elections under UN supervision.
Interview, Luanda, Angola/
The Washington Post, 10-7:(A)7.

Julius K. Nyerere
President of Tanzania

5

People say the Soviet or Cuban presence in Angola and Ethiopia poses a great problem, but they ignore the proliferation of French troops all over Africa. People continue to believe that we belong to Europe.
World Press Review, July:49.

WHAT THEY SAID IN 1981

Harry Oppenheimer
South African industrialist

1

If you think of private enterprise as building a better, more prosperous and fairer [South Africa], then the most important part of all is that black people should have major opportunities in private enterprise . . . To avoid a revolution in South Africa, we've got to take substantive steps not only toward social justice but toward the sharing of power within a period of five years.

Time, 6-15:45.

Olara Otunnu
Ugandan Ambassador/
Permanent Representative to the
United Nations

2

[Criticizing the U.S. policy of not choosing between black and white in South Africa]: The choice is between the forces of apartheid which have brutalized and dehumanized the vast majority of South Africans and the forces that seek to set them free. How can a country that professes democracy [the U.S.] remain neutral between an oppressive system which has deprived 80 per cent of the citizens of their basic rights and a movement of people that seeks to restore these democratic rights?

Before UN Security Council, New York, Aug. 31/
The New York Times, 9-1:8.

Raymond Parsons
Chief executive, South African
Association of Chambers of Commerce

3

[Saying neighboring countries are dependent on the South African economy]: If South Africa sneezes, the rest of southern Africa catches a cold . . . They can neither afford to apply sanctions against South Africa [to protest apartheid], nor afford to see sanctions imposed on it. South Africa has for some years lived with, and adjusted to, the threat of sanctions and trade embargoes. Businessmen and the public sector have long ago prepared contingency plans

to protect the economy at any vulnerable points.

Chicago Tribune, 3-9:(1)2.

Muammar el-Qaddafi
Chief of State of Libya

4

[On the intervention of Libyan troops in Chad]: We declare that the fate of the Chadian people and that of the Libyan people has become one common fate forever . . . we tell France and the whole world that Chad is linked to Libya, Libya to Chad, by destiny, geographically, humanly, historically, futuristically, by security, and economically.

The Washington Post, 3-20:(A)27.

5

[On the recent dogfight between U.S. and Libyan warplanes over the Gulf of Sidra, which Libya claims as its territorial waters and which the United States says is international waters]: We are warning the peoples of Sicily, Crete, Turkey and all the states of the Mediterranean that if America again attacks the Gulf of Sidra, then we will intentionally attack the nuclear depots in their countries and cause an international catastrophe. We are ready to die for the Gulf of Sidra. We will make the Gulf of Sidra into a new Red Sea with our blood.

At rally celebrating 12th anniversary of
overthrow of King Idris, Tripoli, Libya, Sept. 1/
Los Angeles Herald Examiner, 9-2:(A)4.

6

I can tell you why America calls me the most dangerous man. It is part of the political and psychological preparations for the conquest of Libya. America intends to attack Libya and bring it under its domination again . . . There are varying methods, but they all have the same aim of subduing Libya and incorporating it in the American sphere of influence again. To do this, a direct occupation of the country with troops is not necessary. It is enough to overthrow the revolutionary regime and replace it with another, pro-American, regime. That is one

(MUAMMAR el-QADDAFI)

method of American imperialism, and that is what I meant when I spoke of America's plans for conquest.

Interview/Chicago Tribune, 9-27:(2)1.

1

[On U.S. President Reagan's previous career as an actor]: We showed his films on TV because we couldn't believe it was true that such a man was President of America. We rolled about laughing. We keep repeating his films to amuse our people. I have nothing against anyone exercising his profession if it is honest and honorable. What I say is that as an actor Reagan was unsuccessful and third-class, so that he has an inferiority complex, that he seeks to compensate for it by stupid and incalculable actions . . . I am not a third-class actor. I have tradition. I have roots. I am a revolutionary. I have made a revolution. Reagan embodies nothing more than the peak of a capitalist rotten society in which everyone is ready to make any promise so long as he is elected.

Interview/Chicago Tribune, 9-27:(2)2.

2

[Denying charges by U.S. President Reagan that he has sent "hit squads" to assassinate top U.S. government officials]: Reagan is silly, and he is not qualified to lead America as a superpower. He is behaving like a child . . . We are ready to make investigation and to see who is liar, and you will see—Reagan is liar . . . What is the reason [for these charges]: Are you [Reagan] mad? We are a small people who want to be free, want to be non-aligned. We are sure we didn't send any people to kill Reagan or any other people in the world, and we want to see those big lies [exposed].

American broadcast interview,
Tripoli/
"This Week With David Brinkley,"
ABC-TV, 12-6.

Didier Ratsiraka
President of the Malagasy Republic
(Madagascar)

3

I have said in all my speeches that Madagascar is probably the only really non-aligned country. No military battleships can come here . . . Theoretically, I am ideologically closer to the Soviet Union than to the Americans; I admit that. But this question is a strategic, not an ideological, one.

Interview, Antananarivo, Madagascar/
The Washington Post, 3-22:(A)22.

Jerry J. Rawlings
Head of Government of Ghana

4

[On the coup that just installed him as leader of Ghana]: I ask for nothing less than a revolution—something that will transform the social and economic order of this country. I'm not here to impose myself; far from it. We ask for nothing more than proper democracy . . . after two years of nothing but repression.

Dec. 31/Los Angeles Times, 1-2('82):(I)4.

Ronald Reagan
President of the United States

5

[There has been a failure in the U.S. to] recognize how many people, black and white, in South Africa are trying to remove apartheid and the steps that they've taken and the gains that they've made. As long as there's a sincere and honest effort being made, based on our own experience in our own land, it would appear to me that we should be trying to be helpful. Can we abandon a country [South Africa] that has stood beside us in every war we've ever fought, a country that strategically is essential to the free world? It has production of minerals we all must have, and so forth. I just feel that . . . if we're going to sit down at a table and negotiate with the Russians, surely we can keep the door open and continue to negotiate with a friendly nation like South Africa.

Television interview, Washington, March 3/
The New York Times, 3-15:(1)10.

WHAT THEY SAID IN 1981

(RONALD REAGAN)

1

[On recent U.S. naval maneuvers in the Gulf of Sidra, waters Libya claims are her own and which the U.S. considers international waters, and the Libyan-U.S. dogfight which resulted]: We conducted those maneuvers on the basis of what are international waters and that artificial line that has been created. This foray by the Libyans was nothing new. They have frequently harassed our aircraft out beyond that line in the Mediterranean. We decided it was time to recognize what are the international waters, and behave accordingly . . . we periodically send our ships into the Black Sea just for the same reason, just as the Soviet Union sends ships into the Caribbean, just to assure everyone is observing international waters and the rules pertaining to them.

To reporters aboard U.S.S. Constellation off California, Aug. 20/ The New York Times, 8-21:6.

Jonas Savimbi
Leader, National Union for the Total Independence of Angola (UNITA)

2

[On his fight against the Russian- and Cuban-backed regime in Angola]: The great drama of the West in the modern era is its own guilt. Guilt is devouring the values of the West, and it is a tragedy to watch. Colonialism was a historical fact; you cannot deny it. But now it is in the past, and while it is true that colonialism brought with it a form of domination that tried to destroy our values, we learned through colonialism ideas and methods to resist, and we did resist, and we succeeded in gaining our independence. But now, this new form of colonialism is something alien. The Russians and the Cubans, who were supposed to be our friends, and who did give us help in our struggles against the Portuguese, are now bringing [Angola] a new style of slavery.

Interview/ The Wall Street Journal, 2-27:18.

3

[On UNITA's dealings with South Africa]: I want to stress that we are against apartheid. We don't agree with a government that has a constitution based on racial discrimination . . . But people in this region are bound to have some sort of relations with South Africa. It is inevitable. If the South Africans liberalize their own system, it will facilitate those relations . . . But are we to say, as [Tanzanian President Julius] Nyerere does, that black Africa must raise an army to fight the South Africans? The consequences of that would be catastrophic for everybody in this region. We prefer dialogue on the South African issue . . . When people say to us, "You have contacts and trade with South Africa," it is not something we need to apologize about. We all of us feel and hope South Africa will change its internal policies. But the contacts [in any case] will remain.

Interview, Samatango, Angola/ The Washington Post, 7-24:(A)15.

Shehu Shagari
President of Nigeria

4

[On possible U.S. aid to anti-government guerrillas in Angola]: If the United States is willing to support rebels in a sovereign African nation, it would be extremely serious. I don't believe [the U.S.] will do it because it would be very unwise. But if it did, it would be in defiance not only of Angola but of all Africa.

News conference, London, March 20/ Los Angeles Times, 3-21:(I)8.

Ian Smith
Member of Zimbabwean Parliament; Former Prime Minister of Rhodesia (Zimbabwe)

5

[Saying Zimbabwe needs its white population and shouldn't drive it away]: They [whites] have the skills and the capital. I'm not a racist, but it's the story of Africa: Every black country that forces its whites to leave has become a tragedy.

Interview/Newsweek, 3-9:13.

(IAN SMITH)

1

[Criticizing the government of Prime Minister Robert Mugabe]: People who have been loyal servants of this country, people with 20 to 30 years' service, hoping as everybody hopes to get promoted, find themselves superceded by people who have been in the game five minutes, with no qualifications whatever. What do they do? They depart. Anybody would ... [The government is] going out of their way to talk socialism, contrary to what they talked when they came in. They are frightening away foreign investment. They are moving in a direction that is the antithesis of private enterprise. When you see how socialism failed in the rest of Africa, it's a wonder that people can't see that for themselves.

Interview, Salisbury/Chicago Tribune, 9-11:(1)8.

Donald B. Sole
*South African Ambassador
to the United States*

2

[On U.S. pressures on his country to reach a settlement in Namibia and to liberalize the apartheid system in South Africa]: The Reagan Administration is offering some carrot, but there is no doubt in our minds that it is also going to wield the stick. Unlike the [previous] Carter Administration, it believes you get more done if you apply private persuasion, and indeed private pressure, than public rhetoric. What we seek, and what I believe the Reagan Administration seeks, is simply a normalization of relations. We are not asking for any concessional favors at all. What we hope is that because the Reagan Administration approaches foreign policy on a global basis—rather than on a compartmentalized basis as did Mr. Carter—there

will be a greater recognition of the need to maintain stability in southern Africa.

Interview/Los Angeles Times, 9-21:(1)8.

3

[On whether South Africa has a nuclear bomb]: Where would we use a bomb, anyway? Look at the psychological approaches nations take toward a bomb program, which costs a tremendous amount of money. Pakistan wants it because the Indians have it. Arab countries want it because they think Israel has it. South Africa doesn't have that kind of threat. Where would a bomb be useful? If it's some kind of guerrilla war you're talking about, we couldn't use one at all, not in our own country.

Interview/The Christian Science Monitor, 12-3:15.

Helen Suzman
Member of South African Parliament

4

[On the South African Parliament]: It's a funny place. It's insulated. You're almost like a lot of fish floating around in an aquarium while the world is carrying on its business outside. The people here never actually have a confrontation eyeball-to-eyeball with the people who are affected by the laws. You see, it's all done through officialdom. It's the old thing of the messenger and the bad news. No one wants to get his head chopped off for saying: "Look here, things are really bad. They are starving in the [black African] homelands." They say, "Oh, no, no, no. We're giving rations. Really, it's all exaggerated. It's just done for sensational press reports."

*Interview, Johannesburg/
The New York Times, 9-10:6.*

The Americas

John Aimers
National chairman,
Monarchist League of Canada

1

[On a proposed new Canadian Constitution that would reduce ties with Britain]: There is a strong suspicion . . . growing in people's minds that [Canadian Prime Minister Pierre Elliott] Trudeau wants to be the first president of Canada. I must say until recently I felt that this was an extreme position, but I am beginning to wonder if this whole scenario . . . isn't designed to set up some sort of confrontation which will permit him . . . to declare some ridiculous [Unilateral Declaration of Independence] and somehow sever our monarchial connection.

Los Angeles Times, 2-10:(I)11.

Millard Arnold
Deputy Assistant Secretary, Bureau of
Human Rights, Department of State
of the United States

2

[Criticizing the decision of the U.S. to resume military aid to El Salvador]: Obviously, the decision to resume aid has been viewed with great alarm in our Bureau. We're unhappy because that decision has to be viewed in its consequences. We're talking about a country under martial law that faces a serious and growing threat from within, where 11,000 people were killed last year. You've got to say to yourself, this [U.S. aid] isn't going to help any. Anyone with a modicum of intelligence will have to draw the conclusion more lives will be lost.

Washington, Jan. 14/
Los Angeles Times, 1-15:(I)14.

Zbigniew Brzezinski
Assistant to the President of the
United States for
National Security Affairs

3

[The U.S. has] dominated Central America militarily. We at times have exploited it economically . . .   But we are outgrowing that phase of our history . . . If the workers of Gdansk [Poland] have the right to demand a decent wage and decent weekly hours, the peasants of El Salvador and Nicaragua have a right to demand their land.

Before French Institute of International Relations,
Paris, Jan. 12/ The Washington Post, 1-13:(A)8.

George Bush
Vice President of the United States

4

[Whatever the human-rights faults of other governments in Central and South America,] the [Cuban] Communist alternative would condemn the people of those regions to the most repressive form of government. The [Cuban President Fidel] Castro regime is a perfect miniscule model of its sponsor and master, the Soviet government. And the revolution they seek to export is not a revolution of freedom and human dignity; it is a revolution of tyranny and the brutal repression of human rights—including the precious right to worship one's God, the very foundation of Western civilization and culture. To condemn the repressive policies of any nation in Central America, without recognizing that the worst offender of human rights in this hemisphere is Russia's satellite in Havana, isn't simple hypocrisy; it is short-sighted

(GEORGE BUSH)

foreign policy that ill serves the cause of peace and freedom.

At Duquesne University, May 8/
The Washington Post, 5-9:(A)20.

1

Having nothing to offer but revolution, [Cuba] creates other revolutions by destabilizing, by infiltrating, by terrorizing. The Cubans have been caught doing this red-handed over and over in this hemisphere—in El Salvador, in Costa Rica, in Nicaragua, in Guatemala, in Colombia. I find that [Cuban President Fidel] Castro is frequently annoyed by my remarks. I must confess this gives me some pleasure. On the day that Fidel Castro holds free elections in Cuba, I will say something nice about him.

Before Dominican National Assembly,
Santo Domingo, Oct. 12/
Chicago Tribune, 10-13:(1)5.

Jorge Bustamante
Director, Central Elections
Commission of El Salvador

2

[On the elections scheduled for his country next year]: We want to have a nice, clean, free election, and a nice, big turnout. The [guerilla-warfare] violence will not end overnight. The violence is the result of more than 100 years of injustice, of the great difference between the rich and the poor, the result of the lack of education, the loss of hope, the lack of faith in the future. We must have a revolution. And the revolution must start with a free election.

Interview, San Salvador/
Los Angeles Times, 12-29:(I)6.

Aristides Calvani
Former Foreign Minister of Venezuela

3

If a Marxist regime installs itself in El Salvador, it will represent a profound unbalance in the area. It is most important for international

Marxism to triumph in El Salvador, because it permits them to establish the beginning of a bridge. They intend to have a Marxist government in Nicaragua, too.

The Washington Post, 1-17:(A)21.

Oscar Camilion
Foreign Minister of Argentina

4

[On the U.S. arms embargo against his country because of Argentina's alleged violations of human rights]: We can live with it, though we prefer to put aside this small hindrance. It is not a very friendly initiative. We hope to re-establish normal relations with the United States. The United States is a traditional friend and it is an important country with which we have lots in common. [But] we are more interested in establishing fraternity inside Argentine society than in diplomatic negotiations and small problems with other countries because of so-called human rights. We Argentines will reach our goal of national conciliation. We will create reasonable stability in our institutions, and the world will sooner or later accept the way we Argentines find to live with ourselves.

Interview, Buenos Aires, April 9/
The New York Times, 4-13:4.

Jorge Castaneda
Foreign Minister of Mexico

5

[On criticism of his country's recognition of the anti-government guerrillas in El Salvador]: We are not legitimizing the guerrillas. We didn't create the guerrillas. But they are a reality. They control part of the territory, and they have the support of a substantial part of the population . . . The deterioration of the situation in El Salvador has been particularly bothersome over the past year. We have observed the violence resulting from the civil conflict. We have witnessed over the past two years the uncontrolled activity of groups identified with the official government apparatus that have liquidated hundreds of thousands of persons, frequently

WHAT THEY SAID IN 1981

in a bestial fashion. We cannot remain alien or insensitive to this suffering.

> News conference, Mexico City, Sept. 4/
> The New York Times, 9-5:3.

Fidel Castro
President of Cuba

1

[Saying the U.S. is threatening a blockade of Cuba, which it says is shipping arms to the rebels in El Salvador]: They are trying to find other ways to wipe us off the face of the map. We will fight for each piece of our territory, to the death, in case imperialism attacks us. We will not resist the symbol of liberty if it is offered to us, but we will not retreat [in the face] of aggression. [The U.S. is] threatening the patriots of Salvador and hatching aggressive schemes against that country. The U.S. is supporting or propping up most corrupt dictatorships on our continent to establish brutal domination, and Cuba will not be brought to its knees.

> At Soviet Communist Party Congress, Moscow,
> Feb. 24/The Washington Post, 2-25:(A)14.

2

It is a lie that there are Cuban military advisers in El Salvador [helping the Salvadoran guerrillas against the government]. It is a lie that part of the weapons supplied by the Soviet Union for our own defense is being redistributed to Central America. It is a lie that Cuba is supplying weapons and ammunition to Salvadoran patriots. The channels for it do not exist, and Salvadoran patriots have been fighting for months with their own resources, or with weapons they wrest from the enemy. Lies, lies, nothing but lies. [But] it would not be immoral or censurable to provide weapons to a people whose sons and daughters are being brutally annihilated if it were within our possibilities.

> At meeting of Interparliamentary Union,
> Havana, Sept. 15/Los Angeles Times, 9-16:(I)18.

Vinicio Cerezo Arevalo
*Secretary general, Christian Democratic
Party of Guatemala*

3

[On next year's scheduled Presidential election]: We require two conditions from the government to contest the election. First, an end to repression by underground right-wing groups; and second, legal reforms in the electoral system to guarantee that the people's vote will be respected . . . If we lose this opportunity, Guatemala is going to have a civil war like that in Nicaragua and El Salvador. [The right-wingers in the current government] are the hardest people in Central America. Their strategy is to present the [U.S.] Reagan Administration with just two choices—leadership by the extreme right or extreme left . . . We accept and respect the fight of the [Communist] guerrillas; but the changes they want are not the ones we want. We want a pluralistic society. They want a totally socialistic society.

> Interview, Guatemala City/
> The Christian Science Monitor, 8-26:13.

Pedro Chamorro
*Co-editor, "La Prensa,"
Managua, Nicaragua*

4

[On Nicaragua's Sandinista government]: They do not grant freedom of assembly to all parties—only to the Sandinistas. They stop all others from meeting. They have confiscated many industries in the private sector—including some not formerly owned by the [deposed] Somozas. They have attacked all the independent media. They have established close connections with the Soviet Union. They practically idolize Cuba. They say that someone needs to teach us "the Cuban way." They regard [Cuban President] Fidel Castro as if he were the leader of the world. They have created a climate of hate. The Nicaraguan revolution [which installed the Sandinistas] was a united effort of all classes to get rid of a dictatorship. Class hatred started only after the revolution. Now the bourgeoisie feels threatened and doesn't want

(PEDRO CHAMORRO)

to invest. There has been a brain drain. This revolution is not democratic.

Interview/World Press Review, July:27.

James Cheek
Assistant Secretary for Inter-American Affairs, Department of State of the United States

1

[On U.S. policy in El Salvador during the current guerrilla warfare there]: A lot of people think we're trying to impose some American democratic system on El Salvador, and it's true. We believe in a democratic process as a way of ordering national affairs. The democratic process is pluralistic; it allows all views to come forward and freely be expressed. And when you have fragmentation and such sharp divisions, how—except through a pluralistic system—can everyone be heard? The negotiations that the left talks about is that, well, let's let the Marxists and the Christian Democrats and the Socialists sit down and decide everything. But there's a lot more—there's a whole private sector out there. Most of the labor movement in the country is independent of either the left of the government or the right.

Interview/Los Angeles Herald Examiner, 8-1:(A)4.

Claude Cheysson
Foreign Minister of France

2

[On U.S. policy in Latin America]: There will be cases where there will be differences [between U.S. and French policy] because you [the U.S.] will be tempted to jump to the conclusion that because a country has relations with Cuba, or because its prime minister has a beard and dresses in a funny paratrooper commando uniform, we should not be on speaking terms with them. We don't accept that. That is much too simple.

Interview/Time, 6-29:34.

Rafael Cordova Rivas
Member, ruling junta of Nicaragua

3

[Nicaragua's] GNP in the financial year just ended was 10 per cent higher than 1977-78—the best year under [the late President Anastasio] Somoza—but we still do not have money for arms. Not one cent of our budget will be spent on arms. But if the Soviet Union wants to send arms, including tanks and planes, we will gladly accept them. If the United States sends us tanks, we will accept them, too. We feel threatened because Honduras has 12 new . . . tanks sent by the U.S. and a small but modern air force with well-trained crews. There are 5,000 former members of Somoza's National Guard in Honduras near the Nicaraguan border and some elements of the Honduran Army support them. We have no defense arms. We have no tanks. We have no military planes. We have only three helicopters, two of which are broken and the third doesn't fly very well.

*News conference, Los Angeles, June 14/
Los Angeles Times, 6-5:(I)17.*

Arturo Cruz
Nicaraguan Ambassador to the United States

4

[On the Sandinistas government in his country]: All this revolutionary sloganeering is not what the peasants want, not what the people want. People sneer and make jokes. It backfires. The government is in the hands of intelligent, honest patriots. I have never questioned that or their deep sense of honor. But they need to revise some of their political views. It is difficult for young revolutionaries to recognize the very, very widespread dissension that exists here. There is a great difference between enemies and political adversaries, and this is not always understood. The Sandinistas need to make the transition from being soldiers to being political leaders. They need to recognize that political opposition should not only be tolerated but is indispensable for a stable society. If they do not, they run the risk of being thrown out of power.

Interview, Managua/Los Angeles Times, 5-27:(I-A)9.

WHAT THEY SAID IN 1981

Kenneth M. Curtis
United States Ambassador to Canada

1

[On U.S.-Canadian relations]: The United States has got to develop better machinery for dealing with bilateral issues. Problems no longer develop at the leisurely pace they used to, and we are not fully geared to giving these issues the day-to-day attention they ought to have . . . What is confusing is that there may be good signals coming from [the Department of] State, but then Commerce or Treasury gets into the act at the eleventh hour . . . It is not only confusing but can be misinterpreted as some kind of bad faith on our part . . . We have to be more sensitive. Our intentions are fine in 99 per cent of the cases. We're not out to try to give Canada a bad deal, but we are a little clumsy in how we proceed.

Interview, Ottawa/The New York Times, 1-17:6.

Hatuey de Camps
President, Chamber of Deputies,
Dominican National Assembly

2

The small nations of the Caribbean aspire to survive, to assure their peoples a quality of life a little better than what they have, reducing the degree of social injustice that prevails in the great majority of our nations. The peoples of the Caribbean don't aspire to the role of great powers or to divide the world into zones of influence. The military presence of one or another great power, transforming the Caribbean into a battlefield, is a phenomenon we question because we've suffered the fruits of such situations.

Before Dominican National Assembly,
Santo Domingo, Oct. 12/
The New York Times, 10-13:3.

Miguel d'Escoto
Foreign Minister of Nicaragua

3

We have made it a priority to make every effort to reach an understanding, a *modus vivendi*, with the United States. We don't expect the

[U.S.] Reagan Administration to like our revolution, but at least to accept it as an irreversible reality, and to respect it. We want a new relationship of dignity and respect and not one of docility and servility.

Managua, Aug. 12/The New York Times, 8-13:3.

Jorge Diaz Serrano
Director, Pemex
(Mexican state oil company)

4

What you can say is that we [Mexico] have a lot of petroleum; we are actually floating on a sea of oil. We are beginning to live up to our geographic shape: as the horn of plenty. It is all a new experience for a country that for so long seemed so poor. Now it is a question of using all this wealth wisely. Getting it out of the ground is no real problem. Putting the revenue to good use and making sure that the country grows in the most orderly way possible is our big dilemma. Here we have few guidelines, except for countries that have allowed oil to dominate too much. So we flounder a little and hope our answers prove correct.

The Christian Science Monitor, 3-17:11.

Jose Napoleon Duarte
President of El Salvador

5

[Calling for free elections to end the guerrilla war in his country]: We are not willing to negotiate [with the rebels] any position in the government because the only people who have the right to determine positions in the government is the Salvadoran people through elections. But what we are willing to do is to find a way to supervise the whole electoral process. All the political parties would register, including all the extreme leftist parties who are willing to incorporate themselves and drop their arms . . . We are going to request from the Organization of American States not only to send us a protocol mission, but to send us contingents from all of the Americas to come and inspect and to really make these free elections.

News conference, San Salvador, March 4/
The New York Times, 3-6:4.

(JOSE NAPOLEON DUARTE)

1

[On the guerrilla war in his country]: Whether this is another Vietnam does not depend on us. It depends on what the others do. If the Cubans, the Russians, the Chinese and the United States want to come here and fight, this will be another Vietnam. But for that to happen, they will have to finish off all the Salvadorans. Here, struggling alone to solve our own problems is the only thing we will accept. The masses were with the guerrillas a year ago. There is no question that there is misery in this country, but now we have created an alternative and taken away the guerrillas' support. We're struggling here for democracy.

Interview, San Salvador, Feb. 20/
The New York Times, 2-21:4.

2

[Criticizing France and Mexico for their recognition of two left-wing guerrilla groups fighting in El Salvador]: Mexico and France are asking the people of El Salvador to overthrow their government. They are telling us that all we are trying to achieve here means nothing. But what is even worse, by this action and from this moment on any nation can now recognize any anti-government terrorist group in any country—yes, even in Mexico, which has a few problems of its own . . . Our country is caught up in a continuous cycle of violence—first from the left, then from the right-wing death squads. That's why this action by Mexico and France is highly irresponsible. I am sure they have not thought out what the consequences will be. There will be a reaction from the right, more violence, more killing, more suffering. Why can't these nations just leave us alone?

Interview, San Salvador/Chicago Tribune, 9-3:(1)9.

Thomas O. Enders
Assistant Secretary for Inter-American Affairs, Department of State of the United States

3

[El Salvador] is divided between the insurgents and a great majority that opposes the extreme left's violent methods and foreign ties. It is divided between an equally violent minority on the extreme right that seeks to return El Salvador to the domination of a small elite and a great majority that has welcomed the political and social changes of the past 18 months. The insurgents are divided within their own coalition between those who want to prolong their ill-starred guerrilla campaign and those who are disillusioned by their failure to win the quick military victory their leaders had proclaimed inevitable; between those who despise democracy as an obstacle to their ambitions to seize power and those who might be willing to engage in democratic elections. Finally, the vast majority of Salvadorans in the middle are also divided—over whether to emphasize the restoration of the country's economic health or the extension of the country's social reforms; between those who honor the army as one of the country's most stable and coherent institutions and those who criticize it for failing to prevent right-wing violence; between those who see the need to develop participatory institutions and those who maintain that there is no alternative to the old personalistic politics . . . we believe that the solution must be democratic, because only a genuinely pluralistic approach can enable a profoundly divided society to live with itself without violent convulsions, gradually overcoming its differences.

Before Washington World Affairs Council, July 16/
The New York Times, 7-17:5.

Jose Figueres Ferrer
Former President of Costa Rica

4

[Agreeing with U.S. support of the government in El Salvador]: Now that for the first time in a long time the U.S. has finally taken an interest in what's going on down in Central America, I think it would be to our disadvantage if it stopped. The U.S. has intervened down there all the time either by commission or omission, unfortunately mostly by omission or not caring. So I would prefer to have an American presence. Look, the U.S. is practically at

(JOSE FIGUERES FERRER)

war with the Soviet Union and what you're seeing [in El Salvador] is the possibility of a government that will be friendly to the Soviet Union [if the Salvadoran guerrillas win]. So I don't blame the U.S. I approve of the shipment of arms, but only to the extent necessary to stop the shipment of arms from Cuba.

Interview, Chicago/Chicago Tribune, 5-18:(1)1.

1

I fought with all my might [against] the Batista dictatorship [in Cuba], and I don't regret it. I would rather have [Cuban President Fidel] Castro's kind of dictatorship, which has a dose of idealism, than a stupid kind of military dictatorship like Batista. Of course, Fidel's a psychopath. He is incompetent, but he has had enormous advantages by converting himself into a tool of the Soviet Union so that he has received more foreign aid than all the rest of Latin America. So when I hear people talk about how great he is, I remember the amount of aid he receives and the amount of authority he wields. If I could wield one-tenth of the authority he does, well, I'm not short of ideas about what to do in handling the economy of Costa Rica. But I have always faced the limitations of the law and democratic principles.

Interview, Chicago/Chicago Tribune, 5-18:(1)4.

Rowland C. Frazee
Chairman, Royal Bank of Canada

2

If we [Canada] continue to be so isolationist as to believe we can build a healthy economy without attracting and welcoming foreign capital and investment, we will see more projects delayed, down the drain or—more accurately—down south [in the U.S.]. We'll see more jobs lost, the Canadian dollar fall still further, the price we pay for imports increase. The notion that foreign ownership is bad ownership, and that we can penalize it retroactively, as contained in the Federal government's National Energy Program, is living dangerously.

It is damaging Canada's reputation abroad, and is fomenting bickering at home, just when we should be pulling together.

At Royal Bank stockholders' meeting, Montreal/ The Wall Street Journal, 3-6:22.

Carlos Fuentes
Author; Former Mexican Ambassador to France

3

[Criticizing U.S. military support for the government of El Salvador, which is fighting a civil war]: How can you ask the political opposition [to the Salvadoran government] to accept peaceful methods when their spokesmen and militants have all been brutally silenced by [government] guns? Who will come out to parley while the [government] death squads are abroad? . . . Perhaps [the U.S.] will come to understand that by helping the military in El Salvador they help Communism in El Salvador. That by identifying the Soviet Union with the revolution in El Salvador, they hand the Soviet Union a moral victory that belongs only to the Salvadoran people. And that even if Cuba and the Soviet Union did not exist, there would be a revolution in El Salvador. And that if it were true that arms flow into El Salvador from Hanoi and Havana and Managua and should then cease to flow, the civil war would continue in El Salvador because it depends on historical factors that have nothing to do with Communism . . .

At The New School, New York/ The Washington Post, 5-3:(C)4.

Alexander M. Haig, Jr.
Secretary of State of the United States

4

[On the guerrilla war in El Salvador]: A well-orchestrated international Communist campaign designed to transform the Salvadoran crisis from the internal conflict to an increasingly internationalized confrontation is under way. With Cuban coordination, the Soviet bloc, Vietnam, Ethiopia and radical Arabs are furnishing

(ALEXANDER M. HAIG, JR.)

at least several hundred tons of military equipment to the Salvadoran leftist insurgents. Most of this equipment—not all but most—has entered via Nicaragua . . . I want to emphasize that [the] government in El Salvador is a coalition, headed by a true Christian democrat, Napoleon Duarte. It includes moderate military and independent civilians . . . The extremist left has thus far failed to topple the existing government in El Salvador. The revolutionaries' recent large military operation has failed. We have also seen the dwindling support in the popular sector for the revolutionaries.

Briefing to foreign ambassadors, Washington, Feb. 17/The New York Times, 2-21:5.

1

[On U.S.-Cuban relations]: I think [Cuban President Fidel] Castro has a choice to make. If he is going to persist in training, supplying arms, strategizing for the forceful overthrow of regimes in the [Western] Hemisphere, it is going to be extremely difficult if not impossible to initiate a dialogue with him.

Before Senate Subcommittee on State Department Appropriations, Washington, May 1/Los Angeles Herald Examiner, 5-1:(A)5.

2

Americans do not have the luxury of avoiding concern about violations of international law or interventionism by the forces of Marxism-Leninism anywhere in the world. It is all the more critical when it occurs in this hemisphere, which is of such strategic significance because of its proximity, Central American oil resources and the Panama Canal. Since 1978, Cuba, with the support of the Soviet Union, has embarked on a systematic campaign of increasing interventionism against its neighbors. Cuba no longer makes any pretense of respecting the sovereignty of other countries. Instead, Havana calls the leaders of violent opposition groups together, forges unity pacts among them,

trains their men, provides arms and sends them back to mount a violent challenge to legitimate governments.

Interview/U.S. News & World Report, 12-21:22.

Moises Hassan
Minister of Construction of Nicaragua

3

There is a common interest among us [in Nicaragua]. We all know how fragile we are, how fragile is our independence. Libya, Algeria, Nicaragua, The Palestinians have known what it is to be the subjects of foreign powers or their representatives. I think this is probably difficult for a country like the United States to understand because it has never suffered very much. It must be difficult for a normal American to comprehend how a country feels that for many years has seen itself as a subject. We know that we are a weak country, economically and militarily. Independence is not completely achieved. We know that the major powers don't want to recognize that we are free.

Interview, Managua, Nicaragua, July 17/ The Washington Post, 7-19:(A)18.

S. I. Hayakawa
United States Senator, R—California

4

[On Mexican workers who cross the border to find jobs in the U.S.]: As long as there is a wide economic disparity between the U.S. and Mexico, we will have millions of Mexican nationals crossing the border to find gainful employment. If we closed the border completely, an impossible task, Mexico would become a pressure-cooker filled with unemployed hungry citizens.

Los Angeles Herald Examiner, 4-10:(A)11.

Jesse A. Helms
United States Senator, R—North Carolina

5

I've felt that we made a tragic mistake in terms of Nicaragua and [not supporting Presi-

WHAT THEY SAID IN 1981

(JESSE A. HELMS)

dent Anastasio] Somoza [who was ousted in a civil war in 1979]. Somoza perhaps was not 100 per cent to the liking or 90 per cent or 80 per cent to the liking of a lot of Americans. But we see now that he was jolly well better than whatever was in second place in terms of freedom in this world, and we found out too late what the [conquering] Sandinistas were all about.

TV-radio interview/"Meet the Press,"
National Broadcasting Company, 3-1.

Deane R. Hinton
United States Ambassador to El Salvador

1

No one would pretend the human-rights situation [in El Salvador] is what it should be, neither the military commanders I have talked to nor the civilian members of the junta, but they are trying. I will continue to pursue human-rights cases, particularly those cases involving American citizens. But I will do it quietly, without planning any news conference to denounce anything or anybody . . . We have made perfectly clear the commitment of the United States government to see to it that the junta is not taken over by an armed insurrection from Havana, from Managua [Nicaragua] or anywhere else . . . Democratic elections that result in a legitimate government is clearly the best political solution that anyone can think of. It would produce a government of a kind this country hasn't seen in 50 years.

Interview, San Salvador, June 16/
The New York Times, 6-17:9.

2

[Saying free elections are the best way to settle the current guerrilla war in El Salvador]: The elections will indicate very clearly that the vast majority of the people of this country are in favor of something different than these five or ten or fifteen thousand misguided individuals [the rebels] that are trying to destroy the country. Once it becomes clear that these people who are on this destructive course are without

support, then it is a question of time. The ultimate outcome is perfectly clear. How are they going to go around the world saying they represent the people of El Salvador if the people of El Salvador are on record as supporting somebody else?

Interview/
The Washington Post,
8-31:(A)1.

Edward M. Kennedy
United States Senator,
D—Massachusetts

3

[On U.S. involvement in the guerrilla war in El Salvador]: We must . . . insist on progress toward a mediated settlement, and the rejection of any movement toward a military dictatorship. The United States must not encourage a coup in any way. And we must make it absolutely clear that we cannot and will not sustain any dictatorship with our foreign aid. A settlement is vital to our national interest, and we must act to advance our own fundamental values of human rights.

News conference,
Washington, March 6/
The Washington Post,
3-7:(A)11.

Jeane J. Kirkpatrick
United States Ambassador/Permanent
Representative to the United Nations

4

[On the guerrilla war in El Salvador]: The [U.S.] Reagan Administration would like nothing better than to see a civilian and democratic government in El Salvador. Everyone would like to see El Salvador pacified. We would all like for the people of El Salvador to be permitted to choose their rulers. That is the only political objective the current [U.S.] Administration has—that and the objective of making certain that the guerrillas do not by force of arms deny the people of El Salvador that

(JEANE J. KIRKPATRICK)

choice. No one would like anything better than to have the decision left to the people.

At debate on El Salvador, Washington, Feb. 26/
The New York Times, 3-8:(4)2.

Marc Lalonde
Minister of Energy of Canada

1

[On his country's plan to "Canadianize" its energy industry, so that foreign ownership will be no more than 50 per cent]: Quite clearly, our view is that the oil and gas sector is a strategic one for this country, and no country worth its salt in modern times would tolerate the degree of foreign ownership and control that exists in the Canadian petroleum industry, where last year over 80 per cent in sales and 72 per cent of the assets were foreign-owned, and where 17 out of the 25 largest corporations were foreign-owned and controlled, and where not one of the first 10 corporations was a Canadian-owned and controlled company.

At dinner for correspondents, Ottawa/
The Washington Post, 8-9:(F)2.

Carlos Lemos Simmonds
Foreign Minister of Colombia

2

[On Cuban aid and encouragement to Latin American guerrilla groups]: It used to be that when one talked of intervention in Latin America, it brought to mind the image of marines landing on our beaches. But the interventionism of today is of another style. It's a more cunning form. It pits men against their own compatriots. It gives them arms and training and sends them back to their countries to topple democratically constituted governments.

August/The New York Times, 8-13:3.

Clarence D. Long
United States Representative, D-Maryland

3

. . . sending [U.S.] military aid to El Salvador is unnecessary. The government of El Salvador

in January defeated a "final offensive" by the leftist guerrillas without our help. The national uprising that the insurgents expected failed to materialize. Their offensive was a total failure. Why not let well enough alone? . . . If we send a lot of military down there, we're likely to revive the whole resentment of gunboat diplomacy, Yankee imperialism, dollar diplomacy. Our intervention may well lead to a situation where the adversaries in El Salvador would, as in Vietnam, concentrate on hating us. That, certainly, is not in our national interest.

Interview/U.S. News & World Report, 3-16:31.

4

[On El Salvador]: The problem is not so much that the [guerrilla] war's at a stalemate. The problem is that the economy's at a stalemate. The land reform was carried out in a bad way. The cooperatives don't work . . . A billion dollars left the country before they could slam the door. It's a repressive regime, and we just don't know how to keep them from stealing our money. I don't know what the solution is, but I do know that the U.S. Treasury is going to be the target of a ripoff; and if we stay in there, we're going to end up being the enemy.

Interview/The Christian Science Monitor, 7-14:6.

Jose Lopez Portillo
President of Mexico

5

While I do not wish to overstate achievements, it would be foolish to ignore the fact that now, at the beginning of the 1980s, Mexican society is better fulfilling its social, political and economic responsibilities and that our most cherished goals have been achieved: national conciliation and public confidence; political democracy; and liberty and peace in the streets, at work and at school. Few countries can make the same claim. We have only to look around us and compare. Let us appreciate the value of what we have, for there are many others who only realized its worth once they had lost it.

State of the Nation address, Sept. 1/
The New York Times, 9-22:35.

WHAT THEY SAID IN 1981

(JOSE LOPEZ PORTILLO)

1

The great powers have moved beyond their own geographic areas and now stand at economic and ideological borders. I believe that, most particularly, the Caribbean is an East-West frontier between the United States and the Soviet Union. The change in the depiction of the problems of Central America is also noticeable. Even 10 years ago, a conflict, a revolution or a *coup d'etat* in Central America—if it deserved any attention in the North American press—was [presented as] a caricature in which a man in a big *sombrero* held a rifle and was doing something curious, comical. Now it is eight [newspaper] columns, and the problem of El Salvador is a problem of East-West confrontation. This means, in effect, that the problems of development are problems of world compromises.

Interview, Mexico City/Parade, 10-4:5.

William Luers
United States Ambassador to Venezuela

2

[On Venezuela]: Here is a nation firmly opposed to authoritarian regimes of the right and left . . . a nation that believes that its own identity as a democracy is enhanced by the strengthening of pluralism and liberty elsewhere.

Los Angeles Times, 2-17:(I)9.

Richard G. Lugar
United States Senator, R—Indiana

3

I support [the U.S.] giving additional [military] training assistance to the existing government in El Salvador because it appears to offer our best hope of bringing about economic reforms and some improvement in the lives of the bulk of the people there. To fail to give the Duarte government an opportunity to succeed—it is barely hanging on at the moment —would be a disservice to the people of El Salvador. Those who are very suspicious of the

Duarte government have some obligation to produce a better alternative.

Interview/U.S. News & World Report, 3-16:31.

Mark MacGuigan
Minister of External Affairs
of Canada

4

[On the guerrilla war in El Salvador]: When it's a question of arms shipments, our position is one of opposition to the shipment of offensive arms, whether by ourselves or by other countries, to states which are in a situation of internal disorder. Beyond that, I don't think anyone should look to us for profound insights on what is happening in El Salvador or what should be done. It is not an area of vital interest to Canada, unlike the Commonwealth Caribbean . . . It's not an area in which we feel any commitment to solve the problem . . . So we don't have a close knowledge of the situation there. We don't know, for instance . . . to what extent the junta is responsible for right-wing violence which is occurring, to what extent the rebel movement is controlled by Communists. We know there are Communists in it. We know that Communists normally do seek to control a movement in which they participate, but we don't know if they control this one. So we're taking what is, in effect, a very modest position.

To reporters, New York, Feb. 4/
Los Angeles Times, 3-5:(I)7.

Paul N. McCloskey, Jr.
United States Representative,
R—California

5

[On U.S. policy toward the guerrilla war in El Salvador]: El Salvador is not worth fighting for, in my judgment. There would be no way of justifying the [U.S. President] Reagan rhetoric [about supporting the Salvadoran government] . . . today, if the Administration did not perceive what is happening in El Salvador as a Soviet-U.S. confrontation, like the 1962 Cuban missile crisis. The fact that we would get in-

(PAUL N. McCLOSKEY, JR.)

volved on one side or another in a three-way fight in a Central American country cannot be explained other than that the State Department must feel it has very tangible evidence that this is a Soviet effort through Cuba . . . I don't think Congress is willing to go along with huge amounts of military or economic aid to a faction in El Salvador for the purpose of keeping El Salvador stable.

Before Los Angeles World Affairs Council,
Feb. 26/Los Angeles Times, 2-27:(I)20.

Edwin Meese III
Counsellor to the President
of the United States

1

[Saying U.S. President Reagan will take a tough stand on countries that export subversion]: It's time that Cuba and the other nations that seek to subvert other countries wake up to the fact that we have a new Administration, a new national resolve, and we will take the necessary steps that are needed to keep the peace any place in the world, and that includes El Salvador . . . We're talking about not precluding any particular [U.S.] course of action, and we're talking about taking those steps that are necessary to prevent subversion, to prevent the expansion of Communism . . . When it's clear that you are going to take those kinds of steps that are necessary, and the people in Cuba and other places see it's to their self-interest not to continue in their course of action, then I think we are going to have a different reaction from those countries than we had in the past.

Broadcast interview/
"Issues and Answers," ABC-TV, 2-22.

Francois Mitterrand
President of France

2

The people of [Latin America] want an end to the oligarchies which, enforced by bloody dictatorships, exploit them, force them to live in unbelievable conditions. A minority of the population controls most of the wealth. How can we be surprised by popular uprisings? It is not a question of Communist subversion, but a refusal to put up with misery and subservience. The West would be better advised to help these people rather than to try to contain them under the boot of repression. When they cry for help, I would prefer it if [Cuban President Fidel] Castro were not the only one to hear them.

Interview/Los Angeles Herald Examiner, 7-2:(A)4.

Jacques Yvan Morin
Vice Premier of Quebec, Canada

3

[On his province's law making French the official language]: You have to realize that over 80 per cent of the province is French-speaking. About 13 to 14 per cent is English, and the rest are various ethnic groups including Italian, Greek and Portuguese. What we've done is make sure the majority would no longer be compelled to speak—at work, at least—a language [English] it didn't know. We also decided all children of immigrants would go to French schools, as is the rule in all civilized countries. If you were an immigrant and moved to the [United] States, you wouldn't go to a Greek or Italian public school. You'd go to one in the language of the country. It's the same here . . . Really, the English-speaking of Quebec have greater rights and privileges than any minority in any part of the world. They also have their own hospitals, media, colleges and social services. We think Quebec has been more than fair to the English-speakers, but being fair doesn't mean disappearing ourselves. We must be fair to the majority as well.

Interview/Chicago Tribune, 11-29:(1)10.

Julian Nava
Former United States Ambassador
to Mexico

4

[Criticizing those Americans who are against U.S. backing of the Salvadoran government in

(JULIAN NAVA)

the guerrilla war in El Salvador]: I am often surprised by the naivete, fed by ignorance, on the part of well-meaning Americans who can't draw the distinction between a genuine domestic desire for radical reform and a social revolution greatly inspired and supported by Russian-bloc countries. Anyone who doesn't see the difference and the danger of an extension of Russian control is out of his mind or is a fraud.

Interview, Los Angeles/Chicago Tribune, 6-8:(4)9.

Daniel Ortega Saavedra
Member, ruling junta of Nicaragua

1

We have insisted many times on the need for a real dialogue with the United States, a dialogue of respect. Up to now, what we find in the United States with the current [Reagan] Administration is an attitude that is disrespectful to our people and our government. [The U.S.] has been the parents of the [deposed] Somoza dictatorship, and now they're telling us they'll give us aid if we behave ourselves. By that, they understand that we submit ourselves to the policies of the United States and act with the same spirit as the slaves of the United States. This we can't accept.

News conference, Havana, Cuba, April 19/
The New York Times, 4-21:4.

Augusto Pinochet Ugarte
President of Chile

2

[On the previous government which was overthrown in his coup in 1973]: The lamentable trilogy of demagoguery, statism and Marxism reached its worst extreme in our fatherland with this last government of the republic. Many today have forgotten how, during the Marxist government, the most characteristic values of our nationality were threatened or sneered at. The free spirit was threatened by imminent totalitarianism. Strong, just and impersonal authority had disappeared, giving way to anarchy. The judicial spirit was destroyed by a

government that despised legality. The sentences of our courts were ignored in a systematic way. All economic private initiative was suffocated by socialist collectivism . . . It was necessary to gather all the reserves of our patriotism, to impede this fall into the abyss with the intervention of the armed forces. More than seven years have passed, with some painful days, and Chile is now an internationally open country with the great spirit created by her better times.

At inauguration of new Constitution, Santiago,
March 11/The Washington Post, 3-12:(A)23.

Ronald Reagan
President of the United States

3

[On a proposal to allow Mexican nationals to cross freely into the U.S. for work]: I'm very intrigued by a program that's been suggested by several border-state Governors and their counterparts in the Mexican state on the other side of the border . . . [Mexico has] an unemployment rate that is far beyond anything —a safety valve has to be there that we're calling it "illegal immigration" right now. What these Governors have come up with, and I'm very intrigued with it, is a proposal that we and the Mexican government get together and legalize this—and grant visas—because it is to our interest also that the safety valve is not shut off and that we might have a breaking of the stability south of the border . . . At the same time, that [easy entrance] would make these people in our country—an employer could not take advantage of them and work them at sweatshop wages and so forth under the threat of turning them in. They, at the same time, then, would be paying taxes in this country for whatever they earned. They would be able to go legally back across the border, if they wanted to, and come back across. And I'm very intrigued with that.

Interview, Washington/
The Christian Science Monitor, 3-13:23.

4

[On U.S.-Mexican relations]: In a world filled with neighbors who resort to violence, neigh-

(RONALD REAGAN)

bors who've lost sight of the shared values and mutual interests, the good-will between Mexico and the United States is a blossom whose beauty we meet here to cherish and protect . . . [I] pledge that this Administration will sincerely and diligently strive to maintain a relationship of mutual respect and cooperation between our two nations, and the decisions which affect both sides of our border will be made only after the closest consultations between our governments.

Welcoming Mexican President Jose Lopez Portillo, Washington, June 8/ Los Angeles Herald Examiner, 6-8:(A)4.

1

[On U.S. support for the government of El Salvador in its fight with leftist guerrillas]: We know better than to engage in armed intervention; gunboat diplomacy could turn off a lot of friends. But we are very supportive of the [President Jose Napoleon] Duarte government in El Salvador. And we're doing everything we can with our other allies in Central and South America to bring about a peaceful solution by way of the election which Duarte is ready to hold. The great threat is coming from the left, and there's no question that it is exported: Revolution has been exported from Cuba and even has a Soviet hand in it. We are trying to launch a Caribbean initiative, which will also include Central America—and we have Mexico and Canada and Venezuela allied with us in this plan—to create a viable economy in those countries. We want to find out what assets can be developed and what can be done to erase the social and the economic problems that make them susceptible to this export of revolution. There is a great support among most of the Latin American nations for our position, and great criticism on the part of those nations of [President Fidel] Castro's Cuba for doing what he is doing.

Interview, Washington/ U.S. News & World Report, 12-28:27.

Arturo Rivera y Damas
Acting Archbishop of San Salvador, El Salvador

2

[On the guerrilla war in his country]: When I came to the archbishopric I tried to locate myself in the center, taking a critical distance as much from the government junta as from the Democratic Revolutionary Front. But also I've tried to point out, with emphasis, that the church needs to concern itself with justice and that this justice be realized among our people— that our peace ought not to be a peace of the cemeteries but one that would try to confront the roots that cause there to be no peace . . . If, instead of going ahead with the reforms, the government steps backward, I'm sure that you have a new explosion of desperation because of the unbearable situation. But that would be in the case that the reforms don't continue. They are responses to real problems and therefore the causes of injustice are being resolved, although partially, and this certainly would play a part in lowering popular tensions.

Interview, San Salvador/ The Washington Post, 3-9:(A)19.

Carlos Romero Barcelo
Governor of Puerto Rico

3

Our island stands in dramatic contrast to Cuba as a model for developing countries throughout the Caribbean and Latin America. Less than 50 years ago, Puerto Rico was known as "the poorhouse of the Caribbean." The level of poverty was shocking. Today we have the highest standard of living south of the Rio Grande.

Before Senate committee/ The Washington Post, 6-21:(A)14.

Andres Rosental
Deputy Foreign Minister for North American Affairs of Mexico

4

The United States sees Russia behind every bush. We have our doubts that the Soviet Union

WHAT THEY SAID IN 1981

(ANDRES ROSENTAL)

is trying to gain a beachhead in Central America ... What has replaced the old right-wing regime in Nicaragua is basically the solution for all of Central America. Why? Because it has brought the left-wing guerrillas into the government, and the private business sector is still in operation along with the media and academia. By isolating Nicaragua and maintaining a wishy-washy foreign policy toward the new government there, the U.S. is making the same mistake it made with Cuba—it is making it turn to the Soviet Union for help.

Chicago Tribune, 2-1:(1)11.

Jaime Santiago
Economist, University of Puerto Rico; Former Director of the Budget of Puerto Rico

1

Puerto Rico is living today under a mirage of economic affluence [while] its real economic sectors are in deep trouble. [Only U.S. Federal funds have] prevented the collapse of the island economy ... A new economic strategy is badly needed to put the economy on the path of a strong self-sustained growth. This will require a substantial change in the economic and political relations between the island and U.S.

The Washington Post, 6-21:(A)14.

Edward P. G. Seaga
Prime Minister of Jamaica

2

[On last year's election in which he defeated his socialist challenger]: Our election wasn't the only one that resulted in setbacks for Cuban and Soviet expansionism in the area. There were seven such elections in the Caribbean in 1980 alone and all of them had the same effect. Ours was just the most dramatic and best known, because we were fighting the proponents of Cuban expansionism and Marxism and defeated the principal protagonist. Our elections and the elections in the other Caribbean countries were fought because we as a

people felt very strongly about our position. We took the position that we did electorally for our own purposes, not to please any other country [such as the U.S.].

Interview/Chicago Tribune, 8-2:(2)1.

3

Prior to the U.S. involvement in El Salvador there was the involvement of Cuba in the supply of arms to El Salvador, and of that we have absolutely no doubt. The supply of arms to the guerrillas in El Salvador was the first move to achieve this polarization. The U.S. has moved to restore the balance from a situation of imbalance that was created by the arms from Cuba. In doing so, it has acted in its own interest and it has acted in the interest of people who want to see the center party, the moderate government, succeed over the extreme left or the extreme right.

Interview/Chicago Tribune, 8-2:(2)2.

Walter J. Stoessel, Jr.
Under Secretary for Political Affairs, Department of State of the United States

4

Our actions with regard to El Salvador have as their goal the reduction of violence and instability in order to facilitate a peaceful transition to an elected government. This is the goal of the Salvadoran people and of their current government, headed by Christian Democratic President Jose Napoleon Duarte, which we strongly support ... The United States cannot stand idly by while a reformist government comes under attack by externally advised and armed guerrilla groups that lack popular support. If we fail to make clear that the external encouragement of violence and instability in El Salvador will have serious costs, we insure that other countries seeking domestic solutions to domestic problems will find their efforts thwarted by guerrilla groups advised and armed from abroad. In turn, our failure to respond adequately to externally supported attempts to overthrow governments committed to reforms

(WALTER J. STOESSEL, JR.)

and to electoral solutions would cause other friendly countries to doubt our ability to help them resist assaults on their sovereignty.

Before Senate Appropriations Committee,
Washington, March 13/The New York Times, 3-14:5.

Pierre Elliott Trudeau
Prime Minister of Canada

1

[Criticizing a proposal by several provincial Premiers that would permit any province to declare that an amendment to the Federal Constitution did not apply to its territory, even though the amendment might be passed by two-thirds of the provinces and the Federal Parliament]: I believe there is a different view of Canada in the minds of many of those Premiers and in our minds . . . I think some of them see Canada as a confederation of shopping centers. I don't. I think there is such a thing as a national will, from which none of us can opt out.

Television interview, April 16/
Los Angeles Times, 4-18:(I)8.

Julio Cesar Turbay Ayala
President of Colombia

2

When we found that Cuba, a country with which we had diplomatic relations, was using those relations to prepare a group of guerrillas to come and fight against the government [of Colombia], it was a kind of Pearl Harbor for us. It was like sending ministers to Washington at the same time you are about to bomb ships in Hawaii . . . It's evident that Cuba has turned more active in exporting revolution. I have no proof that it is furnishing arms to guerrillas elsewhere in the region, but it is not difficult to conclude that no other country in the area has the capacity or the interest in arming these groups. In the majority of these countries, the choice is not between democratic alternatives but between representative government and extremist dictatorship. The fact that Cuba was

willing to intervene here tells us that she will do the same elsewhere in the region.

Interview, Bogota, Colombia, August/
The New York Times, 8-13:3.

Guillermo Ungo
President, Democratic Revolutionary
Front of El Salvador

3

[On his party's guerrilla war against the Salvadoran government]: The Salvadoran people are giving an example of heroism, decision and courage. We cannot stop our military struggle, because, if we did, the extermination of the people would be even greater . . . People generally believe that peaceful methods are synonymous with democracy, while armed insurrection is undemocratic. But this is pure fiction in a country like ours that has lived an anti-democracy where "peaceful methods" were instruments of domination, repression and control.

Interview, Mexico City/
The New York Times, 1-29:4.

Vladillen M. Vasev
Minister Counsellor,
Soviet Embassy, Washington

4

[On charges that the Soviet Union has been supplying arms to anti-government rebels in El Salvador]: The Soviet Union is not concerned with arms shipments to Salvador. The Soviet Union is not involved, and you can't pin it on us . . . We do ship armaments to Cuba as a matter of Soviet-Cuban relations. We do ship arms to Ethiopia as a matter of Soviet-Ethiopian relations. But I flatly deny that there is any Soviet supply of arms to the guerrilla forces in Salvador.

Interview, Feb. 14/
The New York Times, 2-15:(I)7.

Jorge Rafael Videla
Former President of Argentina

5

[On his just-ended Presidency]: Upon assuming control of the government in March 1976,

WHAT THEY SAID IN 1981

(JORGE RAFAEL VIDELA)

we received a prostrate country, one which with the daily effort of all Argentines, we succeeded in standing on its feet. And today, with pride, we hand over a country that is marching forward. We took a country that was in chaos, and today we deliver it in order; a country that was near anarchy, which today we deliver with authority; a country that was stagnating, which today we deliver with growing progress; a country that was violent, which today we deliver in peace.

At inauguration of new President Roberto Viola,
Buenos Aires, March 29/
The Washington Post, 3-30:(A)15.

Roberto Eduardo Viola
President of Argentina

1

We believe we are already within a democratic system [in Argentina]. Some factors are still missing, like the expression of the people's will, but nevertheless we still think we are within a democracy. We say so because we believe these two fundamental values of democracy—freedom and justice—are in force in our country. There are, it is true, several conditioning aspects as regards political or union activity, but individual freedom is nowhere infringed in an outstanding manner.

Interview, Buenos Aires/Time, 7-20:40.

Robert E. White
United States Ambassador
to El Salvador

2

[Saying Nicaragua and Cuba are involved in infiltrating arms to rebels in El Salvador fighting against the government]: I think we have evidence that Cuba is involved. The arms that have come here from Nicaragua, many of them, are Soviet and are traceable to Cuba. Clearly, the evidence, and there is evidence, that Nicaragua has permitted its territory to be used as a transfer point for arms into El Salvador changes the nature of the insurgency movement here

and makes it clear that the insurgency movement is dependent on outside sources.

To newsmen, San Salvador, Jan. 14/
Los Angeles Times, 1-15:(I)14.

3

. . . El Salvador is not lost. And El Salvador's not going to be lost unless we change our policy in a negative way. I can guarantee personally and professionally that there's no possibility of the left taking over during the next six months without major foreign intervention. I say that because of the support that the center has gained through the reforms and because of the weakening of the left. The leftist guerrilla movement is running out of steam. And it will lose as long as the government maintains its reformist, revolutionary-change posture. Militarily, the leftist guerrillas have never launched and sustained a battle for more than 24 hours. There's no case on record where they actually have seized and held any kind of population center. Their strategy is to kill people, blow up buildings, create chaos and break the country economically. The problem is that the right is also trying to break up the country economically and drag it down. Businessmen who stayed in the country and who are cooperating with the government receive death threats regularly from the exiled right-wing community because they're trying to make the economy work. The real danger in El Salvador is a takeover by the extreme right.

Interview/U.S. News & World Report, 1-26:37.

Robert E. White
Former United States Ambassador
to El Salvador

4

The idea that Latins are not capable of democracy is just racist nonsense. The Latin Americans are prefectly capable of democracy if we [the U.S.] want to assist democracy; but if we place ourselves against democracy and on the side of an oppressive military, then democracy is going to fade away. And this is the great contribution of the human-rights

(ROBERT E. WHITE)

policy of the [former U.S.] Carter Administration, which I will defend forever. That policy gives you a litmus test to distinguish between people who are anti-Communist, only because it serves their purposes to stay in power, and people who share authentic Western values—such as El Salvador's [Jose] Napoleon Duarte.

At debate on El Salvador, Washington, Feb. 26/
The New York Times, 3-8:(4)2.

Andrew Young
Former United States Ambassador/Permanent Representative to the United Nations
1

[On U.S. charges that Salvadoran guerrillas are receiving arms from such countries as Cuba and the Soviet Union]: It may be true that arms are being shipped in from other people. I have no way of knowing that. I'm not denying that.

But the fundamental injustice is that 14 families own 80 per cent of the land [in El Salvador] . . . To look at that as just fighting Communism is a mistake.

Interview, Los Angeles, Feb. 24/
Los Angeles Times, 2-25:(I)7.

Leonid M. Zamyatin
Director, International Information Department, Soviet Communist Party Central Committee
2

[On the guerrilla war in El Salvador]: The Soviet Union does not provide El Salvador [rebels] with arms. It never has. It never will . . . When the [U.S.] State Department invents white papers that repeat lies many times [about Soviet arms supplies], the lies do not then become the truth.

At briefing for reporters, Moscow,
Feb. 25/The New York Times, 2-26:6.

Asia and the Pacific

Malcolm Baldrige
Secretary of Commerce
of the United States

1

[Saying Japan must open up its markets to U.S. products]: The Japanese are great about talking about free trade and so forth, but it's something that we've got to be able to call truly a two-way street. We're free-trading and they're not. It's going to be difficult in the future for us to do it that way . . . In recovering after World War II, they grew up with a fierce loyalty to Japanese products. But now Japan's got to realize that they could be the second-largest economy in the world next to us very soon, and when you get to that size, this island mentality . . . just isn't big enough for them.

Interview, Washington, Nov. 6/
Los Angeles Times, 11-7:(I)1,5.

Leonid I. Brezhnev
President of the Soviet Union;
General Secretary, Soviet Communist Party

2

[On why his country sent troops into Afghanistan in 1979 and why they are still there]: Imperialism launched a real undeclared war against the Afghan revolution. This also created a direct threat to the security of our southern frontier. In the circumstances, we were compelled to render the military aid asked for by that friendly country. We will be prepared to withdraw with the agreement of the Afghan government. Before this is done, the infiltration of counter-revolutionary gangs into Afghanistan must be completely stopped.

At Soviet Communist Party Congress,
Moscow, Feb. 23/
The New York Times, 2-24:4.

3

If Soviet-Chinese relations are still frozen, the reason for this has nothing to do with our position. The Soviet Union has never wanted, nor does it now want, any confrontation with the People's Republic of China. Our proposals for normalizing relations with China remain open, and our feelings of friendship and respect for the Chinese people have not changed.

At Soviet Communist Party Congress,
Moscow, Feb. 23/
The New York Times,
2-24:4.

Harold Brown
Former Secretary of Defense
of the United States

4

In the Far East, the Soviet gains in relative military power have been more than offset by the deterioration in the Soviet political position. This includes the development of an implacable—and, by People's Republic of China declaration, eternal—Chinese hostility toward the Soviet Union; much closer relations between the U.S. and China; and the major deterioration in relations between Japan and the Soviet Union deriving in large measure from the Soviet occupation of the northern territories. What undoubtedly seems to the Soviets to be at least an incipient alliance among the U.S., China and Japan must rank as a major disaster in Soviet security policy.

At conference sponsored by
Independent Commission on Disarmament
and Security Issues, Paris/
The New York Times,
11-15:(4)5.

Zbigniew Brzezinski
*Professor of Government, Columbia University;
Former Assistant to the President of the
United States (Jimmy Carter) for
National Security Affairs*

1

The American-Chinese relationship has created a new international situation in which there is emerging a coalition—not a formal alliance—among the United States, China, Japan and Western Europe. This is an objective reality and has to be recognized as a new and important development in world affairs.

*Peking, July 19/
Los Angeles Times,
7-20:(I)13.*

George Bush
Vice President of the United States

2

[Addressing Philippine President Ferdinand Marcos]: We stand with the Philippines; we stand with you, sir. We love your adherence to democratic principles and to the democratic processes. We will not leave you in isolation . . . It would be turning our backs on history if we did.

*Manila, June 30/
Los Angeles Times,
7-1:(I)15.*

3

[On criticism of his recent remarks lauding Philippine President Ferdinand Marcos, despite human-rights violations in that country]: You have to point to the positive side of things instead of the negative. I am familiar with what the left says and what the critics say. Our Administration adheres to human rights. But what we don't believe in is selectively pounding away on our friends, especially those that are moving more and more toward democracy themselves.

*News conference, Honolulu, July 1/
Los Angeles Times, 7-2:(I)8.*

Cao Xiao
*Member, Central Committee, Communist
Party of China; Chairman, Taiwan
Democratic Self-Government League*

4

We believe that all Chinese everywhere want to see the nation [the mainland and Taiwan] reunited and on its way toward becoming a rich and powerful country, realizing a dream we have had for centuries. This creates a great pull on Taiwan to return to the motherland, a pull that may be hard for a foreigner to understand but that strikes a chord in the heart of every Chinese, whether on the mainland, or Taiwan or abroad.

*Los Angeles Times,
4-27:(I)1.*

Jimmy Carter
Former President of the United States

5

My country accepts the fact that there is only one China, and Taiwan is part of it. However, this is still a very difficult and sensitive issue, but one to be resolved by the Chinese people without interference from my country. I know that there have been forthcoming proposals from the Chinese leadership to the people of Taiwan [on the island's reunification with the Chinese mainland], and we will watch the response with interest.

*Peking, Aug. 27/
Los Angeles Times, 8-28:(I)11.*

6

I see China with some obvious economic difficulties—a billion people and many economic resources not yet developed—but it is addressing these problems frankly and I think effectively. My own conviction is that China's influence in the world will be steadily increasing. It's economic, political, military and cultural influence is spreading, I believe beneficially, throughout the world.

*To reporters, Shanghai, Sept. 3/
Los Angeles Times, 9-4:(I)8.*

Chiang Ching-kuo
President of Nationalist China (Taiwan)

1

We will never negotiate with the Chinese Communists. For the Communists, peace talks are actually another form of war—political war, psychological war and propaganda war. Peace talks are, in fact, a political bomb. In terms of Communist strategy, peace talks are a type of poison that will kill us gradually.

Los Angeles Times, 1-29:(I)12.

Chun Doo Hwan
President of South Korea

2

I am happy to say that [U.S.] President Reagan gave me firm assurances that the United States has no intention of withdrawing American forces from Korea. I am pleased that the present level of the United States military presence will be maintained. This makes a vital and indispensable contribution not only for peace in Korea, but peace and tranquility in the Northeast Asian region.

At White House farewell ceremony,
Washington, Feb. 2/
Los Angeles Times, 2-3:(I)1.

3

We are striving to create [in South Korea] a political order in which more freedom will provide the opportunity for social development . . . [There is] no magic formula for maintaining political and social stability. When domestic order and stability are in immediate danger, it is necessary to take firm measures to affirm government authority [such as the recently lifted martial law]. But I know too well that genuine stability can be achieved only when the majority of the people accept the legitimacy of the government and support its decisions.

Before National Press Club,
Washington, Feb. 3/
Los Angeles Times, 2-4:(I)12.

4

[On his offer of negotiations with North Korean President Kim Il Sung]: I made my proposal as an unconditional offer of a dialogue. This is prompted not because there were hopeful signs. On the contrary, the North is as hostile toward us as ever. But we are maintaining peace at a considerable cost to ourselves and our allies. To make war less likely, it is important that I meet with Kim Il Sung. He has experienced the Korean War and has personal recollections of that war. If he should die, his son would take over. Now, here we would have a man who does not know what fear means, does not know the horror of war.

Interview/Time, 4-3:71.

5

Our constitutional history is full of instances of politicians behaving not as public-minded persons but as self-serving persons who spent practically all their public tenure preparing for the next election. Constitutional crises, political repression, illegal amassing of wealth, influence-peddling, cunning maneuvers to curry favor with the voters, factional infighting—all these ills stemmed mostly from politicians' obsession with getting re-elected. All must realize that the people will never tolerate a National Assembly plagued by such ills.

Before National Assembly, Seoul/
The Christian Science Monitor, 5-4:23.

Deng Xiaoping
Vice Chairman,
Communist Party of China

6

The essence of bourgeois liberalism is opposition to leadership by the Party. Without Party leadership, there would be no socialist system. Both Party leadership and the socialist system should be improved, but bourgeois liberalism and anarchy are impermissable... We will adhere to the policy of letting "a hundred flowers bloom and a hundred schools of thought contend" and persist in handling contradictions among the people correctly. However,

(DENG XIAOPING)

this does not mean that criticism . . . should be made of tendencies of bourgeois liberalism. Adherence to these policies cannot be separated from the need for criticism and self-criticism.

July/Los Angeles Times, 9-1:(I)5.

Malcolm Fraser
Prime Minister of Australia

1

[On why Australia has such close ties to the U.S. when its roots are in the United Kingdom]: There are many reasons. We're both Pacific countries; the United Kingdom is not. The United Kingdom in large measure has withdrawn from direct involvement in Southeast Asia; the United States remains very much involved. A larger part of new investment has come from the United States than from Britain. We've got many defense arrangements with the United States. But perhaps more than any of that, it was the United States with whom we were most closely involved during the last World War. It was United States activity that prevented Australia from being invaded. That led to a very close relationship which has been built on a bedrock of common interests. The emotional and traditional relationships with Britain remain very strong and they cannot be replaced. But the practical relationship is coming to be more with America than with Britain.

Interview, Chicago, July 1/
Chicago Tribune, 7-6:(1)1.

Indira Gandhi
Prime Minister of India

2

[On the unrest in her part of the world]: Little did we imagine that the cold war could so soon reassert itself. The thaw was short-lived. Military alliances are now being refurbished. The danger of armed conflict increases. Europe and America are conveniently and subtly transferring their problems to Asian soil. The Atlantic has polluted not only itself but also the Pacific and Indian Oceans.

At meeting of non-aligned nations,
New Delhi/The New York Times, 2-12:3.

3

One of the consequences of the revival of the cold war is the setback to the process of building regional stability through patient negotiations and gradual enlargement of cooperation among neighboring countries. India is deeply concerned that the cold war is being extended to its neighborhood with the inevitable consequences of mounting tensions. Perseverance over the last few years had yielded some promise of regional harmony. We are seeking peaceful solutions to bilateral problems through discussion, hoping thus to reduce recourse to armaments. All of a sudden, the acquisition of sophisticated military equipment [by Pakistan from the U.S.] is being preferred to the security that friendship alone can bring.

At Commonwealth Heads of Government
meeting, Melbourne, Australia, Sept. 30/
The New York Times, 10-1:3.

William Ginn
Lieutenant General, United States Air Force;
Commander, U.S. forces in Japan

4

[Japan's armed forces] have a very limited capacity today in all areas to defend Japan against even the most limited kind of conventional attack . . . I believe it is incumbent upon all those [Japanese] who love Japan to point out that this great nation is in some danger . . . of gradual diminution of its freedom and prosperity [by Soviet intimidation]. The facts [of Soviet aggressive intentions] are there to see— but they must look. It is vital that Japan be able to repel conventional aggression and protect its vital sea lanes in its immediate area. That [capability] will allow us [the U.S.] to do a better job farther out from Japan.

At Foreign Correspondents Club, Tokyo, July 8/
Los Angeles Times, 7-9:(I)12,13.

Valery Giscard d'Estaing
President of France

5

[On the Soviet military involvement in Afghanistan]: The solution [to the Afghanistan

(VALERY GISCARD d'ESTAING)

problem], in my view, is to convene a conference of all countries accused or suspected, rightly or wrongly, of interfering in Afghanistan's internal affairs. First, those that are obviously intervening, that is the Soviet Union; those that are alleged to be intervening, such as Afghanistan's neighbors, Pakistan and India; and those alleged to be supporting them. Then the permanent members of the [UN] Security Council —France, China, the United Kingdom and the United States—and at the same time the countries of the region. India has an obvious responsibility in that part of Asia. And, in a form yet to be defined, the Islamic community, which has followed the issue with special interest. The conference would not be to determine Afghanistan's status—that approach has been tried and has failed for all sorts of reasons—but to end foreign intervention in that country, with each state pledging to do so simultaneously and in a verifiable manner so as to permit the Afghans to restore their country to non-aligned status.

News conference/
The Christian Science Monitor, 2-10:23.

Andrei A. Gromyko
Foreign Minister of the Soviet Union

1

Attention is attracted by the ever-increasing closeness between Washington and Peking. Who would object to the desire of two countries to have normal relations? Nobody, of course. The question is what is the basis of that. In this particular case, the basis is openly hostile toward many states and, above all, the Soviet Union. It is hostile to the cause of detente.

At United Nations, New York, Sept. 22/
The New York Times, 9-23:6.

Hahm Pyong Choon
Former South Korean Ambassador
to the United States

2

There is a suspicion throughout the area that the U.S. may be tempted to strengthen

Japan as a [military] surrogate. That plays on the "ugly Japanese" syndrome. It conjures up the nightmare—an image out of hell—of the swaggering Japanese. Many countries here have already had to deal with a militarily humiliated Japan dominating us by its economic power. On top of that, are we now to have a militarily powerful Japan? Don't try to impose Japan on us. We have our historical hang-ups, too.

Time, 3-23:55.

Alexander M. Haig, Jr.
Secretary of State-designate
of the United States

3

[On U.S.-Chinese relations]: I think it's awfully important that we recognize that the situation is fundamentally one of strategy. It's a strategic relationship that is the underlying motivation for normalization of relationships with the People's Republic of China. It doesn't mean in any respect that we have a convergence of interest and values. I have said that the challenge of this decade facing us is the necessity, on the one hand, to conduct our policies in such a way that the People's Republic of China recognize that there is some value in a normalization of relationships with the United States; that we are reliable. And on the other hand, not permit this normalization process to result in a situation that my European friends describe as poking sticks in a polar bear's [Russia's] cage. And clearly, this is a balancing act of some importance.

At his confirmation hearing before
Senate Foreign Relations Committee,
Washington, Jan. 11/
The New York Times, 1-11:(1)12.

Alexander M. Haig, Jr.
Secretary of State of the United States

4

[Criticizing Vietnam's occupation of Cambodia]: . . . our efforts [to remove Vietnam] are crucial to the Khmer [Cambodian] people,

(ALEXANDER M. HAIG, JR.)

who have suffered for over a decade from a succession of horrors: civil war, genocide, invasion, starvation and colonization. The position of the United States is clear: We believe that the world community has an obligation to assure that these horrors be ended and that they not be inflicted upon the Khmer people again. Their right to choose their own government and to live in peace and dignity without coercion whatsoever must be restored and guaranteed . . . For our part, the United States has no intention of normalizing relations with a Vietnam that occupies Cambodia and destabilizes the entire Southeast Asian region. We will also continue to question seriously any economic assistance to Vietnam—from whatever source—as long as Vietnam continues to squander its resources on aggression.

At United Nations, New York, July 13/
The New York Times, 7-14:6.

1

The Soviet Union has occupied Afghanistan since 1979. The Afghan's religion, culture and national life are in danger of destruction. One fifth of the entire nation has been exiled. The people of Afghanistan cherish their freedom. They are not going to give up their struggle. But why are the voices of conscience among us which cry out against this aggression so muted? Vietnam, which inspired such widespread concern in the West not long ago, has enslaved its southern population, has seized Kampuchea [Cambodia] and now threatens the peace of Southeast Asia. Where are the demonstrations [in the West] against these outrages?

Before Berlin Press Association,
West Berlin, Sept. 13/
The New York Times, 9-14:8.

Lang Hancock
Australian mining industrialist

2

Australia is not a democracy. It is controlled, first of all, by the bureaucracy, secondly by the

trade-union leaders, thirdly by the media, and fourthly by the big manufacturing lobbies. Underneath them are the so-called elected representatives of the people.

Interview, Perth, Australia/
The Christian Science Monitor, 7-27:(B)12.

Noor Ahmad Husain
Director general, Institute of Strategic Studies, Islamabad, Pakistan

3

[Supporting the U.S. sale of F-16 fighter planes to Pakistan]: The F-16s will slow down the air violations [across the Afghanistan border]. They will strike the fear of God [in our neighbors]. We can react with our present aircraft, but it isn't the same thing. What's more, it's going to be good for the morale of the Air Force and the country. As a front-line state, we certainly don't want to use these things for aggression, but we certainly can't objure the right of self-defense. The Russians respect people who can hit back—basically they're bullies. Once they know they can get hurt, they are twice as careful.

The Christian Science Monitor, 11-12:3.

J. B. Jeyaretnam
Member of Singaporan Parliament

4

[On his recent election victory to become the first member of Parliament not of the party of Prime Minister Lee Kwan Yew]: It's simple. The PAP [Lee's party] lost touch. They alienated themselves from the ordinary people. The PAP is not responsive to their needs. I love ordinary people. The government thinks it's only the elite—the clever chaps—who matter now. The people are fed up to the teeth with the government.

Interview, Singapore, December/
Los Angeles Times, 12-5:(I)10.

Kiyoaki Kikuchi
Deputy Foreign Minister of Japan

1

Although we [Japan and the U.S.] are allies, there is no doubt that in the trade and economic fields we are competitors. So if the United States asks us to moderate our exports to the American or third-country markets, because Americans are less competitive, then we simply say no. They cannot ask us to moderate our competitive edge just because we are political allies. Last year was unfortunate because the economic and trade issues became involved in the Presidential election [in the U.S.], where they had no place . . . we made no agreements to restrain exports, because we are sure we are not doing anything wrong.

Interview, Tokyo/
The Christian Science Monitor, 1-20:17.

Kim Ip Sam
Vice president, (South) Korean
Federation of Industries

2

[On suggestions that South Korea is a tightly controlled dictatorship]: That's nonsense. We're not angels, of course. But this is basically an open society where we can say and do what we want. As to the economy . . . well, we have to export to survive. Government officials can't do that. Military men can't do that. How can you sell products in uniform? So in order to survive we must export; and in order to export, this country will basically have to be a free economy.

Interview, Seoul/
The Christian Science Monitor, 3-17:(B)9.

Kim Young Sam
Former leader of banned New Democratic
Party of South Korea

3

[On the imminent first Parliamentary elections to be held under South Korean President Chun Doo Hwan's regime]: The elections are, unfortunately, meaningless under these cir-

cumstances because there is no real opposition. Chun decides who comes out to run in these elections, so what difference do the elections make? . . . Even during the Korean War we had relatively free Presidential elections. Consider how basically anti-Communist the South is. We understand Communism, we know what it means in practice, so let their spies come and 90 per cent of our people will automatically turn them in. For the Korean people, what really matters is that the North is Communist and the South stands for democracy and freedom. That's supposed to be the real difference, and if we lose that, what do we have? People hoped in the spring of 1980 that we would move toward democracy; they had real hope. Now look where we are. If there are three people gathered together, no one will talk. Even if there are two, unless they are really close, they are frightened to say what they think. That's absolutely different from [the late President] Park Chung Hee's time. Of course, just before Park's death things were a little taut here, but now there's simply no chance to speak out.

Interview, Seoul/
The New York Times, 3-25:4.

Bob Komer
Under Secretary for Policy, Department of
Defense of the United States

4

The American taxpayer has been paying unconsciously for the defense of Japan. We provide the nuclear umbrella; we provide the high-seas capability; we're defending their oil. They need it a hell of a lot more than we do. Yet they are spending only nine-tenths of 1 per cent of their gross national product on defense. I'm embarrassed for the Japanese. I would think the Japanese honor would not allow them to be so supine.

Interview, Washington, Feb. 13/
The Washington Post, 2-14:(A)3.

Liu Ta-jen
Spokesman for the
Foreign Ministry of Taiwan

1

[Criticizing the U.S. decision to sell arms to China]: We are deeply concerned over this unfortunate decision because it is not in the interest of peace and stability of the East Asian and Pacific region. We see no benefit but harm out of this, to both the United States and all the free nations in this region.

Taipei, June 17/
The Washington Post, 6-18:(A)34.

Salvador P. Lopez
Former Foreign Minister of the
Philippines; Former Filipino Ambassador
to the United States

2

In the eyes of Filipino intellectuals, America is to be feared, distrusted, even to be angry about. In military and economic power, you [the U.S.] are frightening. You impinge on our lives every moment of the day, every day of the year. We love you and we hate you. We know you so well. We are so close to it: The plurality and openness of your civilization and culture, your passion for individual freedom, I love this. But about the military bases, I'm not too happy. Your multinationals [corporations] are very clever, cunning and subtle. You don't exploit us so crudely. It is more subtle but no less effective. Other countries exploit us, too, but we expect better from the Americans.

Interview/
The New York Times Magazine, 5-24:58.

3

[Criticizing U.S. Vice President George Bush's statement in support of Philippine President Ferdinand Marcos]: Through Mr. Bush, America is making the same tragic mistake it made in Iran supporting the Shah and in Nicaragua supporting [the late President Anastasio] Somoza. You think you are promoting America's national interests. Haven't you learned from your own history that dictators come

and go but the people stay? Are you really taken in by all this hoopla [the re-inauguration of Marcos]? [The U.S.] has a special moral obligation to the Philippine people. From the turn of the century, you stayed here 50 years to teach us democracy. Is this the democracy you wanted us to learn? You put your national interests on very shabby foundations.

Interview. Manila, June 30/
Los Angeles Times, 7-1:(I)15.

Adam Malik
Vice President of Indonesia

4

We've always seen a danger from both the Soviet Union and China. For a long time we were not sure which was the most threatening. However, since the Vietnamese invasion of Cambodia and the Soviet invasion of Afghanistan, we realize the immediate threat is from the Soviet Union.

Time, 3-23:55.

Mike Mansfield
United States Ambassador to Japan

5

I think Japan can, should and will do more in [its own] defense, but they will do it in their own time, at their own pace and in view of the realities that confront them. Japan must open its markets further, even though the Japanese market is not as closed as we say nor is the U.S. market as open as we think. It will take time, but I think we should understand that bluster and demands and pressure could very well be counter-productive. In my opinion, the way to cope with the Japanese is to exercise patience and understanding . . . and also express appreciation for what they have done for us . . . We have use of some of the best bases in the Pacific, rent-free. If we weren't out here, with the approval of the Japanese government, how far back eastward would we be and what facilities would we have? Japan gives the United States, voluntarily, $1-billion a year to help defray the costs of keeping 46,000 American military personnel in Japan. I think that sum will be increased . . . The most important relationship in the world—bar none—is that between Japan and the United States, because the next century will be the century of the Pacific. It will depend on the Japanese-American foundation, which has to become stronger, more enduring and unbreakable in the years and the decades ahead.

Interview, Tokyo/
Los Angeles Times, 11-27:(I-A)1,3.

Edmund S. Muskie
Secretary of State of the
United States

1

With respect to [the Soviet invasion of] Afghanistan, I think we should continue our sanctions: They are working; they are imposing a cost on the Soviet Union; and they are a response to continuing aggression by the Soviet Union. That aggression has not in any degree ebbed. The Soviets don't control more than 10 per cent of the territory of Afghanistan. Pacifying the countryside is a daily problem with them. And they are obviously organizing themselves to continue the effort over a period of years and not months. So the cost must continue to be imposed.

Interview/
U.S. News & World Report, 1-26:29.

Charles H. Percy
United States Senator, R—Illinois

2

I don't think the Soviets would have gone into Afghanistan had they known the price they would have to pay—the grain embargo [by the U.S.], the Olympic boycott [by a number of Western countries], and trade restrictions on electronics and other items . . . In my judgment, the Soviets will find a way to withdraw their forces from Afghanistan, and that will help the [U.S.-Soviet] climate.

Interview with reporters, Washington, Feb. 19/
Los Angeles Times, 2-20:(I)13.

Qian Junrui
Director, Institute of World Economy
of China

3

Ours [China] is a socialist economy and will remain so, and that means we will have a centrally planned economy. But the planning must be sound; it must be scientific; it must be based on a realistic assessment of our resources and our capabilities, not just political goals we may have and the desires of individuals . . . Gradually, when we have an economic infrastructure, such as a strong banking system, we will begin to shift the emphasis from readjustment to reform of the economy. Decentralization was not the way out of our current problems, and even the strongest advocates of reforms that use the market as an economic regulator recognize this now.

Interview/Los Angeles Times, 1-26:(IV)6.

Sinnathamby Rajaratnam
Deputy Prime Minister of Singapore

4

Since the U.S. cannot meet the threat [of Soviet expansion in Southeast Asia] on its own, what is needed in Asia is a collective defense system including the U.S., the Association of Southeast Asian Nations . . . Australia, New Zealand and Canada, with South Korea and China as components. The Japanese, too, must contribute their share to the security of this area. They have got to get away from their old policy of saying, "We'll make the Toyotas; you provide the defense umbrella." [But] the U.S. must play the leading role. No one country here can do that itself. America must definitely not delegate regional defense to Japan and China.

Time, 3-23:55.

Didier Ratsiraka
President of the Malagasy Republic
(Madagascar)

5

[On the Soviet invasion of Afghanistan in 1979]: For me, it's not an invasion. I speak only of an entry of troops. There is a military treaty

(DIDIER RATSIRAKA)

of assistance between Afghanistan and Russia. What is the use of a treaty if, when you need the help, you cannot utilize it?

Interview, Antananarivo, Madagascar/
The Washington Post, 3-22:(A)22.

1

[Saying he does not favor a U.S. naval base on the Indian Ocean island of Diego Garcia]: Bases for me are exactly contrary to peace. You can't say on one hand we want the Indian Ocean to be a zone of peace and at the same time construct new bases costing millions of dollars, like at Diego Garcia. It's contradictory. That's why we're asking for the dismantlement of the bases. It happens that the bases are American. If they were Soviet, I would say the same thing. By asking the Americans to dismantle their bases we are at the same time preventing the Soviets from building bases.

Interview/The Washington Post, 3-26:(A)19.

Ronald Reagan
President of the United States

2

[Objecting to the use of the term "Afghan rebels" when speaking of the forces fighting against the Soviet invasion of Afghanistan]: Sometimes I think the Soviet Union has been successful in their propaganda with getting us to use terms that semantically are incorrect. Those are freedom fighters. Those are people fighting for their own country and not wanting to become a satellite state of the Soviet Union, which came in and established a government of its own choosing there, without regard to the feelings of the Afghans. And so, I think they are freedom fighters, not rebels.

Broadcast interview, Washington/
"World News Tonight," ABC-TV, 3-10.

3

[On the U.S. decision to sell arms to China]: . . . I don't know how the Soviet Union will react.

But all we have done is go to the People's Republic of China—we've wanted, and I've said for a long time, to improve relations with them, move them to [the] same status of many other countries, and not necessarily military allies of ours, in making certain technology and defensive weapons available to them. And I think this is a normal part of the process of improving our relations there.

News conference, Washington, June 16/
The New York Times, 6-17:13.

Michita Sakata
Former Minister of Defense of Japan

4

The newspapers are full of stories that the new Reagan Administration [in the U.S.] wants Japan to take on a larger share of the defense burden in the western Pacific. I am concerned about something much more fundamental than burden-sharing. That is our ability to defend *ourselves* against enemy attack—in other words, the credibility of our existing Self-Defense Force . . . Our logistics, our support devices, our communications are all sadly inadequate. I would say we have a Self-Defense Force that has only 50 per cent of the over-all capability it should have. Until it does, we are not a credible defense force and we are not even pulling our own weight, let alone sharing the burdens of others.

Interview/
The Christian Science Monitor, 2-13:4.

Jovita Salonga
Former Senator in the Philippine Congress

5

Let me say right away that I agree with [Philippine President Ferdinand] Marcos and his technocrats when they say that eight years of martial law—from 1972 to 1980—were years of economic growth and expansion. We are not only exporting sugar, lumber, coconut, copper and pineapples—we are also exporting a lot of bananas, semiconductors and even rice. Our [gross national product] has gone up . . . In theory, per capita income has gone up . . . In plain terms, we as a nation have the capability and the po-

(JOVITA SALONGA)

tential to build a good and just society if only the gross national product were to be divided equitably. Unfortunately, this is not the case. Government figures show that 83 per cent of Filipino families earn less than $1,000 a year and another 12 per cent less than $2,000. If those figures are correct, then the conclusion is inevitable: Ninety-five per cent of Filipino families earn less than the minimum required in order to have a decent life . . . Our so-called New Society today is neither just nor compassionate . . . Only a minority at the very top have been the direct beneficiaries of martial law and one-man rule—namely, architects of the so-called New Society and their close relatives and associates, the new set of oligarchs, the old set of oligarchs that decided to accommodate themselves to the demands of the New Society, the transnational corporations, their subsidiaries, affiliates and retainers.

At Assumption College, Manila, March/
Los Angeles Times, 4-22:(I-A)5.

Norodom Sihanouk
Exiled former Chief of State of Cambodia

1

Personally, I do not like to cooperate with the Khmer Rouge [Cambodian Communists]. They have killed many of my compatriots, my children, my grandchildren and my in-laws. It is terrible to have to cooperate with such monsters. But the non-Communist Cambodians in West Europe, in North America, in Thailand and also the Cambodians fighting the Vietnamese inside the country are putting heavy pressure on me [in the fight to oust the Vietnamese occupiers of Cambodia].

Interview/Time 3-2:53.

Son Sann
Leader, Khmer [Cambodian] People's
National Liberation Front;
Former Prime Minister of Cambodia

2

[On his struggle against the current Cambodian government]: We are here [in the U.S.]

to make an appeal to the people and the government of this great nation, the defender of freedom and of human rights. The Khmer Rouge [also fighting against the Cambodian government] are abundantly helped by a Communist power [China]. The Vietnamese [who back the current government] are receiving enormous quantities of aid from another Communist big power [the Soviet Union]. We, the non-Communists and nationalists, have not received any appreciable aid from the West. We are here to ask you not to help any individual but to help an entire people who support the Khmer People's National Liberation Front in its struggle to save what is left of this people.

To reporters, Washington, Dec. 3/
The New York Times, 12-4:8.

Sun Yun-suan
Prime Minister of Taiwan

3

We certainly hope the relationship between the U.S. and the Republic of China [Taiwan] can be improved, just because [U.S.] President Reagan knows our situation better than any other President, has visited here twice and has many friends here. The least thing we could ask is that our two nations implement the [Taiwan Relations] Act faithfully . . . The first priority is the sales [to Taiwan] of defense arms . . . This is a most important subject. Everyone's concerned here. The sincerity of the United States government to improve the defensive capability of my country is at stake. The spirit of that act was not faithfully observed.

Interview, Taipei, Taiwan, Jan. 23/
The New York Times, 1-25:(1)11.

Zenko Suzuki
Prime Minister of Japan

4

Under our "peace constitution," Japan will stick to a purely self-defensive military structure.

(ZENKO SUZUKI)

Although Japan is a great economic power, it will not become a great military power. And we will not possess weapons which threaten other neighboring countries.

To American reporters,
Tokyo, April 28/
Los Angeles Times, 5-3:(I)1.

J. R. D. Tata
Chairman, Family Planning Foundation
of India

1

[On over-population in India]: It is to me a matter of dismay and despair to find that this grievous threat to our very survival as a nation is still ignored in our country and that most people seem to be reconciled to the inevitability of the continued excessive growth of our population. If America could spend $25-billion in 10 years to put a man on the moon, India could make a more realistic allocation for such a vital sector as family planning.

The New York Times, 5-26:4.

Margaret Thatcher
Prime Minister of
the United Kingdom

2

[Defending Pakistan's request for U.S. military aid]: If I had Soviet troops near my frontier and they had just recently occupied the country [Afghanistan] just beyond that frontier, I would want the means to defend myself . . . Until we have arrangements for the Soviet Union to withdraw from Afghanistan, we shall never regard the situation as normal, we shall never accept the Soviet occupation of Afghanistan, and we shall look at every activity of the Soviet Union accordingly.

News conference,
New Delhi, India, April 17/
Chicago Tribune, 4-18:(1)4.

Cyrus R. Vance
Former Secretary of State
of the United States

3

[Criticizing the U.S. decision to sell arms to China]: It seems to me that we were pushing these arms on them rather than any felt need on their part to have lethal weapons. [This decision] was neither sound nor well-timed. It was a very bad mistake. It was needlessly provocative [toward the Soviet Union] and smacked of bear-baiting rather than well-thought-out policy. It runs counter to the objective of diplomacy —influencing others in dealing with a subject you are concerned with.

Interview, New York, June 22/
The New York Times, 6-24:1.

Caspar W. Weinberger
Secretary of Defense
of the United States

4

We necessarily are concerned that Japan's capability for self-defense at this point remains short of what is clearly required. We [the U.S.] spend six times more of our economic wealth on defense than does Japan. We believe that Japan can take the necessary steps to increase her own self-defense capabilities, knowing that this requires a greater contribution of economic resources . . . The United States will continue to provide the nuclear umbrella and offensive striking power on Japan's behalf. [But] the increasing threat to Japan, and to freedom everywhere, clearly requires significantly greater self-defense efforts in the northwest Pacific area. [However,] we do not urge any assumption of overseas military responsibilities upon Japan.

Before Commonwealth Club, San Francisco,
April 28/The New York Times, 4-29:7.

Leonard Woodcock
United States Ambassador to China

5

There is no reason why the United States and China should not be friendly nations. There are no national antagonisms between us. We

265

WHAT THEY SAID IN 1981

(LEONARD WOODCOCK)

obviously share a common concern about Soviet expansionism in Asia and generally around the globe. China certainly cannot hope to accomplish the goals it has set over the next 20, 30, 40 years without stability in East Asia. Stability in this area is also highly important to us because of its impact on world stability, so we share that same basic strategic strength. Even in an area like the Korean peninsula where we are, to some extent, on opposite sides, I feel that both countries have a strong shared interest is seeing stability instead of new turmoil.

Interview, Peking/
U.S. News & World Report, 2-9:34.

Ye Jianying
Chairman, Standing Committee,
National People's Congress of China

1

[On his country's proposed reunification with Taiwan]: After the country is reunified, Taiwan can enjoy a high degree of autonomy as a special administrative region, and it can retain its armed forces. The central government will not interfere with local affairs on Taiwan. Taiwan's current socio-economic system will remain unchanged; so will its way of life and its economic and cultural relations with foreign countries. There will be no encroachment on the proprietary rights and lawful right of inheritance over private property, houses, land and enterprises or foreign investments.

Broadcast address to the nation, Peking,
Sept. 30/Los Angeles Times, 9-30:(I)6.

Taroichi Yoshida
President,
Asian Development Bank

2

Development in Asia is an investment in the 21st century. U.S. aid will enlarge the frontier for the American people. The United States has not only been a strong supporter of the Bank but a stalwart along with Japan, Australia and other major donors. It is very difficult to

quantify the benefits to the U.S., but they are obvious. Asia is one of the most promising areas in the world, not only politically but economically. To raise a very sound groundwork for future development of this area would be a benefit to the U.S. and world peace. The Asian people are very pragmatic and stable in their way of thinking in various fields. We should keep this area in a stable relation with the world. Asia is very dependable.

Interview/
The Christian Science Monitor, 4-28:(B)16.

Zhao Ziyang
Premier of China

3

[Saying the U.S. should not forget that Taiwan is an inseparable part of China]: Now that [Ronald] Reagan has become [U.S.] President, we intend that relations between China and the United States should continue to expand. Don't let those relations stop improving, much less deteriorate [through possible upgrading of U.S. ties to Taiwan]. . . . The execution of U.S.-China relations must strictly preserve and closely follow this basic principle [of China-Taiwan oneness]. Any wavering from this principle [by the U.S.] will be considered interference in the internal affairs of China and will cause a serious setback to relations. China does not want this to happen.

News conference, Bangkok, Thailand, Feb. 1/
Chicago Tribune, 2-2:(1)4.

4

[On the division of Korea]: The continued existence of this abnormal situation is the result of the presence of United States troops in South Korea and the wanton intervention of the United States in the internal affairs of Korea. This is a major factor in the instability of Northeast Asia. We maintain that the internal affairs of a country ought to be settled by the people of that country themselves and no foreign intervention is allowed. The Chinese government and people firmly support the just position of the Korean people calling for the withdrawal

(ZHAO ZIYANG)

of the United States troops from South Korea and opposing the creation of "two Koreas."

At banquet in his honor, Pyongyang, North Korea, Dec. 20/The New York Times, 12-22:3.

Mohammed Zia ul-Haq
President of Pakistan

1

I have no misconceptions about my personal position. I am a military—call it, in Western terminology—a dictator. I am a self-assumed head of state of Pakistan. But I offer to my Western friends, and to some extent my critics inside Pakistan, that fortunately the position of the present regime has been accepted. Once the job is done, we will leave it to the people. I haven't contracted for the whole of my life that there is only one person, named Zia ul-Haq, who can rectify the situation. It is not so. I have a limited role. Once we have created an environ-

ment, then we hope to give an opportunity to the people to elect their own representatives. And that is my ultimate aim: for the peaceful transfer of power from the military to elected civilian representatives.

Interview, Islamabad/ U.S. News & World Report, 9-21:46.

2

[On his country's relations with India]: We are a smaller country, but we have peculiarities of our own. We are autonomous and we are a respectable nation. We will respect the Indians and we will demand that much respect as is due to a respectable nation. But if India wishes that it can treat Pakistan like Bangladesh, Nepal, Burma, then they are very well mistaken, because they can't have that from Pakistan unless they break the bones of 84 million people and ride on us, which they can't do either.

Interview, Islamabad, Oct. 16/ The New York Times, 10-18:(1)14.

Europe

Boris Aristov
Soviet Ambassador to Poland

1

The Soviet people are convinced that the Polish nation . . . will be able to solve the complicated tasks and assure the pulling of the country out from [the current labor] crisis . . . A record of nonsense and lack of responsibility was set by militaristic circles in the United States who see in detente an obstacle to their aggressive plans. Attempting to justify the arms race, NATO has been spreading in a perfidious way some insinuations on alleged military danger [to Poland] from the Soviet Union, and the foreign policy of the socialist countries is being distorted. The enemies of Poland have tried to use the temporary difficulties and some failures as well as errors to attack socialism [in an effort to undermine Soviet-Polish friendship by] weakening of the socialist commonwealth and breaking it up from inside.

*At ceremony marking 36th anniversary of
Soviet-Polish friendship pact, Warsaw,
April 21/Los Angeles Times, 4-22:(I)12.*

Raymond Aron
French journalist and professor

2

[Saying the Western European allies are suffering from varying degrees of "Finlandization" —accommodating the Soviet Union]: What we are seeing today in Europe is what has happened so often before in the past. The great army arrives at the border with trumpets blaring and flags flying. The people take note of its strength,

the sacrifice required to repel the army, then accommodate themselves to "the new reality."

Time, 3-23:36.

Humphrey Atkins
*British Secretary of State
for Northern Ireland*

3

[On whether, in the wake of IRA member Bobby Sands' death from his prison hunger strike, Britain should give in to demands of other IRA prisoners for political status]: No. We come right up to the matter of principle. Is murder [by the IRA] any less murder because the person claims he had a political motive? The answer is no. We have seen . . . the funeral of a man who took his own life, either by his own decision or on the instructions of those who felt it was useful to their cause that he should die. Whatever the reason, it was a tragedy that he should have added his name to the list of those who have died in Northern Ireland as victims of a campaign which can contribute nothing to the resolution of historic and deep-seated problems of this province.

Chicago Tribune, 5-10:(1)6.

4

[On the IRA]: You have a group of people whose declared objective is to take over the government of both Northern Ireland and Ireland. They first seek to destroy the government of Northern Ireland, and then the government of Ireland, and then set up a socialist dictatorship. They are trying to do it by force because

(HUMPHREY ATKINS)

they know they cannot do it by democratic means. They've been trying to do it by force for 10 to 12 years now, and they are failing.

Interview/The Washington Post, 9-8:(A)16.

George W. Ball
*Former Under Secretary of State
of the United States*

1

A lot ot people in Europe are disturbed by the saber-rattling they have heard and continue to hear out of Washington. It scares the bejesus out of the Europeans, and they go to the streets, shouting that a bunch of lunatics is running things in Washington. What's worrisome to me is that for the people in the streets, who often aren't that numerous, there are enormous numbers at home who feel exactly the same way.

Time, 11-30:39.

Raymond Barre
Prime Minister of France

2

[On the recent election of Socialist Party leader Francois Mitterrand as President of France]: [There will be] deterioration of the domestic and international situation of our country . . . The day will come when the French people, learning from experience, will turn away from illusions and myths and return to the realm of realism and progress with courage and confidence.

May 11/Los Angeles Times, 5-12:(I)1,10.

David Basnett
*General secretary, General and
Municipal Workers Union (Britain)*

3

[Criticizing British Prime Minister Margaret Thatcher's economic policy]: Mass unemployment isn't a result of government policy. Mass unemployment *is* the government's policy . . . Talk of economic recovery in the current cir-

cumstances is a confidence trick, a device to deflect the mounting pressure of public opinion for a fundamental change in policy.

The Wall Street Journal, 8-26:28.

Terence Beckett
*Director general, Confederation of
British Industry*

4

[On British Prime Minister Margaret Thatcher's economic program]: This government's over-all policy is good and is providing us with a great many benefits. We wholeheartedly agree with the need to bring down inflation. As a result of this government's policies, wage settlements are coming down, we are getting very much improved productivity, we are getting acceptance of shop-floor changes we were never able to get before. Many of our firms are telling us they're getting performance from their suppliers in a way they haven't had in a long time. But still, it's all a question of balance. The government's policy has been to concentrate perhaps a little too much on monetary aggregates. The recession has gone a lot further and a lot deeper than it expected; the pound has risen far more than expected; interest rates have remained at a very high level longer than expected. And as a result, industry has borne a disproportionate share of the burden. There are a great many things the government could do to help that it isn't doing.

*Interview, London/
The Wall Street Journal, 2-3:26.*

Tony Benn
Member of British Parliament

5

The real question in Northern Ireland . . . is can Britain maintain a standing army in Northern Ireland and hope to solve the problem? Now, there is a view, and I hold it very strongly, that the partition of Ireland was a crime against the Irish people and that the legitimate objective for the country [Britain] is to bring about conditions where the Irish

WHAT THEY SAID IN 1981

(TONY BENN)

people can solve the problems themselves. The partitition took place without the consent of the majority of people in Ireland in 1920. It was imposed on Ireland by the British government. The British government, in my view, has no long-term future in Ireland. The problem has to be solved there and that may involve a new look at it. Indeed, in my opinion, it must involve an international initiative. British troops cannot solve the problems of Ireland, and almost everybody in Britain is coming to realize that now.

BBC interview, May 12/
Chicago Tribune, 5-21:(1)10.

1

[Calling for unilateral nuclear disarmament for Britain]: We do not believe that an American President, whom we did not elect and cannot remove, should have the power of peace and war by firing missiles from our airfields.

Time, 6-1:38.

2

[On the increasing left-wing slant of his Labor Party]: What's happening is not some left-wing takeover of the Labor Party. Rather, the Party is moving back to its original socialist roots. People who vote labor should know that if we win we'll get Britain out of the Common Market, get rid of American nuclear bases, get back to full employment, and expand the public service.

The New York Times, 9-20:(4)3.

Christoph Bertram
Director, International Institute of
Strategic Studies, London

3

[On the consequences if peace protestors succeed in forcing NATO to abandon installation of new nuclear missiles in Western Europe]: The consequences would be very disturbing for East-West arms control. NATO would

be forced to give up its modernization program without the Soviets having to give up anything on their side. It would also strengthen a tendency toward unilateralism in the United States. The Americans might conclude that they would have to act regardless of what the Allies say, and European influence on American policy would be diminished. It would give rise to a lot of disturbing strains in the alliance.

Chicago Tribune, 11-15:(1)19.

Mario Biaggi
United States Representative, D—New York;
Chairman, Ad Hoc Congressional
Committee for Irish Affairs

4

[On the death of IRA hunger striker Bobby Sands in a Northern Ireland prison]: The intransigence of the British government throughout this matter is to be condemned. They have displayed arrogance in their spurning of world pleas—including the Pope's—for a humanitarian resolution.

May 5/Los Angeles Times, 5-6:(1)31.

William Borm
Founder, Free Democratic Party
of West Germany

5

[Calling for the removal of U.S. nuclear missiles from West Germany]: We are like ships in a convoy, passing through a dangerous sea. But we in Europe are not only in a convoy, we are on the same ship. If our flagship, the United States, heads toward the icebergs [war with the Soviet Union], like the *Titanic*, it is not necessary that we follow. We want to go to the same destination, but avoid the icebergs.

Chicago Tribune, 11-15:(1)1.

Willy Brandt
Acting chairman, West German Social
Democratic Party; Former Chancellor
of West Germany

6

Neutralism [for West Germany]? I don't think there is anything to it. "Europeaniza-

270

(WILLY BRANDT)

tion" . . . is something which one should regard as a serious element in developments we are going through. There is a growing feeling that we must rely upon ourselves, in cooperation and friendship with the United States. But the Americans ask us to make more progress in getting together and taking more of our [own] responsibilities. The vast majority would say there can be no neutralism. Neutralism in the political and security field would mean to cut links with the United States, which we do not want to do, and would also endanger our good relations with our most important partners in Europe, especially France. That we just do not want to do. Something which is interpreted as pacifism or neutralism has to do partly with worries which I understand very well and partly with the feeling that we must get back to more responsibilities for Europe. The European element is more important than what some of our friends call neutralism.

Panel discussion, Bonn/
The New York Times, 6-21:(4)3.

Leonid I. Brezhnev
President of the Soviet Union;
General Secretary, Communist Party
of the Soviet Union

1

[On the unrest in Poland]: [Counter-revolutionaries] are trying to do everything to block the advance of socialism, to erode it from inside. For that purpose they are using any means, such as economic pressure and blackmail, false propaganda, flattery and demagogy, support and encouragement of counter-revolutionary forces where they exist, and many other types of subversive activities . . . But Polish Communists, with the support of all genuine patriots, will be able, one would assume, to give the enemies of the socialist system a fitting rebuff.

At Czechoslovak Communist Party Congress,
Prague, April 7/
Chicago Tribune, 4-8:(1)1.

The unbridled nuclear arms race in Europe is becoming lethally dangerous for all European people. In order to start in some way the practical solution to this problem, we propose that, for the time being at least, a line be drawn under what exists to put an end to the further deployment of new and replacement of both Soviet and NATO medium-range nuclear missiles stationed in Europe. This includes, naturally, the American nuclear forward-based systems in that region. The moratorium could be valid until a permanent treaty is concluded on the limitation and, still better, on the reduction of the above-mentioned nuclear means of both sides in Europe. Naturally, our proposal for the moratorium is not an end in itself. It has been made with the intention of creating a more favorable atmosphere for talks. We regard as the objective in this question . . . precisely the reduction by both sides of the amount of nuclear means accumulated in Europe. This is quite possible to do without worsening the conditions of security of either East or West.

At Czechoslovak Community Party Congress,
Prague, April 7/
The New York Times, 4-8:6.

3

[On the U.S. decision to produce the neutron bomb]: I shall say with all responsibility that we shall not remain indifferent to the appearance of such weapons in the arsenals of the United States and other NATO members. If this happens, the Soviet armed forces will be in the possession of a proper counterbalance to such weapons . . . As far as the Soviet Union is concerned, we have never sought and we are not seeking military superiority . . . To set oneself the aim of becoming stronger than all others, to lay claim to world leadership—all this has already taken place in recent history [during the Nazi era in Germany] and the outcome of such attempts is well-known.

At luncheon honoring visiting Vietnamese
Communist Party leader Le Duan, Moscow, Sept. 7/
The Washington Post, 9-8:(A)1,18.

WHAT THEY SAID IN 1981

(LEONID I. BREZHNEV)

1

[Saying some Western leaders have talked about "limited nuclear wars" in Europe]: The result is that the possibility of using nuclear weapons in a "European war theatre" is being raised to the level of a military doctrine. As if Europe, where hundreds of millions of people live, is already condemned to become a stage for war. As if it were some kind of box of tin dolls that deserve no better fate than to be dissolved in the furnace of nuclear explosions. We are deeply convinced that the plans to deploy the new American nuclear missiles in Western Europe, and especially on the territory of the Federal Republic [West Germany], which will be aimed at the Soviet Union, threaten to create a danger such as has never been seen before. People sense this danger clearly and are certainly waiting for everything to be done to eliminate it.

Bonn, West Germany, Nov. 23/
The New York Times, 11-24:4.

Zbigniew Brzezinski
Professor of government, Columbia University;
Former Assistant to the President of the
United States (Jimmy Carter) for
National Security Affairs

2

[On the Solidarity independent trade-union movement in Poland, which is now being suppressed by martial law in that country]: In the longer run . . . I think the problems that the Polish Communist system has run into—inefficiency, demoralization, lack of motivation . . . increasing pressures for self-expression from a more literate working class—are going to be felt in the Soviet Union as well. There is, if you will, an historic time lag at work here and I don't know whether it's a decade or two decades; but what has happened in Poland could easily already be happening in the Baltic republics, in certain portions of the western Ukraine, maybe in those parts of the Soviet Union where the working class is now in the third generation and is somewhat politically

mature. That, of itself, is not enough to make it into the kind of crisis that Poland went through. But in a decade or two, it could become quite widespread.

Interview/The Washington Post, 12-20:(B)4.

Lasse Budtz
Member of Danish Parliament; Member,
Parliamentary Committee on Defense.

3

[On his country's reluctance to support defense spending]: We are not exaggerating the problem of getting public opinion to support any increase in the defense effort. The Danish voters simply do not believe very deeply in the need for increases in defense, or even that Denmark can be defended. This is reflected in all parties in Parliament. We are not indifferent to the problem, but we have to deal with very inert public opinion where defense is concerned.

Los Angeles Times, 4-5:(I-A)4.

McGeorge Bundy
Professor of history, New York University;
Former Assistant to the President of the
United States (John F. Kennedy and Lyndon
B. Johnson) for National Security Affairs

4

[Calling for a scale-down in NATO plans to deploy advanced missile systems in Europe to counter a Soviet build-up of SS-20 missiles]: The SS-20 did not and does not give the Soviet Union any nuclear capability against Europe alone that she did not have in overflowing measure before a single SS-20 was deployed. Not only were the existing SS-4s and -5s, though old and cumbersome, entirely adequate in themselves for threatening a nuclear attack on Europe, but, what is much more important, every long-range Soviet strategic missile that can reach the U.S. can also hit Europe . . . If the Soviet Union should ever reach a political determination to strike Europe without striking the U.S., it would have all the weapons it needed without the SS-20s. Any danger there may be of any such action is quite literally independent of the existence of the weapon [the SS-20]

(McGEORGE BUNDY)

that the West has spent so much time advertising . . . Soviet nuclear procurement policy is not so sensible that we should imitate it blindly, nor so threatening that we need to believe our own enormous forces are weak. A strategic modernization much more modest than [U.S.] President Reagan's recent proposals can meet the needs of both ourselves and our allies, with or without new land-based missiles in Europe. The [NATO] alliance today needs economic progress and political self-confidence more than it needs weapons, and among weapons it needs conventional more than nuclear reinforcement.

At New York University sesquicentennial conference/
The Christian Science Monitor, 11-18:23.

George Bush
Vice President of the United States

1

[On the appointment of three Communists to French President Francois Mitterrand's Cabinet]: Our European allies are sovereign nations and the decision on how they are governed rests with their citizens and with their elected representatives. However, the position of the United States on the subject of Communist participation in the government of our allies is well-known. This participation is bound to cause concern.

Paris, June 24/
Los Angeles Times, 6-25:(I)8.

Leopoldo Calvo Sotelo
Prime Minister of Spain

2

[Advocating his country's joining NATO]: Military blocs exist, though we all would prefer to live without them. But as long as there is a wall in Berlin, the government and the government party know on which side of it they want to be.

Debate in Parliament, Madrid, October/
The New York Times, 10-30:6.

Frank C. Carlucci
Deputy Secretary of Defense
of the United States

3

Like the East-West balance, the relationship between the United States and Western Europe also has shifted dramatically over 30 years. The United States no longer produces and consumes 50 per cent of the world's GNP. Europe is no longer shattered, impoverished and disunited. Indeed, Western Europe's total GNP exceeds that of the United States. In this situation, the United States cannot be expected to improve and strengthen U.S. forces in Europe, unless other allies increase their contribution to the combined defense effort. Nor can the United States, unaided, bear the burden of promoting Western interests beyond Europe.

Before Western defense specialists, Munich, Feb. 21/
Chicago Tribune, 2-23:(I)2.

Santiago Carrillo
Secretary general,
Communist Party of Spain

4

[Arguing against Spain joining NATO]: What does Spain have to offer NATO? Just targets for atomic weapons. There is a profound crisis in NATO, resistance to deploying new missiles, resistance even in America's most faithful ally, West Germany. And at this moment of crisis, Spain chooses to join NATO, without conditions.

Debate in Parliament, Madrid, October/
The New York Times, 1-30:6.

Lord Carrington
Foreign Minister of the
United Kingdom

5

Opponents of nuclear weapons in Europe say that Western planning is now based on fighting and winning a nuclear war. This is mistaken. In any nuclear war there would be only losers. NATO's nuclear weapons . . . are designed to prevent war . . . The unilateral-disarmers in my country say that other states

273

(LORD CARRINGTON)

would follow suit if Britain disarmed . . . but disarmament by example does not work. The Soviet Union has explicitly rejected unilateral steps . . . The movement for European nuclear disarmament has called for a nuclear weapon-free zone from Poland to Portugal. This is unfortunately a delusion . . . Soviet nuclear weapons can reach Western Europe from beyond Poland—indeed, from beyond the Urals. What would there be to stop the Soviet Union from threatening nuclear war? The same movement says it hopes to extend its activity to the Soviet Union. How do they propose to set about that? Look at the persecution of the [Soviet] people who tried not to urge disarmament but merely to monitor their country's compliance with the Helsinki Final Act . . . Regarding the claim that we face the choice of being red or dead: This, too, is highly misleading, because there is in fact a third alternative. It is the one that Western Europe has pursued successfully for half a lifetime: to prevent war and remain free.

Lecture, Oct. 27/
The Washington Post, 11-6:(A)30.

Charles
Prince of Wales

1

[On his role as Prince during the decades before he can become King of England]: [It] is to try to set an example, to help push people along, to be encouraging, to warn, to advise, amuse. Everything to give people pleasure and a sense of purpose in life, a sense of satisfaction, and a sense of feeling they have done something useful by congratulating them and generally being seen to show interest when it's deserved. It all, I hope and feel, goes toward trying to make as happy a society and country as possible.

Radio interview/
The Washington Post, 7-29:(B)2.

Claude Cheysson
Foreign Minister of France

2

[The Atlantic Alliance] is the basis of our foreign policy. Not only because we are committed to it but also because we stand for the basic principles that protect man and the humanistic development of the kind of society in which we believe. It's the way to oppose any totalitarian progress. With that goes a defense commitment. We are not members of [the military structure of] NATO. We do not intend to change the former policies. We are not going to be a part of the integrated NATO system. But we'll keep on building and modernizing our defense forces, in particular our independent deterrent [nuclear] power.

Interview/Time, 6-29:34.

3

[On the effects of having Communist ministers in the French Cabinet]: If our allies tell us something about it, we shall answer, "It's none of your business." That must be very clear. But the fact that they have fear concerns us, of course. It would be an important question if we were dependent on the Communists for a majority [in the National Assembly]. Then they would be in a position to—blackmail may be too strong a word—but to put pressure on us. If we have the absolute majority, Communists in or out make no difference.

Interview/Time, 6-29:34.

4

[On French foreign policy]: There are a number of cases where we can play a useful role in settling disputes in parts of the world. In such cases our intention is never to work alone. There will be no more cases where you hear of a "French initiative." We will try to support the countries in the region which have some authority. It's not by chance that in August I have gone to Mexico, Algeria and India. We consider these typical of the countries we would be very anxious to support when they think

(CLAUDE CHEYSSON)

something should be done in a region where they have authority.

Interview, Paris/
The Wall Street Journal, 9-1:24.

Jacques Chirac
Mayor of Paris; Gaullist candidate
for President of France

1

The President [Valery Giscard d'Estaing] thought he could campaign simply on the place of France in the world and on his action for peace. Then to his surprise he was attacked on unemployment, both by [Socialist candidate Francois] Mitterrand and myself. And again his trip to Warsaw [in May, 1980, after the Soviet invasion of Afghanistan] to meet [Soviet President Leonid] Brezhnev came under fire. That for him was the last straw. Giscard and his people are beginning to lose their nerve. They are shooting in all directions. It is a bad sign.

To reporters/Los Angeles Times, 4-22:(I)8.

Warren M. Christopher
Former Deputy Secretary of State
of the United States

2

We must never underestimate the importance of our [European] allies. Their combined economic output equals ours. If there were a military crisis in Europe, they would supply most of the manpower. To keep that alliance strong, we must be ready for whatever strategy the Soviets choose to pursue, and that requires military preparedness and political resolve.

Before Young Lawyers' Section,
American Bar Association, Aug. 8/
Chicago Tribune, 8-18:(1)11.

Peter Corterier
Member of West German Parliament; Leader,
Bundestag Defense and Foreign Affairs
Committee

3

What we are seeing is the emergence in West Germany of a new, entirely post-war genera-

tion of young political activists. These are young people who more or less grew up with detente and West Germany's *ostpolitik* [eastern policy], without any real awareness of the sacrifices and effort that went into a strong defense in NATO which was the basis of those policies. Now they see the economy slowing down, detente turning sour and all that, and they have a vague idealistic feeling that we could get back on track simply by doing away with nuclear weapons, saving on defense, making new accommodations with the East, and so on.

Los Angeles Times, 3-23:(I)16.

Milovan Djilas
Author; Former Vice President
of Yugoslavia

4

[The leaders of Yugoslavia] must open themselves to democratic opinion and change. If they do not do this, they will go toward more and more crises, a more and more chaotic situation . . . If this stagnant, oppressive regime continues, Yugoslavia will face difficulties, including her unity. It will not be tomorrow, but the prospects are not bright . . . The collective leadership is not efficient. They have power, the power of the police and the army, but not efficient government. They maintain the cult of [the late President Josip Broz] Tito, changing nothing in their ideas. And inefficiency and stagnation continue.

Interview, Belgrade/
Los Angeles Times, 4-22:(I-A)2.

Lawrence S. Eagleburger
Assistant Secretary for European Affairs,
Department of State of the
United States

5

[On the possibility of European nations refusing to deploy modernized American medium-range nuclear missiles because of popular opposition in those countries]: We would lose our credibility with the Soviets, while demonstrating that they have a veto over NATO

WHAT THEY SAID IN 1981

deployment decisions. We would raise a doubt in the mind of many Americans who would not understand why our allies are less committed to their security than is the United States. And worst of all, we would all be profoundly uncertain of our future ability to take difficult decisions together.

June/The New York Times, 8-29:2.

Erhard Eppler
Member of presidium, Social Democratic Party of West Germany; Former West German Cabinet minister

1

[Addressing an anti-war rally against U.S. nuclear missiles being stationed in West Germany]: The peace movement shows that the old nations of Europe are more than chess figures on the board of the world powers, both world powers . . . Here in this country, we celebrate the courage of the Poles who do not want to be directed [by the Soviet Union] how they should live. Is it so bad if we do not want to allow ourselves to be told how we have to die? The Europeanization of Europe takes place not only on the Vistula [a river in Poland] but also on the Rhine.

At anti-war rally, Bonn, West Germany, Oct. 10/ San Francisco Examiner & Chronicle, 10-11:(A)1.

Kenan Evren
Head of military government of Turkey

2

I want to underscore that Turkey will return to the parliamentary democratic system. This shall be done not because the West wishes it, but because it is a system that best suits Turkey and is [suited] to the Turkish nation and the wishes of the Turkish people themselves. It was [Kemal] Ataturk [founder of the republic] who said the democratic system is best suited to Turkey. Since we are his sons and took over from him, we shall see to it his wishes are realized.

Interview, Ankara/The Washington Post, 5-29:(A)26.

Garret FitzGerald
Leader, United Ireland Party (Fine Gael)

3

The ending of the Northern Ireland tragedy [Catholic-Protestant violence] and the resolution of this centuries-old conflict will . . . be the principal objective of any government that I lead. I am, through my mother, directly connected with the Protestant tradition in Northern Ireland, and I believe that I have inherited and developed a sympathy for the susceptibilities and problems of the community. I came into politics for two reasons—to help promote the economic development [of Ireland] and to work for the resolution of the conflict between my father's and my mother's people . . . We in the south must create the conditions here that make attractive some form of agreed Ireland, some form of [north-south] arrangement to which we could all agree and which could lead eventually to unity by consent.

Interview, Dublin/ Los Angeles Times, 6-25:(I-B)3.

Colette M. Flesch
Vice President of Luxembourg

4

Washington has used the language of force, and inevitably it has been listened to, in Europe and the rest of the world, to the great satisfaction of some; but it has not fully been understood by all, even among friends of the United States. This change of tone has undoubtedly affected communications between the U.S. and the Soviet Union, but it has also complicated relations between the U.S. and Europe. What do Europeans complain about?: The U.S. does not respect the [Atlantic] Alliance's rules of the game and does not give the Europeans a fair chance to take part in the decision-making process. The U.S. is not interested in a balanced cooperation, based on an equitable compromise. It refuses a medium road and wishes to impose its views upon its European allies. The U.S. takes risks. This, of course, it is free to do, but only as long as it does not put its allies in jeopardy. Thus, some Europeans feel that they are

(COLETTE M. FLESCH)

being treated in a way that is not dissimilar to that in which the Alliance's enemies are; and they come to wonder whether the language of force is not also directed toward Western Europe.

At Fletcher School of Law and Diplomacy,
Tufts University/
The Christian Science Monitor, 12-3:27.

Michael Foot
Leader, British Labor Party

1

[Critcizing those Labor Party members who threaten to leave and form a new, more-moderate party in the face of a turn to the extreme left by Labor]: We want everyone now in the Party to stay in the Party. We should be fighting against this anti-human Tory government and its cruel economic policies, not against one another.

The New York Times, 2-1:(4)5.

Jean Francois-Poncet
Foreign Minister of France

2

[Western Europe should] stop thinking of the United States as the shield behind which they can lay down their burden of responsibilities. They have to stop heaping continuous, contradictory criticism on the United States, complaining one day that it is weak and the next that it is over-confident, rejecting its involvement yet fearing its disengagement. [On the other side,] Americans complain that the Europeans are hesitant, weak and divided, that they are incapable of action. But when we do act, for example in the Middle East, Americans often say that our moves are ill-timed or out of place. The United States sometimes acts as if unity were synonymous with uniformity.

At Fletcher School of Law and Diplomacy,
Tufts University, Feb. 26/
The New York Times, 2-27:4.

John Kenneth Galbraith
Professor emeritus of economics,
Harvard University

3

[On the election of Socialist Francois Mitterrand as President of France]: I'm acquainted with Mitterrand and I think you should keep in mind the old French saying, "The more things change, the more they remain the same." Mitterrand's election was partly a reaction to the free-market principles of Premier Raymond Barre, which have caused considerable suffering in some of the industrial areas of France . . . But there will be no radical change in French economic policies. France is run by its civil servants, and they don't change.

Interview, San Francisco/
San Francisco Examiner & Chronicle, 5-17:(Review)4.

Richard N. Gardner
United States Ambassador to Italy

4

Four years ago I was distressed to find how much Marxist-Leninist thinking had penetrated the high schools, universities, the intellectual press, the arts and culture [in Italy]. The penetration was greater than with any other [U.S.] ally . . . [But now] the Communists are on the defensive for the first time, and I hope they stay that way . . . There is no country in the world where the common man retains greater affection for the United States and what it stands for than Italy . . . It is gratifying that the new [Reagan] Administration [in the U.S.] is signaling its recognition of the very great importance of Italy in the Atlantic Alliance. Whether measured in terms of its geopolitical position, its political and economic importance, or its real contributions to the Alliance, Italy deserves to be in the inner circle of the Alliance.

Interview, Rome/Los Angeles Times, 2-11:(1-A)4.

Valery Giscard d'Estaing
President of France

5

[On socialist Party leader Francois Mitterrand, who is running against him for the Presi-

277

(VALERY GISCARD d'ESTAING)

dency]: . . . whether he wants to or not, whether he knows it yet or not, Monsieur Mitterrand is also speaking on behalf of the Communists. If Mitterrand is elected, it will be Communist order or Socialist disorder.

Campaigning, Dole, France/Time, 5-11:40.

Alexander M. Haig, Jr.
Secretary of State-designate
of the United States

1

. . . we are not facing the inevitable, inexorable supremacy of Marxist-Leninism as a system. Quite to the contrary; it is a profound historic failure. If one measures the success of the Soviet brand of Communism, we find economic shortfalls that are increasing in severity over the last three or four years; we find it an agricultural basket case in a historic sense. Despite the fact that Soviet leadership has driven larger and larger segments of their population into agriculture, the consequences have not been remunerative. We find growing demographic problems within the Soviet system as non-Soviet populations begin to thrust for greater autonomy and a greater voice in the conduct of Soviet policy. We find that transmitted into the Eastern European zone of influence.

At his confirmation hearing before
Senate Foreign Relations Committee, Washington,
Jan. 10/The New York Times, 1-11:(1)12.

Alexander M. Haig, Jr.
Secretary of State of the United States

2

Every night I pray that [Soviet President Leonid] Brezhnev stays healthy and alive for a good while to come—at least until we have caught up [militarily] with the Soviet Union. Because if he goes suddenly, I believe that the young ones waiting in the wings will take over. They have never known war; to them, Stalingrad is the title of a movie. They have never known poverty such as the world experienced during the Great Depression. They are in a very expansive mood, and the longer they wait their turn, the better off we all will be.

At dinner celebrating his confirmation by the Senate/
Time, 3-16:13.

3

The Soviet Union shows clear signs of historic decline. Observers of the international scene have concentrated far too long on the difficulties of the West. Just consider the view from Moscow: The Soviets have made no headway with China and are forced to maintain over 50 divisions on the Chinese border. The conquest of Afghanistan has proven to be neither easy nor cheap. They are pouring $200-million a day in aid into Hanoi to prop up the Vietnamese, who are themselves bogged down in Cambodia. The Soviets confront an impossible dilemma in Poland. Their ideology has failed, and they know that the Polish people may well resist direct or indirect suppression. Clearly, the costs of Soviet foreign policy are growing, and no easy solutions are available. This may be having an impact even on the Soviet domestic situation. Consumers who have nothing to buy with the savings are becoming restive. Soviet leaders, I think, are beginning to recognize that the system itself is in trouble.

Interview/U.S. News & World Report, 5-18:29.

4

This thriving city [West Berlin] is a superb example of the success of the West . . . there is an alternative on the other side of the Berlin Wall [in East Berlin]. It is a sad spectacle—a revolution that has lost its appeal. Slogans that once moved men now bore them. Institutions that purportedly offer hope for millions instead oppress them. Cynicism and pessimism are pervasive. Writers, artists, poets, philosophers—the creative spirits of society—have fled westward in unprecedented numbers, unable to be heard in their own countries.

To West Berlin press corps,
Sept. 13/
Chicago Tribune, 9-14:(1)8.

(ALEXANDER M. HAIG, JR.)

1

[In the event of a European conflict with the Soviet Union,] there are contingency plans in the NATO doctrine to fire a nuclear weapon for demonstrative purposes to demonstrate to the other side that they are exceeding the limits of toleration in the conventional area, all designed to maintain violence at the lowest level possible.

Before Senate Foreign Relations Committee,
Washington, Nov. 4/
The New York Times, 11-5:4.

2

[On the public demonstrations in Europe against deployment of nuclear weapons there]: We are witnessing in Europe today a convergence of several groups. Some people are concerned about the environment, while other people fear Soviet power. Still others are worried about nuclear weapons and nuclear energy. All of them are anxious about threats to peace. But this does not mean that our European allies are going "neutral" or that they are abandoning NATO and the policy and strength that has preserved our freedom. The [Soviet] invasion of neutral Afghanistan and the violation of neutral Sweden's territory by a Soviet submarine should dispel the illusion that neutrality confers immunity.

Before House Foreign Affairs Committee,
Washington, Nov. 12/
The New York Times, 11-13:4.

Denis Healey
Deputy leader,
British Labor Party

3

[On the recent rioting in British cities]: Britons will never feel safe again in their homes and streets until the policies that have produced unemployment and decay have been reversed . . . The government must take action to offer our youngsters hope, and take it now before next week's unemployment figures send another wave of despair across our land.

July 12/ The Washington Post, 7-13:(A)20.

4

[On his concern about extreme leftists taking over the Labor Party]: Too often those who demand more democracy in the Labor Party want exactly the opposite, a system in which a small minority of self-appointed activists deny the vote to the average Party member. Ordinary decent men and women whose support we should be able to take for granted are worried stiff that our Party has been taken over by the bully-boys who howl down free speech at Party rallies, who reject the ballot box in favor of violence on the streets.

The New York Times, 9-4:2.

Edward Heath
Former Prime Minister of the
United Kingdom

5

[Criticizing the economic policies of British Prime Minister Margaret Thatcher]: It is imperative in our present economic circumstances, both national and international, that we should make a completely fresh assessment of Conservative [Party] economic policy. Many of us [Conservatives] have remained almost silent for a long time on these matters, perhaps for far too long, in order that the dire consequences of the present dogmatic policies could be more widely recognized. We were hoping that they would bring about a more pragmatic approach to economic affairs. [But the increase in the minimum interest rates from 12 to 16 per cent,] the still further increase in unemployment and the numbers of liquidations which are bound to follow, the rise in mortgage rates together with the hardship and personal bankruptcies associated with them, all indicate that the situation is getting worse, not better, and that the policy has become more dogmatic, not less so.

Manchester, England, Oct. 6/
The Washington Post, 10-7:(A)11.

WHAT THEY SAID IN 1981

John Hickey
Sociologist, New University of Ulster
(Northern Ireland)

1

The whole atmosphere [in Northern Ireland] is heavily influenced by the fact that you constantly see troops in the streets, which is not something that most societies have. You can be stopped frequently at road blocks; you can have your cars searched; when you go into a store, you're often searched. One of the tragedies about this is the fact that if you live in that situation long enough, you come to regard it as being normal. Your expectations of what life ought to be like drop all the time, so you get used to a way of life that should not be acceptable in any civilized modern society. And it's producing a generation of children who don't know anything else. What sort of trouble it is going to cause in the future when those children grow up to be adults, nobody knows.

Interview, Los Angeles/
Los Angeles Herald Examiner, 7-15:(A)2.

Johan J. Holst
State Secretary,
Foreign Ministry of Norway

2

There is a growing frustration and anger caused by the lack of progress in efforts to curb the accumulation of nuclear arms taking hold in West European society. Unless public confidence can be restored in the feasibility of arms control and the credibility of NATO's commitment to pursue it, there is a serious danger that social consensus behind prudent defense policies may disintegrate, leading to polarized social strife and general crisis in the relationship between state and society in Europe. It seems doubtful whether international stability is attainable in a climate of instability at the national level about the proper approach to security.

At conference sponsored by Independent
Commission on Disarmament and Security Issues,
Paris/The New York Times, 11-15:(4)5.

Erich Honecker
First Secretary,
Communist Party of East Germany

3

The day . . . when workers in the Federal Republic set about transforming [West Germany] into a socialist society the question of unification of the two German states will appear in a completely new light. There can be no doubt about what our decision will be in that situation.

At East German Community Party conference,
East Berlin/Chicago Tribune, 3-24:(1)8.

Geoffrey Howe
Chancellor of the Exchequer
of the United Kingdom

4

We [the Thatcher Administration] came to office at a time when the British economy had been declining for many years relative to the other industrial economies, with both inflation and unemployment on a rising trend over a period of years. We had to tackle long-standing and deep-seated problems. But we recognized—unlike some of our predecessors—that the power of government to secure economic success was limited. Our strategy was therefore to create the right conditions for a return to steady growth. First, inflation had to be controlled. Second, the supply side of the economy had to be improved by reducing the burden represented by the public sector and by removing unnecessary controls. We have made good progress in both. The British economy has shown a chronic tendency to experience higher inflation rates than most other industrialized countries. This means we must put the defeat of inflation first, ahead even of the important goal of reducing the burden of taxation on the supply side of the economy. It would be criminal to slacken off at this stage, despite the high level of unemployment—which has risen partly from the world recession and the oil price-rise and partly from excessive increases in U.K. wages.

Before Association of American Correspondents,
London/The Christian Science Monitor, 4-22:23.

280

Gustav Husak
First Secretary,
Communist Party of Czechoslovakia

1

[On the unrest in Poland]: All those who are attempting to use events in Poland for instigating an anti-socialist campaign must be reminded of our clear standpoint. That is, that the protection of the socialist system and the achievements of its peoples are not only the concern of each socialist state but also the joint concern of all the states of the socialist community.

At Czechoslovak Communist Party Congress,
Prague, April 6/
The Christian Science Monitor, 4-7:1.

Wojciech Jaruzelski
Prime Minister of Poland

2

[On Poland's current labor unrest]: I am calling on all trade unions with an appeal: Let us stop all strikes. I am asking you for three months of honest work, 90 days of calm, to put some order in our economy. Forces of evil have been attempting to penetrate [the new independent union] Solidarity and lead it toward false positions, anarchy and derailment of socialism. People in the new unions should not let themselves be pressured. Further destructive activities may lead to conflict and to a fratricidal war . . . the government has the Constitutional rights to defend its system. We have enough power to halt those people and processes that slow progress down. Destruction must be stopped and stopping it is not only the duty of the government but of all Poles, including Solidarity activists.

Broadcast address to the nation, Warsaw, Feb. 12/
Los Angeles Herald Examiner, 2-12:(A)4.

3

[On anti-Soviet tendencies in Poland during the current labor unrest]: It would be difficult to imagine the functioning of our economy and the scale of economic paralysis without Soviet aid. In view of this, we have to be sharper in our assessment of the wave of anti-Sovietism . . . An end must be put to the deepening anarchy, hooliganism, anti-state and anti-Soviet excesses, as well as to mocking disregard for the law and accepted customs.

Before Parliament, Warsaw, Sept. 24/
Chicago Tribune, 9-25:(1)5.

Wojciech Jaruzelski
Prime Minister of Poland; First
Secretary, Polish Communist Party

4

[Announcing martial law in his country to counter the activities of Solidarity, the independent trade union]: Our country is on the edge of the abyss. Achievements of many generations, raised from the ashes, are collapsing into ruin. State structures no longer function. New blows are struck each day at our flickering economy. Living conditions are burdening people more and more . . . Strikes, strike alerts, protest actions have become standard. Even students are dragged into it . . . it cannot be said that we [the government] did not show good-will, moderation, patience [in dealing with Solidarity], and sometimes there was probably too much of it. It cannot be said the government did not honor the social agreements. We even went further. The initiative of the great national understanding was backed by the millions of Poles. It created a chance, an opportunity to deepen the system of democracy, of people ruling the country, widening the reforms. Those hopes failed . . . I declare today the Army Council of National Salvation has been constituted, and the Council of State obeying the Polish Constitution declared a state of emergency at midnight on the territory of Poland . . . The Army Council of National Salvation is not a substitute for the constitutional government. Its only task is to protect law in the country, to guarantee re-establishment of order and discipline. That is the way to start coming out of the crisis, to save the country from collapsing.

Broadcast address to the nation,
Warsaw, Dec. 13/
The New York Times, 12-14:8.

WHAT THEY SAID IN 1981

(WOJCIECH JARUZELSKI)

1

In our socio-economic system there is room for self-managing and really independent trade unions—independent of the state employer but also independent of the manipulations and terror of irresponsible politicos. There is room for workers' self-management. The rich variety of forms of social, scientific and cultural life is not contradictory with the intentions of the authorities.

Broadcast address to the nation, Warsaw, Dec. 24/
The New York Times, 12-25:6.

Roy Jenkins
Former Chancellor of the Exchequer
of the United Kingdom

2

[Criticizing British Prime Minister Margaret Thatcher's economic program]: All the experience of the last two and one-half years shows that the government is chasing a mirage. It is trying to reduce the public-sector borrowing requirement [budget deficit] by creating recession. But the effect of the recession is to make the government's financial position worse . . . In short, experience shows that it is impossible to get the deficit significantly down by digging deeper into a recession. It's like getting your car stuck in the mud: If you put your foot on the accelerator, your wheels spin and you dig in deeper. You have to go back and take a run—get out of the particular rut you're in.

Interview, London/
The New York Times, 11-5:29.

John Paul II
Pope

3

[Addressing Polish union leader Lech Walesa on Poland's current labor-government confrontations]: Everyone has praised the particular maturity that Poland's society and especially the workers' movement has shown in handling and resolving the difficult problems before them in a critical moment for the coun-

try . . . [The actions of the unions and the government have been] free of violence and domination, seeking solutions through reciprocal dialog and fundamental motivations and taking account of the common good. May you always be accompanied by the same courage as at the start of your initiative, but also by the same prudence and moderation.

Vatican City, Jan. 15/
Chicago Tribune, 1-16:(1)5.

Juan Carlos
King of Spain

4

[Saying there should be greater dialogue between Spain's military and civilian authorities]: It should remain clear that this is not aimed at establishing a military influence that will condition indirectly national political activities. On the contrary, we should try instead to assure that politics is not obsessed by military influences after the grave events of February 23 [an attempted military coup], but that the sentiments of those in the armed forces are known and weighed.

Addressing the supreme councils of the armed forces,
Madrid, March 24/
The New York Times, 3-25:4.

Stanislaw Kania
First Secretary,
Communist Party of Poland

5

[Criticizing attempts to establish an independent trade union for farmers]: We register our categorical opposition to all attempts at inciting the countryside, of sowing anarchy or creating a political opposition. There is no room in the Polish countryside for a political opposition of an anti-socialist character, because there is no room for a struggle that is not in the interests of agriculture or farmers and workers.

Before Polish Communist Party and
United Peasant's Party, Jan. 11/
The New York Times, 1-12:1.

(STANISLAW KANIA)

1

[On current labor unrest in his country, led by the independent trade union Solidarity]: We have come face to face with manifestations of anarchy, with instances of diarchy, with the transformation of an organization which claims itself to be a trade union into one far removed from what is laid down in its statutes. We cannot ignore, let alone accept, the fact that at the behest, certainly not of the workers but of instigators as they were called here, Solidarity is being steered in the direction of a political opposition. This is a fact which concerns us enormously.

Feb. 2/The Washington Post, 2-4:(A)1.

2

[Addressing members of the Soviet Communist Party on the current labor unrest in his country]: . . . we wish to assure you, comrades, to assure all our friends, that we have enough will and strength to prevent counter-revolution in Poland. Poland was and remains a socialist state, a true ally of the Soviet Union and an unbreakable link in the socialist community. We are grateful to the Communist Party of the Soviet Union and to the Soviet people for their fraternal assistance and support, for their understanding of our situation and their confidence that our Party and people will be able to solve our problems independently.

At Soviet Communist Party Congress, Moscow, Feb. 24/The New York Times, 2-25:3.

3

The country is in a very dramatic situation. The most accute reflection of this is in the lack of basic commodities in consumer markets, and the social dissatisfaction which this creates . . . The main thing now is to establish law and order in the country, to denounce and struggle against foreign forces, which are increasing tension, indulging in demagoguery and misinformation, and trying to set up an authority alongside our authority and against our authority. Such a state of affairs cannot be continued in Poland without putting Poland in jeopardy.

At Polish Communist Party Congress, Warsaw, July 20/Los Angeles Times, 7-21:(I)11.

4

[On Solidarity, the independent Polish trade union]: The Solidarity union has become a field of penetration of forces of the extreme right, a refuge for all Polish reactionary elements, a testing ground for counter-revolutionary forces and groups that do not conceal their goal is to overthrow socialism.

Before Polish Communist Party Central Committee, Warsaw, Oct. 16/The New York Times, 10-17:3.

John Kelly
Foreign Minister of Ireland

5

[On the turmoil in Northern Ireland]: We have expressed disappointment that our urgent words to London have not had a better response. But what is to be said of the IRA? They and their satellites try to harangue this [Irish] government into attitudes and gestures that they think will advance their aims. The reason they take this trouble with the government is that they know it is recognized and seen, in the outside world, as the lawful government of this state . . . But when the government condemns their violence, their crude contempt for human life, their ruthless indifferences to the wishes of most Irish people, suddenly the government's legitimacy counts for nothing, and its authority is the subject of insult . . . This government says to the IRA: Call off your campaign of violence, cease the shooting and the bombing and the intimidation; halt the wicked cruelties that have shamed and disgraced the name of Ireland and its flag.

The Washington Post, 8-18:(A)20.

WHAT THEY SAID IN 1981

George F. Kennan
*Co-chairman, American Committee on
East-West Accord; Former United States
Ambassador to the Soviet Union*

1

The foreigner who has to deal with the Soviet government often has the impression of being confronted, in rapid succession, with two quite disparate, and not easily reconcilable, Soviet personalities: one, a correct and reasonably friendly personality, which would like to see the relationship assume a normal, relaxed and agreeable form; the other, a personality marked by a suspiciousness so dark and morbid, so sinister in its implications, as to constitute in itself a form of hostility. I sometimes wonder whether the Soviet leaders ever realize how much they damage their own interests by their cultivation of it.

*At Second World Congress on Soviet and
East European Studies, Garmisch, West Germany/
Chicago Tribune, 2-15:(2)1.*

Andrew Knight
Editor, "The Economist" (Britain)

2

[On terrorist and Fascist activity in Europe]: It is remarkable that such movements are not widespread, considering what Europe has been through since 1974. Terrorists were then building up in Germany, and subsequently in Italy, and there was a fear of polarization with Fascist groups on one side and left-wing terrorists on the other. Germany has traditionally been a hothouse for extremist movements, left and right. That country's maturity in the past six or seven years is remarkable. When there is an election in Germany, 90 per cent of those qualified to vote do so voluntarily. Italy is equally remarkable. When you think of the non-government that Italy has had for years, and how the Italian people have come to hate the Red Brigades, it is a wonder Italy is still there in one piece. This says something about European institutions, which have shown themselves more durable than many people would have thought. But for how long, if the economic gale continues—that's another question.

Interview/World Press Review, April:24.

Spyros Kyprianou
President of Cyprus

3

[On the division of his country into Greek and Turkish sectors]: The continuing impasse is having most adverse effects on both Greek Cypriots and Turkish Cypriots. In the first place, the existing artificial division of the country is proving very harmful. The political uncertainty is not creating the right climate for economic growth, for political stability is an essential prerequisite to any kind of economic venture. Moreover, the continuing conflict causes both communities to waste energy and resources which could otherwise have been channeled to productive purposes. The protection of the problem has adverse effects for the West as well. It poisons relations between Greece and Turkey, two members of the Western alliance, because of the ethnic links between these two countries and the two [Cypriot] communities.

*Interview, Nicosia/
The Christian Science Monitor,
4-9:(B)5.*

4

A solution [to the Greek-Turkish conflict in Cyprus] will come only when Turkey withdraws its soldiers and allows Cypriots themselves, of both Greek and Turkish ancestry, to work out their differences. The bulk of the Turkish troops that invaded Cyprus in 1974—some 30,000 now—still occupy almost 40 per cent of our island. About 200,000 Greek Cypriots—nearly one third of the total population of the island—are now refugees, forced to leave their homes in the Turkish-occupied areas. Turkish settlers are being brought in to colonize those areas—which indicates Turkey's eventual goal may be annexation of the occupied area. In short, Ankara's aim, until now at least, is not to seek federation, as it claims, but a solution of a partitionist nature. This undercuts any chance for a just and lasting settlement.

Interview/U.S. News & World Report, 12-21:30.

Joseph Luns
Secretary General,
North Atlantic Treaty Organization

1

The basic aim of the alliance [NATO]—to preserve peace and the way of life of the Western democratic countries—has not changed. But the world of today is more complicated than it was when NATO was conceived and negotiated. Then, it was more or less bipolar, with the great menace of the Soviet Union overshadowing everything. Now it is much more complicated. It is multipolar, with all sorts of problems like the North-South problem; problems of countries trying to get dwindling resources like oil; the very active and dangerous new religious nationalism; and finally, there is the fact that the Soviet Union is taking advantage of its vastly increased military power to infiltrate and occupy regions which lie outside its perimeters. Having said that, I would be against extending the NATO frontiers because . . . the East-West conflict and the protection of the countries of the alliance against possible Soviet aggression are still central to the alliance.

Interview, Brussels/
Chicago Tribune, 1-19:(1)4.

2

There is a certain irony, which may not be entirely surprising, that the much-quoted detente is now contributing in a not inconsiderable way to a negative influence on the internal cohesion and solidarity of the [NATO] alliance partners. I might even say that this was one of Moscow's goals when it helped to initiate detente more than 10 years ago . . . What is worse, all too little has been done to destroy the illusion, eagerly disseminated by the Soviets, that detente is irreversible.

At military conference, Munich, Feb 22/
The New York Times, 2-23:2.

3

[On Soviet pressure on Poland due to the labor unrest there]: Acts of intervention, including the use or threat of use of military force, are incompatible with the professed Soviet desire for peace and disarmament and are inconsistent with the Helsinki Final Act and the United Nations Charter. Any Soviet intervention would pose a serious threat to security and stability and would have profound implications for all aspects of East-West relations. In particular, [NATO] ministers agreed that the Soviets would gravely undermine the basis for effective arms-control negotiations if they were to intervene in the internal affairs of Poland. Poland must be free to decide its own future.

Statement by NATO defense ministers read in Bonn,
West Germany, April 8/Los Angeles Times, 4-9:(I)8.

4

[On public demonstrations in Europe against deployment of new nuclear missiles there]: As a European myself, I can readily sympathize with the anxieties that the issue of theatre-nuclear force modernization has aroused on this side of the Atlantic. What I am unable to sympathize with, however, are the defensive, almost apologetic tactics many allied governments have adopted in treating those anxieties. These tactics have in my view mainly served to ensure that the issue, which was bound to be difficult enough anyway, would become a major threat to trans-Atlantic unity, which it has.

Before North Atlantic Treaty Association, London,
Sept. 30/The Washington Post, 10-1:(A)21.

Georges Marchais
Secretary general,
Communist Party of France

5

[On France's new Socialist President Francois Mitterrand's appointment of a number of Communists to his Cabinet, but in less-influential positions]: I would be a hypocrite if I were to try to hide that we would have preferred to go into the government in a more comfortable situation from the point of view of our influence. Some will call this capitulation. I call this the continuation and the development of the Communist Party's policy.

Time, 7-6:33.

WHAT THEY SAID IN 1981

Pierre Mauroy
Prime Minister of France

1

[Saying his Administration is going to decentralize government in France and return more power to cities and regions]: We must rid ourselves of what remains of Napoleon's *ancien regime*. The men of the chateaus are gone now. We must accomplish the historic task of creating a republic of citizens.

The New York Times, 7-17:1.

2

[On his Socialist government's plan for nationalization of key industries]: Nationalization will not be a statification. We shall protect the identity and autonomy of the national companies thus created. They will enjoy full responsibility as companies, being called on to act on their own initiative at national level as well as international level. The government is aware of the completeness and liveliness of these groups. Its concern is not to dismantle them but to [make them] prosper.

*Before National Assembly, Paris/
Los Angeles Times, 7-20:(IV)6.*

3

[Saying France intends to produce its own neutron bombs and not rely solely on those of the U.S.]: France's policy is not at all neutralist . . . France intends to remain faithful to its allies, with the United States in the forefront . . . The government is perfectly aware of the fundamental contribution for the balance of forces of American deterrence. But how can we miss seeing that the American deterrence is designed to protect the United States for sure, the Western camp of course—and not only France.

*Before Institute of High National Defense Studies,
Paris, Sept. 14/The Washington Post, 9-15:(A)1,17.*

4

The [French economic] crisis will not solve itself. It will be overcome only with a formidable industrial adaptation and social mutation. It is up to the heirs of the first proletarians thrown at the foot of steam engines to achieve the emancipation permitted by new technology.

*Before Parliament, Paris/
The Washington Post, 9-20:(A)25.*

Bernadette Devlin McAliskey
Northern Irish republican activist

5

There is no deed of the British government, no matter how low, that would shock the people of [Northern] Ireland any more. They have tried everything from famine to genocide, and that [convicted IRA member] Bobby Sands is still in prison is no surprise to me. If there is a civil war in this country in the next week, 90 per cent of it will have been started by the press out of sheer boredom. All they want to know is whether Bobby Sands is going to die [from his prison hunger strike]. Iran isn't so exciting any more. Maybe [you in the press] will go to El Salvador next to whet your appetite.

*To reporters, Toome, Northern Ireland/
Los Angeles Times, 5-4:(I)8.*

Harold McCusker
Member of British Parliament from Northern Ireland; Deputy leader, Official Unionist Party of Northern Ireland

6

When [convicted IRA activist] Bobby Sands ran for the seat in [Parliament] in April, 30,000 people voted for him. He was in the Maze Prison, on a hunger strike. People [by voting for him] maybe wanted to save his life. I could at least understand the vote. But four months later, 31,000 people go and vote for [Owen] Carron, who openly supports terrorism. Well, Protestants ask why they should now object to illegal activities by their own people [in the face of IRA terrorism]. Protestants have watched 10 hunger-striker funerals since May. IRA gunmen fired shots over the coffins. Only once did police and Army chase them. So Protestants don't like calls for the same Army and police to crack down on any Protestant paramilitary activity. They are fed up.

Interview/The Christian Science Monitor, 12-16:3.

Constantine Mitsotakis
Foreign Minister of Greece

1

We have said many times to the Turks there is no solution to resolve our differences except by arbitration or a decision of an international court, since to divide the Aegean [Sea] between the two of us is practically an impossible task . . . The problem of Cyprus is at the base of all our differences. Without Cyprus, the other problems probably wouldn't exist.

Interview, Athens/
The New York Times, 2-16:3.

Francois Mitterrand
President-elect of France

2

[On his election victory]: Frenchmen and women have chosen the change I proposed to them. Only the entire national community can respond to the demands of the present times. I shall act with resolution in order that, true to my obligation, the nation finds the path toward the necessary reconciliations. We have much to do together. I make no distinctions between our people. I shall have no other ambition but to justify their confidence. This victory in the first place belongs to the forces of youth, the forces of labor, the forces of creativity, the forces of renewal, which have united in a great national upsurge for employment, peace, liberty—the themes of my campaign which will also be true of my term in office.

Victory statement, Chateau Chinon, France,
May 10/Los Angeles Times, 5-11:(I)1.

Francois Mitterrand
President of France

3

[On his appointment of several Communists to his Cabinet]: The American reaction is their business. The decision is mine. The more that the decisions of France are free, the more France will be respected . . . People have written that [U.S. President] Reagan is angry. So what? If Reagan sneezes, so what? I'm not going to stand at attention . . . The Americans are far away, and they don't understand our developments. All this is a momentary mood . . . It is obvious that the Communist Party has goals that are different from mine. But the Communist ministers [in the Cabinet] are not there to carry out their Party's goals . . . I don't want to surrender to specters. Those [Communists] who voted for me are French people like the rest. Must I give in to historical antagonisms? . . . I want to make history by moving forward.

To reporters, June 27/
The Washington Post, 6-28:(A)19.

4

[On his plan, as a Socialist, for nationalizing French industry]: France is not such a large country. Where there are monopolies, economic interests in the hands of one person, one family, one group, they have absolute control; and if this involves key sectors of the economy, the disappearance of internal national competition becomes a very serious matter for the state, the nation and democracy. I would add that whether to nationalize or not is a matter which concerns our own internal policies and nothing else. In any case, I am not planning to collectivize the economy of France. I merely wish to restore to national ownership what belongs to the nation, nothing more.

Interview, Paris, June 1/
The New York Times, 6-4:6.

5

My position on East-West relations is simple: The defense of peace requires a world balance of power—an obvious statement—and a sufficiently balanced situation in Europe. I shall therefore always be in favor of what is required to maintain such a balance of power. That is why I was the first political leader of France to protest, as a Member of Parliament, against the installation of [Soviet] SS-20 missiles on the Russian-German border. When I was running for the Presidency, the Americans were not very much in my favor, but rather worried;

(FRANCOIS MITTERRAND)

the Soviets were not very much in favor, but rather worried; the German government was not very much in favor, either. Luckily, the French people were of a different opinion.

Interview, Paris, June 1/
The New York Times, 6-4:6.

1

[On a trend toward neutralism in West Germany]: Neutralism is a word that must not be used lightly. As far as I am concerned, I try to understand. And I understand the West German reaction, because West Germany is a country loaded with nuclear explosives that are not under its control. This contradiction is difficult to bear. It gives rise to a series of questions about which a Frenchman must speak with caution. Nations that have [their own] nuclear capability find it easier to avoid such crises than nations that have none and that feel themselves prey to the decisions of others.

Interview, Paris/Time, 10-19:57.

Walter F. Mondale
Former Vice President of the
United States

2

In the last nine months [under the Reagan Administration] the United States has dangerously mismanaged relations with our European allies. We have sown doubt and confusion about our ability to act as a full partner with Europe. After careful study, I am convinced that the alliance is in more trouble today than at any times since the North Atlantic Treaty was signed.

Before Foreign Policy Association, New York,
Oct. 20/The Washington Post, 10-22:(A)25.

Edmund S. Muskie
Former Secretary of State of the United States

3

There's constant effort to read Soviet intentions. I don't think the conclusions ought ever

to be static, because they can be affected by internal developments in the Soviet Union as well as external events. That's a dynamic state of elements and pressures that one ought never to lose sight of. They're not 10 feet tall. They do have internal problems, economic problems. They don't have unlimited ability to challenge us or the rest of the world; and sometimes when we act as though we thought they did, our reactions to their behavior tend to be excessive and unrealistic. It's a very dangerous game, a very delicate game. I can't think of a question I found more troublesome in these eight months [being Secretary of State] than the occasions—and there were many—on which we considered what are Soviet intentions next. We constantly monitor their troop dispositions, troop movements, military exercises; and when they emerge in a new area in different dimensions and large dimensions, we have to be concerned about what they might lead to, and what we need to be in a position to do in response. And it's a worrisome business.

Interview, Washington/
The Washington Post, 2-1:(C)5.

Alec Nove
Director, Institute of Soviet and
Eastern European Studies,
University of Glasgow

4

[On the upcoming generation of Soviet leadership]: There are two theories on the subject: One is totally pessimistic: The up-and-coming generation are isolationist conservatives—"little Stalins in the provinces," as some people call them ... They will not be particularly aggressive internationally, my contacts say. But they will be backward-looking, hostile to reform, and unimaginative. But I have also heard the following: In the [Communist] Party apparatus there are some bright, intelligent people who cannot now express their ideas. They are patiently waiting for their opportunity, and many bright ideas will surface once the octogenarians are out of the way. Personally, I believe that both theories are true. But the bright people will not be holding the

(ALEC NOVE)

top *political* jobs. So I think there will be a struggle between the conservatives and the reformers in the next generation.

Interview/
Forbes, 10-12:50.

Ruairi O'Bradaigh
President,
Provisional Sinn Fein
(political branch of Irish Republican Party)

1

[On how he would like to see the Northern Ireland problem solved]: The Catholics in the north are the "blacks," but the Protestants are only the poor whites. The rule in the south [the Republic of Ireland] is neo-colonial, with imperialist puppets running things. We want to disestablish both states—in the north and south. But that doesn't mean we want civil war. The ideal solution is a phased English withdrawal from Ireland and the creation of a new federal socialist system which would give each of the four traditional Irish provinces [Ulster, Connaught, Munster and Leinster] its own parliament and each local community control of its own affairs. The unionist-minded people would still have a working majority in the historic nine-county province of Ulster . . . The means of production, distribution and financial exchange must be controlled by the people and administered democratically. Finance, insurance and key industries must be brought under state control, as well as agriculture and fisheries. An upper limit will be placed on the amount of land any one individual may own. Larger tracts will be taken over and leased to groups of families to be run on cooperative lines. Private enterprise will still have a role to play in the economy, but it will be much smaller than it is today. Multinational corporations will not be allowed to have a controlling interest in Irish industry.

Interview, Dublin/
Los Angeles Times, 5-7:(I)8.

David Orr
Chairman, Unilever, Ltd.

2

If we [British] just sat back and relied on the benefits of North Sea oil, we could live quite comfortably until the oil wells dried up toward the end of the century. But that would be absolutely the wrong thing to do. The benefits of North Sea oil and the beneficial effect on our balance-of-payments situation do give us breathing space through which we should set about the task of restructuring industry and making ourselves more competitive. Then, when North Sea oil runs out, we should have an industrial base which can be strong and efficient. In a perverse way, North Sea Oil gives us something of a problem, because the very fact of having it and a strong balance of payments is likely to keep the pound strong for years to come—and that strong pound, which has helped to reduce the rate of inflation, does make the problem of being more competitive a difficult one. Those industries that are exporting or competing against imports are finding the battle pretty tough, with a rate of exchange that some people claim is over-valued and certainly which has stayed strong in the face of quite high inflation.

Interview, London/
U.S. News & World Report, 3-2:30.

Ian Paisley
Member of British Parliament from
Northern Ireland

3

[Announcing the formation of a Protestant militia in his fight to keep Northern Ireland within the United Kingdom]: Hundreds of men, all of whom own legally held firearms, are solemnly pledged and determined that Ulster will not be delivered bound into the hands of its enemies or the clutches [of those] to whom our faith and traditions are hateful. We will stop at nothing if any attempt is made to hand the loyalists of Northern Ireland over to the enemies of our country.

Los Angeles Times, 2-7:(I)14.

(IAN PAISLEY)

1

We have an unholy trio—the Thatcherite government [in London], the Dublin government, and the IRA. They all have the same goal: to bring us [Northern Ireland] into an all-Ireland Republic. That will never be. Over our dead bodies only.

*Church sermon, Belfast/
Los Angeles Times, 11-30:(1)9.*

Andreas Papandreou
Prime Minister-elect of Greece

2

[On the Socialist victory in the just-concluded Greek elections]: Change is necessary for the survival of the Greek nation and the Greek people. I am truly proud that the option of change has been endorsed in such a democratic way by the vast majority of the Greek people . . . We will make change tangible; it will show its face right away and without delay. We will not lead the country into any adventure.

*Athens, Oct. 18/
The Washington Post, 10-19:(A)1.*

3

Greece is a highly centralized country. We have a very powerful central government, a huge bureaucracy. Our objective is to decentralize, to give more powers to local government, and at the same time take such measures as are necessary to turn our various public enterprises from budgetary deficit operations to successful cost-minimizing operations.

*Interview/
The Washington Post, 10-20:(A)11.*

Andreas Papandreou
Prime Minister of Greece

4

[Saying his country's continued participation in NATO and the presence of U.S. military bases in Greece are subject to negotiation now

that he has been elected Prime Minister]: We have no desire to take our country into any adventure. We are not prepared to move unilaterally. And this really means that we shall start negotiations . . . The Atlantic Alliance refuses to guarantee our frontiers from the east. It protects them only from the north. But there is no visible threat from the north, while during the last seven years there have been many problems with Turkey . . . We are against [U.S.] bases [in Greece], that's clear. At the same time, we recognize that America is a superpower . . . and we do recognize, also, that it would be foolish to move toward a confrontation between Greece and the United States.

*Broadcast interview, Athens/
"Issues and Answers," ABC-TV, 10-25.*

Timothy Raison
*Home Office Minister of State
of the United Kingdom*

5

[Supporting a tightening of the U.K. immigration laws affecting former British colonies]: We have got finally to dispose of the lingering notion that Britain is somehow a haven for all those countries we once ruled. Our new citizenship law will reflect the reality of today's world rather than our imperial past.

The New York Times, 2-8:(1)3.

Miecsyslaw Rakowski
Deputy Prime Minister of Poland

6

[On the emergence of the independent Solidarity trade union and the unrest in Poland that followed]: As a result of the events that occurred in Poland, we have differentiated what we describe as "Polish Socialism." It is too early to say that we have already created something new. So far in Poland we have just disassembled or damaged the old structures, but the new ones have yet to be constructed. The world will look upon us as idiots if we do not create a cohesive, efficient and working economic system. So far, the world admires Polish ideas. But you cannot earn a single dollar from

(MIECZYSLAW RAKOWSKI)

the export of ideas, and we have been known as exporters of ideas for a few hundred years. To be an example for other countries, more is needed. We need high productivity, good work organization and an effectively operating state system.

Interview, Warsaw/
The New York Times, 5-10:(4)3.

1

. . . the radicals within Solidarity [the independent Polish trade union] are quite numerous. They were born under conditions of struggle. They can't—perhaps don't want to—proceed from fighting to dialogue. Their goal is to destroy the government. They cannot exist without fighting . . . I wish that Solidarity would finally understand that it is in their own interests to cooperate with the government. If they drag us to the bottom, they will go to the bottom as well. For there is no way that Communists are going to give up power here and allow Solidarity to start ruling.

Interview, Warsaw, June 6/
The Washington Post, 6-7:(A)24.

2

[The current economic and labor crises in Poland could] assume a permanent character and both the authorities and the public will get used to it. It will become a permanent way of life in which we constantly talk about getting out of the crisis, while doing nothing to release ourselves from its grips. The threat to our country and national existence need not necessarily have a violent nature. It may instead be gradual, doing the job just as thoroughly . . . We may get used to the shortage of basic goods and persuade ourselves that work is not what matters most, that other countries must take care of our well-being and that our specialty is celebrations and debates.

At Polish Communist Party Congress,
Warsaw, July/
The Washington Post, 8-10:(A)21.

Ronald Reagan
President of the United States

3

The American people and the U.S. as a whole would react to the utmost of our capabilities and would fully commit our resources to the defense of Western Europe. Our friends and allies in Europe should understand that this commitment will not diminish while I am President.

Interview/The Washington Post, 2-23:(A)23.

4

. . . it is impossible—and history reveals this —for any form of government to completely deny freedom to people and have that go interminably. There eventually comes an end to it, and I think the things we're seeing, not only in Poland but the reports that are beginning to come out of Russia itself about the younger generation and its resistance to long-time government controls, is an indication that Communism is an aberration—it's not a normal way of living for human beings. And I think we are seeing the first beginning cracks, the beginning of the end.

News conference, Washington, June 16/
The New York Times, 6-17:13.

5

Twice in my lifetime, I have seen the peoples of Europe plunged into the tragedy of war. Twice in my lifetime, Europe has suffered destruction and military occupation in wars that statesmen proved powerless to prevent, soldiers unable to contain and ordinary citizens unable to escape. And twice in my lifetime, young Americans have bled their lives into the soil of those battlefields—not to enrich or enlarge our domain but to restore the peace and independence of our friends and allies. All of us who lived through those troubled times share a common resolve that they must never come again. And most of us share a common appreciation of the Atlantic Alliance that has made a peaceful, free and prosperous Western Europe in the post-war era possible. But to-

(RONALD REAGAN)

day, a new generation is emerging on both sides of the Atlantic. Its members were not present at the creation of the North Atlantic Alliance; many of them don't fully understand its roots in defending freedom and rebuilding a war-torn continent. Some young people question why we need weapons, particularly nuclear weapons, to deter war and to assure peaceful development. They fear that the accumulation of weapons itself may lead to conflagration. Some even propose unilateral disarmament. I understand their concerns; their questions deserve to be answered. But we have an obligation to answer their questions on the basis of judgment and reason and experience. Our policies have resulted in the longest European peace in this century. Wouldn't a rash departure from these policies, as some now suggest, endanger that peace? From its founding, the Atlantic Alliance has preserved the peace through unity, deterrence and dialogue.

At National Press Club,
Washington, Nov. 18/
The New York Times, 11-19:9.

1

[On the imposition of martial law in Poland in a crackdown on the activities of the Solidarity independent trade union]: It would be naive to think this could happen without the full knowledge and the support of the Soviet Union— and we're not naive. We view the current situation in Poland in the gravest of terms, particularly the increasing use of force against an unarmed population and violations of basic civil rights of the Polish people ... The Polish nation, speaking through Solidarity, has provided one of the brightest and bravest moments of modern history. The people of Poland are giving us an imperishable example of courage and devotion to the values of freedom in the face of relentless oppression ... Two Decembers ago, freedom was lost in Afghanistan [when the Soviets invaded that country]. This Christmas it's at stake in Poland. But the torch of liberty

is hot. It warms those who hold it high. It burns those who try to extinguish it.

News conference, Washington, Dec. 17/
The New York Times, 12-18:16.

Bernard W. Rogers
General, United States Army;
Supreme Allied Commander/Europe

2

In some [Western European] nations, one senses stirrings of neutralism. Also, in the United Kingdom, Netherlands and FRG, we again see anti-nuclear demonstrations, which we had hoped were a thing of the past. These anti-nuclear movements often have strong unilateralist overtones, reflecting a false belief that if we set the example for the Soviets by unilaterally disarming, they would somehow feel morally compelled to follow suit. To me, this is very naive, and I believe that history is on my side. But growing unilateralism is worrisome. In this regard, if the [Atlantic] Alliance fails to show the necessary resolve—as perceived by the Soviet Union—that the greater threat requires a greater effort and that it will make the requisite security arrangements to protect the West's freedom of actions, values and way of life, I am concerned that we may see in Western Europe an environment comparable to what existed just before World War II. If the European situation deteriorates to that point, the Soviet Union might well accomplish its objective of dominating Western Europe without firing a shot.

Interview/
U.S. News & World Report, 6-15:25.

Helmut Schmidt
Chancellor of West Germany

3

[Criticizing attacks on his support for NATO deploying medium-range missiles in Europe]: ... stop letting it be suggested as if the Americans are our enemies and the Russians our friends. We Social Democrats stand without ifs and buts for the alliance with the U.S.

Before Bavarian Social Democratic Party members,
Recklinghausen, West Germany/
The Wall Street Journal, 5-18:4.

(HELMUT SCHMIDT)

1

[On the U.S. and West Germany]: We owe security, our freedom, also our cosmopolitanism [to the Atlantic partnership]. The basic rights in our Constitution—many people are not aware of this—stems only in part from German and European tradition. The greater part stems from the tradition of liberty which was founded in the United States of America more than 200 years ago.

Before Parliament, Bonn/
Chicago Tribune, 9-27:(1)4.

Peter Shore
Member of British Parliament; Labor
Party spokesman for economic affairs

2

[On Prime Minister Margaret Thatcher's new austerity budget]: It is a budget of unemployment. It is a budget for the accelerated decline of industry and the economy. Undeniably, it is a budget of failure.

Before Parliament, London, March 11/
The New York Times, 3-12:(1)3.

Romuald Spasowski
Polish Ambassador to the United States

3

[Saying he has asked for asylum in the U.S. because of the Polish government's martial law crackdown on the Solidarity labor movement in his country]: A week ago, a state of war has been imposed upon Poland, a state of war against the Polish people. Under the umbrella of the military, specially trained units and security police began an unprecedented reign of terror . . . This carefully orchestrated and direct crackdown is not an internal Polish issue. This is the most flagrant and brutal violation of human rights . . . At this very moment, when you [Americans] sit in front of your TV sets, evil forces crash on Poland and its deeply patriotic and religious people. Think about those Poles. Try to imagine their lot when you listen every day to the news; remember, they

are best sons and daughters of my country, those workers, those students, those intellectuals. A new chapter of Poland's struggle for independence and human dignity has opened a week ago. We will never give up. The only solution to the tragedy is a political solution, by dialogue. Nobody can put in prison 36 million people and make them slaves in the very center of Europe. Violence and oppression will only aggravate the situation, and history proves that they are bound finally to collapse.

Washington, Dec. 20/
Los Angeles Times, 12-21:(I)8.

Axel Springer
West German publisher

4

[On anti-Americanism evidenced in recent West German public protests against deployment of new nuclear missiles in that country]: Some of [the protestors] are motivated by an irrational fear of war, by a fright of the atom as a weapon and also as a source of energy. Other motives are gullibility vis-a-vis Soviet intentions, or misconception of America, or the deceptive hope that neutralism could become the cure-all to remove Germany from its dangerous position on the dividing line between East and West. But turbulent and frustrating as such demonstrations and their manifestations are, they do not give the real picture of the state of mind of the German people. According to a public-opinion poll taken [recently], 70 per cent of the people are absolutely opposed to such demonstrations. Of the remaining 30 per cent, more than two-thirds are unsure of their decision. I know from my own observations and from all public-opinion polls of recent weeks and months that an overwhelming majority of the people in my country would stand up and be counted for a continuation of American-German and German-American cooperation and friendship. Like you, we Germans are not for a policy of confrontation, but for a policy of strength, with the final aim to reduce armaments on both sides.

At Boston University/
The Christian Science Monitor, 10-27:23.

WHAT THEY SAID IN 1981

Franz Josef Strauss
Premier of Bavaria, West Germany

1

With [U.S. President] Reagan's election, the American voter has made a decisive choice for change. The Europeans, in their own interest, must take over their share of the load, and the political leadership here and in other European countries must stop turning over the responsibility for defense to the Americans while leaving detente and trade with the East bloc to themselves. The Atlantic Alliance will not be able to hold together if the Europeans concern themselves principally with their welfare states while the Americans forgo many domestic political projects in order to make everyone's security their highest priority.

At rally, Passau, West Germany, March 5/
The New York Times, 3-6:4.

Adolfo Suarez
Prime Minister of Spain

2

[Announcing his resignation]: My political power has eroded during my nearly five years as Prime Minister. No other person, during the last 150 years, has for so long democratically governed Spain. But the building of a system of liberties, a new model of social coexistence, and a new model of the state, has been at the expense of my political forcefulness. I think it has been worth it. But I do not wish to see this democratic coexistence become, once again, a paranthesis in the history of Spain.

Broadcast address to the nation,
Madrid, Jan. 29/
The New York Times, 1-30:1.

Margaret Thatcher
Prime Minister of the United Kingdom

3

If we are safe today, it is because America has stood with us. If we are to remain safe tomorrow, it will be because America remains powerful and self-confident. When, therefore, the Americans face difficulties, we need to say to them more clearly: "We are with you" . . .

Winston Churchill said at a Pilgrims dinner in 1932: "There is one grand, valiant conviction shared on both sides of the Atlantic, that together there is no problem we cannot solve." It is still a fitting and living message for the Prime Minister of Britain to carry to the President of the United States.

Before Pilgrims Society, London, Jan. 29/
Los Angeles Times, 1-30:(I)15.

4

[Saying she will hold firm to her tough economic policies, despite criticism that they are not helping stem the British recession]: It's like a nurse looking for a patient with sympathy and says, "Never mind, dear, there, there, lie back and I'll look after you," or the nurse who says, "Now come on, shake out of it. It's time you put your feet to the ground and took a few steps. Now get back and take a few more tomorrow."

The New York Times, 2-8:(12)33.

5

[On the Soviet Union]: I make no dispassionate assessment of my potential enemy, his objective, his methods—and I don't believe the Soviet Union changes its objectives; it merely changes its methods. I may not know its motives, but I know the fantastic proportion of its gross national product that it puts into armaments. I know that being in a substantially landlocked country, with most of its supplies coming across land, it does not need such a big, big navy. It does not need so many submarines. Why, then, is it doing these things? I know that, although it growls at Europe for stationing cruise missiles, it's got the most modern theatre-nuclear weapons in the SS-20. I know that they marched into Afghanistan; I know they are in Hungary, Czechoslovakia. They've got Cuban surrogates in Angola. I know that they've given help to both Somalia and Ethiopia. I know that there have been problems in the Caribbean, problems in Central America. Why? It is actually culpable if a [Western] leader does not make an assessment of that. That's

(MARGARET THATCHER)

not hawkish—I hate those jargon things. That's doing your duty by your countrymen.

Interview, London/Time, 2-16:36.

1

[On Britain's membership in the EEC]: We've had our quarrels with Europe. They were justifiable. I believe we are through them. Who would rejoice if Britain came out? The Warsaw Pact countries. They would have their tight alliance and would see that the democracies could not work together in peace. We can and we do. Of course there will be difficult times—the closer the family is, the more virulent the quarrels.

Interview, London/Time, 2-16:36.

2

[On U.S.-British relations]: Today, once again, our sense of common purpose and common resolution is being tested. It will not be found wanting. The message I have brought across the Atlantic is that we in Britain stand with you. America's successes will be our successes. Your problems will be our problems. And when you look for friends, we will be there.

Washington, Feb. 26/
Los Angeles Times, 2-27:(I)11.

3

[On criticism of her new high-tax budget]: Now, what really gets me is this—that it is very ironic that those who are most critical of the extra tax are those who were more vociferous in demanding the extra expenditures. What gets me even more is that, having demanded that extra expenditure, they are not prepared to face the consequences. I believe this government has taken the wise and moral course, and I will challenge anyone who takes the contrary view. So when people say that this is a no-hope budget, I can only say to them that this budget is the only hope for Britain's sustained and genuine revival.

At luncheon for small-business leaders, London,
March 11/The Washington Post, 3-13:(A)20.

4

[On her proposed bill that would tighten U.K. citizenship requirements for nationals of former British colonies]: Each and every country has a right to determine who shall be given citizenship. Every country has exercised that right to a very much greater extent than Britain has. We have half a million British citizens who came from India. Before countries criticize us too much for having a nationalities bill, they should also look to see what other countries of the world have.

Before Indian Parliament, New Delhi,
April 16/The New York Times, 4-18:4.

5

[On IRA activist Bobby Sands, who is on a prison hunger strike to try to gain recognition as a political prisoner]: There can be no question of political status for someone serving a sentence for crime [illegal possession of firearms]. Crime is crime. It is not political, and there can be no question of granting political status. I understand that Mr. Sands is still on hunger strike, and I regret that he has decided not to come off it.

News conference, Saudi Arabia, April 21/
The New York Times, 4-22:4.

6

[On the current riots in cities around her country]: [The unrest] has nothing to do with deprivation. We've poured money into housing, school buildings. In Liverpool, we put twice as much into industrial aid as in any previous year. We've poured in extra teachers with extra pay, extra social workers. I think somehow we've misled ourselves into thinking that having done all that, we would be able to solve the problem. It hasn't . . . I'm concerned with getting certain moral values right. If you don't live with discipline, you'll get some kind of anarchy breaking out somewhere.

Interview, London, July 17/
San Francisco Examiner & Chronicle, 7-19:(A)17.

WHAT THEY SAID IN 1981

(MARGARET THATCHER)

1

[On criticism of her stringent economic policies]: The tough measures this government has had to introduce are the very minimum needed for us to win through. I will not change just to court popularity. Indeed, if ever a Conservative government starts to do what it knows to be wrong because it is afraid to do what it is sure is right, then's the time for Tories to cry: Stop. But you'll never need to do that while I am Prime Minister.

At Conservative Party conference,
Blackpool, England, Oct. 16/
Los Angeles Times, 10-17:(I)31.

Gaston Thorn
President, Commission of the
European Communities

2

There is no tension yet in European relations with the United States [because] the [U.S. President] Reagan Administration is enjoying a kind of political honeymoon with European opinion. But there is anxiety. People are anxiously asking, "When do you think the Reagan Administration will start adapting its policies to help us? By Christmas? By next Easter?" . . . the United States generally seems to be saying, "Wait until Uncle Sam is better, then we can look after your [European] sickness—if you're still around to take the medicine."

Interview, Brussels/
The Washington Post, 7-9:(A)15.

Yvon Toussaint
Editor, "Le Soir," Brussels

3

Belgium has the peculiarity of always having coalition governments. Because our electoral system never produces a clear majority from either the left or the right, the resulting coalition cannot carry out decisive policies. This had many advantages in the past when the conditions—particularly the economy—were good. It permitted taking into account all the dif-

ferent shadings of Belgian public opinion. But now that conditions have worsened, we are beginning to ask whether such a system paralyzes political activity. In any case, Belgian public opinion feels that even if we change Administrations, the situation won't change. Another factor is the strength of pressure groups. They can block any measure that is disagreeable to an appreciable segment of the population. So the Administration must keep running just to stay in place.

Interview/World Press Review, August:31.

Pierre Elliott Trudeau
Prime Minister of Canada

4

[On Poland's current martial-law military government instituted to suppress the Solidarity free trade-union movement]: There is no doubt [that] if there is a civil war in Poland, there is a very good chance the Soviet Union would intervene because it couldn't allow a civil war on its border. Therefore, everything which would prevent a civil war is for me a positive step. If a military regime [in Poland] prevents a civil war, I can't inherently say it is bad.

News conference, Ottawa, Dec. 18/
Los Angeles Times, 12-25:(I)12.

Andy Tyrie
Leader, Ulster Defense Association
(Northern Ireland)

5

[On the Catholic-Protestant violence in Northern Ireland]: The attacks on the police and the killing of people . . . are answered by plastic bullets [from the authorities]. There is a war going on here, and we want it fought with real bullets.

Newsweek, 5-25:59.

Lech Walesa
National chairman, Solidarity
(independent Polish trade union)

6

[Supporting the independent labor movement in his country]: I know we can have a big

(LECH WALESA)

achievement and can even go ahead of Japan in efficiency of work [if workers are treated decently]. Because everything will be checked by the workers—every little screw—because the workers will say, "Look, that's my money" . . . Before, our unions were good. But now a group has come to power that has built itself nice little houses [and doesn't pay attention to us. We want] unions in which we can have some power and decide what to do ourselves, to man them ourselves, and not just have the government give us orders. We want to do it ourselves and not be put down by the government.

In film about the Polish labor movement/
The Christian Science Monitor, 1-22:3.

1

[On his union's strikes and other pressure against the Polish government on behalf of workers]: Whatever we are doing here is forced upon us by life. We don't want to go on striking anywhere. But we are constrained to do so. We are not afraid; even if we should lose—it's better to fall standing upright than to go ignominiously backward.

Interview, Warsaw/
Los Angeles Herald Examiner, 2-4:(A)4.

2

I am not a diplomat; I am not a master of ceremonies and even less an intellectual. I am an uncouth man, a worker. I have never read a book in my life, and I am a man with a goal to reach, so I don't give a damn for certain things. Not for the books, not for the interviews, not for the Nobel Prize and even less for you [the interviewer]. I have no complexes. I don't. Neither toward the generals, nor toward the prime ministers, nor toward you. I can give a punch on the desk of the prime minister, I can leave a general in a lurch without saying good-bye, and as for you I can do the same.

Interview/The Washington Post, 3-8:(C)1.

[On whether Communism has failed in Poland]: It depends on the way you measure the concept of good, bad, better, worse. Because if you choose the example of what we Polish have in our pockets and in our shops, then I answer that Communism has done very little for us. If you choose the example of what is in our souls instead, I answer that Communism has done very much for us. In fact, our souls contain exactly the contrary of what they [the communists] wanted. They wanted us not to believe in God, and our churches are full. They wanted us to be materialistic and incapable of sacrifices; we are anti-materialistic, capable of sacrifice. They wanted us to be afraid of the tanks, of the guns, and instead we don't fear them at all.

Interview/The Washington Post, 3-8:(C)4.

4

[On whether the Soviets could forceably crush Solidarity]: Impossible. I'm not and have never been afraid of this. You can defeat a man, defeat a nation. But you can't force a man to work. They [the Soviets] would need three men wearing stars to watch each one of us to force us to work . . . and we would still find a way to avoid it.

Interview, Gdansk, Poland/
Los Angeles Herald Examiner, 4-12:(A)1.

5

[Saying a Soviet invasion of Poland to crush the labor unrest there is unlikely]: If anybody tried to overcome us by force, it would not be very beneficial . . . but even if this were the case, we would act. We would put up a stand and no one would charge us with cowardice . . . I think we have enough wit and intelligence to know how far we can go [in demanding reforms from the Polish government]. We realize what the realities are, but we are also aware that we have no other choice. What has happened since August [the government's agreeing to Solidarity demands] cannot be simply canceled

(LECH WALESA)

or deleted. And we shall not permit a foreign hand to delete it.

Broadcast interview/
"Good Morning America," ABC-TV, 5-1.

1

. . . the Poles are capable of settling their own internal affairs by themselves and among themselves. It is in the common interest that external intervention should not become an obstacle to the process of consolidation now going on in Polish society. Our union was born out of protest. Using the traditional method of workers' struggle—demonstrations and strikes—it contributed in a definitive way to launching a profound transformation of the social and political life of the country. There is no area which has remained unaffected by this process of renewal. Even though we are aware this is only the beginning of these changes, no one in Poland has any doubt as to the fact that there is no way back to the previous methods of ruling the country and governing its economy. The principles of social justice, democratic freedoms and independent action that are the guidelines of Solidarity transcend the frontiers between states, blocs or systems. They are the common property of the labor movement.

Before International Labor Organization,
Geneva, June 5/
The Washington Post, 6-6:(A)1.

2

We [Solidarity] should not *speak* politics, we should *make* politics. I believe that confrontation [with the authorities] is unavoidable. The next confrontation will be a total confrontation. Now we need some time to survive a little longer and then we can win. We shall regain authority as a union when we give food, cigarettes and so on to the people. The government has offered only stupid propaganda. We see more clearly that without political solutions nothing can be achieved. The whole war will be won by us. He who gives food to the people will win.

To union printers, Aug. 20/
Los Angeles Times, 8-21:(I)8.

Thomas J. Watson, Jr.
United States Ambassador
to the Soviet Union

3

[On the Soviet Union]: Lots of people say that when the post-war leadership comes along —people without parents who grew up in the revolution, without memories of World War II —then things [in the Soviet Union] will change. I don't think things will change . . . This is one of the most stable governments and unlikely-to-change people on the face of the earth. There is no hope of collapse, no hope of change. What there may be hope of is a little better ability on the part of the West to understand them, and perhaps a little better ability on their part to understand us.

Interview, Moscow, Jan. 14/
The Washington Post, 1-15:(A)7.

Caspar W. Weinberger
Secretary of Defense
of the United States

4

I saw the Soviet prison wall, that great monument to Soviet realism which stretches all the way from the Balkans to the Baltic. Other empires in the past have built walls to keep their enemies out, but the Soviet empire needs walls to keep its own population in.

Rome, April 9/
The Washington Post, 4-10:(A)26.

5

[If the Soviets invade Poland to quell the independent labor movement there,] it should convince most North Atlantic Treaty Organization countries that collective negotiations with Russia for the reduction and limitation of arms—strategic and otherwise—are futile. Outright invasion would expose their so-called

(CASPAR W. WEINBERGER)

peace offers to be quite phony and would offer the rest of the world little reason to conclude that it can profit from negotiating with the Soviets on any matter—or trusting them at all.
Interview/
U.S. News & World Report, 4-13:46.

Shirley Williams
Member of British Parliament

1

[On the current riots in cities throughout Britain]: I believe that the challenge that faces Britain is every bit as difficult and serious as that faced by the United States in the 1960s. A very great deal depends on whether we have the imagination and the vision to respond in the way the U.S. did, [with] major programs to improve race relations, improve cities and fight poverty.
Broadcast debate, London, July 8/
The Washington Post, 7-10:(A)14.

2

[On the alliance between her new Social Democratic Party and the Liberal Party]: Our supporters and yours now not only hope to break the rigid mold of British politics, we are suddenly ablaze with the realization that it can be done. The grim choice [between the Conservative and Labor parties] lays on us the heavy responsibility of offering an alternative.
At Liberal Party Conference, Llandudno, Wales, Sept. 16/The Washington Post, 9-17:(A)24.

Kaare Willoch
Prime Minister-elect of Norway

3

[On his Conservative Party's recent victory in the national elections]: Norwegians are not tired of the welfare state. But they know you cannot pay for a welfare state without economic growth, and you cannot have economic growth with taxes as high as ours.
Interview, Oslo, Sept. 14/
The Washington Post, 10-12:(A)19.

Manfred Worner
Chairman, Defense Committee,
West German Bundestag

4

Anti-Americanism in Europe is bound to pave the way in the United States for anti-Europeanism and can lead to American isolationism—this time not of America's own choice, but forced upon her by the Europeans. And without the United States, a policy of preventing war by deterrence based upon the balance of forces is impossible either in or for Europe, so that security cannot be guaranteed . . . "Rather red than dead" is a pseudo-alternative. A war-prevention policy which is effective by reason of its credibility offers the assurance that there is no necessity to be either red or dead. Thirty years of practicing a policy of military balance are perhaps no proof that that concept has always been and still is the right one, but they are pretty good circumstantial evidence.
At conference sponsored by Independent Commission on Disarmament and Security Issues, Paris/
The New York Times, 11-15:(4)5.

Leonid M. Zamyatin
Director, International Information Department, Soviet Communist Party Central Committee

5

It is not accidental . . . that the imperialist forces are now striving to saturate Western Europe with medium-range missiles, but also to take advantage of developments [labor unrest] in Poland in order to weaken the socialist community, to try to undermine somehow from within, through Poland, the defense potential of the Warsaw Pact countries. Such is the policy of the imperialist powers, and certain forces, including those in the Federal Republic of Germany, are now trying to profit by this.
Broadcast address, Moscow, June 20/
The New York Times, 6-21:(1)6.

The Middle East

Abdullah ibn Abdul Aziz
Commander,
Saudi Arabian National Guard

1

. . . there is another government [in the U.S.] that influences American policy. There is a government within the government in the U.S. I am sorry to say this, but it is widely believed here that American policy is really run from Tel Aviv [Israel]. I would like for the American people to understand who really runs their government. When we look at the American people, we admire them as peace-loving, intelligent, industrious and accomplished. But we see certain elected representatives who want to impose policies that contradict U.S. interests . . . We hear constantly that the Soviet Union and Communism constitute the greatest danger to the Middle East. But as a friend, I tell you that you Americans constitute the greatest danger. The reason is your total alliance with Israel. The Arab masses feel abandoned by the U.S. and find it convenient to look to the Soviet Union instead. The policies of the U.S. often make it difficult for your friends to maintain that friendship.

To U.S. businessmen and editors, Riyadh/
Time, 11-9:18.

James Abourezk
Former United States Senator,
D—South Dakota

2

There's no way that the whole [Arab-Israeli dispute] is going to be settled without the eventual result being an independent Palestinian state—and I don't know how that's going to happen unless the United States and Israel begin talking to the PLO. Israel says it won't talk to the PLO because they're murderers and terrorists. That's hogwash. The United States talked to the Vietnamese all during the Vietnam war. There were negotiations going on and they were killing Americans left and right. How do you end a war unless you negotiate with your opposite party?

Interview/
Los Angeles Herald Examiner, 7-31:(A)12.

James Akins
Former United States Ambassador
to Saudi Arabia

3

[Saying the U.S. should not seek closer ties to Iran now that they have released 52 Americans held for over a year]: We've been humiliated. To say everything is back to normal would be catastrophic, not only in the Mideast, but around the world. Nations must not humiliate the U.S. with impunity . . . [Iran is] not the most important [nation] to us [in the Middle East]. Saudi Arabia is the most important. Iraq is a close second. I won't downplay Iran's significance. It is an important country because of its strategic location. We must have a friendly government there, clearly. But we don't. To bow and scrape before the mullahs now is no way to bolster our position.

Interview/U.S. News & World Report, 2-2:35.

Yasir Arafat
Chairman, Palestine Liberation Organization

4

[On the killings of unarmed Israeli women and children during PLO attacks]: I am against

(YASIR ARAFAT)

it, but it happens. But you have to ask these citizens, why are they living in my homeland? [By] living there, they are participating in this tragedy, they are participating in this crime with their government . . . Let them withdraw from my homeland.

Interview/Los Angeles Times, 6-23:(I)10.

1

There is this biased stand by the American Administration, which completely ignores the American people's interests in this area by giving this spoiled Israeli baby limitless support with military, financial and diplomatic help and even with the very latest technology —weapons and instruments to continue aggression against our people and occupation of our land. They are using these weapons now, I am sorry to say, with Pentagon approval in active attacks not only against the Palestinians but against the Lebanese, to threaten the Syrians and, lastly, against the Iraqis. And we don't know who will be the next target.

Interview, Beirut/Newsweek, 7-6:40.

2

[Israeli Prime Minister Menachem] Begin and his master in Washington [U.S. President Reagan] must remember that we will not accept losing. We are human beings, too. They have to remember that the blood of our women and children is precious, too. We are not against anybody. We want to live in peace in [an] independent state.

*News conference, Beirut, July 21/
Los Angeles Herald Examiner, 7-21:(A)4.*

3

To achieve peace [in the Middle East] we must have a permanent and just solution which recognizes the Palestinians' right to establish an independent state, to self-determination and

their right to return to their homeland and Jerusalem.

*News conference, Beirut, July 25/
The Washington Post, 7-26:(A)15.*

4

[Addressing the U.S. on its arms supplies to Israel]: Stop sending bombs, cluster bombs, fragmentation shells, napalm, F-4s, F-14s, F-16s, Phantoms, Lance rockets, laser weapons, rockets to the Israeli military junta. We [Palestinians] are human beings and not an experimental field for the new weapons, and we have the right to live as human beings, not as rabbits for hunting.

*To Japanese reporters, Tokyo, Oct. 14/
The New York Times, 10-15:8.*

5

[On Israeli's assertion that the PLO is a terrorist threat against it]: Do you think anybody can believe their big lies? *They* are the huge military power in this area, including nuclear bombs. They have 23 to 25 nuclear bombs. This means one for every Arab capital and the rest for the Palestinians. Can you imagine it? Who needs the [security] guarantees now? The Arabs are in need of these guarantees. The Palestinians are in need of these guarantees. Don't forget that within one month, two Arab capitals [Beirut and Baghdad] were raided by the Israelis.

*Interview, Beirut, November/
The Wall Street Journal, 11-12:27.*

Moshe Arens
*Member of Israeli Knesset (Parliament);
Chairman, Knesset Committee on
Foreign Affairs and Security*

6

[On Syria's war against Christians in Lebanon]: What is happening is that Syrians, with characteristic brutality . . . are trying to destroy that factor which resists Syrian domination of Lebanon. The Syrian objective is also clear— to control Lebanon and turn it into a satellite or, perhaps, a part of Greater Syria. Our com-

(MOSHE ARENS)

mitment, together with other Western countries, is not limited to the population of south Lebanon. It also includes the rest of Lebanon.
Chicago Tribune, 4-6:(1)2.

1

[On U.S. criticism of Israel's destruction of an Iraqi nuclear reactor which Israel says would have been used to produce nuclear bombs]: I think it [the criticism] is unfortunate, and I hope that after some discussion with the United States there will be more understanding of the position Israel has taken. I think that all Israeli citizens can breath a sigh of relief, and I think that all the citizens of the civilized world can breath a sigh of relief now that the Iraqis cannot build atomic bombs.
June 9/The Washington Post, 6-10:(A)17.

2

So far, there has been a very significant gap between the Israeli and Egyptian positions [on Palestinian autonomy]. The Egyptians have been looking for an autonomy framework that, in effect, will assure eventual Israeli withdrawal from Judea and Samaria [the West Bank] and the Gaza Strip and a return to the 1949 armistice lines. Israel is looking for the opposite—an autonomy framework that will assure continued Israeli presence in these areas . . . a difference in direction of almost 180 degrees . . . It's not hard to understand why it would be difficult to find a meeting point to close that gap.
Israeli radio interview/
Chicago Tribune, 10-23:(1)5.

Hafez al-Assad
President of Syria

3

[Criticizing U.S. policy in the Middle East]: We must ask what hope could be attached to a policy which has so deteriorated in its hostility to the Arabs as to become explicitly governed

by the policy of Israel. The United States doesn't want friends in the Middle East, it wants lackeys and agents and satellites, like [Egyptian President] Anwar el-Sadat.
Before Palestine National Council,
Damascus, April 11/
The New York Times, 4-12:(1)6.

4

[On Israeli's criticism of his country's deployment of anti-aircraft missiles in Lebanon]: Israel feels free to attack our forces in Lebanon, which are legitimately present there. But if we provide our forces with defensive weapons, which is what our missiles are, Israel says we have no right to defend ourselves. Our missiles are deployed in places near the Syrian border and they cannot strike targets inside Israel. These missiles can strike only low-flying planes which attack our forces. We wish no war, but if we are attacked by Israel, we are prepared to defend ourselves.
Interview, Damascus, May 20/
The New York Times, 5-21:4.

Tark Aziz
Member,
Revolutionary Command Council of Iraq

5

Any coordination [of nations] in the Arab Gulf will not be strong and able to defend the area from foreign intervention without Iraq. We don't want to impose this fact on our brothers in the Gulf. We don't want to behave nervously. We know that whenever there is a real danger in the area, everybody will look to Iraq, what Iraq is doing. This is the reality of things . . . There is no immediate Soviet danger to the Gulf area. The danger to the Gulf area was created by the Iranians . . . by the expansionist policies of Iran in the time of the Shah and in the time of [Ayatollah Ruhollah] Khomeini . . . The Shah planted the seeds of crisis in the area when he pretended to play the role of policeman . . . We are not against American military preparations against the Soviet Union, and we are not against Soviet military pre-

(TARK AZIZ)

parations against America. This is big-power business. But they shouldn't make our lands a theatre for their conflict.

Interview/The Washington Post, 4-24:(A)40.

George W. Ball
Former Under Secretary of State
of the United States

1

The current Camp David peace process—with only Egypt, Israel and the U.S. participating—is far too narrow to permit any solution to the Palestinian issue. Palestinians must be directly involved. That means all parties must ultimately sit down at the peace table with the Palestine Liberation Organization. No other solution exists . . . The PLO is not going to acknowledge the existence of Israel in advance of negotiation. It's perfectly clear that Israel is not going to promise flexibility on the West Bank or Gaza Strip in advance of negotiation. The only way you break a deadlock is simply to negotiate. That's the overriding responsibility of the United States. The issues can't be resolved without negotiation. In countless situations through history, nations still vowing to destroy one another sat down and worked out a peace. It can be done in this case, too. But they must talk.

Interview/
U.S. News & World Report, 8-31:33.

2

[Supporting Reagan Administration plans to sell AWACS planes to Saudi Arabia]: We cannot ask Saudi Arabia to join with us in the defense of the region and then refuse them the means to defend themselves. That's totally contradictory. This AWACS sale is a litmus test for the Saudis. They have a huge country, surrounded by potential enemies. They will not understand if we say to them: "You can't have the means that are essential for you to defend yourselves." It's a test of American *bona fides* in the Middle East.

Interview/
U.S. News & World Report, 8-31:34.

Abolhassan Bani-Sadr
Exiled former President of Iran

3

[Iran's spiritual leader, Ruhollah] Khomeini, since he has been in power has become a slave to power. Our economy is more dependent than in the Shah's time. Freedom is worse off than under the Shah. There is no freedom of the press or expression. Arbitrary acts, executions, imprisonment, torture, are daily events. It is hell.

Interview, Paris/
Sna Francisco Examiner & Chronicle, 8-2:(A)18.

Mehdi Bazargan
Member of Iranian Parliament;
Former Prime Minister of Iran

4

[Criticizing the rule of Iran's spiritual leader Ayatollah Ruhollah Khomeini]: It is regrettable that we should have to admit that a terrifying fire has started in our dear country and is threatening the nation, the government and religion. There are not many who are prepared to fight the fire, and some are trying to intensify and spread it. Girls and boys—those who support or are affiliated [with the opposition to Khomeini's rule] or those who are non-aligned and neutral—are being sacrificed in the streets and revolutionary courts for fair criticism and deviation.

Before Parliament, Teheran, Oct. 7/
The New York Times, 10-9:3.

Menachem Begin
Prime Minister of Israel

5

[Criticizing West German Chancellor Helmut Schmidt's suggestion, after a trip to Saudi Arabia, that his country has a moral commitment to the Palestinians]: From a moral point of view, Schmidt's statements certainly rank as the most callous ever heard. It seems that the Holocaust has conveniently slipped his memory and he did not make mention of a million and a half small children murdered, of entire families wiped out. The German debt to the Jew-

WHAT THEY SAID IN 1981

ish people can never end, not in this generation and not in any other. The entire nation cheered on the murderers as long as they were victorious. But what do we hear? We hear of a commitment to those [the Palestinians] who strove to complete what the Germans had started in Europe.

At political rally, Jerusalem, May 3/
The New York Times, 5-5:6.

1

[Criticizing France and West Germany for their support of Palestinian rights]: [The French] have forgotten the slogans of the revolution—*liberte, egalite, fraternite*—and in Germany they have forgotten the crime against our people. They are greedy and have only two goals—to sell weapons expensively [to the Arabs] and to buy [Arab] oil cheaply. They have no principles, no heart, no memory; nothing else interests them.

At political rally, Jerusalem, May 3/
Los Angeles Times, 5-4:(I)17.

2

I, Menachem Begin, the son of Zeev and Hasia Begin, do solemnly swear that as long as I serve as Prime Minister, we will not leave any part of Judea, Samaria, the Gaza Strip or the Golan Heights.

At celebration of Israeli independence, May 7/
Los Angeles Times, 5-10:(I)9.

3

[Speaking of Syrian President Hafez al-Assad on the Syrian missiles recently deployed in Lebanon]: Mr. Assad, you went to what is called brinkmanship, or as we say in Hebrew, the brink of a chasm. Withdraw [the missiles]. It will not make you lose any prestige or honor. We do not want that. It will be in your honor, because you will be serving peace. There is no greater honor than to serve peace. Therefore, retreat from the brink. Take out the missiles.

They do not belong there, where you put them. And take your soldiers and withdraw from the Mount of Sannin. Let us renew the status quo ante, and all humanity will breathe freely once again.

Before the Knesset (Parliament), Jerusalem,
May 11/The New York Times, 5-12:6.

4

[Saudi Arabia] is one of the most corrupt states in the world. It's not really a country; it's a family. Four thousand princes and princesses getting billions of dollars and not knowing what to do with them.

To reporters, Jerusalem, May 18/
The New York Times, 5-19:3.

5

[On Israel's destruction of an Iraqi nuclear plant]: We are convinced from the information at our disposal that they could have produced three, four or five [nuclear] bombs . . . and [Iraqi President] Saddam Hussein is just the person who could have done it because he murdered at his own hand his political adversaries. And you must understand that for the last two years I have been living in a nightmare. I used to see groups of little children who asked me questions and greeted me, and I knew that these children might be victims of an atomic bomb . . . We will withstand all the reaction [the criticism by other countries of the raid on the plant], becaus? what we did was defend ourselves . . . We warned the French; we told them not to continue to supply the Iraqis with this equipment [for building the plant].

Israeli radio interview, June 8/
The Washington Post, 6-9:(A)11.

6

[On criticism of Israel's recent bombing of PLO offices in Beirut, which resulted in many civilian casualties]: We will not cease our fire on the civilian population in Lebanon if the [PLO] terrorists build headquarters or bases near or within civilian populations. We will

(MENACHEM BEGIN)

continue to attack such headquarters and bases, and the responsibility for it falls on those who position themselves within civilian areas.

Los Angeles Herald Examiner, 7-20:(A)4.

1

I have many thoughts about the Saudis and I don't hesitate to repeat them. Because from that country came the call for holy war against Israel. That means they are trying to destroy Israel. Saudi Arabia gives hundreds of millions of dollars to the terrorist PLO. And although Saudi Arabia is afraid of the Soviet Union and Communism, they support the PLO, which is an agent of the Soviet Union . . . The danger to Saudi Arabia is from within. This is a country corrupt in its soul, in its body politic. It is absolutely corrupt, and it is an implacable enemy of Israel. It calls for *jihad* [holy war]. This is Saudi Arabia.

Interview, Jerusalem, July 30/
The Wall Street Journal, 7-31:20.

2

As far as [Egyptian] President [Anwar] Sadat is concerned, yes, I do believe he wants peace . . . I wouldn't say that about all of his advisers. There are some advisers who until this very day actually oppose the peace treaty and Camp David agreements [between Egypt and Israel] . . . But still the ruler of Egypt—the real ruler— is President Sadat. We signed a peace treaty. Some people—cynics—call it a piece of paper. But I am an old man—an old Jew, 68 years old —and I have worked for my people for more than 50 years. And in those 50 years, I have learned from experience that cynicism isn't to be equated with wisdom. It is cynical to say that a peace treaty is a piece of paper that can be torn into shreds. It cannot. It is a very serious document.

Interview, Jerusalem/
The Wall Street Journal, 7-31:20.

3

[Criticizing U.S. delays in delivering fighter planes to his country because of Israel's recent air raids on Lebanon]: [The embargo on the planes] is absolutely unjustifiable, and a wrong was done to Israel, and I am only glad that now it is going to be righted. The planes embargoed in America are Israeli planes. They are made in the United States but they were acquired or bought by Israel, and it was done by contract . . . When you contract for certain items, and you sign that contract, then the owner of those planes, or any other weapons or anything else, is the acquiring country, not the country which sold the planes.

To reporters, Jerusalem, Aug. 16/
Los Angeles Times, 8-17:(I)7.

4

[Rejecting demands that Israel dismantle Jewish settlements in the occupied Arab territories]: Jewish settlement in Eretz Israel is not only our irrevocable right, it is an integral part of our national security. Any demand to remove or cease settlement is rejected and shall be rejected.

Before the Knesset (Parliament), Jerusalem,
Nov. 2/Chicago Tribune, 11-3:(1)8.

5

[On American criticism of Israel's annexation of the Golan Heights]: I say again to our American friends: We shall continue to be allies, but no one will dictate our lives to us, even the United States of America. We are talking about our very lives on the Golan Heights, about our lives and our future and the welfare of this nation. No one will push us back to the borders of June 4, 1967—no one, no people, no power will succeed in pushing us back to those borders, borders of bloodshed, borders of provocation and aggression. [When Syria possessed the Golan Heights,] spurred on by their deep and abiding hatred they would open fire, from the Heights, on our towns and villages, instituting a reign of blood and terror throughout the area. Their targets were man, woman and child—and the attacks took their toll in

(MENACHEM BEGIN)

killed and wounded. [And] from the historical point of view, the Golan Heights were and will remain an integral part of the land of Israel.

Before the Knesset (Parliament), Jerusalem, Dec. 14/The New York Times, 12-15:9.

1

[Criticizing the U.S. for suspending its strategic-cooperation agreement with his country as a protest over Israel's annexation of the Golan Heights]: You [the U.S.] won't frighten us with punishments. He who threatens us will find us with our ears deaf. You have no right to punish Israel and I object to the use of this word . . . Now you are boasting again that you are "punishing" Israel. What sort of talk is this, punishing Israel? Are we a vassal state of yours? Are we a banana republic? Are we 14-year-old boys who, when we don't behave properly, get their knuckles rapped? . . . Kindly inform the [U.S.] Secretary of State that the Golan [annexation] law will remain in force.

Addressing U.S. Ambassador Samuel Lewis, Jerusalem, Dec. 20/ Los Angeles Times, 12-21:(I)1.

Eliahu Ben Elissar
Israeli Ambassador to Egypt

2

[Saying Egypt has blown hot and cold in its attitude toward Israel since the two countries established relations one year ago]: We were ready to dance in the streets when the Egyptian flag was raised in Israel. But the Egyptians had not spent their lives dreaming of seeing the Israeli flag in Cairo. That was the beginning of the asymmetry, and it has continued to this day.

Time, 3-9:33.

Avigdor Ben-Gal
Commander, Israeli armed forces in the northern district along Lebanese and Syrian borders

3

[On the fighting in Lebanon between Syria and Lebanese Christians]: Lebanon is the only one of our bordering nations that has not crystallized politically. Our aim, as I see it, is to influence the molding of its image. The way is cooperation with the Christian minority. The Christians want aid for survival. They see themselves as a patriotic elite; they want to be free of the [Syrian] occupation and establish a Christian Lebanon. We also want a Christian Lebanon, not hostile, free of the Syrian army.

Interview/The New York Times, 4-26:42.

Joseph R. Biden, Jr.
United States Senator, D—Delaware

4

[Arguing against the U.S. selling AWACS to Saudi Arabia]: This massive sale of some of our most technologically advanced weaponry would render some of our most important military secrets vulnerable to compromise. If a future change in government or policy should replace the present friendly Saudi regime with an unfriendly Saudi government, the AWACS planes, along with the tanker aircraft and advanced air-to-air missiles proposed in this sale, could threaten U.S. forces in the region as well as those of friends like Israel. The Saudis have made it clear that at some point they expect to operate the AWACS independently of any American participation. The result in the future could be that we would find ourselves looking down the barrel of our own gun in the Middle East.

At Senate Foreign Relations Committee hearing, Washington, Sept. 17/ The New York Times, 9-18:6.

Yehuda Z. Blum
Israeli Ambassador/Permanent Representative to the United Nations

5

[On his country's recent destruction of an Iraqi nuclear reactor]: In destroying the Osirak reactor, Israel performed an elementary act of self-preservation, both morally and legally. Israel was exercising its inherent right of self-defense, as understood in general international law and as preserved in Article 51 of the United

(YEHUDA Z. BLUM)

Nations Charter . . . Iraq has in recent years entered the nuclear armaments field methodically and purposefully, while at the same time piously appending its signature to international instruments specifically prohibiting it from doing so.

At United Nations, New York, June 12/
Los Angeles Times, 6-13:(I)8.

Leonid I. Brezhnev
President of the Soviet Union;
General Secretary, Soviet Communist Party

1

What is happening in the Middle East is profoundly tragic and dangerous. One miscalculation, and the flames of war could sweep the entire Mideast region. And it is not known how far the sparks of this fire could scatter. [Tension in the Persian Gulf area] is being sharpened because Washington is trying to bring gross pressure on Iran and organize intervention against the Afghan revolution. The strain is aggravated by the unprecedented concentration of military forces of the United States in the entire region.

Broadcast address to the nation,
Tbilisi, U.S.S.R., May 22/
The Washington Post, 5-23:(A)1.

2

One power, the United States of America, would like to get its hands on that region [the Middle East]. That power, it seems, regards the wealth of the Middle East as if it were in Texas or California, while the other power, the Soviet Union, has no such claims whatsoever.

Chicago Tribune, 6-15:(1)7.

George Bush
Vice President of the United States

3

[Supporting U.S. President Reagan's plans to sell AWACS planes to Saudi Arabia]: If these planes were a significant threat to Israel, we wouldn't be selling them to Saudi Arabia. It's that simple. Those who say otherwise are ignoring the fact that President Reagan is one of the best American friends Israel has ever had. We will stand by Israel. But at the same time we cannot—we will not—ignore our friends and vital interests elsewhere in the Middle East.

At National Press Club,
Washington, Oct. 9/
The Washington Post, 10-10:(A)2.

Robert C. Byrd
United States Senator,
D—West Virginia

4

[Arguing against the Reagan Administration's plan to sell AWACS planes to Saudi Arabia]: I am deeply concerned over the precedent established by the proposed AWACS sale to Saudi Arabia. The assurances provided the Congress by the Administration do not address these concerns adequately. We do not have a treaty relationship with Saudi Arabia. We do not have any defense arrangement with Saudi Arabia. Yet, the Saudis have rejected any suggestion that the U.S. will exercise joint command and control of the AWACS system. If the Saudis are as concerned as is the United States in maintaining their security against external threats, then I think we have a right to determine what technology, if any, should be sold them and under what conditions that technology is to be transferred . . . As long as the Arab-Israeli dispute is pushed into the background, this sale does not make any sense. Rather than contributing to stability in the region, I fear it will only raise the threshhold of tension. I am concerned that we are fast approaching the point where we are handing over grenades to potential adversaries in the region with the pins already pulled.

Before the Senate, Washington, Oct. 21/
The New York Times, 10-22:6.

WHAT THEY SAID IN 1981

Frank C. Carlucci
Deputy Secretary of Defense
of the United States

1

The threat to vital Western interests in key areas, such as the Persian Gulf, can be met only if all concerned share the burden and find new ways to make greater contributions in support of our common interests. Western Europe's stake in the security and stability of the Persian Gulf is enormous and well-recognized. What is perhaps less well-understood is the great contribution the Western European members of the [Atlantic] Alliance could make to help protect the security of this region so vital to them.

At military policy conference,
Munich, Feb. 21/
The New York Times, 2-22:(1)8.

Lord Carrington
Foreign Secretary of the United States

2

I make no apology for my firm belief that no good will come of pretending that the PLO can be ignored, or that they do not have a very wide measure of support amongst the Palestinians, both inside the [Israeli-] occupied [Arab] territories and elsewhere.

London/The New York Times, 11-6:3.

Jimmy Carter
Former President of the United States

3

[On 52 Americans just released after being held hostage by Iran for more than a year]: One very serious fact is becoming evident, and that is that our Americans in Iran were mistreated much worse then has been previously revealed . . . Iran, in my judgment, and the people responsible in Iran for this criminal act, ought to be condemned by all law-loving, decent people of the world. It's been an abominable circumstance that will never be forgotten.

Wiesbaden, West Germany, Jan. 21/
Los Angeles Times, 1-22:(I)1.

4

[On his handling of last year's American-hostage crisis in Iran]: I've thought about it a lot. It was one of the more difficult events of my life. And I still don't see a better series of decisions, even in retrospect, that I could have taken than the ones I did take at the time. I think it came out well in the end. Our nation's integrity was honored. Its interests were protected. The hostages' lives were spared. Their freedom was restored. I suffered politically, which is not of great moment in the historic scope of things. The lesson to be learned is how badly the Iranians suffered. I doubt if any kidnapers ever paid a more horrible price than the Iranians did.

Interview, Xi-an, China, Aug. 29/
The Washington Post, 8-31:(A)10.

5

We can't speak for Israel, but I think a simultaneous acknowledgment of the PLO and that Israel has a right to exist, and our dealing with the PLO would be certainly something that I favor. Many of the PLO leaders are very moderate in abhorring terrorism and violence. I don't see any possibility of the Palestinian world, and the Arab world, of acknowledging any other leadership for the Palestinians other than the PLO.

Interview aboard Air Force One, Oct. 11/
Chicago Tribune, 10-12:(1)1.

6

[Criticizing the U.S. Reagan Administration on its handling of the Egyptian-Israeli Camp David agreement]: I can certainly understand why any [American] President does not personally join the discussion, but it is almost inconceivable that neither the Secretary of State nor any other high [U.S.] negotiator has been assigned to help implement the Camp David agreement. I have been listening with great personal concern to the confusing statements from Washington. We are a signatory of the Camp David accords. Have we abandoned this commitment? If not, do we only have a casual

(JIMMY CARTER)

interest in the ongoing peace talks? Do we recognize the catastrophic consequences of a failure? Is this another abrupt change from more than a decade of bipartisan commitment? These questions cry out for answers.

Before Council on Foreign Relations,
New York, Dec. 17/
The New York Times, 12-18:4.

Claude Cheysson
Foreign Minister of France

1

[On the recent Israeli destruction of Iraq's nuclear reactor]: We are proud to be friends of Israel. We shall do everything we can to help Israel to live in peace within the borders recognized by the international community. This cannot be affected by one act. But that act—which also killed a Frenchman—was against international law. Israel must be in a position to live one day with open borders, with normal cooperation with its neighbors. The more such acts occur, the more difficult it will be to progress along such lines . . . We also support the rights of the Palestinian people. In history, each time the rights of people have been ignored, there has been rebellion after rebellion—and no peace. We are guilty in a way because we felt in 1948 that if we could give a decent life to Palestinians in refugee camps, that would be the answer. This was a most shortsighted perspective.

Interview/Time, 6-29:34.

Warren M. Christopher
Former Deputy Secretary of State
of the United States

2

[On his recent successful negotiation for the release of 52 Americans held hostage by Iran for over a year]: I think they [Iran] finally reached a point where the cost of retaining the hostages outweighed the alleged benefits of keeping them . . . I think they developed finally a willingness, but it was coupled with a massive

national ambivalence that caused them to get up to the edge and then pull back, time after time.

Broadcast interview, Los Angeles/
"Face the Nation," CBS-TV, 1-25.

Geula Cohen
Leader, Yehiya Party of Israel

3

[On the assassination of Egyptian President Anwar Sadat and its effect on the Israeli-Egyptian Camp David accords which provide that Israel withdraw from occupied Sinai]: The very fact that one bullet can cancel an agreement is a sign that not only the withdrawal, but all these procedures, must be stopped. There is no doubt that this incident confirms all that we have been saying. There is no stability in this region, and one cannot make an agreement which is dependent on a non-democratic regime and one man.

Jerusalem, Oct. 6/
The New York Times, 10-7:1.

Alan Cranston
United States Senator,
D—California

4

[Arguing against the proposed U.S. sale of AWACS to Saudi Arabia]: Because of its very small size, Israel—to preserve its security—must have the ability to make a pre-emptive strike against an aggressor. That's not a very pleasant reality, but it is imposed upon Israel by circumstance. These sophisticated radar planes, by permitting pinpoint surveillance of the Israeli Air Force, could wipe out Israel's ability to mount such a pre-emptive strike . . . A true pre-emptive strike should be employed only when a nation has irrefutable evidence that another nation is about to attack it. One purpose of intelligence gathered by an AWACS is to foreclose that option to an enemy.

Interview/
U.S. News & World Report, 5-18:67.

WHAT THEY SAID IN 1981

Moshe Dayan
Former Foreign Minister and former
Minister of Defense of Israel

1

We [Israel] don't have an atomic bomb now. But we have the capacity; we can do that in a short time. We are not going to be the first ones to introduce nuclear weapons into the Middle East, but we do have the capacity to produce nuclear weapons. And if the Arabs are willing to introduce nuclear weapons into the Middle East, then Israel should not be too late in having nuclear weapons too.

Interview, Jerusalem, June 24/
The New York Times, 6-25:1.

Alan Dixon
United States Senator, D—Illinois

2

[On U.S.-Iran relations now that the 52 American hostages have been released after being held in Iran for over a year]: Nobody is more upset than Alan Dixon. But it might be in the best national interest to continue military aid. Iran doesn't like the Soviet Union, either, and we may need Iran as a buffer between us and the Soviets. I think we should treat Iran the same as we treat all foreign nations. We should be decent and understanding . . . Our main concern should be the best national interests of the United States.

Washington, Jan. 21/Chicago Tribune, 1-22:(1)6.

Ephraim Evron
Israeli Ambassador to the United States

3

Unlike the United States, which views Saudi Arabia as a moderate country, as it were, we see it as a confrontation country, a country that has been involved in all the wars against Israel and that has been a party to all—political and military—hostilities against Israel to this date. As a result, we view with concern the United States courting of Saudi Arabia, or, if you like, the tightening of relations between the United States government and Saudi Arabia.

Israeli radio interview, Washington, October/
The New York Times, 11-1:(1)10.

Ismail Fahmi
Former Foreign Minister of Egypt

4

[Criticizing the U.S. sale of AWACS planes to Saudi Arabia]: The AWACS already in Saudi Arabia have not helped to defend Saudi airspace. Everyone knows the Israelis penetrate it up to eight times each month with impunity. I am not against the Saudis acquiring four, five, or even 10 AWACS planes if they want them for prestige purposes. But regarding [U.S. President] Reagan's statement that the deal will boost the chances of peace in the Middle East—personally, I doubt it. On the contrary, I believe Israel will now become even more intransigent, and force Reagan to give them either two or three AWACS of their own, or some other sophisticated equipment, to balance the deal with the Saudis. And if Reagan doesn't do this, then the only way he can prove he is not anti-Israel—or anti-Semitic in their terms—would be to espouse the Israeli point of view on any Palestinian settlement.

Interview, Cairo/
The Christian Science Monitor, 11-4:4.

Saud al-Faisal
Foreign Minister of Saudi Arabia

5

[On the relative importance in the Middle East of the Arab-Israeli conflict and Soviet influence in the region]: We would put priority on the Israeli conflict. That is the basic cause of instability and insecurity in the region . . . As for the Soviet Union, undoubtedly the perspective of the United States toward the Soviet Union is different from any other country's perception because of the position of the U.S. vis-a-vis the Soviet Union.

Farewell remarks after meeting with visiting U.S.
Secretary of State Alexander Haig, Riyadh, April 8/
The Wall Street Journal, 4-9:2.

Willard Gaylin
Social psychiatrist; President, Hastings Center
of the Institute of Society, Ethics
and Life Sciences

1

[On whether the U.S. hostages recently released by Iran are heroes]: I find the use of the word heroism peculiar at best. It is not only wrong, it is mischievous. I think it places an unfair burden on these people . . . Heroism implies choice and action. These people didn't have any choice. Yes, they were victims, maybe even martyrs. But this was a situation the opposite of heroism, a situation that involves humiliation, impotence and abandonment of responsibility.

The Washington Post, 1-31:(A)6.

Ashraf Ghorbal
Egyptian Ambassador to the United States

2

[Calling on the U.S. to take action against Israel for that country's just-announced annexation of the Golan Heights]: What about you [the U.S.]? What are you doing? . . . You are a sovereign and a superpower. Show us your teeth. Show *them* your teeth . . . We have been in the preaching business for three years with our Arab brothers, [urging them to] do it the way we did it [peaceful negotiations with Israel]. But when Israel annexes the Golan, what is there to negotiate? Isn't Israel defeating her own argument? What is Israel leaving to the other countries to negotiate about? . . . The issue is to get Israel out of its isolation into peace in the area. We have been trying to help Israel. But so far they have given us a most difficult time.

To reporters, Washington, Dec. 16/
Los Angeles Times, 12-17:(1)17.

Barry M. Goldwater
United States Senator, R—Arizona

3

[Supporting the U.S. sale of AWACS planes to Saudi Arabia]: The time has come when the defense of Saudi Arabia, like it or not, is far more important to America than the defense of any other Arab country in the Middle East. AWACS is a vital element in that. Saudi Arabia and the Indian Ocean are the most strategic pieces of real estate in the world. If Soviet power ever gains domination over the Indian Ocean and the Persian Gulf, we'll be through as a world power.

Interview/
U.S. News & World Report, 5-18:67.

Alexander M. Haig, Jr.
Secretary of State of the
United States

4

The broad strategic issues raised by Soviet imperialism are the fundamental reality that Arab-Israeli disputes must be related to. An exclusive preoccupation with the Arab-Israeli dispute would not remove overriding strategic dangers that those of us who share common values—Arab and Jew, and America and other Western nations—have got to confront. Now, this does not mean that the urgency in the search for an Arab-Israeli agreement is to be subordinated to the broader East-West concerns, but rather that these are mutually reinforcing concerns that must be dealt with in parallel. But never with an exclusive preoccupation. In the past we have had a tendency to do that.

Interview, Washington/Time, 3-16:24.

5

Our friendship with Saudi Arabia is not based solely on its role as an oil supplier. Saudi assistance has been important to states breaking away from the Soviet embrace, and to strategically important countries such as Sudan and Pakistan. Saudi Arabia has played a crucial role in the negotiations on Lebanon and in the formation of the new Gulf Cooperation Council. We expect Saudi cooperation in fostering peace and stability to broaden as the security environment improves. It is against this background that the proposed [U.S.] arms sales to Saudi Arabia must be seen. Their arms will in-

(ALEXANDER M. HAIG, JR.)

crease Saudi Arabia's ability to defend itself; they will directly assist U.S. forces deployed in the region, just as U.S. AWACS do now; and they demonstrate our commitment to assist the Saudis against more severe dangers.

Before Senate Foreign Relations Committee,
Washington, Sept. 17/
The Wall Street Journal, 9-21:30.

1

The elements of our policy in the Middle East are integrated into a balanced strategy which recognizes that the peace process and security cooperation reinforce one another. If our friends are more secure, they will be more willing to take risks for peace. And if they make progress toward resolving their differences, they will be more willing to cooperate with us and with each other against threats to their security. It is essential to demonstrate that we can implement such a strategy, one that takes full account of the complex facts of the Middle East. That is why we are vigorously supporting the autonomy talks in partnership with Egypt and Israel. That is why we are moving ahead with security assistance to countries threatened by Soviet and Libyan aggression. That is also why we are pursuing strategic cooperation with other friends in the Middle East and Africa who can assist our efforts in the region.

Before House Foreign Affairs Committee,
Washington, Nov. 12/
The New York Times, 11-13:4.

Saadun Hamadi
Foreign Minister of Iraq

2

[On Israel's destruction of his country's nuclear reactor]: . . . the region has moved further away from the just and durable peace which the international community is insistently calling for. The responsibility for this setback falls upon the state which has supplied Israel with military, economic and technical assistance, providing it with nuclear capability and

the maximum degree of armaments. That country is the United States. It is that unlimited support and assistance that has enabled Israel to commit its repeated aggressions, to refuse to recognize the rights of the Palestinian people and to persist in its policy of territorial expansion. To us, the people of the Arab countries, the Israeli act adds another proof that the Zionist entity, being based on a Fascist ideology, does not believe in a just and durable peace. Its main concern is territorial expansion through the use of blind force and aggression whenever that is possible.

At United Nations, New York, June 19/
The New York Times, 6-20:4.

William D. Hartley
Chief Middle East correspondent,
"U.S. News & World Report"

3

Oil obviously gives America a vital interest in the [Middle East]. But securing that interest is going to be a tough job as long as the U.S. is seen by the Arabs as unequivocally backing Israel. Despite all the other problems, the Arab-Israeli conflict is uppermost in Arab eyes. With the exception of such nations as Syria and Libya, most Arab states are basically pro-Western and conservative. They'd like to be closer to America, but they cannot afford to be so openly as long as the U.S. backs Israel. They don't want to appear as traitors to the Arab cause . . . The Arab-Israeli conflict is an obsession with the Arabs—more important than any Soviet threat. They aren't going to look kindly on the [U.S.] Reagan Administration if it says that any other issue is more important. The U.S. must broaden the peace process by bringing in other Arab states. Countering Soviet influence implies that Washington wants the cooperation of Arab nations. But to get that cooperation, it must work hard to solve the entire Arab-Israeli question. And it must be done in a way that moderate Arabs can accept, without leaning toward Israel.

Interview/
U.S. News & World Report, 3-16:37.

Mansour Hassan
Minister of Information of Egypt

1

[Criticizing Israeli Prime Minister Begin for his establishment of Jewish settlements in occupied Arab territories]: The whole importance of the autonomy idea [for Palestinians] is the evacuation of the Israeli occupation forces, the dismantling of the Israeli civilian authority in the occupied areas, the establishment of a Palestinian entity. Mr. Begin is not making it easy for Arab leaders to have hope in the fruits of a peaceful situation . . . Mr. Begin has grounded [Egyptian] President Sadat's initiative and dealt with the situation in a shrewd, calculating way. If Israel were more positive on the peace process, I'm sure that all the Arabs we call moderates would have fallen in line by now.

The New York Times, 3-8:(1)10.

Hussein I
King of Jordan

2

[On why he refused to permit former U.S. Secretary of State Henry Kissinger to visit Jordan on his recent swing through the Middle East]: I personally don't feel at ease about giving Henry Kissinger any role in any new political effort in this region or its vicinity or with regard to our issue. We are still suffering from Henry Kissinger's blunders to this day. We have suffered enough from them.

Interview/
Los Angeles Herald Examiner, 1-14:(A)4.

3

[Saying he will not take responsibility for West Bank Palestinians]: The peace process in the Middle East is completely bogged down for the time being, and the situation is very dangerous. The Israelis want me to play the role of policeman to protect their occupation and their sovereignty, and I'm not going to play that game.

Interview/The Washington Post, 1-18:(A)20.

4

What we hope for, and wish most, is for the United States to be free to act on its principles and ideals to resolve the [Arab-Israeli] problem according to the traditions which made it the greatest nation of the world in our time . . . What we want to find out is how much the United States is still able to contribute toward the establishment of a just peace. Or, on the other hand, has it already taken a course that puts it on one side in this conflict [the side of Israel]: —fully, totally, irrevocably? If the latter is the case, then it is obvious the United States has compromised its ability to make a contribution.

Interview, Amman, Sept. 22/
The Washington Post, 9-23:(A)22.

5

I am aware that the Camp David agreement [between Egypt and Israel] is regarded in the United States as a great and historic achievement. For our part, we see the failure of Camp David not in what it did but in what it failed to do. We rejoice in Egypt's recovery of Sinai and, as we have repeatedly said, we are anxious to attain a final comprehensive settlement which Israel and all her neighbors can enjoy for all time in our part of the world, where the security of all can be guaranteed. Israel made a deal with Egypt, trading territory for peace. The same principle must apply to all others, particularly to the Palestinians, in terms of their full rights over their now-occupied national soil. Under such conditions, I would suggest that a real, lasting, secure peace is Israel's for the asking.

Before Los Angeles World Affairs Council, Nov. 6/
Los Angeles Times, 11-7:(I)7.

6

[Calling for the internationalization of Jerusalem]: The Almighty in his wisdom did not make Jerusalem that important and touchy a point in the hearts and souls of all of us—Jews or Christians or Moslems—except to offer us a challenge to learn how to respect each other and live together. Jerusalem must be the essence of peace, a symbol of peace. It cannot be a political capital of a state.

Broadcast interview, Los Angeles/
"Face the Nation," CBS-TV, 11-8.

WHAT THEY SAID IN 1981

Saddam Hussein
President of Iraq

1

All Arabs must realize that even if all the Arabs were to recognize so-called Israel now with secure borders, including all the occupied Arab territories, and were to respect this state and remain committed to their obligations or capitulate to Israel, the Zionist entity would not accept a state which forbids it to continue expanding at the expense of Arab sovereignty, but would interfere even with roads someplace in Saudi Arabia and ask that their directions be changed under the pretext that they pose a threat to the Zionist entity, that they are a military threat or something which Israel cannot accept [as the Iraqi nuclear reactor which Israel recently destroyed on the pretext of self-defense]. They will ask the Arabs to cancel the study of chemistry, physics, mathematics and astronomy in the curriculums of their colleges and high schools because they give the Arabs knowledge in the military sphere, thus threatening Israel's security. Israel's interference will be such as to ask for the change of Amirs and to replace them with others, to change kings and to replace them with others, to change ministers and to replace them with others. Israel's demands may even go to the extent of asking that an elementary-school principal be replaced because he brings up his students in a national and pan-Arab way. They will even try to make the Arabs rewrite their history or write it in a new direction, including the Prophet's history.
Addressing his Cabinet, Baghdad, June 23/
The New York Times, 6-24:6.

2

Any nation which wants peace and security and respect for people of the world . . . should help the Arabs in one way or another to build atom bombs, which Israel already possesses.
Baghdad/Newsweek, 7-6:39.

Malcolm Kalp
Former American hostage in Iran

3

What's my view about them [Iranians]? Buy Iraqi war bonds, that's my view . . . Most of those people have just climbed down out of trees. They have no concept of Western civilization, of culture . . . I'd pay them back out of a B-52 bomber, that's one way I'd pay them back. I'd give them $8-billion worth of bombs.
To reporters, Wiesbaden, West Germany, Jan. 24/
The Washington Post, 1-25:(A)21.

Jack Kemp
United States Representative,
R—New York

4

[Addressing Secretary of State Alexander Haig, and saying the same standards of relationship with the Soviet Union—linkage to Soviet actions—should be applied to U.S. relations with Saudi Arabia]: [The Saudis] are opposed to Camp David, opposed to [Egyptian President Anwar] Sadat, have declared a *jihad* [holy war] against Israel. They are anti-Israel and anti-Egypt and also anti-United States. They are arming the PLO daily. What you say about the Soviets goes double for the Saudis.
At House Appropriations Subcommittee on
Foreign Operations hearing, Washington, April 28/
Los Angeles Times, 4-29:(I)7.

Abdul-Halim Khaddam
Foreign Minister of Syria

5

[On Israeli Prime Minister Menachem Begin's demand that Syria remove its anti-aircraft missiles from Lebanon]: We're ready to do battle if Begin translates his threats to deeds. The missiles will not be removed under Israeli or any other pressure . . . We reject the concept that Israel has any right to dictate security regulations in Lebanon or to control its skies.
Interview/Chicago Tribune, 5-6:(1)2.

Salah Khalef
Deputy to the chairman,
Palestinian Liberation Organization

1

[Calling for political pressure to force the U.S. to recognize and sympathize with Palestinian rights]: To us now, it's not a matter of putting a box of explosives to blow up an American building or something like that. What we mean are things like boycotting American products and stirring up Arab public opinion. When we talk about hitting at American interests, we don't mean grenades, only in political terms. We hope there will be a change in American policy toward us. As long as that policy has not changed, we will be hostile to the American Administration and its interests.

Interview, Beirut/
The New York Times, 4-28:4.

Khalid ibn Abdel Aziz
King of Saudi Arabia

2

Our loyalties must be neither to an Eastern bloc nor to a Western bloc. The security of the Islamic nation will not be assured by joining a military alliance nor by taking refuge under the umbrella of a superpower, but by our trust in God, our self-confidence and by a tightly woven unity.

At Islamic summit conference, Taif, Saudi Arabia,
Jan. 25/The Washington Post, 1-26:(A)6.

Khalid ibn Sultan
Director of Projects and Planning,
Army Air Defense Command of Saudi Arabia

3

We are aware that the raw materials of the Middle East and Africa have an essential importance to the Soviets and their allies. In the short term, they would like to control them to deprive the U.S. and the Western industrial nations of these vital resources. In the long term, they want them for themselves against the time when their own resources are diminishing. Unfortunately, my personal prediction is that we might be faced with the necessity of relying on these very people, with ideologies so foreign to us, because of the problems we face in the U.S. arms sales [such as the dispute in the U.S. over whether to sell AWACS planes to the Saudis].

Before Los Angeles World Affairs Council,
Sept. 10/Los Angeles Times, 9-11:(I)23.

Ruhollah Khomeini
Spiritual leader of Iran

4

The danger of Communism is not less than that of Western capitalism, and the Iranian nation should resist the conspiracies of both powers. Once again I remind you of the American danger in the world, especially in the region and in Iran. All those united against the Islamic Republic are linked with America.

Message read by his son on second anniversary
of the Iranian revolution, Teheran, Feb. 11/
Los Angeles Herald Examiner, 2-11:(A)4.

5

[Saying his country is a stable nation despite the recent rash of political assassinations]: Where else in the world would an assassinated prime minister be so quickly replaced? Where else would the power transition be so smooth? . . . Eight assassination attempts [have] been made on Presidents of the U.S.A., the biggest capitalist state, and four have been killed. If stability could be destroyed upon a President's assassination, then the U.S.A. should have lost its stability, too. [U.S. President] Reagan was attacked at the very outset when he took over. Well, the United States didn't plunge into chaos and should not have. Compare our country with other countries. Which country is more stable than ours? Where does another prime minister take over right after one is assassinated? . . . Iran is one of the most stable countries. The explosions and things like these show that it is stable. If it was unstable then these acts would not have taken place.

Addressing the government, Teheran,
Sept. 7/Chicago Tribune, 9-8:(1)1.

WHAT THEY SAID IN 1981

Jeane J. Kirkpatrick
*United States Ambassador/Permanent
Representative to the United Nations*

1

[On Israel's destruction of an Iraqi nuclear reactor]: It is precisely because of my government's deep involvement in efforts to promote peace in the Middle East that we were shocked by the Israeli air strike on the Iraqi nuclear facility and promptly condemned this action, which, we believe, both reflected and exacerbated deeper antagonisms in the region, which, if not ameliorated, will continue to lead to outbreaks of violence. However, although my government has condemned Israel's act, we know it is necessary to take into account the context of this action, as well as its consequences. The truth demands nothing less . . . I do think that one has to recognize that Israel has reason for concern, in view of the past history of Iraq, which has never signed a cease-fire or recognized Israel as a country . . . Nonetheless, we believe the means Israel chose to quiet its fears about the purposes of Iraq's nuclear program have hurt, and not helped, the peace and security of the area. In my government's view, diplomatic means available to Israel had not been exhausted and the Israeli action has damaged the regional confidence that is essential for the peace process to go forward. All of us with an interest in peace, freedom and national independence have a high stake in that process. Israel's stake is highest of all.

*At United Nations,
New York, June 19/
The New York Times, 6-20:4.*

Teddy Kollek
Mayor of Jerusalem

2

[On Jerusalem]: We are like ants constructing a beautiful anthill in the hope that no one will destroy it with a stick. But if that happens, we will build it beautifully again.

*World Press Review,
August:47.*

Bruce Laingen
*Former Charge d'Affairs,
United States Embassy, Teheran, Iran*

3

[On the current political system in Iran, under the Ayatollah Ruhollah Khomeini]: . . . it is a system that cannot endure. As presently constituted, it is incompatible with the requirements of a modern state. And to some extent, at least, Iran is that, thanks to the forced-draft efforts of the [late deposed] Shah to introduce and impose modernism on a state, on a society and on a culture that had a long way to go to reach the 20th century, in many respects. The [current] structure of government provided by the Islamic constitution is so complex as to be virtually impossible to implement in any effective, efficient manner. It has a built-in destiny for administrative inefficiency and lack of progress, out of which change is inevitable.

*Interview, Bethesda, Md./
The Washington Post, 3-1:(C)3.*

Paul N. McCloskey, Jr.
*United States Representative,
R—California*

4

[Saying that, although the Soviet Union could probably defeat the U.S. with conventional forces in the Persian Gulf area, the U.S. should be willing to use nuclear arms to defend that region]: . . . what we've got to make clear to the Russians is this: "You have to kill Americans if you're going to take this kind of military action; and if you kill Americans, we have the power and the ability for a nuclear response." That is the deterrent, the nuclear response following a conventional [-arms] defeat. The American people must show a clear determination to engage in both conventional and nuclear warfare to protect the Persian Gulf in order to prevent the danger of Soviet intrusion.

*Before Los Angeles World Affairs Council,
Feb. 26/Los Angeles Times, 2-27:(I)3.*

(PAUL N. McCLOSKEY, JR.)

1

. . . the Israeli lobby is the most powerful lobby in America today, more than the Mormon Church, the right-to-life people, the Moral Majority or the National Rifle Association. It has completely unbalanced our foreign policy . . . I fear we may be led into war by supporting everything that [Israeli Prime Minister Menachem] Begin does. We should speak out against him.

Interview/Los Angeles Times, 7-20:(I)15.

Francois Mitterrand
President of France

2

I am a friend of Israel, and I shall do nothing to endanger Israel's existence nor the means to exist. But I do not think it is realistic to pretend that the Palestinian problem does not exist. I know what their [Israel's] objection is: They say that they do not want an additional state in the Middle East. They would be prepared to envisage a Jordan-Palestinian solution, like before the Six-Day War when the West Bank was called Transjordan. I am not telling them what they should do, because I am in favor of bilateral negotiations between opponents. I am simply saying that it is normal that the Palestinians should have a homeland where they will build, as they please, the structures of a state. I remain the friend of the Israeli leaders because I have always been very frank with them and they know that I would not pursue policies which would harm them.

Interview, Paris, June 1/
The New York Times, 6-4:6.

3

[Criticizing Israel for destroying an Iraqi nuclear reactor]: Even though there is a latent state of war between Iraq and Israel, it is not acceptable for a country, however just its cause, to settle its disputes by military intervention, which is patently contrary to international law. I can only express my reprobation for [Israeli Prime Minister Menachem] Begin's initiative. Of course, I would consider the matter differently if it were shown that Israel were in real and present danger because of the possible diversion by Iraq of nuclear technology for military purposes. But that has not been demonstrated, to say the least . . . I have very warm feelings about the historical achievements of Israel and about its culture. I know the magnitude of its sacrifices. I admire the abilities of its people and I want to guarantee its existence, its means of existence. Mr. Begin might have noticed as much. Yet, the first thing he did was reduce the accumulated capital of confidence. Too bad. That will not change my opinion on the fundamentals. I remain true to my options. When we asked for condemnation [of Israel for the raid] at the Security Council . . . we condemn the raid, not Israel. We criticize the action of its leaders. We do not request sanctions against its people. And we remain open for any friendly agreement, any peaceful settlement, for anything that will contribute to good relations with Israel in the context of respect for basic principles.

Interview, Paris, June 16/
The Washington Post, 6-18:(A)21.

Khalid Mohieddin
Leader, National Progressive Unionist Party of Egypt

4

[On Egyptian President Anwar Sadat's arrest of religious extremists and leftist and rightist opposition figures]: By doing this, the President is not going to the roots of the problem but [is] trying to use this opportunity to fight national opposition elements in the country. This will not serve either political stability, democracy or the spirit of the rule of law. Everyone who reads the names of the detainees will understand the aim of the campaign.

Interview/
The Washington Post, 9-4:(A)20.

Ali Akbar Moinfar
Former Minister of Petroleum
of Iran

1

Criticizing the increasing hold on the country by spiritual leader Ruhollah Khomeini and his party]: If today the single-party system is not resisted, we must wait for a severe and dreadful dictatorship like those of the Communist countries but with an Islamic color and flavor; and getting rid of it will be far more difficult than getting rid of the monarchist regime [of the late Shah].

Before the Majlis (Parliament), Teheran/
The Washington Post, 6-21:(A)18.

Daniel P. Moynihan
United States Senator,
D—New York

2

[Criticizing the U.S. Reagan Administration's plans to sell AWACS planes to Saudi Arabia]: This is a tragic decision the Administration has made . . . It is just the worst kind of arms system to introduce into the Middle East, which has too many arms as it is. In 1977, when Iran seemed a stable ally, the Carter Administration proposed to sell seven AWACS to Iran—to the Shah. The Congress said no, don't do it . . . Now, if we weren't willing to sell to Iran at that time—and how wise we were [since the Shah was later deposed]—how about the Saudis? The Saudis are certainly a friendly country, a country whose defense we must assist. That's why we have four AWACS there now in Saudi airspace . . . The difference is that we are operating them. And if the Saudis need this kind of information, fine; we can give it to them. I see no reason in the world why we shouldn't have such airplanes in that part of the world. But if they were given to a country such as Saudi Arabia, which in all the preceding wars against Israel has never been able to contribute any arms to the other Arab countries because it hasn't had any . . . this time, with this kind of equipment . . . they will have to . . . join them.

TV interview/
The Washington Post, 9-6:(C)6.

Hosni Mubarak
Vice President of Egypt

3

I think you can feel democracy yourself here in Egypt. We are still correcting the concept of an opposition. To me an opposition should be for the sake of the country and the people and not just for itself. An opposition should analyze a project, see its pros and cons, come out with a better alternative before opposing any project. Opposition for the sake of opposition will not help anybody. We have only been practicing democracy for three or four years and it's a matter of time to fully understand it. We are putting together the pieces for a mature democracy in our country. It is going to take some time.

Interview, Cairo, July 15/
The Washington Post, 10-11:(C)4.

4

[On the Arab world's view of the Camp David agreement between his country and Israel]: Believe me, most Arabs, especially the moderate ones, are not against our initiative, because all of us agree on this treaty. We never differ. Only the rejectionist camp, which contains Syria, Libya, Algeria, Iraq and South Yemen. They have very strong influence and threaten other Arab countries to freeze their relations with Egypt. But most Arab countries, excluding this rejectionist camp, have no objections to our initiative. They are fed up with this [Arab-Israeli] problem. They also want to live. They want to stop spending money on arms for Syria and those other places. It is a very good thing for Syria to keep this problem alive and to take money from the oil-rich Arab world.

Interview, Cairo, July 15/
The Washington Post, 10-11:(C)4.

Hosni Mubarak
President of Egypt

5

[Criticizing those in the U.S. who oppose selling AWACS planes to Saudi Arabia]: The only thing I'm critical of with the [U.S. Reagan] Administration is the AWACS. Why don't you

(HOSNI MUBARAK)

give them to the Saudis? They are your closest friends. They raised their production of oil for you . . . Then, you don't give them the AWACS to defend their country and your interests in this area. This policy should make all your friends have a big question when you refuse this to your closest friend. What are you going to do with your other friends, then?

Interview/Los Angeles Times, 10-12:(I)17.

1

[On his policies as he takes over from the assassinated Egyptian President Anwar Sadat]: To all those who exploit the freedom of the people, I say the fire of the people is stronger, and the supremacy and respect of the law is above all. To all those who think of violence and greed, none of them will escape severe punishment. We shall not turn our back on our decisions, for Egypt is and shall remain stable . . . Camp David [accord between Egypt and Israel], and the peace with Israel, will continue in all its letter and commitment. We shall continue the autonomy negotiations to put the Palestinians on the beginning of the road to get their lawful rights. Brothers and sisters, our loss [of Sadat] is catastrophic; our situation is critical. But we shall not surrender. We will remain loyal to our principles. We will build and not destroy; we shall protect and not threaten; we will safeguard and not squander.

Inaugural address, Cairo, Oct. 14/
The New York Times, 10-15:4.

Behzad Navabi
Minister for Executive Affairs
of Iran

2

[On the just-signed agreement between the U.S. and Iran freeing 52 American hostages held by Iran]: We managed to run in the dirt the nose of the world's biggest oppressor and superpower, thus forcing it to submit to the demands of our Majlis [Parliament]. Obviously, it was very difficult to lay the ground for this, and in certain cases we encountered stiff resistance. However, with God's help and the people's assistance, we managed to face up to them [the U.S.] and break their resistance.

Radio address to the nation, Teheran, Jan. 19/
Chicago Tribune, 1-20:(1)10.

Hisham Nazer
Minister of Planning of Saudi Arabia

3

[On whether a government overthrow, such as happened in Iran when the Shah was deposed, could happen in his country]: The problems in Iran weren't caused by economic development, but by the lack of it. Iran had a huge navy, but no houses. [Saudi Arabia has tried] to create a middle class, [which is] the basis for political stability. [The typical Saudi] is a person who didn't have a house; now he has a house. He didn't have a school; now he has a school. He didn't have a job; now he has a job. Do you think this person will want to upset the system?

Interview, Taif, Saudi Arabia/
The Wall Street Journal, 1-30:23.

Robert G. Neumann
Former United States Ambassador
to Saudi Arabia

4

[On U.S. Reagan Administration plans to sell AWACS planes to Saudi Arabia]: . . . the real meaning of the AWACS is a closer collaboration between America and Saudi Arabia. Saudi Arabia has only 5 million people or a 1-million manpower pool—out of which come the total requirements for the military, the administration, business and the professions. There is no way in which Saudi Arabia could have a very large military force of any kind. So the key to the situation is American and Saudi forces working closely together. That also means that the equipment has to be compatible. The Saudis have made it clear that if we do not sell the AWACS to them, they will go to the British system.

Interview/Los Angeles Herald Examiner, 9-7:(A)9.

WHAT THEY SAID IN 1981

Richard M. Nixon
Former President of the United States

1

[On opposition in the U.S. to the sale of AWACS planes to Saudi Arabia]: We know, the Saudis know, and everyone in the Middle East knows that if it were not for the intense opposition by [Israeli Prime Minister] Begin and parts of the American Jewish community, the AWACS sale would go through. This is a cold fact that opponents of the sale, whatever their own particular reasons, must take into account.

The New York Times, 10-6:4.

Michael Novak
*Chief United States Delegate to
United Nations Commission
on Human Rights*

2

Human rights mean respect for human beings, recognition of each other's dignity. They mean cooperation, mutuality, negotiation. They mean the voice of reason. Yet in my first days within this Commission, imagine my shock when I heard, as I did in this room, so much hatred, so many lies, such squalid racism, such despicable anti-Semitism—all in the sacred name of human rights.

*At UN Human Rights Commission debate on
Israeli policy in occupied Arab territories,
Geneva, Feb. 6/The Wall Street Journal, 3-18:22.*

Bob Packwood
United States Senator, R—Oregon

3

[Arguing against the sale by the U.S. of AWACS planes to Saudi Arabia]: I went back and reread the arguments of the 1978 debate [in the Senate about the sale of F-15 fighter planes to the Saudis, which was approved]. I was struck by how we were told again and again at that time that we had to agree to the sale because it would make Saudi Arabia a moderating influence in the Arab world and induce it to help the Middle East peace process. When I began to analyze it, I asked myself what had they really

done for peace in the time since except to denounce the Camp David [Egyptian-Israeli] accords, break relations with Egypt and finance the Palestine Liberation Organization. They've done everything they could to wreck the peace process. *We* passed the test of U.S.-Saudi relations in 1978, and we've not had in return a Saudi commitment to the peace process. Until we do, I don't want to sell them any more equipment. It's as simple as that.

*Interview, Washington/
The Washington Post, 10-18:(A)7.*

Amos Perlmutter
*Professor of political science and
sociology, American University, Washington*

4

[On U.S.-Iranian relations following the recent release of 52 American hostages held by Iran]: Iran's political and territorial integrity is vastly more important than our quarrels with any specific regime. That means we must sit with whatever regime is in power in Teheran. We should draw distinctions between the regime, which we detest, and the territory itself. In that respect, we have to isolate the mullahs somewhat and assist moderate forces that may eventually replace them. But even before that happens, we have a major role to play. One day, there will be a regime in Teheran that will bring back stability and reason to the nation. Until then, potential dismemberment of Iran constitutes the greatest single political, military and economic threat that America faces today . . . Iran is the most strategic piece of real estate in the Middle East, commanding the entire Persian Gulf. It is imperative that neither the Soviet Union nor Iraq [which is currently at war with Iran] have an opportunity to carve it up.

Interview/U.S. News & World Report, 2-2:35.

Muammar el-Qaddafi
Chief of State of Libya

5

Escalating the [Arab] national counterattack against U.S. imperialism, represented in the form of American military bases in Egypt,

(MUAMMAR el-QADDAFI)

Somalia, Oman and Palestine, means we have to establish bridges with the liberation movements in these countries and prepare to fight together against this imperialist tide . . . In fact, we have established bridges with the Omani liberation movement and the national salvation front of Somalia, and we should be prepared to give them all the aid they ask for to fight along their side against America and these foreign imperialist bases.

Before Libyan revolutionary committees/
The Washington Post, 3-6:(A)19.

Yitzhak Rabin
Member of Israeli Knesset (Parliament);
Former Prime Minister of Israel

1

[On the assassination of Egyptian President Anwar Sadat]: . . . [former U.S. President Jimmy] Carter contributed to the downfall of the Shah [of Iran], and the [U.S.] Reagan Administration contributed to the downfall of Sadat. The same way as Carter by his insistence on human rights undermined the regime of the Shah, in the present [Reagan] Administration one can detect clear signs of moving away from the Camp David [Israeli-Egyptian] agreements. The United States did not show interest in the implementation of several aspects of the agreements, including the autonomy talks . . . The Camp David agreements are in abeyance, and the American Administration moved its emphasis from Egypt to Saudi Arabia instead of worrying about autonomy [for Palestinians on the West Bank]. There is no doubt in my mind that this shift in emphasis weakened Sadat's position in the Arab world as well as inside Egypt.

Oct. 6/Los Angeles Times, 10-7:(I)4.

Massoud Rajavi
Exiled leader of Iranian Mujahedin
(opposition to current Iranian regime)

2

For us, nothing is more valuable than independence. This means that we don't want to be independent only of the U.S., Britain, France or Iraq, but also of other foreigners—including the Soviets. It has been a general reality in Iran that we have been under the historical domination of America for 25 years. Will people forget this? No. But that does not mean the Mujahedin wants to gain independence from the U.S. and sell it to the Soviet Union.

Interview, Auvers-sur-Oise, France/
Time, 9-14:45.

Ari Rath
Editor and managing director,
"Jerusalem Post"

3

[The Camp David framework] is the only positive Middle East development in the past 30 years, and today the Egyptian-Israeli relationship has a global dimension. Take the most recent near-clash on the Syrian border. One of the main reasons the Syrians finally decided not to pursue this—not even to the point of a skirmish with Jordan—is that neither Israel nor Egypt would have tolerated it. Camp David will not only survive; it will have to expand to take in Jordan and to get the blessings of the Saudis.

Interview, New York/
World Press Review, February:28.

Ronald Reagan
President of the United States

4

I think that we have . . . a moral commitment for the present to see that the state of Israel has a right to continue living as a nation. I believe that, and think that we're morally bound to that. But beyond that, I think it's also a two-way street. I think that Israel, being a country sharing our same ideals, I think democratic approach to things, with a combat-ready and even a combat-experienced military, is a force in the Middle East that actually is of benefit to us. But I also feel that morally the United States should do everything it can, in an even-

(RONALD REAGAN)

handed manner, to bring peace to the Middle East. Now this, based on our first commitment, means that we have to get over the hurdle of those nations in the Middle East that refuse to recognize the right of Israel to exist. Peace will come when that first step is taken. Now, a few of them have—as Egypt did, and [Egyptian President] Sadat, who I think is one of the great statesmen for doing that. As to the West Bank, I believe the [Israeli] settlements there—I disagreed when the previous [U.S. Carter] Administration referred to them as illegal; they're not illegal. Not under the UN resolution that leaves the West Bank open to all people—Arab and Israeli alike, Christian alike. I do think, perhaps, now with this rush to do it and this moving in there the way they [the Israelis] are, is ill-advised because if we're going to continue with the spirit of Camp David to try and arrive at a peace, maybe this, at this time, is unnecessarily provocative.

Interview, Washington, Feb. 2/
The New York Times, 2-23:6.

1

Israel and America may be thousands of miles apart but we are philosophical neighbors sharing a strong commitment to democracy and the rule of law. What we hold in common are the bonds of trust and friendship—qualities that in our eyes make Israel a great nation. No people have fought longer, struggled harder or sacrificed more than yours in order to survive, to grow, and to live in freedom. The United States and Israel share similar beginnings as nations of immigrants, yearning to live in freedom and to fulfill the dreams of our forefathers. We know Israelis live in constant peril. But Israel will have our help. She will remain strong and secure and her special character of spirit, genius and faith will prevail.

Addressing Israeli Prime Minister Menachem Begin
on his visit to Washington, Sept. 9/
The New York Times, 9-10:4.

2

[Defending his proposal to sell AWACS planes to Saudi Arabia]: By building confidence in the United States as a reliable security partner, the sale will greatly improve the chances of our working constructively with Saudi Arabia and other states of the Middle East toward our common goal—a just and lasting peace. It poses no threat to Israel, now or in the future. Indeed, by contributing to the security and stability of the region, it serves Israel's long-range interests. Further, this sale will significantly improve the capability of Saudi Arabia and the United States to defend the oil fields on which the security of the free world depends ... An objective assessment of U.S. national interest must favor the proposed sale. And I say this as one who holds strongly the view that both a secure state of Israel and a stable Mideast peace are essential to our national interests.

News conference, Washington, Oct. 1/
The New York Times, 10-2:10.

3

I have to say that Saudi Arabia we will not permit to be an Iran [where the government was forcefully overthrown] ... There is no way, as long as Saudi Arabia and the OPEC nations there in the East, and Saudi Arabia's the most important, provide the bulk of the energy that is needed to turn the wheels of industry in the Western world—there's no way that we could stand by and see that taken over by anyone that would shut off that oil.

News conference, Washington, Oct. 1/
The Washington Post, 10-2:(A)12.

4

[On assassinated Egyptian President Anwar Sadat]: Anwar Sadat, a man of peace in a time of violence, understood his age. In his final moments, he, as he had all during his days, stood in defiance of the enemies of peace, the enemies of humanity. [To those enemies of peace] who rejoice in the death of Anwar Sadat: In life, you feared Anwar Sadat, but in death you must fear him more; for the memory of this good and brave

(RONALD REAGAN)

man will vanquish you. The meaning of his life and the cause for which he stood will endure and triumph.

Washington, Oct. 8/
The New York Times, 10-9:7.

Anwar el-Sadat
President of Egypt

1

[On the 1978 Camp David agreement between Egypt and Israel]: No one has the right to detract from it or obstruct its path. We shall not allow any interference with that sacred process, for it has become an invaluable part of the heritage of mankind.

Before European Parliament, Luxembourg,
Feb. 10/Los Angeles Times, 2-11:(I)15.

2

[Criticizing Syrian President Hafez Assad for increasing Syria's military intervention in Lebanon]: Today he is not placing Lebanon alone, but Lebanon and the Arab world and the whole of the Middle East in a cyclone. And nobody knows how this will end up. Israel got involved four or five days ago. Who opened the gates? The deeds of the Syrians and the [indifferent] attitude of the Arab world and the leaders of Lebanon. We all as Arabs are responsible for that. This opened the gates for the Israelis . . . Let's take a united Arab position and save our reputation as Arabs. Today the Arab name is in the mud; it is at its lowest ebb.

Cairo, May 2/The New York Times, 5-3:(1)3.

3

[On Egypt and Israel's cooperation over the last few years]: We had to demonstrate that peace between the Arab states and Israel, peace between the Palestinians and the Israelis, is not only possible, but it is the only rational option. Today, peace has become the strongest reality in the Middle East, no matter what roadblocks we have to surmount, because the formidable

barriers of fear and distrust have started to crack. [Now] we are asking all nations of the world to talk to the Palestinian people and their representatives, endorsing every cease-fire and encouraging a more stable Middle East, telling both the Palestinian people and the Israeli people that they should sit together and talk together to settle their problems without shooting out their grievances.

At Georgetown University, Washington, Aug. 8/
The New York Times, 8-9:(1)6.

4

[Egypt will] give every facility the United States would need to reach any Arab Moslem state in case of any emergency, because I don't want to see repeated what happened in Afghanistan [the Soviet invasion of that country]. This is a crucial commitment, because Egypt is the middle of the world between three continents: Africa, Asia and Europe. It means that the United States will have every facility to reach every country from Egypt to as far as Indonesia.

Interview, Washington/
San Francisco Examiner & Chronicle, 8-16:(A)23.

5

[On his crackdown on religious and other opponents of his policies]: From now on I shall have no mercy. There can be no half solutions because the issue now is Egypt, its safety, its image and its unity . . . This is not religion, this is obscenity. These are lies, criminal use of religious power to misguide people. We shall not tolerate that any more. The time has come for firm and decisive action . . . All who have participated, encouraged, directly or indirectly helped, or in any way been involved, be they lawyers, journalists, academics, politicians or religious leaders, I shall have no mercy on them—never.

Before Parliament, Cairo,
Sept. 5/
San Francisco Examiner & Chronicle,
9-6:(A)1,24.

Nadav Safran
Professor of government,
Harvard University

1

The potential sources of destabilization in Saudi Arabia grow out of the fact that Saudi society is undergoing a massive social transformation in a very short time . . . No society has gone through that kind of transformation without an upheaval. But the historical record also shows that such an upheaval can take generations to materialize. Saudi Arabia can go on for 10 to 15 years without problems—and it can blow up tomorrow.

The New York Times, 10-18:(1)12.

Pierre Salinger
Correspondent, ABC News

2

[On the recent release of 52 American hostages held by Iran for more than a year]: Why did so many efforts to free the hostages fail? What was the underlying reason that the nation many considered to be the most powerful on earth could not convince a nation in revolutionary distress to hand back its diplomats? The reasons are multiple and fundamental . . . there is no evidence, even today, that people in the United States government ever really understood the mentality and motivations of Iran. As a corollary to that, there is no evidence, either, that the leaders of Iran understood the United States. The dialogue between the United States and Iran represented a massive culture gap. We based our thinking on traditional Judeo-Christian tenets. And what we professed was a respect for international laws. But in the eyes of the Iranians, international law was a creature of the West . . . But misunderstanding was not the only reason for failure. There were other vital causes for the constant disappointment in the hostage negotiations. With only a few small exceptions, the American government spent most of its time trying to get the hostages out by negotiating with the very people in Iran who could not release them . . . There are those in America who believe that the United States should have walked away from the hostage

crisis. They point out that the Iranians are used to haggling in the bazaar. And their argument is that it takes two to haggle. And if the Americans had refused to deal, the Iranians would have come running after them. But the Americans are not used to the idea of sacrificing human life. And this negotiating tactic would have been unacceptable to the majority of the American people. So we negotiated. And in the end, we freed the hostages. Their return home was a victory of the human spirit, but not a victory for America.

Television broadcast/Chicago Tribune, 2-2:(1)7.

Elias Sarkis
President of Lebanon

3

[Calling for a curb to PLO military activity in his country]: The activists of the Palestine resistance from the land of Lebanon alone provide Israel with an opportunity to intensify its attacks on the south of Lebanon—when it wishes and in the manner it wishes—while the world stands impotent. Can we continue to be observers . . . [of] such a situation, which could destroy the south of Lebanon, indeed Lebanon itself, in addition to the fact that there is intimidation by the Palestinian military presence in violation of its commitments toward Lebanon?

At meeting of Organization of the Islamic Conference,
Taif, Saudi Arabia, Jan. 28/
Los Angeles Times, 1-29:(I)5.

Saud al-Faisal
Foreign Minister of Saudi Arabia

4

[Criticizing Israel's recent destruction of an Iraqi nuclear reactor]: What would be the state of the world if the United States and the Soviet Union could act as Israel? Israel is more capable militarily [than other Middle East countries]. Now they don't want Arabs to have defensive weapons. Soon we will find that the concept of Israeli security means they will bomb a university in Saudi Arabia on the logic

(SAUD al-FAISAL)

that a scientist there could make weapons to attack Israel.

American broadcast interview, Jidda, Saudi Arabia/
"Issues and Answers," ABC-TV, 6-14.

Helmut Schmidt
Chancellor of West Germany

1

Germans who themselves are seeking national self-determination cannot allow themselves not to recognize the demand for the self-determination of the Palestinians. The Palestinians are not the only ones [in the Middle East] who throw bombs.

Broadcast interview, April/
Los Angeles Times, 5-4:(I)17.

2

For me it is a tragedy of Greek proportions that after 2,000 years the Jews were finally again able to found their own state [Israel] and that it doesn't seem possible to consolidate and secure it in understanding with its [Arab] neighbors. Some day the Israelis have to recognize that the Palestinians have the right to decide about their own future, about who is to represent them. No one but the Palestinians themselves can decide this. And if they should form a state, or decide to do so, they would at least have to decide about that. They must have the right to organization as a state. And some day the Palestinians have to recognize that the Israelis, like any other people in the world, also have the right to live as a state within recognized, secure borders. And if the two of them would only approach each other with the awareness that they both have ahead of them something to recognize about the other, then a great deal would be gained. But so far they haven't even recognized each other as partners in a dialogue.

West German broadcast interview, April 30/
The Christian Science Monitor, 5-7:4.

Herbert Scoville, Jr.
President, Arms Control Association;
Former Assistant Director, Arms Control and
Disarmament Agency of the United States

3

[On Israel's recent destruction of an Iraqi nuclear reactor]: There's no question in my mind the Iraqis were trying to build up the capability of having a nuclear weapon, and obviously that's a terrible thing. We should do everything we can to stop it. But [what Israel did] is not the way to do it. That's just madness. If anything, it's going to make matters much worse. Here are the Israelis, whose hands certainly aren't clean in this particular area. Everything I know makes me believe they have nuclear weapons of their own. And [for them] to sit there and say, "We have the right to destroy any nuclear installation of yours which is potentially a weapons installation," is just asking for retaliation back.

Interview/The Washington Post, 6-14:(A)3.

Yitzhak Shamir
Foreign Minister of Israel

4

Saudi Arabia does not deserve the title of "moderate." This state has participated in all the wars against Israel. It orchestrated the conference which declared *jihad* [holy war] against us. It is the major financier of Palestine Liberation Organization terrorism. It worked persistently and aggressively against the peace process.

The Washington Post, 3-24:(A)17.

5

[On Israel's destruction of an Iraqi nuclear reactor]: The decision to destroy that reactor was taken only when it became absolutely clear that Iraq was on the verge of producing nuclear bombs, the principal target of which would have been Israel. People in all parts of the world, including the Middle East, are sleeping more soundly today, secure in the knowledge that this particular reactor has been removed. [The reactor] had to be destroyed before

325

WHAT THEY SAID IN 1981

it was to become operational in the summer of 1981, for its destruction at a later date would have brought about radioactive fallout endangering the civilian population of Baghdad.

At United Nations, New York, Oct. 1/
Los Angeles Times, 10-2:(I)4.

Hisham Sharabi
Professor of history,
Georgetown University

1

The United States is seen by more and more people in the Arab world as cynical, manipulative and coercive. They see it as treating the area and its people only in terms of its own interests and in terms of its anti-Soviet crusade, with hardly any regard to the aspirations and interests of people involved. The United States today may have many friends among the ruling elites of the Arab world, but it has less and less friends among the Arab people. Some Arabs wonder whether it is an accident that the stereotyping of Arabs in the American media grows daily more aggressive and that the public attitude toward everything Arab becomes more and more hostile. How is one to explain U.S. alliance, presumably to protect American interests in the world itself, with the occupier of Arab lands [Israel]? How is one to account for the lionization of precisely the one Arab leader whom Arabs almost universally regard as a Quisling [Egyptian President Anwar Sadat]?

At symposium sponsored by Georgetown University's
Center for Contemporary Arab Studies/
The Christian Science Monitor, 7-27:22.

Ariel Sharon
Minister of Defense of Israel

2

I believe that the starting point for a solution [to the Palestinian problem] is to establish a Palestinian state in the part of Palestine that was separated from [what was to become] Israel in 1922 and which is now Jordan. Some 80 per cent of the population of Jordan is Palestinian.

Most of the prominent members of the government are Palestinian Arabs—the same Arabs who are living in Galilee, in Nazareth, in Haifa. The only strangers are the members of the Hashemite Kingdom [ruled by King Hussein] . . . I don't mean that if we had a Palestinian state in Jordan we would have good neighbors. There would be bitter conflict, but the conflict would be over territory, not over the right [of Palestinians] to exist as a nation. King Hussein is not a partner in the Camp David talks. I don't mind who takes over Jordan.

Interview/Time, 10-5:33.

3

[Criticizing the U.S. Senate vote to approve the sale of AWACS planes to Saudi Arabia]: AWACS is part of a bigger problem, that of the supply of sophisticated American arms to Arab countries. The United States is supplying weapons to Iraq . . . They don't do it directly; they supply them through the Saudis and the Jordanians. The fact they are supplying these very sophisticated weapons puts us in a very difficult situation. They say the United States must supply weapons to the Arabs. We will accept that. But why must they be the most sophisticated weapons?

Before United Israel Appeal, Oct. 28/
Los Angeles Times, 10-29:(I)7.

Saaheddin Shazli
Exiled leader, Egyptian National Front

4

[On Egypt's new President Hosni Mubarak, who succeeded the assassinated Anwar Sadat]: We will use violence to topple Mubarak. We will continue . . . until we topple that regime and establish democracy . . . Our main target is the establishment of democracy, by which I mean parliamentary government where the President has very, very limited powers, and the real power is vested in the party leader who gets a majority in Parliament.

News conference, Tripoli, Libya,
Oct. 12/
The Washington Post, 10-14:(A)20.

William H. Sullivan
Former United States Ambassador
to Iran

1

[On U.S.-Iran relations now that Iran has freed 52 American hostages it had held for over a year]: Clearly, the Soviets' intention is to drive as sharp a wedge as they can between the United States and Iran and at the same time try to enfeeble the Iranian nation. The irony is that, despite the outrage the U.S. feels toward Iran, it is in our national interest to preserve the territorial integrity of the nation. I would not expect the Soviets to militarily attack Iran like they have Afghanistan, but I am sure they are already busy agitating tribal factions against Teheran.

Interview/The Christian Science Monitor, 1-22:10.

Ghassan Tueni
Lebanese Ambassador/Permanent
Representative to the United Nations

2

[On Israel's recent bombing of Iraq's nuclear reactor]: Condemnation [of Israel] is not sufficient. The international community, and America in particular, must find it possible to put an end to Israel's license and sentiment of impunity. Israel, not the atom, must be harnessed for peace.

At United Nations, New York, June 15/
Los Angeles Times, 6-16:(I)11.

Caspar W. Weinberger
Secretary of Defense
of the United States

3

The umbilical cord of the industrialized free world runs through the Strait of Hormuz into the Arabian Gulf and the nations which surround it. That area [because of its importance in the shipping of Middle East crude oil], Southwest Asia and the Gulf, is and will be the fulcrum of contention for the foreseeable future. The Soviet Union will almost certainly become a net energy importer. This, coupled with their economic necessity for eventual access to the Gulf oil basin, is their long-range objective of denying access to oil by the West. We cannot deter that effort from seven thousand miles away. We have to be there. We have to be there in a credible way.

Before Senate Armed Services Committee,
Washington, March 4/
The New York Times, 3-5:10.

John C. West
United States Ambassador to
Saudi Arabia

4

[Saying U.S.-Saudi Arabia relations could suffer if a way is not found to include the PLO in Middle East peace talks]: We've got to find a basis for the participation of the Palestinian people, including the PLO, if we are going to get a realistic possibility of solving the Palestinian problem. I think we have been engaged in a holding action and our time has run out. As of now, [U.S.-Saudi relations are] as good a relationship as it has ever been. But it is a very tense and tenuous relationship. That creates a real problem for [U.S. President] Reagan and his Administration. Frankly, [the Saudis] are waiting for the new Administration to take some steps to solve the two basic issues of Middle East peace [the Palestinian problem and the status of Jerusalem]. If the Reagan Administration doesn't do that, then for a variety of reasons, some of which the Saudis themselves can't control, the relationship is going to deteriorate, and it could deteriorate very quickly and very badly.

Interview, Jidda, Saudi Arabia/
Los Angeles Times, 1-30:(I)9.

5

Can [an Iran-style revolution] repeat itself here in the Kingdom [of Saudi Arabia]? My answer would be no. The culture here is stronger than most people give it credit for, and although modernization has brought strains and tensions, the system has been flexible enough to adjust to the tensions of the times. There is a commitment here to stability, tradition and continuity.

The New York Times, 3-25:6.

WHAT THEY SAID IN 1981

Ahmed Zaki al-Yamani
Minister of Petroleum and
Minerals of Saudi Arabia

1

[On why his country has been a moderate in the OPEC block when it comes to increasing the prices of its oil exports]: . . . raising prices with no controls or restraints would not have been in favor of certain OPEC countries and specifically Saudi Arabia. If we were to force the Western countries to invest large sums of money in alternative energy resources, it would take seven to 10 years to bring about some results of these investments, which would reduce oil demand to a level that would affect Saudi Arabia, which at that time would not find enough markets to sell its oil to meet its economic demands. Other countries have a clear interest in obtaining the largest possible income in dollars for each barrel for the short period it can sell for . . . If I were an Algerian, I would no doubt wish that the price of oil today reach $100 a barrel—even if I brought the world economy down. Because no matter what happens to the world, they must buy this oil from me regardless of how much I encourage them to look for alternative energy sources, because these alternatives will not be achieved for at least 10 years, and at that time I don't care . . . [But] the interest of the Kingdom of Saudi Arabia is that we extend the life of oil to the largest extent possible to allow us to build our economy in the most diversified manner, including industry and agriculture.

At University of Petroleum and Minerals,
Dhahran, Saudi Arabia, January/
The Christian Science Monitor, 2-5:6.

2

We believe that the Soviets are a threat [in the Middle East], but we believe that the Israelis are a threat much greater than the Soviet threat. We believe that the Israelis are the entry of the Soviets to our area. If you solve the [Arab-Israeli] problem and enforce peace in the area, by this you stop the Soviets from their invasion, the way they are doing it so far . . . The real security for the Israelis is peace. We are ready for that. We

are asking for this. We are dying to get it. It's only their arrogance which is stopping the whole thing, and we hope something might change in the future. We are extending our hands for that . . . We don't want anything more than [what the UN Security Council resolutions call for]. And those resolutions call for the withdrawal [by Israel] from the occupied territories, including Jerusalem, and the identity of the Palestinians to solve their problem and give them their self-determination right. When this happens, I think everybody will be happy. Peace will prevail, and the Israelis will live a different type of life, as a nation living there forever.

American broadcast interview/
"Meet the Press," NBC-TV, 4-19.

Zayed bin Sultan al-Nuhayan
President of the United Arab Emirates

3

Our conception of [Persian] Gulf security is one in which the countries of the Gulf are allowed to live peacefully and securely without interference from foreign powers, and without the great powers trying to determine the area's fate . . . The central role which Western and other countries can play to ensure stability in the Gulf and in the Middle East lies in their work toward a just and lasting solution to the Palestinian issue and in putting an end to the continuing Zionist [Israeli] aggression against Palestine and Lebanon.

Interview, May/
The Christian Science Monitor, 5-26:10.

Mordechai Zipori
Deputy Minister of Defense
of Israel

4

[Criticizing the U.S. plans to sell AWACS planes to Saudi Arabia]: It is a very, very unpleasant decision. Israel will fight it, as it has in the past and will in the future, by appealing to the [U.S. Reagan] Administration and the American public . . . We are reaching a stage where the burden is becoming too heavy to bear. We would have expected a little more

(MORDECHAI ZIPORI)

understanding from friends on matters that could harm our defense capability.

Israeli radio interview, April 22/
Chicago Tribune, 4-23:(1)2.

1

[Criticizing U.S. suspension of delivery of four F-16 fighter-bombers to his country because of Israel's recent bombing of Iraq's nuclear reactor]: Every partnership is based on an agreement which each side reads as it wishes. It is clear that the state of Israel, and certainly its defense establishment, is not happy with the decision taken by the United States. We tend to view this more as a lack of understanding, which, after the matter has been explained, will see the previous situation restored. Relations between the United States and the state of Israel are above and beyond such mishaps . . . Israel doesn't equip itself with any weapons for parading purposes. All the weapons that we possess are for

the purpose of defending the state of Israel. And what constitutes the defense of the state of Israel shall be determined only by the government of Israel, and not by any other state, not even the most friendly one.

Radio interview, Jerusalem, June 11/
The New York Times, 6-12:1.

Edward Zorinsky
United States Senator, D—Nebraska

2

[On whether he should vote for or against President Reagan's plan to sell AWACS planes to Saudi Arabia]: I feel that on the facts and on the merits, the vote should be in opposition to the sale. But underlying all that is the ability of a President of a country to be able to conduct [foreign] policy in the future with the support of his own people and also of the Congress of the United States. And that's what concerns me. Am I contributing [by a "no" vote] to the removal of his ability to do just that?

To reporters, Washington, Oct. 28/
The Washington Post, 10-29:(A)4.

War and Peace

Leonid I. Brezhnev
President of the Soviet Union;
General Secretary,
Soviet Communist Party

1

[Denying U.S. President Reagan's charge that the Soviet Union believes a nuclear war can be won]: [The] thoughts and efforts of the Soviet leadership, just as of the Soviet people as a whole, are directed at preventing nuclear war altogether, at eliminating the very danger of its outbreak. It is dangerous madness to try to defeat each other in the arms race and to count on victory in nuclear war . . . if there is no first nuclear strike, then consequently there will be no second or third nuclear strikes. Thereby, all talk about the possibility or impossibility of victory in nuclear war will become pointless. The question of nuclear war as such will be removed from the agenda of the day.

Interview/Chicago Tribune, 10-21:(1)8.

Jimmy Carter
President of the United States

2

It's now been 35 years since the first atomic bomb fell on Hiroshima. The great majority of the world's people cannot remember a time when the nuclear shadow did not hang over the earth. Our minds have adjusted to it . . . Yet the risk of a nuclear conflagration has not lessened . . . The danger is becoming greater. As the arsenals of the superpowers grow in size and sophistication and as other governments—perhaps even, in the future, dozens of governments—acquire these weapons, it may only be a matter of time before madness, desperation, greed or miscalculation lets loose this terrible force.

Farewell address to the nation, Washington, Jan. 14/U.S. News & World Report, 1-26:34.

Yi Chazov
Director-general, National
Cardiology Research Center, Moscow

3

Some of the military, public functionaries and even scientists are trying to diminish the danger of the nuclear arms race, to minimize the possible consequences of a nuclear war. Statements appear that a nuclear war can be won, that a limited nuclear war can be waged, that humanity and the biosphere will still persist even in conditions of total nuclear catastrophe. This is an illusion which many of them do not believe themselves and which must be dispersed.

At Congress of International Physicians for the Prevention of Nuclear War, Warrenton, Va., March 20/The New York Times, 3-21:8.

Alexander M. Haig, Jr.
Secretary of State-designate
of the United States

4

There are more important things than peace. There are things that Americans should be willing to fight for . . . In the nuclear age, the responsibilities are awesome, but there are things worth fighting for.

At hearing on his confirmation before Senate Foreign Relations Committee, Washington, Jan. 9/Los Angeles Times, 1-10:(I)19.

Gary W. Hart
United States Senator, D—Colorado

5

For nearly 40 years, nuclear weapons have posed the gravest threat to our security; today, they are becoming an immediate threat to our survival. For nearly 40 years, nuclear weapons have had the power to render war unthinkable;

(GARY W. HART)

today, there are those who think about a limited nuclear war—and think it can be won. For nearly 40 years, our nation has sought to lead the world away from the abyss of nuclear war; today we have managed—incredibly—to cast aside that sense of purpose . . . Today there are almost no restraints on the nuclear arms race between the superpowers. The spread of nuclear weapons world-wide is unchecked. And major governments lack the will to pull us back from the edge of the nuclear abyss.

The Washington Post, 11-15:(C)6.

George F. Kennan
Co-chairman, American Committee on East-West Accord; Former United States Ambassador to the Soviet Union

1

No one will understand the danger we are all in today unless he recognizes that governments in this modern world have not yet learned how to create and cultivate great military establishments, particularly those that include the weapons of mass destruction, without becoming the servants rather than the masters of what they have created. Modern history offers no example of the cultivation by rival powers of armed force on a huge scale that did not in the end lead to an outbreak of hostilities. And there is no reason to believe that we are greater, or wiser, than our ancestors.

At Second World Congress on Soviet and East European Studies, Garmisch, West Germany/ Chicago Tribune, 2-15:(2)5.

2

Once our people begin to accept that a given war is inevitable, they behave in ways that make it inevitable, whether they were right in their initial assumption or not.

Interview/ The Washington Post, 5-24:(C)3.

Gene R. LaRocque
Rear Admiral, United States Navy (Ret.); Director, Center for Defense Information

3

There can be no winners in a nuclear war; and there's been no Presidential statement from the Soviet Union, no top leaders who ever suggested you could win a nuclear war. On the contrary, their leaders have all said that a nuclear war will be disastrous for all sides. [Yet] the United States has embarked on a limited nuclear war-winning strategy . . . We can't control the Russians in a nuclear war. And therein lies the fundamental fallacy of the idea that you can fight and control a [nuclear] war. Once nuclear weapons begin to fall, communication will be blanked out . . . There will be no way to control a [nuclear] war once it starts.

Interview/ Los Angeles Herald Examiner, 6-9:(A)12.

Hugh L'Etang
Physician; Editor, "The Practitioner" (England)

4

[Nations may be at the mercy of a few individuals in government] whose idiosyncrasy exerts not only a disproportionate influence but one with frightening implications. I'm impressed by the way wars are caused, or at least not stopped, by minor officials who seem to wield a great deal of personal power without responsibility. Many of these officials are not violent, aggressive or psychopathic, but they may have the everyday failings of vanity, self-importance and even stupidity.

At conference on possible causes of a third world war/ Los Angeles Times, 1-18:(I)4.

Ronald Reagan
President of the United States

5

. . . peace is the highest aspiration of the American people. We will negotiate for it, sacrifice for it; we will not surrender for it—now or ever. Our forebearance should never be misunderstood. Our reluctance for conflict should not be misjudged as a failure of will. When action is required to preserve our national security, we will act. We will maintain sufficient strength

(RONALD REAGAN)

to prevail if need be, knowing that if we do so we have the best chance of never having to use that strength. Above all, we must realize that no arsenal or no weapon in the arsenals of the world is so formidable as the will and moral courage of free men and women. It is a weapon our adversaries in today's world do not have. It is a weapon that we as Americans do have.

Inaugural address, Washington, Jan. 20/
Los Angeles Times, 1-21:(I)16.

Eugene V. Rostow
Director, Arms Control and Disarmament
Agency of the United States

1

The wall between conventional and nuclear war can never be impermeable. Small wars can become big ones at least as readily as in the days when archdukes were assassinated at Sarajevo and Danzig was the center of world concern. It is now apparent that arms-control agreements are hardly worth having if they make the world safe for conventional warfare, terrorism and the movement of armed bands across international borders.

Before English-speaking Union,
London, Nov. 30/
The Washington Post, 12-9:(A)31.

Jonas Salk
Medical researcher; Founding director,
Salk Institute, San Diego, Calif.

2

The absurdity of an atomic war is so obvious that we can't possibly allow it to happen. If we are so ingenious as to be able to solve all sorts of other problems, then we surely have the ingenuity to find a way to avoid war.

Boston/Los Angeles Times, 1-11:(I)2.

Helmut Schmidt
Chancellor of West Germany

3

. . . peace is a state that continually must be renewed among states—by means of keeping and restoring balance on the lowest possible military level, by means of negotiations and

pacts, by creating mutual trust, by cooperation. Balance is an indispensable precondition. But balance alone is not enough. It is also necessary to talk to each other.

State of the Nation Address
before Parliament, Bonn, April 9/
The Washington Post, 4-10:(A)25.

Herbert Scoville, Jr.
President, Arms Control Association;
Former Assistant Director, Arms Control and
Disarmament Agency of the United States

4

I don't think nuclear war is survivable. I don't say you wouldn't save some lives by civil-defense measures, and it's certainly important to evacuate the President and top military people to work out a way of ending the war. But the disaster would be so great, I don't even think civil defense is a worthwhile effort. It's much better to put one's effort to avoid nuclear war altogether.

Chicago Tribune, 2-25:(1)16.

John G. Tower
United States Senator, R—Texas

5

The next war will be a come-as-you-are event. Either we're ready or we're not.

Nation's Business, July:27.

Dmitri F. Ustinov
Minister of Defense of the
Soviet Union

6

The Washington Administration is increasingly using blunt instigatory vocabulary. Its high-ranking representatives declare with cynical disregard for the destinies of peoples that "there are things more important than peace," and a so-called "limited" nuclear war is not only possible but even acceptable. Statements of this kind are dangerous in themselves. But when they come from people vested with the administration of the state in one of the world's biggest powers, the danger becomes particularly serious.

At Kremlin rally on eve of anniversary of
the Russian Revolution, Moscow, Nov. 6/
The New York Times, 11-7:4.

PART THREE

General

The Arts

Ansel Adams
Photographer

1

I've always had that feeling in photography that when you learn something you have an obligation to pass it on, so maybe I have a fixation with that. I spend an awful lot of time teaching and working with museums, writing. I often wonder if I hadn't done things like that, would I have been a better photographer? I think I would have been a worse one. I think I might have exposed more acres of film; but people who go out and make photographs constantly really don't have that much in the end. Of course, a lot of people are surprised that I give away my secrets. I don't have any secrets. The process is basically very simple, and the secret can't be explained anyway, if there is one. It's a secret that I don't know the answer to myself.

Interview, Carmel Highlands, Calif.
Los Angeles Herald Examiner, 1-4:(A)2.

Ronald Berman
Professor of literature, University
of California, San Diego

2

The main policy for the [National] Endowment [for the Arts] seems to be to spread money around rather than to create serious art. Money is spent on geographic rather than artistic principles, going to as many Congressional districts as possible. Money is also diffused according to race, region, sex and the like. The primary aim seems to be to get money from the Federal government to as many satisfied customers as possible. Consequently, much of the money has been spent unwisely.

Interview/
U.S. News & World Report, 7-13:63.

Theodore Bikel
Actor; Member, National
Council on the Arts

3

[Criticizing the Reagan Administration's plans for cutting funding of the National Endowment for the Arts]: The Los Angeles Symphony won't go broke. It's the small theatres, the small dance companies that depend on that Federal dollar. A lot of those might simply disappear. They can't go and ask elsewhere for money unless they have that Federal dollar. The Federal dollar is a Federal Good Housekeeping Seal of Approval for them.

The Washington Post, 2-18:(B)6.

4

[On the U.S. Reagan Administration's planned cutbacks in funding for the arts]: The only word that comes to mind regarding the cutbacks in the arts is "punitive." I see the survival of the arts, and my place within it, as more than just a spiritual involvement but a place to fill one's life with meaningful things—with content and beauty.

Interview, Connecticut/
San Francisco Examiner & Chronicle,
4-19:(Datebook)31.

Robert Brustein
Artistic director, American Repertory
Theatre; Director, Loeb Drama Center,
Harvard University

5

Though I don't feel positive about the overall culture picture, I am optimistic about a number of American artists who just plug away regardless of the circumstances. If our better institutions are allowed to survive and these continue to be responsive to artists, serious

335

WHAT THEY SAID IN 1981

(ROBERT BRUSTEIN)

culture will endure. There's a certain stubborn-ness and obstinacy about American artists. They are working on the last frontier in America: the frontier of the imagination. The arts attract many creative people seeking new forms as a kind of space travel of the mind. As long as they persist, there is still hope for the arts. In the meantime, I worry about the state of the soul of most Americans who are exposed to the mass arts because these tend to be soporific and debilitating.

Interview/
U.S. News & World Report, 6-29:67.

William F. Buckley, Jr.
Political columnist;
Editor, "National Review"

1

[Saying he backs Reagan Administration cuts in funding for the arts]: I am here to say the evil thing about current controversies over funding as the Reagan Administration pro-poses to slash government aid to the arts. I would have to reject the notion that there is a clear mandate for the use of public money to facilitate risking adventurous artistic enter-prises. My guess is to the extent they have merit, they will surface . . . I doubt that there are unrecognized geniuses in this world. I tend to doubt that they are unrecognized because the public sector hasn't exercized itself strenuously enough to discover them. My guess is that the impulse to compose, the impulse to perform, the impulse to devote oneself to a lifetime of humiliation . . . is the result of an inner urge. And it is difficult to assuage that urge by public participation . . . We live on the assumption that the majority of the American people sanc-tion what the government does . . . the notion that 51 per cent [of the people] has the right to tell 49 per cent that they don't have to listen to music, they don't have to attend the mu-seums—but they must pay for them—strikes me as an interesting but not entirely plausible philosophical compromise.

Before American Symphony Orchestra League,
Dallas/Los Angeles Times, 6-22:(VI)3.

Chuck Close
Painter; Master's graduate, art department,
Yale University

2

[Saying today's art students have higher ex-pectations than when he was in school in the early 1960s]: I didn't expect a lot of things to happen for me. I always knew that I would have to find a way of supporting myself and my art. When I was in school, the Frank Stellas, the Andy Warhols, were making it; but it was not clear to what extent they were going to make it. We've since seen more and more peo-ple have more and more success at a younger age, and this has raised expectations among students. They now believe that you can make a living from art. What was a surprise for me became expected by the next generation of artists.

The Christian Science Monitor, 1-26:17.

Michael Crichton
Author; Motion-picture director

3

I think concern about violence in art is legitimate. We don't really know how many people are affected by it. They may be directly affected, or it may serve as a release valve. But in any case, I don't think you can completely divorce art from the society which is its con-text. We live in a violent society, and our art will reflect this.

Interview, New York/
The Christian Science Monitor, 4-1:(B)11.

Elaine de Kooning
Painter

4

Art has been hijacked by non-artists. It's been taken over by bookkeeping. The whole thing is so corrupt. But I suppose that's okay. For artists, everything is grist for the mill. Artists are like cockroaches; we can't be stamped out.

Interview, Los Angeles, April 13/
Los Angeles Times, 4-16:(VI)3.

THE ARTS

Lawrence K. Grossman
President, Public Broadcasting System

1

[On proposed U.S. government cutbacks in funding for the arts]: In making the long-overdue repairs to our economy, we are slashing away at the very institutions that make our civilization worth saving—our schools, libraries, museums, arts, scholarship and basic research. All are in serious financial trouble today, as is public television . . . What we are used to thinking of as culture and education have never been left totally to the marketplace and never can be. The new telecommunications technologies—cable, disc, direct broadcast via satellite—left entirely to their own devices will far more likely produce prize fights a lot faster than prize dramas, and centerfolds before serious music.

News conference, June 9/
Los Angeles Times, 6-11:(VI)1,10.

Al Hirschfield
Artist

2

I don't believe there's any more progress to be made in art or morals. No one will make a drawing better than those in the caves of Altamira, nor will anyone write better in English than Chaucer or Shakespeare. Form changes, true. But geniuses are rare and exist in about the same percentage as always. And compulsory education doesn't make more or greater poets than the Arabs at the wall who wrote the *Rubaiyat.* What progresses today is technology.

Interview, New York/
Los Angeles Times, 7-26:(Calendar)4.

Francis Hodsoll
Chairman, National Endowment for the Arts of the United States

3

[President Reagan] comes out of the arts community, as everybody knows. Since he's been in office, he has created a task force for the arts and humanities to explore ways in which we could improve [private] support for the arts. He's the first President to create an ambassador-at-large for cultural affairs. He is also con-

tinuing and, I would say, strengthening, the practice by some past Presidents of using the White House as a place to honor arts and artists. It seems to me the President has gone a long way toward negating the perception [that he does not support the arts] that may have existed at the beginning of his Administration.

News conference, Los Angeles, Dec. 8/
Los Angeles Times, 12-10:(VI)5.

Thomas P. F. Hoving
Consultant on cultural affairs;
Former director, Metropolitan Museum of Art, New York

4

The future of the arts in America is good. Only government can really get in the way. I don't worry about government interference; I worry about government's trying to help too much. That can lead to over-bureaucratization and a certain dullness . . . In the final analysis, government can help the arts without spending any more money. People in arts-related government posts should come to work each day saying, "What can I do to encourage the arts—*without* spending money?" [For example,] the [national arts humanities] endowments could support a domestic arts-indemnity act that would insure traveling museum exhibitions against loss. This would enable the riches of great museums to go to smaller places in the country without the burden of insurance premiums.

Interview/U.S. News & World Report,
12-29('80)/1-5('81):83.

Pontus Hulten
Director, Georges Pompidou Center, Paris

5

I belong to the generation of Rauschenberg and Tinguely. We had a dream of bringing art out of confinement, which many identified with museums; I myself thought it applied more to galleries. I wanted—it sounds stupid—to bring art and life together, something like that. Rauschenberg said it better: The museum of the future is to be in the little crack between art and life.

Interview, Paris/The New York Times, 2-22:(2)27.

WHAT THEY SAID IN 1981

Ada Louise Huxtable
Architecture critic,
"The New York Times"

1

You may have been hearing rumors about the death of modern architecture. The wake is being held in the better art and cultural journals. I do not agree . . . Modern architecture united revolutionary theory and technological development for an unprecedented, far-reaching and unsurpassed creative and cultural synthesis. It offered the most cohesive, innovative, expressive and universal art-form since the Renaissance. And it created masterworks to stand with any of the past.

The Christian Science Monitor, 7-8:23.

Yousuf Karsh
Portrait photographer

2

. . . the face is a terrible challenge for me [to photograph]. The face is just an introduction to the problems and depths of what goes on in the heart and mind of a person. If I can photograph people's thoughts, I am so fortunate.

Washington/The New York Times, 10-6:8.

Lewis H. Lapham
Editor, "Harper's" magazine

3

[In the U.S.] we have money, we have commerce, we have good people—[but] we have no art. Why not? So we go to Europe to hire dancing-masters. And the result is a lack of confidence on the part of the American sponsor and donor. Try to go to a board of directors and explain music or poetry or something—no way. You have been relegated to the position of woman, child or homosexual. Clearly, you are not a serious person. You are somebody who is vaguely creative and your work is praised in the same way that the daubs on nursery-school walls are praised for their "creativity." But it's essentially not a serious undertaking. The artist in America is not a serious person—not in the sense of Sophocles, for example, who was a general, or Rubens, who was an ambas-

sador. It's something for the kids. Humor them. Keep them happy. And the National Endowments are a form of humoring them. These are irresponsible people who must be paid off, and we have to do something with them. I think this kind of patronage has a debilitating effect and that the less of it there is, the better off the country will be. The reduction of patronage of this kind on all levels would bring about a rejuvenation of the American cultural enterprise.

At symposium sponsored by International Center for Economic Policy Studies, New York, June/ The Wall Street Journal, 7-17:27.

Jim Melchert
Director, Visual Arts Program,
National Endowment for the Arts
of the United States

4

[Supporting government funding of the arts]: When we're talking about art, we're talking about investigation. And if they can support the exploration of outer space, they should be able to support exploration of inner space— the human experience—as well. And that's what poets and painters do.

Interview, Washington/ The Washington Post, 7-26:(G)4.

Joan Mondale
Chairman, Federal Council on the
Arts and Humanities

5

I mentioned [to former NEA head Nancy Hanks] that the NEA had been criticized for giving too much to performing arts [and not enough to other areas of the arts] . . . She said you have to lead from strength. And that is what she did all those years. She made the Endowment strong and glamorous and acceptable and desirable. What [current NEA Chairman] Livingston Biddle has been able to do is fill in the other areas that aren't necessarily glamorous. Dance is booming. The theatre is strong. Those are glamorous people. They're celebrities, superstars. But how many people know the names of our foremost American paint-

(JOAN MONDALE)

ers? Not many. And crafts? Forget it. So I've had a little bit of bias in that direction.

Interview, Washington/
The Washington Post, 1-18:(H)6.

Henry Moore
Sculptor

1

. . . all the arts are to help both the viewer and the artist himself to develop a particular sense. I mean, painting and sculpture are for the eyes, and for people who are sensitive in their eyes, to learn and to experience and to get pleasure—not earn a living, nothing to do with the practical side. Art is not practical, and shouldn't be practical. Art is not to earn a living. It's to make the difference between us and animals, like cows. I mean, a cow doesn't stop and look at a field and say, isn't it a beautiful green. Painting and sculpture are for the painter and sculptor to develop his interest and his visual side. Music is for the hearing side of life. Literature is to develop our sense of language and meaning. And all of them are there to make life more interesting, more wonderful than it would be without them. And this is what one tries to do with one's own work. Every day one notices something that you didn't probably notice the day before. And in that way the artist helps other people to have a short-cut toward appreciating and enjoying something in life that, without the artist's help, they might not have noticed.

Interview, Much Hadam, England/
Saturday Review, March:46.

Harold Prince
Stage producer-director

2

[On the argument that tax dollars should not be spent for high culture that appeals only to a small minority]: It's offensive to me that anybody would refer to high art as art for a small audience. That's like saying it's only for the rich folks. While rich folks historically have

endowed and supported art, the appreciators of art certainly don't come from the privileged class. It isn't the privileged few who jam the museums, the concert halls, the regional theatres, the off-Broadway theatres. High art is for all the people. Critics of Federal support ought to realize that the effect of art in a community is not immediately measurable. We're talking about a spiritual contribution—the quality of a state of mind, of inner dignity, of harmony, of the soul. Art even extends beyond the boundaries of a specific place to the whole world. That may sound very high-flown, but I believe it.

Interview/
U.S. News & World Report, 7-13:64.

Ronald Reagan
President of the United States

3

[Saying the arts should stop looking to government for financial support]: In this country, we have maintained by voluntary contributions more musical groups, more orchestras, more ballet and opera companies, more non-profit theatre and more cultural institutions such as libraries than all the other countries in the world put together.

At celebration on behalf of Ford's Theatre,
Washington, March 21/
The Washington Post, 3-23:(C)1.

Nicola Rescigno
Artistic director and conductor,
Dallas Opera

4

Generally speaking, the whole picture of art . . . is in a downward trend. Our generation has been so fantastically productive in science, because the brain can do so much. So we've had a preponderance of fabulous happenings, but not in the artistic fields for 20 or 25 years. Popular taste is definitely going down, and the critics forget what happened 10 years ago!

Interview/
Opera News, November:12.

WHAT THEY SAID IN 1981

David Rockefeller
Chairman, Chase Manhattan Bank

1

I feel public [government] support for the arts is justified, though certainly one can debate the exact level. I would hope that industry would increase the level of its charitable giving, but I'm not so sure it's realistic to think that corporate giving will make up for all the cutbacks by the [U.S.] Federal government—they're pretty significant. I think the result is going to be that some art institutions are going to have a tough time for the next few years.

Interview/
Los Angeles Herald Examiner, 4-4:(A)7.

Arthur M. Schlesinger, Jr.
Professor of humanities, City University of New York

2

[On Reagan Administration plans to cut Federal support for the arts]: There are those . . . who applaud this result because they regard Federal subsidies for the arts as "indefensible." If a cultural institution cannot pay its own way in the market, they contend, then it has no economic justification and, if no economic justification, no social justification. This argument implies that only those activities that pass the box-office test are worth pursuing. But one can almost argue the reverse more persuasively: that the most precious institutions in our society—our schools, universities, libraries, museums, opera houses, hospitals, churches—are precisely those that do not pay their way. Surely a society as rich as ours can afford to divert some of its abundance to activities that enrich our culture even if they fail the box-office test.

At awards ceremony of American Academy and Institute of Arts and Letters, New York/
The New York Times, 7-18:17.

Josep Lluis Sert
Architect

3

There is a negative attitude among the general public toward modern architecture that is both human and understandable. The majority of "modern stuff" is vulgar and cheap-looking, monotonous, identified with "box-like," flat facades and roofs, curtain walls, etc., which are repeated for miles, the same in every city . . . For too many years architects have . . . usually ignored the human values of livability which should have been given priority . . . [But] the modern city has not been built . . . The great historical event that the appearance of modern architecture represents, its wide acceptance and world-wide influence, is too recent to be judged. There is no doubt that new directions are emerging . . . Modern architecture is not dead. It has not yet followed its full course. If you have a sense of history and compare it with other great changes in different periods, you will find it is still young and very much alive.

Accepting the gold medal of the National Institute of Architects, Minneapolis/
The Washington Post, 5-23:(C)9.

Maxim Shostakovich
Exiled Soviet orchestra conductor

4

[On government control of arts in the Soviet Union]: Everything that sounds pessimistic is rejected. Even a woman who is painted carrying a hundred pounds of potatoes on her back has to be depicted as smiling optimistically. That applies to music, too. The [Communist] Party wants to express through culture that everyone is satisfied.

Chicago Tribune, 5-18:(1)7.

Beverly Sills
General director, New York City Opera; Former opera singer

5

Any cutback [in Federal aid] for the arts is a tragedy. The Federal funds generate a lot of extra money. The government's attitude can be catching in terms of foundation and private giving. It could be contagious, and is dangerous.

Feb. 19/The New York Times, 2-20:14.

(BEVERLY SILLS)

1

I don't think the arts should be exempt from government budget cuts] . . .if we get the same cuts as everyone else, that's fine . . . if people want beauty in their lives, they're going to have to work and pay for it.

Interview/
"W": a Fairchild publication, 6-19:22.

Peter Ustinov
Actor, Writer, Director

2

When things are going badly in the world, the arts usually flourish because they play a greater part in alleviating depressed spirits and give people an interest other than their daily grind. A great many fresh things, for example, came out of America during the Depression. Russia just after the revolution was frightfully fertile in artistic manifestations of all sorts. By contrast, when things are going well there seems to be less to write about; at least the audience is less receptive, because they don't really need the arts so much. Some call the interest in the arts in bad times an escape, but it isn't necessarily that at all. It may be a method of achieving understanding about why we are upset about what is taking place.

Interview/
U.S. News & World Report, 3-9:46.

David White
Executive director, New York Dance Workshop; Member, Policy and Grants Panels, National Endowment for the Arts

3

[Criticizing Reagan Administration plans to cut funding for the National Endowment for the Arts]: All across the board you are seeing a fabric that took 15 years to weave simply un-

ravel before your eyes. Somewhere along the line, it will affect the fates of dance companies from American Ballet Theatre all the way down to the smallest independent artist . . . Over the last 2½ years, the 10 major dance companies in this country paid back to the government, in the form of withholding taxes and such, approximately twice as much as they received. Washington has been clearly making money off its arts programs . . . The reductions in arts funding are regarded as "a strategic act." The Administration hopes that people will perceive this cut as directed toward the rich, so as to make more palatable the cuts directed toward the poor, in the form of food stamps and CETA jobs. But the perception is false. It is based on a misconception of how much the arts have become part of the fiber of our national life, on some misbegotten belief that they exist for the pleasure of some "elite."

Interview, San Francisco/
San Francisco Examiner & Chronicle,
5-3:(Scene)8.

Sidney Yates
United States Representative,
D—Illinois

4

[Criticizing the Reagan Administration's planned cuts in the funding of the National Endowments for the Arts and the Humanities]: I don't think the Congress will accept such a low priority for the arts and the humanities. [OMB Director David] Stockman says that the Endowments have hindered business from contributing to arts organizations. He doesn't understand how it's worked in the past. The Endowments have been the trailblazers for contributions from business, not the other way around. I think if the Endowment cuts its contributions, so will business.

The Washington Post, 2-18:(B)6.

Journalism

Karim Aga Khan
Muslim religious leader
and newspaper owner

1

We have all heard of twin cities. Why not twin newspaper companies and news organizations between the industrial world and the developing world? These could provide mutually beneficial exchanges of managerial, technological and editorial experience and news . . . It is imperative that standards of reporting be elevated as well. A complaint that the North reports the South superficially, condescendingly, sometimes inaccurately and without proper social, cultural, economic and political background often has real validity. This is what brought the Third World together in the first place. Many of these countries thought that the industrial world, largely because of its press, was receiving a distorted image of their young nations and their cultures . . . There is, therefore, a need to rethink how we select and train the all-important foreign correspondents and foreign editors. This new approach must demonstrate to the developing nations that the media and government of the industrial world are prepared to recognize the legitimacy of many of the Third World complaints, that they are ready to re-examine their own performance and to respond in practical terms to the needs of the press in developing nations.

Before General Assembly of International
Press Institute, Nairobi, Kenya/
The Washington Post, 3-8:(C)6.

Les Aspin
United States Representative,
D—Wisconsin

2

I've never had a press conference. I don't think press conferences work worth a damn. You can't control the way the story comes

out. Somebody will ask a cockamamie question and that will be the story. If you're an "information story," it's hard to get it across in a press conference. A well-lobbied study and press release are worth 20 press conferences.

Interview/The Washington Post, 6-7:(D)4.

Burton Benjamin
Senior vice executive producer,
CBS News

3

I don't think technology means a damn [in TV news]. When Samuel F. B. Morse, the inventor of the telegraph, was in his dotage, they awakened him from sleep one night and said to him, "Mr. Morse, the telegraph has just reached Texas!" And he said, "Well, what did Texas have to say?" It's the same thing with television news. I don't care if reporters have antennae growing out of their heads; it's useless if they don't have something to say.

Los Angeles Times, 7-6:(VI)8.

Hubert Beuve-Mery
Writer and editor;
Founder, "Le Monde," Paris

4

French journalists don't have the same sense of civic responsibility American journalists have. Our access to information is not as wide as theirs . . . French journalists hesitate to become detectives.

World Press Review, October:50.

Benjamin C. Bradlee
Executive editor, "The Washington Post"

5

[On the revelation that this year's Pulitzer Prize-winning article by *Washington Post* reporter Janet Cooke was a fabrication by the

342

(BENJAMIN C. BRADLEE)

writer]: It is a tragedy that someone as talented and promising as Janet Cooke, with everything going for her, felt that she had to falsify the facts [in her story about an 8-year-old heroin addict]. The credibility of a newspaper is its most precious asset, and it depends almost entirely on the integrity of its reporters. When that integrity is questioned and found wanting, the wounds are grievous, there is nothing to do but come clean with our readers, apologize to the Advisory Board of the Pulitzer Prizes, and begin immediately on the uphill task of regaining our credibility.

April 15/The Washington Post, 4-16:(A)1.

James S. Brady
*Press Secretary to the President
of the United States*

1

I see myself as the Press Secretary for the nation. People say you can't serve two masters. That's right. I have only one master—that's the President. But I serve the President best by serving the press best. Where that comes out is that if you serve the President and the press, you serve the nation. The job here is to facilitate the conversation between the President and the people.

*Interview, Washington/
The Christian Science Monitor, 3-17:3.*

Tom Brokaw
*Broadcast journalist; Co-host,
"Today" show, NBC-TV*

2

I went straight from college into broadcasting, but I always wanted to be a reporter. This generation [of TV newspeople] just wants to be stars. They're more familiar with the hot comb than with an idea. If there had been no TV for me, I would have gone into print. These people would go into acting.

Newsweek, 3-9:53.

3

When I go out to talk to people, I proselytize about the news business, about the press, and I really talk about the idea that television's part of the spectrum but that it cannot stand on its own, from their point of view. If you are to be well-informed, you must use television in conjunction with magazines, newspapers, whatever—because there are some things they can just do better. Even if we [in TV] were to do a very sophisticated job of reporting economic matters, for example, it would still require the foundation of good print journalism to make the final connection.

*Interview, New York/
Los Angeles Herald Examiner,
6-14:(E)2.*

Zbigniew Brzezinski
*Professor of government, Columbia
University; Former Assistant to the
President of the United States
(Jimmy Carter) for National Security Affairs*

4

[The news media] will have to be taught the habit of analyzing and thinking through the meaning of events, and some willingness to engage in the difficult intellectual effort to understand and convey nuances. I would frequently give speeches or make statements [while in office] of an analytical kind. Invariably, in briefing newsmen, I or my colleagues would be asked: "What's new in it?" If you told them: "Well, this is an attempt to explain the meaning of America's position in the world—to emphasize a number of continuing themes underlying American foreign policy," they would ignore it. What they find appealing are the "either-or" presentations of world issues, "good guys" versus "bad guys," "hawks" versus "doves," and personal gossip and power plays. Paradoxically, our chief guarantee against simple-mindedness and uniformity is the freedom of the press, and here one has to hand a bouquet to the mass media. For while they are great purveyors of simplistic notions about a complex reality, they tend to be highly effective watchdogs against empty sloganeer-

WHAT THEY SAID IN 1981

(ZBIGNIEW BRZEZINSKI)

ing, corrupt practices, docility and uniformity. One of the great strengths of the American polity is its pluralism and the diversity of its perspectives; and these are both represented and fostered by the media.

Interview/
The New York Times, 4-22:25.

Carol Burnett
Entertainer

1

[On her libel suit against the *National Enquirer* for alleging that she was drunk in a restaurant]: Words, once they are printed, they've got a life of their own. Because it was in print, it will never, ever, not be a part of me. When I am dead and gone, it will be in my files—newspapers and libraries keep files—and my kids, my grandkids, my great-grandkids can look it up. I really know—I know—that most people believe what they read; and that hurts.

Testimony at the libel trial, Los Angeles/
Chicago Tribune, 3-22:(1)8.

Frank Campbell
Minister of Information of Guyana

2

Surveys have shown that the ratio of news from the developed and the developing countries in major U.S. dailies is 11 to 1 in favor of the industrial world. About a quarter of all news from the Third World was about violence, disasters and negative things, whereas the equivalent figure for the developed countries was under 10 per cent. So the majority of people in the world are doing things which are unknown to the U.S. reader. Britain, which has one-sixth of the population of Africa, accounts for nearly 60 per cent of American overseas correspondence. The 44 countries of Africa have only 4 per cent at most. Now, your editors say that if they were to write about events in a little country like Guyana which are not disasters or violence, people will not read their

paper. So commercialism is the basis of international journalism.

Interview/The New York Times, 2-15:(4)3.

Jimmy Carter
Former President of the United States

3

What hurts as a President responsible for a nation is to see the superficialities and inaccuracies of the press. A few well-known reporters or columnists will print a story that they *know* is a lie. They'll hear a rumor and publish the story as a *fact* without taking five minutes to call me or the Secretary of State or [Press Secretary] Jody Powell and ask, "We've heard this. Is it true?" When I've invited these people to the White House for supper or for an extended conversation, I've said, "You have the authority to call me personally, and I'll get on the phone and tell you whether or not the report is true." They don't *want* to call. Because if they hear a scandalous story, or one that's provocative, they don't want to see it made accurate or see it killed . . . I'm not talking about all of them. I'm talking about some few of them. And when they do run an inaccurate story, they *never* apologize.

Interview, Plains, Ga./
Parade, 7-19:7.

Turner Catledge
Former vice president and executive editor, "The New York Times"

4

[American journalism today is] in pretty darn good shape and I'm pretty well satisfied. Sometimes we fight a bit too much, like the First Amendment was about to be totally erased, which it isn't. I don't like some of the intrusions on objectivity. But over-all, we're changing with the times and we're still getting out the news, and that's about all you can ask for.

Interview, New Orleans, March 13/
The New York Times, 3-17:8.

Walter Cronkite
Anchorman, CBS News

1

[On the influence of broadcast journalism]: The power is just part of the facts of life that we have to live with today—the power being simply that it goes to such a large number of families. The polls show that most of the people are getting most of their news from television. That unloads on television a responsibility that's almost impossible for us to discharge. We can, in that half hour Evening News broadcast, certainly give a lot of people who cannot or will not read a better view of their world than they would have had otherwise. But for another large portion of the public, we're not giving them nearly enough to properly exercise their franchise. And we never will be able to, even if we went to an hour or did more documentaries. You're still expecting people to sit still and watch that material for a long period of time; and the tolerance level has got to be reached at some point for how much people can sit and watch of news or public programming. I think the answer is that, besides watching television news and listening to radio news, they've got to read newspapers. They've got to read magazines. They've got to read books.

Interview, New York/
Los Angeles Herald Examiner, 1-18:(F)4.

2

A good deal of my acceptability has been that I have maintained this air of impartiality which I feel is essential to do this job properly. I wouldn't think of doing anything else. But that doesn't mean I don't have deeply held feelings and thoughts about many major issues of the day. Some of them are conservative, some liberal, some radical. But I've always held them back and I think one in my position should. You and I know that we journalists are capable of having the deepest feelings about subjects and still be able to write totally impartial pieces. That is what separates us from other crafts. If there is any definition of professionalism—and sometimes there is a question as to whether we are a profession, a craft, or a trade—I think we can claim we are professional because of that one ethical consideration: the ability of journalists to write the facts as nearly as they can be determined and set aside their own prejudices and biases in doing that job. It's very much like a lawyer defending a known criminal. We have the same ethical consideration. Why should we challenge our readers and viewers out there? Why should I strain my credibility, my objectivity, by flaunting my beliefs in some things that don't make any difference anyway?

Interview, New York/
The Christian Science Monitor, 3-6:19.

3

[On his imminent retirement as anchorman, after 19 years]: There's no question—anybody leaving something they've done and loved for such a long time as I have is bound to miss it. A guy comes off the police beat and gets a promotion to city editor, but he never gets over the feeling that he'd like to be back on the beat. I suffered that when I moved here from being a foreign correspondent . . . what I hope I'll be remembered for is that I kept the faith on journalistic ethics and principles . . . and perhaps brought an aura of journalistic professionalism to a business which is always in danger of crossing the line into show business.

Interview, New York/
The Christian Science Monitor, 3-6:19.

4

When people ask if [TV newspersons] Barbara Walters, Dan Rather or any of us are worth seven-figure salaries, I have to ask: compared to what? Compared to a lot of fine newspaper people, certainly not. Compared to teachers and the salaries they get, certainly not. But compared to other people from whom the networks and local stations are profiting— rock-and-roll singers, for instance—certainly yes. So you've got to consider the milieu in which we operate.

Interview/U.S. News & World Report, 3-16:46.

WHAT THEY SAID IN 1981

Steve Dunleavy
Metropolitan editor,
"New York Post"

1

We take very, very careful note of what we do. We watch who's buying the paper and why. I see who's reading the paper on the subway, and what they're reading. We get feedback from our circulation drivers on what sells. We listen to what the people have to say, the strap-hangers, the policemen and the firemen and their wives. The point is, we have a formula, and I know a lot of journalists sneer at our formula, but it works. Our formula is publishing stories that have emotion in them, and we do it with a rifle shot, not a shotgun blast. People like to buy something they can feel, something that affects their heart and their pocketbook.

Interview/
The Washington Post, 9-8:(A)2.

James B. Edwards
Secretary of Energy
of the United States

2

The liberal media in Washington have too much influence on American thought. And the rest of the press just picks that up, instead of doing their own work. *The New York Times* and *Washington Post* aren't stalwart, conservative-thinking institutions. They believe in the Ted Kennedys and the Tip O'Neills. They're the ones who got America in the shape it's in today.

Before Greater Columbia (S.C.) Chamber
of Commerce, May 26/
The Washington Post, 5-28:(A)3.

Osborn Elliott
Dean, Graduate School of Journalism,
Columbia University; Former editor,
"Newsweek" magazine

3

In recent years, we have seen journalism and its practitioners denounced as nay-sayers and n'er-do-wells—those "nattering nabobs of nega-

tivism" conjured up by that malefactor of ill-begotten wealth, that far-right Honorable [former Vice President] Spiro Agnew. And we have seen journalism apotheosized, in the Watergate years, as the protector of all that is good and the exposer of all that is evil. The truth, alas, lies somewhere in-between. I would argue that one of the unfortunate residues of Watergate is that very knee-jerk negativism that Agnew chose to magnify, and to find so galling. Too often these days, reporters bring too much suspicion to their jobs—suspecting that anyone in a position of power is there for some ulterior motive. There is a fine line that separates unhealthy cynicism from the skepticism that is so essential to the journalist's trade.

To his students/
The Wall Street Journal, 1-23:22.

Jules Feiffer
Political cartoonist

4

As a citizen, I was despondent over [President] Reagan's election. But as a professional cartoonist I was overjoyed. The Republicans have four years to deal with the country, and I've got four years to deal with them. I think I'm in a better position.

Los Angeles Times, 1-18:(Calendar)3.

Fred W. Friendly
Professor of journalism, Columbia University;
Former president, CBS News

5

[The news media must guard against] a reporter perpetrating a hoax in the interest of success or fame, an editor sloppy or slothful in permitting it to get into the paper or onto television, and Congress, the courts or the regulatory agencies so upset that they push the pendulum back to the point where press freedoms are endangered . . . We [in the U.S.] have the only truly free press in the world, and there are two ways we can lose it. One is by sins of omission, things we don't do. The other is by commission, the things we do badly.

Interview, New York/Los Angeles Times, 6-8:(VI)5.

346

(FRED W. FRIENDLY)

1

[On the recent case in which the *National Enquirer* was found guilty of printing a story on entertainer Carol Burnett which she claimed was untrue]: I understand the *National Enquirer* is very rich and able to pay the [substantial] damages. But let's turn that around to the "Friendly Daily" in Rhode Island. I have a big scoop, but my lawyers say that if we print it, we may be sued and lose because of what happened in the Burnett case. I don't print it because I'm afraid. Who loses? Not me. The public. That's as bad as prior restraint . . . Here I am, 65½ years old, with most of my enemies behind me, defending the *National Enquirer*. I don't give a damn about the *National Enquirer*, but I do care that if there's a First Amendment, it's for the sleaziest of newspapers. There's a marvelous line by Justice [Harry] Blackmun who said, "In this country we have opted not for a responsible press but for a free press." He was right.

Interview/Chicago Tribune, 7-1:(1)16.

2

I care a lot about the First Amendment, but . . . because they [journalists] are Constitutionally Accountable—with a big "A"— to government, doesn't mean that they are not accountable—with a small "a"—to . . . their readers . . . When newspapers get on their high horse and say, "We're different from everybody else; we are accountable only to ourselves," and that's somehow what the Constitution of the United States says, that's almost a blasphemy.

Los Angeles Times, 9-23:(I)26.

David R. Gergen
Assistant to the President of the United States for Communications

3

. . . I feel the moment you walk out there and lie to the press, that you're finished. God forbid the day would come when you felt you had to do it in the national interest. I do place very high stakes on the national interest, and there might come that [moment]. But I think the next day you'd quit. Or whatever. You wait a decent interval and leave. I just think you're of no value to the President at that point, and you're of no value to anyone else. So I think [Deputy Press Secretary] Larry [Speakes], [Press Secretary] Jim [Brady] and I and the others that have shared that podium all feel you will not draw the line, you will not lie.

*Interview/
The Christian Science Monitor, 9-2:(B)4.*

4

The press is more balanced than 10 years ago, and it is not as ideological. There are exceptions, of course, but in general I find that journalists have gone through the same metamorphosis on public policy as the rest of the country. They have become more disillusioned with the promises of big government of the '60s and more willing to consider the possibility of private enterprise as a solution. You can see as much evidence of the country's swing to the right on the editorial pages of our major newspapers as in the public-opinion polls. Take *The Washington Post*, for example. Ten years ago, one would have hardly expected that newspaper to support decontrol of oil prices. And yet both it and *The New York Times* are now ardent supporters of decontrol. Our major newspapers are less predictably liberal on economic issues. And obviously there has been a flowering of good conservative columnists.

*Interview/
U.S. News & World Report, 12-7:25.*

Ellen Goodman
Political columnist

5

[On winning a Pulitzer Prize for her column]: You win it on a Tuesday and then on Wednesday you have to get up and do it [the column] all over again. It's not like winning it for a play or something that's done. In this business you can never rest on your laurels. Journalism

WHAT THEY SAID IN 1981

(ELLEN GOODMAN)

is always work in process. You're always as good as your next column.

Interview, Chicago/
The Christian Science Monitor, 11-10:18.

Charlton Heston
Actor

1

It's a curious thing. Somehow, television [news] anchormen have come to be perceived as pundits. They're *actors*, for God's sake. They don't make all that stuff up. They just read it. Any good actor could read the evening news *cold* better than some of those guys do it after years on the job.

Interview, Washington/
The Washington Post, 6-9:(B)7.

Warren Hinckle
Former editor, "Ramparts" and
"Scanlan's" magazines

2

What journalism is all about is to attack everybody. First you decide what's wrong, then you go out to find the facts to support that view, and then you generate enough controversy to attract attention.

Interview, Washington/
The Washington Post, 10-8:(C)1,17.

Ruth J. Hinerfeld
President, League of Women Voters

3

[Criticizing TV networks for projecting election winners before all polls are closed, which could deter some people from voting]: The race to project victories may increase network ratings, but it may also have serious and harmful effects on voter confidence in the integrity of the election system and in the value of an individual vote.

Before Senate Rules Committee,
Washington, May/
The Christian Science Monitor, 5-11:2.

Norman Isaacs
President, National News Council;
Former newspaper editor

4

Once a story is written, it is graven in stone. It may be 100 per cent incorrect, but the reporters will refuse to concede any point, even a factual error . . . In addition, much local reporting is abominable and even slanted. There is not enough strong editorial control.

U.S. News & World Report, 6-29:72.

Stephen D. Isaacs
Editor, "Minneapolis Star"

5

[On the embellishment and fabrication of newspaper stories by over-ambitious reporters]: The kind of journalism most of us were brought up to practice and adhere to is affected by the knowledge that what gets people ahead is flash and the page-one byline. Without the byline, the piping of stories wouldn't happen.

U.S. News & World Report, 6-29:72.

Gene F. Jankowski
President, CBS Broadcast Group

6

[Saying the Fairness Doctrine should be repealed]: I would say that the First Amendment should apply to everybody. Certainly, it is clear that broadcast journalism does not have the full First Amendment protection that print journalism has, perhaps because for many years electronic journalism was looked upon as a second-class citizen. The time has come to recognize that this must change. The First Amendment should apply 100 per cent to both media. After all, fairness goes along with being a good journalist. There is no reason to believe that broadcast journalists would be any less fair than print journalists . . . Journalists are responsible for covering events, and responsible journalists try to do the best job they can. Whether they work for a television station or for a newspaper, journalists still live by that rule. In fact, for them to do it any other way is to underestimate the intelligence

(GENE F. JANKOWSKI)

of the American public. Because I think if either a newspaper or a television station continually tried to present only one side of the events, the public is smart enough to recognize, "Hey, I'm not getting a fair shake when I read that paper or listen to that station. So, I'll go elsewhere."

Interview/The New York Times, 10-18:(4)10.

Tom Johnson
Publisher, "Los Angeles Times"

1

The fact is that many in our profession have been guilty of conflicts of interest, have been guilty of irresponsible and prejudicial reporting . . . We investigate conflict of interest on the part of public officials. Yet too many media executives are reluctant to acknowledge their own conflict of interest when they take editorial positions on legislation or community projects that can affect their own company's holdings . . . We insist on greater access to government, to the courts and to corporate board rooms. But too many of us apply a double standard when inquiries are made into the probity of our own action. The common dismissal of such inquiries is, "We stand by our story" . . . Until we are as open as we expect others to be, the public will continue to regard us as one powerful institution doing battle with other powerful institutions—and also as having a dubious advantage because of our unique Constitutional protections.

Address sponsored by Washington Journalism Center, Washington, Dec. 8/ Los Angeles Times, 12-9:(I)11.

David Landau
Legislative counsel,
American Civil Liberties Union

2

We take issue with the broadcasters' claims that their First Amendment rights are infringed upon [by the Fairness Doctrine]. It's the public that owns the airwaves. It's their First Amendment right to have a diversity of viewpoints presented to them.

Sept. 17/Los Angeles Times, 9-18:(I)1.

Billy Martin
Baseball manager, Oakland "Athletics"

3

Dealing with the press is [the] toughest [part of being a manager]. The regular press is all right, the guys who follow the games and know how to ask questions. But it's hard for me to deal patiently with a writer who hasn't done his homework. You see, I do mine, and if they haven't done theirs, it bothers me. They come around once in a while, ask a dumb question and stick a microphone in my face. I make them take that mike back, and sometimes, I'll admit, I deliberately give them a dumb answer to their dumb questions.

Interview/Los Angeles Times, 3-3:(III)6.

Robert C. Maynard
Editor, "Oakland Tribune";
Pulitzer Prize juror

4

One of the things that's happening is that we give [Pulitzer Prize] awards for a big blockbuster effort, for a grand expose, for that exotic piece of journalism, but not for the sustaining effort. It's become distorted. We look for things to write that will knock the socks off the Pulitzer board. What the public wants is for us to practice solid journalism for the sake of society.

San Francisco Examiner & Chronicle, 5-17:(B)11.

5

[On the revelation that a Pulitzer Prize-winning story by a writer for *The Washington Post* was a fabrication by the writer]: True, it hurts [journalism] more when it happens to *The Post*, and the boom is certainly louder. But don't tell me that something like this couldn't be pulled out by any of us. Anybody

349

WHAT THEY SAID IN 1981

(ROBERT C. MAYNARD)

[in the newspaper business] who thinks they couldn't be fooled is a fool.

The Washington Post, 4-24:(V)1.

John McMullan
Executive editor, "Miami Herald"

1

[On the Pulitzer Prize for journalism]: I'm appalled by the development of prize factories at some newspapers. I consider prizes a pox, a consumer of time . . . I'd rather get 1,000 new readers than a Pulitzer.

San Francisco Examiner & Chronicle, 5-17:(B)11.

Walter F. Mondale
Vice President of the United States

2

[When you're in public office,] you've got to trust [the press]. There's no alternative. You're going to get some bad stories when you don't deserve it. But to be suspicious and distrustful is a cancer. You've got to work with the system and keep respecting it. I've seen suspicious politicians, and it always hurts them more than it does anybody else.

Interview/The Washington Post, 1-20:(A)21.

Rupert Murdoch
Newspaper publisher

3

[On those who question his desire to buy the financially ailing *Times* of London]: It is most important that everybody engaged in *The Times* realizes that however important it is as a national institution, it is also a business . . . Nothing is a greater guarantee of [editorial] freedom and independence than if we have a viable publication . . . People seem to think

they are doing me a favor in allowing me to take on something that is losing 13 million pounds a year.

Before British House of Commons Education Committee, London, Feb. 11/ The New York Times, 2-12:6.

Ralph Nader
Lawyer; Consumer-rights advocate

4

[Arguing against repeal of the broadcasting Fairness Doctrine]: You and I or anybody else can get together and buy a newspaper, even if it's just a mimeograph machine in the basement. But we can't get together and put up a transmitter and start broadcasting. When somebody sets up a newspaper, it's theirs. The readers don't have a property right in a newspaper. But the public airwaves began in the public domain. A certain portion is given to the licensee to use for private profit; he becomes the trustee for a public property right. Now the broadcasters want to turn it into a total private-property monopoly system. The broadcast spectrum is allocated, and allocated for good reason. It's a public trust. It's just like the Mississippi River.

The Washington Post, 10-8:(C)13.

Christopher A. Nascimento
Cabinet Minister of Guyana

5

The argument offered that the Western press is "free from control," meaning governmental control, is misleading and simplistic. Mass media empires, especially in the United States and United Kingdom, which own, control and dominate the press and broadcasting throughout the Western world and internationally, make a mockery of Milton's plea in his *Areopagitica* for a "free and open encounter." These empires represent the very antithesis of the idea of "press freedom" offered by men like Descartes and Locke. It is true that most Third World media organizations, as is the case of Guyana, are owned and financed by their governments. Most Third World countries are at

(CHRISTOPHER A. NASCIMENTO)

a stage of economic development when there is often no other alternative, unless it be foreign ownership. But there is no logical argument as to why commercial control of the media is inherently any less evil than political control.

Before Rotary Club of Guyana/
The Christian Science Monitor, 12-18:23.

Richard M. Nixon
Former President of the United States

1

[On the revelation that a Pulitzer Prize-winning story by a *Washington Post* writer was fabricated by the writer]: I think it was very unfortunate for that to happen in Washington because *The Post* is the major paper in the nation's capital, and the free world's capital, and it should set an example for responsible journalism. And this was perhaps as irresponsible an example of journalism as you could find, and I hope *The Post* does a better job in the future.

Charlottesville, Va., April 22/
The Washington Post, 4-23:(A)3.

Laurence O'Donnell
Managing editor,
"The Wall Street Journal"

2

[On the revelation that this year's Pulitzer Prize-winning article by reporter Janet Cooke of *The Washington Post* was a fabrication by her]: I think the interest in the story [about an 8-year-old heroin addict] is how just such a thing was printed. My suspicion is that Jan Cooke is not going to be remembered, specifically, for this by as many people who will remember that a great newspaper in America printed a blockbuster story that won a Pulitzer Prize and the next day found out the story wasn't true . . . People feel the press plays a very large role in shaping society. They feel sometimes the press takes very heavy-handed positions toward the rest of us mere mortals, telling them how to think and making sweep-

ing judgment calls on what is right and what's wrong.

The Washington Post, 4-17:(A)3.

Michael J. O'Neill
Editor and executive vice president,
"New York Daily News"

3

[On recent instances of fraudulent articles by newspaper reporters, including one at his paper]: We, and perhaps some other newspapers, have allowed some of these young reporters and columnists too much freedom and have probably not supervised them as closely as we should have. I think, first of all, that one of the faults on our part was to have been too permissive at the editing level about what went in and what did not go in. And secondly, people like me were less-alert than we could have been.

Interview, New York, May 9/
The New York Times, 5-11:12.

Everett C. Parker
Director, office of communications,
United Church of Christ

4

[Saying the Fairness Doctrine should be retained]: It's because the Fairness Doctrine is there that when people complain of a legitimate fairness abuse, in most cases the station says, "Oh, sure, we'll make your views available on the air." If there were no Fairness Doctrine, stations would tell them, "Get lost. It's our prerogative to say what we want." For the most part, then, the Doctrine is quietly there, getting in the way of nobody speaking on the air, but protecting the little guy who doesn't have the power the networks have to say what they want. The success of the rule is [seen] in the fact that you don't have thousands of fairness complaints going into the Federal Communications Commission all the time.

Interview/
The New York Times, 10-18:(4)10.

WHAT THEY SAID IN 1981

Mike Peters
Political cartoonist

1

The main mission of the editorial cartoonist is to be like the kid who stands on the side of the street during the parade and says, "Hey, the Emperor has no clothes!" That's not what our strength is; that's what our job is. Our biggest strength is that we have the chance to imprint a visualization on people's minds that they will not easily forget. Not many people can remember editorials about Lyndon Johnson and the Vietnamese war, but they can remember the David Levine drawing of LBJ lifting up his shirt—and underneath is the scar of Vietnam on his chest. If visuals are good, they'll always be remembered.

Interview/U.S. News & World Report, 6-22:56.

Dan Rather
Anchorman, CBS News

2

[On the pressure on him to be Number 1 in the TV ratings after taking over the anchor chores from veteran Walter Cronkite]: I had no idea [the pressure] was going to be what it was. In human terms, nobody can see and hear that much written and said about himself, and not be aware of it. I do worry some because so much attention is given to the superficial aspects of broadcasting—who's up and who's down. All that counts, but is far less important than maintaining a standard of good, solid journalism.

Interview, New York/
Los Angeles Herald Examiner, 5-8:(A)7.

Harry Reasoner
Correspondent, CBS News

3

[Saying that if he ran CBS he would close the Washington news bureau]: I don't suppose that could ever happen, but it does seem to me that we journalists have fallen into a trap, a pattern. When some news story happens, we go over and talk to Senator Proxmire about it,

whether it's a hurricane or the Medfly. It's easy. The crew knows the way. There's hard-line current to plug in. We have a pretty good idea what the Senator will say, no surprises. I suspect with the energy crisis and ecology and inflation, we have to stay in Washington. But I also suspect that the real energy crisis is not in Washington, it is out there somewhere, and someone with a reporter's feelings ought to go out and look for it.

Interview, New York/
Los Angeles Times, 10-1:(VI)1.

William Rees-Mogg
Former editor, "The Times," London

4

[On the recent sale of *The Times* to Rupert Murdoch, owner of several sensationalist newspapers]: Do I regret the new era? Well, it's not the way I would do things . . . The clearest sign of excellence in a newspaper is the fearlessness to write about things that are boring, but important. *The Times* will shift perceptibly but not dramatically to a high-adrenalin paper, and the process may be good for it.

Interview, London/
The Christian Science Monitor, 3-12:13.

Morley Safer
Correspondent, CBS News

5

I subscribe to the theory of journalism that says reporters should follow a story the way sharks follow an ocean liner . . . The weakness of television journalism has been that instead of being the sharks, we were the dolphins, preceding the ship of state with a wink and a smile, performing our little electronic tricks, showing the way . . . We should go with the story as far as it can take us. [Politicians] should be kept on the rack constantly, maybe even from birth.

Lecture, University of Southern California,
March 17/Los Angeles Times, 3-19:(VI)11.

Ned Schnurman
Executive producer, "Inside Story,"
Public Broadcasting Service;
Former associate director,
National News Council

1

If there has been a failure [in modern journalism], it's that there has been a glamorizing of investigative reporting and new journalism, of "point-of-view" journalism . . . When I was a young reporter, bylines were given very rarely. Now there are promotions, with pictures of the reporters. This personality thing isn't altogether healthy.

Interview/
The Christian Science Monitor, 5-15:5.

Sam Simon
Executive director, National
Citizens Committee for Broadcasting

2

[Arguing against repeal of the broadcasting Fairness Doctrine]: In terms of the political reality, [if the Fairness Doctrine is repealed] the broadcasters will have the absolute right to decide which candidates are given coverage, and they will be able to support any candidate they want. Imagine how that will fundamentally change the political structure of this country. We'll have three [political] parties: ABC, CBS and NBC.

The Washington Post, 10-8:(C)13.

William J. Small
President, NBC News

3

[On criticism that projection of election winners by TV networks before all polls close could deter some people from voting]: Broadcast projections have never been demonstrated to have any measurable effect on either voter turnout or voter choice. The reasons people vote or fail to vote are many and complex. It would be wrong and simplistic to conclude that this decision hinges significantly on the words of television news commentators.

Before Senate Rules Committee, Washington, May/
The Christian Science Monitor, 5-11:2.

Tom Snyder
Broadcast journalist; Host,
"Tomorrow" show, NBC-TV

4

I don't feel that the stories I've covered in my career have been of great significance. While the greats in broadcast journalism were covering wars and [political] conventions, I was covering protest marches and fires, city-council meetings and mayoral races—more local and regional stuff. Great journalism is when you dress up in a uniform and go over to Afghanistan and identify yourself with the natives there.

Interview, New York/Playboy, February:77.

William F. Thomas
Editor and executive vice president,
"Los Angeles Times"

5

We [journalists] all know we're supposed to be honest. We all know we're not supposed to take free gifts from people who could be perceived as influencing what we do . . . If you don't know . . . those things when you come here, then you don't deserve to be here. I don't like . . . codes of ethics . . . and other things like that, which I think would look like we're denigrating the people we're handing them to. I don't like to be treated like a child . . . and that's what those codes of ethics seem to say to me . . . It's insulting. I've never seen a written code of ethics that wasn't so damned obvious that it was clear that you were doing it more for its outside PR value than for any inward impact.

Los Angeles Times, 9-23:(I)25.

Ted Turner
Chairman, Turner Broadcasting System;
Founder, Cable News Network

6

[On why he started CNN]: [The major networks are] the worst pollutants this country has ever seen. The network news is nothing more than a headline service of the most spectacular things that happened during the day . . . I didn't watch much TV news before I

WHAT THEY SAID IN 1981

(TED TURNER)

started [CNN] because I didn't need to see any more charred bodies. It was too depressing.

Before Advertising Club of Cincinnati/
The Washington Post, 1-16:(C)2.

Mike Wallace
Correspondent, CBS News

1

I don't think there's anything wrong with drama in a news program, nothing wrong with confrontation of a hostile interviewee. On the contrary, I think it makes for interesting, provocative, useful journalism.

Interview/
The Christian Science Monitor, 5-1:23.

Tom Wolfe
Author, Journalist

2

One of the best things that happened to me in newspaper work was the fact that I was never able to get a column. I think a column, like a beat, is confining. Unless you have tremendous energy like Jimmy Breslin, a columnist finds himself more and more writing off the top of his head. When you read a columnist who writes about something he's read, something he's seen on television, something that happened around the house, then you know he's really an exhausted man. He has no more material.

Interview, Beverly Hills, Calif./
Los Angeles Herald Examiner,
1-4:(California Living)6.

Literature

William Abrahams
Senior editor, Holt, Rinehart and
Winston, publishers

1

[On being an editor]: One is picky at first, and then one finds the pickiness moves on. If you carp and criticize, editing's very well-chosen. [But] if you are totally intolerant, you shouldn't be in publishing . . . [because] there is a real danger of becoming totally cynical. I would quit if I became cynical.

Interview/
San Francisco Examiner & Chronicle,
5-10:(Review)11.

Eric Ambler
Author

2

. . . there aren't too many serious novels written now. There are some bad good novels, and a few good bads. Philip Toynbee once said that I was good bad, in danger of one day becoming good good. Perhaps he meant it as a compliment. By the way, I'm not claiming that my books become great novels through the passage of time. I'm simply saying they have some relevance in a social context. Most serious novels today have very little social context.

Interview/
The New York Times Book Review, 9-13:3.

3

There was a time when writers could grow with a publisher, but no more. I spent many years with Alfred Knopf, but I left him when he was taken over by Random House. I'm with Farrar, Straus now because it is about the only publisher not owned by a conglomerate. The business has become known—as Knopf said

once—as a mining business. It is very different now. I don't really think it is possible any longer for people to become professional novelists as I did. They can't survive.

Interview, Los Angeles/
Los Angeles Times, 11-1:(Calendar)25.

Martin Amis
British author; Former literary editor,
"The New Statesman"

4

American writers are celebrated in the sense no English writer is. The idea of an English writer doing what [J. D.] Salinger did [becoming a recluse to avoid publicity] would make us die of laughter because in England you don't get anybody to bother you. No one would *dream* of going up to an English writer and saying, "What do you think of Vietnam?" I think it makes American writers more ambitious, and that's a healthy thing because they tackle bigger subjects. There's a fatal sort of quiet about the English novel: You get these finely tuned little novels about middle-life crises; you don't get *Humboldt's Gift*, a big essay on American literary life, or *Good as Gold*, an examination of American politics. English writers don't sound off the way they do in America.

Interview/The New York Times, 8-20:23.

William Anderson
Poet

5

When I write poetry, I'll write it down, or a tiny bit of it, and then have to depend on the reader to bring his own feelings, moods and memories to the act of reading the poetry. And this act is considerable art in itself. To read

(WILLIAM ANDERSON)

poetry or literature with attention is a marvelous thing to be able to do—to respond, to live and be moved by this subtle world you've created about you. But the difference between the poet and everyone else is the difference of capacity and the direction of desire. You also have to love words and make games and puns of words and language. You must want to do it. And the more you want to do it, the more you will find yourself doing it. If you look at the nature of poetry and what you are doing, that helps. Poetry is made up of rhythmical sentences, with words joined together in a charged language. In choosing words, the poet has an effect on people and can bring them to a marvelous state of delight, contemplation and peace.

Interview, London/
The Christian Science Monitor, 9-30:20.

Terrel H. Bell
Secretary of Education of the
United States

1

[Saying schools should not require students to read books that may be contrary to the principles on which the student is being brought up by his parents]: My argument is that you need to have freedom of speech, you need to have freedom to read. I'm not one of those book-burners. But I think you need freedom *from* a few things, including vulgarity or crudity of speech, if they insult your sensibilities and the standard of the home from whence you come . . . if I have strong religious persuasions about [a certain kind of book, and a teacher requires it,] then I don't have freedom *from* that book, you see. Now, that's the other side of having freedom to have access to it. And all of us say, "My, let's not go in and burn the books." But what about forcing the minority individual . . . who comes from a home where they feel their youngsters at that age should not be exposed to that kind of literature? And if the state says, "We have a compulsory-attendance law, and you must send your child to school," and if the state says, "We have a state textbook-adoption system and therefore the school must use the book we've adopted," [then it's wrong] . . . I don't think that ought to be required reading or you don't pass English I, and if you don't pass English I, you can't graduate. Now, supposing you were teaching a literature class and I were the parent. If you presented me with a list and over here are the required readings, and over here are the optional ones, and you say, "Pick 3 out of these 15 optional ones," [then] my children and I could get away from *Slaughterhouse-Five* if we wanted . . . Read James Joyce if you want to. As for me, I wouldn't make it required reading in *my* class; [but I] certainly wouldn't want to join the ranks of those who would charge in, rip it off the shelf and throw it in the bonfire. But that's the point I made—that there ought to be freedom *from* speech as well as freedom *of* it.

Interview, Washington/
The Christian Science Monitor, 3-25:(B)2,3.

Bruno Bettelheim
Psychologist

2

. . . all studies of reading achievements have shown that the best predictor of reading achievement is the literacy level of the parents. Habits are formed in the home by copying one's parents. It's not enough that the parents read; they must enjoy it as well. If parents don't *enjoy* reading or say what was gained from it, children may learn to read signs and labels and ads on television, but they do not grow into literate persons—that is, they never find reading meaningful or gain important values from reading.

Interview/The Washington Post, 7-19:(C)5.

Charles Bukowski
Poet

3

[On why he doesn't give many poetry readings]: I like to be hated and loved all at once. That's why I enjoy giving readings, sometimes,

(CHARLES BUKOWSKI)

because the haters scream, the lovers scream, and I do my work and collect my money. I guess I am closer to the street people than I am to anybody, and when you get anybody who is a little higher, he becomes a mark. So that's why you have to lay low, do your work and just be quiet. Do your screaming in the pages but don't let them see you too often. Once the artist starts mixing with the masses, the artist becomes the masses.

Interview, Los Angeles/
Los Angeles Times, 1-4:(Calendar)6.

Anthony Burgess
British author

1

We have reached the point where a book's longevity depends not on its merits but on how it is marketed—a rather awful thing. I think, cynically, that if the book is selling well in the U.S. it is because it is very long. Americans do not buy books they can read at one sitting; they feel cheated. A thick book, solid as a piece of furniture, one you can set aside to read some day—namely, never—guarantees success there.

Interview/World Press Review, December:34.

James Clavell
Author

2

Because of screenwriting, I'm visually trained. I get energy into the page. *King Rat* I wrote in a mews house in London. One room, really, and garden. Very closed-in, and so is the novel. But that worked because the Japanese are closed-in people; the Japanese are contained in themselves. *Tai-Pan* I wrote in a house on Woodrow Wilson Drive in the Hollywood Hills, which also worked. Looking out at the hills, one side was Sodom and one was Gomorrah. *Shogun* I did in Canada in a 40x30-foot living-room in the midst of a typhoon. Absolutely perfect.

Interview, Los Angeles/
Los Angeles Times, 4-19:(Calendar)5.

Michael Crichton
Author

3

[Saying he will keep his future projects to himself and not speak about them beforehand]: That's because every time I drew up any sort of plan, I proceeded to do something else. And since I ultimately abandon anywhere from one-third to one-half of my writing projects, I've now stopped talking about what I'm going to write until I've actually done it.

Interview/
The New York Times Book Review, 2-8:30.

Pat Golbitz
Senior editor,
William Morrow & Co., publishers

4

The editor is like a midwife. You do everything to ensure a healthy birth, but you can't give the baby blue eyes.

The Wall Street Journal, 6-22:16.

Francine du Plessix Gray
Author

5

The Great American Novel is a provincial, inflated macho contest. Such euphemisms as the great Swiss novel and the great Colombian novel do not exist. Pressure from society to write the Great American Novel has caused more harm to the American [young writers] than all the marijuana in India and all the cocaine in Beverly Hills.

At Yale University, Oct. 20/
The New York Times, 10-22:20.

Graham Greene
Author

6

A writer must have enormous patience. A writer must clearly realize that his profession will cause him pain and sometimes leave him in solitude . . . One of the most painful sensations is when you cease to be a young writer and feel the burden of age. It is dangerous to start

357

WHAT THEY SAID IN 1981

copying oneself, as Hemingway did. Don't start to write if you don't feel compelled to do so . . . Don't write without a sense of necessity. But if the urge persists, you should be aware that a hard life lies in store. Maybe a writer's profession will make your life more comfortable, but no external comfort can ease your suffering from inner failures.

Interview, Antibes, France/
World Press Review, October:39.

Lars Gyllensten
Secretary, Swedish Academy; Member,
Nobel Prize awards committee

1

[On criticism of the judging and selection of winners of the Nobel Prize for Literature]: We are aware of the criticism and the mistakes that may have been made in the past. And of course, there is no such thing as a world's best writer. But a full year's research goes into the selection process, and we do try to survey a wide range of writers . . . One must accept a kind of pragmatic procedure and look to the fundamental idea in Alfred Nobel's will as a whole. It was a matter of encouraging science in literature and of disseminating them in an international perspective for the benefit of mankind, but not of handing out empty status awards.

Los Angeles Times, 8-10:(I)1.

Evan Hunter
Author

2

[On how he finds writing after many years at the craft]: Easier in terms of being able to bring off a scene, execute whatever I visualize. More difficult in that I'm trying to keep it fresh. It's as if you're starring in a Broadway show that has been going on for years and you've got to develop tricks to keep it fresh. Otherwise, you end up a hack. There are enough of those around.

Interview, Los Angeles/
Los Angeles Times, 5-14:(V)29.

John Irving
Author

3

. . . I believe that a writer has an adversary relationship with his publisher . . . If someone has applied himself to an art for 15 or 20 years and they've gotten good at it, and they're expected to do something else to support themselves while the [publishing] industry that sells this craft supports itself very well, something is badly wrong. Morally wrong . . . The problem is that publishing has never been a business. If it's to remain honorable, its first obligation is to publish those things with complete support and integrity which it knows are not going to make the money.

Interview, Putney, Vt./
The Washington Post, 8-25:(B)9.

4

Writers are skilled. Poets, too, and composers. But it is never good enough to simply do well at what you do. I've written enough to be aware there are people who gun for you because you're successful. The world isn't free of mean-spirited people, especially in the literary world. There are some people who disliked [his book, *The World According to*] *Garp*, and others who disliked it because it was widely successful. It's the old elitist attitude. There are a lot of people who resent writers who are popular—especially writers who are serious and who become popular.

Interview, Cambridge, Mass./
Los Angeles Times, 9-13:(Calendar)29.

Erica Jong
Author

5

. . . I grew up in a time when most important American novels were written by men. Most distinguished women writers tended to write in male-dominated prose. They did not write books that only a woman could have written. My generation of young female writers discovered its own character and found that we could dictate the form and content of our own

(ERICA JONG)

fiction. It was given to my generation to come along and show that we had sexual feelings. It was given to my generation to assert that territory of honesty which had long ago been established by men.

Interview, Weston, Conn./
Writer's Digest, June:22.

1

There is a sense that poetry comes from the intuitive part of the brain. It is much more pleasurable and euphoric than writing a novel. You feel that you are tapping into the source of unconscious creativity. Nearly every poet that you talk to will tell you that it is, in a sense, an automatic process. Writing a novel is a much more conscious thing. It's a daily job. You go to your desk at nine in the morning and work until three or four. I would say that one day out of· ten you feel euphoric and the words just fly off of your fingers. The other nine days you wonder how the hell you are going to move your heroine from one place to another and what adventures will take place along the way. You find that a good part of your day is taken up inventing and devising, and that most of the time you don't think it is any good.

Interview, Weston, Conn./
Writer's Digest, June:24.

Alfred Kazin
Critic; Professor of English,
Graduate Center, City University
of New York

2

There are a great many talented writers working now. After all, we've had writers recently like Nabokov. We have writers now like Beckett, Bellow, Solzhenitsyn. Terrific writers. But this is an obvious point: In an age where people spend a great many evenings looking at television, and in which the visual—whether in movies or in advertising—fascinates them, they don't get the same thing out of reading. The

people who applauded Dostoyevsky had no other way to find out what was happening in the world except to read a book. Today, they turn to [TV personality] Barbara Walters.

Interview, New York/
The Christian Science Monitor, 1-28:(B)7.

Galway Kinnell
Poet

3

When you look at poetry of the past, it does seem that it's very often characterized by a rather amazing, to us, knowledge of many aspects of life. I think that's one way in which contemporary poetry seems deficient. Contemporary poetry often looks as though it's written by a person who's relatively ignorant with respect to the world and the processes of the world—someone who has read a lot of poetry, perhaps, and studied and written a lot and has a certain verbal expertise but who is in some profound way out of contact with ordinary things.

Interview, Laguna Beach, Calif./
Los Angeles Times, 9-27:(Calendar)7.

Judith Krantz
Author

4

. . . it's unfair to use the fact that I promote a book to make it seem as if it is a triumph of hype over substance. Almost all writers these days work hard at promotion, but no one can promote a book into the Number 1 spot on the best-seller list. A book has to sell itself, because, very simply, people want to read it. When a first novel by an unknown, like *Scruples*, becomes Number 1, it isn't because of promotion!

Interview/Book Digest, February:27.

Judith Krug
Director, Office of Intellectual Freedom,
American Library Association

5

[On groups that are trying to ban certain books from libraries]: I could sense an increase in the pressures since last spring, but it really

WHAT THEY SAID IN 1981

(JUDITH KRUG)

took off last November [on election day]. I don't know if it's a coincidence or if this is the wave of the future . . . It's not just the anti-sex-education people. All sorts of people are trying to keep out things that they don't approve, including feminists and anti-feminists, blacks, Jews, single-issue groups . . . I will not buy the people who come to me and say, "I'm not a censor, but this book is awful." I will not buy the argument of a higher good. There is no higher good than the First Amendment.

The Washington Post, 1-31:(G)1.

Louis L'Amour
Author

1

[Saying his stories of the Old West have authentic background details, and that among other things he uses actual diaries from the period]: When I start to write a story, I don't have to imagine what happened; I *know* what happened. I know what these people were thinking. I know what they did when a wagon broke down. I have it all right in front of me. Before I write a story, I saturate myself with these diaries to the point that what I write will be naturally correct . . . When I write about a cave or a creek, it's there. I've been there to see it. When one of my characters uses a certain herb to heal a battle wound, it's actually there, right where he picked it. I didn't invent it or have it magically transported there. When I write, I take a slice of history and place my characters there to react to the situation at that time. This is, after all, our history. Hundreds of years from now, our stories of the West will be tinged with mysticism, as are the stories of other ancient heroes like Robin Hood of England and the Shah Rama of ancient Iran.

Interview, Los Angeles/
Los Angeles Herald Examiner,
3-1:(California Living)6.

Lewis H. Lapham
Editor, "Harper's" magazine

2

My idea of a writer is that the writer is more interested in what he is trying to say than in how he looks when saying it. For some people, they're so filled with their idea and they want to explain and show and teach and reveal or whatever word you choose. And it's this, whatever it is, outside of themselves, that is more important than their own style or their image or their own preoccupation. So that they get taken out of themselves and become preoccupied with the subject at hand. And those are usually the good ones. The not-so-good ones are the ones that are always concerned about *me*. Me, me, me. Right? And the result is that it's always much easier to edit a good writer than a bad writer. The good writer always is much more willing to take changes, advice, cuts, suggestions, revisions and so forth than the bad writer. And the reason is that the good writer is interested in what it is that he's trying to say. And any way that it can be said better or made clearer or more specific or concrete or effective or powerful, he is grateful to you for that.

Interview, New York/
The Christian Science Monitor, 5-27:(B)3.

Norman Mailer
Author

3

I think [the novel is] the most difficult of all the forms I've tried. I've always been fond of journalism, but I don't respect it in the same way because I think it's easier. Artists always have a kind of regard for virtuosity, and although the fact that something is easier doesn't therefore mean it's a lessor form, deep down I think most artists feel that if it's hard you respect it more . . . The thing that makes the novel so hellishly difficult is that you have to elucidate a story from the material. If you make a mistake, then you may not discover it until the book is done and you're looking back on it 10 years later. It's very much like chess in a funny way. Good chess players always speak

(NORMAN MAILER)

of the best line of continuation. They can analyze a game afterward and really replay the points of no return and see whether a knight should have been moved to another box. In the novel, you're left wondering.

Interview, New York/
Saturday Review, January:46,48.

1

I have a distrust of the literary world which is not dissimilar to the kind of distrust a red-neck who starts to write has of the literary world—which is that they are all fancy double-talking phonies up in New York. My view is somewhat more sophisticated, but I think that the literary world is a very dangerous place to be in if you want to do an awful lot of writing because it's almost necessary to take on airs in order to protect yourself in that world. In a way, you can't handle yourself skillfully unless your airs are finely tuned . . . [Ernest] Hemingway committed suicide working on those airs. He took the literary world much too seriously, and he's almost there as a lesson to the rest of us: Don't get involved in that world at too deep a level or it will kill you and kill you for the silliest reasons—for vanity and because feuds are beginning to etch your liver with the acids of frustration.

Interview, New York/
Saturday Review, January:53.

Colleen McCullough
Author

2

Most critics believe that a book that makes a lot of money can't possibly be very good. But the darlings of the critics so often don't last, and people who were never the darlings wind up the darlings of tomorrow. That's a judgment that won't come till I'm dead, so I don't worry about it.

Interview, Beverly Hills, Calif./
Los Angeles Herald Examiner,
10-18:(E)2.

Scott Meredith
Literary agent

3

Writers hop from publisher to publisher mainly because of the size of the dollar, and their loyalty tends to be more toward the agent than toward either the publisher or editor. Editors are no longer father-confessors. Most are more concerned about bringing in the bacon than in trying to rewrite the bacon.

Interview/
Los Angeles Herald Examiner, 1-27:(B)1.

Leonard Michaels
Author

4

I have the worst possible habits as a writer. I can't write page two until I'm satisfied with page one, so I rewrite page one 25 times, then page two, and meanwhile I'm dying to get to page 30. What I publish is usually pretty thin and ecologically sound, but the paper I waste getting to it is equivalent to a small forest.

Interview, Berkeley, Calif./
The New York Times Book Review, 4-12:31.

Harold T. Miller
Chairman, Houghton Mifflin Co.,
publishers

5

[On the large sums of money an author can get for paperback, foreign, TV and movie rights to his books]: You try to bring a young author along, but there isn't as much incentive to keep on doing that when by the time he reaches the usual break-even point, about his third or fourth book, he's likely to sell it on the auction block.

Los Angeles Herald Examiner,
1-27:(B)4.

Jonathan Miller
Producer, Director, Writer

6

I think there is the feeling on the part of television writers and film writers generally that

WHAT THEY SAID IN 1981

(JONATHAN MILLER)

people exist in novels the way you and I exist in Los Angeles. But as you know, we can be easily taken out of Los Angeles and moved to San Francisco or London or anywhere. There's the feeling that people exist in novels as if the novel was a box out of which you could pluck the characters and put them into something else—a play, a film. Where of course, in fact, the greater the novel, the more indissolubly connected with the novel they are. Actually, they are made out of the prose that describes them. Once you merely remove the speeches assigned to them, snip off the connective tissue of prose in which they are set, you actually destroy them. Because they are not made up of anything other than the descriptions the author has made of them. In a third-rate novel, the prose is negligible and the speeches detachable and that way you can easily separate the characters from the book. They are taken out as if the novel is nothing but a container.

Interview/
Los Angeles Times, 7-26:(Calendar)48.

Toni Morrison
Author; Editor, Random House, Inc.,
publishers

1

First novels, poetry, combined forms and experimental forms are not forthcoming from established publishers. They don't "earn out" —meaning the break-even point is never met. It's not profitable . . .   That situation is devastating to all writers . . .

At "Black Literature in the '80s" forum, Columbia
University/The New York Times Book Review,
2-22:3.

2

[Writers are] toys held in contempt by publishers. We're little toys to be played with by kings who love us when we please and dismiss us when we don't.

At American Writers Congress meeting, New York/
Los Angeles Times, 10-22:(V)4.

David Niven
Actor, Author

3

I write by the seat of my pants. I start with a vague foundation which then becomes an incomplete tiny cottage. And then I go back to paint the house different colors and to put in a flowerbed. I'm totally untrained. I remember the night I mailed off the manuscript for *Go Slowly*. I'd gone to bed and was reading Evelyn Waugh's diaries in which he said he had given up adverbs because they were worthless to a writer. I didn't know what an adverb was, so I rushed to a dictionary. Suddenly I realized every other word in my manuscript was an adverb and I couldn't sleep for a week.

Interview, San Francisco/
San Francisco Examiner & Chronicle,
12-6:(Datebook)34.

Joyce Carol Oates
Author

4

I think what's so great about reading and writing novels—the whole literary adventure— is that it allows us entry into other people, that one gets inside the consciousness of marvelous characters like Dostoyevsky's three brothers and the shadowy fourth. When I read V. S. Naipaul, suddenly I feel that I am inside the soul of a Trinidadian. If I read a novel by a Pole, I can see on the inside of a Pole in a way which I can't be just by reading a newspaper. I feel that if a writer has a function, it is to bear witness to different personalities and attempt to dramatize them from the inside. The people I really admire—Henry James, James Joyce, Flaubert and Dostoyevsky—don't feel that they know all the answers, and their art is an exploration. I don't think that novelists should be dogmatic. Certainly I don't feel that inclination. I want to understand people. Joyce felt that any moral dogma in the novel was a perversion, that one should not impose that kind of vision on a work of art.

Interview, New York/
Los Angeles Herald Examiner,
8-25:(B)4.

(JOYCE CAROL OATES)

1

Reviewers are somewhat more gentle with beginning writers. Most beginning writers are called "promising," for a few years. Most books get mixed reviews. People whose books sell in the millions are people whose books don't get reviewed. I don't think it matters as much as we would like to think.

Interview, Princeton, N.J./
San Francisco Examiner & Chronicle,
10:11:(Review)10.

George Plimpton
Author

2

As a writer, one always looks for confrontation, people who are being driven to some sort of limit. Georges Simenon once wrote that he always put characters on the end of limbs and then would start cutting the limb off to see how they behaved out there, under pressure.

Interview, Los Angeles/
The Christian Science Monitor, 8-12:(B)22.

V. S. Pritchett
Author, Critic

3

[On the current widespread use in literature of language that used to be considered obscene]: There are plenty of old obscene books and some of them were very good, but they were generally rare editions and were not popularly read. They were introduced with more grace, or with a certain air of learning, or belonged to satire, which has a great deal of license. One can't say totally that this present freedom is a bad thing; it sometimes is and sometimes isn't. There are certain words which do shock me, especially if they're in the wrong context. I think it is a matter of context. One must also be able to write a sentence which interests, or pleases, to do which requires a great deal of skill.

Interview, Vanderbilt University/
The Wall Street Journal,
6-12:24.

Philip Roth
Author

4

I was struck by what happens to be a celebrated writer there [in Eastern Europe] and what happens to a celebrated writer here [in the West]. The differences, from my point of view, were almost comically vivid: In my situation, everything goes and nothing matters; in their situation, nothing goes and everything matters.

Interview, New York/
The New York Times, 5-11:17.

Gordon A. Sabine
Professor of journalism, Virginia Polytechnic Institute and State University

5

People who want to censor books aren't really censoring books; they are censoring people. They presume to be protecting folks when in fact they are restricting them. Reading is an enlarging and expanding activity, not a restricting one. If I don't get a chance to read something when I need it, it's not just library circulation figures that are hurt; it may be something inside me that suffers. The censor is trying to predict the reaction of a potential reader to a book. But we have found that you just can't predict that.

Interview/
U.S. News & World Report, 6-1:64.

Mary Lee Settle
Author

6

New York is just a trading post [for writers]. You pack your skins together and load them on your back and trek into the city. You stay awhile, you bargain, and after the bargaining is over, you get drunk. But then you leave; you go back into the country to get more skins . . .

WHAT THEY SAID IN 1981

(MARY LEE SETTLE)

[In some countries,] if you step out of line [as a writer] you go to jail. [In America,] we can print anything we want, so long as someone will publish it. The tyranny here is a tyranny of commercialism, of indifference to quality, a tyranny of literary fads and fashions.

At University of Virginia, April 18/
The Washington Post, 4-20:(C)1,9.

1

[On what she calls "prefabricated pop books" being published today]: Distributors say, "That's what people want." My answer is, if you are presented in a food store with only rice, potatoes, cabbage and grits, that's what you will buy if you are hungry. How can the distribution industry say that that is what people want if they present a potatoes-and-grits choice to book buyers?

At American Writers Congress meeting, New York,
Oct. 11/The New York Times, 10-12:15.

Isaac Bashevis Singer
Author

2

I believe in storytelling, and dislike commentary by the author. The events must speak for themselves. A fiction writer who tries to explain his story from a psychological or sociological point of view destroys his chances to endure. I have expressed this idea with the words: Events never become stale; commentary is stale from the very beginning. Commentary has almost destroyed the literature of our present century.

At University of California, Los Angeles/
Los Angeles Times, 6-15:(V)3.

3

The worst mistake a writer can make [is to] bore his audience in the name of some higher purpose. In art, as in love, the act and the enjoyment go together.

Lecture at Library of Congress, Washington,
Nov. 2/The Washington Post, 11-4:(B)15.

Mickey Spillane
Author

4

[Saying he is a writer, not an author]: I don't rewrite a word. I'm no bleeder. Agonizing is for authors, not writers. Writing is like show-business—the second word is the important one. The first word brings you fame, but the second brings you fortune.

Interview, Murrells Inlet, S.C./
People, 7-27:54.

D. M. Thomas
Author

5

Serious work can come only from your psyche. You go along for years, and then all of a sudden there comes a divine spark and it all works. All I can do now, as I write, is hope and pray that it will strike again.

Interview, Hereford, England/
Los Angeles Herald Examiner, 3-26:(B)6.

6

The only place where poets are taken seriously is behind the Iron Curtain. They're either killing them or celebrating them, but at least they buy their books.

Interview/"W": a Fairchild publication, 3-27:4.

7

There is an inevitable connection between an author's hangups, his personality and what he writes. But if there's one grain of art, that redeems everything. It is like the radium that Madame Curie found in the pile of rubble. Art is like that.

Interview, Oxford, England/
Los Angeles Herald Examiner, 5-9:(A)7.

P. L. Travers
Author

8

[Saying she shuns publicity]: So many writers like to be movie stars. I'm not a bit like

(P. L. TRAVERS)

that. I'm absorbed entirely in what I'm doing, and in life. What's a writer, anyway? Just somebody who scribbles. I don't think they're any more special than someone who cooks. I'd rather the writing be known than me.

Interview, London/
Chicago Tribune Magazine, 11-15:37.

John Updike
Author

1

[On the practice of remaindering books, clearing out stock at discount prices]: It's never occurred to me to feel in any way abused by this. The run of a trade book seems to be briefer and briefer. There's that one golden moment when you're on the front tables of the bookstores. I don't know how long it lasts now—a couple of weeks, a couple of months at best? Then back you go. It's just part of the generally slightly crasser flavor of publishing. It is true that my early books were never remaindered that I can remember prior to *Couples*. But then I think it was feasible to print in smaller runs. Now the style seems to be a whopping big one—then pray it will move. Of course, often it doesn't move in that quantity.

Chicago Tribune, 3-22:(Book World)2.

2

There's a crystallization that goes on in a poem, which the young man can bring off, but which the middle-aged man can't. It saddens me that, for whatever reason, I can't or don't write much of it any more. Nor do I write as many short stories as I used to, or write them with the same ease—that sense of just being like a piece of ice on a stove. I feel myself being pushed toward the novel as my exclusive metier, in part because I'm no longer as adept at the shorter form as I was. It may be a kind of muscular thing that also makes ballplayers retire at 40. Certainly writing is, among other things, a kind of athletic achievement—just the mental quickness, the ability to combine thoughts

simultaneously. Also, I think that any achievement, and especially artistic achievement, is born partly out of the illusion that what you have to do is important and that you can do it. And one of the powers of youth might be the power of conjuring up this illusion. Once you start to doubt whether something is worth doing, there's a terrible tendency not to do it.

Interview, Georgetown, Mass./
Saturday Review, October:20.

Gore Vidal
Author

3

I'm not interested in the middle-class, middlebrow novel which is 90 per cent of what's being done now. It seems to me that that sort of thing is done so much better by soap operas and movies like *Kramer vs. Kramer*. These books are always teaching morals in a very crude way —identity crises, mature relationships, sacrificing all for love. It's very difficult for a writer like myself who doesn't share these prejudices.

Interview, New York/
The Christian Science Monitor, 3-16:(B)6.

4

. . . I do sometimes despair about the future of the novel. They all seem to have been written by English teachers for English teachers to be read in college English classes. And ever since the days of Sir Walter Scott, we have been in the grip of the weighty moral novelists. I've been saying for years that Louis Auchincloss is an important novelist who has been dismissed by critics because he supposedly writes about an insignificant group of men on the Eastern seaboard. What the critics don't realize is that these are the men who are running the country.

Interview, Chicago/
Chicago Tribune, 4-14:(1)14.

Kurt Vonnegut, Jr.
Author

5

[Criticizing those who try to ban certain books from school libraries because of content

(KURT VONNEGUT, JR.)

or language]: All these people talk so eloquently about getting back to good old-fashioned values. Well, as an old poop I can remember back to when we had those old-fashioned values, and I say let's get back to the good old-fashioned First Amendment of the good old-fashioned Constitution of the United States—and to hell with the censors! Give me knowledge or give me death!

At American Writers Congress meeting, New York/
The Washington Post, 10-12:(D)3.

Robert Penn Warren
Poet

1

[On why he writes]: Why do you scratch when it itches? It's a compulsion. It's an irritation. I know a thousand stories, everybody knows a thousand stories. But only one cockleburr catches your fur and that subject is your question. You live with that question. You may not even know what that question is. It hangs around a long time. I've carried a novel as long as 20 years. And some poems longer than that. Sometimes a line will hang around for years. I started writing *Audubon* back in 1940. I threw it away as no good entirely. It *was* no good. I was stuck with some narrative sense in it, but it had no narrative sense, except a biographical one. And then one morning when I was helping to make a bed . . . I was holding one side of the sheet and I suddenly remembered one line from the version I had written 20 years before: "Was not the lost Dauphin; was only"—and that became the first line of the new poem.

Interview, Fairfield, Conn./
Saturday Review, July:38.

Elie Wiesel
Author

2

For me, writing isn't an occupation, but a duty. I write as much to understand as to be understood.

Interview, New York/
The Christian Science Monitor, 6-24:(B)7.

Tom Wolfe
Author, Journalist

3

Good reviews are much better than bad reviews, on practically every level. But when you write something like *From Bauhaus to Our House*, or *The Painted Word*, or *Radical Chic*, for that matter, and you get general agreement [from critics] . . . well, somehow that would mean you haven't said anything very novel, very original. And in some way, I guess I just can't stand the idea that, somewhere, somebody might pick up something I've written and just not give a damn.

Interview, New York/
The New York Times Magazine, 12-20:47.

Harry Zehner
Professor, Department of English,
Marymount University,
Tarrytown, N.Y.

4

[On literary plagiarism]: When T. S. Eliot used other writers' lines, he did so because he saw himself as perpetuating certain literary traditions; commenting on them, as it were. Today, writers are just ripping each other off because they don't want to work at their craft. Besides, I think they know the American public doesn't really care what's original, as long as it's entertaining.

Chicago Tribune, 1-22:(2)2.

Larzer Ziff
Professor of English,
Johns Hopkins University

5

[On "faction," the literary blending of fiction and factual history]: . . . ultimately what it's doing is helping to define certain truths that cannot be determined by mere chronology or historical sequence. Some writers apparently see history as so repetitive and so devoid of reason that they choose faction as a way of getting at underlying patterns . . . So, just as some people try to find meaning through transcendental meditation, gurus or drugs, some writers try

(LARZER ZIFF)

to find it by rearranging historical truths . . . Contemporary novels present fact as fiction

because fiction is often the higher reality, not limiting and arbitrary like historical truth.

Interview/
The New York Times, 7-16:18.

Medicine and Health

Christiaan Barnard
Heart-transplant surgeon

1

[On euthanasia]: I think it's stupid not to legalize it. It's stupid because of our sanctioning of other forms of putting people to death without any reservation. Things like war and capital punishment and liberalized abortion. It's absolutely ironic and hypocritical to let our countries spend billions of dollars to train people for one purpose only, to kill people, and to spend billions of dollars on sophisticated machines which have one purpose only, to kill people. Yet when the doctor asks to terminate the life of a terminally ill patient, you're horrified. I think we should get our priorities straight . . . all this revolves around God's concept of life. But what is that? I don't know it. You don't know it. But I doubt it very much if God's concept of life is a patient who's just barely breathing and whose heart is barely beating. Even God must think that life in this case has already ended. So maybe euthanasia is not taking life, even from the way that God thinks about life.

Interview/Los Angeles Times, 3-18:(1-A)4.

2

I've realized that we judge medical results incorrectly. If you go to a medical meeting and a doctor should talk about replacement of heart valves, he always talks about how many patients survived. He never tells you about how the survivors lived. In transplantation, you think it's been a failure because you heard only about the deaths. But you have never considered how well people have lived for two or three years after transplantations. And as a result of this, I realized that we are viewing medical treatment with a wrong goal in mind. The aim is an improvement in the quality of life, not in the prolongation of life. Modern medicine and modern technology are applied mainly to extending the existence of a patient, not to improving the quality of his life. This kind of medicine can be very inhumane. Any medical approach to a problem has a limitation, and once you've reached that, the duty of the doctor then is to allow the patient to have a good death, a comfortable dying.

Interview/Los Angeles Times, 3-18:(1-A)4.

Ruth Behrens
Director, Center for Health Promotion,
American Hospital Association

3

[On the increasing involvement of businesses in the health of their employees]: A number of things contribute to why businesses have become interested. The over-all national interest that people now have in their health is beginning to spread to executives in businesses. Businesses and hospitals that are interested in the movement often have someone high up who is personally committed to this type of life-style. It also can improve employee morale. They believe that healthy employees are more productive and there will be less absenteeism and fewer sick days. Also, with health-care benefit costs increasing, they see the potential for keeping employees healthy and decreasing the rate of increase in those costs.

Chicago Tribune, 11-17:(4)13.

Baruch Blumberg
Associate director for clinical research,
Institute for Cancer Research, Philadelphia

4

Increasingly, we find causes of hospitalization are related to illnesses that doctors cannot

(BARUCH BLUMBERG)

prevent, such as alcoholism and drug abuse. These illnesses are a consequence of the individual's own activity. Doctors can make a contribution to dealing with such problems, but really there's not a great deal they can do to prevent them. Responsibility resides with the individual.

Interview/
U.S. News & World Report,
4-6:45.

Alfred M. Bongiovanni
Professor of pediatrics and obstetrics,
University of Pennsylvania

1

[On being asked, at hearings on proposed abortion legislation, just when human life begins]: I have learned since my earliest medical education that human life begins at the time of conception. I submit that human life is present throughout this entire sequence, from conception to adulthood, and that any interruption at any point throughout this time constitutes a termination of human life.

Before Senate subcommittee,
Washington, April 24/
Chicago Tribune, 4-25:(1)3.

Edward N. Brandt, Jr.
Assistant Secretary for Health,
Department of Health and Human Services
of the United States

2

The level of health in this country is good and getting better . . . Many of our elderly are survivors—survivors of diseases that would once have killed them: stroke, heart disease and others. [The increased life expectancy] reflects the virtually unprecedented declines in mortality in the age groups over 65 that we have been experiencing since the late 1960s.

News conference,
Washington, Dec. 3/
Los Angeles Times,
12-4:(I)1.

Robert N. Butler
Director,
National Institute on Aging
of the United States

3

Most gerontologists feel the natural or inherent genetic limit for human beings is about 110 years. In this country, life expectancy at birth is 73 if you lump men and women together. We have dramatically increased life expectancy since the turn of the century, when men expected to live to 46 and women to 48, but we still have 37 years to add before expectancy matches the maximum life span . . . So far, we haven't found any biologic reason *not* to live to 110.

Interview/
U.S. News & World Report,
8-24:35.

Rhonda Copelon
Lawyer,
Center for Constitutional Rights

4

[On the current controversy over legal abortions, of which she is a proponent]: One has to recognize that underlying the drive [against abortions] is a religious-moral position. When you enact a law at the behest of a religiously motivated movement, you have the potential for the most extreme application. A good example is Prohibition, which started with an attack on public drunkenness and ended up making Constitutionally illegal the most minimum form of alcoholized beer. It ended up trying to impose a morality through a criminal statute which had been given the force of the Constitution. That is a real danger. Most of the people who want to treat abortion as a severe crime want to see all abortions ferreted out . . . I think the underlying motive is an attack on women, on their right to self-determination which is at the core of being human, and on their right to be sexual apart from procreation. If there is no abortion, every act of sex is an act of fear.

Interview/The New York Times, 4-19:(4)14.

Norman Cousins
Senior lecturer, School of Medicine,
University of California, Los Angeles;
Former editor, "Saturday Review"

1

I can't overestimate the importance of attitudes and confidence [in a heart-attack victim], because, you see, the body manufactures cholesterol under conditions of apprehension and stress. There are many things involved in heart attack. Just looking at cholesterol alone is not enough. Your ability to be confident about your recovery, your ability to experience joy, the ability to have fun, the ability to work, your ability to look forward to things—these things are an essential part of bringing about the balances in the body. Attitude is not a substitute for treatment any more than treatment is a substitute for attitude. [But] if medical science has 10 points to bring to the encounter, then the individual has 10 points to bring to the encounter. The important thing to see is how close you can get to 20 points.

Interview, Los Angeles/
Los Angeles Times, 5-11:(V)5.

Michael Crichton
Author; Physician

2

[On his being a physician-turned-author]: It's sort of understood that a large percentage of people who go to law school will not be practicing lawyers. But medicine, at least when I was in it, was thought of differently—it was revered in a certain way that made leaving it much like leaving the priesthood.

Interview, New York/
The New York Times Book Review, 2-8:30.

Lewis A. Engman
President, Pharmaceutical
Manufacturers Association

3

When a [drug] company discovers a promising new compound, it must patent it right away or risk losing it to a competitor. The patent is generally issued within two years, and

the 17-year term begins to wind down right away. But the drug at the time of the patent issuance is almost never ready for the market. On the average, it takes seven to 10 years of development and testing to secure [FDA] approval. Which means that effective patent life is 17 years, less seven to 10, or about half as long as Congress originally decided was required to provide innovators adequate investment incentives. [As a result,] we've created a situation where the incentive for building a better mousetrap is twice that for coming out with a new drug to cure cancer. That's an incredible state of affairs.

Los Angeles Times, 12-28:(IV)5.

Indira Gandhi
Prime Minister of India

4

My idea of a better-ordered world is one in which medical discoveries would be free of patents and there would be no profiteering from life or death. Affluent societies are spending vast sums of money understandably on the search for new products and processes to alleviate suffering and to prolong life. [But drug manufacturers are driven by] profit, fierce competition and recourse to hard-sell advertising.

Before World Health Organization,
Geneva, May 6/The Washington Post, 5-7:(A)16.

Carolyn F. Gerster
Physician; Former president,
National Right to Life Committee

5

[Arguing against abortion]: The statement that "life begins at conception" is not a religious dogma but a biological fact. If one is prepared to give a woman the unrestricted right to kill her unborn daughter, one had better be prepared to some day give the daughter the unrestricted right to kill her aged mother. Euthanasia has followed abortion as the night follows day.

At Senate Separation of Powers Subcommittee
hearing on a bill to ban abortions,
Washington, June 18/
The New York Times, 6-19:9.

Ira Glasser
Executive director,
American Civil Liberties Union

1

. . . the whole [abortion] dispute in my view is a religious dispute and always has been. [The anti-abortionists'] view is that the fetus, from the moment of conception, is the moral equivalent of a human being and that, therefore, an abortion, even 30 seconds after conception, is the equivalent of murder. Now, if they're right, if the fertilized egg is a human being, then abortion is murder, and it's really no different than killing a child who is six months old. But if you don't believe that, it's not very different than pulling a tooth. The question of whether the fertilized egg is alive is not the question. It's alive like the tooth is alive. It's alive like an insect is alive. It's alive like a bacteria is alive. Or a plant. The question is not: Is it alive? The question is: Is it a human being? When you abort an egg, is it the same as killing a baby?

Interview, New York/
Los Angeles Times, 12-4:(I-A)7.

Jere Goyan
Former Commissioner, Food and Drug
Administration of the United States

2

Drug companies have a tendency to try to sell drugs and not to convey information . . . Too often the wrong drug has been given to the wrong patient at the wrong time and in the wrong amounts . . . Too much drug therapy has been atrociously irrational.

Interview/
Los Angeles Herald Examiner, 6-22:(A)9.

Robert Hartman
Economist, Brookings Institution

3

[Saying President Reagan should not exempt Medicare from his proposed Federal spending cuts]: Medicare is as important as Medicaid if you want to stop spiraling costs and excess utilization of health resources. In

the long run, the only way to curb government medical costs is to require patients to pay a share. Cost-sharing has to be part of the system now. And Medicare would be more amenable to cost-sharing than Medicaid, which is a program for the poor.

The Christian Science Monitor, 3-25:5.

Lawrence Hatterer
Psychiatrist, New York Hospital-
Cornell Medical Center

4

The degree of polyaddictiveness is not known by the public. But the concept of being "high," whether on drugs or some activity that triggers the release of brain chemicals, is becoming part of our ethos. Kids who complain they're bored, that life is dull, are reflecting society's idea that normal levels of activity or sensation are undesirable. We have the sense that nobody should be uncomfortable—ever.

Interview/The New York Times, 1-27:17.

Henry J. Hyde
United States Representative,
R—Illinois

5

. . . abortion is the killing of an innocently inconvenient human life. If human life is precious in our society, it ought to be protected from extermination, whether for sociological, economical or any other reason. We legally protect snail darters [fish], wild birds and dolphins—even lawn grass. The unborn child is particularly vulnerable and needs protection.

Interview/
U.S. News & World Report, 5-4:31.

Julius Jacobson
Surgeon; Pioneer in
microvascular surgery

6

[On his being an innovator]: I was taught early on that half of what's in the textbooks is wrong—if you only knew which half. If you're not constrained by existing knowledge and

371

(JULIUS JACOBSON)

don't have the idea that what you do is the best that can be done, you've got the mind-set to be an innovator.

Interview, New York/
Chicago Tribune, 3-22:(1)6.

John Paul II
Pope

1

Science and medicine offer a message of hope and commitment for all of humanity. If only a minimum part of the budget for the arms race would be devoted to this cause, important successes could be achieved to alleviate the conditions of many suffering persons . . . Mental illness, which affects about 3 per cent of the world's population, must be given special consideration because it constitutes the gravest obstacle toward the realization of man.

New Year's Day address, Vatican City, Jan. 1/
Los Angeles Times, 1-2:(I)11.

2

[Arguing against abortion]: It is the task, the duty, of the church to reaffirm that procured abortion is death. It is the killing of innocent creatures. In consequence, the church considers any legislation favorable to procured abortion as a very grave offense to the primary rights of mankind and to the divine commandment, "Thou shalt not kill."

Vatican City, May 10/
Los Angeles Times, 5-11:(I)9.

Edward M. Kennedy
United States Senator,
D—Massachusetts

3

[Criticizing Reagan Administration plans to transfer Federally supported health programs to state and local governments]: These Federal programs were developed precisely because states and local governments were either unwilling or unable to meet basic health-care needs. The Administration's proposals contain no assurance that Federal dollars would

be spent to meet health-care needs. They contain no assurance that funds will be targeted to the poor and the under-served. They contain no assurance that services by the states with Federal funds meet minimum quality standards. In short, the Administration's legislation is nothing more than a formula for writing a blank check.

At Senate Labor and Human Resources Committee
hearing, Washington, April 2/
The New York Times, 4-3:10.

Alan Levin
Professor of dermatology, University
of California, Berkeley

4

We are allergic to the 20th century. The increased use of petrochemicals has created disease states which result in depression, lack of motivation, increased irritability; and these factors then would lead to reduced productivity, financial stress and also crime . . . We see men and women with this disease and we call it acquired allergy.

San Francisco/
Los Angeles Times, 6-14:(I)3.

Stuart B. Levy
Professor of medicine and micro-
biology, Tufts University Medical School

5

[Saying there is an over-use of antibiotics today]: In this country, doctors prescribe antibiotics for everything, including ailments such as the common cold, for which the drug is not effective. Antibiotics are added in animal feed. In Third World countries, antibiotics are available without prescriptions and used as a cure-all.

News conference, Boston, Aug. 4/
The New York Times, 8-6:8.

Jean Mayer
Nutritionist;
President, Tufts University

6

If you look at different populations of the world, they don't have the same spectrum of

(JEAN MAYER)

diseases as they get older. It gives one hope that one can eliminate disease . . . When Japanese move to this country [the U.S.], their disease patterns change. The longer they live here the more they have exactly the same distributions of cancer as Caucasian Americans. So factors associated with mode of life, and probably with nutrition, influence whether people develop cancer of the stomach or cancer of the colon or cancer of the breast or don't develop cancer at all . . . The same thing is true for hypertension. If you look at a map of the world, the prevalence of hypertension is so clearly associated with salt intake . . . In some of the islands of Japan where salt intake is much higher [than in the U.S.], 40 per cent of the population is hypertensive.

Interview, Chicago/
Chicago Tribune, 8-4:(1)8.

Eugene McCarthy
Physician, New York Hospital-
Cornell Medical Center

1

[On "second-opinion programs," which require two medical opinions on the necessity for surgery before insurance companies will pay]: We now feel that we could target these programs at just six or seven much-performed procedures—like hysterectomies and knee, back, cataract and bunion surgery—with a much more dramatic yield in operations not done and money saved . . . There is one more benefit. When a second-opinion program is started, there is usually a drop of 8 to 15 per cent in surgical benefits paid—just because of the "sentinel effect," the fact that doctors recommending surgery now know another doctor may be looking over their shoulder.

New York, Feb. 2/
The Washington Post, 2-3:(A)12.

Karen Mulhauser
Executive director, National Abortion
Rights Action League

2

The right to choose abortion is a moral position. There has never been any causal relation-

ship demonstrated between the availability of legal abortion and the decline in morality [in society]. Indeed, it is immoral to force a 12-year-old victim of incest to continue a pregnancy and, as a child, to raise a child. It is immoral to force a couple who knows that the woman is carrying a seriously deformed fetus to bring that child into the world. Also, it is immoral to force any woman who is unwillingly pregnant and in desperate need of medical care to continue her pregnancy.

Interview/U.S. News & World Report, 5-4:32.

Barbara Nichols
President,
American Nursing Association

3

Nursing basically is just tough work. You can become physically fatigued from the physical work and psychically drained. When you add to that work a work environment that treats nursing as a series of tasks that anyone can do, you begin to understand why so many nurses are leaving the workforce. There is a lack of acknowledgment of the contribution and knowledge nurses make not only to patient care but also to the quality of life.

Los Angeles Times, 2-11:(I-A)7.

John T. Noonan, Jr.
Professor of law, University of
California, Berkeley

4

[On abortion]: The terrible fact [is] that Americans are now killing their own offspring on a scale exceeding that of any . . . The taking of the life of the unborn cannot be private. It is a social act. Multiplied one million times a year, it is a social act amounting to atrocity.

Before Senate Constitution Subcommittee,
Washington, Oct. 5/
Los Angeles Times, 10-6:(I)9.

Humphry Osmond
Professor of psychiatry, University
of Alabama, Birmingham

5

One reflection of the change in doctor-patient relationships is the increase in suits against doctors. The ironical thing is that the most

(HUMPHRY OSMOND)

skilled doctors, the technically brilliant chaps, get the worst suits against them—in part because so much more is expected of them. Many of these physicians are often extremely brusque. The great surgeons very frequently relate rather curiously to their patients. But if you feel that Doctor X is going to save your life, you are not likely to worry about whether he has nice manners. Over-all, medicine is not built on very sensitive and imaginative persons. I don't go to the most sensitive physician I can find if I want some special and important procedure; that person's sensitivity and kindness might lead him to overlook important things in my condition.

Interview/U.S. News & World Report, 9-28:66.

Bob Packwood
United States Senator, R-Oregon

1

[Criticizing anti-abortion activists]: These modern-day Puritans are convinced they are right, as convinced as Cromwell, and they are prepared to impose on us, if they can, their view of God's will. It is a dangerous and pernicious theology, and those who hold it—if they are successful in this effort [to outlaw abortion]—will not stop until they have imposed upon us a restriction of all of our liberties with which they do not agree.

Before Senate Constitution Subcommittee,
Washington, Oct. 5/
Los Angeles Times, 10-6:(I)9.

Itzhak Perlman
Violinist

2

[On being in the wheelchair as a result of polio when he was a child]: When you are in a wheelchair, people don't talk to you. Perhaps they think it's contagious, or perhaps they think that crippled legs mean a crippled mind. But whatever the reason, they treat you like a thing. I will be traveling, with someone pushing my wheelchair, and when we come to the passport station the officer will ask, "Where is his pass-

port?" I always make sure that I have my passport with *me*, and I look up at him and say, "*I* have my passport." I make him talk to *me*.

Interview, New York/
The Washington Post, 3-19:(D)14.

Joseph A. Pursch
Corporate medical director, Comprehensive Care Corp.; Former chief of alcohol rehabilitation services, U.S. Naval Regional Medical Center, Long Beach, Calif.

3

[Alcoholism is] epidemic. It's also a communicable disease. You can communicate some illnesses by transmission, like germs on towels and coffee cups, and kissing and making love. But alcoholism is much more communicable. People teach it to each other and they raise their children to become alcoholics. Hardly anyone ever encourages anybody to go out and get VD or meningitis or tonsilitis or scarlet fever, but people do encourage each other to get into alcoholism. They push drinking by having drinking traditions, by having "happy hours," by meeting with all the girls at 4 o'clock right around the corner . . .

Interview/
San Francisco Examiner & Chronicle,
4-26:(Sunday Punch)7.

4

Alcoholics and problem drinkers are being treated, but they are being treated for alcohol-related problems—gastroenteritis, liver disease, heart muscle ailments, broken bones, burns—rather than the underlying disease, alcoholism. The average alcoholic spends a lifetime in and out of hospitals for alcohol-related problems, but is almost never treated for alcoholism.

Interview, Washington/
Chicago Tribune, 9-3:(I)15.

Ronald Reagan
President of the United States

5

I happen to believe [that] in abortion we are taking a human life . . . [California has] a law

(RONALD REAGAN)

that says that if someone abuses or mistreats a pregnant woman to the point of causing the death of her unborn child, that individual would be tried for murder. We know that the law of the land gives an unborn child the right to inherit property, and the law protects property rights. Isn't it time we determine if there was some question, if you found a body on the street and you didn't know whether it was dead or alive, wouldn't you opt on the basis that it was alive and not start shoveling dirt on it? This is what I feel about the other [abortion]. Until we determine and make, to the best of our ability, a determination of when life begins, we've been opting on the basis of that, "Well, let's consider they're not alive." I think that everything in our society calls for opting that they might be alive.

News conference, Washington, March 6/
Los Angeles Times, 3-7:(I)7.

Julius B. Richmond
Surgeon General of the United States

1

. . . lower-tar, lower-nicotine cigarettes appear to provide some small protection to the smoker, assuming the absence of changes in smoking behavior. We can accept this as reasonable advice to the individual smoker, but we cannot accept this as a societal answer to the smoking issue. Only by reducing the numbers of smokers in our population can we hope to reduce significantly the illness and death which smoking brings about.

News conference, Washington, Jan. 12/
Los Angeles Herald Examiner, 1-13:(C)8.

John Roach
Roman Catholic Archbishop of
Minneapolis; President, National
Conference of Catholic Bishops

2

[Condemning abortion]: The horrors of nuclear war, though hardly fantasies, are possibilities at present. But the horror of legalized permissive abortion is tragically real. Nearly nine years after the Supreme Court decision of 1973 initiated this carnage, who can doubt that it is time to say, "Enough!" Human dignity and human rights are mocked by this scandal. The concept of just law is mocked by the evasions used to create and continue it.

At National Conference of Catholic Bishops
meeting, Washington, Nov. 17/
The New York Times, 11-18:12.

Leon E. Rosenberg
Chairman, department of human
genetics, Yale University
School of Medicine

3

[Testifying as to when actual human life begins, at hearing on possible abortion legislation]: Some people argue that life begins at conception, but others say that life begins when brain function appears, or when the heart beats, or when a recognizable human form exists in miniature, or when a fetus can survive outside the uterus, or when natural birth occurs. There is no single, simple answer. If I am correct in asserting that the question of when actual life begins is not a scientific matter, then, you may ask, why have so many scientists come here to say that it is? My answer is that scientists, like all other people, have religious feelings to which they are entitled. In this instance, I believe they have failed to distinguish between their personal biases and their professional scientific judgments.

At Senate subcommittee hearing on abortion,
Washington, April 24/
The New York Times, 4-25:9.

James Schoenberger
President, American Heart Association

4

. . . it is realistic to expect we may be able to prevent heart disease. Deaths due to heart disease have gone down 25 per cent in the last 10 years. Deaths due to stroke are going down 5 per cent a year. It is clear to me that stroke is an entirely preventable disease, for the most

(JAMES SCHOENBERGER)

part, and this will probably some day be a rare disease in this country. At a decline of 5 per cent a year, it isn't going to take very long to become rare ... Other diseases will become more troublesome as heart disease becomes less of a problem. In certain age groups, the lines are already crossing between cancer and heart disease. Cancer is now the most important cause of death in some younger age groups and may become so in some of the older groups ... It's not difficult to predict that the cancer rate is going to go up as the population ages and doesn't die of heart disease ... To me, this is not a good trade-off. We'll not stop our efforts so that you can die of heart disease. The answer is to get people to live as long as they can with their hearts and to continue to work on the cancer problem.

Interview, Chicago/
Chicago Tribune, 2-11:(1)4.

Richard S. Schweiker
Secretary of Health and Human
Services of the United States

1

The future of health care under the Reagan Administration can be described in two words: competition and prevention. Restoring competition to the health industry and preventing disease before it strikes will be two themes central to our policies ... We cannot allow health costs to keep climbing, because we simply cannot afford to pay the bill ... This Administration is committed to trying something new. We intend to loose the forces of the market to make the health-care system more competitive. We believe competition will prove to be the single greatest force for controlling prices ... [On the prevention side,] by taking simple steps—by not smoking, by using alcohol in moderation, by eating a proper diet and getting the proper amount of exercise and sleep—a 45-year-old man can expect to live 10 or 11 years longer than a person who does not make these choices. We must convince people how to take control of their own health,

how to adopt habits that can make trips to the doctor less frequent. Prevention should be in the minds of every American, and at the heart of every health-care institution.

At conference sponsored by
"The National Journal," Washington, June 11/
The New York Times, 6-12:8.

Henry Siegman
Executive director,
American Jewish Congress

2

[Criticizing a proposed bill in Congress that would restrict abortions]: These amendments take sides, or would allow the government to take sides, not between a moral and an amoral approach [to abortion], but between two conflicting moral approaches that are equally grounded in profound religious conviction. The proper role of government in a free society is to allow different religious traditions to inculcate their own beliefs with respect to abortion, and to leave that final decision to the woman, answering to God and conscience.

Before Senate Constitution Subcommittee,
Washington, Nov. 5/
The Washington Post, 11-6:(A)3.

Albert Szent-Gyorgyi
Nobel Prize-winning scientist;
Scientific director, Institute for
Muscle Research, Woods Hole, Mass.

3

The whole cancer field, for as long as I can remember, has been centered on coming up with a quick cure for the disease. This is plain nonsense. You see, the cell is like a very involved watch. The watch is made up of hundreds of little wheels and parts. First you must know how it is put together, how it works. But in cancer, nobody ever asks that. In spite of all the noise about cancer and the enormous expense, practically no *cancer* research is done in this country ... The emphasis has shifted to the environment, which is very interesting. But this is also not *cancer* research. To research cancer means to go into the cancer itself and

(ALBERT SZENT-GYORGYI)

find out what is wrong with it—with the electrons. But practically no one does that.

Interview/
The Saturday Evening Post, Jan.-Feb.:28.

Sarah Weddington
Lawyer; Former Assistant to the
President of the United States
(Jimmy Carter)

1

[Arguing against a bill that would ban abortions]: You have not heard from the family of the 11-year-old girl in Nebraska who became pregnant and had to have an abortion last month, but who might not have had that choice if this bill were law. You have not heard from the Virginia mother who is watching her child die an agonizing death from Tay-Sachs disease, who is pregnant again, and who, if this bill were law, would face the possibility of condemning another infant to the same torture.

At Senate Separation of Powers Subcommittee
hearing on abortion, Washington, June 18/
The New York Times, 6-19:9.

Gail Worden
Executive vice president,
American Hospital Association

2

Aside from the cost-containment issue, the availability of nurses to take care of patients is the largest problem for hospitals today. The problem exists generally across the country and is critical in some areas. If they don't have sufficient staffing, hospitals are closing units. In some cities, there's a waiting list to get into hospitals, so patients often have to delay surgery.

Los Angeles Times, 2-11:(I-A)7.

377

The Performing Arts

MOTION PICTURES

Robert Aldrich
Director

1

Those guys who come along and catch lightning in a bottle with one hit film and become overnight geniuses, they make me laugh. If they don't tell you that success has to do with timing, over which they have no control, selling, over which they have no control, and the mood of audiences around the world, over which they have no control—then they're idiots.

Interview, Los Angeles/
Los Angeles Times, 10-11:(Calendar)25.

Woody Allen
Actor, Director, Screenwriter

2

[Saying he must strike a balance between artistic and commercial film work]: With films . . . you need millions of dollars of other people's money. In other words, I'm not asking 20,000 people to buy my things; I'm asking 20 million. So I try to walk that balance. Now, [director] Ingmar Bergman works in Sweden and works with a state-owned financed thing, and he can write something about death and medieval Sweden, and if a hundred people come and see it, he'll just go on to the next thing, the state having lost $200,000. But I don't have that situation. I'm in a popular medium. So I try to walk that line, to do good stuff that doesn't succumb to commercial demands. But I have to keep one eye, or one toe, in the commercial world.

Interview, New York/
Chicago Tribune, 5-31:(6)22.

Nestor Almendros
Cinematographer

3

Cinematography is not an art in and of itself. It is part of an art. For an art to be an art, it has to be independent of anything.

The Hollywood Reporter, 9-11:(S)14.

Robert Altman
Director

4

The old moguls were avaricious and profit-oriented. But at least they were smart enough to know they had to develop what they would eventually prey on. The new studio people aren't that smart. You'd never hear of [Humphrey] Bogart if he had come along five years ago, because who'd move him carefully from picture to picture and develop his talent and image? Nobody. The film companies have forgotten their responsibility to nurture the talent they make their profit from. If I came along with an innovative project like *M*A*S*H* today, I know I'd never get it off the ground. Everything is in the hands of accountants now, who look at nothing but the bottom line.

Interview, New York/
The Christian Science Monitor, 11-12:22.

Michelangelo Antonioni
Director

5

A talented individual—director, actor, writer, composer—can still express his world view in an industrial structure as complex as the cinema . . . John Huston is a born *auteur*, a man who reflects his own universe in the disparate themes, who can take over the in-

(MICHELANGELO ANTONIONI)

dustrial machinery and make a few errors. Orson Welles thinks of himself as much more than the *enfant terrible* of American film, just as [Ingmar]Bergman is much more than an enigmatic philosopher.

Interview/World Press Review, June:58.

Marvin Antonowsky
Vice president in charge of marketing, Columbia Pictures

1

The Western became obsolete when space became the new frontier. The old frontier is dead. Kids have no interest in it. As long as kids are buying tickets, there will probably never be another successful Western.

Los Angeles Times, 6-7:(Calendar)5.

Alan Arkin
Actor

2

When recently have you heard anyone in Hollywood say it doesn't matter how much money a film makes? In the '50s and '60s, there were people in the film business taking responsibility and taking chances . . . Now I get the feeling no one's interested in anything that doesn't either make $80-million or win an award.

Interview, New York/
Los Angeles Times, 8-7:(VI)6.

Samuel Z. Arkoff
Producer; Former chairman and president, American International Pictures

3

[On the competition motion-picture theatres face from pay TV, cassettes, etc.]: All these new gadgets are home gadgets. The young want to get out of the house. No matter what lures the proprietors of the new media may extend, there is a tribal instinct for the young to congregate together. These deep-seated instincts take young people out of the house and into the

theatre. They are and will remain [theatres'] best customers.

At ShoWest convention, Reno, Nev., Feb. 9/
Los Angeles Times, 2-11:(VI)4.

Robert Benton
Director

4

The cost of [making] movies is astronomical now, and that's dangerous. It makes it difficult to take creative risks. If it continues, fewer pictures will get made. With stakes so high, directors can't afford to fail. I just don't know how Hollywood will bounce back. The person who comes up with the answer has my nomination for the Nobel Prize.

Time, 3-30:71.

Bruce Beresford
Australian director

5

[On the difficulty of selling films, like his current *Breaker Morant*, to U.S. film distributors]: If something is not immediately exotic, they don't want to know. They see a film about modern Australia and they complain about the accents. And it's hard enough to get a film like *Breaker Morant* shown over here [in the U.S.]. It has won a lot of awards, but you've practically got to win the Nobel Prize to get a film on in the States. I remember showing *The Getting of Wisdom* to some American exhibitors at the Cannes Film Festival. They asked who was in it. I said, "No one you've ever heard of." They asked what it was about. I said a girls' school. They asked where's the sex. I said there wasn't any—and it was goodbye.

Interview/Chicago Tribune, 5-17:(6)15.

Ingmar Bergman
Director

6

I do not make masterpieces. I am a craftsman making tables and chairs for other people. They have to choose if they will use them. If

(INGMAR BERGMAN)

one of the pictures I have made has given only one human being something for his life, I would be happy. If people use my pictures some way, it doesn't matter if they have made them angry. They have become emotionally involved. That is what I am after.

At Southern Methodist University seminar/
Los Angeles Times, 5-12:(VI)2.

Bruno Bettelheim
Psychologist

1

Since the moving picture is the central art of our time and the most authentic of all American art, my conclusion is that only the moving picture can give us the myths we need to guide us and to permit us to find satisfaction in life, despite all the existential unhappiness to which all men are heir.

Delivering American Film Institute's
Patricia Wise Lecture, Washington/
Los Angeles Times, 1-9:(VI)4.

Theodore Bikel
Actor

2

I approach a film by way of remembering what live performing is about. It's difficult to perform to a camera crew and no live bodies that would react with a sigh, sob or laugh. It's especially true of comedy, when you're working for a laugh that may come six months later.

Interview, Connecticut/
San Francisco Examiner & Chronicle,
4-19:(Datebook)31.

John Boorman
Director

3

. . . making any film is a process of discovery in its own right. There is no way of doing it but to feel your way. You are constantly groping forward, finding and discovering. Shooting

for me is an agony. It could be pleasurable but for the pressure of time and money. With every minute that passes, you mentally hear the meter ticking away.

Interview, London/
The New York Times, 2-22:(2)17.

4

The success-failure syndrome [in Hollywood] exerts such enormous pressure. After doing *The Deer Hunter*, Michael Cimino couldn't really go off and make a small Western. The system insists he turn it into an epic. You either fail dismally or succeed beyond your wildest dreams. [Francis Ford] Coppola has to keep trying to top himself in order to hang onto his reputation as a whiz kid. Stanley Kubrick was one of the first it happened to. I was having lunch with Jack Nicholson while he was making *The Shining* with Stanley. He said: "It's so exhausting. We did 147 takes of one shot today. With Stanley, I always try to peak at around take 40." You get a similar problem with stars. The more you pay them the less they do. And the expenses multiply. A $3-million star has to have his own makeup man, who makes twice as much as the set's makeup man, who then demands a raise. When [Marlon] Brando was doing *Superman* he wouldn't memorize lines. In that scene where he talks to the baby, they had a television monitor behind the baby's head, so he could read the lines. On one take, the baby reached behind his head and hit the switch that turned off the television. Brando never changed his tone, just started saying, "And if baby turns off the television set, daddy won't be able to read his lines."

Interview/
The Washington Post, 4-12:(H)2.

Mel Brooks
Actor, Director, Screenwriter

5

You've got to risk a lot of critical wrath sometimes because your job [as a film-maker] is not to please the critics. Your job really is to please the public, the paying audience. I think critics

THE PERFORMING ARTS—MOTION PICTURES

(MEL BROOKS)

are hamstrung. I don't think they can get as fair an assessment of a film as they think. After all, they get in for nothing; they don't wait on line; so they don't even have the pre-conditioning that is necessary to appreciate a film. I think the social flux [of going to the movies] is very important. The critics don't buy candy or popcorn. They don't sit with the bubbling mob of youngsters that sits there waiting to devour the comedy on the screen. And so their critical view of it all—well, is it fair to say they're a little too critical?

Interview, New York/
Chicago Tribune, 6-7:(6)5.

1

. . . comedy has a lot more immortality, a lot more durability than drama. D. W. Griffith made *Birth of a Nation* [in 1915], but you try to find it playing somewhere [today]! I can show you 20 comedies made at roughly the same time that you can see [today] in movie houses and pay more for—from Chaplin's *City Lights* to Keaton's *The Navigator* to anything that Laurel and Hardy made. I mean, comedy may not be recognized in its time, but it always has more *cachet* and more real value than any drama ever made. Any drama! I mean, I love *The Maltese Falcon*, but it will never stand up over time to Chaplin, Buster Keaton, the Marx Brothers, or to Laurel and Hardy.

Interview, New York/
Chicago Tribune, 6-7:(6)5.

Dyan Cannon
Actress

2

There are so many fables about actors. Actors are supposed to be children and very emotional and out of control. And it's just the opposite. Actors have to be able to call on any emotion like this [snaps fingers]. They're far more disciplined than most people are trained to be.

Interview, New York/
The Christian Science Monitor, 6-17:(B)8.

Charles Champlin
Arts and book critic, and former
film critic, "Los Angeles Times"

3

[On why he gave up being a film critic]: . . . there are not enough movies around to strain the intelligence of a geranium. There is a desperate lack of passion in the film-making process. I don't see anyone running a studio who has any passion for the creative process, or, for that matter, any creative control. It's not that they have granted that control to directors; they have simply surrendered it out of terror and ignorance.

Interview, Los Angeles/
"W": A Fairchild publication, 7-17:8.

Susan Clark
Actress, Producer

4

The worst thing about producing is sitting around whistling, calling your friends for lunch while you wait for the writers to write. And you're the whipping-boy on the production; you get whipped a lot. Nobody gives you a chair; nobody asks you if you'd like coffee, no union supports you.

Interview, Los Angeles/
Los Angeles Times, 1-6:(VI)8.

James Coburn
Actor

5

[On acting]: I take in all the impressions and information [about the character]. And when the time comes for action, I just let it go. It's "jazz" acting. It's like when Sarah Vaughan sings a song. She sings the lyrics, but she doesn't sing it exactly the way it was written. It bears her style. That's the way it is with [acting] roles. Each character has a style. Once you find out the character's style, it becomes really simple. With jazz, you have to know the chord structures, the form of the thing. But when you

381

WHAT THEY SAID IN 1981

stand up there and sing, you don't think about it. You just let it flow.

Interview, Los Angeles/
Chicago Tribune, 11-11:(1)17.

Francis Ford Coppola
Director, Screenwriter

1

We don't make "movies" any more in Hollywood, any more than they make "cars" in Detroit. A Chevy is the same as a Buick is the same as an Oldsmobile. The era of handmade cars is over, and the era of handmade movies is soon about to be over. The cost of making films is going up so fast that the only way the film companies can survive is to make their movies so predictable that they can move them out like so many units in an assembly line. I mean, a good movie coming out of this country right now is really an accident and a testament to the survival instincts of the talents who made it.

Interview, Los Angeles/
Chicago Tribune, 2-8:(6)12.

George Cukor
Director

2

If the scene is not there on paper, you [the director] can do all the fiddling in the world, and it won't work. Good writers are the most important thing, or I should say good dramatists. Good writing isn't enough. Often you read something that's impressive on the page, but it doesn't play. I find when I work with a really good script, it carries *me* along. Incidentally, I don't believe in improvisation. I find it excrutiating.

Interview, Beverly Hills, Calif./
The New York Times, 10-4:(2)14.

Catherine Deneuve
French actress

3

We European actors are not as conscious of career as Americans appear to be. Here [in the

U.S.], it seems, there is a lot of pressure to make choices which will shape a career. But with us, a career is something you realize you have when you look back.

Interview, Beverly Hills, Calif./
"W": a Fairchild publication, 4-10:10.

Sandy Dennis
Actress

4

A lot of acting is embarrassment; people are embarrassed to do things. Once you get over that, and you can make an ass out of yourself in rehearsal or anywhere, then you have the ability . . . It's when you feel foolish that you hold back in acting.

Interview, Washington/
The Christian Science Monitor,
8-26:(B)12.

Brian De Palma
Director

5

When you work in an art-form, you're very aware of what its primary strengths are. And I think film is one of the few mediums in which you can deal with sex and violence; you can't really do it on television or on stage. So they're elements to be explored in film. Whether you want to paint with those colors is up to you. But because of my very sort of formalistic training, I sometimes go for what is the strongest, most vivid color on the palette, which in the case of movies is violence. It plays very strongly, and I can do it very well. I don't think you can work with all these colors on the palette if you start trying to decide if something's a good color or a bad color. Either you do it well or you don't do it well.

Interview/
The New York Times, 7-19:(4)22.

Barry Diller
Chairman,
Paramount Pictures Corporation

6

[On the escalating costs of film production]:
. . . it's not the dozen or so big-budget pictures

(BARRY DILLER)

that are the problem. The problem is not the movie of size and scale you decide to take a risk on because you believe in it. Taking risks is what I do for a living. The problem is not with the size but with outsize, with pictures that should cost $4-million and now cost $14-million. Everyone complains about the inflationary spiral. But when a contemporary movie shot by a relatively unknown director takes 110 days to shoot, that's not an inflationary spiral. That's a travesty of management. United Artists lost more money on their insignificant little pictures all together than they will on [the very expensive] *Heaven's Gate*. What Paramount is trying to deal with now is the $16-million movie that should have cost $6-million. We have to attack this problem now, or in three years there will be so much blood on the floor you won't be able to mop it up. It may take an industry disaster to enforce efficiency at some studios . . .

Interview/
Los Angeles Herald Examiner, 3-24:(B)4.

Robert Duvall
Actor

1

A script is just words on a page. There's an expression like "a pound of behavior is worth a ton of ideas," or something like that. An actor takes those ideas and lifts them off a page and transforms them into behavior. My life is geared toward behavior. I need to make something happen at that moment. I want to see people thinking on film, thinking thoughts on film. A balance between real life and movie life.

Interview, New York/
The New York Times, 10-25:(2)15.

Clint Eastwood
Actor, Director

2

[On the film *Heaven's Gate*, which was withdrawn from release by United Artists for re-editing after it had gone millions of dollars

over budget]: What I wonder is what would have happened, in a case like that, in the old days? What would Jack L. Warner or Harry Cohn have done? They would've been down there when the guy was $100,000 over budget, saying, "Take a hike, kid." Nobody does that now. I asked one studio exec one time about a picture he was having similar problems with. "Why don't you get in there and express your opinion that the film ought to run two hours instead of four?" He said, "Well, we don't want to get a reputation for tampering with a film-maker's work." "That's very noble," I said, "and being a director myself, I hope you never want to tamper with *my* work. But I also hope that if I come to you and say, 'I want to make a three-hour film, I've got about an hour's worth of material here'—well, I hope you'll kick me in the side of the head.

Interview, New York/
The New York Times, 1-11:(2)15.

Blake Edwards
Director, Screenwriter

3

[Saying he wants complete control of his films, including distribution and advertising]: I know they [the studios] have answers to that . . . that a film-maker hasn't good business sense. Bull. I'm a terrific businessman. And we are beginning to see more outside interests, who would not interfere in the making of a picture, perfectly willing to put up millions and millions of dollars. Hopefully, they'll get a hit; but if they don't, they'll at least get a tax-write-off. More and more, you're going to see the studios as we know them becoming more impotent because that money is coming from elsewhere.

Interview, Iver Heath, England/
"W": a Fairchild publication, 7-17:9.

Douglas Fairbanks, Jr.
Actor

4

[The] Golden Age of the '30s in Hollywood was horrible; horrible in the sense that oligar-

383

chical tyranny—as exercised by the mostly pin-headed studio chieftains—is horrible.

Interview, Saratoga Springs, N.Y./
Los Angeles Times, 4-19:(Calendar)16.

Federico Fellini
Director

1

I am a story-teller. I want to say a story about myself, my dreams, strange things, lies, the combination of sincerity and fantasy, auto-biography and complete invention, with the desire to astonish, to make love, to move, to put in some philosophies, some doubts. Anyway, I make a picture because I sign a contract. I take an advance; I don't want to give it back. That is the real reason.

Interview, New York/
San Francisco Examiner & Chronicle,
4-19:(Datebook)18.

2

[His advice to young film-makers]: To try to do what they have in their own mind. To not believe in other directors. To not believe in the producer. To try to do what they want to do, if they have something to say. To be-lieve in what they think. To not be tied to theology, to commercialism, or to the audience. Just to be completely and dangerously free.

Interview, New York/
Chicago Tribune, 6-28:(6)2.

Sally Field
Actress

3

All I ever wanted to do was act. Sometimes, these days, you get so caught up in finding properties and in who the director will be—and then who will get along and who'll do the rewrites, and about the budget and what it will be and how and where the money will come from—that you forget why you're here. You

forget that you're here because you wanted to act. That's all.

Interview, Los Angeles/
Los Angeles Times, 12-21:(VI)8.

Milos Forman
Director

4

The way one perceives a book and a film are totally different. You read a book in the privacy of your room. You are the boss; you set the pace and rhythm of your reading. In the movie house, you can't do that. When you make a film, you realize that the audience will be powerless to stop it, or flip back to refresh their memories, or skip the boring parts. They are at the mercy of your storytelling. If you want to keep their attention for 2½ hours, you have to *follow* the story. Whatever doesn't contribute to the main plot-line has to be sacrificed. You make the choices instinctively. Only then do you analyze them rationally.

Interview, New York/
The Christian Science Monitor, 12-10:19.

Lillian Gish
Actress

5

[On the old silent film, *Napoleon*, which was just re-released]: It was made more than 50 years ago and it is still great. After all, only 5 per cent of the world speaks English. Silent films are universal. Everybody can understand them, and there is a world market for them without dubbing. And with music as well. There was full orchestra for the *Napoleon* screening, just as there used to be for many of [director D. W.] Griffith's films when they played the old movie palaces. If directors were brave enough now, like Mr. Griffith was, they'd be doing silent films again. Only recently I saw the movie *Black Stallion*, and there was a mar-velous 30-minute sequence without dialogue which went beautifully. You can't keep silent films from coming back . . . They are the uni-versal language. I'd just like to see them come back while I'm still here.

Interview, New York/
The Christian Science Monitor, 2-13:19.

Jean-Luc Godard
French director

1

[In the film industry,] there is no curiosity about trying new ways. The industry does no research. It's like a runner who never trains or a doctor who never practices but who operates once every two years or so. Pity the poor patient.

Interview, Los Angeles/
Los Angeles Times, 1-22:(VI)2.

2

Good movies are made only when a country is in bad shape. Why were so many fine Italian movies—like Roberto Rossellini's *Rome* and *Open City*—made in the years just after World War II? Why Italy and why then? The Italians had nothing. Their only hope for legitimacy was the creation of a totally new image to relay to the rest of the world. Now Poland is in turmoil. Consequently there are 10 good Polish movies right now. In contrast, I am not sure there is even one good American film.

Interview/
World Press Review, April:61.

Richard Harris
Actor

3

[On film-industry executives]: Those insensitive businessmen sit up there and they claim that they can speak with the voice of the American proletariat from their tables at Ma Maison and Chasen's [restaurants], where they have two-hour lunches at $350 a lunch, all on expense accounts, and go back in their Rolls Royces to their enormous mansions in Beverly Hills and they weekend in Palm Springs, and they can tell us what the taxi-driver wants to see, what the shopkeeper wants to see, what the secretary wants to see? They've lost touch. They've totally lost touch.

Interview, Boston/
The Washington Post, 8-30:(K)8.

Buck Henry
Director, Screenwriter

4

[On producers]: . . . I'll never understand why anyone wants to produce a picture. It's a hard and difficult grind. You have to talk to a whole lot of people I wouldn't dream of talking to about a lot of things I wouldn't ever want to talk about. There's another thing. A producer has to think about just one thing—the picture—for months on end, and that's very unhealthy. Any job that requires you to think about one thing in one light for a long time must be unhealthy. I'd never, ever, want to produce a movie.

Interview, Los Angeles/
Los Angeles Times, 1-4:(Calendar)25.

Katharine Hepburn
Actress

5

. . . as far as acting goes, it's got to be great. That's my motto, anyway. You've got to aim for the top of the mountain because you'll never get a quarter of the way up, in any event. There are just too many things in the way. But if your performance satisfies just the director, if you don't set a really high standard for *yourself*, you're never going to be very interesting because people are perfectly content to have you get off at a way-station. They couldn't care less. The only person who cares is yourself. So you *have* to be damned good, to get noticed or appreciated! And no excuses!

Interview, San Francisco/
After Dark, October:30.

John Huston
Director

6

[Saying he does not like the Hollywood way of life]: I don't like the things that one does, particularly. There are people here that I like very much. But it's never appealed to me as a way of life. I don't like talking about motion pictures, necessarily, and speculating on who's going to get what part. The behavioral habits

WHAT THEY SAID IN 1981

(JOHN HUSTON)

of actors don't enthrall me. And I think there's a tendency on the part of picture-makers to cannibalize themselves. You begin to make motion pictures about motion pictures. To me that's a bore.

Interview, Beverly Hills, Calif./
Saturday Review, January:14.

Glenda Jackson
Actress

1

There were performances I have given that were dreadful. You can't say that the film was bad but I was good. If the film was dreadful, then I was dreadful, too. Would I like to go back over the last 10 years and excise any of them? The answer is no. Whenever I chose them, I chose them for entirely valid reasons—either because I liked the script or I liked the director or the actors. I'm certainly not ashamed of any of [those films]. I wouldn't go so far as to say that I'm proud of all of them. I have gotten things that weren't particularly good scripts that I thought could become good with the right director or the right performance, and didn't. But I've had some very educational failures and I think I've managed very well not to get stuck in a box. I think it's only by trying what you suspect you cannot do that you improve.

Interview, New York/
The New York Times, 3-22:(2)4.

Fay Kanin
Screenwriter; President, Academy of
Motion Picture Arts and Sciences

2

Film is the world language. Movies speak, people to people, in a way nothing else can. Every time I go to Washington I say that the movies of a nation are its greatest ambassadors. That is certainly true of American films.

Daily Variety, 10-26:15.

Larry Kasdan
Screenwriter

3

The idea that you've got to have a huge hit . . . comes from the media and it comes from megahits. Look at Woody Allen. His movies have all made money. They haven't made enormous money, but he works on material that interests him, so he winds up making interesting movies, and the thing is, he doesn't use stars. An interesting movie will draw an audience big enough to pay for itself. But since the conglomerates took over the movie business, they don't understand about small profits. They understand, but it doesn't interest them. The reason they got into the movie business, one of the reasons, was that they saw these enormous payoffs on a small investment. That looked like a dream business to them. Well, it hasn't worked out that way; and when you look at movies from a business point of view, you're dissatisfied all the time.

Interview, Los Angeles/
The Christian Science Monitor,
1-21:(B)9.

Irvin Kershner
Director

4

[On the high costs of making films today]: I never think of my pictures as big or small. I could have shot [The] Empire [Strikes Back] for one million [instead of $25-million]. It would have been a different picture, but it would have been a picture . . . The trouble with most West Coast [film] executives is, they don't want to make films simply earning their money; they want only *winners*. With everything they do, they want to "bust through." They expect you to keep raising the ante [in film costs]. It is standard wisdom here that the man with the zillion-dollar flop is very much more respected than the man with the modest success.

Interview/
The New York Times,
1-18:(4)20.

Akira Kurosawa
Director
1

I don't think film-makers should talk about themselves or their work. They should only express themselves in their films. I still have much to say—in film—and, in fact, when I die, I prefer to just drop dead on the set.
Interview/
The New York Times, 10-4:(2)21.

Jennings Lang
Producer
2

Nowadays you are kidding when you use the word "producer." One guy here is producing three movies and he's never been behind a Moviola. Harry Cohn, whether he could read or write, knew every aspect of his pictures. He wasn't out there buying Aspen or a Pepsi franchise. He was an Indian chief and he knew the reservation.
Interview, Los Angeles/
Los Angeles Times, 11-22:(Calendar)3.

Angela Lansbury
Actress
3

Acting is really understanding other human beings. It has to do with trusting humanity. Once you've learned this, the audience will get any message you wish to send them; and when you feel that the message has been received, it's a heavenly sensation.
Interview, Los Angeles/
Los Angeles Times, 6-21:(Calendar)50.

Eva Le Gallienne
Actress
4

I like to play things that I have to *become.* If I only played myself, that would be a bore. Acting has to take you outside of yourself. But one can't generalize about acting, you know. In any case, it can't be taught.
Interview, New York/
The New York Times,
1-11:(2)1.

Jack Lemmon
Actor
5

Actors are lucky. They can be a little sadder than the average person under any circumstance, or under circumstances that would never bother the average person. By the same token, they can appreciate and see things—that other people won't see—that are quite beautiful. They retain a capacity for excitement. Sensitivity and intelligence go hand in hand. I never met a really good actor who was dumb.
Interview, Los Angeles/
Playboy, June:194.

6

I have a theory about acting, about how healthy it is. I believe that there are an awful lot of actors who may be emotionally screwed-up—but if they weren't actors, they would be *so* screwed-up that they'd be locked away. I think that acting is a tremendously healthy process. Its main appeal is that we'd all *like* to do it. We all do it as children, but as we grow up we are taught that we're not supposed to do it.
Interview, Beverly Hills, Calif./
The New York Times Magazine, 7-12:32.

Mervyn LeRoy
Director
7

. . . they don't make love stories of beauty much any more. Now they make different kinds of love stories. I don't find them so romantic. Now they make films they shouldn't make. I don't go to see many of them. It's like the grocery business: It isn't always easy to find good apples . . . It depresses me when I think back to how great the movie business used to be as compared to now. I hate the violence and all the blood. It's not necessary if you have a good story to tell. I hate all the four-letter words. We didn't need them in my day. We still don't need them. Everyone wants to see love stories, but now they show all the sex. I like a good sex story if it's clean and done with good

(MERVYN LeROY)

3

taste. But there's a thing about romance. You have to know when to stop, to let the audience imagine the rest.

News conference, San Francisco/
San Francisco Examiner & Chronicle,
6-14:(Datebook)36,37.

Jerry Lewis
Actor, Comedian

1

[Saying the Motion Picture Academy should acknowledge comedy]: The Academy is based on the picture business and the picture business started with the Keystone Kops. We [comics] got the attention of the world through this nonsense called slapstick. How do you not acknowledge comedy? I'm looking for nothing more than respect for our art-form. It must be fairly special if only that many people do what I do. But you've got to remember the Academy is the most snobbish body in life. It would be so much more elegant in the eyes of the public if it would think sometimes emotionally. We're in a highly sensitive, emotional business and they brush that under the rug.

Interview/Los Angeles Times,
3-22:(Calendar)23.

Sidney Lumet
Director

2

[On the difficulties of transferring stage plays to the screen]: Plays always struggle against leaving their natural habitat, and the better the play the harder the struggle. Each play that I've translated to film has required a different approach . . . All melodramas, you see, are improbable. But the key to their success on film is to make them seem possible. And the only way to do that is to more solidly legitimize the characters and their actions than is necessary onstage.

Interview, New York/
The New York Times, 5-10:(2)1.

. . . the movies have gone brainless. And what scares me is that it's probably the audiences' fault—not Hollywood's—because Hollywood is just catering to a taste. It's depressing and alarming. In the final analysis, it doesn't matter how brilliantly a *Raiders of the Lost Ark* is done—and Steven Spielberg *is* a brilliant director. Here, and in things like *Superman II*, what we're dealing with is infantile behavior —comic strips and Saturday-afternoon serials. I don't care how respectful the homage is, it's idiocy. There's nothing wrong with anyone's childhood. But there's something wrong with *staying* in it.

Interview, New York/
The Christian Science Monitor, 8-13:18.

Louis Malle
French director

4

During the last 20 years in Europe, film has been recognized as art. I'm not sure this step has been reached here [in the U.S.]. It's possible in Europe to be a successful artist without necessarily being extremely successful commercially. Here, it's basically much more in the hands of the accountants—there is an obsession with the hit, the blockbuster, which means the ultimate goal is for you to come up with a picture that will please everybody. I've always worked the opposite way. I've been more interested in—not in displeasing people, but in disturbing, provoking them. I want to force them to ask questions.

Interview, New York/
The New York Times, 6-28:(2)15.

James Mason
Actor

5

To me, mimicry is a very important part of acting. It is the basic of acting, in fact. You can mimic in very simple terms, as children mimic their parents. Or it can be performed in a very complicated manner, insofar as you have to mimic not only the superficial sur-

(JAMES MASON)

face of the character, but also his mind as well, which encompasses his emotional experience and his aspirations and his knowledge. All these things you have to understand and put them together in one lump in his [the character's] mind, and then proceed to mimic it. Yes, his mind too; you have to do that to be him, you see. But it doesn't mean that you yourself have to be him. So I've never had the least temptation to allow my personal life or behavior to be infected by this imagined person whom I professionally mimic from day to day.

Interview, Washington/
The Christian Science Monitor, 2-4:(B)2.

Walter Matthau
Actor

1

When people talk about comedy as opposed to serious, I wince, because comedy *is* my serious. I'm very serious when I do comedy; I'm even more serious than when I'm doing drama. Comedy should have an emotional foundation. I make my points better when people can laugh at something and then become enlightened.

Interview, Los Angeles/
The New York Times, 8-16:(2)15.

Malcolm McDowell
Actor

2

Technique is 80 per cent of [acting]. It isn't very romantic, I realize, but there it is. This notion of the pure performance, the inspired performance—it's a myth, spread by people who are willing to believe that actors are artists but can't accept the premise that actors *think*. It's *all* thinking, for God's sake. A good actor might do one pure performance in a lifetime. I had mine in *If . . .* thirteen years ago. Don't ask me how I did it, because I haven't got a clue. It was totally intuitive, and it was never like that again. Everything that came after was tainted by technique. And once you begin to

have technique, there's nothing to do but develop more and more, to make it so good that it begins to erase itself. That's the central paradox of an actor's life. I go through hell now to achieve through technique what used to happen automatically.

Interview, New York/
Esquire, April:42.

Kristy McNichol
Actress

3

I don't believe in Method acting. When I'm on the sound stage and not in front of the camera, I feel just like any other bystander. I'll be running around or getting a Coke or playing catch with someone. I never go into my trailer and think about getting into the right mood for my big scene. I can be right in the middle of throwing a ball in the air when they call me for a scene, and I can shift gears in a second. When I'm on the set, I'm totally there. I know everything that's going on; I'm aware of every camera angle. But the moment I step off the set, I'm a different person.

Interview, Los Angeles/
The New York Times, 9-20:(2)21.

Mike Medavoy
Executive vice president,
Orion Pictures Corporation

4

Obviously, I don't believe in the demise of the American movie theatre because that would mean the demise of the American movie business. The audience for movies has always been the young audience. They go out on a date. It's the experience. Now, if you were to tell me that everyone in America is going to have a 35mm projector and a large screen at home, then I might say there could be a drop-off [in theatre attendance]. The truth of the matter is that people like to go to the movies. It's an event. People have been predicting this demise for years. My guess is that we're going to wind up with even larger [theatre] screens and a return to the movie palaces.

Interview, Burbank, Calif./
Los Angeles Times, 6-17:(VI)4.

WHAT THEY SAID IN 1981

Roger Moore
Actor

1

I suppose, to the general public, this is a glamour industry. They feel there's something glamorous about actors, which isn't true at all. You put on a new pair of shoes and your feet hurt and you stand in the sun doing the same scene twenty times over. I mean—where is the champagne and caviar?

Interview/Cosmopolitan, January:163.

Paul Newman
Actor

2

I'll tell you one thought I've had in my old age: The corruption of the American actor. I always knew it happened to others, but I never knew until now that it could happen to me. It's not the money; I don't have to worry about money. It's that you start thinking of yourself as a "movie star" rather than as an actor.

Interview/
The Washington Post, 2-1:(K)1.

3

I used to spend 85 per cent of my time reading [for pleasure]. Now I spend 85 per cent of my time reading for business [looking for suitable scripts for filming]. I think my perceptions about film are pretty good. But the fact is, there simply isn't much good stuff around. So what's an actor to do? You can stop working. But you have to keep the instrument tuned. So you take the best there is and hope for the best. And you always start with the idea that it's going to end up pretty good.

Interview, New York/
The Christian Science Monitor, 12-3:22.

Jack Nicholson
Actor

4

. . . it's important [for actors] to admit that, in terms of the amount of time you spend in front of the camera, you do more bad work than you do good—otherwise there'd be no need for Take Eight. There's a point when you must admit that you're not the perfect master of the living, breathing, walking, standing-still and being fabulous.

Interview, Los Angeles/
Los Angeles Times, 3-15:(Calendar)39.

David Niven
Actor

5

I've had a grand career playing officers, dukes and crooks; and I get down on my knees and thank God for letting a not-very-good actor survive after all these years. The reason I've survived is because movies are typecast. I'm always asked to play people I'm capable of playing. I don't do Chinese laundrymen or Cossacks.

Interview, San Francisco/
San Francisco Examiner & Chronicle,
12-6:(Datebook)34.

Sven Nykvist
Cinematographer

6

I came home from the studio several weeks ago and turned on the TV. I saw a movie dubbed into English that looked very interesting. I could tell the actors were Swedish and thought it was probably a picture that Ingmar [Bergman] made with another cameraman he worked with a lot, Gunnar Fischer. I liked the lighting and the composition very much. It looked different, and suddenly, when the next scene began, I realized it was a film that I had photographed—*The Virgin Spring*. The second I knew it was my work I was watching, I became very critical. The lighting was no good. The compositions were wrong. I kept looking and only found things I didn't like.

Interview, Los Angeles/
Los Angeles Herald Examiner,
1-25:(California Living)7.

Peter O'Toole
Actor

1

What alarms me most about film-making is that I am handed a script, and I accept the assignment. Then when shooting begins, suddenly the script is full of yellow, pink and blue pages that consist of rewrites. If you're an actor like me, you have spent a great many hours in study preparing for your role, and suddenly you find yourself [trying to sell] the producer the original story that he sold you. It's bizarre.

Interview/
Los Angeles Herald Examiner, 1-23:(A)17.

George Peppard
Actor

2

An actor is a series of instruments. If you want a violin, if you want a cello, if you want a trumpet, he can give you these things. But he has to know what you want.

Interview/
San Francisco Examiner & Chronicle,
8-30:(Datebook)51.

Daniel Petrie
Director

3

On a film, I always rehearse two weeks . . . I hope that I will impress the cast in that time that I will be a good guide and a good audience for them. Because that's what a film director is: an audience of one. That rehearsal period is an opportunity to examine the text very carefully, to find out if all the lines work for the actors. But if this kind of exploration and discussion took place on the sound stage, you'd die!

Interview, Los Angeles/
Los Angeles Herald Examiner, 8-16:(E)5.

Christopher Plummer
Actor

4

[On being an actor]: You certainly must throw yourself into another aspect of life, or

interest, in order to save your sanity. And if you do that, it's really the most delightful profession to be in. Because the world itself, looking at it today, is not particularly fascinating. At least we [actors] have that escape to go to, and earn good money at it. We travel all over the world; we're treated like bloody royalty wherever we go, whether we deserve it or not. We see the world and get paid for it, and have fun.

Interview, Washington/
The Washington Post, 9-22:(B)11.

Sidney Poitier
Actor

5

. . . I'm not being offered worthwhile parts; hardly any actor is being offered worthwhile parts. Our most popular, and in some cases our best, actors are reduced to playing mindless, unimportant, dumb, one-dimensional roles. I haven't been stretched as an actor in over 10 years. But what film actor has? Burt [Reynolds], Clint [Eastwood], Dustin [Hoffman], [Paul] Newman, [Robert] Redford—none of them are working anywhere near their true potential. They're constantly working beneath themselves. Because the material just isn't there.

Interview, Beverly Hills, Calif./
Los Angeles Times, 2-8:(Calendar)33.

Charlotte Rampling
Actress

6

I don't want to be only in the incestuous world of film. I am not specifically writing, taking photographs or making music, but these are all the things I like to do. The work of an actor is to absorb life, live different experiences. Otherwise, you are going to repeat yourself. You are not going to create something new each time.

Interview, Croissy, France,
The Washington Post, 1-23:(B)3.

391

Christopher Reeve
Actor

1

. . . here we are, as actors, charged with the responsibility of representing people as they really are. Well, how do you know your subject if you don't mingle, if you don't stay involved? You don't see the world very closely from the tinted window of a limousine. One of the big traps of celebrity status is that you think like a celebrity rather than a normal person. Two generations ago, it was easier to describe a "star" —with all the glitzy openings and limousines pulling up and people dripping in mink. They were supposed to be beautiful, magical people all the time, even off-screen. And they were stars because the combination of their on-screen life and off-screen life made them interesting. Nowadays, stars are actors first, and all the good ones have theatre [stage] credits up to their elbows and are really quite nondescript outside their working hours. If [Robert] De Niro walked in here and sat in a corner, no one would notice him. Whereas if Clark Gable or Betty Grable walked into a room, it was, *well, hello.* I kind of enjoy today's atmosphere. I don't think it's obligatory to be a *slob*, nor do I think it's particularly attractive; but I do like the fact that we're respected for ourselves and not victimized by studio publicity machinery.

Interview, New York/
Chicago Tribune Magazine, 6-7:47.

Karel Reisz
Director

2

[On translating a book into a film]: It is a vain hope to think you can say the same thing in a film that you can in a book. You and the screenwriter have to apply your own imaginations and make something that is coherent in film terms. In film, you have no description, no ability to get inside people's minds, and a completely different time span. With such different ground rules, of course, you have to start again. But there are certain basic things in the work that you preserve, because that's

what made you want to do it in the first place.

Interview, London/
The New York Times Magazine, 8-30:48.

Ralph Richardson
Actor

3

When I'm mastering a part, I'm collecting. It's extraordinary: There's a man sitting next to you doing something, and you'll say, "Ah, that's exactly what I want!" I mean, you're not looking for it, but you're finding it. Your unconscious mind is searching everything you see. It's like turning over a dustbin and saying, "Ah, that's the very thing!" [In shaping a role,] sometimes the walk comes first; and sometimes it's the last to come. Sometimes it's the eye. Sometimes it's the voice. It enters, bit by bit, the realization of being a character. And it happens more or less by accident. It's at rehearsal, by doing it over and over again, you find that suddenly you find it.

Interview, Washington/
The Chritsian Science Monitor, 6-24:(B)3.

Susan Saint James
Actress

4

I'm hardly ever first choice for [a] feature film. Nobody wanted me for *Love at First Bite* . . . Up to the last minute they were doing makeup tests to see if I was pretty enough. I said, "Listen, you guys, I'll *act* beautiful." They don't seem to realize that if you hire an actress to *play* beautiful, she'll *look* beautiful. Whereas if you just hire a beautiful girl who can't act, you'll get nothing.

Interview, Los Angeles/
Los Angeles Times, 10-25:(Calendar)25.

Susan Sarandon
Actress

5

When you act—if you really act—you've got to get in touch with all the parts of you that

(SUSAN SARANDON)

you don't necessarily like, that you're not real proud of, that frighten you. They're your devils, demons. And getting rid of them is what makes it interesting. It's the fear you have of yourself, of what you might be letting loose—that's the thing.

Interview, New York/Parade, 6-21:4.

Martin Scorsese
Director

1

Films over seven years old have lost their effectiveness because the color is fading. The negative can fade in 12 years. Most of the prints made during the 1950s on the Eastmancolor Kodak color-positive process are already shot. Everything is disappearing, and no one cares. It's an outrage. Making movies has become like writing on water.

At symposium, University of Southern California/ Los Angeles Times, 4-5:(Calendar)3.

Simone Signoret
Actress

2

I get very stupid when somebody asks me how I prepare a role . . . I think the less you analyze a role, this mysterious adventure, well, the better. The person you're playing is a kind of tenant who lives *chez vous* [in you]. There's an expression, putting yourself into somebody's skin—that's absolutely false. It isn't a character that you're going into; it's the *character* that enters *your* skin, installs itself in *yours*, lives in *yours*. And while it's happening you can't talk about the character because it would be him or her that would do the talking.

Interview, Auteuil, France/ The New York Times, 5-3:(2)15.

Maggie Smith
Actress

3

I think films are totally baffling. It's desperately hard. When you're on stage you have the

time to gather yourself together. If you have a performance that evening, you have today to prepare. In filming, you have to be ready when *they're* ready. To have a film career you really have to *want* a film career. It's greedy to want both [stage and film]. I would choose the stage if I had to.

Interview, Paris/ Los Angeles Times, 1-3:(II)11.

Steven Spielberg
Director

4

I think a director has to earn . . . freedom. Having been a bloody veteran of the era of over-inflated [film] budgets, I can tell you there really is something good to be said for the days of David O. Selznick, when there were healthy collaborations between producers and directors. I probably sound like the enemy, but there are some directors who definitely have to have a very strong hand working with them.

Newsweek, 6-15:64.

Donald Sutherland
Actor

5

. . . I see the actor [not] as a vehicle for the director's ideas, but rather as a catalyst who carries his fantasy a little further and refines it. But the film is the director's. It's like being a concubine. It's wonderful to work for someone and satisfy him. That's why actresses so often fall in love with and marry their directors. When Robert Redford told me he was delighted with my performance in *Ordinary People*, I couldn't speak for a day.

Interview/After Dark, March:31.

Gay Talese
Author

6

When you see a serious [film] like *Breaker Morant*, that's an event to be celebrated. But too often today they make movies that are like comic books—and I never was a fan of comics—

WHAT THEY SAID IN 1981

and cater to people with an adolescent mentality even though some of them may be 60.

Interview/
"W": a Fairchild publication, 8-14:12.

John Travolta
Actor

1

When you go to Hollywood, and I'm talking about the Hollywood people, not the physical place, there is nothing to talk about or to do other than the movie business. You *are* your last picture there. You are what your last picture made at the box-office, and everyone around you is whatever his or her last picture made. It is so incestuous that all I can say is that when you go there you feel insecure and when you go away from there you feel secure. I feel I'm a fairly secure person, but when I go there, I feel insecure. It's like a vibration or an aura that is everywhere there. So it's not a preference for me to be there. When I'm there I find myself reading the box-office figures in *Variety* and caring about that. But when I go to another city or come here, none of that seems as important. There are other things to talk about. And I really believe that to be a balanced person you can't overdose on your profession.

Interview, Santa Barbara, Calif./
Chicago Tribune, 7-19:(6)21.

Francois Truffaut
French director

2

The American cinema, traditionally, has this notion of a goal to be achieved. And it is achieved, after great dangers and difficulties. All over the world spectators have found great pleasure in these things. But this kind of theme is not possible in Europe. We have a skepticism about goals being attained. We think goals are illusory. We don't conceive of the individual embarked on a great enterprise. We don't make pictures about taking 5,000 steers across the

country. So what do I do? I take sentiments to the end instead of enterprises.

Interview, Paris/
The New York Times, 10-11:(2)24.

3

Far too much nonsense is written about film directors. Directors are important, of course, but so are screenwriters. I would like to see a great deal more written about the people who write for films. In film schools today everyone you talk to says he wants to be a director, which is a very vague ambition and one that is difficult to achieve. Those wanting to be screenwriters have a better chance. At least they can produce a script for you to read and you can judge their talent immediately. Come to think of it, I don't even like the word "direct." It's too pretentious, too military-sounding. I don't direct actors; I put them on the right track.

Interview, Los Angeles/
San Francisco Examiner & Chronicle,
12-13:(Datebook)25.

Peter Ustinov
Actor, Director, Writer

4

Film-making is really an industry only in the United States and, perhaps, in India. Because it is an industry and obeys the norms of Detroit, somebody produces a highly successful picture like *Easy Rider*, about two people crossing America on motorcycles, and immediately this seems to be a magic formula. People start producing pictures about two individuals crossing America on sand yachts, on their knees, on foot, on gliders. They all flop, and nobody can understand why one was successful and the others weren't. Over-all, the state of the film industry in the U.S. depends on the moment.

Interview/
U.S. News & World Report, 3-9:46.

Jack Valenti
President, Motion Picture
Association of America

1

[On the advantages of motion-picture theatres over pay TV and other home video entertainment]: The large screen, far bigger than any home screen can possibly be; incomparable sound, stereo sound; and the enticement of a lively, clean, spacious, attractive entertainment place; the embrace, the glistening a film gets in your motion-picture theatres. Most people don't want to be held hostage in their living-room no matter how convenient the entertainment available. They want to have a social experience with friends outside where they live. There is a large and durable market in this land for watching films in theatres. But you [theatre owners] are obliged to seek out audiences by offering in your theatre an epic viewing experience not to be found in the home.

At ShoWest convention, Reno, Nev., Feb. 9/
Los Angeles Times, 2-11:(VI)4.

2

Every country is looking for two things: a national airline and a movie industry. It's easier to get an airline. The only way you build a movie industry is through talent—this sourceless asset that one cannot command to be born. You cannot by edict, bayonet or nuclear threat force somebody to make a good movie.

Interview, Washington/
The Washington Post, 7-8:(C)4.

3

. . . the movie business is very simple—yet there is a terrifying complexity to it. The simplicity is: If you make movies people want to see, they will go no matter what. The complexity is: It is incredibly difficult to make a good movie people want to see.

Interview/
Los Angeles Herald Examiner, 9-21:(B)6.

Jan-Michael Vincent
Actor

4

The hardest thing for me to do as an actor is to keep my dignity. So many producers treat actors like trained apes. Not all of them, but enough to make you start to wonder if you're not really like that. The best way to deal with it is to produce your own films . . . The thing is, you have to decide as an actor whether you want to be lazy and just be an actor or if you want to go to work . . .

Los Angeles Times, 1-3:(II)5.

Hal Wallis
Producer

5

There aren't so many real producers now as there were in my day. We had [Irving] Thalberg, David Selznick, Pandro Berman. Today, the producers are actually promoters, people who come from nowhere with a package they've put together—they've optioned a book or married a star and then they package it to the major companies. I think a lot of problems in the business today stem from the fact that these producers don't oversee the whole development, shooting and editing of a picture. Why, I've heard of instances when some of the new directors who are around have interpolated sequences which took three weeks to shoot that were never in the script. Those things just shouldn't happen.

Interview, Los Angeles/
Los Angeles Herald Examiner, 3-20:(D)7.

Raquel Welch
Actress

6

Movie-making is getting to be a lost cause. There is confusion among people in power at the studios, among the people who call themselves producers. There is confusion between movie-making and show business. Movie-making is an art; it takes real knowledge and creative perception. The show-business part

(RAQUEL WELCH)

comes later. First, you have to have something to show.

Before students and press, University of California,
Los Angeles/Los Angeles Times, 2-7:(II)6.

Orson Welles
Actor, Director

1

There's been some talk . . . about directors as if they were a separate breed. I believe that all directors are actors, just as I believe most writers are actors. After all, directors are a very new invention, dating back, I believe, only two centuries in the theatre . . . All of us in this profession of the film are actors, and the director is partly an actor because he plays so many roles. But none of them are really important, except to be the element that's absent in the making of the movie, and that's the audience. The terrible burden of the director is to take the place of that yawning vacuum. His job is to preside over accidents, and that's an important one.

At Hollywood Foreign Press Association dinner
in his honor, Beverly Hills, Calif., Oct. 18/
Daily Variety, 10-20:4.

Billy Wilder
Producer, Director, Screenwriter

2

It used to be that if you needed a few bucks you'd go out to Hollywood and steal some by writing. Screenwriting was not even as respectable as writing for the pulps. But if you had written a book, they paid attention. This is because motion-picture moguls didn't believe in anything but already-printed words. That meant somebody else liked the story first, so the mogul was off the hook. It hasn't changed a whole lot. They still don't read. They want talk, talk, tell me a story. I think if William Shakespeare came to Hollywood they'd ask him to tell them the plot of *Midsummer Night's Dream*. Mr. Shakespeare's agent, Meyer Mishkin, would sit next to him as he told the

story, and toward the end Shakespeare would say, "Then he'd say, 'To be or not to be,' or something like that—only better."

Interview, Culver City, Calif./
Los Angeles Times, 3-29:(Calendar)2.

3

Studios [today] have lost their personality. In the past, if you walked into a movie after the credits, you knew instantly whether it was a Warner Brothers picture or an MGM picture. Studios had their own handwriting; you recognized the ensemble players, and the sets of each studio had a distinctive style to them. Now studios have become more or less Ramada Inn motels; you move in, you move out. It is all very gypsy-like. You even have that unheard-of thing, a co-production between two studios like Paramount and Disney. That could never have happened in the past because the studio heads were sworn enemies; you had to keep Jack Warner and Louis B. Mayer apart or they would get into a fist fight. Those were the good old days.

Interview, Los Angeles/
The New York Times, 12-6:(2)21.

Michael Winner
Director

4

Audiences like to be emotionally aroused. Relief of emotion is what movies are all about, and it's a hair's breadth whether that's exhibited as a scream or a laugh. In fact, the most serious people to direct are comics. I think I have laughed less on the set directing comedy than directing tragedy. *Death Wish* and *That's Entertainment* both came out in the same year, and the same people went to both pictures. You didn't have the sadists and perverts going to one picture and the nice people going to the other. They appealed to different sides of the psyches of the same people.

Interview, Los Angeles/
The Hollywood Reporter, 8-31:2.

Shelley Winters
Actress

1

The whole film industry is sick. It's a miracle they ever make a good movie. It's all anti-hero. Who's making the great moral films like *The Bicycle Thief?* The main theme today in pictures? The bad triumphs over the good. Well, that's why people don't go to the movies.

Interview, London/
Los Angeles Herald Examiner, 3-11:(D)4.

Jane Wyman
Actress

2

The younger [actors] I have worked with kind of "wing it." And you can't wing it, because then you're depending upon your own personality and you're not in character at all. These younger actors really don't have the background and the discipline that we had—all those years and years of it. If we came on a set and didn't know our lines—ho, ho, ho! Yet, I don't blame the kids and I'll tell you why. There's no place for them to get the background that we all had [in the earlier days of the industry]. We were under contract to a studio. My heavens, I did six pictures a year, two at a time sometimes. It was constant discipline under some of the finest directors. And the pros . . . they all helped us kids, saying, "Don't do this and don't do that or you're going to get in trouble." They took the time to do it. And boy, we listened. But now, who's got the time? I feel sorry for the poor little things. I wish there was a way for them to learn. They just have to learn by the process of elimination.

Interview, Los Angeles/
The New York Times, 11-29:(2)40.

MUSIC

Paul Anka
Singer, Songwriter

1

I don't live in the past; I'm a contemporary performer. But a lot of those songs from the '50s had an honesty and a happiness you don't find in music today. They may not have been great songs, but they were done in a happy form and the music wasn't diluted the way it is today. The business was brand-new then. There was no sophistication, no pseudo-intellectualism. People hadn't gone through all the bull and politics they go through now. In today's music, so many other things matter, like what's your deal, and why don't we steal this guy from this label—that kind of garbage. There's no concern for the art. That's what's killing the record business. It's run out of steam. Punk [rock] didn't save it; I don't know whether videodisks can save it. Rock has absolutely taken a nosedive. It's *totally* in the toilet. You've got hardly any good music in terms of musicianship.

Interview/Chicago Tribune, 5-31:(6)14.

Tony Bennett
Singer

2

[Saying he has refused to perform much rock and other contemporary music]: I wouldn't sing the garbage they were peddling. The record companies were forcing artists to take a dive, and I resisted. I thought the only important thing was to be trusted [by the fans]. And I made a stink about it. I still do. Naturally, they [the companies] don't like me; I consider it a compliment. Remember, we're talking about lawyers, accountants and marketing guys; they're in charge of the business. Imagine an industry run by people who don't know anything about the product? . . . there's a tremendous business injustice going on. The record companies have been saying for years that people like me [good-music singers] can't sell, but we keep selling out wherever we go [in live performance]. To me, it's 20 times harder to get people out on the town—and at least that much more expensive—than to get them to buy a record. The truth is the industry *won't* sell the records, not that *we* [performers] can't sell them.

Interview/
The New York Times Magazine, 6-21:26.

Rudolf Bing
Former general manager,
Metropolitan Opera, New York

3

In my view, an opera house must be run by one man who makes the final decisions. I never had a musical director—not that I didn't listen to the musicians. I'm not a musician. I relied on musicians for advice. But the final decision was always mine . . . I don't think you can divide artistic matters from economic ones. There is no artistic decision without economic repercussions, no economic decision without artistic repercussions.

Interview, New York/
"W": a Fairchild publication, 5-18:11.

Alfred Brendel
Pianist

4

Talent is not enough. This is a great misapprehension. There must be persistence and

(ALFRED BRENDEL)

ambition as well. These are qualities which emerge in early childhood. Then there is health, and I am very fortunate in this respect. I have withstood the pressures well. Cortot once said that becoming a successful pianist was largely a matter of constitution. There must also be an ability to communicate—not just musically but with people at large. It is a capacity to make contacts and not be totally hostile toward the rest of the world. Musical communication with an audience can be developed, as mine has over the years . . . One must also have vision, and, again, not just a musical vision. I did not feel the need to reach the top within a few years. I felt my talent should have time to develop. I have also profited from a basic sense of curiosity. I am a skeptic. I believe nothing I haven't examined myself. Finally, one must learn how and on what to concentrate one's energies.

Interview, New York/
The New York Times, 5-3:(2)34.

Anthony Burgess
Author

1

Developments in music foreshadow the future. The future of our society can be heard in today's music, which can be elegant and structured but can express only states of chaos and anguish, never the stability of belief. This discontent, this withdrawal by the individual, was born with Beethoven and Berlioz and continued with Boulez, Berio and John Cage. There is nothing better than contemporary music to make us realize what we have lost.

Interview/
World Press Review, December:35.

Sarah Caldwell
Director,
Opera Company of Boston

2

I am used to working from the point of view of creating movement, visual images, a se-

quence of impressions which the music will function with. A lot of that is like making a good soup: You put in a little salt, taste it, put in a little more. It's an empirical thing; you recognize the dosage when you hit it. If you have added too much of one ingredient, you recognize that, too, because it suddenly becomes ludicrous.

Interview/Saturday Review, January:26.

Richard Cassilly
Opera singer

3

The greatest pleasure in singing for me is physical. I was always athletic, involved in any sport; and opera is very much like a football field. You are totally involved, physically and emotionally. Add the music to that, and it's incredible. The applause is important, because you find out whether or not you pulled it off, how many people really believe you killed Desdemona . . . The acting aspect keeps me in this business more than anything. Some roles are known as "acting roles," in the sense that there is lots for the actor to do. Captain Vere, for instance, is a tortured man. That's fun, and in a way it makes the job easier. In roles like Radames, a stilted, one-dimensional man who says silly things, to try to make the character believable is really a compelling acting challenge.

Interview/Opera News, 1-17:29.

James Conlon
American conductor

4

Probably the most basic difference between American orchestras and European orchestras is that the Americans are more technically proficient, but the Europeans play with a greater sense of style. Those may be cliches, but there's an element of truth in them. However, American orchestras have a flexibility that allows them to move from one style to another much more smoothly than European orchestras. To get a German orchestra to play French music well is a problem. They don't

WHAT THEY SAID IN 1981

(JAMES CONLON)

like it. They think it's superficial, and they just don't take it seriously. To get a French orchestra to play the classics well is just as hard. And in Italy, my experience has been that the orchestras consider German music pompous. They feel they need to help it along by lightening it up. English orchestras are more flexible, more like American ensembles.

Interview, New York/
The New York Times, 8-2:(2)17.

Barbara Cook
Singer

1

I'm one of the few people who sings American popular songs who is a true lyric soprano. But I try to sing that music without using the distorted vowel sounds that make most operatic sopranos sound so dreadful. Or at least they sound dreadful to me. You can talk about Joan Sutherland from now till never. But while I can admire certain things she does, to me she's not a singer; she's an incredible trickster. She does what she does most brilliantly, and many people fall at her feet. But I ask for more. Technique can be dazzling, but I want to know how you *feel* about it.

Interview/Chicago Tribune, 2-12:(1)19.

Ileana Cotrubas
Opera singer

2

Nowadays we are talking not about singers but about directors. It's the age of directors, and this is good and bad. There are many good ones coming from the dramatic theatre to the opera, and they will be musical and help us. But there are others coming from the theatre, where they are good, but they do not understand music, they do not love music, music does not say anything to them, to their sensibility. And they will *destroy* many operas. They look *only* at the words and the character, not at the music. And this makes me very, very up-

set, because why have we to accept these directors? No, I don't, because I will not!

Interview/Opera News, 3-28:17.

Sarah Coyle
Executive director, Fine Arts
Music Foundation, Chicago

3

I've been in the chamber-music business for years, and the scene has completely turned around. Chamber music used to be music only for the musicians; now it's music for the listener. In the past, audiences could hear only the old standards—the Beethovens and the Mozarts. Now they demand to hear new composers and intriguing instrumental combinations. And you find a wider variety of chamber-music lovers than ever in the past. My audiences are less and less stereotypical, and there are a lot of people out there enjoying chamber music that you might not expect to see. Young people, blue-collar workers, and other groups that would have been strangers to chamber music years ago, are discovering its charms.

Chicago Tribune, 1-16:(1)17.

Jan De Gaetani
Mezzo-soprano

4

I have found contemporary music very liberating, vocally. I had come to it very innocently, not knowing how hard it was, or that I was supposed to be afraid of it. Most singers are trained to have one sound, which they rely on all the time. There's nothing unhealthy about that, physically, but it is limiting if your whole artistic spirit does not transcend that. I preferred to start somewhere else, with a different point of view. At its best, contemporary music can offer you not only that different viewpoint, but a great deal of information about attack, color, vibrato, differences in resonance —things that, surely, a singer ought to be able to take back to the standard repertory. I like to think that's what I do.

Interview/
The New York Times, 2-1:(2)17.

400

Mario Del Monaco
Opera singer

1

For a tenor to go on singing leads until he is 60, in good condition, is something of an achievement, and I am proud of it. To sing well is not only difficult, one wonders at times whether it is a lost art. However many people may disagree with me, let me tell you that the abuse of *pianos* and *pianissimos* ends by becoming the cancer of a voice. Twice, in my beginnings, I almost lost my instrument [voice] by using this system of reducing and reducing the voice. It works for light voices but not for large ones. A solid instrument must open the larynx a lot, or it loses the support. Listen to Caruso's recordings—he always sang full voice. To make the sound plausible, smooth and mellow is another matter; and this is what I worked for during my entire professional life. It is very much like a person who becomes hooked on remaining thin and eats very little. Eventually the stomach becomes smaller, and to enlarge it again is impossible.

Interview/
Opera News, 1-17:13.

Edo de Waart
Music director, San Francisco
Symphony Orchestra

2

Recordings opened music to a world of people, but at the same time they put a clamp and damper on experiment and growth. They are perceived as being definitive performances. People suddenly have the definitive version in 25 splices. Is that fair to the performer who has to be "up" for an 8:30 curtain and has only one chance to play through a piece? For a young performer, that can be deadly. How can your performance possibly be as poised or as felt-through as one by Klemperer or Furtwangler? They were 60 when they recorded. There is always the constant shadow of having to walk the line with the giants who were at the pinnacle of their knowledge and their spiritual strength.

Interview, San Francisco/
San Francisco Examiner & Chronicle,
9-6:(Scene)14.

3

A music director has to be autocratic, a dictator to a certain extent. I have made many unpopular decisions. It is part of the job. I always say, if you want to be popular, be a guest conductor. I can't do that. It is empty. It doesn't mean diddle. It is like a one-night stand. I prefer lasting relationships. Guest stands do have their advantages, of course. They have given me the uplift of success, reassurance, during periods when things were bad at home in San Francisco. I have cherished such experiences in Chicago and Boston. But you don't learn from guest conducting. No guest conductor can guess the personality of an orchestra. That takes time. So the visitor just does his own thing and hopes for the best.

Interview, Los Angeles/
Los Angeles Times, 10-25:(Calendar)57.

Gwyneth Jones
Opera singer

4

[On how she projects excitement in her singing]: It is a matter of believing in the situation and believing it is actually happening. I study a role, the surroundings, how the characters walk and talk until I find an essence of how they behave. When I make my entrance, it is as if it is happening for the first time. I feel that we all have in us, very often hidden, so many emotions and so many feelings that need to come out. I am always completely immersed in the role. I believe in it completely. But at the same time, you have to control yourself. I am not just wildly emotional. Obviously one has to learn movement, deportment, facial control, vocal control. It is a two-sided thing, in

WHAT THEY SAID IN 1981

(GWYNETH JONES)

that you must be able to control every muscle, yet the most important thing is that it come from the heart.

> *Interview,*
> *San Francisco/*
> *Opera News, 1-31:29.*

Erich Leinsdorf
Orchestra conductor

1

In 1978 [with the Vienna Philharmonic], I did Pfitzner's *Palestrina*, a work I consider unexportable. Yes, unexportable. *Palestrina*, if brought to this country [the U.S.], would lay an egg. Not every type of music, you see, should travel outside its own orbit. Music is not at all an international language. To think so is an error. Like a *vin du pays*, some music should be consumed only at the source.

> *Interview, Los Angeles/*
> *Los Angeles Times,*
> *7-26:(Calendar)60.*

Yo-Yo Ma
Cellist

2

Sometimes I think you cannot really perform until you realize that you must be three people to succeed musically. The first person looks at the music and says to himself, "Play like this, or play like that." This person creates the concept while you are performing. The second person has the muscles. He plays the instrument; he tries to turn the musical ideas into a language of sound the audience can understand. And the third person is the most crucial. He sits out in the audience and listens to the performance. He is the only one who knows what the first two people are doing, and he must constantly monitor the music if the concert is to be a success. Music-making is like this because every audience is different, and no one can succeed by playing the same way for each crowd.

> *Interview, Chicago/*
> *Chicago Tribune, 2-18:(1)18.*

Zubin Mehta
Musical director,
New York Philharmonic Orchestra

3

I never think about the progress of my career because I really believe today's concert looks after tomorrow's, in every sense of the word. Today's concert is really tomorrow's dress rehearsal. And so it goes.

> *Interview/*
> *San Francisco Examiner & Chronicle,*
> *8-30:(Datebook)38.*

Johanna Meier
American opera singer

4

There was a time when if you didn't come to Europe, you were not considered a serious [opera] singer. That no longer exists. The best training in the world is in the United States. American singers are recognized as the best-prepared and the most flexible. I found in my experience with Europeans that they are less willing to try unusual physical work, like singing from difficult positions. They want to sit and stand straight to get their voice out. Americans tend to put a good deal of physical movement into their roles. They have been responsible to a great extent for the increased involvement with opera. There are now new approaches; people are no longer willing to see a fat lady stand up on the stage and just sing.

> *Interview, Bayreuth, West Germany/*
> *The New York Times, 7-23:18.*

Peter Mennin
Composer

5

. . . my wish is that concert-goers, musicians, everybody, would not be concerned with what [music] is ahead of the times, behind the times, or anything like that. They should listen to music for that which arouses them *viscerally*, as well as intellectually. I mean, the enjoyment of music has to be visceral as well. Without that, you're bored. The reason Beethoven and Mozart still give us a great deal of enjoyment

(PETER MENNIN)

is that you get a visceral reaction from the music . . . And that's the difference between a major composer and a minor one, or one that's forgotten along the way. A major composer always means a visceral reaction, a physical involvement. You can't resist that. It's either very beautiful, very dramatic, very elevated . . . And I can't see why contemporary music can't emulate the principle—not the sound, but the principle—of physical involvement.

Interview/
The Christian Science Monitor, 7-29:21.

Gian Carlo Menotti
Composer

1

What I find very sad is that with this incredible interest in the arts in America, the creator is still in last place. People say,"I am interested in music," but they mean they are interested in conductors, singers, instrumentalists. But they couldn't care less who the composer is unless he is dead.

Interview, New York/
The Christian Science Monitor, 6-26:19.

Riccardo Muti
Conductor

2

Some of the opera productions I have worked on have provoked bitter arguments, but out of those confrontations are born ideas and new modes. I have always disdained productions that are easily accepted and pretty much dead the day after opening. The other kind are the ones that are remembered, that mature and spiritually enrich the audience.

Interview/World Press Review, July:62.

Birgit Nilsson
Opera singer

3

Today all the young singers are so incredibly capable. They know everything about music—

a lot more than we did at their age. But even though the schools are so good and everyone so well-educated, there seem to be few really good voices. Maybe they are killing themselves before their time. Everyone wants young singers for television and records. You don't need the true voice for that. You give what you have, and the microphone does the rest. Many are starting to sing Wagner seven or 10 years too early. If you start doing those parts too soon, you kill the voice.

Interview, New York/
The New York Times, 10-11:(2)23.

Gianna Pederzini
Former opera singer

4

[Opera] singing is a profession today. In my era it was a total dedication, which meant giving everything to it . . . I studied five years before I dared to present myself before an audience, and even then I continued to study five more. Now, after [only] months, they are on-stage, cheating the public and ruining their own chances for a distinguished career. Though I get very angry, I know only too well it isn't their fault. Politics play a leading role, and managers, conductors, unions are all severely to blame. So many divine operas are ruined today by directors who insist on seeing political messages where they don't exist.

Interview, Rome/Opera News, 1-10:23.

Itzhak Perlman
Violinist

5

The violin is a klutz instrument. You clutch it with your chin and shoulder, and as soon as you begin to do that, your back starts to hurt. Some players get a terrible rash on their neck or chin from holding a violin. So you try to make yourself as comfortable as possible and get to work on the instrument. But first you have to learn how to control your hands, your arms, your fingers, how to stand, what to do with your elbows. Then you start in on tone, vibrato, which way the bow is going.

WHAT THEY SAID IN 1981

(ITZHAK PERLMAN)

Fiddle players have a tough time and a longer time before they can get results. It may be 10 or 15 years before a violinist can get all these things under control and learn how to get what he wants out of the instrument. Then he can start thinking about the music. A pianist's musical responsibility comes much sooner. Once you learn the notes on a piano, you have to start making music. This may explain why there are so many more pianists than violinists. Of course, as a fiddler, I shouldn't complain about that.

Interview, New York/
.The Washington Post, 3-19:(D)14.

Roberta Peters
Opera singer

1

[On her 30 years with the Metropolitan Opera]: Thirty years—that's a long time. People say, "How do you do it?" I don't know. I've been lucky, but I've also worked hard and studied. And I haven't changed my repertory drastically. I've seen so many singers come and go because a manager says, "Oh, you can do *that!*" The manager wrings them dry and moves on to someone else.

Interview/The New York Times, 2-6:14.

Nicola Rescigno
Artistic director and conductor,
Dallas Opera

2

It's a cliche, but the rapidity of transportation has adversely affected the whole musical picture. I can't understand, for instance, conductors who have three orchestras at once. The giants of the past said it took three and four years, rehearsing every day in one theatre, to get what they wanted. [Today,] I can fly over

the Atlantic and arrive and get some sleep and go out and perform. But if it's a rough trip, and I sleep badly, the performance suffers.

Interview/Opera News, November:12.

Leonard Rosenman
Composer

3

[On writing music for films and television compared with writing for the concert hall]: I don't look down on my experience writing for the commercial mass media, but what I do in it has little to do with music, because the propulsion of film scores is literary. When I say film music is not music, my colleagues get mad; but even when it's done at an imaginative and highest level, it's like fantastic, marvelous wallpaper that's cut to fit, compared to an abstraction by Jackson Pollock. Their functions are entirely different. An understanding of that difference allows me to function in these two fields.

Interview/
San Francisco Examiner & Chronicle,
5-10:(Review)17.

Mstislav Rostropovich
Cellist; Music director, National
Symphony Orchestra-Washington

4

[Conducting is] like boiling water. After a few performances, the boiling becomes a little cooler, and my contact with the orchestra becomes more objective. My best performances are exactly in-between. If I become too cool, then it's not exciting. If sometimes I am too boiled, then maybe the orchestra doesn't take from me my temperature.

Interview, Washington/
The New York Times, 1-18:(4)17.

Andres Segovia
Guitarist

5

When I was young, a small blemish in my playing could be attributed to a lack of maturity.

(ANDRES SEGOVIA)

Today, such a blemish may be taken—indeed, will be taken—as a loss of powers. At my age, I feel the need to prove that I still can. The kind of practicing I do is extremely concentrated. I often say, when I work, the hours are cubic. What I put in one hour is four-dimensional.

Interview, Los Angeles/
Los Angeles Times, 3-1:(Calendar)55.

Roger Sessions
Composer

1

Music has got to be something that comes from you spontaneously. You can know a lot of it and a lot about it—what you might call musical culture—but the music you write still has to be the result of what you have to *say*. There's too much talk about music, too much self-consciousness. Some composers outlive that and others don't. A composer has to be a part of his music, to be totally involved with it. I couldn't write a piece I wasn't in love with—you have to go to bed with it.

Interview, New York/
The New York Times, 3-22:(2)18.

Ravi Shankar
Indian musician

2

Indian classical music today is very healthy, but changes are coming so fast—musically and politically—that I myself sometimes worry. But up to now, all is well. We [in India] have a bunch of really fantastic young musicians . . . Of course, the whole attitude has very much changed . . . Today there is a fascination with speed—*speed*. My guru used to say that playing one note, pulling it and staying there and savoring the effect and the silence that follows it—if it brings tears to your own eyes and to the listener, that is a great artistic achievement. But now, the attention is very much toward virtuosity. But that is good; that is part of the tradition. You can't just play slow things.

Interview, New York/
The New York Times, 4-19:(2)24.

Beverly Sills
General director,
New York City Opera

3

There are no heroic [opera] singers on the horizon—anywhere. I do see some beautiful young lyric sopranos of the Sayao and Bori type. But there are no spectacular bel-canto sopranos. Joan [Sutherland] is the last. And there do not seem to be dramatic voices—no Toscas, Aidas, Leonores. Tenors? It's a freak voice to begin with, and there never have been many great ones around. What I see in America are fine actor-singers.

Interview/
The New York Times, 2-15:(2)10.

Leonard Slatkin
Music director,
St. Louis Symphony Orchestra

4

[Saying there is no discrimination against women becoming members of his orchestra]: Those who come to audition are heard but not seen, because they sit behind a screen. That happens at auditions for other orchestras, but, additionally, our contenders play in an area that is carpeted, so that you can't tell whether the job candidate is wearing high heels or sneakers. As far as women players are concerned, it's their musical measurements we're interested in—not the usual ones.

Los Angeles Times, 4-12:(Calendar)60.

Ringo Starr
Musician;
Former member of the Beatles

5

[The new bands] don't want to change and explore too much, or else they explore in a very narrow band instead of a wide field. Take Devo, say. They're interesting to a very specific portion of the population, and they seem to stay that way rather than try to cover a lot of bases, which is what someone like Elton John did and what I try to do. I'm not aiming just at teen-agers or people in their 20s or 50s or

405

WHAT THEY SAID IN 1981

(RINGO STARR)

90s. I try to hit them all. And the Beatles—we tried to cover everybody, from your daughter to your grandmother. What happens with a lot of bands is that the first album is dynamite, lots of energy. But then you've got to come up with the second one, and that can be hard. We found it difficult, too. I'm not saying that the newer bands are going through anything that we didn't go through. We weren't any less restricted than they are. But we managed to get past that and change constantly. We were exploring all the time. The new bands just want to play safe.

Interview, Chicago/Chicago Tribune, 3-25:(1)14.

Toru Takemitsu
Composer

1

Composing for me is like mapping out a garden. If you walk through a garden, the elements are always the same: paths, rocks, trees, grass. But as you walk through, each element looks different depending on your perspective. Sometimes, when I am composing, I will actually stop and design a garden to help myself along. Instrumental color, notes, rhythms are like the elements of a garden; every new design is a different piece.

*Interview, New York/
The New York Times, 2-13:17.*

Rudy Vallee
Singer, Entertainer

2

Music has gone from white to black since I entered show business. The popular songs that were written in the '20s, '30s, '40s and early '50s were written by veterans—mostly men who'd had experience in life. How can you write a lyric if you haven't really lived life? Another reason why music was better then is that men like Richard Rodgers had the greatest creative minds for unusual melodies. You don't find minds like this very often . . . The kids of today have taken over the music business— most of them very young. Simply because they write and jot down a few notes, they have the idea that they can write songs. Composers now just don't have depth of inspiration for melody. Most of the lyrics of the pop songs you hear today are repetitious. They're almost nursery rhymes, as if written by children—which they are.

*Interview/
U.S. News & World Report, 8-10:70.*

Frank Zappa
Composer, Musician

3

I just take it on faith that the law of averages would indicate that in a country this big [the U.S.], there has got to be at least a handful of people who are capable of writing worthwhile, beautiful, uplifting, valuable music. But you'll never find out about it, because there's no way to hear their music; because the whole music business in the United States is based on numbers, based on unit sales, and not based on quality. It's not based on beauty, it's based on hype and it's based on cocaine. It's based on giving presents of large packages of dollars to play records on the air.

*Interview/
Los Angeles Herald Examiner, 12-6:(A)17.*

THE STAGE

Woody Allen
Actor, Director, Writer

1

What's toughest about writing a play is going from nothing to first draft. But once you write a play, the hardest work is done, and you can get a wonderful production in six weeks. When you watch rehearsals for a play and you see something you don't like, you can make corrections. When you make corrections in a movie, you have to call the actors from all over the world, and then you get the painters and electricians.

Interview, New York/
The New York Times, 4-26:(2)6.

Lauren Bacall
Actress

2

. . . a musical, let me tell you, is *very* tough work. There's only one way to prepare—singing lessons, body work—so you can build up the *stamina. That's* the most necessary quality one must have in a musical. Forget talent—that comes later.

Interview, New York/
The New York Times, 1-14:17.

George Balanchine
Artistic director,
New York City Ballet

3

There is no such thing as a "Balanchine dancer." Someone else invented it. People like to put titles on things so they know what they are. Why can't you be on your own? You are first somebody. My dancers are just good dancers, with well-trained, nice bodies, intelligence, musicality and exceptional technique.

In all the arts it is the same. You need a good violin, with good intonation, to play a Brahms concerto . . . Dancers have to be strong-willed. They must put all their mind and body into it. You can't be half and half. I always say: Only this. Nothing else, or you will not become a very interesting dancer.

Interview/The New York Times, 2-8:(2)1.

Bill Ball
Director, American Conservatory
Theatre, San Francisco

4

When an actor and an audience are united in the last seven minutes of [a] play, when everybody is completely absorbed, what they're united to is universe. That's why they have left themselves behind. Afterwards, you let go, you return back to dualistic living. But oh, how you've changed for having had those few moments of unity.

Interview/
San Francisco Examiner & Chronicle,
10-11:(Datebook)43.

Mikhail Baryshnikov
Ballet dancer; Artistic director,
American Ballet Theatre

5

[On his recent stint at the New York City Ballet, where he was under the tutelage of George Balanchine and Jerome Robbins]: Just being there was an honor for me—as it is for every dancer. I was too secure before. I needed danger. I needed to be a student again. I needed to be coaxed and teased and booed. After too much success, too much adoration, dancers

WHAT THEY SAID IN 1981

(MIKHAIL BARYSHNIKOV)

lose their perspective. They stop experimenting. They harden in their tracks.

Interview, Los Angeles/
Los Angeles Herald Examiner, 2-8:(E)2.

Robert Brustein
Artistic director, American
Repertory Theatre; Director, Loeb
Drama Center, Harvard University

1

The mood of the theatre reflects what is happening in the broader society. The theatre is like a sponge. It always soaks up society's attitudes. What it seems to be soaking up at the moment is the strong conservative impulse in the country. For now, the theatre seems to be in a state of stasis; it's frozen. There's a cautious attitude that is reflected in a fondness for nostalgia and the resurrection of hits of yesteryear, such as *My Fair Lady* and *Oklahoma*. It is also reflected in the passion for the familiar in drama—domestic and realistic works. There's little effort to stretch the imagination of the audience into an area of new experience. In part, this is happening because people who have paid a lot of money to see a play—and you could buy a few shares of IBM with what it now costs to go to a Broadway show—want something guaranteed: Not just sure-fire hits but also something guaranteed not to ruffle or disturb the quiet serenity of the postprandial hours.

Interview/
U.S. News & World Report, 6-29:67.

Alexander H. Cohen
Producer

2

People once viewed the theatre as an important social event, and they dressed up for the occasion. Now they drink cola in the theatre and talk back to the actors. I'm not criticizing; I'm just describing.

Interview/
The New York Times, 5-10:42.

3

Broadway is too successful. Hit shows are running longer, and there are fewer theatres available than in the past. That makes for a major booking squeeze. With space at a premium, the theatre owners may soon be closing shows that are making a profit in order to make way for shows that might do better. There will be no room for the modest success. But let's face it: Broadway is a business. Making bucks is the bottom line.

Time, 10-5:80.

Gordon Davidson
Artistic director, Mark Taper Forum,
Los Angeles

4

The best work is being done *away* from Broadway, boom or no boom. The plays we do [in Los Angeles] could never originate on Broadway, where a play has to be a big hit, or nothing. Broadway deals with numbers—numbers of dollars, numbers of people who attend. It's a business, not an art-form.

Interview/
The New York Times Magazine, 5-10:46.

Colleen Dewhurst
Actress

5

I'm always amazed when a critic says, "Why would so-and-so pick to do this play?" That statement should be cut from every critic's review. It makes the assumption that actors are reading wonderful plays all the time, and that out of six, they reached out and took the wrong one. It's difficult for actors like Gerry [Page] or Julie [Harris] or G. C. [Scott] to be attacked on that level, as though they hadn't used their heads. My main reason and theirs is that we want to come back to the stage—it's what keeps you alive. You get to the point where you have nothing and you just want to go back to work. Sure, I could do a revival every six months, but I also want to do a part that no one else has ever done, and that's very difficult. You read play after play and finally you say,

408

(COLLEEN DEWHURST)

"This one really isn't so bad." You're not saying this is the greatest play ever written. You're saying you think there are possibilities. Maybe it's a writer whose work you have confidence in; maybe you think something magical will happen in rehearsal.

Interview/The New York Times, 2-8:(2)1.

Goran Graffman
Director; Member, Royal Dramatic
Theatre, Stockholm

1

One of the big differences between putting on a play here [in New York] and at home is in rehearsal time. In Stockholm, we rehearse for a longer stretch—anywhere between nine and 12 weeks—while here we had only three weeks and four days. In Stockholm, an actor can go home and think about his part very slowly—you flow into a role; in New York, an actor has to jump right in. That difference gives a different complexion to the play. All the vital questions are directed at me very early by the cast. And I had to come up with the answers very fast. Analysis and blocking out the moves start practically from the beginning. The actors all learned their lines in two weeks. In Sweden, it often takes a month.

Interview, New York/
The New York Times, 3-17:18.

Martha Graham
Modern-dance choreographer

2

[When choreographing,] I often talk all the way through the dancing, almost like underlaying a text beneath the "lines" of the dancers. I don't ask people to portray an emotion—though in time I may tell the dancers what the movement makes me feel—but rather to move in a technically clean, clear fashion, and so *passionately* that you see the essence of the emotion. I do get very angry sometimes, when I feel the dancers are just "marking" things. "When are you going to *dance?*" I'll scream.

You've got to make your body do every movement, if it's the thrust of a shoulder, as if it were being done for the first time, as if you're listening to the ancestral footsteps. An audience isn't going to be satisfied with less than the full creative act.

Interview, Washington/
The Washington Post, 2-25:(B)7.

Simon Gray
Playwright

3

[On how he begins writing a play]: I generally start with a character in a room who says something, and I hope somebody else will say something. I've very little idea what a play is about till the characters begin to emerge, and that means draft after draft.

Interview, New York/
The New York Times, 2-22:(2)4.

Edward Hambleton
Producer, Phoenix Theatre,
New York

4

It isn't a question of a serious play versus a non-serious one. It is that theatre-going today is a one-time event. With the high costs of tickets, people get choosy and, unless it's the theatre experience of the century, they don't go . . . Serious plays take tender love and care, and when you are working in an atmosphere where it is a thousand dollars a minute, it's very difficult to correct mistakes.

Interview/
The New York Times Magazine, 5-10:42.

Richard Harris
Actor

5

The stage is not a fake medium. You can fake movies; God knows I've seen enough of it. You can get up there without an ounce of talent and be made to look good. No way on stage; you're on your own on stage, so you

WHAT THEY SAID IN 1981

have to conquer that medium yourself . . . You can't do it with camera angles; it's you.
Interview, Boston/The Washington Post, 8-30:(K)8.

Rex Harrison
Actor

1

[On how he keeps fresh after doing the same part over and over]: Concentration. Total concentration. Creating another detail. Good acting is an accumulation of details. But I usually give only one or two performances a week that come up to my standards. I'm a chronically dissatisfied perfectionist.
Interview, Boston/
The New York Times, 8-16:(2)4.

Anthony Hopkins
Actor

2

I'm not bored by acting, not at all. But for me, about 10 performances in the theatre are enough. After that, I tend to lose interest. I enjoy the rehearsals, but once the play is on and running I get restless. And I'll tell you something: A lot of actors I know feel the same way. They think that being stuck in a play for months on end is a terrible bore. But nobody will admit it. There's a conspiracy to pretend we enjoy it. Well, I don't. And I don't mind saying it.
Interview, Los Angeles/
Los Angeles Times, 12-20:(Calendar)50.

Glenda Jackson
Actress

3

. . . without the element of danger, you can't have great acting. I don't mean the danger that someone will forget his lines or break his leg. Theatre should be dangerous for the audience as well as for the actors. In a sense, the theatre is a placatory ritual. It puts on the stage the most frightening taboos and tries to answer the questions, "Who are we? What are we doing here?" It recognizes that we're a group of people sitting in the dark, huddled around a fire.
Interview, London/Saturday Review, March:37.

4

[On appearing in a play in New York versus London]: They give you more comfortable surroundings here [in New York], and there are all kinds of comfortable things, like infinitely perking coffee and orange juice whenever you want it. But I think the pressures are greater here than in the West End [of London]. I think you're more ruthless here. I was astounded to find out in the first week of rehearsals that they could just sack any of us. And in the West End a play almost always at least opens, which isn't true here. I must say, the good thing about this town is that they let you know; they don't want you hanging around if they don't like what you've done.
Interview, New York/
The New York Times, 3-22:(2)4.

James Earl Jones
Actor

5

I am a black actor. I'm happy to be recognized. That's why I am an actor. I feel no great need to be in either integrated or non-integrated companies. I think there's a certain folly, too, in the idea of "Negro" or "Afro" theatre. I'm not even sure what it is, since language is what determines doing live theatre, and we're speaking English, and this is still American theatre— theatre that has to address itself to the public at large. And I count myself as conservative and cautious about doing "white" roles, though I tend to do more of them than my peers. I don't feel that actors should have to be diplomats. But if white actors could play "black" roles and learn the essence of what it means to be a black person in America today, and if black actors took on "white" roles, we would not only extend our ability to have experiences that are not our own, which is what you do with

(JAMES EARL JONES)

every role, but the performing of those roles would elevate acting to something more important and enlightening than just entertainment.

Interview, Stratford, Conn./
The New York Times, 8-2:(2)7.

Gene Kelly
Actor

1

You can get away with more in theatre than you can in motion pictures. Dim a light in theatre and you get an effect. Do it in a movie, and someone will think there's something wrong with the projector. A movie is two-dimensional; the theatre is three-dimensional. One is like a painting. The other is like a sculpture.

Interview, New York/
The New York Times, 8-24:(1)16.

Gelsey Kirkland
Ballet dancer,
American Ballet Theatre

2

I used to believe that unless my idea of perfection was fulfilled, I could not perform. I certainly have come to the place where I realize that there are so many things one must adjust to—whether it's the dance floor, or not having enough rehearsal time, or that your partner is injured—that perfection cannot always be achieved.

Interview, New York/
Los Angeles Times, 5-3:(Calendar)56.

Eva Le Gallienne
Actress

3

I think the great trouble with the theatre now is the [ticket] prices. People simply can't afford to go. I think this is a simply dreadful thing. There should be a stop to it. It's got to change; it can't go on and on and on like this.

There's got to be some sort of rebellion. If somebody really had the guts to come out and say, "This has gone too far; we're going to cut our prices right down," I really believe people would be grateful and respond. But you can't get anybody to do it. I would if I were a manager. But then, I've always flown in the face of providence.

Interview, New York/
The Washington Post, 3-24:(B)3.

Elizabeth McCann
Producer

4

. . . there was a time when people would go to see a Julie Harris or a Geraldine Page—regardless of the show. There used to be a following of theatre people who went to see great actors—certainly all the plays the Lunts were in were not of equal caliber. But in this town today, there are no actors with followings. If the play doesn't work, it doesn't matter *who's* in it. With free entertainment on television and the price of theatre tickets, people don't want to just have a lovely evening in the theatre; they want something they can kick and scream about.

Interview, New York/
The New York Times, 2-8:(2)14.

5

. . . New York desperately needs a large-scale subsidized repertory company. Our producers must depend so completely on the ticket buyer—rather than on a partial subsidy—that we must produce what the largest number of people want. I suppose the old saw is still true: "Theatre must succeed as a business, or it will fail as an art."

Time, 10-5:82.

Alec McCowen
British actor

6

What happened to Marlon Brando couldn't happen in England, only here [in the U.S.]

WHAT THEY SAID IN 1981

where the importance of succeeding or failing is so magnified. Al Pacino in Brando's position is tragic, because he can't afford to fail. That's very bad for a career. It's courageous of Pacino to do what he does in this country, to play Shakespeare on Broadway. But to us [British] it just seems logical. The only way you can grow is in front of a live audience.

Interview/
"W": a Fairchild publication, 3-27:4.

Jonathan Miller
Producer, Director, Writer

1

I believe that there is no definitive version of any playwright. The story of immortality of any great playwright is really the story of his ability to invite and survive successive transformations of his work. All productions of Shakespeare are "messed around" productions of Shakespeare. There's absolutely no way in which you can present some sort of original ground-level version of the "real thing," which would give audiences the impression that they were in the presence of what Shakespeare intended. We have very little idea what Shakespeare intended. It's extremely dubious that, even if we knew, we would be able to present that, and whether it would interest a modern audience. Every single production of Shakespeare since the day it was created has consisted of a transformation of Shakespeare. I think that's true of any playwright who outlives his own wildest dreams of posterity.

Interview, New York/
The Christian Science Monitor, 4-17:19.

Michael Moriarty
Actor

2

The theatre [in New York] is owned by the critics. Nowhere in the world do theatre critics hold as much power as they do in this city, and that's not right. I blame the audience and

producers for allowing this to happen—the audiences out of laziness and the producers out of monetary consideration.

Interview, New York/
The Hollywood Reporter, 10-8:10.

James M. Nederlander
Theatre owner

3

Being a theatre owner means you're really in the moving business. You move 'em in, you move 'em out. I've been involved in a lot of flops. No question about it. When you have a show the people don't want, you just close it and go on to the next one. That's about the size of it. Running theatres is also kind of a numbers business. If you have 10 theatres and five shows that are successful, they will make enough money to carry those theatres. If you have one theatre in New York and the show is a flop, you're out of business.

Interview, New York/
The New York Times, 11-29:(2)4.

Trevor Nunn
Artistic director, Royal Shakespeare Company, London

4

By endeavoring to dramatize a work by Charles Dickens, I was trying to find out what had happened to the English theatre in the 19th century, which plummeted into sentimentality and fifth-rate melodramatic nonsense. My theory is that in every age there is something you can call the "going form," so that if Shakespeare had lived in the 19th century, he would have written novels, and if Dickens had lived in the 17th century, he would have written plays.

Interview/
"W": a Fairchild publication, 11-6:12.

Pat O'Brien
Actor

5

Oh, I'm grateful to the movies. After all, they made me a wealthy man and bought me

(PAT O'BRIEN)

the kind of recognition that enabled me to have a long and satisfying career. But the stage is really where I love to be. I get an electric charge out of having a live audience in the house. There's a crackle in the air, a magic that you just don't feel when you're doing retake after retake on a film. The theatre is really a joy. It's so much more of a challenge, you know, to have to keep working on your role, adding a bit here, subtracting a bit there. You lose a laugh one night, and then try to get it back the next, tinkering with your part to figure out what went wrong that time, how to make it better the next.

Interview, Los Angeles/
Los Angeles Times, 8-29:(II)10.

Peter O'Toole
Actor

1

I was deeply pro-stage for many years, and it still is the well. I think it's where we grow. I think we can get easily fossilized on celluloid. Theatre is the only way to know, to grow; no matter how painful it is, you do it, and it's even more rewarding when you get it right.

Interview, Beverly Hills, Calif./
Daily Variety, 1-13:42.

Geraldine Page
Actress

2

If you waited for the perfect part, you'd sit at home and never get a chance to practice your craft. I always hope the play I'm in is a success, but in this business who can tell? So it's futile to turn down something just because you don't think it'll go. If you enjoy working on it, if you learn something—that's what's important in finding a role.

Interview/
The New York Times, 2-8:(2)15.

Joseph Papp
Producer

3

. . . I don't want to depend on any government [for grants and subsidies for the theatre]: I don't believe in that, actually. Nothing makes you feel more independent than getting your money from the box-office, from people putting their money on the line. I know the arts need to be supported. But subsidy on a large scale has its drawbacks. A lot of theatres depend too heavily on the government, and then develop this welfare-recipient mentality . . . [And] there's always that potential [of government interference] with plays, especially when you go into a political period where certain people want to be extremely critical and you have a less tolerant kind of Administration [in Washington]. The more independent you are, the more effective you can be and the more you can articulate.

Interview/
San Francisco Examiner & Chronicle,
10-18:(Datebook)37.

Arthur Penn
Director

4

I believe that a large part of the training in the regional theatres is in imitation of the British style of acting. The British orientation is textual; they start from the language and work toward the character . . . I've been trying to attract [actors] toward the less rigid—more lively, if you will—American style of acting: We start from the character, I think, and work toward the language . . . I think there is a quality of passion to the American actor. I'm certainly attracted to it, and I like to hope that underscoring it is a characteristic of my work. That quality is certainly also present in some British actors, but I tend to feel the mechanical and intellectual process is dominant in the British . . . I believe, and this perhaps is too nationalistic a view, that the American style of acting puts actors quickly in touch with each other, so that their continuous presence in a company, as in England, is not absolutely necessary.

Interview, New York/The New York Times, 3-8:(2)24.

(ARTHUR PENN)

1

Theatre [the stage] is a very warm, close, familial phenomenon. You work with the same group of people day after day. On the other hand, theatre essentially is the playwright's medium. There aren't enough images in the theatre; there isn't that much a director can say, and I miss that aspect. Film, on the other hand, is very transient; people come in, do their work and go. But a film essentially resides in the director's head. I get a great deal of pleasure out of both [film and stage work], but I have always alternated.

Interview/The New York Times, 12-6:(2)18.

Harold Prince
Producer, Director

2

Off-Broadway and the regional theatres—especially the regionals—have become [Broadway's] lifeline. That's where the serious non-musical theatre finds its authors and its audience.

Time, 10-5:81.

Lloyd Richards
Dean, School of Drama, Yale University;
Artistic director, Yale Repertory Theatre

3

As a person participating in the theatre, I've found that none of our work is possible until the playwright does his work. The impulse comes from there; and without that impulse—nurtured and given an opportunity to develop—there is no theatre except the theatre of the past.

Interview, New Haven, Conn./
The New York Times, 1-11:(2)5.

Ralph Richardson
Actor

4

Encouragement to an actor is very helpful, because we can't see. A painter can see his painting; he takes a look at it . . . Van Gogh never

had any encouragement from anybody; he saw his own pictures and his own pictures gave him faith that he was a fine artist. Well, an actor can never see the total impression that he makes. And if a critic who sort of knows something says that your work is pleasing, you feel as if you might be on the right track. Because *you* don't know if you're on the right track or not. I mean, you can have several successes in plays, but not know whether your total work is any good or going wrong, don't you know?

Interview, Washington/
The Christian Science Monitor, 6-24:(B)4.

Diana Rigg
Actress

5

Before I accept anything these days I ask myself three questions: [A] Am I going to enjoy it? [B] Will it extend my range as an actress? [C] If it fails, will I regret it? If the answers come up yes, yes and no, then I do it.

Interview, Mallorca/
Los Angeles Times, 6-7:(Calendar)30.

Jerome Robbins
Ballet master,
New York City Ballet

6

You can't explain how to choreograph. It's unanalyzable. It's like stepping into space, or working on a black canvas and hoping that the part you fill will be strong enough to lead to the next part . . . Choreography is like your thumb-print, your signature. It comes out of your life.

The New York Times, 5-31:(2)20.

Susan Sarandon
Actress

7

[Comparing acting in films with acting on stage]: In a film, you don't have to take responsibility if it's a disaster, because it really has so little to do with you. An actor [in films] has no control finally. In the theatre, it's just the

(SUSAN SARANDON)

opposite. You run the terrifying risk of having an audience tell you if you're right or wrong. At the end of the performance, when you're standing there, and you look out, and people are weeping and laughing and standing up, and you look around, and there's only one other person on stage, I mean there's no doubt that you had something to do with that.

Interview, New York/
The New York Times, 4-3:20.

Gerald Schoenfeld
Chairman, Shubert Organization
(theatre owners)

1

[Criticizing cutbacks in government aid to the arts in the U.S.]: Theatre is a creator of jobs, especially for low-income and minority people. Theatre is an urban renewer and neighborhood stabilizer. The performing arts, by their very nature, generate tremendous amounts of earned income. Unfortunately, people in government don't comprehend this; certainly not on the Federal level. The state and city should certainly have that awareness and make up the slack. Baltimore did it, with the Mechanic [Theatre]. They *bought* the damn theatre. Any place that allows a theatre to be destroyed because of a lack of funds, or that taxes theatre, like Chicago, is completely ignorant about what theatre does for the community and the amount of money it generates, in my judgment.

Interview, New York/
Los Angeles Times, 11-29:(Calendar)57.

Neil Simon
Playwright

2

Writing is an escape from a world that crowds me. I like being alone in a room. It's almost a form of meditation—an investigation of my own life. It has nothing to do with "I've got to get another play." When I go to work in the morning, I read the newspaper first. I don't have the slightest idea of what I'm going to do. I'm in this meditative mood like

being on a high board, looking down to a cold, chilly pool. Then I give myself a little push—the water isn't as cold as I thought. I don't think anyone gets writer's block. I think fear takes over.

Interview, Boston/
San Francisco Examiner & Chronicle,
4-19:(Datebook)35.

3

A writer inhibits himself by not telling the truth. I read many biographies of creative people, especially writers, painters and musicians. If you don't reveal yourself, you're lying somewhere along the way, and it will come out in the work. You don't have to be graphic, but you have to be truthful.

Interview, New York/
The Christian Science Monitor, 10-1:18.

4

If you want to know why [Broadway] musicals do so well so long, just walk down Fifth Avenue. All you hear are foreign languages. Musicals they can understand.

Time, 10-5:81.

Maggie Smith
Actress

5

[On her earliest appearance on stage in London in a play that was a flop]: It didn't worry me at the time. When you start, it's not desperate; one's got a confidence of some kind. You think it will be all right if you know your lines. At the start you have nothing to lose. They're all rushing to see someone else.

Interview, Paris/
Los Angeles Times, 1-3:(II)4.

John Taras
Ballet master, New York City Ballet

6

You learn choreography by doing it. You also learn by what you see. You look in the

415

(JOHN TARAS)

streets, at the cloverleafs on highways that go over and under, at architecture—architecture is very important—at trees, flowers, the terrific designs in French gardens, parades—not that they're as good now as they were before—and, my God, there's no more beautiful ballet in the world than an English coronation. Lord Mountbatten's funeral—terrific—it was organized in three days. Flights of birds, schools of fish—all those wedges, V-shapes, you see them in *Swan Lake*. A horse race, a baseball game—think of the slides in a baseball game.

The New York Times, 5-31:(2)20.

Peter Ustinov
Actor, Director, Writer

1

I like to make them [the audience] laugh, but I prefer the end result to be a smile. It's really the difference between a drinker and a taster. A smile means understanding . . . Laughter is a release, a therapy. A smile is a result.

Interview, Paris/
Los Angeles Times, 5-3:(Calendar)38.

Raf Vallone
Actor

2

The stage is better than films because you have the deepest communication, the most direct communication. The audience is a subject —not as it is in TV or the movies. The judgment of the audience is immediate. In the theatre, legitimate or opera, the collective becomes the individual, and the individual becomes part of the collective. This is a magical sensation that you get nowhere else.

Interview, San Francisco/
Opera News, 2-14:31.

Edward Villella
Ballet dancer

3

[On the "Young People's Introduction to the Dance" programs]: I hate this myth that

children don't understand, that you have to be careful with them. If you give children honesty and quality, they pay attention. And some of the most intent faces in our "Introduction" audiences have been adult. Parents, too, sometimes just think of ballet as *Swan Lake* or *The Nutcracker* at Christmas. We want to remove the veil of mystery. A lot of people still think classical ballet isn't for the average person. But it's a human art-form. It uses the human body. We jump. Everyone jumps. It's just that it's more sophisticated. Look at what we have to do while we jump up into air!

Interview/
The New York Times,
2-6:16.

Robert Whitehead
Producer

4

Culturally, Broadway [today] is impoverished. We have a bunch of girlie-girlie shows and no plays dealing with what we are as a nation. We have no plays that have anything to do with our lives. In the past we had musicals, but we also had a half-dozen fine playwrights each season. Now, the balance has gone over entirely to show-biz.

Interview/
The New York Times Magazine, 5-10:28.

Tennessee Williams
Playwright

5

I'm very conscious of my decline in popularity, but I don't permit it to stop me because I have the example of so many playwrights before me. I know the dreadful notices [Henrik] Ibsen got. And [Eugene] O'Neill—he had to die to make *Moon* [*for the Misbegotten*] successful. And to me it has been providential to be an artist, a great act of providence that I was able to turn my borderline psychosis into creativity.

Interview, New York/
Los Angeles Herald Examiner,
8-13:(B)7.

Lanford Wilson
Playwright

1

Starting a new play on Broadway—that is out of the question, Everything is judged by money. Ordinarily nice people become awful; the atmosphere is hysterical. People lose all perspective. The system is not conducive to creating.

Interview/
The New York Times Magazine,
5-10:46.

Franco Zeffirelli
Director

2

[On directing for the stage]: After 35 years, I can anticipate problems and come up with quick solutions. But I don't believe in planning everything beforehand. I'm Italian, not German. Some directors come to the theatre with everything precisely noted, and they have no regard for the human material. You cannot treat artists like hangers, or dummies, on which you hang your characters. Onstage, I want to put human beings, vitality, all of life's beauties.

Interview, New York/
The New York Times, 12-13:(2)21.

TELEVISION

Steve Allen
Entertainer

1

The men hired to run the [TV] networks are business executives who know about scheduling and strategy, but they don't know much about producing a show, or how to write a good script. Unfortunately, TV is big business, and there's a lot of money to be gained if you're Number 1 . . . [Ratings] don't mean a damn thing to me personally, except that they determine whether I work or not on prime-time. But we all know how important they are to the networks. For example, NBC has me currently doing a series of comedy specials. I think we're turning out the funniest shows of this season. The reviews have been sensational, but no matter how great the shows are, it has nothing to do with whether they stay on the air. The network executives have told me, "The shows are fantastic and we love them, and as soon as the ratings come in we'll let you know if we want you to do any more." It's that simple.

Interview, Los Angeles/
Los Angeles Herald Examiner,
1-11:(California Living)6.

2

[TV] has its own peculiar glamour—and I use that term even though "glamour" doesn't cover the whole phenomenon I'm referring to here. It's like a religious aura or the atmosphere surrounding a political figure who has just won an election, as though his body were giving off invisible rays. Which is why almost any stupid thing on television seems like a big deal.

Interview, Van Nuys, Calif./
Chicago Tribune Magazine, 2-8:24.

3

[There has been] a steady and demonstrable deterioration of the American intelligence, [and one of the causes is television. Watching a half-hour of *Charlie's Angels* is not going to make] a little piece of your brain fall out of your left ear. This won't happen, any more than eating one piece of white bread will make a tooth fall out. [But] 30 years of eating white bread, and the equivalent, will cause you physical harm; [and] 30 years of watching television of the most mindless thought must have, and has had, a destructive effect on the intelligence.

At National Public Radio conference,
Anaheim, Calif./Variety, 5-6:2.

Robert Altman
Director

4

[On the proliferation of cable, pay and other television forms]: The networks try to play it safe, to be bland. But they're too big to make all the decisions about something as diversified as the video outlets will be. The machine, the monster, is going to be so hungry that it'll turn whatever it has to for material. The networks won't be able to monopolize it. Small individual people's groups should be able to get in. It could be like publishing, where you deal with a whole spectrum, and specialization can occur. There could be a whole renaissance.

Interview, New York/
The Christian Science Monitor, 11-12:22.

Lindsay Anderson
Director

5

One of the greatest problems is that the creative process in terms of film or of television

(LINDSAY ANDERSON)

is fearfully expensive. Time is money. Time is also the essence of creativity. Not having enough time necessarily limits the artist's freedom. So that when one makes a video version [of a stage play] in three days, one is working for a purpose but not exactly indulging in a primary creative activity. Video has its own style and personality. But, finally, I think you have to judge any work of art by the experience that it gives, not by theoretical concepts of what is a movie, what is film, what is television, what is tape.

Interview, New York/
The New York Times, 2-22:(2)29.

Roone Arledge
President, ABC News and Sports

1

[Saying television news specials should be exempt from ratings, which compare them with entertainment programs]: Serious news programs are a public service that rarely attract a large audience, and they shouldn't have to compete with light-entertainment programming. Right now, each network is penalized in the weekly averages if it puts on a serious news program. News should be removed from the ratings stranglehold.

The New York Times, 2-12:18.

Danny Arnold
Producer

2

The atmosphere of TV is hostile to fine creative talent. Money is the bottom line. Too much is dishonest. Too much is expedient.

TV Guide, 10-24:29.

Herbert Brodkin
Producer

3

Television now is two things at once. It's the worst it has ever been, and at the same time it is doing some of the best things it's ever done.

I'm speaking of shows like *Roots* and *Playing for Time.* Hollywood applies its formula, but a couple of things always come through if there is a gleam of creative persistence. But most of what television does in the area of drama is despicable; it's criminal. Many of the programs have a strong tie-in to the problems in our society—the encouragement of violence, sex, drugs and disregard for laws.

Interview, New York/
The New York Times, 11-15:(2)39.

Pierre Cardin
Fashion designer

4

. . . it is stupid to say television is bad. You can turn the button off, just as you can put a book down. The book is good for intelligent people. TV is good for the average, the sick and the old. If these people weren't watching TV, what would they be doing? Drinking? Fighting? Doping? TV breaks the solitude. Sometimes people who are not cultured have nothing to say to each other. Television helps the conversation. Like Mercury, television is the messenger of the metallurgy. It brings everything to you—all the gods.

Interview, Paris/
Los Angeles Times, 4-17:(Fashion '81)5.

Norman Corwin
Writer

5

Perhaps the worst that can be said about commercial TV is not that it is a slave to ratings, which it is; or an assembly line for dramatized violence, which is bad enough; or an attic of old movies—but that it is a trivialization of a whole culture. [TV tends] to reduce us, to fragment our concentration, erode our standards, fritter away our native genius and make of our political procedures a kind of National Trifle Association.

At University of Southern California
School of Journalism, May 7/
Los Angeles Times, 5-9:(II)8.

WHAT THEY SAID IN 1981

Michael Dann
Senior adviser, ABC Video Enterprises;
Former vice president in charge of
programming, CBS-TV

1

By 1986, people will be spending as much each month for electronic equipment and programming in their homes as they do now on their cars. Every new house will have a home entertainment room, and it won't be uncommon for a family to spend $200 to $300 a month to buy services ranging from entertainment to information to education.

The Christian Science Monitor, 1-11:(12)52.

Bette Davis
Actress

2

I can't watch series TV these days—they are so awful, all that violence. But the dramatic specials, the [made-for-] TV movies, the special dramas—I tell you, they have the best scripts being written today. Much better than the scripts that become movies.

Interview, Los Angeles/
San Francisco Examiner & Chronicle,
10-11:(TV Week)3.

James E. Duffy
President, ABC-TV Network

3

[On the Coalition for Better Television and the Moral Majority, which are criticizing the sex-and-violence content of TV programming and threatening boycotts of sponsors]: [Their dogma] violates the basic principles of what American democracy is all about. [They are] electronic evangelists using the medium to raise money to attack the medium. The issue is not morality, but power, money and control. [TV is] by far the most careful of the media on matters of sex, violence, and profanity—not to be remotely compared to the content of books, movies, magazines, plays, certainly not to cable [TV] which does in fact carry pornographic programs and movies into the home. [The Coalition's efforts represent] a drive to throw

us back at least a century to outdated notions of Victorian morality. The last thing we need is a new wave of intolerance from either the left or the right.

Before New York chapter, National Academy of
Television Arts and Sciences/
The Hollywood Reporter, 5-19:83.

Jerry Falwell
Evangelist;
Chairman, Moral Majority

4

I object to the [TV] networks using public airwaves to make my living room a cesspool [with their programming]. If someone wants to invite profanity and vulgarity into their homes, there are cable channels available . . . In no way are we talking about repressing ideas, political concepts. We're in no way talking about limiting the opinions or people's moral or social values. We're talking about dirt. We're talking about bedroom scenes, sex and violence that is obnoxious, non-constructive and demeaning to the American moral fabric.

News conference, Washington, April 30/
Los Angeles Times, 5-1:(I)5.

Mark S. Fowler
Chairman, Federal
Communications Commission

5

[The] first and foremost objective is to create, to the maximum extent possible, an unregulated, competitive marketable environment for the development of telecommunications. There is an unbearable arrogance, I think, when an agency acts as if it knows all about how individual technologies ought to operate and how they all should be made to fit into one grand regulatory scheme . . . There is no other single area where the First Amendment concerns are highlighted in such bold relief as in the regulation of those industries whose business is to formulate and communicate ideas. Technological developments are proceeding at such a rapid pace that many definitions of telecommunications services are becoming blurred.

(MARK S. FOWLER)

Unless the [FCC] remains sensitive to these constant changes and their implications, there is a danger that rules perhaps validly applied to one service may be inappropriately applied to another very different service.

At National Cable Television
Association convention, Los Angeles, May 31/
Los Angeles Times, 6-1:(I)3,20.

Fred W. Friendly
Professor of journalism,
Columbia University;
Former president, CBS News

1

[Saying news programs should not be included in weekly television ratings]: When you apply ratings to news, they have no meaning at all. It's as if you took Walter Lippmann and rated him against Popeye. Exempting news programs from ratings is a trick, but it's a benevolent one. If it makes the networks do more serious programming, all the better.

The New York Times, 2-12:(18.

2

The cost of a [TV] documentary—$100,000 in my day, $200,000 today—and the amount of time you spend is so great that people are scared to do complex, serious subjects for fear they'll fail. They would much rather do the simple or sensational story because they know it has a better chance, that it's a sure thing with audiences. I know you can do a program about rape or abortion, and it is quite easy to make it compelling—you've got pictures, you've got drama, you've got the clash of conflicting interests. But if you want to do one on productivity or tariffs or arms control, the chances are that it may not be a big success or have big ratings and you may, in fact, fail.

Interview, New York/
Los Angeles Times, 6-8:(VI)1.

3

Public television and radio are not just viable alternatives. They are options of sanity to the billion-dollar penny arcade called commercial television, which makes so much money doing its worst that it cannot afford to do its best.

At meeting of Public Broadcasting Service,
Cincinnati, June 28/
Los Angeles Times, 6-30:(VI)1.

Michael Fuchs
Senior vice president in charge of
programming, Home Box Office (pay TV)

4

[Comparing pay TV with commercial TV]: . . . the commercial network system is so competitive that it can't give shows a chance to find their audiences, to grow on people. I'd like to think that we will be a little bit less competitive than the commercial networks and will be able to do more specialized things . . . I think one of the things the networks do best is their news-type programming. I think you'll be seeing even more of that. And if we have forced that to happen [through superior entertainment programming on pay TV], I feel *that* is our public service. Maybe we will prove to be the conscience of the networks by making them more competitive. If they are forced to react to the consumer more than they have in the past, I think we will have performed a great service.

Interview, New York/
The Christian Science Monitor, 7-3:19.

George Gerbner
Dean, Annenberg School of Communications,
University of Pennsylvania

5

[On how to control excessive TV violence]: The question is not one of more censorship or less. The networks are 100 per cent self-censored as it is. The question is, on whose behalf is this process operating? Right now it's on behalf of the advertisers who pay the bill to get the maximum audience at the minimum cost,

WHAT THEY SAID IN 1981

and cater to every existing prejudice. The networks should be censoring themselves according to a different value system.

The New York Times, 4-26:(2)25.

Lillian Gish
Actress

1

I think television is killing itself. They're playing down [to audiences]. [The late film director D. W.] Griffith used to say, "Remember, there are more of them out there than there are here, so they know more than we do. Always play the best you can—play up to them, never down." But they're all playing down in television.

Interview, New York/
The Christian Science Monitor, 2-13:19.

John Goberman
Director of media development,
Lincoln Center, New York

2

One of the interesting things that happens when these cultural pay [TV] channels start talking about programming is that they don't seem to realize that there is a vast difference between what's good and bad. The audiences really react to performances that are good and doesn't care at all to watch the stuff that's not very good. So the cultural channels had better be careful. There is the temptation to put together a cultural channel very cheaply with not very good stuff. Staying-power is very dependent upon having the best. "Cultural" is an all-encompassing word that on the surface sounds homogeneous but it is really not at all. Not all "cultural" programming is worth watching. There is a need for the best, and less than that won't fly.

Interview, New York/
The Christian Science Monitor,
4-2:18.

Jane Hershey
Editor-in-chief,
"Cable TV Magazine"

3

The variety of choice offered by cable TV makes it active. You don't have to watch in a droning, passive mood and sit through a hundred things you don't want to see to find something you do want to see. You buy and watch what you want. If you want movies for your children, they're there . . . If you want dirty movies for you and your wife, *they're* there.

Interview/ "W": a Fairchild publication, 3-13:9.

Glenda Jackson
Actress

4

[Television] is a totally boring medium. It does nothing for anybody. Most of what is put on is unadulterated, dyed-in-the-wool rubbish. However, most of the stuff that has been put on television has found its proper home.

Interview, Los Angeles/
Los Angeles Times, 2-12:(VI)15.

5

I think actors are wasted on television. It's the only medium in which the whole is less than the sum of its parts. The actors just go through the motions because that's all they're asked to do. That little screen couldn't contain anything larger.

Interview, London/
Saturday Review, March:37.

Clive James
Television critic,
"The Observer," London

6

. . . awful British TV doesn't have the attraction of awful American TV. You can see how awful American TV might appeal to somebody. Awful British TV—you don't see how it can appeal to anybody. You wonder how it got on the air.

Interview/The Christian Science Monitor, 3-27:19.

Leonard Jason
Associate professor of psychology,
De Paul University

1

The parents may have children who watch too much TV, but the parents may not mind because the television is kind of an instant baby-sitter . . . This is a serious problem, and it must be dealt with in a serious way. A child who is watching so much television that he doesn't engage in peer play, and in relating to children and adults in the real world, is in trouble. He is watching television instead of finding out who he is.

Interview/Chicago Tribune, 2-11:(1)18.

Fay Kanin
Screenwriter; President, Academy of
Motion Picture Arts and Sciences

2

[Comparing television with motion pictures]: . . . television [is] more open to intimate subjects, exploring relationships between people —maybe because television requires less production money and can take more chances on subjects. On the other hand, films are freer; television is less able to be open in the treatment of sexuality, or the use of language. So each medium has its own strength.

Daily Variety, 10-26:15.

Lane Kirkland
President, American Federation of Labor-
Congress of Industrial Organizations

3

It's clear to me that for some years—probably more so in the future—this box [television] is going to dominate American life; it's where people get their information, or what they think is information; that's where they form their impressions. It's profoundly affected American politics—I think to a degree for the worse, but it doesn't matter, it's there. It's molded the kind of personality that seems to be most successful in getting elected. That type of personality may have a little more difficulty governing than getting elected.

Interview/The New York Times, 11-16:12.

Paul Klein
Producer; Former executive vice president
for programs, NBC-TV

4

It's very difficult to get anything new on TV because something new doesn't have a track record, and the programmer who puts it on could get fired if it doesn't work—and it takes a long time for something new to work. The advertisers all say they want things that are new, but they really don't. They want guaranteed circulation [audience].

Interview/
U.S. News & World Report, 12-14:57.

Jack Klugman
Actor

5

[Lamenting the speed required in making a TV series]: When time is the enemy, there is no artistry. Time has got to be the artist's friend. When you're painting a picture, you paint a little today—and then go back the next day and change the color, change the lines. It's a continuation, a culmination of all of your moods, all of your feelings. But if [you've] got to get it out, you're always driving home saying, "Gee, I should have tried that. Why didn't I do this?"

Interview/
Los Angeles Herald Examiner, 2-9:(C)8.

Thomas Kratenmaker
Professor of law,
Georgetown University

6

[On excessive violence on TV]: Any kind of government regulation which tried either to shift the time at which programs were aired, or which banned them altogether because of the fear that they would encourage aggressive action on the part of children, would be un-Constitutional under the First Amendment. That's because the government is required to demonstrate the presence of a clear and present danger that violence will immediately and irreparably ensue from the viewing of such programs by children;

(THOMAS KRATENMAKER)

and because the government has no right to deny to adults the right to receive information, expression, entertainment or other similar speech protected by the First Amendment on the theory that it may harm children.

The New York Times, 4-26:(2)25.

Norman Lear
Writer, Producer

1

Gratuitous sex [on TV]—do we really need young women in bra-less sweaters running and bouncing across a set because someone has said that dinner is ready? Do we need the same young woman jumping up and down in her bra-less sweater when she is told that dinner will consist of lamb chops? "Not lamb chops!" Jump, jump . . . I will never believe that this sort of TV behavior is motivated by the artistic needs of the writer or the director or the actress. It is motivated, primarily—in a long circuitous fashion—by the needs of three networks to win in the ratings . . . By three networks' obsession with the bottom line. An obsession it shares with all of the rest of American business. And that, of course, includes me.

Before Hollywood Radio and Television Society,
Beverly Hills, Calif./
Los Angeles Herald Examiner, 9-17:(D)6.

2

The history of network television teaches that the concentration of most of the resources of broadcasting in three companies results in the kind of fierce competition which invites the kind of homogeneous broadcasting that allows for too little diversity and retards the development of new and competing technologies. With the explosion of new technologies, this history must not be repeated. It would be good for the country to have the dissonant variety inherent in our pluralistic society find its way to the tube—people of all races and religions and life-styles—the hotheads, syba-

rites and ascetics, the mockers and "madmen" —let's have them all.

Before House Telecommunications Subcommittee,
Washington/
The Christian Science Monitor, 12-14:23.

Gene P. Mater
Senior vice president for policy,
CBS Broadcast Group

3

[On the Coalition for Better Television's monitoring programs for excessive sex and violence, and its threat of sponsor product boycotts]: The justification for all this seems to be that a whole array of troubling societal problems will be alleviated, if not eliminated, if only television is changed. Divorce, promiscuity, crime and the like would fade into the background. Never mind that every one of them long predates the introduction of television. Finding a scapegoat is easier than finding a solution.

Before National Academy of Television
Arts and Sciences, New York/
Los Angeles Herald Examiner, 4-10:(A)5.

4

[On moral standards in his network's programming]: It is our belief that social mores do change and they change quite literally on a daily basis to some degree; and rather than have a set of standards listed—you will do this, you may not do that and so on and so forth—we don't do it. We judge, frankly, based on input from affiliates, the letters that we receive, sessions such as this, the columns that you people [in the press] write. But we don't set ourselves up with a set of standards of this is what we are going to project in programming. It may sound simplistic, but basically we're talking about entertaining and informing, and that's exactly what it amounts to; and to come up with a set of biblical standards, or other standards, saying that this is what we're going to do—we don't feel that it is either the duty, the responsibility, or indeed within the prov-

(GENE P. MATER)

ince of the broadcaster to, if you will, educate the American people.

*News conference, Los Angeles, June/
The Christian Science Monitor,
6-26:23.*

Gian Carlo Menotti
Composer

1

I think that opera on television loses as much of a new audience as it attracts. That is because most opera shown on television is so bad. Opera is not for television unless it is written for television. To adapt an opera for television, you need a superb cameraman and a superb director. I frankly believe that most operas are directed abominably, and once you put on television a close-up of a heavily made-up fat singer with her mouth wide open revealing her wobbly tongue and she acts with exaggerated gestures, people will laugh and close the television.

*Interview, New York/
The Christian Science Monitor, 6-26:19.*

Jonathan Miller
Producer, Director, Writer

2

Great novels cannot be dramatized. The transformation of a great novel into a work of filmic art on TV is really self-defeating. The best films are made from third-rate literature. Often something quite cheap and bad has been turned into a classic film, but I can't think of any good film based on a work of art greater than it.

*Interview/
Los Angeles Times, 7-26:(Calendar)48.*

Tad Mosel
Playwright

3

People should consider that the dialogue of TV is just as much an artifice today as it was 30 years ago. The so-called naturalism of Paddy

Chayefsky's *Marty* wasn't more realistic than screenplays that had been written before. It just had a different rhythm, but you'd never hear anyone in real life talk that way. What was emerging was Chayefsky's voice. And the thing that's lacking in screenplays being produced on TV today is an original voice.

*Interview/"W": a Fairchild publication,
9-11:12.*

Bill Moyers
Broadcast journalist

4

Television is the national campfire around which we spend our time. We can laugh at [TV character] Archie Bunker, be enchanted by a drama or a fantasy. But there is no place where the civic life is addressed. In commercial television journalism, the urgency almost drowns out the impact. That's what I'd like to see public television become . . . the place where the significant issues of our time are heard. The place where the conversation of democracy can be heard.

*Interview, New Orleans/
Los Angeles Times, 12-25:(VI)17.*

Victor S. Navasky
Editor, "The Nation"

5

The movie business may have gone through enough structural changes to transcend the residue of values from the blacklist episode [of the 1950s]. But television is different: Shows are still half an hour; you still have sponsors; ad agencies still play an important role; the networks are still there. The same structure is in place, even though there's more independence. I have a feeling that the unwritten laws governing the TV business are not entirely attributable to the millions of dollars at stake. I'm talking about the obsession with ratings, the rules about what you can and can't put on, the great fear that seems to infect some of the people who work in TV. I think these things are partly attributable to the fact that TV was born as a mass medium during the cold-war years.

WHAT THEY SAID IN 1981

So you have to be *careful* all the time . . . The president of the Writers Guild of America once testified before Congress that certain subjects can't be dealt with on TV, in fiction. The Vietnam war was that way for a long time. I don't think box-office is the only reason. It's my intuition that these strictures date back to the origins of television in the cold-war atmosphere.

Interview/
The Christian Science Monitor, 1-22:18.

David Ogilvy
Former chairman, Ogilvy &
Mather, Inc., advertising

1

I've come back [to the U.S.] every year. When I come back, I see things through newer eyes. I've been watching the television and I'm really appalled at the amount of advertising [on American TV]. It seems to me to project a culture which is becoming terribly materialistic. The sound of selling is the dirge of our time . . . In Europe, there are not nearly so many commercials on television—not so much the unrelenting bombardment of commercials which I find so unattractive here. Sooner or later, it will have to be brought under control, probably by the government, for the sake of the immortal soul—the consumer.

Interview, Los Angeles/
Los Angeles Times, 4-2:(IV)1.

Neil Postman
Professor of communication arts and
sciences, New York University

2

Television communicates the same information to everyone simultaneously, regardless of age, sex, level of education or life experience. Therefore, television eliminates many of the important ways that we distinguish between children and adults. For example, one of the main differences between an adult and a child is that the adult knows about certain facets of life—its mysteries, its contradictions, its violence, its tragedies—that are not considered suitable for children to know, or even accessible to children. What television does is bring the entire culture out of the closet, because programs need a constant supply of novel information. In its quest for new and sensational ventures to hold its audience, TV must tap every existing taboo in the culture: homosexuality, incest, divorce, promiscuity, corruption, adultery and terrible displays of violence and sadism. As a consequence, these become as familiar to the young as they are to adults. The new media tend to obliterate classes of people, particularly the difference between what we call adulthood and childhood.

Interview/
U.S. News & World Report,
1-19:45.

Lee Rich
President,
Lorimar Productions

3

I'd rather do a million *Dallas*es than one critically successful *White Shadow* that doesn't get the [ratings] numbers. *Dallas* may be crap—and it won't win any awards—but it's really good crap.

Newsweek, 2-9:94.

Lloyd Richards
Dean, School of Drama, Yale University;
Artistic director,
Yale Repertory Theatre

4

Most of the people going through school today are too young to remember *Playhouse 90* and writer Paddy Chayefsky. They grew up in an era when the TV screenwriter really didn't have a chance to express himself as an artist. There has been very little orginal writing for TV over the past 20 years.

Interview/
"W": a Fairchild publication,
8-28:9.

Sharon Rockefeller
Member of the board,
Corporation for Public Broadcasting

1

[On the Reagan Administration's cutback in funding for Public Broadcasting]: This Administration believes in the private sector picking up the tab for things like public television. I think Walter Annenberg's $150-million gift to CPB was great, but there are very few Annenbergs, and there simply isn't enough private money to fill the gap. Do you know military bands get twice as much money as the proposed cuts for CPB? And what will people think when there is no more *MacNeil-Lehrer* or *Nova?* You can well foresee the possible reaction to budget cuts. Right now it's just too early, but there are always shifting sands in politics. Nothing is permanent.

Chicago Tribune, 8-16:(12)3.

Wayne Rogers
Actor

2

Insecure people can be enormously protective and proprietary about their work. But when you're doing a [TV] show week after week, you can't afford that. I say to people, "I'm not interested in more exposure for myself. I'm interested in the quality. We're all trees, and the forest is the important thing."

Interview/TV Guide, 3-21:32.

James H. Rosenfield
President, CBS-TV

3

[On what TV programming would be like if it gave in to crticism from various pressure groups and critics]: There could be no comedy involving business people, union members, minority-group members, women; and we might as well include doctors, scientists and lawyers in the exempt category as well. In drama, there will be no more violent incidents —no pie-throwing either—to satisfy those concerned with scaring people. There will be no mention of sex, premarital or extra-marital.

No mention of abortion. No talk of rape or child pornography. No character will sympathetically portray feminists. No character will sympathetically portray traditional feminism. All programs, henceforth, have to present only the positive portrayals of all characters. There shall be no negative, humorous portrayals of characters, nor harm threatened to any character. No actor or actress who has ever supported controversial causes shall ever be hired. No program will be based on books or movies that have been criticized by anyone. Nothing will be presented that is unsettling to anybody. Is this the TV picture you want to put on America's screens? . . . Do you think networks could provide 15 hours a day of the sort of programming I've described and still manage to encourage the use of over 65 per cent of all TV sets on each and every night of the week, as they do now? Of course not.

Before TV and Radio Advertising Club,
Philadelphia, Sept. 24/
Daily Variety, 9-25:25.

Boris Sagal
Director

4

. . . a picture means most to a director when he sees it in the projection room. When you see your picture on television all cut up with commercials, your heart just sinks. It's a time of terrible despair, which you learn to live with because this is an advertising medium; you're there to sell Pepsodent.

Interview/
Los Angeles Times, 3-29:(Calendar)3.

Edgar J. Scherick
Producer

5

Fear is so rampant these days [at the networks] with inflation. They're afraid to do anything that isn't a sure thing. So they do blue shows or violent shows, things they think are money-makers. One lesson I have learned across the years is that if you start out to make something because it's going to make money, you'll

427

WHAT THEY SAID IN 1981

(EDGAR J. SCHERICK)

fall flat on your tail. But if you start out to do something because you've got a good feeling about it, the money will come as surely as night follows day.

Interview, Los Angeles/Los Angeles Times, 1-27:(VI)8.

Herbert S. Schlosser
Executive vice president, RCA SelectaVision; Former president, National Broadcasting Company

1

[Comparing television and videodiscs]: We're really in very, very different businesses. Broadcasting is an advertising medium. It fills an enormous amount of hours every day. This [discs and tapes] is much more like the publishing or the record business. People are going to go out and buy that thing they want. What we're beginning to see in the '80s is the coming into the home of many, many different things that are going to give the viewer the option of watching commercial broadcasting, public broadcasting, discs, tapes, playing a game [on the TV set], or pay cable—many, many more things. And we see a great deal of evidence that consumers are willing to commit a great deal more money to that.

Interview, New York/Los Angeles Times, 3-24:(VI)5.

Fred Silverman
President, National Broadcasting Company

2

[Criticizing organizations which encourage boycotting of sponsors of TV programs they consider offensive because of sex and violence]: There are groups today—well-intentioned, I know—who would impose their version of acceptable "speech" and entertainment on the rest of us by abridging this fundamental freedom. Their target now is television. Their method is secondary boycott of advertisers. [If such groups are successful,] the ultimate end of their actions would be a loss of freedom. Not just my freedom as a broadcaster, but your freedom, too, as a viewer. [Groups such as Moral Majority are] tempted to give up our passion for free speech because they think—from their own

particular viewpoint—it is being abused ... Improvement will not come at the expense of freedom. It comes through the exercise of freedom.

Before Hibernian Society, Savannah, Ga./ The Hollywood Reporter, 3-23:1.

Tom Snyder
Broadcast journalist; Host, "Tomorrow" show, NBC-TV

3

[In TV,] it's the win syndrome and the money syndrome. Dollars, revenue. Although most Americans read about TV in terms of what's on the air or who's getting fired, the executive managements of all three networks are really concerned about the financial pages and profits. They all speak in terms of quality TV and being responsive to public need, but what they really respond to are the annual financial reports that are given at stockholders' meetings. That's the bottom line—the money.

Interview, New York/Playboy, February:170.

Aaron Spelling
Producer

4

[On pressures from groups, such as Moral Majority, for the reduction of sex and violence in TV programs]: ... the general public seems to be asking for a change. What I really wonder is whether they are asking for *better* television. If that were really the case, I think that the creative community would be very pleased. Ask me if I would rather live in a society where the networks bought 15 police shows or 15 *Family*s —there is no doubt that I would rather see them buy 15 *Family*-type series. We'll see if that is going to happen. But as far as this Moral Majority is concerned, they seem to hate anything that has *any* action in it. As far as I can see, what they really love is pap ... If the public *really* wants less action shows, then why do they keep *watching* more and more of those very series they are supposed to dislike? ... After all is said and done, *nobody* can speak for the people except the people themselves.

Interview/The Hollywood Reporter, 6-23:6.

Grant Tinker
Chairman, National Broadcasting Company

1

[On whether TV violence has a negative influence on young viewers]: I'm not sociologist enough to be able to answer that in any useful way. But I do think that television can be faulted over the years for a certain kind of bloodless violence, a kind of deathless death [in its programming]. This kind of thing may give an impressionable child the feeling that a blow doesn't hurt, that blood isn't real, that bullets don't kill, etc. If that's true, I think it is one way in which we should clean up our act. However, I think television has already cleaned up its act in many ways. I think it is now much more aware and much more responsible than it was a few years ago. We have people who spend all their time trying to make sure that we don't overstep the bounds. If you are asking if TV is the genesis of violence, I would say it is more likely that television may be reflecting the reality out there, especially in inner cities.

Interview, New York/
The Christian Science Monitor, 1-28:(B)16.

Ted Turner
Chairman, Turner Broadcasting System

2

It has become apparent to me over the years that I have been in this business, that television is having, in my opinion, a tremendously detrimental effect on this country [the U.S.], a tremendously detrimental effect. I think this is mainly caused by a lack of responsibility on the part of the television networks . . . for putting on programs that are representing to the American people the wrong role models. I believe television is primarily responsible for the rising crime rate, the tremendous emphasis on materialism, the breakdown of the family.

Interview, Atlanta/Chicago Tribune, 5-29:(1)1.

Jack Valenti
President, Motion Picture
Association of America

3

In the future, all TV sets will surely be equipped not only with great-size screens, but with stereo sound of clarity and quality that embraces the eye as well as the ear . . . conventional TV viewing will go down. Competitive alternatives will take up the breach . . . The great future war in the home will be how people allocate their personal viewing time. This is the great enigma . . . Within the next 20 years, the caliber of writers, directors, actors, actresses, producers, craftsmen will be visibly larger. Their literacy and education in the cinematic art will be the connecting link between what is created and how well it is done. For the creative society . . . the next 20 years will be the golden era, for all the stuff of technology will cry out for more and more programming to fill the endless caverns of the electronic landscape.

Before World Affairs Council,
Los Angeles/
The Washington Post, 1-25:(H)3.

4

[On criticism of excessive violence in films and TV]: I saw more violence on network news programs during the Vietnam war than I have seen in a lifetime. What are you going to do, shut off the news? Where do you draw the line? A movie might jolt a psychotic into action— or somebody might jostle him in the subway, or be rude to him, and that might also precipitate an action by someone teetering on the precipice. Anything could set him off. We lose tens of thousands of people a year to automobile accidents; should we ban the automobile? We don't even ban handguns, and look at all the people who are killed every year by handguns . . . You pay a price for a democratic society. But I wonder whether those people who clamor for the banning of violent shows might find the Russian model attractive, where the state tells you what you can put on television. You pay another price for the absence of what some people find offensive, and that price is that you give over to the state or another authority the right to make judgments about what should be banned.

The New York Times, 4-26:(2)25.

429

WHAT THEY SAID IN 1981

Henry Waxman
United States Representative,
D—California

1

[On corporate funding of public broadcasting]: If people tend to think well of major corporations for their underwriting, that doesn't offend me. What *is* disturbing—and I have never had an adequate answer to this—is whether a corporation, simply by making a contribution, has a subliminal impact on the kinds of programs public broadcasting will undertake.

TV Guide, 6-20:8.

Donald E. Wildmon
Chairman, Coalition for
Better Television

2

[On his organization's criticism of TV program content]: . . . it's not individual programs, because they change from week to week, that is a concern of mine or I think of other people in the country. What really concerns us is the value system being depicted in those programs. Precisely, a value system that says violence is a legitimate way to achieve one's goals in life. A value system that says violence is a legitimate means to resolve conflict. A value system that says sex is something to snigger at or that you participate [in] with anyone other than your own spouse. A value system that says, instead of intelligence, profanity is the way to enforce what everyone has to say.

News conference, Los Angeles, June/
The Christian Science Monitor, 6-26:23.

3

[Supporting a boycott of companies sponsoring TV programs having excessive sex and violence]: Everything on the air has a message. TV represents behavior modification, or monkey-see, monkey-do. A child sees it and it leaves an impression. But consideration, decency,

honesty, fidelity, hard work—those values aren't there. If I disagree with the values that are there, can't I stop supporting the companies that put them on? Sex and violence exist—and so do going to the bathroom and vomiting; but you don't see them on TV. Where is the TV show about a modern house with decent people?

Time, 6-29:83.

4

[On his proposal for an economic boycott of companies that sponsor objectionable TV programs]: I don't imagine any two people will agree 100 per cent on anything. The problem is, we do have freedom of speech, yes. But freedom of speech works two ways. It works for us as well as the other people [who are against his boycott plans]. Here's our whole premise in a nutshell—and I don't believe you've seen it [explained] in any publication—not *Time*, nor *People*, or any other supposedly objective newsmagazine—and it's as American as apple pie: The networks can show what they want to show. The advertiser can sponsor what he wants to sponsor. The viewer can view any of the three options made available to him by the networks, and only the networks or the local stations tell you what you can and cannot watch. And the consumer can spend his money where he wants to [and buy or not buy a sponsor's product as he sees fit]. Now, I really can't find anything wrong with all of that, can you? Yet a lot of people [his critics] can. We have not asked Congress to pass a single law. Therefor, we're not testing the First Amendment; we're actually preserving it. We're taking our case to the marketplace—which you always do in a capitalistic, democratic society.

Interview/
The Saturday Evening Post,
November:75.

Vladimir K. Zworykin
"Father of television"; Inventor of
the television tube

5

[On television today]: The technique is wonderful. I didn't ever dream it would be so good.

430

(VLADIMIR K. ZWORYKIN)

The color and everything. It is beyond my expectation. [But] the programs! I would never let my children ever come close to this thing. It's awful what they're doing.

Interview on his 92nd birthday, July 30/
The New York Times, 7-31:12.

Philosophy

Mortimer J. Adler
Educator; Former professor of
philosophy, University of Chicago

1

The underestimation of the human intelligence is the worst sin of our time. I've had the most extraordinary conversations with taxi drivers in New York. Or, take a huge dinner party—if you propose to talk about, say, angels or any other basic idea, you can take the conversation away from football, baseball, the stock exchange, inflation. It's easy, because people have minds, and with minds, they like to think.

Interview/
The New York Times, 8-5:18.

Steve Allen
Entertainer

2

. . . contrary to what you might think, I've had my ups and downs. But that's true of all performers and more true of the superstars than anybody. If you were to look at the careers of John Wayne or Bob Hope or Frank Sinatra or Marlon Brando and slice off a 25-year period, you'd find a lot of peaks and a lot of valleys. It happens with anything—a hairdo, a song, a baseball team, a candy bar—that zooms to a peak of popularity so sharply that it goes off the top of the chart and continues onto the wallpaper. There's nowhere to go from there but down. That doesn't mean that you have to go to the other extreme, to the bottom of the chart and onto the carpet. But it does mean that at some point in the future you're not going to be that popular any more. There is that risk, and it would be much better if one had one's choice not to do it that way—to just go on being good and being appreciated, so you can always count on your constituency.

Interview, Van Nuys, Calif.
Chicago Tribune Magazine, 2-8:25.

Sparky Anderson
Baseball manager, Detroit "Tigers"

3

In my opinion, too many people are looking for security when it's already right there with them. I grew up poor, which is one of the best things that can happen to you; otherwise, you're never going to understand or appreciate success . . . The real meaning of success is to be happy with what you are doing and to get up every morning with the idea that you're going to try to make everyone you meet happy. And we don't need booze or marijuana or cocaine to give us courage, because courage is something that comes from within.

The Christian Science Monitor, 2-19:16.

Yul Brynner
Actor

4

I don't believe anything is ever the same. The only way it can be done is to start everything anew. I believe our lives are like that. It applies to us as civilians as well as artists. No two days are ever really alike, if we're intensely aware and searching as I think we ought to be.

Interview, New York/
The Washington Post, 2-15:(K)2.

Zbigniew Brzezinski
Assistant to the President of the
United States for National Security Affairs

5

History is much more the product of chaos than of conspiracy.

Interview, Washington, Jan. 17/
The New York Times, 1-18:(1)3.

Anthony Burgess
Author

6

Hope lies only in the individual—in his capacity for self-construction, for being not

(ANTHONY BURGESS)

only a subject that perceives, a voice that speaks, but also a body of knowledge and values nurtured by the past. Young people are wrong to condemn the past, to believe that by destroying it one is automatically building a better world. I do not mean that the task of education is to hold up the past as an example to new generations. I mean that they should be given a choice: "This is what the past was all about. Now, use your gifts and your freedom to decide knowledgeably what is good and what is evil." There is one thing about the past which makes me strangely optimistic. It can be judged. It can be tamed, digested. Each of us has the capacity to discern what is evil in it and what is good.

Interview/World Press Review, December:36.

George Burns
Entertainer

1

[On being 85 years of age]: I can't get old; I'm working. I was old when I was 21 and out of work. As long as you're working you stay young.

The Washington Post, 1-21:(E)4.

Dalai Lama
Exiled former Chief of State of Tibet

2

Without kindness we cannot survive in this world. Through hatred and anger there is no possibility to achieve compassion, and love is extremely important. The value of kindness is limitless . . . Each of us has the responsibility to serve mankind, to think of mankind, to be concerned for mankind.

At Sanders Theatre, Harvard University/ The Christian Science Monitor, 8-26:(B)7.

John Eccles
Medical educator; Physiologist

3

What worries me [about the world is that] I don't think we've come to terms with the enormous explosion of information . . . of the

way in which each of us is immersed now— you might say, *drowned*—in too much trivial information, so no one thinks any more. It was much better in the days when people could think and talk and get some primitive understanding of their lives. Now this terrible disease of over-information means you are so distracted that you don't know how to think, and most people go through life hardly knowing they're alive.

Interview, Washington/ The Washington Post, 3-15:(F)4.

Federico Fellini
Motion-picture director

4

Any man in any part of the world, not just the Italian, sees in the woman that which he doesn't know of himself. He has been conditioned—forever—to hope that with the woman there is the possibility to discover his other side. The obscure side, like sun and moon. It's a myth that has a great power on the psyche . . . There are myths about women—I am very ignorant, so I can't quote facts in a historical way—but mythologists and archeologists say that before the patriarchal society there was a matriarchy. Men were something like dogs. Procreation was thought to be made by the wind, so they didn't even have that kind of justification for their existence.

Interview, New York/ San Francisco Examiner & Chronicle, 4-19:(Datebook)17.

Joao Baptista Figueiredo
President of Brazil

5

Democracy, even in trouble, is worth far more than any progressive dictatorship.

Political speech, Rio de Janeiro/ The New York Times Magazine, 12-6:126.

R. Buckminster Fuller
Engineer, Author, Designer

6

At the age of 32, I decided that I was either going to commit suicide or discover what a

(R. BUCKMINSTER FULLER)

penniless human could do on behalf of humanity. I decided on the latter and realized that human beings were introduced into the universe for an important reason. They're like bees, you see, bees who go out and get honey without realizing they're also performing cross-pollination. I realized that we are only throw-away, that we've never designed anything, that the universe exhibits a mathematical orderliness which naturally implies a greater intellect at work, and that we are part of that design. Then I made a commitment never to use this knowledge for personal gain or political power. My life has been, as a result, one miracle after another.

At party celebrating his 86th birthday,
Philadelphia, July 7/
The New York Times, 7-9:14.

Armand Hammer
Chairman,
Occidental Petroleum Corporation

1

When people tell me I'm lucky, I like to tell them, "I'm lucky because I work seven days a week, 14 hours a day." You have to have that level of commitment to what you do. You have to work hard, but that alone isn't enough. After all, a lot of people work hard and never get anywhere. You have to be able to recognize a good opportunity when you see one. There are so many opportunites, but people don't always know how to take advantage of them. You have to be willing to take risks. You need courage—that's very important. You can't be afraid of things.

Interview, Los Angeles/
Los Angeles Herald Examiner,
10-11:(California Living)27.

Thor Heyerdahl
Explorer

2

[On the experience of being alone while sailing in mid-ocean]: You feel part of the universe. You have the sky with the stars, and the sea with the plankton, and that's all. You wake up; in a sense, you live. You feel it right through your brain and your body that this is reality. When you come back and live the life of modern man, it isn't reality. It isn't the real thing. We've forgotten the truth about life the way we live today.

Interview/
The Washington Post, 3-8:(K)5.

Joel Hildebrand
Professor emeritus of chemistry,
University of California, Berkeley

3

The finest hours of life are not those spent among large groups of people, but in conversation with just a few, in reading great books, in listening to great music, wandering in a forest of giant sequoia, peering into a microscope, unraveling nature's secrets in a laboratory. The men who have had most to give to their fellow men are those who have enriched their minds and hearts in solitude. It is a poor education that does not fit a man to be alone with himself.

Interview/
San Francisco Examiner & Chronicle,
11-15:(California Living)9.

Ivan Hill
Former president,
Ethics Resource Center, Washington

4

Albert Schweitzer said that, in a general sense, ethics is the name we give to our concern for good behavior. We feel an obligation to consider not only our personal well-being but also that of others and of human society as a whole. If early man had not identified his own welfare with that of others, he could not have survived and mankind wouldn't have developed. In recent books on anthropology . . . cooperation and sharing were given as basic reasons for man's survival. Honesty and ethics are basic, working social principles, not just moral guidelines.

Interview,
U.S. News & World Report, 11-16:102.

Bob Hope
Entertainer

1

Procrastination is the Number 1 cause of tension. It causes more heart attacks and strokes than anything else. You always worry about the things you put off. They're always in the back of your mind, festering and creating anxiety. Suddenly you're overwhelmed by the matters you've neglected, and that's when you're in trouble; that's when you toss and turn at night and start coating your stomach with Mylanta. I'm a great believer in getting things taken care of *fast*.

Interview/
The Saturday Evening Post, October:55.

John Irving
Author

2

Whether in politics or other realms, dreamers are dangerous people, though they may also be enchanting and captivating. If you marry a dreamer, or have one for a child or parent, you are in for a hard time. This person you are attached to can not only get himself or herself in a great deal of trouble, but can make trouble for everyone he or she loves, as the father does in my new novel. He is so likable and means well, but his illusions are so removed from reality that they absolutely jeopardize the lives of those people he most means to protect. Though dangerous, dreamers are also essential. We'd still be in the caves without them; we'd also be able to kill fewer people. We have everything that we have—good and bad—because of them. In the broadest perspective of human history, dreamers are more important than you and I. They change lives, but they also accomplish some great harm.

Interview/U.S. News & World Report, 10-26:71.

Donald Johanson
Paleoanthropologist

3

I don't think we can predict what's going to happen [to the human species] in terms of evolution, My only feeling is that we've been here a very short period of time—though we tend to look at ourselves as invincible because we are cultural animals, because we are supposedly so highly evolved. But since 1945, the species has no longer been invincible. We have the capability to destroy the species itself through nuclear holocaust. And I think that the way the world is posturing itself, there is a strong possibility the species could face self-destruction within the next 100 years. We need to be much more sensitive about our place in nature, because we've *not* been around for very long. Any thoughts of being invincible have to be discarded. Speaking from a strictly evolutionary point of view, there is nothing looking over us, nobody guarding us.

Interview/
Los Angeles Herald Examiner, 4-28:(A)7.

John Paul II
Pope

4

[On human rights and justice]: Even in exceptional situations that may at times arise, one can never justify any violation of the fundamental dignity of the human person or of the basic rights that safeguard this dignity. Legitimate concern for the security of a nation, as demanded by the common good, could lead to the temptation of subjugating to the state the human being and his or her dignity and rights. Any apparent conflict between the exigencies of security and of the citizens' basic rights must be resolved according to the fundamental principle, upheld always by the church, that social organization exists only for the service of the man and for the protection of his dignity, and that it cannot claim to serve the common good when human rights are not safeguarded.

Manila, Philippines, Feb. 17/
Los Angeles Times, 2-18:(I)8.

5

Learn to call white white and black black, evil evil and good good. Learn to call sin sin

WHAT THEY SAID IN 1981

(JOHN PAUL II)

and do not call it liberation and progress, even if all of fashion and propaganada disagree.

Rome, March 26/
Los Angeles Times, 5-14:(I)21.

Erica Jong
Author

1

I still don't much like what marriage stands for in our patriarchal society. The marriage laws in our culture still derive from the notion of women as property. I really believe that the whole nature of the institution as we understand it is evolving in a line with some of things that my generation of women writers have been writing about. I see hope for marriage as it is being reconstructed, but not as it was 10 years ago. If marriage is seen as a woman taking a man's name, trading her sexual services in exchange for a man's keep and selling her reproductive rights for a house, then I think it's horrible. But if you see it as an equal partnership with shared responsibilities, then perhaps the institution can be saved.

Interview, Weston, Conn./Writer's Digest, June:25.

George F. Kennan
Co-chairman, American Committee on East-West Accord; Former United States Ambassador to the Soviet Union

2

The Russians demoralize their young people by giving them too little freedom. We demoralize ours by giving them too much. Neither system finds itself able to provide them with the leadership and inspiration and guidance needed to realize their potential as individuals and to meet the responsibilities the future is inevitably going to place upon them.

At Second World Congress on Soviet and East European Studies, Garmisch, West Germany/
Chicago Tribune, 2-15:(2)5.

Galway Kinnell
Poet

3

Ignorance is a form of devotion. To have little surges of ignorance is very good for us because they restore us in the way prayer does. We all feel that when we lie out on a hillside on a clear and moonless night and look at the stars. It's just natural for the imagination to try to grasp just what all that is up there, and to try to imagine ourselves past what is up there. And then, at a certain point, sooner for some than for others, you are absolutely smitten by a kind of ecstacy of ignorance, which means that you're giving your full devotion, for that moment, to what is.

Interview, Laguna Beach, Calif./
Los Angeles Times, 9-27:(Calendar)7.

Archibald MacLeish
Poet, Playwright

4

[On the recent assassination attempts on U.S. President Reagan and Pope John Paul II]: There was a time when an assassin was at least the Brutus of the play, shouting something about tyrants as the deed was done. Now he shouts nothing because he does not speak the tongue and never heard the word for tyrant and cares for nothing but himself. The victim is the hero now, the statesman with his laughing courage, the Pope with his warm human love. But the murderer is nothing—not a madman even—just a fool. And our generation, degraded by a clatter of unmeaning pain, makes panic of what should be tragedy.

Conway, Mass./
Los Angeles Herald Examiner, 5-15:(A)17.

Charles Malik
Former Lebanese Ambassador to the United States

5

They tell you there is steady progress in history; they tell you modern man is better and happier than any man in the past; they tell you we are more advanced, spiritually,

(CHARLES MALIK)

morally, intellectually, than all the ages of the past. This is all false. In the more important things in life, history does not disclose steady progress. There are a few shining peaks of the spirit, with many intervening sloughs and valleys. Plato, Aristotle, Augustine, Chrysostom, Aquinas, Shakespeare, Goethe, Dostóyevsky— we have nobody comparable to these men in our age. You can live ten lives on them, and the remarkable thing is that they are more relevant to the present than any man in the present. Progress! Fiddlesticks! Who has progressed from the *Psalms*, or from *Isaiah* or Jeremiah, or from the New Testament? . . . Ages are to be compared not by numbers but by the best in them. And the best souls in our age pale before the best souls in the past. The decay of respect for the past, the decay of respect for authority, the decay of the notion of the classics—these are the banes of the age.

At Wheaton College commencement/
Time, 6-15:55.

Billy Martin
Baseball manager,
Oakland "Athletics"

1

I don't flout authority. I *disagree* with it when I think it's wrong. Authority is something of a position. It doesn't mean it's right because they did it a hundred years ago. Maybe they were wrong a hundred years ago . . . I don't disagree with a guy who dislikes authority if he's smarter and has a better answer. If you don't have one, then you'd better listen. A guy should be successful before he voices an opinion. Unsuccessful people should not comment about what is going right or wrong. They've got to prove success before they can say, "Hey, this is right and this is wrong."

Interview/Parade, 4-19:18.

Francois Mitterrand
President of France

2

[As President,] I am not going to let my official duties invade my whole life. Man is like

a tree, which needs to have its roots in fertile topsoil. If only the head is there, without roots in the life-giving soil, then there will be nothing but a mind repeating the same things over and over again in a vacuum, without inventing anything new, divorced from the source of life. Inventiveness requires roots in the life-giving soil. It is by devoting time to solitary thought that I am able to keep my roots in the soil. Failing that, my action would become sterile, ineffective. I must therefore organize my day so as to have time for thought.

Interview,
Paris, June 1/
The New York Times,
6-4:6.

3

I was born during one world war, and when I was 20, I fought in a second world war. I was young at a time when Hitler, Mussolini, Franco, Stalin and a few others were on European soil. All that passes under our eyes proves that we do not live in a peaceful and harmonious world. Everything is a struggle; everything requires courage, effort. There is no response to history without effort, and effort is required because everything is difficult: passions, interests, rivalries, mankind just emerging from pre-history. Just look around us. Yes, history is tragic.

Interview, Paris/
Time, 10-19:58.

Alberto Moravia
Author

4

I think women are more interesting than men . . . women have always been outside society. Men control the society and have a position to protect. And this disables them, makes them afraid. But women are not timid. They don't have to protect themselves the way men do, so they are stronger, less timid.

At University of Southern California/
Los Angeles Times, 5-4:(V)2.

437

Sandra Day O'Connor
Associate Justice-designate, Supreme
Court of the United States

1

. . . I have performed some marriage ceremonies in my capacity as a judge. I would like to read to you an excerpt from a part of the form of marriage ceremony I prepared: "Marriage is far more than an exchange of vows. It is the foundation of the family, mankind's basic unit of society, the hope of the world and the strength of our country. It is the relationship between ourselves and the generations to follow." That statement represents not only advice to give to the couples who have stood before me, but my view of all families and the importance of families in our lives and in our country.

At Senate Judiciary Committee hearing on her
confirmation, Washington, Sept. 9/
The New York Times, 9-10:10.

Alan Paton
Author

2

. . . the word hope and the word optimism, they make me very angry. I had a letter from one person about a television interview I did in Britain. He said he was surprised I was so optimistic. I wrote back and said that's one word I dislike, the word optimistic, because it almost suggests you're being optimistic without grounds. I think hope is something different. I think one can hope without grounds.

Interview, Durban, South Africa/
San Francisco Examiner & Chronicle,
8-2:(Review)13.

Prince Philip
Duke of Edinburgh; Husband of
Queen Elizabeth II of England

3

There is [a] point about leadership: Leaders can only be effective if people want to be led. The present reaction against authority and what is called the Establishment suggests that many people simply do not want to be led.

Interview/
U.S. News & World Report, 2-9:47.

Roman Polanski
Motion-picture director

4

Talent is something you are born with, something that comes naturally, easily. When you take that talent and work and work, pushing it as far as it can go, that is genius.

Interview, Paris/
Los Angeles Herald Examiner, 4-5:(E)10.

Neil Postman
Professor of communication arts and
sciences, New York University

5

The invention of childhood was one of the most humane inventions of the Renaissance. What it did was to make it a cultural principle that we had to nurture and protect children. It promoted ideas throughout society that are important, such as curiosity and malleability and innocence and a sense of continuity and re-creation. These are the qualities that we've come to associate with childhood that are necessary prerequisites for developing into mature adulthood.

Interview/
U.S. News & World Report, 1-19:45.

Nancy Reagan
Wife of President of the
United States Ronald Reagan

6

I sometimes say that 75 per cent of marriage consists of patience and effort. Love is to give and take unstintingly . . . I feel sorry for those who talk about spontaneity and independence, but who ignore patience and effort.

Interview/
The Washington Post, 11-15:(A)17.

(NANCY REAGAN)

1

I think we've done a terrible thing to our young children, to everybody really, in the movies, on television . . . in the news that we give them. We've taken away all their heroes. There's this tendency to tear people down all the time. Why? Why? There's no point in all of that. I'm talking about the things you see on television or you read in the paper. It doesn't seem to me that there is any balance, and I know there are wonderful, courageous, compassionate things that are being done every day of the week that we'll never hear anything about. Kids see the bad side of people, the warts. I think we're doing a terrible thing to our kids.

Interview,
Washington/
Chicago Tribune, 12-21:(1)2.

Ronald Reagan
President of the
United States

2

The years ahead will be great ones for our country, for the cause of freedom and for the spread of civilization. The West will not contain Communism; it will transcend Communism. We will not bother to denounce it; we'll dismiss it as a sad, bizarre chapter in human history whose last pages are even now being written.

At University of
Notre Dame commencement,
May 17/
The Christian Science Monitor,
5-18:13.

Mickey Rooney
Entertainer

3

. . . someone once asked me what I want on my epitaph when I pass away. Just two words—I tried. And that's what this game

is all about, is *trying.* There's the tryers, the criers and the liars.

Interview, New York/
The New York Times,
8-23:(2)18.

Robert Runcie
Archbishop of Canterbury

4

[On marriage]: A marriage which really works is one which works for others. Marriage has both a private face and a public importance. If we solved all our economic problems and failed to build loving families, it would profit us nothing, because the family is the place where the future is created good and full of love—or deformed. Those who are married live happily ever after the wedding day if they persevere in the real adventure which is the royal task of creating each other and creating a more loving world. That is true of every man and every woman undertaking marriage.

At the wedding of Britain's
Prince Charles and Lady Diana Spencer,
London, July 29/
The Christian Science Monitor, 7-30:24.

Jonas Salk
Medical researcher;
Founding director,
Salk Institute for Biological Studies,
San Deigo

5

People are moving from competitive and independent postures toward greater cooperation and conciliation. I even see evidence of such changes in groups that are concerned with pollution, nuclear war, starvation and health. There seems to be almost an instinct on the part of humans to improve not only their individual conditions but those of others as well. We are beginning to realize more and more how we are parts of a whole, and that for fulfillment we need to satisfy ourselves not only as individuals but *also* as members of the human species.

Interview/
U.S. News & World Report, 12-7:72.

Maurice Sendak
Author of children's books

1

There is not an isolated world of the child, separate and apart from an isolated adult world. When I was a child I did not realize that. I used to think that there was an enormous gulf, a Death Valley, between being a child and being an adult like my father. I wondered how you traveled across that territory, and I think all children have that fear. Somewhere along the line in my work, I gained the insight that there is a subtle, complicated interrelationship between childhood and adulthood. To move from one to the other, you don't change the way a caterpillar does to become a butterfly. And you don't have to let go of one and quickly find the other before you can get over to the other side. In moving across, nothing is lost; in fact, you add to what you are. To be a healthy person, you have to be sympathetic to the child you once were and maintain the continuity between you as a child and you as an adult.

Interview/
U.S. News & World Report,
8-31:65.

Richard Sennett
Professor of the humanities,
New York University

2

Our political heritage has led us to believe that there is a relationship between the pursuit of happiness and power. That is a fatal mistake. You can make power more just and credible; you can make it feel legitimate—but you cannot make people enjoy being ruled. Power always hurts. We can't do without a power structure. It binds people together— and they must be bound together. At the same time, it is a restraint. Yet we keep looking for the magic keys that will make people enjoy it. What we should be doing is searching for ways to mitigate the injuries of power so that people will be willing to accept authority as legitimate.

Interview/U.S. News & World Report, 4-27:79.

Isaac Bashevis Singer
Author

3

There's no place a man can escape to now. Like art, life itself is a risk and a hazard in its very nature. It's always fragmentary, never complete. Its validity is in the adventure.

Interview, Washington, Nov. 3/
The Washington Post, 11-4:(B)15.

Margaret Thatcher
Prime Minister of the United Kingdom

4

The Communist countries deny people fundamental freedoms; because they deny them fundamental freedoms, they do not get the economic success which democracies get. If you look, the shortages of food tend to occur in the Communist countries . . . The democracies tend to produce food surpluses, the Communist countries food shortages. Communist countries produce wave after wave of refugees as people try to escape from them. The free-enterprise democracies do not produce refugees —they are the places where refugees go. So we know and fervently believe that our great mission in the world is to try to extend the area to which democracy applies. And we know the way in which Communism works: Once we have got Communism, it is the most difficult thing to shake off.

Broadcast interview, London/
The Christian Science Monitor, 2-2:19.

Warren Thomas
Director, Los Angeles Zoo

5

Animals are a reaffirmation of our own beginning. If we ever really lose touch with the natural, we die a little in ourselves. We lose sensitivity, we lose sense of wonderment. We are then saddled with a world of our own manufacture, which leaves something to be desired. Therefore, when you look at the wildlife of the world, you have to consider it as a legacy—a legacy that does not really belong to us. There's an old African proverb that goes something like this: Our responsibility to the wildlife in

(WARREN THOMAS)

the world now is simply loaned to us by our children. And that indeed is true. You don't own animals at all. We have a zoo-full of animals and, yes, I can show you paper-work to prove we legally own those animals. But animals have no real nationality and no real ownership. You just hold them in trust for another time.

Interview/
Los Angeles Herald Examiner,
5-19:(A)9.

John Updike
Author

1

The lawn! Did you ever look at the lawn in a certain light? And you realize it's this teeming mass of little lives that don't matter and they're going to die shortly, and in every cubic inch there's 100,000 microbes and *they're* dying. I've got really depressed out on the golf course as I looked at yards and yards of grass. Nature is an appalling spectacle! Crushing! So in the midst of this crushing, what shelters are there but bed and church? And maybe a book now and then.

Interview, Georgetown, Mass./
The Washington Post, 9-27:(F)3.

Peter Ustinov
Actor, Director, Writer

2

. . . all of us with disciplines—whether we're scientists or artists or dentists—have a second nationality, which is our profession. When you have a meeting between Western and Eastern dentists, they can forget all about nationalities because they're frightfully interested in the new technique about molars! And it's vitally important to the world that this exists.

Interview, New York/
The Christian Science Monitor,
2-19:19.

Gore Vidal
Author

3

It's as though the human race were programmed for certain cultural developments to happen at a certain point, like an individual human baby: At a certain age, it waddles, then it stands up, begins to talk, reaches puberty and starts to reproduce. I had always thought of the human race as being sort of open-ended, since we evolved out of our friends, the monkeys. Now I am starting to think of it as being more like a sort of very large virus, with a pre-established life-span and strict limitations that are coded right into its basic structure. A virus can live just so long in a host, and then it dies. Is the end of the human race predetermined in just the same way? It has given me a horrible, almost a Calvinistic sense of predestination—everything already determined. The period I studied was 2,400 years ago, and look what we have done since then. There are four billion of us now, with nuclear power and potentials that can hardly be guessed. I can't help wondering whether this includes the potential to destroy ourselves—the certainty of destroying ourselves built into mankind from its origins.

Interview, Washington/
The Washington Post, 5-4:(B)13.

Friedrich A. von Hayek
Economist

4

Inequality . . . is necessary . . . to prompt individuals to do what permits the creation of national product . . . Only those peoples who can feed themselves [should] survive and increase . . . If we guarantee that everyone who is born will be kept alive, we will soon no longer be in a position to fulfill this promise.

World Press Review, June:46.

Robert Penn Warren
Poet

5

[On whether he had come to terms with death]: How do you know? How do you an-

WHAT THEY SAID IN 1981

(ROBERT PENN WARREN)

swer a question like that? Only a fool doesn't think about it. But it's not making terms with death; it's what terms you make with life in relation *to* death. You don't wait for death; you live for death—if you can keep working. That's the horror: being immobilized. Only heroes can survive that. I wouldn't want to have to survive that.

Interview, Fairfield, Conn./
The New York Times, 6-2:10.

Paul Weiss
Professor of philosophy,
Catholic University

1

What takes place in universities now is a variation on what happened centuries ago when scholars had patrons. The patron was not necessarily a man who knew anything; he was a man who had money. If he didn't like your play, painting, music or sculpture, you were out of luck. In light of that, it is extraordinary how many talented people managed to get by without support. Some of the great painters that we recognize now couldn't even get a show around the beginning of this century. They were rejected by the Establishment. There are always a number of people who are doing important things but who are not immediately recognized because they're violating the established categories. In philosophy, it takes about 40 years for an idea to become fairly well-known, but eventually it becomes known and gradually grows more and more conspicuous. Its promulgators become dominant at the same time that the others who were once prominent are ignored.

U.S. News & World Report, 2-2:49.

Elie Wiesel
Author

2

For a long time I didn't want to get married and have a child, for fear of what lay in store for the next generation. So I didn't get married

till I was 40, and my son was born when I was 46. I still fear for him, for us all. Imagine a day when [Libyan leader Muammar] Qaddafi or other madmen have nuclear weapons. And it will happen, which is why I tremble for the whole human race. So you see, I must keep up my running argument with God, but in doing so I must also never let myself forget one thing: It is man to whom He gave the means to achieve ultimate salvation and God's own redemption—the key to the orchard of knowledge.

Interview, Beverly Hills, Calif./
Los Angeles Herald Examiner, 4-7:(C)6.

Tom Wolfe
Author, Journalist

3

I always had the feeling . . . that my parents knew exactly how life should be conducted. They had confidence in the choices they were making and they made us feel that we should have confidence, too. To this day I can't stand to see parents wrestling over the macaroni of their lives in front of a child. My parents must have had tough decisions to make, but I was never called on to bear witness to their anxiety. In Richmond [Va., where he grew up], there just isn't this dwelling on weakness the way there is in New York. Maybe people felt it, but it wasn't considered a proper subject for discussion. To some people that might sound like repression, but I think repression can be a positive value. Negative emotions feed on each other and it's probably better to let some of them remain nameless.

Interview, New York/
The New York Times Magazine, 12-20:48.

Walter B. Wriston
Chairman, Citicorp

4

Values [today] are topsy-turvy. It boggles the mind—the transfer of personal integrity to institutional integrity. Now college students

442

(WALTER B. WRISTON)

have a mixed dormitory—men live on one floor and women on the next—and they sit around worrying about whether or not General Motors

is being honest. When I was in college it was different. We were concerned about personal values. I believe that there are no institutional values, only personal ones.

Interview/The Washington Post, 1-18:(G)9.

Religion

Roger Baldwin
Founder,
American Civil Liberties Union

1

I think the pressures in the United States that come from the so-called Moral Majority and the evangelists will have some impression —they have a lot of money and a lot of votes— but I don't think they'll get far. We've had them with us a long time. I hope there will be some resentment from the established churches in America, who represent a different kind of people—the kind of people you go to church with. The others are the kind you only listen to on the radio.

Interview, Oakland, N.J./
Los Angeles Times, 2-23:(V)5.

Ernest Evans
Post-doctoral fellow, Center for
International Affairs, Harvard University,
Authority on terrorism

2

This world we are living in is so dangerous, there is so much potential for destruction, that I think all religious groups—Christians, Jews, Moslems, Hindus, whatever—have a solemn duty to stress tolerance and love of neighbor . . . the world is just too dangerous a place for the preaching of religious hatred. Five hundred years ago religious wars were terrible. But the survival of civilization was not at stake. Now it is. That's the bottom line.

Interview, Cambridge, Mass./
The Christian Science Monitor, 4-1:(B)28.

Jerry Falwell
Evangelist;
Chairman, Moral Majority

3

[On whether President Reagan will support positions taken by his organization on the state of morality in America today]: What has been done by secular humanists over the past 40 years is not going to be undone in 30 days. But the ball is rolling in the direction of Bible-believing Christianity for the first time in my lifetime. I'm willing to give the President a chance.

At New Religious Rights movement meeting,
Washington/Chicago Tribune, 2-1:(1)12.

4

People today want their preacher to be a man of God, prepared and authoritative, standing in his pulpit declaring, "Thus sayeth the Lord." People are tired of preachers just getting up there, scratching their heads, and saying, "Well, it seems to me . . ."

Chicago Tribune Magazine, 8-16:12.

Jozef Cardinal Glemp
Roman Catholic Primate of Poland

5

The church is there to serve the society in every way compatible with its pastoral role. It must shed light on the questions and stop those who would lead us into darkness. It must always strive for truth and justice.

To reporters, Rome, July 29/
Chicago Tribune, 7-30:(1)2.

Barry M. Goldwater
United States Senator,
R—Arizona

1

[On New Right religious groups that try to pressure public officials]: The uncompromising position of these groups is a divisive element that could tear apart the very spirit of our representative system. I am warning them today: I will fight them every step of the way if they try to dictate their moral convictions to all Americans in the name of conservatism. I'm frankly sick and tired of the political preachers across the country telling me as a citizen that if I want to be a moral person I must believe in A, B, C and D. Just who do they think they are? . . . I am even more angry as a legislator who must endure the threats of every religious group who thinks it has some God-granted right to control my vote on every roll-call in the Senate . . . By maintaining the separation of church and state, the United States has avoided the intolerance which has so divided the rest of the world with religious wars.

Before the Senate, Washington, Sept. 15/
Time, 9-28:27;The Washington Post, 9-16:(A)6.

Billy Graham
Evangelist

2

We as clergy know so very little to speak out with such authority on the Panama Canal or superiority of armaments. Evangelists can't be closely identified with any particular [political] party or person. We have to stand in the middle in order to preach to all people, right and left. I haven't been faithful to my own advice in the past; I will be in the future . . . I want to preserve the purity of the Gospel and the freedom of religion in America. I don't want to see religious bigotry in any form. Liberals organized in the '60s, and conservatives certainly have a right to organize in the '80s. But it would disturb me if there was a wedding between the religious fundamentalists and the political right. The hard right

has no interest in religion except to manipulate it.

Interview/Parade, 2-1:6.

3

There has been an unhealthy tendency toward individualism [among evangelists]—a tendency on the part of some individualists to go their own way. Also, I think we have failed to communicate to the "world church" some of the positive things evangelicals are doing, such as in the area of social work. I have also been concerned because too often we have tended toward superficiality—an overemphasis on easy-believism or experience rather than on true discipleship. We have sometimes offered cheap grace and cheap conversions without genuine repentance. In addition, evangelicals have not tried to capture the intellectual initiative as much as we should. We haven't challenged and developed the minds of our generation. Though there are many exceptions, generally we evangelicals have failed to present to the world great thinkers, theologians, artists, scientists and so forth.

Interview/Christianity Today, 7-17:19.

Richard C. Halverson
Chaplain of the United States Senate

4

I was thankful for the way evangelists got involved in the last [U.S.] election. But I recoil at the way evangelists have become enculturated with secular values—as if the motivation was to put people in public office who would help maintain and increase our standard of living. That is blasphemous.

Interview, Washington/
Chicago Tribune, 2-8:(2)6.

Jesse A. Helms
United States Senator,
R—North Carolina

5

The Moral Majority is criticized by others, but you get out there in the grass-roots and

(JESSE A. HELMS)

see who is supporting a spiritual revival, and you see the heart of America. And I think it is good. Basically, we're talking about faith in God versus secular humanism.

The Washington Post, 2-15:(A)21.

Carl F. H. Henry
President, American Theological Society; Lecturer-at-large, WorldVision International

1

Having lost its biblical moorings, our age stifles its conscience and displays an utterly shameless sensuality. One cannot but note the rampant perversion of sex, the breakdown of family life and the cruelty and inhumanity evident in the ready massacre of fetal life. One must mention also the failure of the great universities to sustain fixed moral values, the inability of humanism to mount ethical resources requiring self-sacrifice, and the widening effort by frontier scientists to gloss over the ethical and moral implications of their experiments by an appeal to mere utilitarianism. Then, too, prime-time television highlights cultural trivialities and poses little challenge to ethical waywardness. Yet I detect a new longing by disenchanted youth—after a spate of sinful living—for personal worth and for lasting love. Some are turning to the life-changing dynamic that revealed religion offers even the most profligate.

Interview/Christianity Today, 3-13:21.

Theodore M. Hesburgh
President, University of Notre Dame

2

[On Pope John Paul II]: If you look at the intellectual legacy of the man—judging him by what he has written—it's clear he approaches things on a philosophical, rather than theological, level. He has said that the strongest thing in a society is the solidarity that pulls people together in a common endeavor. Now, he's going to face opposition in the church and he's going to find people who just want the status quo. And he's going to have to live with people who do want change. I think change is important. One of our great cardinals once said, "To grow is to change, and to grow greatly is to change greatly." Well, John Paul II is going to grow greatly, I believe. He's going to get involved. He cannot, by his nature, be morally neutral.

Interview, University of Notre Dame/ Chicago Tribune, 1-28:(1)4.

3

[On the attempted-assassination shooting of Pope John Paul II]: This insane act should at long last, I believe, turn the world at large against terrorism and make terrorists outlawed on the whole face of the earth. It seems to me there is no semblance of justification for terrorists now that they have aimed at one of the greatest apostles of justice and peace in this world.

Los Angeles Herald Examiner, 5-15:(A)17.

John Paul II
Pope

4

It is especially gratifying to witness how the bonds that unite all those who believe in God have been strengthened in recent years. I am thinking in a particular way of the bonds of dialog and trust that have been forged between the Catholic Church and Islam. By means of dialog, we have come to see more clearly the many values, practices and teachings that both our religious traditions embrace; for example, our beliefs in the one almighty and merciful God, creator of heaven and earth, and the importance that we give to prayer, almsgiving and fasting. I pray that mutual understanding and respect between Christians and Moslems, and indeed between all religions, will continue and grow deeper, and that we

(JOHN PAUL II)

will find still better ways of cooperation and collaboration for the good of all.

Karachi, Pakistan, Feb. 16/
Chicago Tribune, 2-17:(1)1.

1

[Priests and other church people] are not social or political leaders or officials of a temporal power. [But] the church must indeed be attentive to the needs of the men and women of our time. She cannot be indifferent to the problems which they face or to the injustices which they suffer.

Before church people, Manila, Philippines,
Feb. 17/Los Angeles Times, 2-17:(I)1.

2

With legitimate pride, one can state: Whatever the church teaches today on marriage and the family has been her constant teaching in fidelity to Christ. What God has joined together let no man put asunder. [The church] will never dilute or change her teaching on marriage and the family. For these reasons, the church condemns any attempt through the practice of polygamy to destroy the marriage bond. For these reasons, also, the church states clearly that marriage should be open to the transmission of human life. On my part, I owe it to my apostolic office to reaffirm as clearly and as strongly as possible what the church of Christ teaches in this respect and to reiterate vigorously her condemnation of artificial contraception and abortion.

Address to welcoming crowd,
Cebu, Philippines, Feb. 19/
Chicago Tribune, 2-20:(1)5.

Edward M. Kennedy
United States Senator,
D—Massachusetts

3

[On the attempted assassination shooting of Pope John Paul II]: This is a shot that has gone to the soul of the world. The greatest symbol of peace in the world has been struck down by this latest act of mindless violence. Those of us who had the privilege of meeting the Holy Father know him as a warm and caring person. His aura has moved the earth.

Before the Senate, Washington, May 13/
Los Angeles Times, 5-14:(I)3.

Hans Kung
Swiss theologian; Visiting professor,
University of Chicago Divinity School

4

I deeply regret the increasing polarization under the new Pope [John Paul II] and the frightening growth of intolerance. Even more, I regret the silent mass exodus of believers, especially women, out of our parishes. Many bishops don't seem to be aware that they are painting themselves more and more into a corner with their unconditional conformism to Roman doctrine and politics. They are subscribing to a distinct minority view. Of course, the majority isn't always right. However, in Christ's church the majority is right when Jesus Christ, as we know him in the gospels, stands on the majority's side.

Interview/
Chicago Tribune Magazine, 11-29:70.

Martin E. Marty
Professor of history of modern
Christianity, University of Chicago
Divinity School

5

There are an awful lot of good sermons being preached today. But they are no longer the cultural events they used to be. They no longer generate news, not because the sermons are worse but because the context has changed. A generation or two ago, the celebrity pulpit conferred status on the preacher. Today, television confers that status.

Chicago Tribune Magazine, 8-16:12.

WHAT THEY SAID IN 1981

Eugene Pickett
President,
Unitarian Universalist Association

1

[On the future of the Unitarian movement]: We're seeing a turnaround. We have a new sense of hope and optimism. We have more students studying for our ministry than at any time in our history. And one of the reasons is the Moral Majority. We're an alternative [to the Moral Majority], and we want to change the image of the church as a rigid institution . . . I want us to capture something of the spirit of the evangelicals. Most of religion needs revitalization—especially liberal religion . . . We have to remember that our special job as Unitarian Universalists is now what it always has been—to serve as an ethical and prophetic remnant, a "moral minority" which takes as its obligation the preservation of memory and the pronouncement of justice. We must show the way of conviction without arrogance, insight without coercion, and democracy without demagoguery.

Interview, Chicago/
Chicago Tribune, 10-24:(1)6.

John Roach
Roman Catholic Archbishop of
Minneapolis; President, National Conference
of Catholic Bishops

2

The right of religious organizations of varying views to speak [on public issues] must be defended by all who understand the meaning of religious liberty and the social role of religion. But religious organizations should be subjected to the same standards of rational, rigorous presentation of their views as any other participant in the public debate. These same standards of discourse are the ones by which our position should be judged. Neither the rigor of reasonable argument nor the controversy which surrounds the role of religion and politics should make us timid about stating and defending public positions and key issues.

At National Conference of Catholic Bishops meeting, Washington, Nov. 17/The New York Times, 11-18:12.

Robert Runcie
Archbishop of Canterbury

3

[Saying he favors closer relations between Catholics and Anglican communions]: The greatest obstacle is undoubtedly the question of authority. In the Roman Catholic Church it is highly centralized in the papacy. In the Anglican communion it has been widely dispersed. The result is that Anglicans are inclined to think the Roman tradition is too stiff and Latin. The Roman Catholics think our tradition is too vague and Anglo-Saxon. That's what we have to solve . . . In this country [Britain] we have a new hope of achieving unity with the free churches. As for the Orthodox, that's my dearest love because I've traveled a lot in the cause of unity with the Orthodox churches. Organic unity is a long way off, but I rejoice to think we have made some progress.

Interview, London/
Los Angeles Times, 4-18:(I-A)8.

4

[Criticizing "casual" Christian worship]: At present, there is a danger of reducing God to something of a pal and ignoring the harder demands of his word. Some Christian worship is so casual that this aspect of the God and Father of Jesus Christ would seem to have been obscured with shallow *bonhomie* . . . The neighborhood God, jogging with us through life's way, is not the whole truth about the Father of our Lord Jesus Christ. He is a fashionable puppet who fails our imagination as we look into the vastness of space and ponder the mystery of creation.

Sermon, Stevensville, Md., April 25/
The New York Times, 4-26:(1)16.

Alexander M. Schindler
President, Union of
American Hebrew Congregations

5

[Supporting a program to win converts to Judaism from those who have no religious adherence]: The stakes are exceedingly high. There

448

(ALEXANDER M. SCHINDLER)

are 35,000 Jewish intermarriages a year—that makes 70,000 adults and, given our miniscule birthrate, an additional 35,000 children minimally. The total is 100,000 souls up or down each year . . . out of our present [Jewish] population of just under 6 million. Our survival is at stake . . . What we propose here is that we stop bemoaning our fate, once and for all shake off the defensive stance born of a ghetto mentality, and make Judaism a proud, yes, an assertive faith.

At Union of American Hebrew Congregations
meeting, Boston, December/
The Christian Science Monitor, 12-15:8.

Bruce W. Thielemann
Dean of the chapel,
Grove City (Pa.) College

1

There is no special honor in being called to the preaching ministry. There is only special pain. The pulpit calls those anointed to it as the sea calls its sailors, and, like the sea, it batters and bruises, and does not rest. To preach, to really preach, is to die naked a little at a time, and to know each time you do it that you must do it again.

Chicago Tribune Magazine, 8-16:26.

Gore Vidal
Author

2

. . . I like the Jesuits. There's a group I visit every once in a while, and they look into my black heart and I look into their black hearts, and we all get along very well. I mentioned to one of these Jesuits that I favored taxation of religious groups, and later on, after he had expressed his open disapproval of the idea, he pulled me aside and whispered, "Actually, it is a price we would be willing to pay."

Interview, Chicago/
Chicago Tribune, 4-14:(1)14.

Richard E. Webber
Theologian,
Wheaton (Ill.) College

3

In the neo-evangelical circles, we can ask questions, we can doubt, we are more willing to be ambiguous and recognize the complexities of life. But fundamentalists are one-dimensional Christians. There is no freedom to think differently from the common mind. If you don't use the proper shibboleths and condemn the right people, they have grave questions about you. And for them, conversion is not only to Christ but to the cultural indentification in which Christ is presented. People are attached to it with such incredible zeal, it's hard to carry on a civil discussion with them.

Chicago Tribune,
8-23:(2)2.

Elie Wiesel
American Author

4

In Russia, the mystery is that, so long after the revolution, so many of its 10 million Jews insist on being Jews. Religious education is still prohibited there, but when I first visited Russia in 1965, I found a deep thirst for Judaism. There is no explanation except the power of the collective memory of the Jewish people.

Interview, Beverly Hills, Calif./
Los Angeles Herald Examiner, 4-7:(C)6.

Donald E. Wildmon
United Methodist minister;
Chairman, Coalition for
Better Television

5

More than 50 million Americans go to church regularly—but rarely on television [programs]. People make decisions based on Christian principles—but rarely on television. People pray—but rarely on television. Every community in America has local churches and synagogues which contribute to the good of their local

449

WHAT THEY SAID IN 1981

(DONALD E. WILDMON)

communities and this country; but they don't exist on television. The Christian faith has healed the alcoholic, rehabilitated the criminal, rejoined the broken home, helped the teen-age drug addict find purpose and meaning in life, and undergirded the ethics of business people. But you would never know this by watching network television . . . No one denies that all Christians have their faults and failures. Yet all too often, when persons are identified as Christians in [TV] programs, they are characters only to scorn, prompt revulsion, and to ridicule. I cannot remember seeing a program on network television, set in a modern setting, which depicted a Christian as a warm, compassionate, intelligent or gifted human being.

Chicago Tribune, 10-10:(1)8.

Science and Technology

Elie Abel
Professor of communication,
Stanford University

1

[On the new communications technologies, such as cable TV, satellites and computers]: . . . sooner rather than later many Americans will be priced out of the market, debarred from the benefits promised by the new technologies because they cannot afford to pay for them. We may, in short, confront the prospect of media segregated by economic and social class: over-the-air broadcasting for the masses and the newer technologies for the classes. The affluent should be better informed than they are today; the lower orders could be even less well informed.

At "Communications in the 21st Century"
symposium, Richmond, Va./
Los Angeles Times, 4-9:(VI)1.

William Agee
Chairman, Bendix Corporation

2

America is losing its edge in business-related technology . . . Innovation in this country has slowed to a crawl . . . the trend signals a serious problem ahead. The ones to suffer the consequences of our loss of technological leadership today are the general public. More significantly, the ones who will suffer the consequences five and 10 years from now are the young people in this country. They will be hit with the loss of jobs. They will feel inflation and the declining GNP. Perhaps most important, they will experience a loss of national pride, spirit and idealism.

Before Town Hall, Los Angeles/
Los Angeles Herald Examiner, 5-20:(C)7.

Leonid I. Brezhnev
President of the Soviet Union;
General Secretary, Soviet Communist Party

3

I should like to stress that the Soviet Union has been and remains a convinced supporter of the development of businesslike international cooperation in outer space. May the shoreless cosmic ocean be pure and free of weapons of any kind. We stand for joint efforts to reach a great and humanitarian aim—to preclude the militarization of outer space.

At ceremony honoring Soviet cosmonauts,
Moscow, April 17/
Los Angeles Herald Examiner, 4-18:(A)4.

Joel Chaseman
President,
Post-Newsweek Stations (broadcasting)

4

[Criticizing the deregulation philosophy exhibited lately by the FCC in the face of rapidly expanding new technologies]: What are the distinctions among the broadcaster, the telephone company, the cable operator, the newspaper or magazine, the IBM or the Xerox, if each is purveying data to all, or only to some, and if several share the same wire, cable or optical fiber? What public policy should govern? What are the First Amendment protections of each? Which is to be regulated and which not? Which should be licensed Federally and which locally? Which subject to rate regulation and which not? How will the borders of journalism be defined? . . . What of copyrights and program piracy? Who owns data? Who is to say in the coming era which of our records should be released for scrutiny? How tight a castle will your home become when the computers

451

(JOEL CHASEMAN)

of cable company and charge-card outfits speak to AT&T's computer, and together discuss what you've watched, where you've gone, what you've read, the source and size of your income and what calls you have made? The computers will know and they will tell, unless Congress decides that they should not. This is not simply a marketplace to be deregulated and left free to govern itself. This is an open invitation to a corporate police state, free only to those who will monitor our homes and our businesses through the new information and communications system on which we will become increasingly dependent.

Before Town Hall of California, Los Angeles,
Jan. 27/Los Angeles Times, 1-29:(VI)1.

Mary E. Clark
Professor of biology, San Diego
State University

1

In America and other advanced cultures, belief in technology has become a religious faith. We have come to think of ourselves as so technologically clever that we will always be flexible enough to get through any crisis. But in many ways we have become so dependent on technology that we have lost our adaptability. All it takes is a New York blackout or a Three Mile Island [nuclear-plant accident], an oil spill or an invasion of Medflies to show how fragile our relationship with technology really is. We have become its servants rather than its masters.

Interview/
U.S. News & World Report, 8-17:48.

2

Science, and the technology it spawns, provide two kinds of power. First there is power or "mastery" over nature. We have overcome the separation of distance by building cars and airplanes—and the roads and runways needed to operate them. The second use we make of science is the power it gives us over others. Per-

haps the clearest case in point—and one that clearly threatens our survival—is weapons technology . . . we are paying far too much attention to the power that science gives us, and far too little to the wisdom it has to teach us . . . About 100 years ago, the senior Oliver Wendell Holmes said: "Knowledge and timber shouldn't be much used till they are seasoned." We need time to discover and assimilate the wisdom science can teach us before trying to apply the power it gives us. We need to discover a safer, less precarious path into the future. Science does have a valuable role to play, if we could but let it.

Smithsonian Lecture, Washington/
The Christian Science Monitor, 10-26:(B)5.

John Eccles
Medical educator; Physiologist

3

I am an evolutionist, of course; but I don't believe that evolution is the final story. I believe it hasn't solved some very fundamental problems. The genetic code and natural selection explain quite a lot. [But] evolution doesn't explain how I came to exist. It doesn't explain even the origin of consciousness, even animal consciousness. If you look at the most modern texts on evolution, you find nothing about mind and consciousness. They assume that it just comes automatically with the development of the brain. But that's not an answer. If my uniqueness of self is tied to the genetic uniqueness that built my brain, the odds against myself existing are 10 to the 10-thousandth against. It is just too improbable to wait around to get the right constructed brain for you. The brain is a computer, you see. Each of us has a computer and we are the programmers of this computer. You are born, as it were, with this wonderful structure evolution and genetic coding has wrought . . . But the soul is the unique creation that is ours for life. It is *us. We* are experiencing, remembering, creating, suffering, imagining. All of this is processed here with the soul central to it.

Interview, Washington/
The Washington Post, 3-15:(F)1.

R. Buckminster Fuller
Engineer, Author, Designer

1

Humanity has developed a great many badly-conditioned reflexes. One is the idea that technology is something new. [We've come to] think of technology only where *we* began to be the inventors—as machinery of war, or to exploit humanity. I find this anti-technology ignorance very greatly troubling. I say our whole escape [for the future] is through technology.

Interview, Pacific Palisades, Calif./
Los Angeles Herald Examiner, 3-29:4.

John Glenn
United States Senator, D-Ohio;
Former astronaut

2

. . . there was a significance to our landing on the moon [in 1969] that goes far beyond the satisfaction that comes from a dramatic and spectacular victory in international competition. The success of the *Apollo* program gave mankind initial access to the literally infinite resources of the universe. Few Americans fully realize the extent to which the uses of space have already affected our daily lives since we achieved that initial success. Despite the life-enhancing spin-offs from this research, despite the fact that space research and development, even in its infancy, has provided the cutting edge of our technological superiority for almost 20 years, we are not pressing our advantage in space. We are all but abandoning portions of our civilian space program.

At Goddard Memorial Dinner/
The Washington Post, 4-10:(A)19.

3

I look at space as being our entry into a huge laboratory, being able to travel in realms we've never traveled before, new solar patterns, waves. How does the sun form its energy? What can we manufacture in the weightlessness of space that will give us new advantages in computer or job-creation here on earth, new informa-

tion? It's like—you know, throughout all of history we have advanced because we were a curious people. A book, *The American Challenge*, written some years ago by a French author, put it into words I think are more true today than they were then. He said that we went ahead of the rest of the world in a tiny timeframe in history, not because we had waving fields of grain and purple mountains majesty, but because from our inception as a nation we put more into research, inquiry into the unknown; and then when those facts became a pattern and free-enterprise capitalism could pounce on those facts, that's what created jobs, that's what created industry and the new in this country. I see our space program and that kind of research fitting in that mold.

TV-radio interview/"Meet the Press,"
National Broadcasting Company, 4-12.

Dean Kenyon
Professor of biology, San Francisco
State University

4

The more information we get in the field of molecular biology with respect to DNA, the cells, genetic material and the synthesis of protein, the more we can see that this system does evidence a special creation rather than a development by natural means. The genetic code, for example, bears no evidence that it could have originated through natural chemical tendencies. It seems to bear the hallmark of an order that was impressed upon it from the outside—the same way the order of the parts of an airplane are impressed upon it from the outside. There's nothing about the physical chemistry of the airplane that would make you think it could have formed itself.

Interview/
Los Angeles Herald Examiner, 5-8:(A)20.

George Keyworth
Adviser to the President of the United States
for Scientific Affairs

5

Our country has relinquished its pre-eminence in some scientific fields, while others are strongly threatened through efforts in Eur-

WHAT THEY SAID IN 1981

(GEORGE KEYWORTH)

ope, Japan or the Soviet Union. It is no longer within our economic capability, nor perhaps even desirable, to aspire to primacy across the spectrum of scientific disciplines. The constraints of reality require discrimination and vision . . . We must strive to identify those disciplinary areas where vitality is required to support industrial, military [technologies] . . . as well as those with particular scientific promise . . . measured in terms of probability of major breakthroughs.

Before American Association for the Advancement of Science, Washington, June 25/ The Washington Post, 6-26:(A)14.

Morris Kline
Professor emeritus of mathematics, New York University

1

Mathematics is a man-made, artificial subject. It is not *the truth.* Nevertheless, it can make rather remarkably accurate predictions about physical phenomena. In our own age, the theory of relativity is one such example; the atomic bomb is another. Mathematics is the prime instrument—the only instrument— for creating theories and deducing facts about physical phenomena. It enables us to formulate the law of gravitation and laws of motion and to deduce their implications. Using mathematics, we can deduce where the planets are; but mathematics cannot tell us why they are in those orbits and what keeps them there. We say, "Well, the sun's gravitational force maintains them in their paths." But *how* does the sun exert a force on the planets? We don't know. Newton himself could not explain what the force of gravity is. He tried to give a physical explanation and then gave up. In the end, we just don't know why mathematics works as well as it does. We're faced with a mystery.

Interview/ U.S. News & World Report, 1-26:63.

Arthur Kornberg
Professor of biochemistry, Stanford University

2

When we began genetic research, the press generated a lot of fear among the public. People worried about little microbial monsters that would come out and destroy everything. This led to restrictions on research, which still exist in some places. But the financial attractiveness and practical success of the research have dissipated much of the concern— and I want to be sure that restraints on responsible research do not occur again. Certainly, there is always the possibility that the research can be abused and distorted. Any knowledge can be misapplied. Whether scientists engage in improper activity will ultimately depend on the ethics and morality of the community. But if you operate in a climate of fear in which you see only the unfortunate and evil developments, then you simply can't make any progress.

Interview/ U.S. News & World Report, 3-16:74.

Aleksei A. Leonov
Soviet cosmonaut

3

[On the flight of the first U.S. space shuttle]: I personally know both the American astronauts involved in the flight, and definitely wanted to see their spacecraft make a safe landing, and this because I knew that the experiment they had to take was extremely dangerous. This success was a major technological achievment, since it opens up entirely new dimensions in spacecraft flights, especially as to their means of landing. But the more serious question concerns the use these achievements will be put to. For I was overcome by numbness when I heard the American announcement that the [shuttle] *Columbia*'s research mission was not only scientific, but also military.

News conference, Salonica, Greece, April 16/ The New York Times, 4-17:12.

David F. Linowes
*Professor of political economy and
public policy, University of Illinois*

1

The law and social mores have not been keeping up [with technological advancement]. Present-day technology seems to permit man to control everything but technology. What is needed at this time is for the dynamic forces driving innovations to be linked with the values of freedom. The scientific wizardry that jeopardizes a people's freedom and a nation's sovereignty should now be directed to assisting in protecting it. It was President [John] Kennedy who lamented, "Every time scientists make a major invention, we politicians have to invent an institution to cope with it—and almost invariably it must be an international institution." The world awaits the creation of such an institution.

*Before Woman's National Democratic Club,
Washington/Chicago Tribune, 9-9:(1)11.*

Walter R. Lynn
*Professor of civil and environmental
engineering, and director, Program On
Science, Technology and Society,
Cornell University*

2

[On technological risks in society]: People don't mind being accountable for the safety of decisions that they make themselves, but they may want absolute safety in situations where they feel that someone else is imposing a risk on them that they don't want to bear. Such decisions are—finally—political; and if the body politic says, "We're not prepared to bear the burden of that uncertainty," then in a democratic society they have the right to reject it. How safe is safe enough is a value judgment. Scientists are not any more equipped to make value judgments about how safe things ought to be than you and I. It is dangerous to assume that those with technical or scientific expertise are especially qualified to make such judgments. Decisions are made by scientists and technologists—sometimes pre-emptively and sometimes by default—because nobody else is

prepared to do it. On balance, I must say that we've done pretty well.

*Interview/
U.S. News & World Report, 3-30:60.*

Edwin McMillan
*Professor emeritus of physics,
University of California, Berkeley*

3

I'm concerned about the public disaffection toward science. People recognize science as doing great things for their lives. But when it comes to appreciating science and having sympathy for it, they mostly don't. They associate it with the mad scientists making monsters in dimly lit laboratories rather than understanding what the activity of a scientist is really like.

*Interview/
U.S. News & World Report, 4-6:46.*

Marvin Minsky
*Professor of science, Massachusetts Institute
of Technology; President, American
Association for Artificial Intelligence*

4

Some day, either decades or centuries from now, people will have to decide about building extremely intelligent machines. Some will see this as a threat to our species' survival, while others will see them as a natural stage of our own development—not as *them* versus *us* but as a natural step of our own evolution. Does it really matter if our descendants are made of flesh or of silicone or even of something completely different? Perhaps we should only care that they propagate our deepest wishes and aspirations. The modestly intelligent machines of the near future promise only to bring us the wealth and comfort of tireless, obedient and inexpensive servants. But when that other time comes, some people will oppose creating super-intelligence at all, as in Frank Herbert's novel *Dune*, regarding it as a crime to "build a machine in the image of a mind." Others will be more adventurous and argue that man has been what he is for only a few million years.

WHAT THEY SAID IN 1981

(MARVIN MINSKY)

The universe will last about another thousand times that long. What sense would it make for us to stand all that time in just one place in just one form?

Interview/
U.S. News & World Report, 11-2:65.

Walter F. Mondale
Former Vice President
of the United States

1

. . . two basic problems are holding our [the U.S.'] technological potential in harness. We are not funding enough basic research, and second, we are not producing the army of teachers and researchers and scientists we need. Total spending for research and development, as a percentage of gross national product, has declined in the last 15 years. American corporations will spend twice as much on acquisitions this year as on research. And government support is down . . . Although the Japanese population is one-half the size of ours, they are graduating 50 per cent more electronics engineers than we do. Although the need for people with doctorates in computer science is growing, we are graduating fewer of them than we did five years ago. All this adds up to a very worrisome fact. We are neglecting science. By inadequately supporting research, both business and government are deploying resources in a short-sighted way.

November/The Washington Post, 11-13:(A)22.

David Morrison
Chairman, division of planetary sciences,
American Astronomical Society

2

[Criticizing Reagan Administration plans to cut back funding of NASA's unmanned planetary program]: Given its tremendous boost to national pride and prestige, many people don't realize that the entire planetary program uses only 3 per cent of NASA's budget, and all NASA is less than 1 per cent of the Federal budget. Yet this highly successful effort is to undergo more than a belt-tightening. It may be killed outright.

Denver, Oct. 13/
The Christian Science Monitor, 10-15:8.

Bruce C. Murray
Director, Jet Propulsion Laboratory,
Pasadena, Calif.

3

Space is one of the ways to be great in the 20th century. We [the U.S. space program] have been admired throughout the world for our leadership. We have done positive things that have no harmful environmental side effects and enlarge our knowledge. We can say we no longer feel great, and our economy is so bad, and our insecurity so great that all our resources must be devoted to things of now. Like old soldiers, we can just fade away, and the Japanese and Russians can become the leaders. There has to be new projects or the demonstrated capability of our technology will end. We are at a crossroads, and what we decide will tell a lot about what kind of country we are . . . I think the jury is still out.

Interview, Pasadena, Calif./
Chicago Tribune, 8-30:(1)8.

Russell L. Schweickart
Chairman, California Energy Commission;
Former astronaut

4

[On manned space exploration]: We are infants leaving the womb of earth, and the important thing is how we respond to the birth pangs. We don't have the option of climbing back. Our gestation period—our cosmic nine months—is up . . . Our little egg is cracked, and we're seeing the whole cosmos out there. And when the egg is cracked, the chick doesn't take out the Elmer's glue and seal it back up.

Interview, Sacramento, Calif./
The Christian Science Monitor, 4-29:(B)3.

John B. Slaughter
Director,
National Science Foundation

1

I can't say if there is any single innovation taking form right now that will exert as great and direct an impact on our economy as the tractor or the Model T. On the other hand, I can see a host of advances in knowledge that will almost certainly lead to much the same kind of enhancement of our well-being . . . The clear implication of these trends is that yet another generation of far more sophisticated devices will soon be touching all of our lives in much deeper ways than anything we have yet experienced.

At University of Southern California
commencement/
U.S. News & World Report, 6-15:35.

Solomon H. Snyder
Director, department of neuroscience,
Johns Hopkins University
School of Medicine

2

Research is showing that there are powerful genetic and, therefore, chemical influences determining all sorts of features of human nature. Studies of identical twins separated at birth and reunited many years later suggest the importance of genetic make-up. They show that the twins have remarkable behavioral similarities even though they were raised by completely different families. That fits with the intuition of a lot of parents. If you raise children, you can see that each child has a particular way of dealing with the world that is evident almost from birth. I am not arguing that environment and how parents raised you have no influence on behavior; psychological and environmental factors will remain important. But the pendulum is likely to continue swinging toward an appreciation of the considerable impact of genetics in determining personality.

Interview/
U.S. News & World Report,
4-20:76.

Michael I. Sovern
President, Columbia University

3

America's private universities have led the way in scientific innovation—the lion's share of the ground-breaking research has been done in our laboratories, and the majority of America's leading scientists have trained with us, hardly a startling congruence. Recognizing the critical importance of keeping American science in the forefront, the previous [Carter] Administration recommended the expenditure of $75-million for advanced scientific instrumentation—the tools of state-of-the-art research and training. This entire item has been stricken from the [Reagan Administration] budget. Private universities cannot assume these costs. The result will be an inexorable reduction in the effectiveness of both research and training, a further erosion of America's ability to compete.

At Columbia University commencement/
The Christian Science Monitor, 6-17:14.

Clarence A. Syvertson
Director, Ames Research Center,
National Aeronautics and Space
Administration of the United States

4

We spend 28 per cent of the national budget on welfare. We spend .8 per cent for space. That's a 35-to-one ratio. I like to look at it this way: The money we spend on welfare and things like that is money spent on correcting the problems of the past. Because we got ourselves into some problem, now we have to help out the people impacted by it. But space is an investment in the future. Now it seems to me that any intelligent, well-run organization—whether it be a company, a university or a country—ought to be able to spend one-fifth as much on the future as it does on the past. For every dollar we spend on the space program, there have been many studies that show they have returned to the economy far more than the dollar.

Interview, Ames Research Center, Mountain View,
Calif./San Francisco Examiner & Chronicle,
6-14:(California Living)9.

WHAT THEY SAID IN 1981

Albert Szent-Gyorgyi
Nobel Prize-winning scientist;
Scientific director, Institute for
Muscle Research, Woods Hole, Mass.

1

If Louis Pasteur were to come out of his grave because he heard that the cure for cancer still had not been found, NIH would tell him, "Of course we'll give you assistance. Now, write up exactly what you will be doing during the three years of your grant." Pasteur would say, "Thank you very much," and would go back to his grave. Why? Because research means going into the unknown. If you know what you are going to do in science, then you are stupid! This is like telling Michelangelo or Renoir that he must tell you in advance how many reds and how many blues he will buy, and exactly how he intends to put those colors together.

Interview/The Saturday Evening Post, Jan.-Feb.:30.

John W. Young
Commander, United States space
shuttle "Columbia"

2

[On the space shuttle]: There's no question in my mind that the capability to put 65,000 pounds in low earth orbit—to put payloads up there cheaper than we've been able to do it before, not having to throw away the booster —will absolutely revolutionize the way we do business here on earth in ways that we just can't even imagine. It will help develop science and technology. With the space shuttle—when we get it operational—we'll be able to do in 5 or 10 years what it would take us 20 to 30 years to do otherwise in science and technology development.

Interview/
U.S. News & World Report,
4-13:56.

Sports

Muhammad Ali
Former heavyweight boxing
champion of the world

1

[On why he is returning to boxing at age 39]: Everybody knows me. Not just in the West, but in China, in Russia, in Morocco, in Libya. They know me all over the world. I set a goal for myself, to demonstrate to other people what can be done. I do it for them. People tell me not to fight, but they are at the foot of the wall of knowledge and I am at the top. My horizon is greater than theirs. Why do people go to the moon? Why did [the late civil-rights leader] Martin Luther King say he had a dream? People need challenges.

Interview,
Nassau, Bahamas/
The New York Time, 11-29:(1)20.

George Allen
Former football coach,
Washington "Redskins"

2

Coaching isn't just what takes place on Sunday . . . Good coaches are also talent-evaluators—and I'm not talking about just evaluating players but equipment men, film men, switchboard operators, whatever. At Washington, we had the earliest-opening switchboard in the League and the last to close. I used to try other clubs and they'd be closed at five minutes to 5—and those clubs were in last place.

Interview,
Palos Verdes Estates, Calif./
Los Angeles Times, 2-6:(III)10.

Sparky Anderson
Baseball manager,
Detroit "Tigers"

3

I've had five pennant winners, taken the [Cincinnati] *Reds* four times into the World Series and won twice, and I never considered myself a better man because I won. The important thing is to compete and compete hard, but I've never felt that winning was everything.

The Christian Science Monitor, 2-19:16.

Mario Andretti
Auto-racing driver

4

When I began my racing career, I set some goals. I've achieved all of them and some I hadn't planned on. But I still get a burning feeling inside when it's time to race. Everyone's life is full of greed, and my life is full of greed to do more, to win more. To be able to repeat as champion is even sweeter than the first time around, and there's nothing in the world that keeps you going more than pure enjoyment of your work.

Interview, Los Angeles/
Los Angeles Times,
3-1:(III)7.

5

[On whether the dangers of auto racing are overrated]: It's not overrated. The dangers are there. It's real. There's no question about it. As safety-minded as we are, in every respect. As you know, we've been fighting for the safety of circuits, safety of everything. The reason

(MARIO ANDRETTI)

we're doing it is because we're going faster and faster. We're trying to maintain an acceptable standard. Still, no matter how much effort is put into it, it's always going to be a dangerous sport.

Interview/
Los Angeles Herald Examiner, 9-9:(A)11.

Bob Arum
Boxing promoter;
President, Top Rank

1

At this point in history, we are blessed with the greatest collection of American boxers we ever had. They are also well-dressed, well-spoken, with middle-class aspirations. Not so many "dese, dem and dose" guys. They give boxing a very good image.

The New York Times, 2-8:(1)25.

Gene Autry
Owner, California "Angels" baseball team

2

. . . I'm an old union man; I belong to five unions right now. Obviously, I'm not against the players making as much money as they can. I think I've pretty much shown that. But something has to be done before baseball self-destructs. We've got to bring some sanity back to the game . . . If teams in your league are going out and buying up all the big-name players and you don't, then you're going to be in serious trouble. I owe it to the *Angel* fans to field the best team I can. The way the system is set up now, either you go out and bid like crazy or you come up empty. It's crazy and it's got to change. We're not out to cut the players' wages back. I feel strongly the players should be paid the money they deserve. But it's gone too far. The whole system is out of whack.

Interview, Palm Springs, Calif./
Los Angeles Herald Examiner,
3-17:(C)1.

3

[On the current baseball player strike]: I'm on record for saying that if the players struck—that's it, forget the season. As far as I'm concerned, it can be a long one. If we're shut down for the rest of the season, it will be good for baseball. That way, an awful lot of boys wouldn't be back next year, and a bunch of young kids would be coming in. It would be the same with us, the *Dodgers* and all over the league. We [the owners] have listened to the players long enough. We'll begin taking charge. I have a lot of sympathizers among the owners. The All-Star Game, the first four World Series games—they're all for the players' benefit. I say forget them all.

Interview, Palm Springs, Calif., June 12/
Los Angeles Herald Examiner, 6-13:(C)2.

Dusty Baker
Baseball player,
Los Angeles "Dodgers"

4

All great hitters are controlled. The burning desire to always be ready is there, but the coolness of the mind controls everything in the world. And this comes from the universal powers above. Most men fight themselves rather than using their strength to their advantage. This relates directly to hitting a baseball.

Interview, Vero Beach, Fla./
Los Angeles Herald Examiner, 3-18:(D)3.

Harold Ballard
Owner, Toronto "Maple Leafs"
hockey team

5

[Criticizing the over-expansion of the sport, over-paid players, the numerous lawyers now involved in hockey, etc.]: Hockey was not meant to be a Hollywood production. It takes men to play the game, and we should have men running it. Canadians think of hockey as a pure sport. They resent the intrusion of the money and show-biz guys. As a matter of fact, I'd like to form an eight-team Canadian

(HAROLD BALLARD)

league, let all American teams play in their own league, and we'll play them at the end of the season for the Stanley Cup.

Interview, Toronto/
The Washington Post, 3-15:(M)1.

Rick Barry
Former basketball player

1

Basketball has problems today like other businesses have problems. But the product in basketball gets better each year. Talent is so plentiful that every team can get its hands on skillful players. Winning is just a matter of putting together the right combinations.

TV Guide, 3-21:17.

Jacques Barzun
Educator, Writer

2

[Saying that, over the years, baseball has mirrored American society]: Fundamentally, things haven't changed. Baseball still reflects our society; it's just that society has changed . . . When we look at the triumphs of American technology on a large scale, we see the fine workings of a national machinery—everybody in every department cooperating effectively with no gaps in time. It was like the making of a double-play perhaps. Or a relay in which nine men speedily clicked together to achieve a desired result. It's a beautiful thing to observe. But now, the contentions in baseball parallel the enormous unrest in our society—there's more litigation, for example, than ever before. And the star system has gotten out of hand. The teamwork that once marked the beauty of baseball is now scorned, and along with the diminishing appreciation for the rich qualities of baseball, there has developed diminished appreciation for the rich qualities of American life.

Interview/
The New York Times,
5-31:(1)23.

Buzzie Bavasi
Executive vice president, California "Angels" baseball club

3

I come from the old school of baseball and I guess I still live in the past. But you have to learn to change. The people who run baseball and the people who play it are different now. There are 12 or 15 players in baseball today who make as much as I paid the entire *Dodger* team in '53, the year we won the pennant. The most Camp [Campanella] ever made was $36,000, and Jackie Robinson made $39,000. You can't tell me there's a player today 30 times better than Jackie Robinson. In the old days, the Sniders, the Drysdales, the Campanellas—every day they would come into my office and talk baseball. Now the players show up at the park at 5 o'clock. They have other interests —they can afford other interests.

Interview/
Los Angeles Herald Examiner, 5-10:(B)1.

Johnny Bench
Baseball catcher, Cincinnati "Reds"

4

The pressure on a catcher never has been rougher. Enforcement of the balk rule has given runners a big edge on the pitchers. The runners today have artificial turf. They use track shoes. And the young ones seem to run 100 in 9-flat. And the older ones study moves better than ever. If your elbow and your legs are acting up, as mine do, how would you like to throw out Davey Lopes?

Interview, Tampa, Fla./
Los Angeles Herald Examiner, 3-8:(C)1.

John Bishop
President, International Motor Sports Association

5

[Auto] racing sometimes makes super-human demands on those who take part. It commonly pulls out more strength, ingenuity and endurance from a person than he thought possible. Envision the Daytona pits at 3:30 a.m.,

WHAT THEY SAID IN 1981

(JOHN BISHOP)

only halfway through the 24-hour race. You'll see what bone-tired looks like. That's the cue for a car to come in on an unscheduled pit stop, half the body-work gone, oil-line ruptured and a wheel in ruins. Those half-dead mechanics come to life as if they are on camera. [They] get things patched up and the car running competitively again in 10 minutes' time. Or look in on the timers and scorers at dawn. The temperature stands at 25 degrees, the heaters have quit, there's no chance to move around to get the circulation going, and there's no more coffee. You are timing five cars at once, your relief is late, your fingers are freezing, and suddenly the safety car comes out, bunching all the cars up. That's when you discover there is some adrenalin left after all, and the scorekeeping continues without a lapse or an error . . . I'm sure that every driver, official, pit steward, timekeeper, crew chief and mechanic adds to his skills at every event. Just as important, his appreciation of how much he can take or how long he can deliver also grows with each race.

Los Angeles Times, 4-20:(VIII)2.

Jane Blalock
Golfer

1

The thing I like most [about women's golf], and I think it will continue to improve in the next decade, is the quality of golf courses we play. I remember not so long ago we were playing on some cow pastures. We'd get into town, ask where the course was and they'd say, "Go down the road until you see the corner grocery store by the stop sign. Ask them how to get there." And when we got there, even the grocery clerk didn't know where it was. Now we're playing more and more on prestige courses . . . The atmosphere is different, too. The girls used to do all the tournament planning, all the preparation. Now when we arrive the course is roped off and transportation is available. And we attract so much more attention. I don't know how it works, whether the money makes

us more prestigious, or by being more prestigious we attract more money. I remember we used to beg for sponsors. Now they're lined up waiting to come in.

Interview, Palm Springs, Calif./
Los Angeles Times, 4-1:(III)6.

George Blanda
Former football player,
Oakland "Raiders"

2

Things never change in football. It's still blocking and tackling and execution, and having an experienced quarterback who is patient enough to take what the defense gives him.

Interview/
The Christian Science Monitor, 1-14:10.

Jim Bouton
Former baseball pitcher

3

I can't think of anything good to say about [baseball-club] owners, because my experience with them was not good. When I was winning 21 games, they paid me $10,500; I had to hold out the following year for an $8,000 raise. They abused players; they told us that if we didn't like the contract, we could go become a plumber or a gardener. Now I see the owners squawking about selling their ball clubs. Well, if they don't like it, *they* can go into the gardening or plumbing business. Those guys own these teams as a tax dodge. They are allowed to depreciate the value of their players. In effect, fans are supporting the players' salaries. We are all subsidizing them, because when rich owners don't pay their taxes, then we all have to make it up.

Interview/
Los Angeles Herald Examiner, 4-20:(A)4.

4

In high school they called me Warmup Bouton, because that's all I ever did. I didn't expect to make it to the big leagues, so when I

(JIM BOUTON)

finally did, it was a big surprise to me. If you've been a great athlete all your life, you don't appreciate how fun it can be. A lot of players lose perspective; they become convinced they're doing something important. So many people come to watch, and you get paid so much, it must be important. And of course it's not. The more important it becomes to you, the more serious it is. So many players never appreciate the fun and good life they have. I couldn't understand why Roger Maris would have so many problems while hitting 61 home runs.

Interview, Los Angeles/
Los Angeles Times, 4-23:(III)3.

Nick Bremigan
Baseball umpire, American League

1

[On umpiring]: You may have 50,000 people who think you've kicked the play [made an erroneous call] but you never change a call once you've made it, even if you're wrong. Some umpires will take a lot of heat from an angry manager. Others have quick guns. One word that will get a manager ejected quicker than anything is to call an umpire a "homer." They are insulting your integrity by saying you're taking the easy way out and calling the game for the home team. Call an umpire "homer" and it's like waving a red flag in a bull's face.

Interview/
The Christian Science Monitor, 3-25:(B)15.

Paul "Bear" Bryant
Football coach,
University of Alabama

2

I've never won a football game. Coaches don't win games; the players do. My teams won games in spite of me. I mean that. My assistant coaches are more responsible for many of our victories than me, and you could say their wives, too. You've never seen an assistant coach who didn't have a good wife. There

ought to be a special place in heaven for coaches' wives. Every time a player goes there, at least 20 people have some amount of influence on him. His mother has more influence than anyone. I know because I played, and I loved my mama. Then the assistant coaches have an influence on him; his girlfriend has an influence on him; the band and the cheerleaders and his teammates.

Interview, Tuscaloosa, Alabama/
Chicago Tribune, 11-15:(4)4.

August A. Busch, Jr.
President, St. Louis "Cardinals"
baseball team

3

[Criticizing the settlement just approved by owners and players that ended the player strike]: ... in all my years, both business and personal, I have never been more disgusted, angry and ashamed of a situation in which I was involved ... What did we [owners] end up with? If the *Cubs* lose a player to the *Phillies* through free-agency, then possibly I have the honor of giving the *Cubs* my 27th-best player—marvelous compensation. A precedent has been set. A horrible contract has been extended for one year. In return, we have the privilege of increasing players' minimum salary to $40,000 in 1984, with nothing in return regarding pension contributions. We will never again be in a position to get strike insurance. We have made the [player] union our partner ... The owners who forced this settlement by their actions [at the negotiations] in New York sold us out because of their individual problems and egos. There are owners who undermined the Player Relations Committee and shamefully cheated and deceived all of us. They think they are the future of baseball, but believe me, they are not worthy to even carry the briefcase of Walter O'Malley, Phil Wrigley, Horace Stoneman, Bob Carpenter, Mrs. Payson and, of course, my dear friend, John Fetzer. I have been in baseball in good times and in bad, but none so shameful.

At meeting of club owners, Chicago, Aug. 6/
The Washington Post, 8-8:(D)5.

WHAT THEY SAID IN 1981

Al Campanis
Vice president, player personnel,
Los Angeles "Dodgers" baseball club

1

[On whether there will be player changes on the *Dodgers* even though they just won the World Series]: I have a friend who's an architect and he took me to his home . . . It was a beautiful home. You think, "How could anyone want a better home?" But he's telling me, "I need more storage room. This bathroom has to be changed." That's the way it is in a ballclub. I don't think you're ever satisfied. You want to improve it.

Interview/
Los Angeles Times, 10-30:(III)13.

Rod Carew
Baseball player, California "Angels"

2

[On whether he thinks exceptionally high salaries should be the most important thing to players]: No, I don't. You hear athletes say we only have a certain amount of time and we have to take advantage of it and make it while we can. But I enjoy doing what I'm doing. It's something I always wanted to do . . . The only place it can end is if the owners get together and stop it. But these guys [the owners] are fighting each other, trying to outdo each other. So it's going to continue . . . In some ways you can't blame the players for taking as much as they can get because for so many years the owners didn't give a damn about the players. As long as they could get the players to go on the field and get fans in the seats, that's all they cared about. Now it's starting to backfire on them and the players are taking advantage of it.

Interview/
Los Angeles Times, 2-12:(III)1.

Eddie Chiles
Owner, Texas "Rangers"
baseball club

3

[On the current player strike]: We have two major forces here, the owners and the players

and we have to learn to live together because we're dependent on each other. We're all in the same boat. You can't sink half a boat and expect the other half to float on ahead. Right now we're both going down together. The future of baseball is on the line, to a certain extent. How we handle this is going to determine if we come out of it and continue to get better and better, or get worse and worse. A phony, fictitious settlement really wouldn't do anybody any good. It would be a step in a downhill plunge . . . When we let something like this happen right in the middle of a season, then something's gone wrong, and I'm pretty mad about it. We should have been able to handle our problems in a better way. This should have been worked out between the seasons, and if they didn't get it worked out, they shouldn't have started the season. Nobody gains from a strike—the players lose, the owners lose, and the fans lose.

Radio interview/
The New York Times, 7-27:27.

Jocko Conlan
Former baseball umpire

4

[Saying there should be stiffer penalties for abuse of umpires, such as the recent incident in which Oakland manager Billy Martin allegedly bumped and threw dirt on umpire Terry Cooney]: If I had been working [that] game, I would have hit Martin with everything I had . . . [Years ago,] when Johnny Allen barely bumped George Barr after a balk call, [baseball commissioner] Ford Frick gave him 30 days [suspension]. And he wanted to give him 60. He would have given Martin at least 60 days. [But] go back to spring training earlier this year. [Baltimore manager Earl] Weaver pulls a club off the field and causes a forfeit, and gets [only] three days. Up in Seattle, [manager] Maury Wills alters the batter's box and gets two days. Jim Frey at Kansas City kicks dirt all over the umpire, and over in New York, Gene Michael throws his hat and jacket at the umpire, and all they get is a slap on the wrist. You can't build any respect if you don't back

(JOCKO CONLAN)

your umpires any better than that. And without respect, how are you going to run the game?

Interview/
Los Angeles Herald Examiner, 6-5:(B)6.

Howard Cosell
Commentator, ABC Sports

1

[Saying sports has become too important in America]: Everything is totally out of whack. I read a comment by a fan the other day. He said he would not know what to do with himself without baseball [because of the current player strike]. For all I know, he was a steel worker who at one time or another had been on strike, too. Yet he is lost because of the baseball strike, which has absolutely no significance sociologically, philosophically, educationally to this country. With all the vital issues of our existence, we are wrapped up in whether a stupid game is going to be played . . . [And] a new problem has cropped up: fan violence. You can't take your wife or kid to the ballpark now without fear. It is a terrible, terrible thing—contradictory to what sport should be about. But it is a predictable offshoot to our original premise—that the games, the scores, the athletes have become too big, too important. Winning, losing, too important. Out of whack, the whole thing. We have to get a fix on sports in this country soon. More people know [baseball player] Reggie Jackson than the Secretary of State. It's insane.

Interview/
Los Angeles Herald Examiner, 6-19:(B)1,6.

Larry Doby
Former baseball player,
Cleveland "Indians"

2

[On the high salaries of today's players]: Too much education and too much easy money. When I was a kid, it was tough to get a quarter to go to the movies. Now kids have their own automobiles, fat allowances and anything they want. They sign long-term contracts and feel secure for life. Pride and desire are dying qualities. I'll tell you, if I played today, no matter what I made, I'd bust my gut.

Los Angeles Times, 2-4:(II)8.

Angelo Drossos
President, San Antonio "Spurs"
basketball team

3

[On his policy of paying bonuses to his players when they turn in a good performance]: Let me put it this way: You've played three nights in a row, you're really tired, you've been sleeping in beds built for 6-footers when you're 6-9, you're playing a team you know you can beat, *and* you know you're going to make the playoffs. Why *shouldn't* you be paid for really putting out? I don't see a problem with it. The presidents, vice presidents and other executives of many companies have incentive plans tied to the bottom line, the company's profit. It's the American way to compensate people for a job above and beyond what is expected . . . With an 82-game season, the players inevitably are going to let down. They need a goal, motivation, stimulation. That's what I was hoping would happen, and so far it has. Let's face it, the difference between winning and losing in the NBA, especially on the road, is often that little extra push [effort]. Our team is giving us that.

Interview, San Antonio/
Los Angeles Times, 1-20:(III)5.

Leo Durocher
Former baseball manager

4

[On the current player strike]: I'm not for the players and I'm not for the owners, but I think the players are being stupid. Maybe I'm just over the hill and maybe there's something here that escapes me, but I can't see where any group that has a minimum salary of $32,500 a year and meal money of $32 a day has reason to strike. I remember fighting

WHAT THEY SAID IN 1981

(LEO DUROCHER)

my way to the big leagues making $4 a day in meal money and thinking it was great.

Interview/
Los Angeles Times, 7-29:(III)2.

Eddie Einhorn
President, Chicago "White Sox"
baseball club

1

[Saying baseball clubs must improve their promotion efforts to attract fans to the park]: You can't run a baseball team like it was run 20 years ago, 10 years ago, even five years ago. There are many ramifications. The stakes are higher. The competition for the entertainment dollar is tougher. But baseball is probably the last sport to come out of the dark ages of promotion and publicity. I guess they figured they were entrenched and didn't have to do these other things, that they could open a park with a decent team and draw a million. But now, when you see a million won't pay the bills, you'd better draw two million.

Interview, Chicago/
Chicago Tribune, 4-12:(4)1.

2

[Baseball is] show business, and most [club] owners enjoy it for that, and for what it means to be a part of something different like that. You don't go into baseball to make money, I mean big money. You can't. But I also know you don't go in to lose money. I've never heard of an owner selling a team for less than he paid for it . . . There are also financial advantages to being an owner that don't appear in the profit-and-loss statement. It's well-known that you meet people you might never meet otherwise, and it helps your other businesses. Do you think the [New York] *Yankees*, for example, has hurt [owner George] Steinbrenner's shipbuilding company? I doubt it. It's funny, though. Hardheaded businessmen sometimes lose their perspective when they get into something like baseball. A certain, call it romance,

takes over. The same as it does with fans. You think it's not strictly a business. Then something like this [the current player] strike hits, and it knocks you back to reality.

Interview/
The New York Times, 6-21:(1)24.

Dwight Evans
Baseball player,
Boston "Red Sox"

3

[On the current player strike over the owner-compensation issue]: The owners are asking us to surrender benefits that have been given us by the courts, and we're not going to do that. One of the reasons salaries are so high is because owners like Gene Autry of the California *Angels*, George Steinbrenner of the New York *Yankees* and Ted Turner of the Atlanta *Braves* keep giving players thousands of dollars more than they are worth. Well, that's not our fault.

The Christian Science Monitor, 6-15:18.

Jim Fregosi
Baseball manager,
California "Angels"

4

[On the biggest change he has seen in baseball]: Most people would probably tell you designated hitters. But I think the biggest change has been the physical attributes of the players today. They spend the year-around on baseball now. They take care of themselves and work on body-building. Most good ballplayers go into their 30s in very good condition these days. Physically, they used to be nearly through at 30 . . . The players today know their body is their best investment. They know it will make a lot of money for them if they take care of it. So they do—and that's been the biggest change in my time.

Interview/
Los Angeles Times, 3-10:(III)8.

Jim Frey
Baseball manager,
Kansas City "Royals"

1

When a team is not going well, people come up with all sorts of reasons. You start out blaming the weather; then it's the umpires; then the schedule; then bad breaks, bad hops, bloops, missed pitches, whatever. When you get down to blaming the fans, I think you're running out of excuses. Anyway, if you're not going to give credit to all those things when we win, maybe we shouldn't blame them when we go bad.

Interview/
The Christian Science Monitor, 5-19:10.

Carl Furillo
Former baseball player,
Los Angeles "Dodgers"

2

[On the current player strike]: I could see this coming from the time they went to expansion. They didn't have the athletes to fill all the teams, and when owners saw that there were only a few decent players, they started giving money away to them. They created a monster. I blame both sides [owners and players] and their greed for this. And the sucker is the fan; he controls the whole thing. When the players go back, fans should stage a 30-day moratorium and stay away from games. They should say, "The hell with you. Go ahead and play now if you want to." I got a Gold Pass [a lifetime pass to major league games] when I retired, and I haven't used it yet. I wouldn't go across the street to see a game.

Interview/
Los Angeles Herald Examiner, 6-25:(D)1.

Roman Gabriel
Football coach, California State
Polytechnic University, Pomona;
Former player, Los Angeles "Rams"

3

If a [college football] player can't perform in the classroom, chances are he isn't going to give you what you want on the field, either. When we recruit, we look for a lot more than the physical aspects of a player. We also want to know how intelligent he is, what his interests are, and where he rates as a self-starter . . . Anyone who thinks that an education isn't more important than playing any varsity sport isn't very well informed. I saw a lot of this in pro football when I was with the *Rams* and the Philadelphia *Eagles*—dozens of guys who weren't prepared for anything after football because they hadn't gotten their degrees or been to many classes. While it is true that being a former pro will often open doors in the business world that might otherwise have remained closed, nobody stays very long in those good jobs if he doesn't produce.

Interview, Pomona, Calif./
The Christian Science Monitor, 8-21:16.

Ed Garvey
Executive director, National Football
League Players Association

4

The free-agent system doesn't work in the NFL. No free-agent system would work, even if you eliminate compensation and the right of first-refusal. That's because owners share their revenues equally and there is no economic incentive for management to win . . . I think they'd like to win. But will they spend money to win? No! . . . The NFLPA will negotiate for a percentage of gross revenue. That way, when the League grows, we'll be happy to grow with them.

New Orleans, Jan. 22/
Los Angeles Times, 1-23:(II)4.

5

[On why the players feel they are entitled to 55 per cent of the NFL's gross revenue]: Few industries are as labor-intensive as football. There are a few industries that have a smaller investment in equipment, plant and the other things usually associated with businesses. You have to look at the entertainment industry to get something of a parallel—and in entertain-

467

(ED GARVEY)

ment it's not unusual for talent to get this much or more. Look at the automobile business compared to football. The automobile manufacturer must create a new model every year; he has to build plants, hire sales forces, put on national advertising campaigns and other things. He has a lot of costs you don't have in football—and that's about it. Can you think of anything about the NFL that fits the traditional mold of American business? To begin with, the NFL is a monopoly. It strictly controls entrance into it [by either players or owners]. It controls the exit of its employees [by the option clause, etc.] and it controls their lives while thay're in it. They're now paying their players 30 per cent of gross, and we say it should be 55 per cent. That's the argument.

Interview/
Los Angeles Times, 3-25:(III)12.

Steve Garvey
Baseball player,
Los Angeles "Dodgers"

1

[On the current player strike and the issue of free agency and owner-compensation]: I don't think the compensation issue is worth interrupting what might have been the finest season in baseball history. Free agency as it stands now has done three things: One, the game is more popular; two, there is more profit being made; and three, there is an equality of teams in the standings. There is no need for more compensation [for club owners].

Interview/
The Christian Science Monitor, 7-2:16.

Bob Gibson
Former baseball pitcher,
St. Louis "Cardinals"

2

. . . when you let people like Willie Mays and Mickey Mantle get away from baseball, you lose something important. I think every effort should be made to see that that type of person

doesn't slip out of the game. I don't think there's any question the quality of the game has slipped a bit. All these teams have led to a diluting of talent. It wasn't that long ago we had eight-team leagues. Now I can't even tell you how many major-league clubs there are.

At his induction into Baseball Hall of Fame,
Cooperstown, N.Y., Aug. 2/
Chicago Tribune, 8-4:(4)4.

David Graham
Australian golfer

3

[Saying he likes playing in the U.S.]: . . . in America there are a hundred [golfers] who can play. You can make it rich living somewhere else, but nowhere else [but the U.S.] can you *prove* you can play. You need the competition to knock you down and bring you up. You know, it's good to be humble. Golf has to kick you in the mouth now and then to be worth anything. It's good to win the U.S. Open, and then go out the next day and start again from scratch.

Interview, Sandwich, England/
Los Angeles Herald Examiner, 7-15:(C)3.

Bud Grant
Football coach,
Minnesota "Vikings"

4

As coaches, we have no union, no bargaining agent, no protection and no strength to deal from. We are purposely kept in that position by the League. We're resented because we have so much impact on the game: pro football is a coach's medium and always has been. So the League sees us as a necessary evil. We're muzzled . . . and can't say "Boo." Everybody'd be happier if we were clones, like the officials. Everything you say is supposed to be "Positive" . . . If I'd known 25 years ago what I know now, I don't know if I'd have gotten into this profession.

Los Angeles Times, 2-4:(III)1.

Dennis Green
Football coach,
Northwestern University

1

I've been on teams that were used to winning, and if you don't win, all hell breaks loose on those teams. They are outraged. They come back like they have more at stake than the coaches. They get upset if someone fumbles. They get mad if a unit doesn't do its job. What they do is make each other play better. This is what I call a winning tradition . . .

Interview/
Chicago Tribune, 9-20:(4)6.

Pat Haden
Football player,
Los Angeles "Rams"

2

[On unruly sports fans]: Something is wrong with American sports. It's a product of the times. The reaction fans have is like recreational violence. Maybe they figure they pay X-number of dollars, it's their prerogative to do anything. It's everywhere. Little leagues, high school, college. Coaches hit players. We have academic scandals. It is a win-at-all-costs attitude. Until it is changed, we encourage that sort of fan reaction.

Interview/
Chicago Tribune, 9-25:(5)1.

Joe B. Hall
Basketball coach,
University of Kentucky

3

Winning is an obsession at Kentucky. That's not a bad thing. It keeps you on your toes. I feel we have to win here . . . That doesn't mean you have to win a national championship every year, but you have to be a contender. You have to be able to honestly say, at any time, that within two years you'll be contending for the NCAA title.

Interview, Lexington, KY./
Los Angeles Times, 1-28:(III)10.

Ralph Hauk
Baseball manager,
Boston "Red Sox"

4

Everybody seems to think [players are] tougher to handle now because of the [high] salaries. In my opinion, they're no different at all. I have found if a man is a major-league player, he had to have a lot of ability and pride in himself or he never would have gotten there. That kind of player, the minute he gets that uniform on, everything else is bygone.

Interview, Pompano Beach, Fla./
The New York Times, 2-23:30.

Lou Holtz
Football coach,
University of Arkansas

5

. . . players will live up or down according to their expectations. If players think of themselves as dogs, pretty soon they'll start barking.

Interview/
Chicago Tribune, 9-20:(4)6.

Red Holzman
Basketball coach,
New York "Knicks"

6

[On reports that today's players don't take defeat as hard as yesterday's did]: That's true. When I first started to coach in the pros, guys would come into the locker room after a tough loss and break up furniture or brood or act like there was no tomorrow. It was like they had committed a crime by losing. Now, as a coach I certainly don't want my players to take any defeat lightly. But when you're part of an 82-game schedule, you're playing five times in the next six nights, and you're rushing to catch an airplane, I don't think it's too smart to carry those kinds of feelings with you. In that respect, I think today's players handle things a lot better emotionally.

Interview, Los Angeles/
The Christian Science Monitor,
3-5:16.

Frank Howard
Baseball manager,
San Diego "Padres"

1

[Saying there is more to judging a manager than his won-loss record]: The classic example of a manager who shouldn't be graded on wins and losses is Gene Mauch. I've played against Gene's clubs, and watched them for years, and it's clear to me that nobody gets more out of his players. If he's never won, it's because he's never had the talent. You're only as good as the horses that run for you. Some of the potentially best managers ever—Ted Williams for one—just never had the horses.

Interview/
Los Angeles Times, 2-18:(III)6.

Hale Irwin
Golfer

2

Golf is the "only-est" sport. You're completely alone with every conceivable opportunity to defeat yourself. Golf brings out your assets and liabilities as a person. The longer you play, the more certain you are that a man's performance is the outward manifestation of who, in his heart, he really thinks he is . . . You can talk about strategy all you want—what you do when you're a shot ahead or behind—but what really matters is resiliency. On the last nine holes of the Masters or the Open, there's going to come at least one point when you want to throw yourself in the nearest trash can and disappear. You know you can't hide. It's like you're walking down a fairway naked. The gallery knows what you've done, every other player knows, and, worst of all, you know. That's when you find out if you're a competitor.

Interview, Augusta, Ga./
The Washington Post, 4-12:(M)7.

Reggie Jackson
Baseball player, New York "Yankees"

3

The will to win is worthless if you don't get paid for it.

Time, 3-23:84.

470

4

I've batted .450 in the World Series and I've hit .120. I've struck out in the clutch and I've hit the longest home runs you'll ever see. I've made great catches and I've fallen on my face and looked like a fool. I've been picked off, picked on and picked myself back up. Live big, die big. That's my way.

The Washington Post, 10-16:(D)1.

Jimmy Jacobs
Prize-fighter manager

5

The idea of "Does he have a good jaw or doesn't he?" is a myth perpetuated by people who don't know that it is a fighter's attitude, not his chin, that determines who will be knocked out. Fighters that don't want to get knocked out—Rocky Marciano, Muhammad Ali, Sugar Ray Robinson—don't get knocked out. There is a great correlation between attitude and survival. I just don't believe that nature wires the jaw to the brain differently in different men.

The Washington Post, 9-15:(C)2.

Ron Jaworski
Football player,
Philadelphia "Eagles"

6

There definitely are levels that a quarterback goes through. First you wonder if you're good enough to play in the NFL. Then you make it, but wonder if you can become a starter. Then you start for a few years and they say you're not a winner. Then you take your team to the playoffs and they say you're not a Super Bowl quarterback. Then you get there a few times and you get that Fran Tarkenton reputation, and they say you can't win the big one. I've fought my way here [to the Super Bowl], and I want to see if I can have the big game in the big game.

Interview/
The Christian Science Monitor,
1-21:14.

Tommy John
Baseball player,
New York "Yankees"

1

[On criticism that free-agency is ruining baseball]: Some critics have pictured us [players] as greedy and self-centered, intent on grabbing everything we can regardless of the consequences. Nothing is further from the truth. The players are very concerned about the health of the game. But from all we see, baseball is thriving on free-agency. Never in history has the competition been keener. Crowds are bigger. TV appeal is growing. If the baseball owners would open their books and show us that the present free-agency rules are ruining the game, you can bet the players would respond. It would be like Chrysler. When Chrysler started to fold, everybody pitched in to make sacrifices. The workers even agreed to take cuts. It would be the same in baseball if it could be shown that baseball is in danger.

Interview, Ft. Lauderdale, Fla./
Los Angeles Herald Examiner, 3-8:(C)4.

Sonny Jurgensen
Former football player,
Washington "Redskins"

2

When you are in the game, you don't realize what kind of special life you lead. You are spoiled. Everything is done for you. You develop a very narrow view of life. But when you get out, you finally realize it was just a game, nothing more. I worked at it, enjoyed it, but I was playing a little-boy's game as a grown man. It was a lot of fun, but it had to end sometime . . . If you play long enough, you eventually realize why you are being held in esteem, why you are on a pedestal and how soon you can tumble. You realize it's all superficial.

Interview/The Washington Post Magazine, 9-6:19.

Michael Killanin
Former president,
International Olympic Committee

3

[On the boycott by some countries of the 1980 Olympics in Moscow as a protest against

the Soviet invasion of Afghanistan]: Despite the efforts of certain politicians to use the Games at Moscow for political expediency, I believe they in the end were losers. The victors were the Olympic movement, supported by the international sports federations and many national Olympic committees who were completely free to participate in probably the best-organized Games of the modern Olympic era. It is only sad that in some sports, competitors were forbidden to compete or prevented from competing. As always, it is the athlete who suffers when politcians meddle with sport.

At meeting of sports federations and Olympic
committees, Baden-Baden, West Germany,
Sept. 24/The Washington Post, 9-25:(D)3.

Billie Jean King
Tennis player

4

The prize money we get today, of course, is fabulous. Back in 1971 I had to win 19 tournaments to earn $100,000. Now if a player is hot, she can make that much in maybe six weeks. In fact, there is at least one tournament going on somewhere every week, where years ago that opportunity wasn't available to young players trying to gain experience. What we've got now is a system that can perpetuate itself.

Interview, Los Angeles/
The Christian Science Monitor, 2-18:14.

Bill Kinnamon
Former baseball umpire,
National League

5

Athletes don't always make good umpires. They're used to being yelled for, not booed at. A lot of the time they just can't take the loneliness. No umpires are in it for the glory. You're supposed to be invisible until game time. You never get much ink unless the press thinks you made a bad call. Nobody applauds when you call a perfect game. Your satisfaction is internal. You have to be a thick-skinned extrovert. Withdrawn umpires don't last long. The field is your stage, and you turn it on like an actor. No mat-

WHAT THEY SAID IN 1981

(BILL KINNAMON)

ter how big or small you are, when an umpire steps on the field he has to walk nine feet tall. If you look confident, the ballplayers will leave you alone, at least until you make your first mistake.

Interview/
The Christian Science Monitor, 3-25:(B)3.

Eugene V. Klein
Principal owner, San Diego "Chargers"
football team

1

[Supporting NFL regulations requiring League approval for teams to move their franchises from one city to another]: [Without that regulation,] we would absolutely have a traveling circus where there would be no fan loyalty. I for one do not want this to become a fly-by-night Barnum and Bailey traveling circus. Like anything else, we've got to have rules.

Testifying at antitrust trial on the Oakland
"Raiders" proposed move to Los Angeles,
Los Angeles, May 28/
Los Angeles Times, 5-29:(II)1.

Chuck Knox
Football coach,
Buffalo "Bills"

2

I can't think of any profession as insecure as being an NFL head coach. Your fate is never in your own hands. One injury, one bad call, one bad bounce and a year's work can be burned up. They say the breaks all even up in the long run. But how many of us last that long?

Los Angeles Times, 2-4:(III)1.

3

I think "coach" is the right term in football and "manager" is right for baseball. When you think about it, baseball is an individual-type game. You either hit the ball or you don't, and there's not much a manager can do when Dave

Winfield doesn't make contact. On the other hand, football is a team-concept game. The players have to be taught to work together—they have to be "coached."

Interview/
Los Angeles Times, 11-3:(III)6.

Jack Kramer
Tennis player

4

In an individual sport [such as tennis], you can't go out there with soft feelings. You've got to be mean and ornery to be a winner. But what you're looking for is to be mean and ornery inside, but to be very pleasant in your outward things—that's what makes popular champions.

Interview, Los Angeles/
Los Angeles Herald Examiner,
9-6:(California Living)5.

Bowie Kuhn
Commissioner of Baseball

5

[On the trend toward increasingly higher free-agent player salaries and other problems which might bankrupt some baseball clubs]: Ruly Carpenter came into my office in New York about a week ago and said that he felt he would have to sell his Philadelphia [Phillies] franchise. He said that he was worried about the direction the game was going and was pretty well fed up. There were two heavy hearts in the room—mine and Ruly's . . . Some people certainly would be driven out of the game. It doesn't make economic sense to drive out class owners. We can't be sure that their replacements will have the same determination to protect the game's integrity.

Interview, Orlando, Fla., March 8/
The Washington Post, 3-9:(D)8.

6

[Supporting club owners' demands that they are entitled to compensation for a free-agent player in the form of a player from the roster

472

(BOWIE KUHN)

of the team receiving the free agent]: It's necessary for baseball and good for the fans. When a star player moves and you get an amateur back [as is now the case], it's not fair to the fans. You lose a Dave Winfield or a Don Sutton, and you get little back. It's remote. Under our proposal, you'd get a player who can step into the lineup. There's no way it's going to work a hardship on the players. It would not have any effect on Winfield or Sutton, or Darrell Porter. If [New York *Yankees* owner] George Steinbrenner had to give up the 16th player on the *Yankees*, it would not have stopped him from signing Winfield as his left-fielder. And it would not have cost Winfield any money.

Interview, New York, June 25/
The New York Times, 6-26:20.

1

[On the current player strike]: I think there is a public perception that the commissioner somewhere, somehow must have the power to deal with this, to tell the players and owners what to do, and end the strike. That public perception is understandable, considering the considerable powers of the office. But that happens to be the wrong perception. This commissioner—no commissioner—can't tell a labor union not to strike. There has been a popular notion that the commissioner can tell labor leaders and management to stay in a room until they solve the problem. [Player union leader] Marvin Miller would laugh at me if I told him how to bargain . . . The assertion that the commissioner fomented the strike is nonsense. Second, the assertion that the commissioner wanted the strike is nonsense. Third, the notion that the commissioner wanted to break the Players Association, nonsense. I'd be the last guy who would. We need the Players Association. Fourth, that the commissioner should have used some vast powers, like Jupiter, and "Stop this," can't be. And the perception that I, the players and clubs have no interest in the fans is simply not true. One of my greatest concerns

is the fans. In deference to the fans, it's almost like a strike shouldn't happen to baseball. It's like a public utility. But that kind of philosophy overlooks the fact that baseball has an outstanding record with strikes. Few industries have a record so good.

Interview/
Chicago Tribune, 7-26:(4)1,5.

Frank Kush
Football coach, Hamilton (Ont.)
"Tiger Cats"; Former football coach,
Arizona State University

2

Football is a great game. There are a few turkeys in it, sure, but it doesn't change; the basics don't change. The pros are in this for the contract; the [college] kids are in it for the game and the social factor, the recognition in college. Anyone who says different is a hypocrite. That's the problem with the college game today. It's so hypocritical. They try to say the kids are there for an education. It isn't true. Maybe later, when they mature a little, they realize they should get the education. But most of them want to play the game, that's all.

Interview, Hamilton, Ontario/
The Washington Post, 10-4:(D)4.

Tom Landry
Football coach,
Dallas "Cowboys"

3

The biggest misconception about me is that I'm unemotional. I'm not a cheerleader, but I do feel the excitement. You see, concentration is the most important part of my job on the football field. If you're going to do something constructive in a game from a coaching standpoint, you must be completely engrossed in what's going on, not in the emotions of the game.

Interview, Philadelphia/
Los Angeles Times, 1-11:(III)4.

WHAT THEY SAID IN 1981

(TOM LANDRY)

1

The secret to winning is constant management, and that quality comes down from the owner. Our organization has been steady from the beginning. Many of us have grown with it and I think this has paid off. When your organization is constant in football, confidence spreads throughout the whole picture.

Interview, Thousand Oaks, Calif./
Los Angeles Herald Examiner, 7-17:(B)1.

Tom Lasorda
Baseball manager,
Los Angeles "Dodgers"

2

There's no defense for a base-on-balls. There's a defense for anything but a base-on-balls. A guy hits a line drive, takes three steps out of the batter's box, and has a heart attack and drops dead—you can throw *him* out at first base. The next guy walks and drops dead at the plate with a heart attack, and they put in a pinch runner. There's no defense for a base-on-balls.

Philadelphia, May 5/
Los Angeles Herald Examiner, 5-6:(B)1.

Keith Magnuson
Hockey coach,
Chicago "Black Hawks"

3

I've come to the conclusion that every team has a different personality. When you're a coach, the key is discovering that personality and acting accordingly. At the same time, you have to be concerned about the men on your team. If they have a problem, you've got to help them solve it; and, if they aren't playing very much, you've got to encourage them and keep them motivated. And the Number 1 priority always has to be for the team, to win the game that's coming up.

Interview, Chicago/
Chicago Tribune, 1-22:(6)2.

Moses Malone
Basketball player,
Houston "Rockets"

4

With so many players always near the basket, the one thing you can never escape is the physical pounding that comes with getting the ball. Establishing position is part of it, of course. So are strength and good hands. But the main thing is getting yourself into a frame of mind where you can ignore physical punishment, and a lot of centers won't do that . . . unlike a lot of centers, I don't just pick my spots. I go after everything that comes off the boards. Like I said, I'm willing to pay the physical price as often as I have to.

Interview, Los Angeles/
The Christian Science Monitor, 3-4:14.

Ted Marchibroda
Former football coach,
Baltimore "Colts"

5

A coach's most important responsibility is the emotional level of his team. After material [raw talent], that's what wins the most games. But if your material is weak, whether through injury or whatever, then emotion isn't enough. What happens then is that, since nobody wants to face the weaknesses of his players, they blame the bad motivation on the coach. And the less secure the coach's job becomes, the less confidence the players have in him and the less able he is to motivate them. It's a vicious cycle.

Los Angeles Times, 2-4:(III)12.

Billy Martin
Baseball manager,
Oakland "Athletics"

6

There are two things about managing that make it all worthwhile. The first is molding people—frankly, I like to mold them. After they've played for me, they're never the same again. They become an aggressive person, and that's what it takes in any business. I take a

(BILLY MARTIN)

lot of pride in watching my old players keep succeeding after they've left me. Second, managing gives you a place to win. You can't play any more, but you can still win, and winning is everything. There's no such thing as a good loser. There are good winners and bad winners, but no good losers—and you can say that in every language.

Interview/
Los Angeles Times, 3-3:(III)6.

1

Basically, managing is repeating and reminding. You can't say *anything* once to *anybody* and let it go at that. Your coaches and you have to go over everything every day, sometimes every minute—where the outfielders are playing you, how much wind, where's the sun, how many outs. Baseball is a game in which you have to do your homework before the game, sure; but then, you have to keep doing it for nine innings.

Interview/
Los Angeles Times, 3-3:(III)6.

2

I preach pride to my men. They must have pride; they must forget the American dollar sign once they put on that uniform. We had pride with the [New York] *Yankees*, a big thing. The players today are no different than when I played second base for the *Yankees*, except for one thing—now you show them *why* something must be done. It's not sufficient just to *tell* them they must do it. But it's no generation gap; it's a communications gap.

Interview, Scottsdale, Ariz./
Chicago Tribune, 4-1:(6)3.

John McEnroe
Tennis player

3

. . . I think people are crazy to be umpires in the first place. The only way they do a good job

is when they don't get noticed. They shouldn't have 70-year-old men [calling the lines] or people with glasses . . . and that's not to take anything away from people with glasses. But if you're playing for the finals of Wimbledon, you want things to be right. After all, you wouldn't want the Super Bowl decided by one bad call.

Interview, Los Angeles, April 13/
Los Angeles Herald Examiner, 4-14:(C)2.

4

[On his unpopularity because of his bad manners on the court]: I know that all this is never going to change until I completely change the way I act on the court. But that may take years . . . If other players can control themselves over bad calls, I should be able to, too . . . I've got no one to blame for the boos but myself. I wish people knew that I wasn't that bad . . . I know being a linesman [many of whom he has verbally abused] is a thankless job, especially with guys like me around. It's gotten to the point where people just want to get on you. They're waiting. It's sad.

Interview, London, June 22/
The Washington Post, 6-23:(D)3.

John McNamara
Baseball manager,
Cincinnati "Reds"

5

[Criticizing this year's split season, a result of the recent player strike]: [Cincinnati's record the first half counts for nothing. We played one less game than the *Dodgers* and finished half a game behind them. We also had two games rained out after we were leading in both . . . Now [in the second half of the split season] it's sudden death. Either we win the second half or we're gone. Every game is a pressure game . . . How can [baseball commissioner Bowie Kuhn] arbitrarily say that the leaders on June 12th [just before the strike] are the [first-half] winners? There should be no first-half winners. The fairest plan would be to continue the season with everything counting.

WHAT THEY SAID IN 1981

(JOHN McNAMARA)

Then the second-half winner could play the team with the best record over both halves.

Interview, New York, Aug. 29/
The New York Times, 8-30:(1)25.

Dave Meggysey
Field representative, National Football League; Former player, St. Louis "Cardinals"

1

Sports is a reflection of the dominant culture. It's in the hands of the political-corporate-economic system which thinks only in terms of profit. They care nothing about the game, which, ideally, is life-affirming. What we see as a game, owners see as a business. And the game suffers from it. It's like being a farmer who grows food for himself. He's not going to ruin it with petrochemicals. He's going to produce a better product than the agribusiness farmers whose motive is profit.

Interview, Mill Valley, Calif./
Los Angeles Times, 1-7:(III)8.

2

I have always believed the Number 1 priority for the NFL is for the players to gain control over the game they play. When I talk to teams I ask the guys, "Who do you think *is* the NFL?" The athletes *are* the game; they are the reality; they are the NFL. NFL players are the lowest-paid, getting the lowest percentage of gross revenue in the highest-risk sport. The average career of an NFL player is 4.2 years, and his average life expectancy is somewhere around 55 years ... Our idea is simply that the basic structure has to change. This is America-Apple-Pie. It's democracy. The NFLPA and I have finally come together over the issue of percentage of gross revenue. It's the first step to gaining a measure of control over the game they play. It's come to the point that the only way to get that control over their working conditions is to do it collectively.

Interview, San Francisco/
San Francisco Examiner & Chronicle, 12-6:(C)5.

F. Don Miller
Executive director,
United States Olympic Committee

3

The Olympic Games only involve a relatively small number of world-class athletes, but every one of them who is successful motivates thousands of youth. The [1984] Los Angeles Games are going to be very important to the grassroots programs in amateur sports in this country, programs that can be very beneficial to individuals and to society. If you've got that broad base, and the programs for advancement, the elite will come naturally to the top.

Interview/
The Washington Post, 2-20:(E)2.

Marvin Miller
Executive director, Major League
(baseball) Players Association

4

[On the current player strike]: The owners think they can crack the union and force the players to their knees. For two days, we've attempted to negotiate a settlement on the concept of a player pool to compensate for the loss of free agents. The owners' position is that if a club signs a quality free agent, it must expose a valuable player in direct compensation. Our executive board has voted that down over and over ... The problem is simple: The owners pretend they're negotiating, but direct compensation to punish clubs signing ranking free agents is their real aim. They let out stories that they're about to make a big movement. Then they come in to produce a small mouse with 10 problems connected to it ... [The owners] are adamant that every club signing a quality free agent must expose a valuable player as compensation for him, and that's the heart of the matter.

Washington/Chicago Tribune, 7-25:(4)1,2.

Rick Monday
Baseball player, Los Angeles "Dodgers"

5

You go through your baseball life with the realization that your final day as a player is

476

(RICK MONDAY)

going to come. It's inevitable. But life doesn't stop when you leave the game. It's a change in the flow. Unfortunately, a lot of players go through it thinking that baseball on the major-league level is an end in itself. It's something they take for granted, the way people do with youth. But it's not guaranteed. Very few of us get to determine when that day arrives. Most of the time, someone else decides.

Interview/
Los Angeles Times, 9-15:(III)5.

Wilbert Montgomery
Football player,
Philadelphia "Eagles"

1

You know the dangers of the sport. You take a chance every time you're on the field. Life is a chance itself: You can get mugged; you can get hit by a car. When you play football, you accept the dangers. If you love the game, it's worth it. If you don't think it's worth it, it's time to get out. I get great satisfaction from football. I like the thrills and joys of winning, the closeness of the players, the whole learning experience. I like the chance to go places and see things and meet people, things you wouldn't do otherwise. This sort of opens you up and prepares you for life when you leave the game . . . All the hard work, the soreness, the pain, the sweat and tears—you can put them all together and learn a lesson from them and use that lesson in real life. This [football] isn't real life.

Interview, Philadelphia/
The New York Times, 1-19:39.

Edwin Newman
Correspondent, NBC News

2

Sports people take on heroic dimension. Somebody gets the winning hit in the World Series and thousands of people are ready to go mad at the mere sight of him. And it makes a sizable difference to the country . . . Sports

are popular because it is measurable, definable and provable . . . Sports is a very good area in which excellence is still treasured. That is something the country needs very, very badly. One of the great dangers of sports is that it is beginning to take on other aspects of American life. It is becoming more complicated and risks becoming less interesting for that reason.

Interview/
The Washington Post, 7-19:5.

Jack Nicklaus
Golfer

3

Pride is probably my greatest motivation because I can't stand to get beat. But I get beat a lot, of course, and I don't mind losing quite as much if a guy plays better than I do. That's the nice thing about golf: It's such a humbling game. It's the only sport where, if you win 20 per cent of the time, you're the best. In other sports, you must win as much as 90 per cent of the time to be the absolute best.

Interview/
Chicago Tribune Magazine, 6-14:14.

Roger Noll
Economist, California Institute
of Technology

4

[On the financial aspect of professional sports in the face of criticism of high player salaries and other fiscal problems]: Sports are in no danger of going under. The only danger is to the wealth of certain individual owners. There are many more potential buyers [of sports franchises] than there are willing sellers. That, along with rising franchise prices, is a much better indicator of the health of sports than mere profit and loss . . . figures that can't be trusted.
Los Angeles Times, 3-17:(IH)8.

Peter O'Malley
President, Los Angeles "Dodgers"
baseball club

5

[On why the *Dodgers* have for years drawn the biggest crowds in U.S. sports]: One reason

477

(PETER O'MALLEY)

is that this is such an appealing game. But the big reason is that we continue to win. You see this very clearly in our mail. Any time we lose a few games, the letters we get are critical of everything and everybody, from the custodians and groundskeepers to the outfielders. When we win, on the other hand, the mail pours in about how beautiful the park is, how clean, what marvelous landscaping, what great guys the players are. Same team, same park.

Interview, Los Angeles/
Los Angeles Times, 1-17:(III)7.

1

[On player-management friction]: To this point, I don't think the fan has been turned off or upset by baseball's internal struggles. They come out to the ballpark because we've got a great game; to enjoy a period of relaxation they can't get elsewhere; and because baseball is not part of the real world. The fans don't identify with the owners and their problems and I don't expect them to. They've got problems of their own. With them the game and the good time that goes with it is the thing, and I hope that never changes.

Interview, Vero Beach, Fla./
The Christian Science Monitor, 4-2:16.

Bobby Orr
Former hockey player,
Boston "Bruins"

2

The fans still want to see clean, hard checking and hitting, which are part of the game, but I don't think they really enjoy the bench-emptying brawls and long delays . . . I think the National Hockey League is doing a fine job in controlling [player] violence. It's still going to take time, but they're getting away from the fisticuffs with recent rule changes, heavier fines and longer suspensions. The fans today much prefer to see strong skating, puck-control and goal-scoring. And the teams

that can skate and play the team-game are the ones that win.

Interview/
Los Angeles Times, 2-11:(III)1.

Arnold Palmer
Golfer

3

[On why many new golfers lack charisma]: I suppose $300,000 a week does it. I read in the paper in Hawaii one guy saying, "Aw, if I make the cut, I don't have to worry about it. I know I'm gonna make some money." Can you imagine that? I mean that's really unbelievable. It's like doing something that doesn't excite you. Asked for his wish, one of these guys told somebody, "I just want to make the cut every week." You've got to be kidding me. I'd rather win one tournament in my life than make the cut every week.

Los Angeles Times, 3-18:(III)2.

Jack Pardee
Former football coach,
Washington "Redskins"

4

The coach should be allowed to coach and not be shot down from other angles. Let me do my job, not worry about jockeying for position . . . I can't be a figurehead. Don't tell me to win, then say, "But do it this way." Without authority, I don't want the job.

Interview, Unison, Va./
The Los Angeles Times, 2-4:(III)1.

Arthur E. (Red) Patterson
Assistant to the chairman,
California "Angels" baseball club

5

The only thing better than a two-team city is a three-team city. When the *Dodgers* and *Giants* both pulled out of New York the same year [in the 1950s], I well remember the *Yankees'* attitude. They predicted they'd set an attendance record. But a funny thing happened. With [the departure of the two other teams], their

(ARTHUR E. [RED] PATTERSON)

[Yankee] attendance went down . . . Baseball fans love to argue. Arguing creates interest. And interest sells tickets. It's as simple as that. When there were three teams in New York, the chatter of the fans was endless, all over town. *Dodger* fans argued that Snider was better than Mays or DiMaggio and Mantle, and in baseball, you know, a fan can prove anything. When New York had three teams, it was the center of the baseball universe. With the *Yankees* alone it's just another one-team town.

Interview/
Los Angeles Times, 4-3:(III)8.

Hank Peters
General manager, Baltimore "Orioles" baseball club

1

[Criticizing the trend toward long-term player contracts]: In the old days, everything was one year at a time. Next year's pay was determined by this year's play. There was always a minority of players who lacked the proper "intensity," to borrow one of those football words. But now, that minority is growing. Once you've got that big, multi-year contract, I'm afraid there's a tendency to think that your primary goal is not to get seriously injured until the option year of that contract comes up . . . We have a situation in baseball now where the intelligent self-interest of a player and the best interests of his team aren't always the same.

The Washington Post, 8-30:(M)6.

Bum Phillips
Football coach,
New Orleans "Saints"

2

Really, I'd rather have a self-made football player than a natural-made football player. The natural-made player hasn't had to go through the rigors; he hasn't listened to coaches and done a little extra. He does only what you say. The player you win with listens to you,

then runs a few extra yards. If a guy doesn't work for you, I don't care how smart you are, you can forget your football season. I'd rather take a guy with less talent who works, than one with talent who doesn't work.

Interview, Vero Beach, Fla./
Chicago Tribune, 8-23:(4)4.

3

You measure discipline in the fourth quarter of a game, not at midnight in a bar. Rules don't mean a damn thing. Discipline is learning to suck it up when you're behind in the second half. Discipline is executing the way you should in the fourth quarter when you're tired and hurt and want to quit and go home to mama.

Interview/
Los Angeles Times, 9-11:(III)11.

Richie Phillips
Executive director, Major League (baseball) Umpires Association

4

Baseball is in a state of turmoil today. Managers are frustrated because their players are being distracted by the threat of a [player] strike. Last week George Steinbrenner, the principal owner of the [New York] *Yankees*, attacked his players, his managers and umpires. He even complained about umpires' calls in a game the *Yankees* lost in Baltimore. Steinbrenner was in Florida and did not even see the game on television. The owners are now so frustrated they don't know which way to turn, so the umpires are bearing the brunt of the frustrations. Managers berate umpires to incite their players and the fans.

Interview, Philadelphia, June 1/
The New York Times, 6-2:21.

Joe Pisarcik
Football player, Philadelphia "Eagles"

5

[On being a backup quarterback rather than a starter, like the *Eagles'* Ron Jaworski]: You get a lot of satisfaction being on a football

WHAT THEY SAID IN 1981

(JOE PISARCIK)

team. But once you're there, you want to play. And if you play awhile, the only satisfaction is winning and then going to the Super Bowl. But I know that some great players like O. J. Simpson and Gale Sayers never got to the Super Bowl. So I have a lot to be thankful for. Sure, I'd like to be Number 1 [quarterback]. And if anything happens to Ron, I will be. But I look at it this way: Would you rather be president of a company losing $100,000 a year or vice president of a company making $1-million a year?

Interview, Philadelphia, Jan. 16/
The New York Times, 1-17:17.

Gary Player
Golfer

1

I've played golf with all sorts of people. I've traveled more than any sportsman who ever lived. So I have had the opportunity to see the world for myself. And I have concluded that if governments would stay out of sports and let sports organizers run the show, everybody would compete together and therefore have a better understanding of people's attitudes, problems and ways of life. Sports can provide an opportunity for developing relationships that no government-to-government negotiating sessions can provide.

Interview/
U.S. News & World Report, 5-11:68.

Jerry Quarry
Former boxer

2

[Boxing is] a vicious, vicious sport. People get hurt, and some people are never the same again. Still, all some fans go out to see is blood. If they don't see blood, they feel cheated. That's what it is all about: blood and kicking asses. I never liked that White Hope crap; but, to be honest, I never liked boxing, either.

Interview/
Los Angeles Examiner, 5-6:(B)5.

Ronald Reagan
President of the United States

3

A Navy football player once described [football] as the nearest thing to war without being lethal. It is the last thing left in civilization where two men can literally fling themselves bodily at one another in combat and not be at war. It's a kind of clean hatred. You hate the color of his jersey, but there's a mutual respect that develops while you're playing on the field. And also, there is a kind of inner confidence because you've met your fellow man in that kind of physical combat. I know of no other game that gave me the same feeling that football did. That's why you can look at the bench when the TV camera comes over and see the fellows sitting there crying. *I've sat there crying.*

Interview/
The Washington Post, 3-2:(A)10.

Joseph Robbie
Owner, Miami "Dolphins"
football team

4

Crowd violence is probably the ultimate danger to the existence of sports. I perceive that one of the greatest threats to the future of spectator sports of every kind, here and abroad, is deliberate, excessive violence on the playing field, and violent crowd reaction in the stands.

Before House Criminal Justice Subcommittee,
Washington, May 19/
The Washington Post, 5-20:(D)3.

Frank Robinson
Baseball manager,
San Francisco "Giants"

5

What I'm after is a team that will make the routine plays in the field all the time. I don't care about the spectacular play because it isn't going to help you that much. What kills a manager is when one of his infielders boots an easy double-play ball or one of his hitters can't sacrifice the tying run from first to second base

(FRANK ROBINSON)

with the team's power coming up. The point is, if you can't get that kind of execution regularly, you can forget about pennants.

The Christian Science Monitor, 1-19:12.

1

Individuals can't win baseball games and pennants. Only the team wins. To make good in baseball you have to respect your team at least as much as yourself . . . Even if you hit .400. Success comes from thinking "team," thinking "we," "us"—not "me," "I." You don't describe a winning team by the number of stars it has. A winning team is nothing more than the right blend of individuals willing to make sacrifices.

Interview/
Los Angeles Times, 2-25:(III)12.

Bill Rodgers
Champion marathon runner

2

Racing [running] isn't fun. Well, it's half fun and half hellish. It's an intense challenge physically and psychologically. If you want to test your limits, it's great for that. It's such a grind, training and running year in and year out. There's no off-season. It's a hard life-style. But it's been worth it. It has enabled me to live in a beautiful house, to meet great people. I've been fortunate. But I can't downplay how tough it is to push at a high level year after year. When you can't handle it any more, you've got to retire. First, you've got to love running. Then you've got to love the competition. It is an obsession. It is unbalanced. It's way off a normal life. I guess that's true for many athletes at the top level.

Interview, Boston/The New York Times, 4-20:33.

Pete Rose
Baseball player, Philadelphia "Phillies"

3

I want to play all the time. I think the mark of a good player is his consistency. And the only

way a guy can be consistent is to play all the time. I've always said if a manager posted a sign in the clubhouse that read, "A player will be docked 1/162 of his salary," few players would ask for a day off. You'd see a lot of 162-game-a-year players.

Interview, Los Angeles/
Los Angeles Herald Examiner, 5-20:(C)1.

Pete Rozelle
Commissioner,
National Football League

4

[Alluding to the Oakland *Raiders'* fight to move to Los Angeles against the wishes of the NFL, even though such approval is required by League regulations]: What makes the individual teams successful is their membership in the League. If you didn't belong to a league, and just had teams arranging scrimmages against one another, you couldn't expect many people to watch. But you can't have a league unless everybody is willing to abide by mutually agreed-upon rules.

News conference, New Orleans/
The Christian Science Monitor, 1-26:16.

Mike Schmidt
Baseball player,
Philadelphia "Phillies"

5

I'm not thinking of home runs now, which is probably why I'm getting them. If you go up there trying to knock it out of the park, it's usually not going to happen. I have to keep reminding myself that if I just hit the ball solid, make good contact, it will go . . . The ultimate temptation for a long-ball hitter is to go for the home run. I have to fight it all the time. I have to force myself to think contact, not hitting the ball out of the park.

Interview, Philadelphia, Aug. 23/
The Washington Post, 8-25:(D)3.

481

WHAT THEY SAID IN 1981

Tom Seaver
Baseball pitcher,
Cincinnati "Reds"

1

I'll miss it when I stop [playing]. If I don't ever see another airport again, that would be fine. But the game, the game, that I'll miss. The mind-games you play with the batter, the clubhouse, the people in the game. But more than anything, I'll miss the competition. That's what makes it all worthwhile. The money, the fame and the glory are all nice; only a liar would tell you they aren't. But the best part is that feeling when you're in a tight spot and get out of it. That's what I'll miss. That's what I'll remember when I look back.

Interview, Houston/
The Washington Post, 5-17:(N)4.

2

The thing most people don't understand is that pitching isn't the same every time out. Pitching is what you have best on the day you work, and if you can't get your fastball over the plate, then maybe you can with your curve. I've also learned over the years that most hitters' strengths and weaknesses expand and contract, especially if they are in a groove or in a slump. But basically, hitters fall into a pattern, and once you know what they like, you can set them up for the put-out with something else.

Interview/
The Christian Science Monitor, 10-2:16.

Freddie Shero
Former hockey coach,
Washington "Capitals"

3

When you're a coach, you're miserable. When you're not a coach, you're more miserable . . . You can't be happy coaching. If you're happy coaching, you should get out of the game. You've got to suffer. That's what it's all about—constantly trying to improve. If you're happy all day long, you must be an idiot.

Interview/The Washington Post, 11-15:(D)16.

Don Shula
Football coach, Miami "Dolphins"

4

I don't believe in gimmicks. I like to work within the rules and I like to do this with as much poise as possible. You win with strength, not luck, and by how much you accomplish in practice during the week.

To reporters/
The Christian Science Monitor, 8-7:16.

Reggie Smith
Baseball player,
Los Angeles "Dodgers"

5

[On the recent settlement of the player strike]: The owners proved that might makes right. They thumbed their noses at the law. They didn't care that we [players] won free-agency through the legal process, through arbitration and the courts of law that supposedly this country is based on. The law doesn't mean anything; as long as you have power and might, you're right. I don't want to hear [owner representative] Ray Grebey talking that crap that nobody won [the strike]. The owners won. They got compensation [for premium free agents], and we [players] lost money and time for nothing. We struck for nothing.

Interview, Los Angeles, Aug. 2/
Los Angeles Herald Examiner, 8-3:(C)1.

Stan Smith
Tennis player

6

. . . it is important to know everything you can about your opponent. If I can't scout a player myself, then I ask someone on the tour whose judgment I trust to do it for me. What I want to know primarily about an opponent is his style. You know, things like: Does he come to the net? Does he move well? Does he favor one side of his body? What's his second serve like?, etc. [If an opponent changes his normal habits and style,] you have to be ready for that, too; and that's why most game plans

(STAN SMITH)

are flexible. In fact, to save time I usually include two or three alternatives in my preparation for just that reason. Often when a guy gets away from the way he normally plays, it isn't the change so much that causes you to make errors as the feeling that you're not quite sure what you ought to be doing. And while you're thinking about this, he's winning the match. The good players simply don't allow that to happen.

Interview, Los Angeles/
The Christian Science Monitor, 4-22:14.

Harold Solomon
President, Association of
Tennis Professionals

1

[Saying there will be new, stricter rules governing the behavior of players on the courts]: The things guys get away with on the court are outrageous . . . The players want to be reprimanded. They want to be controlled. It's unique in sports that a body of athletes has to ask for rules to govern them. People behave like they do because they know it's easy to get away with almost anything. We don't want that any longer. We're proposing up to six-month suspensions and $5,000 in fines. The players have been pushing for those for 18 months now.

The Washington Post, 7-26:(E)14.

Rusty Staub
Baseball player,
New York "Mets"

2

[On the current player strike]: The normal statement from the uninformed is "How can you [players] be striking with all the money you're making?" They think we should thank God we have it. They're right that we are very fortunate. But we are unusually talented people in the entertainment business, and we are being rewarded for the first time in history at the price the market will bear. You're never going

to have a situation where people [fans] [who are] doing without something—a ride on the subway, the collection of garbage, the milling of steel—are going to respond positively. People are not interested in the facts. They just want to see baseball.

Interview, New York/
The New York Times, 6-20:14.

George Steinbrenner
Owner, New York "Yankees"
baseball club

3

I get mad as hell when my team blows one. But there are five million *Yankee* fans just like me sitting in front of their TV sets with beer and hollering the same thing . . . I want this team to win. I'm obsessed with winning, with discipline, with achieving. That's what this country's all about; that's what New York is all about—fighting for everything: a cab in the rain, a table in a restaurant at lunch time. And that's what the *Yankees* are all about, and always have been.

Interview, Tampa, Fla./
The New York Times, 9-20:(1)23.

Hank Stram
Former football coach,
Kansas City "Chiefs"

4

The life is draining out of the game. Some super-rich guy buys the team and meddles with it. Some jock-sniffer, who's not even a football guy, runs the front office. The assistant coaches are technicians who divide the team up into offense, defense, special teams and kicking game. They're the theorists. And the players are big, strong, weight-trained mechanics who do exactly what they're told. The coach is just the guy standing in the middle holding a clipboard, with nothing to do. Where the hell is the humanity in the game? I remember when guys got into the game so they could express themselves. It was heroic.

Los Angeles Times,
2-4:(III)12.

WHAT THEY SAID IN 1981

Lynn Swann
Football player, Pittsburgh "Steelers"

1

There are two kinds of violence in football. One is a hit that is deliberately, illegally aimed to hurt you. The other is the incidental violence in the pileup—the extra elbow, the little punching and wrestling, the over-zealousness. I've never spoken out against the second kind . . . because the players who do that aren't really trying to get by with something. When I went public with my complaints I was talking about the guys who go for deliberate career-ending hits. I wasn't talking about incidental illegal contact. . . . this is a man's game—one of the few we have. Any time a group of large, well-conditioned men compete in close quarters, there's going to be some pushing and shoving. How much force does it take to stop Earl Campbell? Are three tacklers enough—and do you penalize the fourth for a late hit? Then suppose Earl breaks loose from these guys on the next play? I've seen him do it. You've got to let us play some football.

Interview/
Los Angeles Times, 11-27:(III)16.

Joe Theismann
Football player, Washington "Redskins";
Former player, Canadian Football League

2

The CFL will never compare to the National Football League because it's made up of Canadians who would rather be playing hockey. They're better hockey players than football players, but they aren't good enough to make the grade in their own country, where hockey's Number 1. So they play at their secondary skill. That's a big reason why the quality in Canada is so different. It would be like a major-league player deciding to play in Japan. It's not the same kind of ball.

Interview/Chicago Tribune, 9-20:(4)5.

John Thompson
Basketball coach, Georgetown University

3

[Saying that athletes and their families bear much of the blame for the growing number of

recruiting scandals]: If a girl on the street wants to be flirted with, she will be flirted with. If she doesn't want anyone messing around, no one will mess with her. It's the same with basketball players. If they're being flirted with, it's because they wanted to. The responsibility lies with the kid and with his parents.

Los Angeles Times, 2-23:(III)2.

Lee Trevino
Golfer

4

If an athlete doesn't get mad, he's not much of an athlete. But I've set this happy-go-lucky standard and I try to adhere to it, even though I may be laughing on the outside and seething on the inside. It's what's happening on the inside that gives me my drive, my motivation.

Interview, Los Angeles, Feb. 17/
Los Angeles Times, 2-19:(III)8.

Wes Unseld
Basketball player,
Washington "Bullets"

5

The most dominant ability for a basketball player is to be able to think on the court. Height, strength and jumping ability are important; but if you can think, you can offset your physical liabilities. I guess I'm a real live example of that.

Los Angeles Times, 3-20:(III)13.

Gene Upshaw
Football player,
Oakland "Raiders"

6

I kept reminding our players during the play-offs that the only thing winning does is it lets you play next week. But unless you win the Super Bowl, everything else is down. You can remember the *Steelers* won four Super Bowls, but you never remember who they beat. When you come here [to the Super Bowl] for the first time, you tend to be happy just being here.

(GENE UPSHAW)

But until you win the Super Bowl, you haven't won anything.

Interview, New Orleans/
The New York Times, 1-27:20.

Bill Veeck
Owner, Chicago "White Sox"
baseball club

1

I wouldn't change any way the game is played dugout to dugout. It remains the most changeless thing in our society. But I would insist on some improvements at other levels. First, there would be one set of rules; there would be designated hitters in both leagues or in neither . . . Secondly, there would be one set of umps for both leagues, not two sets with different codes . . . Thirdly, there would be either artificial turf or no artificial turf. I understand the difficulties in inside arenas like the Astrodome. But I firmly feel a baseball park should smell like grass, not an extension of the city streets with cigarette smoke and other odors. The leagues should be realigned. There should be three divisions and a wild card. Emphasis should be on natural rivalries—*Cubs-White Sox, Yankees-Mets, Dodgers-Angels,* Toronto-Montreal, Dallas-Houston. Play in the same time zones; this would save fuel. If we aren't careful, we're going to price family groupings right out of the park . . . In the '60s I spoke to 20 campuses a year. The mood was never to smile. Everything was on speed, action, violence. It was promoted by football, hockey and muggings. Now everybody wants to smile and be happy. Baseball is the answer. It is the island of stability in an unstable world.

Accepting Life Achievement Award of Baseball
Magazine, New York, Feb. 2/
Los Angeles Times, 2-3:(III)3.

Dick Vermeil
Football coach, Philadelphia "Eagles"

2

I don't give a damn for [pre-Super Bowl] parties, ceremonies, celebrations. To me, there's

only one way to enjoy a football game, gentlemen, and that's to win it.

Time, 1-26:55.

Darrell Waltrip
Auto-racing driver

3

In racing, the highs are the highest you can experience and the lows are the lowest you can experience. You can be so high after a win, and you think you've got the bull by the horns. Everybody's pumped up; your sponsors, they're all happy; Junior Johnson is happy; and the fans are happy. You're celebrating and, man! you can't wait to get to the next race. Then you go to the next race and you qualify poorly and the car doesn't run right, the crew is upset and the owner is upset and the sponsor's on the phone wanting to know what's going on. You start to race and you run five laps and the engine blows and you put the car on the truck and go home—and they didn't even know you were there. Everybody is very understanding if you're winning. Nobody understands if you're losing.

Interview, July 21/
The New York Times,
7-22:21.

Tom Watson
Golfer

4

I think there's too much money involved in sports, including golf. Fans don't like to see players make mistakes when they get so much money. They seem to feel [that] if we're paid what we are, we shouldn't make mistakes. But we're only human. The best athletes in the world make mistakes. Athletes are being dehumanized by big salaries, or big payoffs. Consequently, there are no heroes today in sports.

Interview,
Pebble Beach, Calif., Jan. 28/
Los Angeles Times, 1-29:(III)1.

Earl Weaver
Baseball manager,
Baltimore "Orioles"

1

My strategy doesn't mean beans. Most nights, I could stay home. All I can do as a manager is create situations whereby my players can do what they do best. If they do it, then I'm a genius. If they don't, then [sportscaster] Howard Cosell says that I'm going against the book. Who wrote this book anyway?

Los Angeles Times, 4-24:(III)2.

Sonny Werblin
President, Madison Square
Garden Corporation

2

We're [the New York *Knicks*] not going to get into a bidding war in the free-agent [player] market. Basketball has enough trouble with attendance now. In three or four years, every player will become a free agent, and if they change teams it will hurt the game. Players will be moving from one team to another and there will be no loyalty and no players the fans can relate to the way there used to be. A lot of teams are looking for the revenue from cable and pay-TV as the savior, but that help is three or four years away, and by that time a lot of these clubs and owners will be long gone.

The New York Times, 6-14:(1)26.

Edward Bennett Williams
Lawyer; Owner, Baltimore "Orioles"
baseball club

3

I'm basically a capitalist, but I think baseball needs a quasi-socialistic system to survive. Right now, we have the [New York] *Yankees* taking in $27-million a year and the Minnesota *Twins* $9-million. If we allow that to keep up much longer, the rich teams will sign all the good players, competition will wither and our financial problems will be multiplied.

The Wall Street Journal,
4-8:20.

Maury Wills
Baseball manager, Seattle "Mariners"

4

Every team in baseball is weak in fundamentals. That goes for the champion *Phillies* and Kansas City and everybody else. The winners in both leagues are winning with talent. They make as many fundamental mistakes as the bottom teams, but you don't notice their mistakes when they win. So the best and fastest way for us [the *Mariners*] to compete is to learn the fundamentals. That's the way to close the gap.

Interview/
Los Angeles Times, 3-17:(III)10.

Phil Woosman
Commissioner,
North American Soccer League

5

Let's face it. Sports come down to nationalism, and the star system is what sports is about. When the young players in the U.S. and Canada make those teams powers in world soccer, there will be a tremendous increase in attention for soccer [in North America]. The future of the sport rests with the young people who are playing it right now, the players who will create interest, the fans who will come out, having grown up with the sport. We've just got to be patient. People forget that we've [the NASL] gone from Triple-A to major-league in terms of talent the last few years and that's cost a lot of money. I've seen this League go from 17 to five teams [in 1969] and come back. If we have setbacks again, fine; it happens, but we'll come back.

The Washington Post, 5-17:(N)7.

James H. Zumberge
President, University of Southern California

6

[College football is important because it] is probably the most unifying element on campus

(JAMES H. ZUMBERGE)

. . . what academic event could generate 50,000 paying spectators seven times a year? If it was so inimical to the values of the university, one would think that somebody other than the University of Chicago would have done away with it by now.

Interview, San Marino, Calif.
Los Angeles Times, 2-17:(II)2.

The Indexes

Index To Speakers

A

Abdullah ibn Abdul Aziz, 300
Abel, Elie, 451
Abernathy, William J., 76
Abourezk, James, 300
Abrahams, William, 355
Abrams, Elliott, 132
Abrams, Floyd, 174
Adams, Ansel, 119, 335
Adler, Mortimer, Jr., 105, 432
Aga Khan Karim, 342
Agee, William, 451
Aimers, John, 236
Akins, James, 300
Albright, Joann, 105
Aldrich, Robert, 378
Alexander, Benjamin, 105
Ali, Muhammad, 459
Allen, George, 459
Allen, Lew, Jr., 54
Allen, Richard V., 54, 132, 225
Allen, Steve, 418, 432
Allen, Woody, 378, 407
Almendros, Nestor, 378
Altman, Robert, 378, 418
Ambler, Eric, 355
Amis, Martin, 355
Anderson, Bernard, E., 12
Anderson, John B., 183, 225
Anderson, Lindsay, 418
Anderson, Sparky, 432, 459
Anderson, William, 355
Andretti, Mario, 459
Andrus, Cecil D., 119
Anka, Paul, 398
Antonioni, Michelangelo, 378
Antonowsky, Marvin, 379
Arafat, Yasir, 300-301
Arens, Moshe, 301-302
Aristov, Boris, 268
Arkin, Alan, 379
Arkoff, Samuel Z., 379
Arledge, Roone, 419
Armstrong, William L., 76
Arnold, Danny, 419
Arnold, Millard, 236

Aron, Raymond, 268
Arum, Bob, 460
Ashley, Thomas L., 155
Aspin, Les, 54-55, 155, 342
Assad, Hafez al-, 302
Astin, Alexander W., 105-106
Atkins, Humphrey, 268
Auchter, Thorne G., 76
Autry, Gene, 460
Aziz, Tark, 302

B

Babbitt, Bruce E., 155
Bacall, Lauren, 407
Bailey, F. Lee, 174
Bailey, Stephen K., 106
Baisinger, Grace, 106
Baker, Dusty, 460
Baker, Howard H., Jr., 7, 155
Baker, James A., III, 55, 76, 132-133, 183
Balanchine, George, 407
Baldrige, Malcolm, 26, 119, 211, 254
Baldwin, Roger, 183, 444
Balitzer, Alfred, 184
Ball, Bill, 407
Ball, George W., 269, 303
Ballard, Harold, 460
Bani-Sadr, Abolhassan, 303
Banowsky, William S., 106
Barnard, Christiaan, 368
Barre, Raymond, 269
Barry, Marion S., Jr., 217
Barry, Rick, 461
Barzun, Jacques, 461
Basnett, David, 269
Bavasi, Buzzie, 461
Baxter, William, 26
Bazargan, Mehdi, 303
Bazelon, David L., 42
Beard, Edward P., 156
Beckett, Terence, 269
Becton, Julius W., Jr., 55
Begin, Menachem, 303-306

I

J

M

Index to Subjects

A

Abortion—*see* Medicine
Acheson, Dean, 134:4
Acting/actors, 383:1, 384:3, 391:1, 392:4, 393:3, 396:1
  audience, 407:4, 408:2
  black, 410:5
  British, 411:6, 413:4
    London vs. New York, 410:4
  careers, 382:3
  character, style of, 381:5
  corruption, 390:2
  creating something new, 391:6
  danger, element of, 410:3
  delightful profession, 391:4
  director, relations with, 393:5
  discipline, 381:2
  embarrassment, 382:4
  encouragement, 414:4
  European, 382:3
  followings, 411:4
  glamour, 390:1
  healthy, 387:6
  an instrument, 391:2
  intelligence, 387:5
  learning, 397:2
  long runs of plays, 410:1, 410:2
  Method, 389:3
  mimicry, 388:5
  outside yourself, 387:4
  parts, choice of, 390:3, 408:5, 413:2, 414:5
  performance, good/bad, 386:1, 390:4
  potential, 391:5
  preparing a role, 393:2
  as President of U.S., 198:4
  rehearsal, 391:3
  shaping a role, 392:3
  stage vs. films, 380:2, 409:5, 412:5, 413:1, 414:7, 416:2
  standards, 385:5
  stars, 380:4, 390:2, 392:1
  starting out, 415:5
  success, 411:6
  in Sweden, 409:1
  technique, 389:2
  television, 422:5
  treatment of, 395:4
  typecasting, 390:5

Acting/actors *(continued)*
  understanding other human beings, 387:3
  U.S., 382:3, 411:6
  yourself, in touch with, 392:5
Adams, John, 8:2
Adulthood, 440:1
Advertising—*see* Commerce; Television
Afghanistan:
  foreign affairs:
    India, 257:5
    Pakistan, 257:5, 259:3
    Soviet Union, 62:2, 135:4, 139:5, 144:1, 148:3, 150:2, 152:5, 154:2, 254:2, 257:5, 259:1, 261:4, 262:1, 262:2, 262:5, 263:2, 265:2, 275:1, 278:3, 279:2, 292:1, 294:5, 323:4, 327:1, 471:3
    U.S., 307:1
Africa, pp. 225-235
  destabilization of, 226:3
  economy, 225:5
  foreign affairs:
    Cuba, 62:2
    France, 231:5
    South Africa, 225:5, 230:6, 232:3
    Soviet Union, 107:5, 226:3, 315:3
    U.S., 152:4, 154:1
  press, 344:2
  united, 229:2
  See also specific African countries
Age, 433:1
  of chief executives, 28:5, 36:2, 38:1
  of government leaders, 168:3
Agnew, Spiro T., 346:3
Agriculture/farming, 27:2, 33:3
  Communism, 32:2
  family-owned farms, 27:1
  foreign-trade, 34:5
  land, loss of, 219:5
  subsidies/loans, 27:3, 34:1
Air transportation—*see* Transportation: air
Alcoholism—*see* Medicine
Alfred the Great, 65:4
Algeria:
  foreign affairs:
    Egypt, 318:4
    France, 274:4
  oil, 328:1
Ali, Muhammad, 470:5

F

J

O

P

Tennis *(continued)*
  umpires, 475:3
  winning/losing, 472:4
  women, 471:4
Terrorism—*see* Crime
Texaco, Inc., 32:5
Thalberg, Irving, 395:5
Thatcher, Margaret, 187:5, 269:3, 269:4, 279:5, 280:4, 282:2, 290:1, 293:2
Theatre—*see* Stage
Third World/developing countries, 132:1, 143:4
  economics, 143:1
  foreign affairs:
    aid, 137:4, 148:1
    bases, 151:5
    Cuba, 137:2
    Germany, West, 137:2
    Soviet Union, 58:1, 137:2, 141:3, 142:2, 144:2
    U.S., 133:2, 137:4, 141:3, 142:2, 144:2, 147:2, 147:3, 148:6, 153:5
    press, 342:1, 344:2, 350:5
    See also specific Third World countries
Tinguely, Jean, 337:5
Tito, Josip Broz, 275:4
Toynbee, Philip, 35:2
Trade, foreign—*see* Commerce
Transportation, 167:2, pp. 211-216
  air transportation:
    airline not luxury, 214:1
    controller strike, 77:2, 87:1, 94:2, 102:5, 211:2, 212:1, 212:4, 213:4, 213:5, 214:4, 214:5, 215:2, 215:4, 216:5
    FAA, 211:2
  automobiles, 29:1, 32:4, 79:6, 80:4, 90:2
    Chrysler Corp., 29:1, 29:3, 36:1, 212:3, 471:1
    energy aspect, 214:3, 216:1
    Ford Motor Co., 213:2
    foreign competition, 35:3
      Europe vs. U.S., 214:3
      Japanese exports, 211:1, 211:4, 213:3, 214:2, 216:1, 216:4
    foreign manufacture by U.S., 213:2, 214:2
    General Motors Corp., (GM), 212:3, 213:2, 216:1
    government regulations, 213:2, 215:1
    safety/air bags, 215:1
    small, 215:1, 216:1, 216:3
  mass/public, 212:2, 215:3, 219:5
  railroads:
    Amtrak, 213:1
    Conrail, 211:3, 216:2
Truman, Harry S., 158:5, 184:2, 191:3, 194:5
Trying, 439:3
Turkey:
  democracy, 276:2

Turkey *(continued)*
  foreign affairs:
    Cyprus, 284:3, 284:4, 287:1
    Greece, 284:3, 287:1, 290:4
Turner, Ted, 466:3

U

Uganda, 229:1
Unemployment—*see* Labor: employment
Unions—*see* Labor; Poland: Solidarity
United Kingdom/Britain/England:
  actors, 410:4, 411:6, 413:4
  Conservative Party (Tory), 277:1, 279:5, 296:1, 299:2
  defense/military:
    disarmament, 270:1, 273:5, 292:2
    U.S. bases, 270:2
  economy, 82:4, 101:2, 101:3, 277:1, 289:2, 296:1
    budget/taxes, 295:3
    Common Market/EEC, 270:2, 295:1
    inflation, 269:4, 280:4
    interest rates, 269:4, 279:5
    recession, 269:4, 282:2, 294:4
    unemployment, 269:3, 270:2, 279:3, 279:5, 280:4, 293:2
  foreign affairs:
    Australia, 257:1
    Canada, 236:1
    Iran, 321:2
    U.S., 294:3, 295:2
      bases, 270:2
  immigration/citizenship, 290:5, 295:4
  Labor Party, 270:2, 277:1, 279:4, 299:2
  Liberal Party, 299:2
  literature/books, 10:1, 355:4
  oil, North Sea, 289:2
  police, 47:1
  press, 344:2, 350:3, 350:5, 352:4
  Prince of Wales, 274:1
  religion, 448:3
  riots, 279:3, 295:6, 299:1
  social conscience, 10:1
  Social Democratic Party, 299:2
  stage/theatre, 410:4, 411:6, 412:4, 413:4
  television, 422:6
  See also Northern Ireland
United Nations (UN)—*see* Foreign affairs
United States (U.S.)—*see* America
United States Steel Corp., 32:5
Universities—*see* Education: college